THE ENCYCLOPEDIA OF
MOTORCYCLES

THE ENCYCLOPEDIA OF
MOTORCYCLES

GENERAL EDITOR: ROGER HICKS

Published by Silverdale Books
an imprint of Bookmart Ltd
Registered number 2372865
Trading as Bookmart Ltd
Desford Road
Enderby
Leicester LE9 5AD

ISBN: 1-85605-592-2

Editorial and design by
Amber Books Ltd
Bradleys Close
74-77 White Lion Street
London
N1 9PF

Authors: Roy Bacon, Roger Hicks, Mac McDiarmid, John Tipler, Mick Walker
Project Editor: Conor Kilgallon
Designer: Graham Curd

Printed in Singapore

CONTENTS

The Aprilia Moto 6.5, first introduced in 1995. Unusually, the machine was designed by Philippe Starck, better known for his furniture designs. The bike's innovative lines generated a lot of publicity for the Italian company.

An FB Mondial GP racer from the 1950s. Most track bikes from this era used full or 'dustbin' aerodynamic fairings to improve performance. This was Cecil Sandford's championship-winning 250cc machine.

CONTENTS

P&M competition machines from a bygone age. The machines were slower, but the competition was still intense. This picture is from 1913.

INTRODUCTION

Traditionally, an opera army marches two steps forward, then one step back. Motorcycle evolution seems to have followed much the same path, with the addition of numerous sideways shuffles, a good number of spectacular but ultimately pointless leaps into the air, and frequent pauses to bury the head in the sand in the hope that other manufacturers' technological advances would go away.

This is, perhaps, because motorcycles are not entirely rational things; they appeal more to the senses than to the intellect. Who can resist running their fingers across the deep, smooth lustrous paint of a petrol tank? Who can forget the smell of a motorcycle, that amalgam of hot iron and light alloy and petrol and oil and rubber? Who has ridden a motorcycle and cannot remember the warmth of the sun, the almost liquid cold of early-morning shadows, the exhilaration of acceleration and speed, the sudden heart-wrenching fear of falling off?

What is constantly surprising is the way that the features we take for granted have sometimes taken decades to become established. In 1904, Indian motorcycles had twist-grip throttles; but it was not until the 1920s that these came into widespread use, and on the eve of World War II, there were still motorcycles where the speed was regulated by the sort of lever that is still used today on a lawn-mower.

Yet other features are so commonplace that we can barely imagine a motorcycle without them. Take the clutch, for example. Without one, the only way to start the motorcycle is to run alongside and, once the engine catches, to vault more or less gracefully into the saddle. When you come to a dead stop, the engine stalls. And yet, the 'free engine' (as the clutch was also called) was not only unknown at first; even after it had appeared, it was often an option.

Part of the reason for all these variations is that a motorcycle is not a particularly difficult thing to make, especially if you can buy in some of the parts that you need to make it. In business terms, the barriers to entry are low, so anyone can have a go.

COVERAGE

We have tried to be as objective as we can in the amount of coverage that each manufacturer receives. Some, such as BMW, Harley-Davidson and Honda, are so important,

and have made so many models, that we have given them as much space as we could spare. The next level down may be every bit as romantic, interesting and attractive, but either had a shorter existence, or they did not produce as many models: people like Brough Superior or Vincent. They get a slightly shorter entry. Shorter still are the entries for those manufacturers who either made a few technically interesting but still reasonably mainstream models – people like Scott or Hesketh – or who made a broad range of rather less riveting bikes, such as CZ or Francis-Barnett. Then there are those who warrant only a page or half a page, either because they are long gone or because their machines were frankly unexciting or simply strange: the clutchless, five-cylinder radial-engined Megola is perhaps the perfect example of the bizarre. Finally, there are around 2000 manufacturers who really only warrant a few words, and these are described in the columns that run throughout the book on the right-hand pages.

We also have to make a confession: this book is not comprehensive. It cannot be. We have listed more manufacturers than anyone else, but we know that our lists are not complete.

TECHNICAL AND OTHER DATA

You may also feel that we could have treated the technical data differently. Once again, you are right. The trouble is that although some things are readily verifiable – you can generally tell how many cylinders a motorcycle has, for example – there are others that are at best disputable, and at worst, the subject of intended deception by the manufacturers. Disputable figures include things like weight and top speed. Is the weight quoted with a full tank and a tool kit, or without? The difference could easily be 15 to 20kg (30 to 50lb). And where one reviewer ran 210kph (130mph) through a radar gun, another might trust the speedo and say that he had seen 221kph (137mph).

For fairly obvious reasons, we have not weighed each bike ourselves, or actually measured its top speed or power ouput, so the figures we have used have been taken from a wide variety of sources; they should be treated as a good guide, rather than as eternal scientific verities.

Yet another area in

Edward Butler patented his Petrol Cycle in 1884 and was thus the first man to build a vehicle fitted with an internal combustion engine.

which confusion rules is dating. Typically, a company might be formed one year; show its first machine at one of the big shows the year after; start actually delivering machines later in the same year, or even another year on; and then go under a few years later. For obvious reasons, going out of business is rarely given the same publicity as starting up, and besides, production may be sporadic for years afterwards. In some cases, too, a long-established firm might start making motorcycles many decades after it was originally founded: for example, the manufacturers of the Sunbeam, Marston Ltd, started business in 1790. The dates we have given are generally a 'best view'.

A sub-division of this problem is when the same name is used repeatedly. The new company may or may not claim legitimate descent from the original, but if there has been a complete change of management, premises and models, we have counted them as a new company: Indian and Henderson-Excelsior are good examples. With Hesketh, on the other hand, where much the same machine has been made in much the same premises by much the same people, we have disregarded the actual question of whether the company behind the bikes was Hesketh, Hesleydon or Broom Engineering.

MOTORCYCLE DESIGN

A single-track vehicle is inherently unstable: it has to keep moving if it is not to fall over. Even when it is moving, is is not hard to turn it aside from its intended path. An overly high centre of gravity will increase the risk of its tipping over; too small tyres will not grip the road adequately.

Big tyres are more comfortable, and provide a bigger contact patch, but are more susceptible to being deflected by hitting a stone or road-stud on one side. Suspension is vastly more comfortable than a rigid frame, and helps keep the wheels in contact with the road, but unless it is well done, it can allow the wheel to twist.

A bigger, heavier bike is more comfortable in a straight line or on poor roads, but a smaller, lighter bike is more responsive. More power is more fun – this should never be neglected – but power-to-weight ratios may well be better influenced by reducing weight than by increasing power.

As speed increases, the instability of the bike increases: this is to a considerable extent the result of the self-centring tendency of a pneumatic tyre, coupled with the gyroscopic effect of the revolving wheel, though frame design is also important. Rake and trail make steering easier and safer in small quantities, but too much of either can make the bike unresponsive.

There may also be a conflict between assembly and reparability – or even simple maintenance. The sequence of operations that makes sense when you are assembling something in a factory may be a disaster when you come to work on the machine: a classic example was the old Volkswagen Beetle, where you had to remove the engine to change the spark plugs. All this, too, must be considered.

Then there is durability. Some manufacturers build machines that will last practically forever. Others have rust-prone steelwork, electrics that fry, and Nickasil bores that last a long time but cannot be repaired, but only replaced, when they finally do wear out. Old designs tend to be less efficient and produce less brake horsepower than new, but are more comprehensible. The whole business is an endless series of trade-offs, and different riders (and different manufacturers) prefer different compromises.

The Brough Superior was built in England between the two World Wars and was the finest marque of its era; it is still a legend today.

PREHISTORY: BEFORE 1901

The very earliest motorcycles were steam driven, and the oldest that survives – indeed, the first of which clear and unequivocal evidence exists – is a French Michaux 'boneshaker' of 1869 with a Perreaux steam engine mounted slightly alarmingly under the saddle; in the United States, S.H. Roper made something similar, a little later. Another American, L.D. Copeland of Philadelphia, made a steam bicycle (and about 200 steam tricycles) beginning in 1884. One of the few steam machines to enjoy any commercial success was the 1894 Dalifol, French again, with a single-cylinder double-acting side-valve engine.

Famously, Gottlieb Daimler built the first motorcycle to have an internal combustion engine in 1886. Edward Butler's 1884 patent antedated Daimler's (1885), and in 1887 he built a motor-tricycle which was eventually broken up for scrap in 1896.

The first commercially successful petrol-engined motorcycle appears to have been the Hildebrand and Wolfmuller of 1892. The Holden, patented in 1896 was actually built from 1899 to 1902.

The Werner, built in Paris from 1896 had a 217cc De Dion Bouton-type engine, with hot-tube ignition, mounted on the steering head of the bicycle frame, with belt drive to the front wheel: their first design had had the engine over the rear wheel, driving it via a chain and friction roller, but this was not satisfactory. Although the Werner was popular and successful, its high centre of gravity and narrow tyres made it vulnerable to what was, at the time, often referred to as 'the dreaded side-slip'. If it did fall over, the fuel usually spilled, and the hot-tube often set fire to the fuel, resulting in an expensive conflagration.

Hot Tubes and Electric Ignition

A hot-tube ignition is exactly what its name suggests. The tube is heated by an external burner, and protrudes into the cylinder. The fuel-air mixture, already heated by compression, is ignited by the hot tube. The system is adequate only for low engine speeds and very modest compression ratios.

Ruhmkorff coil-and-battery systems were known as early as 1860, and Butler in 1887 used an electrostatic friction generator. After 1895 the choice was between the battery-coil-contact breaker system devised by De Dion Bouton and the magneto: initially the Simms-Bosch low-tension version, then in 1902 the Bosch refinement of the Boudeville high-tension magneto of 1898.

Suzuki, founded in 1952, is now one of the giants of the motorcycle world. This T20 Super Six was the company's first true sports bike.

Werners were so successful, in fact, that they were made under license or simply copied. Even so, there were plenty who preferred clip-on cyclemotors, which motorised an ordinary bicycle. Many were fitted on the front down-tube, just in front of the pedalling bracket or inside the frame. The centre of gravity was much lower than on the Werner, making the dreaded side-slip less likely; and it was this that prompted the New Werner.

BIRTH OF AN INDUSTRY: 1901–15
The New Werner of 1901 is often held up, with good reason, as the first modern motorcycle. The engine is in the right place; it is integrated with the frame; and the whole thing is recognisably the ancestor of the kind of thing we ride today. Of course it had no clutch, and only a single gear, but this would soon be remedied.

A noteworthy feature was the spray carburettor, which sprayed fuel into a venturi in the inlet tract. This was much more predictable than the surface-vapouriser or wick-type systems used in many early machines, where the air was drawn over a small lake of fuel, or past a wick saturated with it, in order to create the fuel-air mixture. By 1903, carburettors of various kinds had supplanted surface vapourisers almost completely.

Drive was still direct and clutchless, but very shortly Phelon and Moore introduced first a countershaft, and then a two-speed clutch gear in 1905. The chain-driven countershaft of 1901 allowed a much bigger countershaft pulley, greatly reducing the risk of slip if the final drive was by belt, though P&M used all-chain drive.

Valve Operation
The earliest engines mostly featured a mechanically operated exhaust valve and an 'automatic' or 'atmospheric' inlet valve, which was sucked open against a weak spring. Although this was adequate for slow-revving engines, mechanically operated inlet valves were needed for higher speeds. These were normally side-valves, though some were overhead valves operated by push-rods: a typical layout, which survived for many decades, was an overhead inlet valve and side exhaust valve, or ioe - 'inlet over exhaust'. Automatic valves had pretty much died out by 1910, though at first, mechanically operated inlet valves were sometimes offered as an extra-cost option.

Very soon the perennial motorcyclists' demand for extra power came to the fore, and this was achieved in a number of ways. Engines ran faster, delivering more power strokes per minute. They were made bigger, delivering more power per stroke, and compression ratios were increased, delivering more power for a given swept volume. Overhead valves allowed more efficient combustion for more power per stroke, and faster filling and emptying of the cylinders, for higher engine speeds. And more cylinders were added.

Extra cylinders had more to offer than mere power. They improved reliability: if one cylinder on a V-twin failed, the other would get you home. They smoothed out the power delivery: instead of one power stroke every two revolutions (in a four-stroke), you could have one per revolution from a twin, and two per revolution from a four. Not only did this make for a smoother engine: it also reduced transmission loading, by providing a larger number of smaller power strokes for a given output, and it allowed higher engine speeds because of better balance and smaller individual reciprocating masses.

The V-twin was the classic choice, because it fitted so neatly into the frame. V-twins were made in a huge variety of sizes including such monsters as the 90-degree V-twin 16bhp JAP of 1908, which was 'square' at 120mm bore and stroke for a massive 2714cc.

Honda revolutionised two-wheeled transport with the C50 Super Cub. It was cheap, reliable and has become the best-selling machine of all time.

The legendary Harley-Davidsons are the epitome of the _Easy Rider_ lifestyle. No other motorcycle or manufacturer arouses such a fanatical following.

A few parallel twins were made (including the 3¼hp Werner of 1905) but this layout would not become really popular for another 30 years or more; the flat-twin, normally mounted in-line with the frame rather than transversely, was much more popular. Douglas was famous for this layout, which offered perfect primary balance. There were also a few fours, the shaft-drive 363cc FN of 1905 being one of the best known. By 1908, Scott offered a two-speed foot-operated gearbox, a clutch, liquid-cooling, a kick-start and telescopic forks – which sounds very modern!

In other words, well before World War I, most of the components of the modern motorcycle were known, and by the eve of the war, they had often been combined to very good effect.

REFINEMENT: 1915–29
At the front lines in World War I, an environment where reliability might literally be a matter of life and death, the most successful and reliable ideas – clutches, gearboxes, kick-starts, high-tension magneto ignition – were rapidly adopted by almost everyone. Fundamental redesigns were rather less widespread, though both Harley-Davidson and Indian made significant changes during the war itself.

When peace came in 1918, much had been learned about motor vehicles and as a result, in the early 1920s, more and more machines featured all-chain drive and three-speed or even four-speed gearboxes, with kick-starts, and the positive-stop foot change was introduced by Velocette in 1925: over the next ten years or so they became standard on all but the most primitive machines.

Increasingly, the Americans joined those who produced the primitive machines, because the motorcycle was being sidelined by the rise of the motorcar. In the first ten or 20 years of the century, Americans had often been at the forefront of motorcycle design, but by the late 1920s their machines were looking increasingly dated.

Singles remained the bread-and-butter of most manufacturers, though fast, powerful new V-twins such as the Brough Superior (1921) were introduced, and big side-valve V-twins were used for heavy side-car haulage. BMW introduced their famous transverse flat-twins in 1923, with more than a nod to the ABC built in Britain by Sopwith from 1918 to 1921. Fours were very thin on the ground, except in the United States, where people needed big heavy machines for long distance riding and could afford them.

HOLDING ON: 1929–49
Throughout the depression years, there was more room at the top of the motorcycle industry than at the bottom. Millions were out of work, but the middle class was far less affected, and among those rare buyers, the well-to-do middle-class riders, there was still a steady demand for Brough Superiors and other 'gentleman's motorcycles'.

This, presumably, was what explained such novel designs as the 597cc Ariel Square Four of 1929 and the Matchless Silver Arrow (400cc) and Silver Hawk (593cc). However, even BMW, whom we now regard as luxury manufacturers, had to cut back. The pressed-steel Star frames, introduced in 1929, looked somewhat utilitarian and would probably have been replaced rather sooner if there had been more money about.

However, there was also a great deal of investment in racing, partly as a matter of national pride and partly as a matter of escapism: the rider on his fifth-hand side-valve plugger could still relate vicariously to racing victories by his bike's manufacturer and his country.

Apart from the supercharged BMWs, both for racing and for record-breaking, perhaps the most interesting racing innovations came from Italy. One was the 499cc Moto-Guzzi 120-degree V-twin, which won the Senior TT in 1935 at 136.6kph (84.68mph), and the other was the transverse-four Gilera 494cc, which covered over 195km (121miles) in

The BSA Rocket 3 was built in 1968, a time when the British motorcycle industry was dominant. Its subsequent decline was swift and painful.

one hour in 1938. Had it not been for World War II, the transverse four might have triumphed a good deal earlier.

The mass market, however, relied on much less exciting machinery. In the early 1930s, ultra-light two-strokes were popular, and after about 1936 there was even the retrograde step of the autocycle, with no gears, but with pedals to make up the deficiency.

Among conventional four-strokes, singles ruled at first, but detachable heads were increasingly commonplace, as were overhead valves and even overhead cams, though side valves were still popular where simplicity and torque were at more of a premium than horsepower. By a process of endless refinement, singles were made to deliver impressive power outputs: the 500cc 'cammy' Nortons delivered 48bhp at 6500rpm in 1939 using low octane fuel and a compression ratio of 7.5:1.

Among twins, the V-formation remained popular at the larger end of the market, either in sporting guise – a 1000cc JAP-engined Brough Superior set a world speed record of just under 274kph (170mph) in 1937 – or, with side valves, as a tradesman's slogger for pulling a sidecar, such as the 1140cc Royal Enfield. BMW continued to refine the flat-twin, and even Douglas began to play

with the transverse layout with the Endeavour, but the parallel-twin also started to give some indication of the success that it would enjoy in years to come Triumph's 1937 Speed Twin was the one that is best remembered.

During this period, the positive-stop foot change became all but universal, except in America and four-speed boxes, often of unit construction, became the standard. Brakes continued to improve, though rigid rear ends were still popular in the interest of economy, weight and handling.

Ducati's beautiful 996R was an evolution of the 916 model, considered by many to be the best superbike of the 1990s.

GOLDEN YEARS FOR GREAT BRITAIN: 1949–69

After World War II, Europe was exhausted and getting back on its feet. The United States was much better off, but here motorcycles were treated much more as fun vehicles than as transport, which meant that the market was proportionately much smaller.

In Great Britain, it took some years for even the major manufacturers to get into their stride again. The break-point came in 1949 with the introduction of important new bikes from Norton and Triumph: the Dominator 500, Norton's first parallel-twin; and Triumph's Thunderbird 650.

The best singles of this seemingly golden age were hypertrophied, one-dimensional machines like the 'cammy' Norton, the BSA DBD34 Goldie and the Velocettes; the parallel-twins were so good when they were introduced that they survived with only modest (though constant) improvement.

In continental Europe, the emphasis was initially on the cheapest possible forms of transport, and an enlightened attitude to mopeds – no test or insurance was required for low-powered vehicles – established a two-wheeled culture that endures to this day. Despite the fact that the Italians soon returned to building fast singles and multis, and although a number of continental manufacturers (such as BMW) continued to develop increasingly outdated basic designs, the real reason why Britain was able to maintain such a commanding position for so long was lack of competition.

When it came to mass transport, the Italians with their low-cost, fully enclosed scooters (the Vespa and the Lambretta) were rather more in touch with the market, and of course the Japanese were taking high-speed, technically advanced engines to unheard of heights. They just weren't selling many outside Japan – yet.

SUPERBIKES AND AFTER: 1969 ONWARDS

Honda's CB750 F1 provides the break-point for our last era. The transverse four would become so ubiquitous in the ranks of powerful motorcycles that it would for a while be known as the UJM, the Universal Japanese Motorcycle. The first big, powerful, mass-produced modern four, it looks surprisingly modest today, delivering a mere 67bhp at 8000rpm. Modest, that is, until you considered the opposition.

The British parallel twins were close to the limit of their development, American V-twins were huge expensive tractors, Italian machines had similar charms to British motorcycles, but many of them cost a fortune or were hopelessly unreliable or both. One of the few really new designs was the stroke series BMWs, but they had to overcome two decades of perception as slow, dull bikes.

The CB750 galvanised the market: Vincent performance (or better) at an astonishingly affordable price. True, the handling of the Japanese bikes was still suspect, but it became a mark of manliness to pretend to have mastered such brutes as Kawasaki's truly terrifying 498cc H1 Mach III (1969), or its 748cc derivative, or the 82bhp Z1 transverse four (1972). Those who actually knew how to ride fast generally preferred a little less power and a little more road-holding.

In parallel with this intense race for more horsepower, Honda (above all) had been waging an advertising campaign to make motorcycles more socially acceptable with their slogan, 'You meet the nicest people on a Honda'. This was not the image that people had, for example, of Harley-Davidson or Nortons or Triumphs.

And, on top of all this, prosperity was rising in much of the world. Although this meant that motorcycles-as-transport was on the wane, it also meant that motorcycles-as-recreation was on the rise.

These three factors – superbikes, the 'nicest people' campaign and prosperity – combined to give us the modern era of very fast, very reliable motorcycles, along with the ever-growing phenomenon of the 'born-again biker', the middle-aged, usually male, rider who goes back to motorcycles after a gap of two or even three decades, with the money to indulge himself.

Power (and prices) at the top of the market soared. Exotic layouts proliferated, even for production motorcycles: transverse sixes from Benelli, Honda and Kawasaki, flat-fours and V-fours (Honda again), in-line fours (BMW), four-stroke triples (BSA, Triumph and Laverda), even flat-sixes (Honda yet again). The one-litre class, long forgotten outside the United States, became once again a standard capacity, and then was enlarged to 1100, 1200, even 1500cc. For a while, there was a voluntary 100bhp limit, but as it was seldom observed, it was soon forgotten. Top speeds became meaningless: quite apart from speed limits, it is very hard to find anywhere that you can ride at the wrong side of 240kph (150mph) for long. But there were good results from all this excess.

These arose principally from an overall improvement of the perception of both motorcycling and its practice: motorcycles are now more socially acceptable than they have ever been. Motorcycle registrations are up; more motorcycles are being sold; there are even new marques coming into production, especially in America. We are arguably at the beginning of a new golden age of motorcycling: these are the good old days.

Putting a roof on a motorcycle is not a new idea, but the individualistic styling of BMW's 125cc C1 scooter made it a very modern urban two-wheeler.

ABC

THE ALL BRITISH (ENGINE) CO was founded close to Brooklands race track in Weybridge, Surrey, England. Initially, the company built engines for planes (aero engines), before moving on to motorcycles in 1912. Granville Bradshaw, who became associated with many other projects over the years, was the main designer, and he was persuaded to produce some special parts for Les Bailey to fit to his 350cc Douglas. The parts included cylinders, overhead-valve gear, pistons and connecting rods, the result running at Brooklands late in the year to set a new kilometre record for the class at over 116kph (72mph).

At the same time, ABC announced a new 494cc, flat-twin, overhead-valve engine, mounted in line with the frame. Both cylinders were directly in line with each other, as well. To achieve this layout, one piston used a normal connecting rod but the other had two rods which spanned the first. This meant the crankshaft had three big end crankpins. There was

A line drawing of the famous ABC twin that began with high hopes thanks to its advanced specification, but failed mainly because of its high costs.

an outside flywheel and gear drive up to the camshaft and on to the magneto, while ball and roller bearings were used for both crankshaft and camshaft.

By 1913, a few ABC machines had been built and two started the Senior TT race but retired, as did other bikes using the ABC engine. Better publicity came in early 1914 when Jack Emerson set new 500cc records at Brooklands using an ABC and shortly afterwards the company introduced a two-model

The Bradshaw-designed Skootamota was one of many post-WWI scooters and better than most with larger wheels and more practical layout.

range, the TT and the Touring. The flat-twin engine was used in both bikes, but the TT version used overhead-valve while the Touring had an overhead exhaust and side inlet. Transmission was all-chain with a three-speed Armstrong gearbox that was actually their hub

gear as normally fitted to the rear wheel but used by ABC as a countershaft box. The frame was conventional but both wheels were sprung using laminated leaf springs, a feature that Bradshaw used on other designs in later years.

Before the outbreak of the World War I, the firm moved to Walton-on-Thames, Surrey, where war work meant production was mainly limited to making engines for the services. However, the company still found the time to make a few motorcycles, and between 1915 and 1916 these machines were fitted with the ABC four-speed gate-change gearbox and spring frame. At the time, these were sophisticated models.

In 1919, the definitive ABC bike appeared, although built by another company, Sopwith Aviation, who were based at Kingston-on-Thames, Surrey. Again designed by Bradshaw, it had an overhead-valve 398cc flat-twin engine set transversely across the frame and built in unit with the four-speed, gate-change gearbox. The engine was light and modern with a short stroke much less than the bore of the turned steel cylinders on which fitted the cast-iron heads with exposed rockers. Inside the crankcase went a one-piece crankshaft with the connecting rods threaded into place before the roller bearings were fitted and then retained. The rods supported short light-alloy

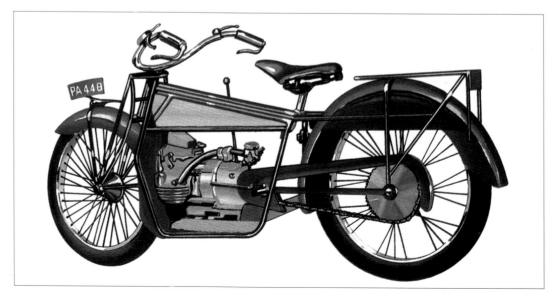

pistons and the gear-driven magneto sat on top of the crankcase. The mixture was supplied from a single carburettor with the manifold warmed by the exhaust.

The engine drove back to the gearbox with a bevel box behind that turned the drive for the chain to the rear wheel. The engine went into a duplex frame spread wide enough to form crash bars. These bars supported legshields which ran down to the footboards. The front wheel was suspended by girders with a leaf spring while the rear wheel moved through pivoted forks with twin leaf springs. Much of this design was revolutionary and orders poured in. However, production problems, such as the troublesome valve gear, delayed its appearance on the market, and it proved expensive to make.

Meanwhile, ABC also produced the Skootamota, one of several scooters to appear just after World War I, and one of the best. Again designed by Bradshaw, it had a simple tubular frame with no suspension and 40.6cm (16-in) wire wheels with external-contracting band brakes for each. The engine sat above the rear wheel and was derived from a war-time flat-twin, reduced to a 124cc single with the cylinder

pointing aft and the magneto clamped to the front of the crankcase in place of the forward cylinder. At first it had an exhaust-over-inlet valve layout but in late 1920 this was changed to overhead-valve, while transmission was by chain to the rear wheel. The fuel tank sat over the engine; a saddle was fixed to a pillar at the front of the engine so the rider was not forced to stand while in motion. Introduced by ABC, it was built and marketed by Gilbert Campling of Albermarle Street, London, until 1923.

While the Skootamota sold well during the brief scooter boom,

This is a 1919 version of the ABC twin with its flat-twin engine, unit gearbox, four speeds and leaf-spring suspension front and rear.

Sopwith were in trouble and by 1921 had gone into liquidation after making about 3000 machines. The demise of Sopwith eventually spelled the end for ABC as well, who stopped production in 1923.

However, the ABC twin engine lived on, since it was built under licence by the French Gnome & Rhone firm in the early 1920s, who produced an improved 494cc version as well as the 398cc model, until 1925.

ABC TWIN
1920

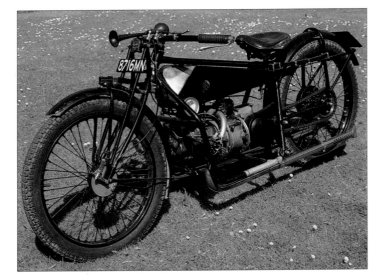

Although the pre-war ABC had a flat-twin engine, it lay along the frame. After World War I, the company proposed to build something which was far more advanced, but kept to the horizontally-opposed engine, with its

inherent good balance and minimal vibration.

To this was added overhead-valves on a short-stroke engine built in unit with the four-speed gearbox. Only in its chain final drive did it lack a feature due to

Little was altered for this 1920 ABC twin with its wide-spaced duplex frame tubes, drum brakes for both wheels but chain, rather than shaft, drive.

appear on the BMW to come in 1923, but it did have rear suspension, something the German firm would not adopt until 1938.

The aim was to build a two-wheeled car; the frame tubes were spread apart to act as crash bars and carry legshields under the footboards. The smooth running made it too easy for it to run too fast, often shedding the pushrods.

The ABC Twin worked well if looked after, but handling could be difficult and it was costly to buy.

Engine: 398cc ohv flat twin, 68.5x54mm, air-cooled
Power: n/a
Gearbox: unit 4-speed hand change
Final drive: chain
Weight: 110kg (243lb)
Top speed: 100kph (60mph)

ABAKO
Germany (Nurnberg) 1923–25: This was a manufacturer of 129cc single-cylinder machines with their own two-stroke engines, Sturmey Archer gearboxes and chain drive.

ABBOTSFORD
England 1919–21: Single-cylinder scooter with two-stroke engine and chain drive.

ABC
England (Birmingham) 1920–24: This assembler used Villiers two-stroke engines, at first 296, and then 247cc.

ABC
Germany 1922–25: Lightweights with their own 149cc two-stroke single.

ABENDSONNE
Germany 1933–34: This assembler used two 98cc Villiers two-stroke singles coupled together.

ABERDALE
England 1947–59: This was a manufacturer of Lightweight/ Autocycles with 98 and 123cc Villiers and Sachs two-stroke engines. It was taken over by Bown in 1959.

ABE-STAR
Japan 1951–59: Maker of two overhead-valve four-stroke singles, originally 338 then 148cc.

ABIGNENTE
Italy 1926: Maker of 345cc two-stroke motor; manufactured in very limited numbers.

ABINGDON
England 1903–33: The original Abingdons had proprietary engines (Fafnir, Kerry, Minerva, MMC) but later the company used its own singles and V-twins. Also known as AKD, Abingdon King Dick, after 1925.

ABJ
England 1949–54: A.B. Jackson made unremarkable lightweights, initially 98 and later 49 and 123cc, which where all powered by Villiers two-stroke singles. They also produced an auxiliary cycle-motor from 1952 onwards.

ABRA
Italy 1923–27: This manufacturer used 149cc DKW single; it later switched to using its own 132cc single.

ACE

ACE WAS FOUNDED IN Philadelphia in late 1919 and only ever built one type of machine: an in-line four. The creation of William Henderson, who had started building similar machines under his own name in 1912, the bike reflected his wish to produce light-weight machines. The new Ace would be agile and graceful, out-performing his older, heavier models.

Detail of the 1924 Ace Four showing the leading-link front forks, typical of the era in the USA. Also visible are levers for clutch and gearchange.

The basic design remained the same as Henderson's old machines, though, with the in-line engine built in unit with a three-speed gearbox where the drive turned for the final drive chain. The engine had a capacity of 1220cc and was of the F-head type with overhead inlet and side exhaust valves operated by the gear-driven camshaft on the right side. The crankcase was split horizontally with three main bearings for the crankshaft, while lubrication was by both splash and pump. A single carburettor went at the rear of the inlet manifold and ignition was by a gear-driven magneto on the left.

A multi-plate clutch took the power to the hand-change gearbox and the whole assembly went into a tubular frame with typical American leading-link forks. As was common practice in the USA at the time, there was only one brake, on the rear wheel, since it was believed that the dirt roads outside towns made a front brake a hazard to use. The bike was painted dark blue.

The machine was soon in production and in the public eye when Cannonball Baker set a new record for the Los Angeles to New York run in 1922. Sadly, the year ended in tragedy when William Henderson was killed while road testing. Arthur Lemon was hired to replace him and further developed the Ace, whose smooth running, power and stable handling made it a strong seller.

In late 1923, the Ace became famous after setting a new speed record. Using a slimmer, lighter and more powerful machine than the normal production model, the bike was timed at over 208kph (129mph), 171kph (106mph) with a sidecar. Among the changes were drilled pistons, connecting rods and timing gears as well as a much narrower fuel tank and tucked-in controls. Although the record was not recognised internationally, the Ace was a very special and very fast motorcycle.

Despite this success, the firm ran into financial trouble and

The Ace Four built by William Henderson in the form of his earlier machines with the in-line engine in unit with the gearbox. This is a 1924 model.

production stopped, as a result of these problems, at the end of 1924. The company restarted twice and even moved location. However, in 1927 it was bought by Indian which continued to build the Ace until 1928 when its own four replaced it.

ADLER

ORIGINALLY ESTABLISHED BY Heinrich Kleyer as Adler Fahrad-werke AG in 1886 to manufacture bicycles, the company began to supplement this business with typewriter production in 1895 and the company name was changed to Adler Werke. Four years later, in 1900, Adler (Eagle) joined the ranks of the automobile pioneers when its first car was manufac-tured, and then in 1902, it tried its hand at motorcycles.

Based in Frankfurt, Adler's first models used French De Dion engines, but the company soon developed its own single-cylinder and V-twin engines. However, its powered two-wheel division did not achieve enough profile and

An early Adler (eagle) single cylinder four-stroke dating from 1906. As with several of the bikes produced at the time, final drive was by belt rather than chain.

from the end of 1907 until the late 1940s, Adler concentrated on pedal cycles, cars and typewriters.

Adler's first new motorcycle design for over four decades arrived in 1950. It took the shape of the M100, and was the work of Hermann Friedrich, Adler's managing director and chief engineer. This was a simple 98cc (50x50mm) two-stroke single-cylinder commuter bike, which was primarily created to help fill the void which existed for anyone needing basic personal transport in post-war Germany.

Obviously the humble M100 was never intended as a performance machine, its top speed being 71kph (44mph), but its ride was well up to the standards of any rival, with a good level of comfort, thanks to a sturdy twin-tube frame and both front and rear suspension. The front was sprung by a peculiar combination of a leading link and blade design employing an internal coil spring, while plungers were used at the rear of the machine.

In 1951 three larger brothers joined the M100: the M125/150 singles and the M200 twin, although the latter appeared late in the year. The 89kph (55mph) M125 (123.5cc, 54x54mm) used a frame of similar design to the 100, whereas the M150 (147cc, 59x54mm) shared its cycle parts with the M200 twin. At the top of the range came the latter bike. In those days small capacity twins were still quite rare and these machines therefore attracted widespread attention. The M200 was an important model for Adler

Introduced at the end of 1953, the NB201 was powered by a 199cc (65x60mm) two-stroke single engine. The machine also had plunger rear suspension.

as it was to lead directly to its most famous series, the M250, from which such companies as Ariel in England and Yamaha in Japan were to take inspiration for the future.

On both the M150 and M200 the suspension system was similar to the smaller models, but more substantial, and used bottom links with a clock-type spring. Not only did the two machines share the same basic frame, forks, suspension (still plunger), 41cm (16ins) wheels and full-width aluminium brake hubs, but the cost-saving modular design policy also went further, including much of the tinware and smaller components. Even the new four-speed gear cluster was shared between the two. Performance

figures were not vastly different at 95kph and 100kph (59mph and 63mph) although the twin had more acceleration, despite being considerably heavier due to its more complex engine.

The new M250 arrived in 1952. It was to become Adler's top seller. All Adler's postwar engines shared an unusual transmission arrangement. The twins employed an engine-speed clutch mounted on the crankshaft outside the primary drive which was by helical gears. But the 98 and 123cc models used an even more unusual configuration. In these models, the engine was mounted off to the right (offside) of the bike with the clutch and the gearbox in line with it to the left. Drive to the rear wheel was taken from a sprocket adjacent to the clutch between the engine and gearbox and concentric with the crankshaft. This particular set-up was an arrangement unique to Adler.

Adler's performance in sporting events was to prove how reliable they were, with truly impresive results in 24-hour endurance racing, the ISDT (International Six-Days Trial) and 100 per cent finishes in many cases, and events such as the Luttich-Monaco-Luttich Rally, where the marque gained much glory. Continuous development saw new front forks on the 150, 200 and 250cc models and a sports version of the larger twin, the MB250S.

Adler was aquired by electrical giants Grundig in 1958; motorcycle production ceased later that year.

Built in the 1960s, this Adler Special featured improvements to the standard machine such as a water-cooled engine, Dell'Orto carbs and Ducati front forks.

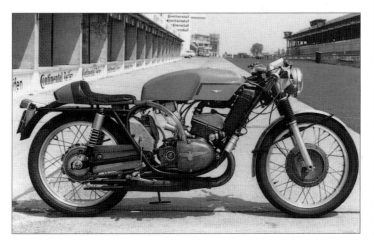

ACCOSSATO
Italy (Moncalieri near Turin) 1973–unknown: This company made limited-production, small-capacity motocross enduro single-cylinder two-strokes with high performance. Models included the CE 80 (1985), producing 21bhp at 12,000rpm from a water-cooled engine.

ACHER
France 1926: This firm was the manufacturer of a 500cc water-cooled two-stroke twin engine.

ACHILLES
Austro-Hungary, later Czechoslovakia (Ober-Politz a.d. Nordbahn) 1906–12: This company made four-stroke singles and V-twins with engines from Fafnir and Zeus.

ACHILLES
Germany 1953–57: The founder of the Austro-Hungarian Achilles, above, moved to Germany after WWII. The new firm began with two-strokes using 147 and 174cc Sachs engines, then made a 48cc two-stroke single.

ACMA
France (Fourchambault) 1948–62: Built Vespa scooters under licence, with 123, 147 and 173cc motors.

ACME
England 1902–22: Until 1918, this firm used bought-in Minerva engines. Following on from this, they built their own 348cc singles and 997cc V-twins. Merged with Rex in 1922.

ACS
France 1980: This was a builder of racing machines, beginning with a 999cc four-stroke triple which delivered 150bhp at 11,000rpm, with the engine a stressed frame member.

ACSA
Italy (Bologna) 1954: A moped with 75cc engine: this was a total commercial failure.

ADLER M250

1952

Adler's first twin of the modern era was the M200 (192cc, 48x54mm) of 1951, which led the marque's most famous model, the M250, launched in 1952. At the M250's heart was a 247cc (54x54mm) piston-port two-stroke parallel twin. In original form this produced 16bhp at 5590rpm with 5.75:1 compression pistons. Externally it differed from the 200, with larger 180mm (7ins) drum brakes and minor details such as silencers and equipment levels. All Adler twins employed an engine-speed clutch mounted on the crankshaft, outside the primary drive which was by helical gears.

The M250, which sported plunger rear suspension and leading-link forks with 'clock' springs, began to make a name for itself in competition events. An M250 won the Warsage 24-hour race for production machines, beating all the 350ccs. In the ISDT

Launched in 1952, the 247cc M250 twin cylinder two-stroke was a trend setting design, and became a successful competition machine.

that same year, four Adler twins started; all four finished (three Golds, one Bronze). The year after, it was five Golds.

In October 1953 the Frankfurt Show saw a customised M250 with fully-enclosed bodywork by Freiss, and the MB250S, a sports version with 18bhp and several changes, such as hi-level exhausts.

The standard model code also changed from M to MB250. For a high performance two-stroke twin, its fuel consumption was high, an average 4 litres/100km (70 mpg).

By the mid-1950s Adler was offering two over-the-counter dirt bikes. Powered by the famous MB250 engine, one was a copy of the factory's ISDT mounts; the other a full-blown motocrosser with 20bhp.

Engine: 247.3cc 2s parallel twin, 54x54mm, air-cooled
Power: 16bhp at 5590rpm
Gearbox: 4-speed foot change
Final drive: chain
Weight: 140kg (283lb)
Top speed: 114kph (71mph)

ADLER RS250

1954

Besides its excellent M/MB250 series of roadster twins, Adler has built limited numbers of competition models: dirt bikes for long distance trials such as the ISDT, a full-blown motocrosser and RS (Renn Sport) racing models in both air- and water-cooled form.

The turbine-smooth 247.3cc (54x54mm) Adler engine was first raced with home-tuned models by Walter Vogel, Hubert Luttenberger and the Kramer brothers. However, the Nurnberg rider Hans Hallmeier was first to use a race-kitted M250

The air-cooled RS (Renn Sport) racing model was based on the M/MB250 roadster. The machine was eventually available in either water- or liquid-cooled guises.

twin, in 1953 at Hannover's Eilenriede Rennen. NSU's world champion, Werner Haas, won the event, but the Adler's speed and acceleration commanded all the press attention. As a result, Adler built a batch of over-the-counter racing models for private sale, based on the standard M250

roadster. The prototype debuted at the Dieburg circuit in 1954 with Herbert Luttenburger. Besides its specially tuned and brake-tested engine (24bhp), most interesting new features were by Jan Friedrich Drkosch: the frame, of lightweight steel tubing; and the suspension, with a swinging-arm with pivoted fork at the rear and two hydraulically-damped leading-link forks up front.

The RS engine was largely the work of Kurt Grosman. He spent a

considerable amount of effort on the gas-flow, experimenting with varying lengths of inlet and exhaust track and expansion chambers. The carburettors were specially imported British Amals. The 1954 RS250 was capable of 193kph (120mph). This was an excellent performance for what was, after all, a production-based engine.

Engine: 247.3cc 2s parallel twin, 54x54mm, air-cooled (some later engines water-cooled)
Power: 24bhp at 7800rpm
Gearbox: 4-speed foot change
Final drive: chain
Weight: 102kg (115lb)
Top speed: 103kph (120mph)

Englishman Richard Williats racing his RS250 at Castle Coombe, April 1963. The bike was powered by a production-based engine.

AERMACCHI

ITALY 1950–78

A 1963 250 Ala Verde being ridden
a the Vandvoort citcuit by
Dutchman Jaap de Jong.

VARESE, A SMALL PROVINCIAL
TOWN only a few kilometres from
the Swiss border, has been a centre
for the Italian aircraft industry
since 1912, when the company of
Nieuport-Macchi was founded
there by Giulio Macchi. I
Nieuport-Macchi grew quickly
during World War I, and continued
– albeit under the fresh title of
Aeronautica Macchi (soon
abbreviated to Aermacchi) – to
concentrate on aircraft in the years
that followed.

At the time, the Varese firm
became one of the major
participants in the legendary
Schneider Trophy series of
seaplane races, and had the
distinction of setting a new world
speed record of 708kph (440mph)
with the MC72 seaplane in 1934.

Unable to resume its aviation
activities after hostilities had
ceased, Aermacchi decided to
begin production of a three-wheel
truck. This was followed by a
decision to join the motorcycle
boom which swept Italy during the
late 1940s. The company realised
that to achieve its aim of

producing an attractive, quality
lightweight, they needed the
services of an established designer.
Their choice was Lino Tonti, who
had been at Benelli and had also
worked on aircraft engines during
the war.

Tonti's first design was an
unorthodox open-frame
lightweight with a 123cc
(52x58mm) two-stroke engine of
full unit construction. The engine

**Ridden by Massimo Pasolini, this
75cc Aermacchi broke several
world speed records in April 1956
Several manufacturers battled for
glory in this type of machine.**

pivoted in unit with the rear
suspension. It sold in reasonable
numbers and also enjoyed some
success in long-distance trials,
such as ISDT. Other models
followed, and in 1955 Tonti

ADER
France 1901–06: Manufacturer best
known for a long-stroke transverse-
mounted V-twin delivering 4bhp;
also made a single with half the
power.

ADM
Spain 1987–: Builds small capacity
two-stroke models, including road
racing machines up to 125cc.

ADONIS
France (Neuilly-s-Seine) 1949–52:
This company made scooters and
mopeds of 48 and 75cc with VAP
engines.

ADRIA
Germany 1912–29: Began with an
auxiliary cycle-motor but in around
1921, introduced a 276cc single-
gear machine, followed in 1923 by
a 282cc three-speed. All had belt
drive.

ADS
Belgium 1949–54: This firm
assembled 98cc autocycles with
Sachs and Ilo two-stroke single
engines.

ADVANCE
England (Northampton) 1906–12:
A range of singles and V-twins
made by Smart and Gainsforth
fiited with engines of their own
manufacture.

AEL
England (Birmingham) 1919–24:
This company was a typical small
assembler – actually a motorcycle
dealer – making motorcycles from
147 to 348cc with Blackburne, JAP
and Villiers proprietary engines.

AEOLUS
England (London) 1903–05: Short-
lived shaft-drive machine with
492cc four-stroke single-cylinder
engine of their own manufacture.

AEOLUS
England (Birmingham) 1914–16:
This company made machines
fitted with their own single-
cylinder two-stroke of 269cc. They
went on to make the Bown.

created a pair of fully streamlined record breakers, powered by a 48 and 74cc engine, both of which featured chain-driven overhead camshafts. Several world records were broken by both machines. Soon after, however, Tonti left Aermacchi and joined FB Mondial.

Alfredo Bianchi was hired to replace Tonti, having previously worked with Alfa Romeo and Parilla; Bianchi had also manufactured his own Astoria engines and complete machines in the 1930s.

His first task was to design a new production model, the Chimera, ready for the Milan Show in late 1956. The machine formed the basis for a whole generation of Aermacchi motorcycles over the next decade and a half, with its pushrod-operated valves and horizontal single cylinder.

A feature of the Chimera was its various panels which enclosed much of the mechanical components. When first displayed at Milan, the Chimera was a 175, but before long, a 246.2cc (66x72mm) version was introduced. The enclosure styling exercise, although futuristic, didn't prove a sales success, resulting in the undressed 'naked' version

being offered. In 1958, a tuned 175 was raced in Italy, before a full racing version, the Ala d'Oro (Golden Wing), was constructed in 1959. Producing some 20bhp, it was good for 161kph (100mph) and became the main rival of the Morini Settebello in national, junior category racing.

A 250 racing version appeared the following year, making its first

An Aermacchi hallmark, the overhead valve horizontal cylinder and head; this example is from an Ala Verde.

appearance at the 1960 Dutch TT, ridden by Alberto Pagani. Impressed with the prototypes display of speed, the management – now jointly owned by the Italians and the American Harley-Davidson company – decided to produce a small batch of replicas for sale to private customers for the 1961 season. In addition, Pagani had been joined by Gilberto Milani as an official works development rider to contest Italian national and selected Grand Prix events.

There were a total of eight road production models in the 1960 model range. These were the Chimera 175 and 250, the Ala Bianca 175, the Ala Azzura 250 (all four were touring bikes), the Ala Rossa 175 and Ala Verde (sportsters) and finally, the Zeffiro 125 and 150 (large-wheel scooters). The top performing machine was the Ala Verde, which the company claimed to be capable of 138kph (86mph) with full road equipment and a standard Silentium silencer.

The remainder of the early 1960s saw a huge increase in production, with the majority of the bikes exported to the USA. Meanwhile, the racing Ala d'Oro models (joined by a 350 after

A 350 Aermacchi Ala d'Oro in action during a classic racing event during the 1990s.

1963) were slowly improved after major reliability problems occurred during 1962.

Although the pushrod flat-single Aermacchi never won a Grand Prix, the type did form an important link between the demise of the traditional heavyweight British single-cylinder racer such as the Norton, AJS and Matchless, and the advent of the high performance, modern two-strokes of the 1970s.

Before Aermacchi themselves made the switch to two-strokes, its overhead-valve racing singles were progressively increased in size between 1968 and 1971, from 382 to 402cc.

The first of the Varese factory's new range of two-strokes arrived in 1967, in the shape of the M125 Rapido roadster. A racing version, with the engine specially developed by the German engineer, Peter Durr, made its race debut in July that year.

Aermacchi's racing two-strokes grew from this version. The first time the world was introduced to a brand new twin-cylinder model was when factory rider Renzo

Pasolini displayed the prototype at the Modena Autodrome, in Febuary 1971.

This newcomer was, however, not the work of Bianchi or Durr, but their successor as chief engineer, William Soncini. He had first begun work in 1969, when the American Harley-Davidson management suggested they needed a 250cc racer to compete with the new TD2 Yamaha.

From 1972 until closure in 1978, Aermacchi traded under the AMF Harley-Davidson name.

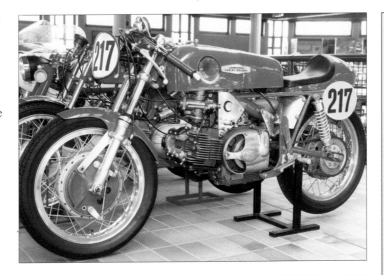

The Ala d'Oro was built in a range of engine sizes from 246 to 402cc.

AERMACCHI CHIMERA   1956

Engine: 172cc ohv horizontal flat single, 60x61mm, air-cooled.
Power: 13bhp at 7000rpm
Gearbox: 4-speed foot change
Final drive: chain
Weight: 122kg (269lb)
Top speed: 110kph (68mph)

Replacing Lino Tonti as chief designer in early 1956, Alfredo Bianchi's first task was to produce a factory machine.

The Chimera (dream) was the star of the 1956 Milan Show with its ultra-modern appearance, but its early promise was never realised

and it was to prove a major sales flop. However, faced with a costly failure in the showroom, Bianchi undressed the bike to create some of Italy's best known sports and racing machines, such as the Ala Verde and Ala d'Oro. Without the Chimera this could not have happened and the machine went on to become a pivotal model in Aermacchi's history.

The use of both steel and aluminium enclosure panelling was a distinct feature of the Chimera, as was the ease with which these various body panels

could be removed. Another notable feature was the near-horizontal single rear shock absorber, although this was not used on the subsequent sports and racing models.

In spite of its ultra-modern appearance, the Chimera's panelling hid a fairly conventional piece of engineering. The 172.4cc (60x61mm) overhead-valve engine featured a horizontal cylinder,

The Chimera (dream) was the star of the 1956 Milan Show, but sales never matched expectations.

AER
England 1931–50: The earliest bikes from A.E. Reynolds were Scott-based specials, but from 1938 to 1940 the AER was a distinct make with 180 degrees, two-stroke parallel twins of 246 and 346cc. It is unclear whether production resumed after World War II, or whether the company went back to specials.

AEROPLAN
Germany (Kohlfurt) 1922–25: This company made somewhat crude two-strokes with DKW engines of 125 and 175cc

AEROS
Czechoslovakia (Kaaden, Bohemia) 1927–29: Assembler of machines with four-stroke 348 and 498cc overhead-valve Kuchen engines, and 250cc Bekamo two-strokes.

AEROSCOOT
France 1953–54: This company made scooters with proprietary 98cc motors.

AETOS
Italy (Turin) 1912–14: This company was a manufacturer of a 492cc V-twin capable of delivering 3¹/₂bhp.

AFW
Germany (Brake, Westphalia) 1923–25: The grandly-named Allgemeinen Fahrzeugwerk assembled 246cc four-stroke singles using Hansa engines.

AGF
France 1948–56: Made lightweights and scooters powered by Ydral engines of 123 and 173cc.

AGL
France 1950: A 250cc racing four-stroke single built by Monsieur A. (presumably G.) Loupia

AGON
Germany (Augsburg) 1924–28: Assembler using a wide range of single-cylinder and twin-cylinder engines, including Bradshaw, Kuchen, JAP and Paque from 172 to 996cc.

AGRATI
Italy 1958–61: This moped manufacturer became better known after its merger with Garelli.

roller bearing big-end, coil ignition, wet sump lubrication, multi-plate clutch, gear primary drive and a four-speed gearbox. Running on a 7:1 compression ratio, maximum power was 13bhp, giving a top speed of more than 105kph (65mph). Although many Italian designers thought overhead camshafts absolutely imperative, Bianchi gave the Chimera pushrod-operated valves, for simpler maintenance and because he believed that overhead-valve layout was not really needed for his machines. For the next 15 years, his overhead-valve horizontal Aermacchi single was as fast as the more complex and expensive machines.

AERMACCHI 125 ALA D'ORO
1968

Although Aermacchi made its name with overhead-valve horizontal single-cylinder road and racing bikes, it also built a considerable number of two-strokes.

One of the most successful was a racer derived from the 1967 M125 Rapido street bike, which featured a tuned version of the

Aermacchi also built two-strokes; one of the most successful was the lightweight 125 Ala d'Oro racer of 1968–70.

same 123cc (56x50mm) piston-ported engine designed by the German engineer, Peter Durr. The original racing prototype

developed 20bhp, exactly double that of its roadster brother.

Intensive testing at Monza in Italy in June 1967 proved that the prototype – still with a four-speed gearbox – lapped faster than the best private Hondas or Bultacos. This led to an early race debut the following month, on the recently-opened Zingonia circuit near Bergamo. Alberto Pagani finished third behind a pair of purpose-built factory bikes, but well ahead of not only the Honda and Bultaco production racers, but also the Motobi and Morini entries.

For the following year, the bike was considerably modified and sported a specially-commissioned double-cradle tubular frame, new cylinder head and barrel, and a new five-speed transmission. The 125 Aermacchi, renamed Ala d'Oro (Golden Wing) after the factory's four-stroke racers, was even more competitive, with power output up to 22bhp.

The company also experimented with an overdrive system (similar to the 1962 Kreidler 50cc racer), featuring no less than 10 gear ratios, five operated by pedal and five by twist grip.

In 1969, the 125 Ala d'Oro produced some excellent results at the highest competitive level, with riders such as Kel Carruthers, Johnny Dodds, Eugenio Lazzarini and Silvano Bertarelli all scoring world championship points. It even won a Grand Prix (something the horizontal single never did) when Dodds rode brilliantly in appalling weather conditions to win the 1970 West German race at the fearsome Nürburgring circuit.

Engine: 123cc piston-port 2s single, 56x50mm, air-cooled
Power: 22bhp at 8000rpm
Gearbox: 5-speed foot change
Final Drive: chain
Weight: 80kg (176lb)
Top Speed: 201kph (125mph)

AERMACCHI 350TV
1971

Engine: 344cc overhead-valve horizontal single, 74x80mm air-cooled
Power: 29bhp at 7500rpm
Gearbox: 5-speed foot change
Final drive: chain
Weight: 140kg (309lb)
Top speed: 160kph (99mph)

The 350 TV, which appeared in 1971, was the definitive Aermacchi overhead-valve horizontal single sports roadster. Even though it was not the last of its type, it was certainly the best. The full Harley-Davidson takeover of Aermacchi the following year spelt the end of the lightweight sports bike, since the American owners favoured the much heavier touring machine, the 350SS, and its trial bike brother, the SX.

There is no doubt that the TV benefited from Aermacchi's involvement in racing, which directly led to the development many of the machine's features. These included hairline steering and super-efficient braking, Ceriani suspension, a five-speed

gearbox and dry clutch, as well as the 344cc (74x80mm) engine itself. Running on a compression ratio of 9:1, it produced 29bhp at 7500rpm. Carburation was taken care of by a Dell'Orto square slide

VHB 30A instrument, with an open polished bellmouth in the best Italian sporting tradition. Other specifications included 6volt electrics (actually the bike's biggest failing), a 60W alternator,

The 350TV, which debuted in 1971, was the definitive Aermacchi overhead valve sports roadster. The machine featured developments derived from Aermacchi's racing programme.

a 14-tooth gearbox sprocket, a 32-tooth rear wheel sprocket, a single exhaust header pipe at the cylinder head branching in two (complete with a pair of Lafranconi mufflers), right-hand (offside) foot change, 'Ace' type one-piece handlebars, matching Veglia instruments and a choice of orange, green or blue paintwork

for the tank, side panels and mudguards.

Out on the road, the 350 TV was a pure Italian lightweight sportsbike, with its graceful lines, slick gear change, full-width drum brakes (a two-leading shoe at the front) aluminium wheel rims, curvaceous tank and racing style saddle. The traditional Aermacchi

'open' frame allowed the rider to make full use of the power, whilst visually the frame allowed a clear view of the neat, compact unit-construction engine.

Mainly sold in Continental Europe, production ceased at the end of 1972 following Harley-Davidson's involvement with Aermacchi.

AERO CAPRONI

ITALY 1947–64

AERO CAPRONI HAD ITS ORIGINS in a group of manufacturing of companies founded in 1908 by Count Gianni Caproni. During the inter-war years, the Caproni group became one of Italy's largest industrial complexes, manufacturing aircraft and cars as well as aero, industrial and marine engines.

After World War II, the Italian motorcycle boom prompted Caproni into manufacturing machines of his own, which also provided a convenient way of converting his factories' wartime output back to peacetime manufacturing. One of these factories was a former aircraft plant in Trento, north-east Italy which was renamed Aeromore SpA. Its products, motorcycles and some three-wheeled light trucks

were marketed under the brand name Capriolo.

The factory's first bike was a 73cc (47x43mm) face-cam design which had the crankshaft running in line with the frame. The bike also used full unit construction, a four-speed gearbox and a pressed-steel, square-section frame.

The machine proved highly successful and led not only to a whole family of Trento-built models, but was also the inspiration for another old Caproni group factory, Caproni-Vizzola, to begin motorcycle production. This company manufactured under its original name, but bought in engines, mainly from NSU in Germany, before ending production in 1959.

At the Trento plant, the Capriolo trademark face-cam engine was

Built by Aero Caproni and sold under the Caprioli brand name, this 125 deluxe used a trademark face-cam engine, which became the basis for a range of lightweights.

further developed and was the basis for a whole new range of sporting lightweights using 98 and 124cc engines. The company also made a 149cc horizontally-opposed twin with shaft final drive, which made its debut at the 1953 Milan Show.

Capriolos also did well in off-road sport, notably the ISDT, in which the Trento marque often provided the Italian squad with bikes.

After declining domestic sales, Aeromore's export drive was also unsuccessful, and their Trento factory was closed in 1964.

AIGLON

LOCATED IN ARGENTEUIL, Seine-et-Oise, Aiglon was one of the earliest French firms to adopt the new Werner layout. As well as producing bicycles, the company also made cars and motorcycles, making use of, and developing, the new internal combustion engine. Their first motorcycle was typical of the period and used a bicycle frame and forks, belt drive, pedalling gear and inadequate brakes. Early machines used a 2hp Mirus engine and other models followed in the years up to World War I, boasting improvements such as a clutch, gears, chain drive to the transmission, proper suspension for the front wheel and

drum brakes. In 1922, Peugeot bought the firm and moved production to Mandeure, Doubs. The company made a range of

models under the Aiglon name, from small two-strokes to large four-strokes.

France had pioneered powered transport on two, three and four

Although badged as an Aiglon, this machine was really a Peugeot from the early-1920s. Re-badging bikes was a habit the firm followed for many years.

wheels and dominated the early use of the combustion engine. As other countries caught up in the 1920s, the French were forced to consolidate and concentrate on their home market. Nevertheless, they continued to build unique motorcycles up to and after World War II. Because of Peugeot's backing, the Aiglon badge was able to survive until 1954, by which time the industry was dominated by a few large firms.

AJS & MATCHLESS

ENGLAND

AJS 1910–67, 1967–73, 1987–
MATCHLESS 1899–1969, 1987–93

THESE TWO MARQUES ARE combined here because, although they began as separate firms, they joined for some years to become AMC, then ended the collaboration, but later both individually had a revival. From the middle of the 1930s right up to the end of the 1960s the two gradually merged, finally only distinguished by badges and colour. However, in

their final days, they were again quite diverse.

This was in the distant future when Joe Stevens and four of his sons went into powered transport at the end of 1900, and then spent the following decade supplying engines to other firms from their Wolverhampton factory. It was not until 1910 that the first AJS made its debut, using the initials of the

elder brother, Albert John. The machine was conventional with a 292cc side-valve engine and either direct belt or two-speeds and chain drive. Enlarged to 315cc for 1912, it was joined by a 631cc V-twin that sold well for sidecar work. Capacities increased and the transmissions improved, their commercial success aided by some achievement in competition. This

was highlighted in the 1914 Junior TT where their light, well-prepared machines were first and second, with two more placed in the first six.

Demand for AJS models increased, but during World War I the range was reduced to just the twin for service use. It continued post-war and in 1920 the firm went back to the Junior TT with new overhead-valve engines. With six entries they started favourite, but five had retired by half distance, while fortunately the last kept going to win by a large margin despite having to push for the last few miles. They did even better at the 1921 TT where their improved machines took the first four places in the Junior, and one of them went on to win the Senior. In 1922 the Junior TT fell to them once again but for the rest of the decade they came second and third.

A 349cc overhead-valve road model finally became part of their range for 1923 at the time when the sporting models had gained the name 'Big Port'. That year also saw the firm branch out into the production of the wireless, using the facilities of the sidecar workshop to produce receiving

During the WWI, the V-twin AJS played its part, usually hauling a sidecar in a variety of forms, including this machine gun and precariously-positioned gunner.

The Matchless Silver Arrow had a narrow-angle, V-twin engine, front and rear suspension but limited performance so only sold slowly between 1930 to 1933.

sets up to 1928. The singles, in 350 and 500cc capacities with side or overhead-valves, ran on with the V-twin that had stretched to 799cc. This took them up to 1927 when their activities extended to producing bodies for the Clyno Nine car, while the racing engines were replaced by new overhead-camshaft units. Built in 349 and 499cc sizes, these had the camshaft driven by chain with a Weller tensioner, the drive enclosed by an aluminium case that also ran forward to the magneto. The machines had four-speed gearboxes but otherwise kept to AJS practice, soon showing that they had potential but needed development.

The camshaft models appeared in the 1928 range which included a 249cc side-valve model for the other end of the market; the first AJS of that capacity. It was during 1928 that they built an experimental in-line, overhead-valve four, which was not taken any further. Early 1929 saw the end of Clyno and the body contract, so AJS turned to making commercial vehicle chassis and in 1930 added the AJS Nine car.

Meanwhile, the motorcycles adopted saddle tanks and the V-twin went up to 998cc. The range contracted for 1930 but did include a 249cc overhead-valve model while some had the engines inclined as was the fashion. Finally, they had a further TT win in the 1930 Lightweight. By 1931 the firm was struggling and the range was extended to interest a different kind of customer. Among the models was a new type with a transverse side-valve 498cc V-twin engine, three speeds, duplex frame and chain drive. Smooth and quiet, it failed to appeal.

During 1931 the firm's financial troubles came to a head and AJS

was wound up and creditors paid in full. It was the end in Wolverhampton, but not for the AJS name or the Stevens family. The name was bought by Matchless, who moved production to their Plumstead works in South London, and became amalgamated with one of the oldest firms in the industry.

Matchless was one of the most important British firms. It had been founded by brothers Harry

The famous initials of Albert John Stevens that graced AJS tanks for so many years. The company has been in existence since 1910 in a variety of different forms.

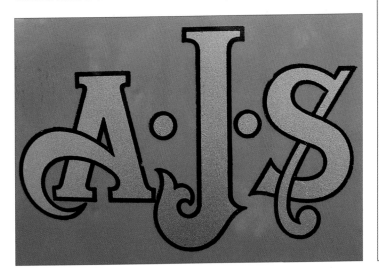

25

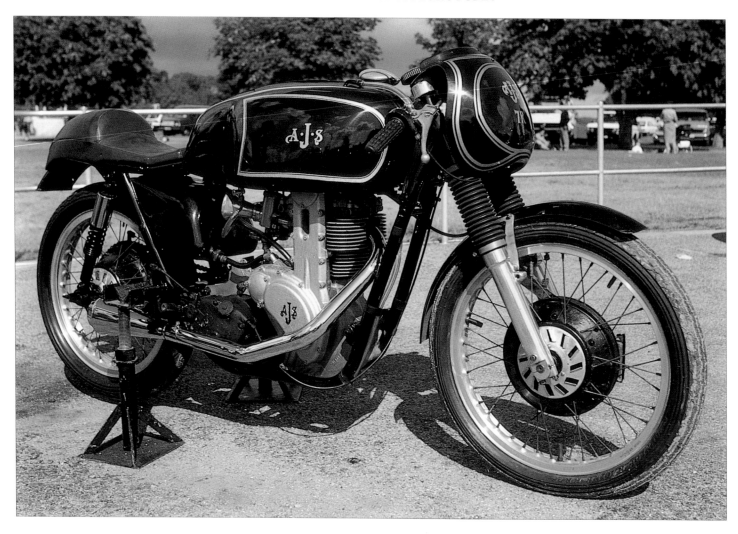

and Charlie Collier, beginning with bicycles and adding power in 1899 with the engine mounted above the front wheel. After further experiments they went into production using a two-and-three-quarters horsepower MMC engine hung from the frame downtube in the fashionable style. Both brothers ran successfully in early competitions and by the mid-1910s were using engines from Antoine, JAP and White & Poppe, as well as offering models with rear suspension.

The brothers were both in the British team for the 1906 International Cup Race that led to the first TT race in 1907, which Charlie won. He was second in 1908, Harry won in 1909 and Charlie again in 1910, giving the firm three of the first four TT races, but in later years they came second and third.

The Matchless range improved and expanded, using various engines, gradually moving to producing a majority of, and then exclusively, V-twins with JAP or

MAG power. This continued during World War I. Following the war, customers had the choice of the two engine makes, rigid frame or rear suspension, with three speeds and chain drive. Both solos and sidecar forms were listed but the latter was the more usual.

A single joined the range in 1923 with a 348cc Blackburne engine and there was an interest in a light touring car with a flat-twin engine but few were built. The next year brought a 350cc overhead-camshaft model, with its vertical drive shaft positioned behind the cylinder, and a 591cc overhead-valve single fitted with a Matchless engine. In 1925 a Matchless V-twin engine replaced the JAP and MAG and other singles were added. This range ran on to the end of the decade.

There was innovation for 1930 in the form of the Silver Arrow designed as a quiet, smooth tourer with a 394cc in-line, side-valve, narrow-angle V-twin engine. It had enclosed valve gear, the oil tank fixed to the front of the crankcase,

three speeds and rear suspension, but lacked performance. The Arrow was followed in 1931 by something more exciting when the firm launched the Silver Hawk with a 592cc narrow-angle V-four engine with overhead-camshafts driven by shaft. It too had a spring frame and was listed for several years, despite the Depression.

The combined AJS and Matchless range took a year or two to settle down and a move to use Matchless engines for most models began in 1933 with their V-twin engines fitted to the AJS. Real collaboration started during 1935 when Matchless introduced their G3 model, which would remain for many years in two or three sizes and with both marque badges. The G3 had a 348cc overhead-valve engine set vertically in its rigid frame to drive a four-speed Burman gearbox with chain final drive. The chain-driven magneto went behind the cylinder with the dynamo underneath it with its chain drive taken from the

The AJS 7R had the pre-WWII chain-driven, overhead camshaft form, but was otherwise all-new and an excellent road racer.

crankshaft. Both electric items came from Lucas, and an Amal carburettor supplied the mixture.

Later in 1935 the G3 was joined by the AJS model 16 that was distinguished from it by its magneto which was positioned ahead of the cylinder. For the next year they were joined by 245 and 497cc versions, listed as G2 and G80 for Matchless and models 12 and 18 for AJS. This format, with sports and competition variants, gradually took over the single-cylinder range with a couple of side-valve versions plus the big V-twins for sidecar work. During this period the Matchless V-twin was also used by other firms, including Morgan cars.

In 1936 AJS introduced an exciting model intended for both road and racing work, using a 495cc V-four engine, initially air-, later water-cooled, form for racing.

AJS and Matchless followed the trend to the vertical twin in 1949 and in time stretched the original 498cc to 646cc and offered it in this off-road G12CS form around 1960.

In 1939 the factory turned over to wartime production to build the G3. In 1941 this became the G3L with the addition of telescopic front forks, which resulted in a light machine that proved better than most at service duties.

After World War II the firm built AJS and Matchless machines at Plumstead in the same format with little to tell one from the other. For some years the magneto position was the main variation, but even that went in time. The firm kept marque loyalty high by

running separate competition teams.

The postwar range comprised two singles for each marque. These were the 348cc model 16M and 497cc model 18 AJS, and the same size G3L and G80 Matchless. All models were based on the pre-war and wartime Matchless with the overhead-valve engine set vertical in the frame, four speeds, foot-change, telescopic forks and rigid frame. Differences amounted to the forward magneto mounting on the AJS and rear for the Matchless, the inscription on the timing cover, tank badges and the colour of the tank lining, with gold for AJS and silver for Matchless to relieve the general black.

Early in 1946 a small batch of competition models appeared with the letter C added to the model code. Changes were minimal with a 54cm (21ins) front wheel, alloy mudguards and suitable tyres. At that time production was everything, so few changes were made to the listed models for a year or two. But AJS was active on the road-racing front and both marques took part in off-road racing events.

AJS were back on the racing scene in 1947 with a 497cc twin

The AMC road single in 348 and 497cc capacities had its origins in pre-war days but by 1955 this AJS 16MS had gained rear suspension and telescopic forks.

ALFA-GNOM
Austria (Wiener Neustadt) 1926–28: Sports racer with 598cc single-cylinder engine; made by Franz and Anton Rumpler, the same firm built the FAR.

ALGE
Germany 1923–31: Motorenfabrik Alfred Geissler built a 173cc two-stroke and four-strokes of 200, 250, 350 and 498cc Also used Blackburne and Villiers engines.

ALIPRANDI
Italy (Milan) 1925–30: Used proprietary 175 and 350cc engines from Moser, JAP and Sturmey-Archer.

ALLDAYS/ALLDAYS ONIONS
England (Birmingham) 190–15: After starting with De Dion Bouton-engined three-wheelers in 1898, this firm entered the two-wheeler market in 1903 with the Matchless (no relation) using their own engine. Renamed Allon in 1915.

ALLEGRO
Switzerland (Neuchatel) 1925–27 and late 1940s to early 1950s: The early series were Villiers-engined two-strokes of 147, 175, 247 and 350cc, and MAG or Sturmey-Archer four-strokes of 250 and 350cc The post-war machines were mopeds and lightweights of 50 to 200cc.

ALLELUIA
France 1920s and 1950s: In the 1920s, this firm made 175cc lightweights. In the 1950s, used other manufacturers' mopeds, re-badged.

ALLON
England 1915–24: The successors to Alldays, Allon built big V-twins (798 and 988cc), good-size singles (499 and 539cc) and a 292cc two-stroke.

ALLSTATE
Austria 1953–63. These were Steyr-Puch scooters and mopeds labelled 'Allstate' for Sears, Roebuck in the United States.

that became known as the Porcupine thanks to its extensive fins. The Porcupine had a chequered race history, but it all came good in 1949 when Les Graham won the 500cc world title. It was only ever a works machine, but in 1948 was joined by a postwar version of the pre-war camshaft model, the 348cc 7R soon known as the Boy Racer, and this was a works and private owner model.

For the 7R the firm retained the chain-driven, single overhead-camshaft engine but moved the magneto behind the cylinder to give it a new line. It was well made and the fully-enclosed valve gear enabled it to keep its oil inside. For the rest, it had a four-speed gearbox, telescopic front forks, pivoted-fork rear suspension and conical hubs with large drum brakes. On the grand prix circuit there were a few successes, including the 1954 Junior TT won by Rod Coleman with a

special three-valve version, but the 7R won plenty of races in private hands.

The road range increased in 1949 with the addition of models with pivoted-fork rear suspension

This G80 Matchless single engine retained much of the early line although the magneto had moved ahead of the cylinder, copying the AJS which always had it in front.

and identified by a letter S in the code. Both sizes and makes were involved to produce the AJS 16MS and 18S plus the Matchless G3LS and G80S. It was also the year when AMC joined the trend to vertical twins with the 498cc AJS 20 and Matchless G9. The engines were in the British style except for having a third, central main bearing, while the cycle side was mainly like the springer singles. The main marque variations were the dualseat and megaphone silencers that went only on the Matchless.

In 1950 the competition models had an all-alloy top half for the engines and springer versions were added the next year as the 16MCS, 18CS, G3LCS and G80CS. Aimed more at scrambles than trials, these springers had fatter, AMC-made rear units that were called 'jampots', the earlier, slimmer ones being known as 'candlesticks'.

This set the range for some years with few real changes, although the Matchless magneto finally moved ahead of the cylinder in 1952. In that year the Porcupine had its cylinders inclined at 45 degrees to become the E95 and the works 7R had an engine with three valves that became known as the 'triple-knocker'. Of more lasting effect was the takeover of the Norton firm by AMC later in the year, although they remained in

Birmingham for a decade. In 1953 the Matchless line added the G45 twin that was a pure racing model comprising a tuned G9 engine slotted into the 7R cycle parts.

For 1956 the whole road range was amended: all the rigid models were dropped, the trials models were in 348cc only and had their own frame, and the scrambles had a short-stroke, all-alloy engine. There was a new frame and cycle parts for the singles and twins with the addition of a 593cc twin offering more power and listed as the model 30 and G11. Further versions of these were added in 1958 combining tuned engines and the scrambles frame to get the street scrambler 30CS and G11CS. By adding the standard fuel tank to these models the firm then had the desirable 30CSR and G11CSR models that were soon known as 'Coffee Shop Racer' machines. That same year also brought alternator electrics to the road models.

For the 1958 road racer there was the machine they had always wanted: the Matchless G50. This was simply the 7R stretched out to 496cc and no one understood why it had taken so long for it to arrive. Less exciting that year was the arrival of the models 14 and G2; 248cc overhead-valve singles that had the illusory appearance of unit construction and lightweight tag. For 1959 more CS versions came plus a 646cc twin in three forms.

An AJS supercharged V-twin racer from 1933. By this time the company had been taken over by Matchless.

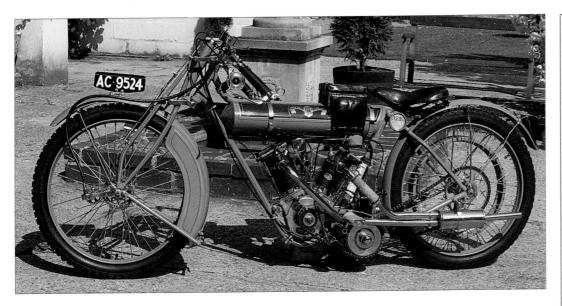

There were new duplex frames for the 1960 road models, along with a 348cc version of the lightweight, coded 8 and G5, with taller engines and better front forks. Changes then became fewer as sales dropped, but a sports version of the 248cc model was added for 1961 when the 646cc CS twin was dropped.

For 1962 the road 350 had its engine revised, while a 248cc CSR was added during the year. The 500 twin was dropped along with the de luxe 650, but there were two Matchless models for the USA. One was the G15/45 with a 750cc twin engine installed in what were mainly CSR cycle parts with some standard ones. The other was the G50CSR, built using a CSR frame and G50 engine with a dynamo clamped to it to enable lights to be fitted.

Late in 1962, AMC moved Norton production to Plumstead which would have a great effect on later developments. The range was thinned for 1963, when the 7R and G50 ceased to be built, and again for 1964 when the road models

were fitted with Norton forks and hubs. In 1965 it saw the addition of 745cc twins: the 33 and G15 in standard and CSR forms, but with the Norton Atlas engine; only the frame and tank were AMC parts.

The AMC days were approaching their end owing to the firm's financial trouble. The year 1966 was their last in their old form, after which the bulk of the range was dropped. There had been one new model for 1966 – the Matchless G85CS scrambler with duplex frame – and this ran until 1969. The standard and CSR models of the AJS 33 ran to 1967 under new ownership, while the Matchless G15 was joined by a CS version and continued to 1969. Production then ceased and the old factory was demolished but neither name vanished.

The AJS name was revived late in 1967 by Norton Villiers for a couple of two-stroke competition machines powered by the 247cc Villiers Starmaker engine. Neither really got off the ground, but for 1969 the scrambler became the Y4 Stormer and was joined by the

A Matchless machine from 1913. This motorcycle raced in the Isle of Man TT that year, and was powered by a 496cc V-twin Swiss MAG-Motosacoche engine.

37A-T trials model of 246cc. Only the Stormer continued for 1970, in various styles and forms.

With the creation of NVT in 1973 the small firm was sold on to Fluff Brown who created the FB-AJS range that ran up to 1981. In 1987, under the name AJS, they returned to building complete machines, effectively the AJS Stormer models, in 247, 368 and 400cc sizes, as before.

Meanwhile, the Matchless name also returned to the market under Les Harris, who built the Triumph Bonneville. He added a single; listed as the G80, it used a 494cc overhead-cam four-valve Austrian Rotax engine, British frame, with Italian forks, front disc brake, rear units, exhaust system and carburettor. Despite the classic image, sales were slow and between 1990 and 1993, it was supplied to special order only.

ALLWYN
India 1972–88: A Lambretta by any other name, 125 to 200cc.

ALMA
France 1949–59. This firm began in 1949 with lightweight 125 and 175cc two-strokes and later went on to make mopeds, lightweights and scooters with (from 1953) Sachs motors.

ALMIDI
Belgium c.1950s: Moped made in the same place that made the bodywork for Dyna-Panhard.

ALMORA
Germany 1924–25: Julius Lowy-designed lightweights with two-stroke engines of 113, 138 and 176cc that could (in theory) be switched to diesel oil once warm.

ALP
England 1912–17: This firm built Moto-Reve machines under licence, as well as a variety of other motors: 199cc four-stroke, 348cc two-stroke and twins (including V-twins) of various sizes.

ALPA PICQUENOT
France c.1956: Two mopeds/autocycles, 49 and 80cc, with two-speed transmission.

ALPHA CENTURI
England c.1967: This company made racing two-stroke parallel twins of 250cc, reputedly capable of 190kph (118mph).

ALPHONSE THOMANN
France 1908–23: This firm made two-stroke autocycles of 98 to 173cc.

ALTA
Wales 1968–71: This Welsh company made motocross and trials bikes powered by Suzuki two-stroke singles, with capacities from 49 to 130cc.

ALTEA
Italy (Milan) 1939–41: Fixed-head 196cc four-stroke unit-construction single capable of 75kph (47mph).

AJS BIG PORT   1923

The name 'Big Port' appeared in 1922 when Tom Sheard won the Junior TT on an overhead-valve model with an exhaust pipe larger than usual. 'Big Port' was not a works name, but was coined by enthusiasts of the road model.

It was always a model in the best vintage style that performed better on the road than it seems it should have done. It looked fragile but was simply light in weight

which enhanced its performance. The flat tank layout made it slim and so easy to flick round bends while the modest power combined with the lack of weight gave it good acceleration. This would keep it with or ahead of the crowd as it simply maintained its speed without effort. In towns, it would potter with the ignition retarded; once out on the road it was up and away before the rest knew it had

gone. The Big Port was only built for a few years, but put the seal on the 349cc AJS reputation as one of the finest of vintage machines.

Engine: 348cc ohv vertical single, 74x81mm, air-cooled
Power: n/a
Gearbox: 3-speed hand change
Final drive: chain
Weight: 95kg (210lb)
Top speed: 135kph (80mph)

AJS S3 V-TWIN

1931

The notion that a quiet, smooth motorcycle would sell well was tried in good and bad times by many firms, and both AJS and Matchless followed this route in the early 1930s. It seldom worked, for it was not what motorcycling was about, except for the high-volume market that had to wait for the moped and scooterette to arrive.

AJS chose to use a 498cc side-valve transverse V-twin engine. For easy access and servicing, the valves were outside the cylinders, so there were two chain-driven camshafts with the points driven from one of them. The crankshaft drove a shaft running back to the clutch and then to the bevel gears that drove the three-speed gearbox, final drive being by chain.

The cycle parts were conventional, but the cradle-frame twin downtubes splayed out to suit the engine type and meet the lower tubes that supported it. Girder forks, wire wheels, drum brakes and a saddle tank with an instrument panel completed the machine. It was a good effort as a design, but it was the wrong time for a luxury tourer. The model was

only listed for the one year, being dropped after the move to Plumstead.

Engine: 498cc sv transverse V-twin, 65x75mm, air-cooled
Power: n/a
Gearbox: 3-speed, hand change
Final drive: chain
Weight: 150kg (330lb)
Top speed: 110kph (65mph)

AJS PORCUPINE

1947–54

Engine: 497.5cc dohc horizontal parallel twin, 68x68.5mm, air-cooled
Power: 54bhp
Gearbox: 4-speed foot change
Final drive: chain
Weight: 140kg (310lb)
Top speed: 210kph (130mph)

The Porcupine was always a works racer, never intended for private use, and was designed during the war as a supercharged twin with the cylinders laid flat to the

ground. With air-cooling and unit construction, it made for a compact assembly with its lightweight mounted low down, well tucked in, along the lines much used by Moto Guzzi. As blowers were banned postwar, the cylinder head had to be revised to take twin carburettors, but otherwise the design remained unchanged.

The 497cc engine had twin gear-driven overhead camshafts and gear drives to the magneto and oil

pump. It had a one-piece crankshaft with centre main bearing and many fine internal details, but the most noticeable external feature was the spiky head fins from which it got its name. The four-speed gearbox was gear driven with chain final drive and the whole unit went into a tubular cradle frame.

The Porcupine never quite fulfilled its promise, although it won the first 500cc world

championship in 1949 with Les Graham. Then came the featherbed Norton and Geoff Duke to dominate. For 1951 the Porcupine lost its spikes. In 1952, the engine was inclined and the model named the E95. It went on until 1954.

Postwar, AJS went road racing with the Porcupine twin, which took its name from the spiky fins of the early engines. Successful in 1949, it was later much revised.

AJS Model 18

1959

The AJS versions of the G3 series of singles always had its magneto in front of the engine in postwar years with Matchless copying this for 1952. Otherwise, the two were very similar except for badges and colours. Both moved on to alternator electrics for 1958 which brought in a cast-alloy primary chaincase, in place of the old pressed-steel type with its sealing problems, while the points went into the timing chest.

After 1958 the engine of the 18 was to have only one more major change which was to go to bore and stroke for 1964, but the cycle side moved on for 1960 with a new frame with duplex downtubes. By 1964 all the road singles were fitted with Norton Roadholder forks and Norton hubs which stayed to the end. The model 18 was accompanied by the 348cc model 16. Both were solid and reliable, excellent for daily transport and weekend trips, using a minimum of petrol, handling well and having good brakes.

Engine: 497cc ohv vertical single, 82.5x93mm, air-cooled
Power: n/a
Gearbox: 4-speed foot change
Final drive: chain
Weight: 179kg (394lb)
Top speed: 140kph (85mph)

While road models lost the magneto by 1960, the off-road versions such as this 18CS kept it, and also the different carburettor with open bell-mouth.

Matchless Silver Hawk

1931–35

While the Silver Arrow was a placid tourer, the Silver Hawk, built as a sports model, was an entirely different matter. It was launched at Olympia, late in

The engine unit of the Matchless Silver Hawk with its overhead camshaft, V-four engine, impressive right-side line and distinctive 'M' tank logo.

1930, at the same time as the Ariel Square Four and, unfortunately, at the height of the Depression. In essence the 592cc Hawk engine was a pair of Arrows, but in place of the side-valve twin there was a narrow-angle V-four with an overhead camshaft driven by shaft and bevels on the right: a most impressive sight. The single carburettor on the left looked less impressive, while the two exhaust pipes ran down on the right-hand side. A dynamo and coil ignition distributor were skew-gear driven from the camshaft vertical shaft and the oil tank for the dry-sump lubrication system was bolted to the front of the crankcase.

The four-speed gearbox was driven by a duplex chain with Weller tensioner and therefore ran at a fixed centre, while the final drive was by chain. Both engine and gearbox went into a Matchless spring frame with girder forks, wire wheels and 20.5cm (8ins) drum brakes. Fully equipped, the

Despite the hard times, there were two new overhead camshaft fours at the 1930 motorcycle show, one the Silver Hawk with a narrow-angle V-engine.

Silver Hawk looked the part but was too expensive for the Depression years. In 1934 the engine was used by OEC for one of their models, and in 1935, Silver Hawk production ceased.

Engine: 592cc ohc in-line V-four, 50.8x73mm, air-cooled
Power: n/a
Gearbox: 4-speed hand change
Final drive: chain
Weight: 170kg (375lb)
Top speed: 135kph (80mph)

MATCHLESS G3
1935–40

This 1935 model was the forerunner of the Matchless and AJS single range that ran on to 1966. It established the layout of the vertical engine, separate four-speed gearbox with foot-change,

cradle frame and wire wheels with drum brakes. During the war it gained telescopic front forks, postwar rear suspension, and later alternator electrics were added, but the line stayed true throughout.

The 1935 G3 was the foundation of the pre-war and post-war single ranges for both Matchless and AJS, being built in three sizes at first, but only two in its post-war guise.

The first G3 was of 348cc and built in Clubman form and had exposed hairpin valve springs and a high-level exhaust system, in keeping with the normal style of the period. Construction was quite conventional with built-up crankshaft, chain drive to the magneto behind the cylinder and dynamo beneath it but rather inaccessible. The electrics were Lucas, the carburettor from Amal, an instrument panel went in the top of the saddle tank and a separate oil tank went on the right beneath the saddle. A cradle frame with duplex downtubes was used up to 1940 when it became a single tube.

Soon after that the telescopic forks arrived to create the G3L. However, well before then 245 and 497cc versions had been added, along with competition and sports models badged as Matchless or AJS. All were fine motorcycles and well finished, but in the end they stayed too long, well after their market had gone. However, it is true to say that few machines led to a production run as long as that of the G3.

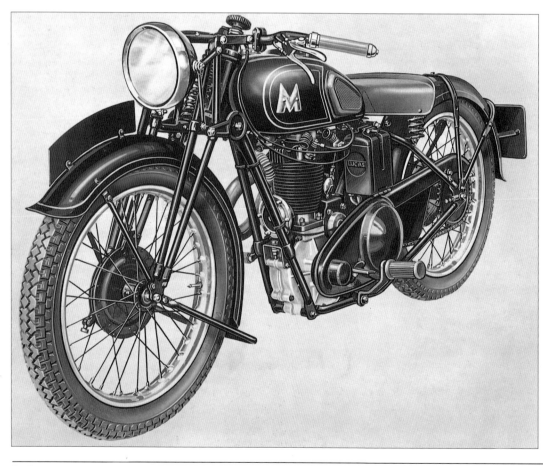

Engine: 348cc ohv vertical single, 69x93mm, air-cooled
Power: n/a
Gearbox: 4-speed foot change
Final drive: chain
Weight: 143kg (314lb)
Top speed: 120kph (72mph)

MATCHLESS G50
1958–63

It was not until 1958 that AMC produced an enlarged 7R for the 500cc class which had been requested since that model appeared. They had built both sizes before the war, but postwar they at

first offered the G45 that was simply a tuned G9 engine in 7R cycle parts. Never really satisfactory, the change from the G45 to the G50 single seemed to make much more sense.

The G50 retained the stroke of the 7R and gained its capacity from an increased bore. It followed the same layout with the single camshaft driven by chain from a half-time pinion in the gear

train to the magneto. An alloy casting enclosed both drives, and as the valve gear was fully enclosed it was an oil-tight engine. It was easy to maintain and used the same four-speed gearbox and

When the 7R appeared in 1948 fans quickly asked for a 500cc version, but had to wait a decade for the new Matchless G50.

cycle parts as the 7R, which was a great asset to private owners running in both classes. This also meant that any chassis changes easily applied to both models,

whose presence helped to boost race entries and add variety to that scene.

This ran on to early 1963 when AMC stopped production. In the previous year they had built the G50CSR, combining the engine with the CSR cycle parts with lights in order to run in the Daytona 200. They proved a point,

for Dick Mann finished second, just 3m (10ft) behind the winner.

Engine: 496cc ohc vertical single, 90x78mm, air-cooled
Power: 51bhp at 7200rpm
Gearbox: 4-speed foot change
Final drive: chain
Weight: 130kg (285lb)
Top speed: n/a

MATCHLESS G12CSR   1959–66

AMC joined the trend to vertical twins in 1949 when they introduced the 498cc AJS model 20 and Matchless G9 with its megaphone silencers and dualseat. Both had overhead-valve engines,

Once AMC started making vertical twin engines they soon progressed to 650cc. The result was the G12 (available in CSR performance guise, below) and the AJS 31 series.

four speeds, telescopic forks and rear suspension. In 1956 they were joined by larger 593cc versions and two years later these appeared in CS and CSR forms. The first was built in street-scrambler mode for off-road work with the lights optional and easily detachable. The second was a high-speed sports machine that combined the tuned CS engine and other parts for fast road use. The suffix letters stood

for Competition Sprung Roadster as far as AMC were concerned, but instantly became 'Coffee Shop Racer' to the rest of the world and stayed that way from then on.

The 593cc twin was short-lived, for 1959 brought a 646cc version in standard, CS and CSR forms plus sports 498cc models for just one year. The larger twins proved fast and popular, being soon offered in a variety of colour finishes with a long list of options that included a headlight cowl for 1962 only. The variety presented a production nightmare despite the common parts, but the G12CSR ran on to 1966, having been joined a year earlier by the G15 series that used the 745cc Norton Atlas twin engine. Alongside them all ran the AJS equivalents.

Engine: 646cc ohv vertical twin, 72x79.3mm, air-cooled
Power: n/a
Gearbox: 4-speed foot change
Final drive: chain
Weight: 173kg (381lb)
Top speed: 180kph (108mph)

AMMON
Germany (Berlin) 1921–25: Fitted motors from various sources including DKW, Bekamo, Baumi and a four-stroke Paque into an unusual pressed-steel frame.

AMO
Germany (Munich) 1921–24: Their 146cc two-stroke delivered less than one hp; the motor which they used was apparently bought in.

AMO
Germany (Berlin) 1950–54: This company made two-stroke mopeds with 48cc Westendarp & Pieper engines.

AMR
Italy (Carsarza Ligure) 1970–83: Competitive motocross bikes with Sachs engines from 125 to 350cc in high-class frames.

AMS
Spain (Malaga) 1954–65: Began in 1954 with Hispano-Villiers two-stroke engines of 125, 148 and 248cc before moving on to a 247cc parallel twin.

ANCON
Argentina 1958: A lightweight with a 100cc Sachs two-stroke motor.

ANCORA
Italy 1923–40: This company began manufacturing with 147cc Villiers two-strokes, then engines of other capacities up to 247 and 350cc, in road, sport and race trim. The factory was bought by Umberto Dei in 1936 and by 1940 engine sizes ranged from 60 to 175cc, the latter machine featuring advanced suspension.

ANDRE
France 1920s: This company made lightweights with a choice of engines: a 175cc two-stroke and 249 and 337cc four-strokes.

ANDREAN
France 1924: An advanced overhead-valve 225cc four-stroke single delivering 10bhp.

AJW

The AJW Wolfhound of 1976 used Italian components, including a Minerelli two-stroke engine. The Wolfhound was one of AJW's last models during a brief revival.

models each year, even though production figures never matched those of the bigger companies.

In the 1930s, model names included the Foxes, Vixenette, Vixen and Flying Vixen. For many years, London dealers Pride and Clarke were AJW's sole agent, but this relative prosperity ended in the late 1930s as the model range was cut back drastically. In 1938,

only the 488cc overhead-valve JAP-engined Flying Fox was sold, although a couple of 249cc Villiers-powered models reappeared for 1939 and 1940.

After the war, J.O. Ball bought the firm, and resumed production in 1948. Two models were available, one a JAP-engined speedway bike. In the early 1950s there was limited production of JAP-powered roadsters, before the supply of JAP engines, except the speedway unit, came to an end.

In the 1970s, the firm imported Giueletta mopeds with AJW tanks and decals. It closed in 1980.

AJW (ARTHUR JOHN WHEATON), a publisher, entered the motorcycling world in the mid-1920s. At first his company mainly built light-weights, but by 1930, the factory was producing no less than 11 models, ranging from the 172cc Villiers-engined BF through to the massive overhead-valve Anzani powered 994cc V-twin.

AJW built their own frames, but everything else, including the engines, was bought in. The best known models were the 172 and

196cc Black Foxes and the 347 and 343cc Silver Foxes. Bigger models included the 500 Double Port, powered by a 498cc JAP engine.

The early 1930s brought the Depression. AJW not only survived, but produced new

AJW built a series of V-twins powered by JAP or Anzani engines. This 1000cc model dates from late 1920s, a period of growth for the company.

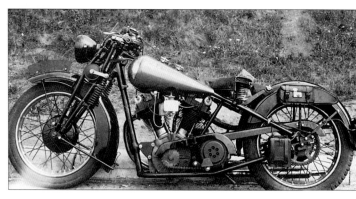

ALCYON

NAMED AFTER A MYTHICAL BIRD of lightness, this early French marque was founded by Edmond Gentil in Courbevoie, Seine,

France. Gentil then took over a number of small firms, including Amor, Labor, La Française, Lapize, Olympique and Thomann.

These companies would merge, eventually to become part of his Gentil et Cie company in its fledgling years.

For its first model, the company followed the new Werner style and used a ZL engine from Zurcher et Lothi. By 1914, it was making machines with V-twin engines, having already successfully manufactured advanced singles with unit construction. During the 1920s, Alcyon produced British-style bikes with side- and overhead-valve engines, separate gearboxes, rigid frames and drum brakes. However, these designs were augmented by adding a front fork that pivoted about the lower crown to compress a spring installed in front of the headstock, a typical sign of French engineering flair. In due course the motorcycles turned over to saddle tanks.

From its pioneer beginnings, Alcyon fitted a rocking front fork controlled by a single spring unit fitted in front of the headstock. Otherwise, this pre-WWI model is typical of its time.

An Alcyon catalogue from the mid-1950s. The machine pictured was a typical product of the firm, with its stylish line, a degree of engine enclosure and modern features for the period.

Digne des plus beaux décors...

During the 1930s, the company returned to unit construction and made some fine, sporting machines with girder forks. These were eventually to replace the older designs.

Postwar, Alcyon bought in their engines from suppliers such as AMC, but their frame and fork designs kept pace with new technology; by the 1950s, their machines had leading-link front and pivoted-fork rear suspensions. There was some degree of panelling, but this was largely unnecessary since the largest model was a 250cc. As with most French firms of that period, Alcyon also produced large numbers of mopeds, scooters and small motorcycles until manufacture ceased in 1957.

ALLRIGHT

GERMANY 1901–27

BASED IN COLOGNE, the firm of Köln-Lindenthaler Motorenwerke AG built motorcycles under various other names as well as Allright. In Britain they were at first imported by the South British Trading Co. of London, and badged as the Vindec Special from 1903, but changed to VS in 1909 to avoid confusion with the native Vindec produced by Brown Bros. Naturally, import ceased in 1914.

Other marque names were Roland and Tiger up to 1907, but all were the same machine and built in the form of that period. Engines came from FN, Kelecom or Minerva and, by 1905, from Fafnir. The bicycle-type frame gained the option of Truffault front

Above: This early Allright, c.1906, was fitted with the Truffault leading-link front fork, band brakes, direct belt drive and pedals, typical of the era.

Below: A 1924 Allright machine fitted with an overhead-valve British JAP engine, separate gearbox and chain drive, typical of the flat-tank era.

ANDREES
Germany (Dusseldorf) 1923–29: This firm began with sporting machines powered by a variety of four-strokes: Blackburne, Bradshaw flat twin, JAP and MAG V-twin. Adding its own 198cc two-stroke in 1928 over-stretched the company.

ANGLIAN
England 1903–12: As well as their own 2½hp Anglian motors, these early machines were available with two-and-three-quarter horsepower engines from De Dion Bouton, MMC, Fafnir and Sarolea, and later with JAP and Blumfield.

ANGLO-DANE
Denmark 1912–14: As the name suggests, these assemblers used English motors (JAP and Villiers).

ANKER
Germany (Bielefeld, then Paderborn) 1949–58: This firm were assemblers of lightweights with Sachs and Ilo engines from 98 to 250cc.

ANTOINE
Belgium (Liege) 1900–10: This company built singles of three to four horsepower and twins of 4½ and 5hp, first with Kelecom engines and then with their own.

ANZANI
France 1906: Although best known as a supplier of proprietary engines, Anzani himself made an improbable propeller-driven motorcycle in 1906 when he was President of the Union of French Aero-clubs.

APACHE
USA (Denver) 1907–11: Braun & Beck made a 597cc inlet-over-exhaust single with a 'backwards' engine where the exhaust was situated at the rear of the engine.

APEX
Germany (Cologne) 1925–26: These models were Sporting two-strokes with 247 and 348cc Blackburne engines.

forks. Band brakes were fitted to both wheels, the rear directly belt driven. V-twin engines were added to the singles and a switch made to

JAP, MAG and Peugeot units, but belt drive was used until the beginning of World War I. After the war, production went on, with

singles and twins in period cycle parts and improved transmissions. In 1923 Allright took over the Cito firm, adding to the range the KG

machine that adopted shaft drive for 1924. Motorcycle production ceased in 1927, although parts were manufactured for others.

ALPINO
ITALY 1945–c.1960

MANY MOTORCYCLE MANUFAC-TURERS went out of business during World War II but Alpino actually started production (in very limited numbers) during the conflict, going into full-scale production immediately afterwards. Its first post-war machine was the 1945 Alpino, a 48cc two-stroke single-cylinder cycle-motor with chain drive and a two-speed gearbox, which could be installed to drive either the front or rear wheel. In 1948, the company made the 48cc Model S, featuring a three-speed gearbox and a top speed of 40 kph (25mph). It also sold the 60cc Model ST.

At the same time, this 60cc engine also appeared in a moped, which seems to have been the basis for a 98cc light motorcycle. By 1951, this engine had grown into a three-speed 125cc with foot-change gears instead of the hand-change design of the earlier model. In the same year, the company produced the 48cc F48 scooter, which had an unusually advanced frame and suspension for both wheels.

By the end of 1953, Alpino had developed a range of models - the very basic Alpetta R48, which had friction drive and no gears, the F48 moped, which rather

confusingly, had a 49cc motor, the Roma, which had the same engine, but two speeds and hand-change, and the F 48 scooter. It also developed two lightweights with 75cc and 125cc engines.

Although Alpino only made small lightweight bikes, they were fast. Andrea Bottigelli touched 128kph (80mph) during a flying kilometre on a specially prepared 75cc. Other riders – Tamarozzi, Cagnazzi, Pennati and Sozzani – also broke records, which included reaching 82kph (51mph) on a 50cc Alpino. Although an impressive achievement, it somehow lacked the drama of the larger machines.

Soon after, a 75cc overhead-cam four-stroke racing machine appeared, though the only four-stroke the company made for road use was the 1955 175. This could top 100kph (62mph), quite an achievement for its time. However, a 1956 development of the 75cc racer could reach almost 120kph (75mph), thanks in part to its four-speed gearbox.

A year later, even the basic T48 moped acquired a four-stroke engine with unit three-speed box and in 1959, the company produced a big-wheeled 75cc scooter and as well as a 50cc mini-scooter.

AMAZONAS
BRAZIL 1978–90

WITH TWO OR THREE EXCEPTIONS, motorcycles and scooters were normally imported into Brazil rather than built there. Amazonas, one of these exceptions, used a Volkswagen car engine as its power unit. This was no great surprise since during in the 1950s, the German company had estab-lished a factory in Brazil to produce their long-running Beetle.

Beetle engines were therefore readily available and Amazonas used either the 1285 or 1584cc

The massive Amazonas from Brazil with its large four-cylinder VW engine complete with five speeds, includingreverse, and VW rear drive unit.

versions in their machines. The motor was an air-cooled four with the gear-driven camshaft located beneath the crankshaft to operate inclined valves by rockers. The plugs were fitted from an angle above and were fired by coil ignition via a distributor.

The four-speed (plus reverse) gearbox was retained. The VW single-plate clutch was also kept, and crudely converted to foot change, the drive going to a VW crown wheel and pinion, and then via a lengthy chain to the rear wheel. The whole package fitted into a massive duplex frame with telescopic forks at the front and

A police version of the Amazonas with the extra equipment, radio, siren, flashing lights and booking forms all fitted to suit the job.

crude plungers at the rear. Cast-alloy wheels carrying large car-type tyres completed the design. This was a massive machine of great bulk and weight.

Performance was poor considering the engine size and handling on the unsuitable, car-type tyres was reserved only for the brave. The controls, other than the clutch, were very heavy. Despite this, and despite a considerable price tag, the machine remained on the market for over a decade.

AMBASSADOR

LOCATED IN ASCOT, BERKSHIRE, England, Ambassador was founded by Kaye Don, an ex-Brooklands driver, who created the firm to expand his post-war business. His first prototype was different to most other firms' designs. It had the lines of a pre-war machine, complete with girder forks, but the engine, built by JAP and also used by AJW, was a 494cc side-valve, vertical-twin, with the carburettor at the front between the exhaust pipes.

The first production lightweight came in 1947 and was a simple machine with a 197cc Villiers 5E engine, three-speed gearbox, rigid loop frame and blade girder forks. It fulfilled the basic transport demands of the time, but in 1949, the company upgraded the bike by fitting the much improved and more modern 6E engine. A version with telescopic forks, called the Embassy, appeared the following year and for 1952, a new model,

the Supreme, boasted plunger rear suspension.

This was followed by the Self Starter model, which had a Lucas starter motor tucked under the front of the tank with belt drive to the engine. Optimistically, due to the bike's small engine, Ambassador also produced a complete Sidecar model which featured Webb girder forks but must have severely taxed the engine. During the year, the whole model range was upgraded. This involved fitting the new 197cc 8E engine, although in real terms, this was hardly altered from the 6E. The following year, the company managed to recognise the

Above: Ambassador built a range of models using Villiers engines and the 249cc twin was used from 1956 for the Supreme model. Later came this Super S.

Below: The 1960 version of the Super S had some rear enclosure and was also listed as the Electra 75, with an electric starter.

need for more power and the Supreme was fitted with the new four-speed 224cc Villiers 1H unit. Another feature of the bike was a new frame with pivoted-fork rear suspension.

The same type of frame was used for the 1955 197cc Envoy. It was this model, along with the Supreme and the 147cc Popular, which comprised the company's range.

Two models, The Three Star Special and the Super S replaced the ageing Supreme and these were joined by an electric-start twin and a 174cc scooter in 1961. A moped with a 50cc Villiers

engine made a brief appearance in 1962 but late that year Kaye Don retired and the firm was sold to DMW. The new owners revamped the range but despite this, production ceased in 1964.

AMERICAN IRONHORSE USA 1990s–

The names of the company's six models for 2000, Slammer, Stalker, Outlaw, Thunder, Classic and Bandit, gives a clear idea of the target market, though style and weight, rather than technical differences, separates the models. The Slammer and the Classic both

Below: The Outlaw is considerably lighter than the Bandit, thanks to smaller mudguards and no panniers, but its main distinguishing feature is the paint job.

weigh an impressive 268kg (590lb), but the Bandit, with its massive mudguards and lockable hard panniers weighs an enormous 351kg (750lb).

Since the maximum permitted gross vehicle-weight for each bike is 500kg (1100lb), this leaves only 159 to 232kg (350 to 510lb) for fuel, rider, passenger and luggage. Fitting relatively tiny fuel tanks was the solution to the weight problem, though this limited the range to 240km (150 miles).

WITH 1573CC (96CID) S&S engines as standard, and 1750 and 1850cc (107 and 113cid) options, machines made by American IronHorse of Fort Worth, Texas are firmly in the Harley-Davidson mould. However, as with all the other so-called 'clones', they have interesting features which set them apart from both the Harleys they initially emulated, and from each other.

In the case of the IronHorse, this included torsion bar rear

Above: The Bandit, the heaviest of a heavy range of motorcycles. The rough, tough outlaw name is somewhat at odds with the portliness of the machine.

suspension, and extreme amounts of plating: brake rotors are not usually candidates for chromium treatment. Although front and rear wheels were standard 46cm (18in) sizes, an alternative 53cm (21in) front wheel was an available option.

AMERICAN QUANTUM CYCLES USA 1997–

A YOUNG AND MODERN company, American Quantum Motorcycles is located in Melbourne, Florida. The company currently manufactures only two machines, namely the Liberty, and its touring sister, the Pioneer, launched in December 1999.

American Quantum Motorcycles describes the Pioneer as 'a product platform' which allows customers to design their own machines through the selection of numerous options. These options can be selected in dealers' showrooms through the internet. The result is the creation of a factory custom

bike which is tailored to individual buyers' requirements.

In some ways, the futuristic production strategy is more interesting than the motorcycle. Such features as fibreglass panniers that follow the lines of the machine do not disguise the fact that it is yet another big V-twin Harley-Davidson look-alike, albeit with four-valve heads. Engine capacities are

Although the company is a genuine manufacturer rather than just an assembler, its bikes still look like Harley-Davidsons.

unremarkable – 1440cc (88cid) and 1573cc (96cid) – and even the bore and stroke are expressed in inches – 35/8x45/8in (92x117.5mm) – for the 1573cc.

Brakes are four-piston discs, one on each wheel, which is surprising on such a large, heavy bike. Despite this, with an initial share offering of eight million dollars in

early 1999, as well as a network of 61 dealers in 2000,, the company is in fact a genuine motorcycle manufacturer, rather than just a copy-cat assembler.

ANCILLOTTI

ITALY 1967–85

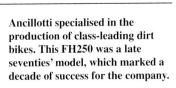

Ancillotti specialised in the production of class-leading dirt bikes. This FH250 was a late seventies' model, which marked a decade of success for the company.

ENRICO ANCILLOTTI COMPANY'S founder was an enthusiast for all forms of motorcycle sport, particularly off-road, so in the late 1960s decided to expand his hobby into a business. The result was a successful enterprise which spanned almost two decades, until bankrupted by the motorcycle recession of the early to mid-1980s.

Like many smaller Italian marques, Ancillotti machines used

engines designed and built out, relying upon bought-in power units by specialist manufacturers, including Hiro and Franco Morini, and the German Sachs company. All were two-strokes, usually with piston-port induction.

Besides motocross and enduro machines Ancillotti also built One-Day trials bikes, like this 1981 CT125. Engines were always bought in from elsewhere.

Motocross, enduro and one-day trial bikes were Ancillotti's main products, but to successfully sell these machines the company had to build reliable bikes capable of winning events. Ancillotti was successful right from the start, although almost all its sales were made in Italy alone. To fully exploit the relatively small Italian market, the company had to build machines for all levels of riding skill, from novices to national champions. Ancillotti's creations were at the front of the field.

Motocross was a major sport during the late 1960s and early 1970s, especially in Italy. In the mid- to late 1970s, it was fashionable to ride enduro bikes on the street, so during this 10-year period, Ancillotti prospered. However, the early 1980s saw a recession. In 1985, Ancillotti, like many other similar marques, was forced to close down.

APRILIA

APRILIA WAS FORMED IN 1956 by Alberto Beggio, the father of today's company president, Ivano Beggio. Initially, the firm focused its activities on the bicycle industry, but in 1960 Aprilia constructed its first powered two-wheeler, a moped. Although the firm's main source of revenue still came from pedal power rather than horsepower, by 1975 it was evident that bicycles were going out of fashion and sales declined. The pivotal point in Aprilia's history came when a faction of workers at the Naole factory near Venice backed a scheme to build a brand new series of motocross racers instead of bicycles. Made with a variety of engine sizes, the new range of models was powered by bought-in motors supplied by Minerelli, Sachs, Hiro and ultimately Rotax. Aprilia's associa-

Above: Using a modified Suzuki RGV V-twin engine, the Aprilia RS250 has become a favourite with sports bike riders; this is a 1996 model.

Below: Instrumentation and LCD displays from a 1999 Aprilia RS250. The rev counter is mounted centrally, underlining the machine's racing pedigree.

tion with Rotax continues to the present day.

Works-supported Aprilia motocross bikes won the national 125 and 500cc Italian championship titles in both 1976 and 1977. This encouraged Aprilia to enter the enduro and, later, trials market, commissioning the world-renowned rider Sammy Miller to advise on the original trials prototype.

By 1981, the company was producing 4500 motorcycles per annum, but the real breakthrough came a year later, when the ST 125 roadster appeared. Sporting a liquid-cooled Rotax two-stroke engine, monoshock rear suspension and modern styling, it proved a massive overnight success. This convinced the company's president, Ivano Beggio, that Aprilia should be selling more street motorcycles. Besides the dirt bikes, Aprilia had until then only sold 50cc ultra-lightweight machines and a range of mopeds.

To achieve its new aim, the Aprilia management looked to the youth market, examining what young people wore, what colours were in fashion, what music they listened to and even what films and television programmes they watched. For example, while other Italian manufacturers complained about the 1986 Italian law making helmet-wearing compulsory, Aprilia began marketing their own helmets in outrageous fashion-conscious designs and colours, so effectively turning a problem into a positive advantage. Another factor in Aprilia's progress during the 1980s was that the average age of its employees was under 30 and even the president was only in his early 40s. The net result of this

Right: The long-awaited RSV Mille (1000cc) 60-degree dohc V-twin superbike was finally launched at the 1997 Milan Show in Italy.

Below: Aprilia have also built and sold custom bikes for many years, like this 1992 Red Rose Classic, to cater to a completely different market to its racers.

ARMAC
USA 1911–13: This firm made one engine (4hp single), fitted into many models, 14 in total.

ARMIS
England (Birmingham) 1920–23: This company used a wide range of proprietary engines from 298 to 654cc: JAP, MAG and Precision.

ARMOR
France (Paris) 1910–57: An offshoot of Alcyon, Armor began by making lightweights with 98cc two-stroke engines and 173cc four-stroke engines; added a 498cc four-stroke single at the end of the 1920s; closed down in 1934; and after 1945 made 48, 98, 125 and (in 1953) 250cc machines before finally being re-amalgamated with Alcyon.

ARMSTRONG
England (London) 1902–05: This, the earliest bearer of the Armstrong name, used 211cc Minerva engines in Chater-Lea frames.

ARMSTRONG
England (London) 1913–14: No connection with the earlier company, this Armstrong used 269cc Villiers two-strokes.

ARMSTRONG
England 1980–87: Briefly owned both COTTON and CCM.

ARNO
England (Coventry) 1906–15: Bright yellow motorcycles with engines of 250, 350 and 500cc.

ARROW
USA (Chicago) 1909–14: Quiet lightweights with their own engine of 1hp or 1¹/₂hp, depending on whom you believe.

ARROW
England (Birmingham) 1913–17: Used Precision and Levis 211cc two-strokes.

was that Aprilia became an icon to the Italian youth.

The company also pursued niche marketing. There were no 'middle ground' machines; the ride-to-work commuter moped had long since been axed. The roadster models were split into three distinct marketing categories: replica racer, Paris-Dakar-style rally bike, or custom cruiser. Although its involvement in motocross ceased in the early 1980s, the company's sporting traditions continued with participation in trials, rallies and, from the mid-1980s, road racing. It even offered replicas of its successful works machines for sale to the public.

By 1986 production was up to 40,000 units, 18,000 of which were in the all-important 125cc sector, which made Aprilia the third biggest seller in the Italian market. This was a fantastic achievement for a company which hardly anyone had heard of a decade before.

The next challenge was to break into foreign markets. Realising that this meant producing new models, Aprilia adopted a five-year plan which cost 60 billion lire (24 million pounds) and was aimed at expanding the model range to include 25 machines, of up to an engine capacity of 1000cc.

Above: By the late 1980s Aprilia was vying for the number one spot in the Italian market. This 1988 125 AFI Replica was part of that drive.

Below: A 1989 Tuareg Wind featured a 600cc four-valve engine made by the Austrian company, Rotax. This machine was a forerunner of the Pegaso (right).

If this was not bold enough, the company also planned to build not only the existing twin cylinder 250cc Grand Prix racer (from 1989 with V, rather than in-line, engine configuration) but also enter the 125 and 500cc World Championship categories. In 1988 the 276cc (76x61mm) Climber rotary valve single-cylinder trials bike arrived, using liquid-cooling, an industry first in this sector.

In 1985, Loris Reggiari, was Aprilia's first works Grand Prix rider, and helped the company develop world-title winning bikes nine years later, when Max Biaggi took the 250cc crown. Biaggi and fellow Italian, Valentino Rossi, became multiple world champions riding Aprilias.

Yet another facet of the Aprilia's success has been its support for a series of one-model (usually RS125 or RS250) championships staged all over Europe.

Back on the road, Aprilla produced its first modern scooter, the 50cc Amico, in 1990. Again, this proved to be an instant success, and gave the company a headstart in the scooter boom of the late 1990s. Other important Aprilia models at this time included the Extrema (a race

A 1994 RS250 being put through its paces. Its handling and braking are racer-like and the machine has many admirers.

Next came a joint venture with Rotax and BMW to build the latter's F650 Funduro four-valve single. Between 1992 and 1999 60,000 sold worldwide.

Dutch two-stroke tuning wizard Jan Wittereen was recruited, developed the existing 125 and 250cc racing models, and brought out a larger V-twin, the RS400V GP racer, in 1994. By the mid-1990s, latest additions included the Suzuki RGV powered RS 250 and the Leonardo scooter with a range of four-valve engines with 124, 150 and 250ccs.

Annual production figures in 1996 exceeded 100,000 units; Aprilia was one of the biggest European manufacturers. In 1997 after launching the RSV Mille superbike, Aprilia now had a range of bikes from 50 to 1000ccs. With the purchase of the Moto Guzzi marque in 2000, the firm became Europe's largest bike builder.

replica), the Red Rose (a custom machine with 50 or 125cc engines) and the Pegaso, which featured 652cc and five valves.

APRILIA 650 PEGASO

1992

The Milan Show of 1991 saw the public debut of Aprilia's five-valve single, the Pegaso. It was one of the first modern bikes, along with some of Yamaha's four-cylinder models, to employ five-valve technology in a production model.

Like Honda's Dominator, Aprilia designers had wanted a motorcycle, which although retaining a visual connection with dirt bikes, was actually a good on-road machine. This was good commercial sense - how many dirt bikes actually get muddy?

In transforming the engine from the old four-valve unit (fitted to the original Pegaso and its earlier Tuareg Wind brother) to the five-valve one, displacement increased from 562 to 652cc (100x83mm). Both the bore and stroke had been changed and there was now dohc instead of sohc, with the cams driven by chain rather than belt as on the earlier motor. This not only gave more outright power but also increased torque. The valves (three inlet and two exhaust) featured a radial distribution. Another major development was from a steel frame to an lighter alloy one.

The 1995 update had been fitted with a more powerful headlamp,

Making its debut at the 1991 Milan Show the 652cc Pegaso features five-valve technology. The bike was a masterpiece.

as well as revisions to the frame, wheel-rim colour (from silver to bronze) and suspension. In 1996 a new stainless steel exhaust appeared.

Towards the end of that year, Aprilia launched the Pegaso 3 with an all-new frame, revised riding position and new styling, camshafts, exhaust system and engine castings. Although heavier, the new Pegaso was a better machine than the one it replaced.

A result of these improvements, the Pegaso became a serious touring bike, so Aprilia introduced a range of accessories, such as

panniers, top box, a centre stand and even an optional rear shock with separate adjustment to satisfy owners' requirements,

Finally in 1999 came the Pegaso Cube. Except for a few new cosmetic changes the machine was much the same as the existing one: just about perfect.

Engine: 652cc dohc vertical single, 100x83mm, liquid-cooled 5v
Power: 55bhp at 8000rpm
Gearbox: 5-speed foot change
Final drive: chain
Weight: 155kg (342lb)
Top speed: 177kph (110mph)

APRILIA RS250

1995

The stunning RS250 is a 250cc V-twin .It is one of Aprilia's best machines. Long-awaited, this bike has proved a major sales success for the Naole-based company.

Using a Japanese Suzuki RGV engine, but re-engineered by Aprilia to its own specification, the 90-degree two-stroke V-twin debuted in 1994.

Press and buyers alike loved it from the outset, with a typical road testers report reading 'The RS is just about the closest you can get to a GP bike on the road'.

Even though the RS250 was almost perfect from the start, some changes have been made to keep the machine up to date. These changes included installing a new CDI ignition module and re-jetting the twin Mikuni 34mm

A classic in sports bike design, the RS250 is a masterpiece of Aprilia engineering.

carburettors for the 1996 version, which have made it altogether easier to ride.

Once the 250cc engine has warmed up to 45 degrees celcius, it is ready for action. It pulls away crisply from 6000rpm, surges with power at 8000rpm and really starts to fly at 9000rpm. This frantic urge continues to build until the 12,000rpm redline, when power simply dies.

The exhaust note changes from a civilised burble to a deep, racer rasp, signalling an acceleration which is strong enough to lift the front wheel off the ground in first gear. This happens without needing to slip the clutch.

Aprilia's superb racer-bred aluminium beam frame provides road-holding and handling abilities

which are good enough to make larger sports bikes seem dull and overweight in comparison. The 40mm inverted front forks and rising rate monoshock rear suspension blend suppleness with superb control and feedback.

Only details such as poorly positioned mirrors, unlacquered graphics and a small fuel tap blemish the RS250's reputation. This particular two-stroke V-twin is a real classic in sports bike design.

Engine: 249cc 2s 90-degree V-twin, 56x50.6mm, liquid-cooled
Power: 60bhp at 12,000rpm
Gearbox: 6-speed foot change
Final drive: chain
Weight: 140kg (309lb)
Top speed: 220kph (137mph)

APRILIA MOTO 6.5

1995

There have been all sorts of motorcycle designers, but until Aprilia hired Frenchman Philippe Starck, never a former kitchen-ware and furniture designer.

When Starck's creation, the Moto 6.5, went on sale in 1995, it certainly generated great publicity. Its styling was very different to the norm and although not to

The Philippe Starck-designed Moto 6.5 was a concept bike which reached production. Although it did not sell in great numbers, it generated a lot of publicity.

everyone's taste, featured all kinds of new details.

The radiator of the liquid-cooled 649cc (100x82.7mm) five-valve, double overhead-camshaft, single-cylinder engine is wrapped around, rather than protruded from, the machine, mirroring the shape of the oval frame and deep tank. The rear tyre, a 43cm (17ins) cross-ply, was completely different to the low-profile sports radials found on most other bikes in the 1990s.

It was remarkable that a company such as Aprilia, with its background in racing and hi-tech, high-performance two-strokes, should have considered building a motorcycle whose appearance was so radical. But whereas many designers' concept bikes don't make it into production, the finished Moto 6.5 largely remained true to Starck's original design. Even more impressively, Aprilia's racing expertise made it an easy machine to control.

Although, ultimately, the machine was not a great sales success, the Moto 6.5 became, and is still, one of Aprilia's benchmark designs.

Engine: 649cc dohc vertical single, 100x82.5mm, liquid-cooled, 4volt
Power: 45bhp at 8000rpm
Gears: 5-speed foot change
Final drive: chain
Weight: 150kg (331lb)
Top speed: 164kph (102mph)

APRILIA RSV MILLE 1998

The RSV Mille superbike was launched in a blaze of glory at the Milan Show near the end of 1997. Its arrival allowed Aprilia to become the only European company with a complete range of machines, from 50 to 1000cc.

The bike owes its existence to the company's amazing growth. At the end of 1996, its turnover was some 800 billion lire (a 32 per cent increase over 1995), selling an amazing 231,000 vehicles, 45 per cent of which were exported. On the track, it had won eight world championships (up to the end of 1997), which helped promote Aprilia's image around the world as Honda had done during the early 1960s.

It also enabled the company to transfer the technical knowledge gained from its racing programme to its standard production models.

The chassis of the new superbike was excellent, but the surprise came with the quality of the engine. For a firm used to dealing with much smaller engines, the 1000cc unit was also

The RSV Mille has proved a big success on both road and track; it can reach 264kph (165mph).

superb. Not only this, but it had an identity of its own. Many other manufacturers, such as Ducati, Honda and Suzuki were fixing their cylinders at 90 degrees. Aprilia set theirs at 60 degrees, enabling them to create a compact, lightweight design. To quell the extra vibration from the narrower of the cylinder angle, the machine sports dual balancer shafts.

The RSV Mille also used dry- rather than wet-sump lubrication.

This allowed the company, to drastically reduce the size of the oil container area below the crankshaft, thus allowing the engine to be positioned much lower in the frame. This also lowered the centre of gravity, producing a bike that handled and performed superbly.

Engine: 997cc dohc 60-degree V-twin, 97x67.5mm, liquid-cooled
Power: 128bhp at 9500rpm
Gearbox: 6-speed foot change
Final drive: chain
Weight: 189kg (417lb)
Top speed: 266kph (165mph)

ARDIE GERMANY 1919–58

BASED IN NURNBURG, Ardie took its name from its founder Arno Dietrich who had formerly been chief designer for the premier company. The first Ardies appeared in 1919 and were 305 and 348cc two-stroke singles with deflector-type pistons. But after Dietrich was killed in a racing accident in 1922 the firm passed into the hands of the Bendit factory and from 1925 used British JAP engines. These ranged from 246 to 996cc, but the best selling models used the 490cc overhead-valve power unit.

Ardie was innovative, using duralumin frames and luxury fittings. In the mid-1930s JAP engines were replaced by Bark,

A 1931 Ardie 500cc side-valve single. Many early models used British JAP engines, before being supplanted by Kuchen and others.

Kuchen, Sachs and Sturmey Archers. To cut costs, Ardie reverted to tubular steel frames. In 1938 Richard Kuchen designed an 348cc overhead-valve V-twin with traverse layout, which never

reached series production. After World War II the company was acquired by the Bertel-controlled Durkopp organisation of Bielefeld. Unlike most smaller German marques, thanks to its engineering

director Dip. Ing. Noack, Ardie built its own engines, in a range of new cross-flow two-strokes, from a 122 to a 344cc twin, which powered their well-engineered commuter bikes.

From 1953, Ardie also built mopeds. After record sales in 1955, the company suffered a decline, like many other German motorcycle manufacturers, finally going into liquidation during 1958.

ARIEL

ENGLAND 1902–70

LIKE MANY OF ITS contemporaries in Coventry in the English Midlands, the Ariel company began life manufacturing bicycles. In 1870, the company's founder, James Starley, with William Hillman, invented the tensioned wire-spoked wheel, which allowed them to build lighter, yet sturdier, bicycles than before. This new device was named Ariel: the spirit of the air.

In 1896, Starley's company merged with the Westwood Manufacturing Company to produce cycle components at the same Selly Oak site in Birmingham, which later housed Ariel's huge industrial complex. The company's first powered vehicle, a quadricycle, arrived two years later. A sort of four-wheeled bicycle, it was propelled by a proprietary de Dion engine mounted above the rear axle. This rather unstable machine was followed by a better three-wheeled version with its engine mounted within the wheelbase.

In 1902, the Starley and Westwood Company was taken

over by Components Ltd, owned by the Sangsters, who could offer far more resources and ambition. The Sangsters became key figures in the British motorcycle industry and were already engaged in manufacturing cars. The first motorcycle built at Selly Oak used a Kerry engine and proved reliable

enough to be selected by the British Auto Cycle Union for the 1905 International Cup Races; a 6hp model ridden by J.S. Campbell averaged 66kph (41mph), the best performance of the event. Ariel later turned to 4hp White and Poppe side-valve engines, eventually building

One of the first powered Ariels was the four-wheeled, de Dion-engined 'Quadricycle' of 1898, shortly replaced by this much stabler three-wheeler.

similar units themselves under licence.

Charles Sangster designed the Arielette, a sophisticated three-speed two-stroke with clutch and kick-start, which might have gone into production if not for World War II. Ariel's first 20 years otherwise featured a succession of largely unremarkable machines, notably side-valve singles and V-twins of 498 and 669cc respectively, and an 998cc inlet-over-exhaust V-twin.

During the early 1920s, the Ariel range extended from a 586cc Blackburne-engined single to a 992cc MAG-engined V-twin, but the quality of its products was beginning to fall behind the best of its rivals'. It was at this time that young Jack Sangster demonstrated that, as well as possessing considerable business acumen, he was a remarkable judge of talent. Within a few years he had enlisted three of the great British motorcycle designers of the time: chief designer Val (Valentine) Page, Bert Hopwood and, in 1927, the great Edward Turner himself.

After being pried away from JAP, Page's first contribution was a pair of singles, a 500cc overhead-valve and 557cc side-valve. Although employing conventional engineering and proving reliable, the newcomers sported sleek and race-like styling, which soon became the norm.

Turner's most enduring contribution to Ariel was the immortal Square Four. Always a proponent of multis rather than singles, he had created the original 497cc overhead-cam design as an

By the late 1950s, Ariel twins were little more than re-badged BSAs, such as this 1958 650cc Huntmaster – essentially a BSA Golden Flash in disguise.

independent engineer working in a machine shop in Dulwich, South London. He hawked it around several manufacturers until Jack Sangster saw its value. In 1930, the resulting prototype, housed in a 500cc 'Sloper' frame, was the sensation of the Olympia Motorcycle Show.

Although the Square Four was not a commercial success, Turner succeeded Page as head of design. He revitalised the Ariel range, most successfully the Red Hunter range of 500cc, and later 350 and 250cc, singles.

After World War II, Ariel was swallowed into the BSA Group.

With Page again in charge of design, their final generation of models took shape. Predictably, these were led by overhead-valve parallel twins. The first of these, the solid but uninspired 500cc KH, sold badly and was withdrawn in 1957. Thereafter, Ariel's big-twin aspirations lay with the 1954 650cc Huntmaster series, essentially a re-worked BSA A10.

If Ariel still had its own identity, it was in the world of trials, where Sammy Miller's exploits on his 500cc single (registration GOV132) became legendary.

Page's other main four-stroke contributions were the 'four pipe'

During World War II Ariel supplied thousands of 'military' 350cc W-NG models to the forces. When peace returned many were sold as war surplus at around £100 ($160).

versions of the Square Four, but most memorable were his two-strokes. Introduced in 1958, the Leader and Arrow range of 250cc twins was a valiant attempt to lead two-strokes away from their utilitarian image. These were effectively the company's last efforts; the Selly Oak plant closed in 1960, and Ariel's identity was engulfed by the BSA empire.

ARIEL RED HUNTER

1939

Widely regarded as one of the best all-rounders of the 1930s, the 500cc Red Hunter single (a Red Hunter twin were also built) was introduced in 1932. It used a derivative of Val Page's overhead-valve single, housed in an elegant chassis. Its instruments were neatly mounted on the fuel tank, much like many Harley-Davidsons today.

Introduced as a 500 in 1932, the Red Hunter survived well into the 1950s with the addition of telescopic forks, although this 350cc version was considered underpowered.

By the time World War II broke out in 1939, the machine was better than ever, having benefited from Ariel's unique rear springing suspension. This rear suspension allowed the Hunter to continue with relatively few changes until supplanted by swing-arm models in 1954. On the rough roads of the time, any form of rear suspension was thought of as a considerable blessing.

An original pre-WWII Red Hunter. This 497cc example dates from 1937. Full valve enclosure followed two years later.

At the Red Hunter's heart was Val Page's solid overhead-valve engine which, by 1939, had developed full valve enclosure, precluding the oily mess criticised on earlier examples. With plenty of 'flywheel' it produced easy, usable power, yet the stroke was not so long as to

prevent it revving reasonably freely.

After World War II, the Red Hunter remained largely unchanged but for the adoption of telescopic front forks. A 350cc version, using identical running gear, proved relatively underpowered.

Engine: 497cc ohv single, 81.8x95mm, air-cooled
Power: 26bhp at 5000rpm
Gearbox: 4-speed foot change
Final drive: chain
Weight: 165kg (365lb)
Top speed: 135kph (84mph)

ARIEL KH TWIN 1948

During the immediate postwar years, and inspired by the success of Edward Turner's 1937 Triumph Speed Twin, every major British manufacturer introduced a parallel twin-cylinder model of their own. Ariel's version, named the KH, was a 498cc machine broadly identical to all the others: four-speed, air-cooled, with overhead-valve and two valves per cylinder. Early examples had cast-iron cylinder barrels and heads, although from 1954, the heads were constructed from light alloy. In the same year, a full double cradle frame with pivoted-fork rear

suspension superceded the earlier sprung-frame design.

Val Page was the designer of the KH who, ironically, had also designed Triumph's first parallel twin, the ill-starred 1933 650cc Model 6/1. And, just as that had been made redundant by Turner's Speed Twin, the uninspired KH could not compete with other twins from Triumph, BSA and its rivals. Although it was a solid and dependable machine, the Ariel twin was not only dowdy in appearance but also sluggish in performance. It reached speeds of a good 16kph (10mph) slower than

its contemporary Triumph T100. The model was discontinued in 1957.

Engine: 498cc ohv parallel twin, 63x80mm, air-cooled
Power: 25bhp at 5750rpm
Gearbox: 4-speed foot change
Final drive: chain
Weight: 188kg (415lb)
Top speed: 132kph (82mph)

The Val Page-designed 498cc KH was Ariel's response to the demand for twins. Introduced in 1948, production lasted until 1957. This is a 1952 example with iron head.

ARIEL SQUARE FOUR 1954

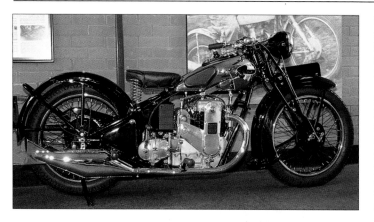

Edward Turner's enduring four was without doubt one of the most imposing British motorcycles ever produced. Essentially comprising two vertical twins on a common crankcase, the Square Four employed paired transverse crank-shafts, geared together at their centres. A single chain-driven overhead camshaft controlled the valves and the wet-sump

crankcases split horizontally, a sophisticated practice common now, but actually later spurned by Turner. In its original 497cc form this was an astonishingly light and compact powerplant, but as it grew to 596 and ultimately 996cc, its character completely changed.

However, the 'Squariel', as it was affectionately known, had one major weakness. The cylinder

Edward Turner's original light alloy, overhead cam 500cc design for the Square Four of 1932 was a far cry from the 1000cc elephants of later years.

head was prone to distortion, since the rear cylinders sat in the heat shadow of the front ones, and early attempts to race the four, albeit in supercharged form, were plagued by 'head warping'. Although a normally-aspirated version managed to take the coveted Maudes Trophy by covering 1126km (700 miles) in 668 minutes, its overheating and the inefficient 'cruciform' inlet tract always imposed a limit on the engine's performance.

In 1937, a revised range of fours appeared. Available in both 597 (the 4F) and 997cc (4G) form, these bikes featured pushrod valve actuation in place of overhead-cam, vertically-split crankcases and, partly to suit sidecar use,

much heavier flywheels. The 4G produced 38bhp at 5500rpm. In 1939, plunger rear suspension was added. After the war, the 600cc version disappeared, and by 1948 the 1000 had telescopic forks and was some 15kg (33lb) lighter, thanks largely to a light alloy cylinder head and block.

In 1954 the final Square Four arrived, Val Page's MkII 'four-piper'. By this time power had risen to 45bhp but this meant that the engine was becoming over-stressed. Plunger rear suspension was also retained in an age when swinging forks were becoming commonplace on machines of similar price.

Engine: 997cc ohv square four, 65x75mm, air-cooled
Power: 45bhp at 5500rpm
Gearbox: 4-speed foot change
Final drive: chain
Weight: 220kg (485lb)
Top speed: 166kph (103mph)

The last Square Four rolled off the Selly Oak production line in 1958, although a much revised development, the Healey 1000, came from Redditch in the mid-1970s. In 1962 the BSA group developed a prototype replacement for the Squariel, similar to the Leader, powered by a 696cc overhead-valve four-cylinder engine, and laid on its side, but it never reached production.

ARIEL LEADER AND ARROW   1958

With its pressed steel beam frame and unit construction twin-cylinder two-stroke engine, Val Page's 1958 Ariel Leader was unlike any motorcycle seen before. Cosmetically, the fully-enclosed bodywork bestowed lines that were clean and easy to keep clean. Fairly light and agile, with lively performance, it was tidy, quiet and functional but radical, too. The engine, inspired by the German Adler twin, employed an in-unit four-speed transmission driving a chain to the rear wheel. Power delivery was smooth and responsive, although

The Leader (such as the 1962 version pictured) and its sporting derivative, the Arrow, were innovative two-stroke designs.

petroil lubrication remained a necessary chore. As well as a generous standard specification, an extensive range of options was available.

In 1959, the Leader was joined by a sports version, the Arrow, which was faster and more conventional looking. It kept the same frame, with the fuel tank under the seat, in the same way as

Honda's Gold Wing. The Arrow weighed 27kg (60lb) less than the Leader, with the later 'super sports' Golden Arrow developing 4bhp more for a top speed close to 126kph (80mph). There was also a 197cc variant. Racing derivatives achieved moderate success.

Engine: 249cc parallel twin two-stroke, 54x54mm, air-cooled
Power: 16bhp at 6400rpm
Gearbox: 4-speed foot change
Final drive: chain
Weight: 163kg (360lb)
Top speed: 113kph (70mph)

ARISTOS

THE ARISTOS, DESIGNED BY Johannes Passler, was first shown at the Berliner Salon in Germany in 1923 and appears to have been sold for for a year or so afterwards. It is the best known of a trinity of machines (the other two were the Sterna and the Menos) which looked very similar, even down to a bizarre striped paint job. Both the Sterna and the Menos are often reported as renamed Aristos machines, but equally, they are sometimes reported as being manufactured before the Aristos, so there is some confusion here. The design seems to have owed a certain amount to the earlier and more successful Mars.

Pressed-steel frames, instead of the usual brazed-up tubular constructions, are cheap to build well, are very strong and can

provide varying degrees of enclosure for the mechanical parts as well as protection for the rider. Unfortunately, at this time, these frames were often produced by companies interested in producing radical designs, but which were usuallly under-funded and ill-

organised, so the concepts were never fully developed. Radicalism in frame design was often accompanied by ill-judged radicalism elsewhere.

The Aristos was no exception. The 614cc longitudinally-mounted side-valve flat twin was water-

The improbable striped paintwork of the pressed-steel frame of the Aristos gives the impression of an Edwardian bathing suit.

cooled, with twin radiators, one each side of the rear wheel. This proved an excellent place for them to collect mud, but not ideal for cooling, even when clean. The seat height was extremely low, little more than 50cm (20ins), which made for a wonderfully low centre of gravity but also promoted a certain feeling of vulnerability. In combination with the footboards, the riding position made for a 'monkey on a stick' riding position for anyone of average height. At least the transmission – three-speed, hand-change, with chain final drive – was reasonably conventional.

ARMSTRONG

HARRY HOOPER, CHAIRMAN of the industrial giant, Armstrong Equipment, the automotive suspension specialist based on Humberside, nothern England, wanted to increase his company's product range. He viewed motor-cycles as a suitable candidate, and put in a bid to buy the ailing Triumph Workers co-operative, Meriden, in 1980. The bid failed, but only a month later, Armstrong were able to take over Cotton, who

had recently gone into voluntary liquidation.

Before Cotton's demise, its boss, Terry Wilson, had forged links with Austrian engine producers Rotax as well as Bolton suspension specialist, Mike Eatough, to build a race-winning 250cc in-line two-stroke twin.

After a boardroom struggle to establish control of the company, Armstrong continued this racing development programme and

The 1982 Armstrong CM36 350cc in-line twin produced 90bhp. The machine used a variety of bought-in, high-quality components.

signed up ex-Spartan designer Barry Hart as chief engineer. Hart's two-stroke expertise and Armstrong's money ensured the new enterprise got off to a winning start, with Steve Tonkin not only winning the 1982 Isle of Man TT Junior (250cc) class, but also

taking his third British Championship the same year. Flushed with success, Armstrong announced its intention to enter the road machine market, and envisaged the introduction of 250, 350, 500 and 750cc street bikes.

To compliment the 250 racer, a brand new Hart-designed 350 twin was built. This machine, again an in-line (tandem) twin, but with entirely new horizontally split crankcases, used 64mm bore aluminium cylinders with a hard chrome lining. Retaining the Rotax 54mm stroke, the new power plant featured Omega pistons, Motoplat electronic ignition and 36mm Mikuni carburettors. Output was an impressive 86bhp, with 90bhp on tap by the time production began in 1982.

As development on the CM 36 350 twin continued and its performance increased, the team thought they had a potential world-beating racer on their hands. Unfortunately, these championship-winning dreams were ended when the sports governing body, the FIM, axed the 350cc class at the end of the 1982 season. Armstrong continued with the 250, but it was never quite as good as the 350.

In 1984, a new twin-spar carbon-fibre framed 250 GP bike,

to be ridden by Niall Mackenzie and Tony Head, with ex-Grand Prix rider Chas Mortimer as team manager, was unveiled.

A year later, Armstrong announced a 500cc three-cylinder engine, again the work of Barry Hart. This new motor featured a bore and stroke of 62.5x54mm respectively, and developed 120bhp at 11,000rpm. Other features of the triple included rear-facing exhausts, a six-speed gearbox, reed-valve induction and power valves on the exhaust. But the 500 did not come up to the expected standard during track testing, resulting in Barry Hart leaving the company.

Armstrong meanwhile built a number of off-road bikes, including motocross, enduro and even a trials bike. They tendered for military contracts, but the Canadian-based Bombardier firm won the contract to supply bikes to the British Army. Failing to secure this contract signalled the end for Armstrong.

Armstrong thought they had a potential world-beater on their hands; but the 350cc class was axed in 1982.

ASCOT PULLIN

ENGLAND 1928–30

CYRIL PULLIN, THE FOUNDER of the company, was an ex-rider who won the 1914 Senior Isle of Man TT and became involved in designing motorcycles.

His Ascot Pullin, introduced in late 1928 as 'The New Wonder Motor Cycle', was short-lived as it suffered major development problems in 1929.

The innovative Ascot Pullin that tried to do too much at once with special unit construction engine and gearbox, pressed-steel frame and many other features.

AUTO-BI
USA 1902–12: Made small bikes and enclosed-engine machines with 1½ and 2½hp E.R. Thomas engines.

AUTOBIROUE
France 1957: Lambretta-based scooter, which may have entered series production.

AUTO-BIT
Japan 1952–62: Overhead-cam 250cc single.

AUTO-ELL
Germany (Stuttgart) 1924–26: Light sports bikes with a 142cc Grade two-stroke.

AUTOFAUTEUIL
France 1905: Precursor of the scooter, with enclosed 427cc 2¾hp motor and chain drive.

AUTOFLUG
Germany (Berlin) 1921–23: Initially, a step-through with 117 and 122cc two-stroke engines, then a conventional machine with 129 and 146cc Bekamo two-strokes.

AUTOGLIDER
England (Birmingham), 1919–22: A Villiers 289cc two-stroke single sat above the front wheel of this scooter-like machine.

AUTOPED
USA 1915–21: A 155cc four-stroke single sat above the front wheel of the American original. Also built under licence by CAS (Czechoslovakia) and Krupp (Germany) the latter with 200cc.

AUTOSCO
England (London) 1920s: Brown and Layfield built this scooter. Different sources give the engine size as 117 and 180cc.

AUXI
Switzerland early 1920s: Auxiliary cycle motor of 135cc, with belt or chain drive.

AVADA
The Netherlands 1950s: This company built 49cc mopeds and may have survived until 1964.

The machine itself bristled with innovation, starting with the 496cc overhead-valve unit construction engine, set horizontally, with a three-speed gearbox placed above the crankcase. Ignition was by gear-driven magneto and lubrication was dry sump.

The engine was fitted into a frame built from steel pressings, with similar forks, and the mechanics were hidden under pressed covers. Wire wheels with drum brakes were specified, but interconnected and with hydraulic actuation.

There were fixtures and fittings as befitted a fully equipped tourer, down to a windscreen and wiper. Unfortunately, it did not handle well and was slow. As a consequence, few motorbikes of this model were sold.

Pullin then announced that a sidecar was to be introduced to go with his motorcycle. Its manufacture would used pressed-steel sides, ends and floor, which would all be welded together to create a rigid monocoque. The motorcycle had a sprung sidecar wheel with hydraulic brake

The pressed-steel front forks of the Ascot Pullin were styled to match the main frame. Also visible is the instrument panel over the handlebars, all part of the full equipment package available on the machine.

system. This feature, too, eventually proved to be just as short-lived.

By the end of 1929, the receiver was called in. Ascot Pullin was eventually closed down a year later, in 1930.

ASTORIA

ITALY 1934–36 AND 1947–57

DURING THE 1930s, the Italian tax system was changed to promote the use of motorcycles. The new system allowed for engine enlargement from 175 to 250cc. This new size stimulated consumer demand and manufacturers started producing light, cheap and more powerful machines. Astoria followed suite, initially responding to demand in 1934.

In their first year, the company used 249 and 499cc overhead-valve Ajax engines imported from AMC, really British AJS units under a different name. Both were of conventional construction with magneto ignition and dry-sump lubrication, mounted upright in the frame with a separate gearbox. Girder forks, drum brakes, full electrics and a saddle tank

completed the bikes' specification. As import tariffs rose in 1935, the firm started using Italian-built engines but production ceased in 1936.

The Astoria name returned after the war and they initially produced a few 500cc machines using materials left over from their pre-war factory. Transport was in great demand, so almost everything was

pressed into service, regardless of age, capacity or condition.

Once up and running, the firm turned to other power units, mainly small 250cc two-strokes, although they also used some overhead-valve four-strokes. In true Italian tradition, these engines had unit construction and the machines soon boasted front and rear suspension.

AUTOMOTO

FRANCE 1901–62

Above: The engine of a 1932 Automoto, the year after Peugeot acquired the firm but still using its own 500cc engine.

THE COMPANY FIRST PRODUCED the Chavanet car in 1898 but moved on to motorcycle production in 1901 under the

Automoto name. Initially using its own copy of a De Dion engine, they later started buying in engines from many sources. The machines

Above: An early Automoto with an advance water-cooled engine. The rigid forks, direct belt drive and cycle front brake were typical.

Automoto produced were typical of infant motorcycle industry, but soon developed. After World War I, Automoto built a series of models that, although heavy, fulfilled a demand for sturdy, long-lasting machines. Both side-valve and overhead-valve engines were used along with Peugeot two-stroke units from 175 to 350cc. These units drove two- or three-speed gearboxes and were fitted into rigid frames with girder forks, wire wheels and drum brakes.

The firm continued manufacturing through the 1920s, adapting to new developments, but in 1931 was taken over by Peugeot. Although Automoto continued producing its prosaic models in the style of the decade, some were fitted with Peugeot engines. The range included a 100cc velomoteur.

Postwar, the company used French AMC and British Villiers engines along with some from other European countries. They expanded the velomoteur class to include 51 to 125cc machines and a started a new cyclomoteur category, limited to 50cc. All others over 125cc were classed as motocyclette. Few exceeded 250cc thanks to the French tax system.

AVRO

ENGLAND 1905–26 AND 1957

A.V. ROE, FAMOUS FOR building aircraft, liked his motorcycles to have exceptional weather protection and he pursued this idea for half a century.

As early as 1905, he designed a motorcycle with extra large mudguards and by 1913 had a design for a vehicle in which the rider sat low, legs either side of a Douglas flat-twin engine. He also specified Druid forks, wheel steering, rear suspension, a lengthy 183cm (72ins) wheelbase, and outrigger wheels to keep the bike upright when at a stop.

It was 1922 before Roe was in the news again when he built the Avro Mobile with low seating, full rider enclosure, a 349cc Barr & Stroud engine, three-speed Albion gearbox and all-chain drive. The frame was sheet steel formed into a channel section, while the chassis had front and rear suspension controlled by quarter-elliptic springs, hub-centre steering, 30cm (12ins) disc wheels and drum brakes. The initial full enclosure on the lines of a 'bicar' was later revised into the form of a 1950s scooter. The machine had a bonnet and screen at the front, a seat, and storage space in the tail. However, the aim of full rider-protection was compromised to some extent.

The machine was road tested in 1926, by which time the designer had become Sir Alliott Verdon-Roe. In the same year he introduced the Ro-Monocar, which used a 343cc Villiers engine, a three-speed gearbox and shaft and worm drive to the rear wheel. He used almost full enclosure and the result was similar to the earlier Avro Mobile. The machine was afterwards renamed the Saro Runabout to promote the new Saunders-Roe company. Later the firm produced a similar Arro model.

The Avro Mobile of the 1920s displaying the weather protection theme the designer pursued from 1905 but which never caught on.

None of these designs caught on but in 1957 another attempt saw the arrival of the Avle Bicar with a Velocette 192cc LE engine, gearbox and rear axle. The LE concept of a side-valve, flat twin engine with good balance and minimal vibration – coupled with the extremely quiet exhaust, all built in unit with the gearbox and using a shaft drive – fitted in well with the Verdon-Roe ethos. Only one was ever made, and Verdon-Roe had to admit that the discomfort of getting wet and spending time getting into special clothes counted for little to riders who liked the wind in their face and the noise of the exhaust. However, BMW introduced a scooter with a roof 40 years later.

AVAROS
Netherlands, late 1950s: This company made a 150cc fully enclosed scooter and 49cc mopeds.

AVANTI
India 1982–93: This firm made 49cc mopeds and a 150cc scooter.

AVENIR
Belgium 1956–unknown: Mopeds with 49cc two-stroke engines.

AVIS-CELER
Germany (Hannover), 1925–31: Avis-Celer made sports machines (the name means 'fast-bird'), first with Villiers two-strokes of 172 to 346cc and then with 347 and 497cc MAG engines, though the racers used JAP 248, 348 and 498cc engines.

AVOLA
Germany (Leipzig) 1924–25: Avola used frames from Defa (Deutsche Fahrradbau GmbH) and engines from DKW (145 and 173cc).

AVON
England (Croydon) 1919–20: Villiers 347cc two-strokes powered these machines.

AWD
Germany (Dusseldorf) 1921–69: For his production motorcycles (he also built racers), August Wurring used a wide range of proprietary engines before WWII, and Sachs and Ilo engines afterwards. There was also a scooter in the 1950s.

AWO
East Germany (Suhl) 1950–61: Confusingly, the AWO 425 was a 250cc overhead-cam single. Later came a 49cc scooter (1955) and the 425S, a 250cc two-stroke (1957), and finally 250 and 350cc overhead-cam singles. During the 1950s, the name changed to Simson.

AYRES-HAYMAN
England (Manchester) 1920: This was an unusual machine with a 688cc Coventry-Victor side-valve flat twin. Inadequate finance led to its demise.

AZA
Czechoslovakia 1924–26: Lightweights powered by 147cc two-strokes.

AZZARITI
Italy 1933–34: A pioneer of desmodromic valve operation, these had 173 and 344cc engines, the latter with a 180-degree crankshaft.

BAILEY FLYER

THE EARLY DAYS OF MOTORCY-CLING brought a number of unusual machines to the market, most of which had a short life. The Bailey Flyer was one of those and, as with so many small manufacturers, the fate of the bike and the company was eventually decided by external events.

McLeod Manufacturing of Portland, Oregon, started production of the machine but this was later taken over by the Bailey-Flyer Autocycle Company of Chicago, Illinois. The machine was unusual because it was powered by an F-head, flat-twin 1000cc engine set along the frame. The flat-twin layout was already a popular one thanks to its perfect

primary balance and much-reduced vibration. The English company, Douglas, used it almost exclusively, Harley-Davidson and

Indian used it to some extent and BMW staked their reputation on it for some six decades. What really set the Bailey Flyer apart was the

Innovation by small firms seldom succeeds and so it was with the Bailey Flyer as a flat-twin engine with shaft final drive was just too much for buyers.

shaft drive to the rear wheel which required two sets of bevel gears to turn the transmission line. A two-speed gearbox was used this set-up and the clutch was installed in the rear hub, a location also used by the Austrian Puch firm for some models. The rest of the machine used conventional parts, but its unusual layout harmed sales.

The USA's entry into World War I spelt the end of production, and after the war was over, the firm disappeared.

BARIGO

FRANCE DID NOT STOP building large motorcycles in the postwar era; they simply concentrated on the small. In time, the larger machines became high quality products sold in niche markets – and so it was with Patrick Barigo. He bought in an Austrian Rotax unit and, at first, concentrated on machines for enduro, desert raid and super motard events.

The Rotax name was well established with off-road manufacturers. The 500cc, water-cooled, single-cylinder, four-stroke engine had twin overhead-camshafts and four valves fed by

twin carburettors. It was soon enlarged to 598cc and drove a five-speed gearbox.

Barigo added top-quality components within a light, strong frame that offered good handling. This, combined with the tractable engine, made the machine an excellent choice for the longer distance events, such as the tough Paris-Dakar rally.

For the 1990s, the company added a road model, based on the existing competition bike, but modified to suit the street. It changed the wheels, tyres and suspension, but kept the alloy

Above: The Barigo road model featured most of the major features of the off-road machine but with full fairing.

Left: Out on the track with the Barigo, complete with its twin exhaust systems. This machine was a high-quality product.

frame, upside-down forks, large ground clearance and sump guard for the engine unit. In came better lights, indicators, cockpit fairing and mirrors, as well as a change in the styling.

Barigo presently continues to make both models, easily able to update and incorporate alternatives to the standard specification in order to suit customer requirements.

BARR & STROUD

ENGLAND 1921

BEST KNOWN AS AN ENGINE SUPPLIER to many motorcycle firms, Barr & Stroud did build one complete motorcycle to act as a test bed for their design. This differed from most others by using a sleeve valve which combined reciprocating and partial rotating movements to align the ports that controlled the gas flow in and out of the cylinder. The engine capacity was 348cc and the sleeve was moved up and down and from side to side by a peg assembly attached to the half-time gear driven from the crankshaft. Further gears ran up to the rear-mounted magneto.

The Barr & Stroud engine also differed from convention in that the cylinder and the upper crankcase half were cast as one, with a separate cylinder head with front exhaust and rear inlet ports. An oil pump went on the outside of the timing cover while the general appearance was similar to contemporary engines.

For road use, the engine was installed in a 350cc AJS frame complete with Brampton Biflex forks, three-speed gearbox and all-chain drive. In this form, it performed well during 1921; it was decided to put it into production from November that year. It was later joined by a 499cc

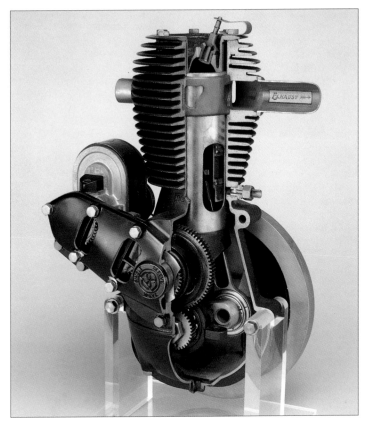

single and a 999cc V-twin but in time, the inherent problems of the sleeve-valve engine marked the demise of its commercial life. The original still survives.

A cross-section of a Barr & Stroud engine showing the sleeve valve that controlled the gas flow and its differing construction from convention.

BARRY

WALES 1904–05 AND 1910

THIS UNUSUAL MACHINE WAS BUILT in Barry, South Wales and made a brief appearance in late 1904 at the Stanley Show in London. Its special feature was a rotary engine, a flat-twin of around 200cc that had a fixed crankshaft while the rest of the engine rotated around it. This allowed the cylinders and heads to manage without cooling fins but made the induction and ignition system much more complex.

The two cylinders had mechanically operated side-valves and spark plugs fired by an induction coil and battery. The mixture was fed from a single carburettor into the centre of the crankcase and thereafter to a gas storage reservoir with further pipes to carry it out to the cylinders. This reservoir was balanced by the

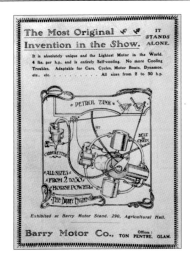

exhaust chamber with two further pipes connecting it to the exhaust ports. An aluminium cover enclosed the engine which was

A 1905 advertisement for the Barry rotary engine unit which gave some idea of its unusual layout. Complete machines were built and the design did lead to a later radial engine.

mounted in a modified heavy-duty bicycle frame with twin downtubes, between which the engine revolved. Rigid forks, pedals and belt final drive completed the machine.

Early in 1905, a lower engine position was tried and the sides of the engine cover fully perforated. It remained an unusual motorcycle engine. In 1910, much better engineered, it was the subject of a patent in the names of W.A. Richards and C.R. Redrup; the latter became known for a radial engine in later years.

BAT

ENGLAND 1901–25

'BEST AFTER TEST', the slogan ran, but the name seems to have come from the company's founder, Samuel Batson, who had been a keen cyclist for many years, before becoming interested in motorcycles. He sudied their construction, patented some important improvements in 1901, built a complete machine to demonstrate them, and the hawked his ideas around manufacturers.

None were interested, so in 1902 Batson set up his own manufacturing business in Penge, South London. During a trial, his new machine, ridden by F.W. Chase, was soon setting records, hence the slogan. The bike used a typical De Dion engine but a sprung sub-frame was available as an option. The next year, the engine was changed to an MMC (with no pedals) though water-cooling and Minerva engines were later introduced.

T.H. Tessier joined the firm in 1903 and broke many records riding BAT machines. In 1905, he bought the company and switched to JAP, Stevens and Soncin engines. For road use he made singles and V-twins, with either rigid or sprung frame, which was

actually a sub-frame that carried the saddle and footrests.

Tessier started using JAP engines exclusively and competed in the first 1907 Isle of Man TT, but retired. The next year saw Harry Bashall finish second on his BAT in the twin-cylinder class; that was the marque's best there.

By 1908, the BAT became known for its comfort and speed while it met with success at Brooklands race track where its build suited the circuit. The range expanded with the addition of a two-and-a-half hp lightweight model alongside larger singles, all with mechanically operated inlet valves. The twins still used the older automatic-inlet-valve type. Racing versions were listed while the firm also produced sidecars and a quadricycle in the form of a motorcycle with sidecar, but with two steering front wheels.

To alleviate production problems, the company reduced the range to just three models for 1910, a three-and-a-half hp single and two twins. A two-speed P&M gear was listed but by 1912 was replaced by a countershaft gearbox with kick-starter and clutch in the rear hub. The singles were dropped

for 1913 when the TT model had overhead-valve and the 8hp one all-chain drive. The year before World War I saw more models, all V-twins with variations of transmission, while the marque continued its sporting success.

During the war, some machines were sold to Russia but eventually motorcycle production gave way to shell-case manufacture.

The company returned in 1919 with 6- and 8hp V-twin models with three speeds and chain drive, but the machines were built from

A typical BAT model from 1913 with a 770cc JAP V-twin engine, leading-link forks and choice of belt or chain transmissions. It also had a neat cylindrical tank.

pre-war spares. A 4hp V-twin was added and in 1922, Tessier's sons took over. A two-and-three-quarters horsepower single joined the twins, the company became BAT, and bought Martinsyde in 1925, whose two V-twins were added to the BAT range for their final year.

BATAVUS

NETHERLANDS 1932–76

The aesthetics of Batavus' last moped, made in 1976, were as awkward as the frame's geometry was unconvincing, although rider accessibility was good.

SOME SAY THAT the bicycle is king on Dutch roads and, indeed, Batavus was originally a bicycle manufacturer. The Rijwiel-en-Motorenfabriek Batavus company, based in Heerenveen, began selling bicycles in 1904, producing its own models in 1914.

Its first motorcycle came out in 1932, powered by a 98cc Villiers two-stroke engine. Models followed using Sachs, Ilo and Villiers power-units of 74, 98, 100 and 150cc.

After World War II production of small motorcycles resumed, using Ilo and Villiers motors of 148 and 200cc, but from 1950, Batavus made mopeds for commercial purposes. Its

motocross and enduro machines used Sachs engines.

By 1969, Batavus was flourishing, acquiring the Dutch moped manufacturer Magneet and taking over the Phoenix, Fongers and Germaan moped brands in 1970. Magneet had been a bicycle maker which started making mopeds; Fongers was almost as old as Batavus, and made FN-powered motorcycles; Germaan was founded in 1935 and made lightweight motorcycles that used small-capacity Villiers, Ilo, Csepel and Sachs engine and, in the late 1950s, built the Achilles Capri under licence, marketing it as the Germaan Capri.

However, by 1976 the bottom had fallen out of the moped market, and Batavus stopped production the same year. The Indian market leader TVS continued to make Batavus mopeds under licence from 1976.

BEARDMORE PRECISION   ENGLAND 1920–25

DURING WORLD WAR I, F.E. BAKER LTD. of Birmingham, well known for its Precision engines, developed an advanced machine powered by a 349cc two-stroke built in unit with a two-speed gearbox. It was launched in 1919 and named after the engine, but in early 1920, became the Beardmore Precision, following an association with the giant William Beardmore engineering group.

Frank Baker's engine was along conventional two-stroke lines although the pumped lubrication system, in which the magneto drive chain doubled as an oil conveyor, was novel. The gearing, too, was imaginative; sprockets at either end of the crankshaft connected through-chains to differing-sized sprockets mounted on a countershaft. Gear selection was via expanding clutches. The engine and gear were contained in aluminium casings as a complete unit.

The engine was fitted to cycle parts which were a mixture of pressed steel and tubular construction, the petrol tank acting as top tube of the frame and heavy, deep-section mudguards doubling as stressed supports for both wheels. These were fully sprung, by a rocking-action fork at the

The first Beardmore machines had a 349cc two-stroke engine built in unit with its two speed gearbox. This is the 1921 Sport version.

The model C Beardmore Precision differed from most other bikes in that its engine was built in unit with the three-speed gearbox.

front and cantilevered arms at the rear, both controlled by multiple leaf springs. Large alloy footboards swept upwards at their front ends to become legshields, the whole presenting an unconventional yet practical package.

Unconventional also meant odd and the machine did not find favour with the buying public, particularly as the 349cc engine lacked power. A sports version without the rear springing was tried in 1921, before the arrival of a 598cc side-valve model with a true three-speed gearbox in unit.

This went into the sprung frame and added power, but didn't address the appearance problem.

A sleeve-valve 348cc engine from Barr & Stroud with three-speed gearbox and choice of transmission followed and a team of three machines was entered in the 1922 Senior Isle of Man TT, all equipped with a new 496cc sleeve-valve engine. These all retired, but later in the year, a replica model appeared with either sprung or rigid frame and a revised link-action girder fork. This was exhibited at the 1922 motorcycle show along with a two-speed 348cc sleeve-valve. A sports version of the latter came in 1923 and was followed by a 246cc sleeve-valve in a tubular frame.

The 246, 348 and 596cc sleeve-valve models were manufactured into 1924, when Frank Baker left the firm and experimental racing machines were entered for the TT; a 250cc overhead-valve with leaf spring controlled valves and an overhead-cam 350 single with four valves, two carburettors and shaft-driven camshaft. Neither brought success, but the overhead-valve 250, with coil-valve springs, was added to the range for 1925 which, together with its earlier sleeve-valve equivalent, and the 348 and 596cc machines, were the marque's last. Beardmore worked with cars for some years; Baker soon had a new marque under his own surname.

BEESTON

HARRY LAWSON WAS A BUSI-NESSMAN who made money during the bicycle boom and then turned to motor vehicles with the aim of buying patent rights to gain control of the industry. He created firms and bought into others; Beeston was his second flotation of 1896.

The company's first machine was a tricycle, with a copied De Dion one-and-a-quarer horsepower engine mounted behind the rear

axle which it drove by gears. It had a surface carburettor, hot-tube ignition at first, and followed cycle practice. The tricycle was soon followed by a quadricycle, essentially the same machine, but with a front-fork assembly with two wheels and seat between them. The firm also built a motorcycle with a one-and-three-quarters horsepower De Dion-type engine located ahead of the rear

wheel. The petrol tank was mounted above the engine and the front frame was taken from a conventional bicycle but with a detachable top tube to convert to a ladies' machine.

Right: Power for the Beeston tricycle was provided by a copy of a De Dion engine, mounted behind the rear axle, which was driven by gears.

Left: The Beeston, as with other early primitives, was essentially a heavy-duty tricycle fitted with an engine, crude transmission, fuel tank and ignition system.

This design ran at 43kph (27mph) at a test track in 1897, but the firm had little faith in the motorcycle, preferring to promote the tricycle. One of these ran in the Emancipation run to Brighton held late in 1896 and early in 1898 the type was demonstrated to the Prince of Wales at Sandringham and ridden by the Duke of York.

However, the tricycle was not popular and the Beeston firm closed down in 1901.

BEKAMO

THIS MAKE WAS BUILT in Berlin and used an advanced 129cc two-stroke engine with a pumping piston in a second cylinder in the base of the crankcase. In some versions this piston controlled the inlet phase as well as increasing crankcase compression, while two transfer ports passed the mixture to the combustion chamber above the main piston with its deflector top.

The machines were designed by Hugo Ruppe, who had earlier worked for DKW, and at first had a wooden frame. This was soon changed for a simple tubular one with light girder forks. Final drive was by chain and some engines had fan cooling with a

cowl over the cylinder to direct the air. Bekamo licensed other firms to produce their engine and among these were Böhme, Eichler, MFZ, TX and Windhoff, while they also sold engines to still more firms.

By 1925 they were out of funds but by then were linked to a Bekamo plant in Czechoslovakia, having supplied them with machines and then engines only. These went into TX frames that had a massive top tube that also acted as petrol and oil tanks. Up to

Bekamo used an advanced 129cc two-stroke engine with pumping piston. This was used by other firms and also built under licence.

1925 the Czech plant at Rumburk was an assembly line for the Bekamo, using a 124cc version of the engine, but when the Berlin

plant closed, all the facilities were transferred and from then on the Czech factory continued in business until 1930.

BENELLI

IN 1911, THREE BROTHERS opened a small workshop in the Adriatic town of Pesaro. From these humble beginnings came one of Italy's most famous and longest-enduring marques.

Initially, the workshop concentrated on general mechanical repairs to automobiles, motorcycles and even firearms. Soon, however, the Benelli brothers began to carry out limited manufacturing of their own. They started producing components for cars and aircraft, a process which accelerated with the outbreak of World War I.

At the end of the conflict in 1918, the family applied their engineering skills to a new field. In Italy, as throughout the rest of Europe, there was a rapidly growing requirement for cheap mechanical transport. Benelli designed and built a 98cc two-stroke auxiliary engine to be fitted to a conventional bicycle.

As with the later French Velosolex, the engine was mounted in the front of the steering column, above the front

A Benelli 125 Trail bike, made in around 1978. Power for the machine came from a single cylinder piston-port two-stroke engine.

wheel. However, the unit was too powerful for the frame, so the company designed a stronger one and the first Benelli motorcycle was conceived. Introduced in 1921, the machine featured girder front forks, magneto ignition, a two-speed gearbox and chain final drive.

At this time, five of the Benelli brothers were involved with the workshop, and the youngest, known as Tonino, rightly saw himself as a future racing star. Beginning in 1923 with the Italian Grand Prix at Monza, Tonino went

The jewel-like 231cc 254 (pronounced Two Fifty-Four) of 1981, featured a four-into-two exhaust system. It also came with cast alloy wheels.

on to score victory after victory. He retired, became a self-appointed factory test rider, but was killed during a testing session in 1937.

By the mid-1930s Pesaro had grown to become one of the famous big five (Pentarchia) of Italian bike industry (with Garelli, Moto Guzzi, Gilera and Bianchi).

B.A.M.
Germany (Aachen) 1933–37: The Berliner-Aachener Motorenwerk was a front which allowed the sale of Belgian FN motorcycles in the Third Reich. All were singles: 198cc two-strokes, 346cc side-valve and 500cc side-valve and overhead-valve.

BAMAR
Germany 1923–25: This company assembled small numbers of motorbikes using engines from companies such as Alba, Baumi, DKW, Gruhne and possibly others.

BAMO
Germany 1923–25: The initials stand for Bautzener Motorradfabric Staubingen & Klingst; this company assembled bikes with 148 and 173cc DKW engines.

BANSHEE
England (Bromsgrove) 1921–24: Banshee used several proprietary engines including Blackburne 347 and 497cc, Bradshaw oil-cooled 346cc, sleeve-valve Barr & Stroud 347cc, and Villiers 269cc.

BARDONE
Italy (Milan) 1938–39: Bardone manufactured heavy 499cc overhead-valve unit-construction singles.

Benelli's racing success had really begun with the introduction of a 172cc (62x57mm) overhead-cam single. A double overhead cam version with square 60.5x60.5mm bore and stroke dimensions came in 1932, and in 1935, a larger displacement 248cc (62x78mm) development.

By the middle of 1938, almost every mainland European factory, as well as AJS and Velocette in England, had embraced supercharging as a way of increasing performance on the race circuit. Benelli were no different and not only converted their existing double overhead-cam 250 singles (Irishman Ted Mellors won the Isle of Man Lightweight TT in 1939 on the normally aspirated version), but also constructed a superbly crafted, jewel-like, four cylinder 250, which put out 60bhp. Unfortunately, the outbreak of war intervened, and the FIM then put a ban on superchargers. These exciting projects never reached their full potential.

The war also destroyed the Benelli works, and with no production facilities, the marque was unable to make a quick return to the market, unlike rivals such as Moto Guzzi and Gilera. Not only this, but there was a family dispute

A 250cc overhead cam racer similar to the one used by Ted Mellors to win 1939 Lightweight TT at an average speed of 118kph (74.25mph).

which saw one of the brothers, Guiseppe, depart with his sons Marco and Luigi to establish the Motobi company. Nevertheless, as early as 1946, the remaining brothers brought their pre-war racers out of hiding and proceeded to do battle with their old rival, Guzzi. Then in 1948, the former Benelli rider Dario Ambrosini

rejoined the Pesaro company as its number one rider after a spell with Guzzi.

In 1949, the FIM instituted the new World Championship series; Benelli and Ambrosini responded by finishing runners up in the 250cc series, going one better the following year, taking the championship by winning every

A 1932 Benelli 175 Sport, with a 172cc single overhead camshaft engine and four-speed transmission. It could reach 120kph (75mph).

round except one. But in 1951, after wining the opening round in Berne and finishing second in the TT, Ambrosini was killed during

The engine from Benelli's 250cc overhead cam street bike of 1939. It was an impressive unit which was also built in 500cc form.

practice for the French GP. Benelli withdrew from racing, and did not re-appear in an official capacity until 1959.

On the production front, the Pesaro factory really only began to get back to normal in 1950. At the Milan Show that year they displayed pre-war designs such as the 500 and 250cc four-stroke singles together with a new 98cc two-stroke. A year later, the 98 became a 125cc, called the Leoncino (little lion), which was built in both two-stroke and four-stroke forms. One of the two-stroke 125s later won fame

following its victory in the 1953 Giro d'Italia (the Tour of Italy), ridden by Leopoldo Tartarini (later boss of Italjet).

Another important Benelli of the early 1950s was the 250 overhead valve Leonessa (Lioness) parallel twin. Together with the Leoncino, this machine had a long and successful production run throughout the 1950s.

In 1959, two important things happened. Benelli returned to racing with an updated version of the long-running double overhead-cam single (with Geoff Duke, Dickie Dale and Silvio Grassetti)

Benelli's innovative four cylinder, water-cooled, dohc, 250, super-charged racer of 1939. The FIM's ban on supercharging after WWII made the engine obsolete .

and production started on a brand new 172cc (62x57mm) overhead-valve unit single, available in either Turismo or Sport guises.

In 1961 Benelli celebrated its 50th anniversary, then following the death of Giuseppe Benelli, Motobi and Benelli merged their concerns, although confusingly, Motobi models continued to be marketed for many years.

1960 saw the arrival of Benelli's second four cylinder model, which was tested by Bruno Spaggiari that year, although it was not until 1962 that the 246.3cc (44x40.5mm) was ready to race.

Two years later the machine won its first GP, with new signing Tarquinio Provini aboard. Meanwhile, the company had been busy building a larger 343cc (51x42mm) version for the 350 class. Later still, in 1967, a 491cc model made its debut. But none of these racing machines, one of which powered the Australian Kel Carruther to the 250cc World Championship in 1969, was enough to halt Benelli's commercial decline, and the firm was taken over by the Argentinian industrialist, Alejandro de Tomaso, in late 1971.

At that time, Benelli had a mixture of series production models, including a whole range of mini-bikes, various Motobi-inspired overhead-valve horizontal singles and the relatively new 643cc (84x58mm) overhead-valve, five-speed Tornado parallel twin, reaching 169kph (105mph).

The first thing de Tomaso did after the takeover was instigate a total revision of the range. Only the mini-bikes (for the American market only) and the Tornado were continued and a new 124cc

BARNES
England (London) 1904: Barnes was an obscure firm which used proprietary engines from MMC, Minerva and possibly others.

BARON
England (Birmingham) 1920–21: This company was an assembler which used Villiers 269cc and Blackburne 348cc engines.

BARONI
Italy 1958: Officine Meccaniche Moto Baroni made mopeds and lightweights with 50cc engines, and a 175cc four-stroke lightweight.

BARRY
Czechoslovakia 1932–39: J. Friedrich Drkosch built a 248cc racing overhead-valve single. The 1938 launch of a 100cc two-stroke lightweight was unfortunately overtaken by the advent of World War II.

BARTALI
Italy (Florence) 1953–61: In 1953, Bartali made a 158cc two-stroke and in 1955, they made a sports version, as well as a racer. In 1956, they produced a moped and a 175cc four-stroke and in 1957, they went on to produce a 124cc two-stroke. In 1958, a motocross version appeared.. However, the programme looked over-ambitious.

(42.5x44mm) and 231.4cc (56x47mm) Japanese-inspired piston-port two-stroke twins were introduced. There was also a 120.6cc (56x49mm) single cylinder trail model. The Japanese influence continued with the introduction of the prototype 750 Sei (Six) – yes, six-cylinder – at the end of 1972. Many saw this as Benelli upstaging the Japanese. Unfortunately, it took another two years to reach limited production, and was joined by a pair of four cylinders: a 500 and finally, in 1975, by a 350. A year later, the definitive machine of the de Tomaso era, the 254 (250-Four) appeared. But this, like the 250 two-stroke twin, had a capacity of only 231cc (44x38mm). Together with a similar Moto Guzzi-badged bike, the 254 was the world's first modern 250cc-class production bike.

Below: The 1980 254 (Two Fifty Four). Its engine was built by Moto Guzzi, as both Benelli and Guzzi were then owned by De Tomaso.

Other multis were to follow at the end of the decade. These came in the shape of the four-cylinder 654 (603.94cc, 60x38mm) and the six-cylinder 900 Sei (906cc, 60x53.4mm).

The recession of the early 1980s severely affected Benelli's production, and by the end of decade the company was sold again. The new company was only interested in 50cc machines for the home market and so their ownership was short-lived and towards the end of the 1990s, yet another owner was in place.

The 750 Sei (meaning six cylinder) made its debut in 1972, but took a further two years to reach production, not coming onto the market until 1974.

The new company made substantial resources available for the development of new models. First came a family of modern scooters. Then the announcement was made in 1999 that a four-cylinder superbike, aptly named the Tornado, was planned to appear early in the new millennium.

BENELLI 250 SUPER SPORT

1936

Engine: 247cc ohc vertical single, 67x70mm, air-cooled
Power: 16bhp at 6500rpm
Gearbox: 4-speed foot change
Final drive: chain
Weight: 136kg (300lb)
Top speed: 113kph (70mph)

In the mid 1930s, the Pesaro company developed plunger rear suspension which first appeared in 1936 on the new 250 Super Sport, and later on 250 and 500 models.

At the Milan Show in early 1938, the Motor Cycle described the 250 single as being 'very English in appearance' and it was.

In the mid-1930s, Benelli developed plunger rear suspension. This innovation made its debut on the new 250 super sport model in 1936.

With dimensions of 67x70mm to give 247cc, the engine had the camshaft drive (by a train of gears) on the offside with points ignition and dynamo lighting. In typical Italian fashion, there was a rocking gear pedal on the offside for the four-speed gearbox. The 250 usually had hairpin valve springs soft enough to be changed by hand. The engine had twin port heads and on some machines the exhaust system incorporated a lever to put its baffle out of action, giving the rider a softer note for town or a sporting rasp for open country. The lubricating oil was carried in a ribbed forward extension of the crankcase. On some models, a small oil-cooler was mounted on top of this, set between the duplex front downtubes of the frame.

The overhead-cam Benelli's were seen as more sporting than Bianchi and Gilera road-going models. Only Moto Guzzi offered machines with similar performance for highway use.

BENELLI 500 GRAND PRIX

1970

The first four-cylinder Benelli, a water-cooled supercharged 250 racer, arrived in 1940. Then came the war, and following the FIM's decision to ban the supercharger, the bike was never properly raced.

In 1960, the Pesaro concern produced another four, again a racer, but air-cooled and obviously without a supercharger. Like its predecessor, the new engine followed the classic engineering layout, with its four cylinders set tranversely across the frame. There were double overhead-camshafts with a central gear drive, and a geared primary drive between the first and second cylinders, on the nearside, to reduce overall width.

The 246.32cc (44x40.5mm) engine originally produced 40bhp at 13,000rpm. Ignition was by battery coil, but this was soon axed in favour of a magneto, located at the front of the crankcases. A multi-plate dry clutch was employed on the nearside of the unit construction engine and gearbox assembly, which had six-speeds. There was also considerable experimentation with

the lubrication system. At first, the oil tank was mounted on the rearside, then it was placed in front of the fuel tank, before finally being relocated under the crankcase.

First appearing at Imola in spring 1962, the machine was fast, but more development was needed, a process that continued until the end of 1963, when Benelli signed Tarquino Provini from Morini. The 1964 machine was much lighter and had seven gears but Provini was still beaten in the Italian Senior Championship by his replacement at Morini, the young Giacomo Agostini.

A year later, the four was further improved with new crankshaft, heads and gearbox. Power output was 52bhp at 16,000rpm. Later in 1965, the company introduced a larger-engined 322cc (50x40.6mm) model. From this came a 343cc (51x42mm) version, with four-valves-per-cylinder.

Provini retired through injury and his place was taken by Renzo Pasolini for 1967. At Monza in September 1968, Benelli wheeled

The 500 Four Grand Prix was the final development of Benelli's racing fours. A 1970-type machine is illustrated here.

out a pair of bigger 494.6cc (54x54mm) fours for Pasolini and Mike Hailwood.

The glory the company sought finally came in 1969 when the Australian Kel Carruthers won the 250cc world title, the last time a four-stroke achieved this in the 250cc class. Following his success, Benelli could not race the four in the 250 category as FIM rules now permitted a maximum of two cylinders and six gears.

The 350 and 500 models continued into the 1970s, their first appearance coming with Walter Villa on a revamped 350 four in the 1973 Italian GP at Monza.

Engine: 494.6cc dohc straight four, 54x54mm air-cooled
Power: 82bhp at 11,000rpm
Gearbox: 6-speed foot change
Final drive: chain
Weight: 120kg (264lb)
Top speed: 264kph (164mph)

BARTER
England 1902–05: The engine on this machine had no conventional crankshaft and the con rod went straight to the rear axle.

BARTISCH
Austria 1925–29: Production of these advanced singles, the first of which (1925) was a chain-drive overhead-cam 348cc, and the second (1928) a bevel-drive overhead-cam 498cc, was limited by lack of financial resources.

BASIGLI
Italy (Ravenna) 1952: This was a water-cooled triple which probably did not proceed much beyond prototype stage.

BASTERT
Germany (Bielefeld) 1949–55: Bastert made lightweights, mopeds and scooters using 49, 98, 125 and 150cc two-stroke engines bought-in from Ilo and Sachs.

BAUER
Germany (Klein-Auheim am Main) 1936–54: Pre-war, this company made bicycles with cycle motors; postwar, they made 123, 147 and 173cc Sachs and Ilo two-strokes. Attempting to build their own 'backwards' (exhaust at the back) overhead-valve 250cc single in 1952 was a mistake and so after 1954, the firm went back to manufacturing bicycles.

BENELLI 900 SEI

1980

The 900 Sei was the ultimate development of the Benelli six cylinder series. It was built between 1980 and 1987.

In 1971, the Benelli family sold their firm to the Argentinian industrialist, Alejandro de Tomaso. This change of ownership introduced a new era of Benelli street bikes. In an attempt to both upstage the Japanese and pull off a publicity coup for his new acquisition, de Tomaso created a flagship six-cylinder model. This was a 750, built to show the world what Benelli was capable of.

The Sei (Six) was a typical Italian luxury engineering creation. Its single-cam, six-cylinder engine was a logical, almost obvious choice, resembling the configuration of its four-wheel, 12-cylinder counterparts at Ferrari, Lamborghini and Maserati. Like them, Benelli's 750 was expensive, but lacked style. In fact, apart from six magaphone exhausts that crowded the rear wheel, the Sei's

styling was conservative, possibly even bland.

The Benelli's engine design owed more to Tokyo than to Turin, but the prototype still created a sensation when it was launched in 1972. Maximum speed was around 185kph (115mph), with factory sources claiming 71bhp at 8500rpm from the 748cc (56x50.6mm) across-the-frame six cylinder engine.

By the time the 750 Sei entered production in 1974, Honda's development of its own six, the CBX, was well underway. Benelli responded by bringing out the larger 900, featuring 906cc and a bore and stroke of 60x53.4mm. This was no mere larger bore and restyled machine; instead it was virtually a brand new bike. The engine was much stronger, with items such as the crankshaft and gearbox, unreliable on the earlier six, replaced with new components. The appearance of the motorbike was also considerably different, with a six-into-two exhaust and a bikini fairing. Maximum speed was in excess of 209kph (130mph) but production of the motorbike ceased altogether in 1987.

Engine: 906cc ohc straight four, 60x53.4mm, air-cooled
Power: 80bhp at 8400rpm
Gearbox: 5-speed foot change
Final drive: chain
Weight: 220kg (485lb)
Top speed: 215kph (133mph)

BENELLI 900 TORNADO

2000

The 900 Tornado uses a famous Benelli model name from the early 1970s. But whereas the earlier machine used a 650 overhead-valve parallel twin engine, the heart of the new Tornado boasts more cubic capacity and an extra cylinder as well.

Although the first production Tornado features a 898.4cc (85.3x52.4mm) engine size, Benelli is planning an entire family of units, of various displacement sizes.

The cylinders are vertical, and the 12 valves (four per cylinder) are inclined at 15 degrees, and driven by a chain on the nearside (left) of the cylinder block.

The crankshaft is timed at 120 degrees to provide a natural 'big bang', enabling optimal traction for the rear wheel for both street and racing uses. A balancer shaft is fitted to iron out vibration, while the integrated ignition and injection system has been

A Benelli for the 21st century. The 900 Tornado uses a liquid-cooled dohc three-cylinder engine. The headlights and cockpit fairing are ultra-modern.

developed to use either three or six injectors.

The lack of a front-mounted radiator offered the design team greater freedom to create a large 13-litre (793cid) airbox without affecting petrol-tank capacity.

The absence of a front radiator also helps to achieve optimum weight distribution. Furthermore, the engine is a stressed member of the frame structure, contributing to considerable overall rigidity. The frame itself is made in chrome-moly steel (front) and cast aluminium (rear), providing attachment for the single rear shock absorber. The steering head angle is adjustable.

Other details include: 43cm (17ins) tyres, triple discs, racing

quality helical five-spoke wheels (front three-and-a-half, rear six section), an aluminium swinging arm, and a wet multi-plate clutch with anti-locking device. There is also a six-speed cassette-type gearbox.

Engine: 898.4cc dohc triple 85.3x52.4mm, liquid-cooled
Power: 140bhp at 11,500rpm
Gearbox: 6-speed foot change
Final drive: chain
Weight: 185kg (408lb)
Top speed: 280kph (174mph)

BERNADET

FRANCE 1930–34 AND 1947–59

Above: The postwar Bernadet scooter was designed with an unusual style for its headlight and was built with a variety of engines, up to 250cc.

BERNARDET, RUN BY THREE BROTHERS, hardly chose the best time to go into business – the terrible Depression of the 1930s – but offered a range of models from 100 to 500cc, using French engines from Chaise and Train. The rest of the machine was conventional for the period but production was limited.

The brothers' late-1947 scooter was a shrewd product with a 125cc Ydral two-stroke engine driving a four-speed gearbox installed by the rear wheel without suspension. Full enclosure and an apron completed the scooter image. Then in 1950 came a larger

model with 250cc Violet split-single, two-stroke engine, rear suspension and a spare wheel. In 1951, this changed to a fixed front mudguard with the headlamp on the apron. Two years later, the firm manufactured a Texas version of the 250 with American-style saddlebags and fringed seats.

In 1954, Bernardet introduced the 50, later 85cc, Cabri, and the Guépar followed, but by 1959 the company had folded.

Below: The Texas version of the 250 Bernadet scooter with its American style saddlebags, tassels and fringed seats, although the position of the spare wheel reflected normal scooter practice.

BERNEG

ITALY 1955–61

BERNEG WAS A REMARKABLE but short-lived company, and their story illustrates how advanced design is not sufficient for success; good business-sense and financial backing are also crictial. Otherwise, Berneg might well have been able to rival Honda, whose name was built on the same lines: manufacturing parallel twins when no one would contemplate making anything other than a single, and using developments such as overhead-cams, light alloys and well-chosen gear ratios

to build small, light, but powerful, bikes.

The name came from Paride Bernardi and Corrado Negrini, who joined forces in Bologna in the early 1950s. Their first machine, the Iridea (reputedly designed by Alfonso Drusiani), was a 158cc four-stroke parallel twin with an overhead-cam driven by duplex chain in a light-alloy head. Primary drive (by chain) went to a four-speed foot-change gearbox, and then again by chain to the rear wheel. The tubular

frame featured telescopic forks and rear suspension, and the bike had a top speed in excess of 100kph (62mph).

It remained in production for two years, followed in 1957 by the Fario, reported as 174 or 185cc. Mechanically like the Iridea, it came in two versions: the basic model, good for 105kph (65mph); or the Gran Turismo, which could reach 120kph (75mph). At the end of 1959, a still faster Sport model was built, but in 1961 the company went bankrupt.

BETA

ITALY 1948–

FOUNDED BY GIUSEPPE BIANCHI in Florence in 1948, the company expanded rapidly as postwar demand for motorcycles was high. By the early 1950s, Beta had an impressive nine-model range, including the Mercurio and Orione. These two machines

A state-of-the-art enduro-style Beta released onto the market in 1998 with monoshock rear suspension.

featured overhead-valve engines, 153cc (58x58mm) and 199.5cc (64x62mm) respectively. The company also made the semi-racing MT (Milano-Taranto) 175. This machine used a specially tuned 172cc (59.5x62mm) version of the touring TV two-stroke model and was capable of 132kph (82mph).

Beta managed to survive the 1960s, at a time when many of the smaller Italian marques failed.

In the last decade, Beta has been a major force in the trials world, particularly with English rider Dougie Lampkin.

During the following decade, trade picked up, helped by the company's entry into the off-road sector, where it built a number of specialised motocross, enduro and trials bikes. But roadsters were not forgotten and, as early as 1974, Beta offered a five-speed 48cc two-stroke trial model.

The late 1970s brought a new 125cc model, offered in either touring or sport guises. The sport version had a specification that included cast-alloy wheels, dual-disc front brake, clip-ons and an expansion-type exhaust.

After being widely exported to a large number of countries,

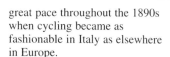

including the USA and Britain, Beta has transformed itself in recent years to become an important dirt bike manufacturer, winning several world championships in the trials section of the sport with the British rider Dougie Lampkin.

BIANCHI

ITALY 1897–1967

ONE MAN WAS FAR OUT in front during the pioneering days of the Italian motorcycle industry: Edoardo Bianchi. Born in July 1865, Bianchi was brought up in a

Milanese orphanage, but from an early age showed a remarkable aptitude for engineering matters.

In 1885, at the age of 20, he set up a small machine shop for

bicycle manufacture. Bianchi moved to larger premises in 1888, when he produced the first Italian vehicle (a bicycle) with pneumatic tyres. The business expanded at a

great pace throughout the 1890s when cycling became as fashionable in Italy as elsewhere in Europe.

In 1897, he tested a French de Dion single-cylinder engine mounted on a tricycle. Although it caught fire, he was still the first Italian engineer to produce a motorised vehicle.

In 1901, the first prototype motorcycle appeared, going on sale the following year. The production version was the first Bianchi vehicle to be constructed entirely out of components manufactured within its Milanese factory, including a 2hp engine built under licence from de Dion.

The famous Bianchi marque badge. In the first half of the 20th century Bianchi was one of Italy's most famous companies, before fading away in the 1960s.

In 1905, by which time it was also producing automobiles, the company was incorporated as Edoardo Bianchi and Co and turnover increased dramatically year on year.

These developments had been greatly assisted by the opening of a vast new plant in 1902 in Via Nino Bixio, Milan, which produced better models, including a much-improved single with such luxuries as magneto ignition, leading-link front forks and belt drive. In 1905, a new design of Traffault fork appeared and by 1910 a brand new 500cc model made Bianchi the envy of every other manufacturer in Italy.

During the World War I, Bianchi concentrated on building aero engines, but also supplied a 649cc V-twin engine and a purpose-built C75 military model. These were manufactured in considerable numbers, and when hostilities were ended, the V-twin was increased in size to 741cc.

However, it was not until 1920 that Bianchi began to take a serious interest in speed events. That year, Carlo Maffeis, riding a 500cc V-twin overhead-valve model, established a new flying kilometre world record of 124.9kph (77.6mph) on a stretch

One of Bianchi's top sellers between 1914 and 1919 was this 498cc ioe (inlet over exhaust) single. After this period, the company began making much faster bikes.

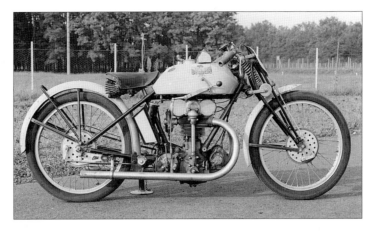

of road near Gallarate. Even then it was not a full factory-backed effort, as the engine was prepared by Carlo at his brothers', Miro and Nando, workshop. But by the mid-1920s, it had become necessary for Bianchi to counter the challenge made to its sales by the likes of Moto Guzzi and Garelli. The result was a brand new 350-class machine designed by Mario Baldi.

Baldi's design featured a 74mm bore and 81mm stroke, giving a displacement of 348cc. It had double overhead-cam driven by bevel shaft and spur gears. The camshafts and coil valve springs were completely enclosed in an oil-tight compartment, a rare feature in those days. Named the Freccia Celeste (Blue Arrow), it was fast and reliable, winning the long-distance Milano-Taranto, the Lario race, and the Italian Grand Prix at Monza.

Bianchi's Freccia Celeste (Blue Arrow) dohc 348cc single dominated Italian racing during the late 1920s. Its star rider was the legendary Tazio Nuvolari.

The legendary Tazio Nuolari, who had started with Garelli, was recruited to the Bianchi team, with riders like Varzi, Arcangeli and Moretti. Nuolari first rode the Bianchi in the 1925 Italian GP and won, at record speed, despite starting last on the grid with a push start and his leg in plaster! Until the end of 1930, the double overhead-cam Bianchi dominated Italian racing.

Baldi was also responsible for designing a new supercharged 492.69cc (52x58mm) four-cylinder racer which debuted in 1939. Due to the war and the FIM's ban on supercharging, this machine never reached its full potential.

BD
Czechoslovakia (Prague) 1927–29: Breitfeld & Danek built high-quality 490 and later 350cc unit-construction double overhead-cam singles. Production continued after 1929 as Praga, with shaft drive.

BEADING ENGINE CO
USA (Farmington, Michigan) 1949: This company made an auxiliary cycle-motor.

BEASLEY
England 1955: This motorbike was a racer with double overhead-cam 125cc engine twin.

BEAUFORT
England (South Twickenham) 1923–26: The Argson Engineering Company made invalid carriages, and also used their 170cc two-stroke single engine in a motorcycle.

BEAU-IDEAL
England (Wolverhampton) 1905–06: Beau-Ideal was an assembler which used Clement, JAP and Minerva engines.

BEAUMONT
England (Leeds) 1919–23: This firm used Wall 269cc two-stroke engines and Blackburne 349cc side-valves. They may also have built several prototype(s) with a Redrup three-cylinder radial, effectively a transversely-mounted flat twin with a single sticking up from in the middle.

Postwar, Bianchi concentrated most of its efforts on selling its range of two- and four-stroke commuter bikes for a transport-starved Italian domestic market. And although the factory did take part in trials and long-distance races, it was not to make a Grand

Bianchi team members and their machines (note the sidecar!), line up before doing battle in the 1935 ISDT.

Prix return until the end of the 1950s.

This return was headed by Lino Tonti, who became head of the Bianchi racing and development department in 1958. Tonti, previously with Aermacchi, FB Mondial and Paton, immediately designed a new 250 engine for either road-racing or motocross. Produced in both 174 (65x52.6mm) and 248cc (77x53.4mm) forms, these twin cam singles were more successful on dirt than on the road.

Tonti then created a series of double overhead-cam parallel twins ranging from 249.45 through to 498.06cc between 1960 and 1964. These were ridden by several riders including Derek Minter, Bob McIntyre and Reno Venturi with varying degrees of success.

But this was effectively the end and motorcycle manufacture stopped in 1967. Today the Bianchi name survives as a bicycle builder, owned by industrial giant Piaggio.

BIANCHI FRECCIA CELESTE RACER

1925

The Bianchi Freccia Celeste (Blue Arrow) single was designed by Mario Baldi and dominated Italian racing from 1925 until 1930. Baldi's design featured 348cc engine (74x81mm/2.9x3.2ins) and had double overhead-cams, driven by a bevel shaft and spur gears. A rarity in those days was that the camshafts and coil valve springs were completely enclosed in an oil-tight compartment.

Lubrication was by the dry-sump method, in which a gear-type pump was used; there was a separate oil tank was under the seat. An auxiliary oil supply to the overhead-camshafts came from a small tank on top of the fuel tank. A multiplate dry clutch transmitted the power output to a three-speed gearbox, in semi-unit with the crankcase, and there was the period tank, mounted hand level for gear changing.

This model's success was due to reliability, speed and the Bianchi team, of which Tazio Nuvolari was a member. Proof of the bike's

The Bianchi team at the 1928 Italian GP at Monza. From left to right, the star riders for the marque: Nuvolari, Zanchetta and Moretti.

sturdiness and endurance is the fact that it won all three of Italy's premier speed events: the long-distance Milano–Taranto, the TT-like Lario race and the Italian GP.

Nuvolari had begun his career aboard Garelli two-strokes, but was recruited into the Bianchi team, with the likes of Achille Varzi and Amilcare Moretti. Nuvolari made his Bianchi debut at the 1925 Italian GP, where he

was forced to take a position at the rear of the grid with a pusher. He was hampered by a plaster cast following a car accident on the same circuit in the previous week. Undeterred, Nuvolari, riding a Freccia Celeste, overtook the entire field to win the race at record speed, faster, in fact, than the majority of the 500s!

From that moment on, until the end of 1930, the Bianchi double

overhead-cam single totally monopolised the 350cc class in Italy. Nuvolari won the Italian Grand Prix again in 1926, 1927 and 1928. In 1929 he became the first man to lap Monza at over 145kph (90mph).

Engine: 348cc dohc vertical single
Gearbox: 3- or 4-speed
Weight: n/a
Top speed: 150kph (93mph)

BIANCHI TONALE   1954

Designed by Sandro Columbo, the Tonale (Tone) debuted in 1954. This is a 1962 175 model.

The Tonale (Tone) first appeared in 1954 and was designed by Sandro Columbo. Its main production series was a 175 (174.7cc, bore and stroke 60x61.8mm) sports roadster which produced around 8bhp, giving it a maximum speed approaching 112kph (70mph). But from this seemingly humble design came a raft of more specialised machines for road racing, motocross and record-breaking.

The racing version was constructed in two engine sizes: the standard 175 and a larger 220 (219.6cc, bore and stroke 65x66mm). In this latter model, the original chain-driven overhead system was replaced by three gears, known as the 'tre bottoni' (three buttons). Built between 1954 until 1956, the 220 was capable of 160kph (100mph).

The Cross 175 and 200 models were purpose-built motocross

bikes developed from the Tonale. Like the road racers, these were built in the mid-1950s, not to be confused with the later dirt racers designed by Lino Tonti.

Shortly before the Milan Show opened in November 1957, Bianchi hit the headlines after breaking a series of speed records at Monza with a specially built 175 Tonale encased in an aluminium streamlined shell. The machine, which could reach speeds of 193kph (120mph), was derived from the standard production Tonale, but employed a number of special components from the racing versions. Running on alcohol, with a compression ratio of around 10:1, maximum power was 17bhp at 8000rpm.

Because of the full enclosure, which was extremely narrow, there was almost no steering lock, so the machine had to be moved manually using a metal bar which slotted through the streamlining. A pair of air intakes looked after engine cooling, while the weight, complete with enclosure, was 120kg (265lb). The wheels carried 43cm (17-ins) tyres; only the rear one was equipped with a brake.

The production 175 Tonale was one of Bianchi's best sellers until manufacture of the motorcycle ceased in 1967.

Engine: 174cc, sohc single, 60x61.8mm, air-cooled
Power: 8bhp at 7000rpm
Gearbox: 4-speed foot change
Final drive: chain
Weight: 116kg (256lb)
Top speed: 111kph (69mph). Racing
219cc model: 161kph (100mph)

BE-BE
Germany (Berlin) 1923–27: The Berlin-Burger-Eisenwerk built their own 112cc two-stroke.

BECCARIA
Italy (Mondovi) 1924–28: Beccaria and Revelli made unremarkable bikes with Villiers 350cc two-strokes or side-valve and overhead-valve Blackburne engines, and Sturmey-Archer gearboxes.

BECCARTA
Italy 1925–28: This firm has a very similar history to Beccaria; the name may be a misprint.

BECKER
Germany (Dresden) 1903–06: Pioneer using Fafnir V-twins and their own singles.

BEFAG
Germany 1922–24: The Badischen Albertus Fahzeugwerke was one of several who failed to make a success of the Julius Lowy engine that could (in theory) be run on diesel after warming up on petrol: the engine was of 113 and 176cc.

BEHAG
Germany 1922–25: The Bremener Eisenhandels AG, an iron and steel works, made a limited number of motorcycles with JAP side-valve engines of 348 and 490cc. They possibly also made a two-stroke of their own design.

BIANCHI RASPATERRA MOTOCROSS

1960

Built in three engine sizes (250, 350 and 400cc) the Raspaterra (ground-scraper) series of motocross bikes was the work of Lino Tonti and closely related to the 318cc MT61 military motorcycle of the same period.

All three Raspaterra models were outwardly similar, using the bevel-driven twin cam single-cylinder configuration. The two larger engine sizes were the most popular, the 400cc (82x74mm) being simply a larger-bore version of the 350cc (77x74mm). The bikes were fitted with small megaphones with reverse cones, and although high revving, also offered a good spread of power lower down the scale.

The 250 version appeared first when factory tester and motocross rider Vincenzo Soletti used it in a number of excellent performances. Engine features included ekektron crankcases, twin-plug ignition, and on the 250 version, an engine which was safe to 10,000rpm, an

Bianchi factory rider Carlo Caroli, on his single cylinder Raspaterra (ground-scraper) during the 1960 Swiss Motocross Grand Prix.

amazing figure at the time for a four-stroke dirt bike. Soletti's performances earned him the 1959 250cc Italian Motocross Championship aboard the double overhead-cam Bianchi.

The motocross machines enjoyed a number of victories in Europe. A sole example of the Raspaterra, a 400, was exported to Terry Hill (a leading race sponsor of the era) in Belfast, Northern Ireland, in March 1960 and used for both motocross and grass track events at selected meetings throughout the province.

Engine: 400cc dohc single, air-cooled
Power: 22bhp at 6000rpm
Gearbox: 4-speed foot change
Final drive: chain
Weight: 180kg (398lb)
Top speed: 129kph (80mph)

BIANCHI 350 DOHC TWIN RACER

1961

Designed by Lino Tonti, the double overhead-cam parallel twin racer began life in 1960 as a 250cc, and soon after, was given a bigger 350cc engine.

Tonti's twin concept comprised an engine built in unit with a six-speed gearbox, mounted in a lightweight frame with a series of small-diameter tubes and an oval-

section brace from the top of the steering head to the centre section of the frame.

The engine featured a built-up crankshaft, while a train of gears ran up between the cylinders to

Created by Lino Tonti, the dohc twin cylinder Bianchi won the Italian title in 1964.

drive the camshafts. Electron alloy was employed for the cam boxes, clutch housing and integral oil sump; the crankcase, cylinder barrels and heads were aluminium alloy. Each head featured dual spark plugs, firing simultaneously due to a pair of Bosch 6volt double-ended coils aft of the steering head.

The larger-engined model debuted with Brambilla at the Monza Italian Grand Prix in 1960. and was obviously much more competitive than its 250 brother.

For 1961, Brambilla was joined by Scottish riders Bob McIntyre and Alastair King. The early part of the season was dogged by poor reliability, but in the Dutch TT the Bianchi twin performed well with McIntyre against MV's Hocking. Hocking won by the narrowest of margins.

McIntyre was signed by Honda in 1962, but in February 1963 the ex-MV rider, Remo Venturi, signed for Bianchi. With a 500cc version of the twin, success came at last: Venturi challenged MV Agusta in the world championship series; the 500 twin with 72bhp at 10,200rpm won the 1964 500cc Senior Italian Championship title.

Bianchi ceased motorcycle production and racing in 1965.

Engine: 350cc dohc parallel twin, 64x52.5mm, air-cooled
Power: 51bhp at 11,000rpm
Gearbox: 6-speed foot change
Final drive: chain
Weight: 127kg (280lb)
Top speed: 210kph (135mph)

BIG BRUTE

CANADA 1990–

BEISTIGUI HERMANOS (BH) Spain 1956–unknown: This was a moped that remained unchanged for many years.

BEKAMO Czechoslovakia 1923–30: Subsidiary of Bekamo (Berlin), initially with smaller (124cc) engines and the petrol tank in a big top tube. A 174cc engine arrived in 1927, and a 247cc engine arrived in a conventional frame in 1929.

BENOTTO Italy 1953–57: This company began with 49cc mopeds. In 1954 they added 150cc Dragon and 100cc Condor. In 1955, Benotto made Vulture 125cc and Centauro Gran Sport 160cc. They were apparently all two-stroke engines, some or all from Ilo.

BERCLEY Belgium (Brussels) 1905–09: A technically advanced machine and one of the earliest vertical parallel twins, this was a 616cc with mechanically-operated inlet and exhaust valves.

BERESA Germany (Munster) 1923–25: Beresa built small numbers of unimaginative singles with JAP and Blackburne 350 and 500cc engines.

PUTTING FOOLISHLY LARGE ENGINES into Norton Wideline Featherbed frames was a fine old custom. Alternatively, there is the option of building a motorcycle around a Chevrolet (mainly small-block) V8. This is the premise upon which the Big Brute was founded. The machine was built in Ontario, Canada by API-Racing Inc.

The company made its name by 'breathing on' Chevrolet engines for dragsters and street rods; it then entered the motorcycle business.

The all-aluminium ZZ4 has radical cams, big valves, a 10:1

Above: A Big Brute Special – though to be accurate, all Big Brutes were pretty much specials, built to their buyers' requirements.

Below: Truth in advertising: the bikes are indeed, big brutes. The reverse gear on this machine is a necessity.

compression ratio, trick crankshaft and pistons to produce 355bhp at 5250rpm from a normally aspirated 5.7-litre (350cid) engine. Various kinds of supercharged motors were also available, as were bigger engines, up to 8.25 litres (502cid).

At 477kg (1050lb), the V8 Big Brute really does live up to its name. Even the 'baby' V6, producing a mere 210bhp in its normally aspirated form and weighing only 448kg (985lb), is over twice the weight of a 'normal' motorcycle. The two-speed automatic transmission is all that anyone could reasonably ask for with so much power on tap,

and the Avon 230 38cmx20cm (15x8-in) round-section rear tyre means there is some chance of being able to steer round corners, though the manufacturers recommend a square-section tyre for maximum traction, especially with the V8.

Unsurprisingly, the promotional literature concentrates more on the bikes ability to turn heads rather than on its nimble handling, light weight or general practicality. It is, in effect, a drag bike that has been converted to (barely) street legal form.

Despite its enormous size, the machine is surprisingly easy to ride. Seat height may be specified

as either 66cm or 71cm (26 or 28ins), and ground clearance under the frame is specified as 13cm (7ins). Very large twin discs at the front, and a single disk at the rear, mean that it stops as well as goes. After all, the bike doesn't weigh much more than many conventional big tourers.

Available information on the machine's performance (and even specification) is sometimes conflicting. For instance, the 'fat bob' tanks are listed as 23 litres (6 US gallons) in one place, and 26.5 litres (7 US gallons) in another. However, it is is not surprising to find conflicting information of this sort available for a custom

machine that can be ridden as anything from a dragster to a tourer.

The machine is, of course, sold primarily as a 'cruiser', which for this bike's purposes is probably best defined as a machine that draws admiring glances whether it is moving or not, has more power than its riders could ever use and which is not primarily intended as a means of transport.

From an engineering point of view, it is one of the more convincing car-engined V8s. However, due to its size and sheer power, the Big Brute is still a long way from the mainstream motorcycling market.

BIG DOG

'WE ARE NOT A TECH INDUSTRY. We are the motorcycle industry.' These words from Big Dog CEO Sheldon Coleman sum up the company's philosophy perfectly. It likes to build motorcycles and does not want anyone telling it how to do it. Intriguingly, this is the same Sheldon Coleman of the Coleman Company, a Fortune 500 company noted for its first-rate camping products.

Like a number of the other American manufacturers who started to produce Harley-Davidson lookalikes, Big Dog's early fortunes were founded on the failure of Harley-Davidson to meet the burgeoning demand of the early 1990s. Countless 'performance' and 'special' parts were already available for making these machines go faster or turn corners better, or look different, or give a more comfortable ride, and it was easy to start assembling whole bikes from scratch.

Big Dog quickly found that they could produce their own designs, while still using an outmoded 45-degree V-twin. The 1750cc (107 cid) engines come from S&S and TP Engineering, with Big Dog rocker-boxes, lifter blocks and cam covers. This is really badge engineering, but not too different from what George Brough used to do with JAP and Matchless engines in his immortal Brough Superiors. The promotional material describes the engines as 'built at Big Dog' but they are not manufactured completely in-house at their factory in Wichita, Kansas.

Other components are optional, such as a TP Engineering/Andrews gearbox with oil-bath primary chain drive, S&S carburettor, Works Performance shock absorbers, Performance Machine brake callipers, or Big Dog's own 40-cm (16-ins) wheels, front forks and various cycle parts. As with most of its competitors, Big Dog places great stress on its paint facilities, and on the fact that you can have any colour or design that you want.

There are also a number of clever touches, such as an electronic attachment that flashes the brake-light three times when you first brake, the better to attract

Big Dog avoided much unpleasantness in naming their machines. This 'Bulldog' is tame compared with some other manufacturers' model names, such as 'Violator'.

the attention of the person behind you.

The Big Dog Vintage Sport, with its rubber-mounted engine, is representative of the six models (the others are Wolf, Bulldog, ProSport, Husky and Pitbull) and weighs an impressive 260kg (615lb) dry. Rather surprisingly, no mention is made in the manufacturers' specifications of the actual power output of the

engine with its slightly under-square 101x108mm bore and stroke and 9.6:1 compression ratio. Presumably, like a Rolls Royce, the answer is 'sufficient'; and equally presumably, it is sufficient because large engines can be tuned to produce a lot of power without being particularly stressed.

The low seat height and foot-boards emphasise the bike's low-speed appeal, and although reviews refer to a three-digit top speed, they also talk about 113–130kph (70–80mph) cruising.

It is, in short, a quintessentially American machine, appealing to enthusiasts of the Harley-Davidson.

BIMOTA

ITALY 1973–

THE ADMIRABLE PRINCIPLE behind Bimota motorcycles was to combine the handling flair of Italian chassis and suspension dynamics with the power and reliability of Japanese four-cylinder engine technology.

Even when the Japanese started producing machines that rivalled the Europeans in terms of handling in the 1980s, Bimota still managed to survive. The niche it occupies caters for riders who want exclusive sporting machines, often with innovative engineering features, built from the best materials and components available.

The firm's founder was Massimo Tamburini, a one-time central-heating engineer who had already built a reputation as a specialist motorcycle builder with a 750cc Honda-engined racing bike in 1973. A combination of his surname and those of his business partners, Bianchi and Morri, contrived to make up the name 'Bimota'.

Predictably, the emphasis was on racing, and Tamburini created a bike based on the Yamaha TTZ350 two-stroke twin, which was good enough to clinch the 350cc World Championship in 1980. In another

discipline, Charlie Williams proved the Bimota could be as effective in endurance racing.

This led to the production of road-going frames marketed as kits to be fitted with Japanese engines. Bimota launched its first complete road bike, the Suzuki GS750-powered SB2, in 1977. It was considerably lighter than the standard Suzuki GS750 and some 32kph (20mph) quicker as a result, with far better handling. This was in part due to the monoshock rear suspension that was years ahead of its time, and moving the fuel tank to a location under the engine, which lowered the centre of gravity.

The next machine was the spaceframe KB1, which could be specified with either a 903 or 1015cc Kawasaki double overhead-cam four-cylinder

Above: Bimota's S6BR was powered by the 1074cc 16-valve four-cylinder Suzuki GSX-R motor.

Below: Bimota's DB1 of 1986 proved to be the company's salvation. It was powered by the Ducati 748 V-twin, which created a bond with the Bologna firm.

Racing was in the blood at Bimota, and Virginio Ferrari took the Formula 1 title in 1987 on the Yamaha FZ750 powerd YB4. Left is the YBS, a sports derivative.

in the early 1980s, found salvation in the shape of the Ducati V-twin engine, which powered the DB1. Although a relatively conventional machine, its Italianate recipe proved an enduring success.

Meanwhile, Bimota's racing activities continued unabated. The company's biggest achievement was winning the Formula 1 Championship in 1987, when Virginio Ferrari rode a Bimota YB4 powered by a Yamaha FZ750 engine.

By 1990, Tamburini had departed to join Cagiva, and Pierluigi Marconi became chief engineer. He maintained the company's reputation for producing the unexpected; the result of his novel thinking over the previous decade was the Tesi (Thesis) which went into production in 1991. Its most

unit. Unusually, its rear monoshock was horizontally mounted, and it also featured variable steering geometry. This was created by means of eccentric upper and lower steering head bearings, which enabled adjustments of 9.9cm–11.9cm (3.9–4.7ins) to be made.

Chassis innovations like these established Bimota as an innovative concern offering hand-built, high-quality machines. The

inevitable result was that Bimotas were very expensive to build and this was reflected in their price. As so often happens to small-volume niche market manufacturers, Bimota frequently found itself over-extended, and during a crisis

Right: Bimota's state-of-the-art YB9 was based around a light-weight alloy beam-frame, and was aimed at the conventional sports bike market.

Below, right: The KB1 from 1979 was available with two Kawasaki dohc fours, mounted in a spaceframe chassis, and featuring variable steering geometry.

Below: Peeping out from behind a plethora of plastic fairings is the aluminium beam frame of Bimota's sports two-seater, the Bellario.

remarkable feature was hub-centre steering, in which the front wheel was mounted within a twin-sided swinging arm that operated a monoshock suspension unit. In common with all hub-centre systems, the idea was that handling benefited from separating braking and suspension forces, which conventional telescopic forks cannot do. But the Tesi was plagued with teething troubles and potential buyers, put off by the high price, preferred to stick with

the more conventional SB6 model using the Suzuki GSX-R1100 motor. While the Tesi was good for PR, it did not stop Bimota from going its own creative way, and during the 1990s, investing in the development of a 500cc Vdue engine. Unveiled in 1997, this was a direct-injection two-stroke V-twin mounted in a lightweight frame with 110bhp. It was typically radical for Bimota but there were serious fuel-injection problems, and it was withdrawn from sale.

There were six other machines on the Bimota stock list, however, using proprietary Suzuki, Yamaha and Ducati engines. The company bounced back with the naked Mantra, something of a departure for the firm that liked its bikes to be fully-faired. Late in 1998, Bimota was bought by Francesco Tognon whose formula was to return to Bimota's fundamental product line. The resulting DB4 used the Ducati 900SS engine with Mantra's ultra-light chassis.

BIMOTA TESI 1990

The Tesi (Thesis) first appeared as a prototype at the 1982 Milan Show, and appeared on the race track in 1984. The specification was extremely radical, a Bimota hallmark. Early versions used Honda V4 power units fitted in carbon-fibre frames, real cutting-edge technology at a time when even Formula One racing cars were not yet using carbon-fibre chassis. The steering on the early Tesi was controlled by hydraulics.

By the time the Tesi went into production in 1990, the chassis medium had switched to aluminium alloy, and consisted of a pair of machined plates bolted around the top half of a tuned 904cc fuel-injected eight-valve Ducati V-twin engine. Above this

was a subframe composed of small-diameter tubing, which served to support the fuel tank, seat, fairings and handlebar pivot. The Tesi had an alloy swinging arm front and rear, which gave it a strangely symmetrical appearance. The double-sided rear unit looked conventional enough, containing an eccentric chain adjuster on the right-hand side, but the front one

Left: The most radical feature of the Tesi 1D was its alloy swing-arm front suspension and steering arm.

Below: Bimota came out with the prototype Tesi in 1982 using Honda V4 power, but the 1D version shown here ran with a tuned 904cc Ducati V-twin.

gave the Tesi a strange appearance. The front wheel rotated around a large-diameter hollow hub which contained a spindle attached to the swingarm at either side. At the centre of the spindle was a vertical pin, which was attached to the hub by bearings that provided steering movement, and a steering arm on the hub was connected to the handlebars via a linkage. To some extent the width of the front fork as it emerged from the lower part of the fairing restricted the bike's steering lock.

The front brakes were applied by an equally complex-looking torque arm. Suspension damping was by coil-over monoshocks, carried in-board above the frame. The advantage over conventional telescopic forks was that the latter compresses under braking, so that road shocks cannot be absorbed so well, and the steering geometry changes as the machine's attitude alters in corners. The Tesi's set-up passes the forces directly backwards to the frame, whereas a normal steering head that accompanies telescopic forks transmits severe braking forces high up in the frame. The idea was that the Tesi frame could therefore be a more minimal structure, and thus lighter.

Engine: 904cc fuel-injected 8v Ducati V-twin
Power: 118bhp
Gearbox: 5-speed foot change
Weight: 188kg (414lb)
Top speed: 266kph (165mph)

BIMOTA YB10 SUPERLEGGERA

1996

THE ITALIAN COACHBUILDER, Touring of Milan, responsible for some of the most exquisite car bodies from the 1930s to the 1950s employed the suffix 'Superleggera', meaning lightweight. This was a reference to its exclusive method of using a tubular spaceframe and aluminium panels to create the lightest possible structure. With similar justification, Bimota used the same suffix for its exquisitely detailed YB11, although it might just as easily have applied it to a number of its

Bimota launched its super-light YB10 in 1996, powered by the 1002cc Yamaha ThunderAce engine, clad in one-piece fairing with carbon-fibre mudguards.

machines. Bimota's stock in trade was always to produce lighter, shorter and faster bikes than the big-name high-volume competition could manage. Like Touring of Milan, Bimota chassis are handmade. The YB10 appeared in mid-1996, using the Yamaha Thunderace liquid cooled 1002cc two-cylinder four-stroke engine. This 20-valve powerhouse was accompanied by high-quality cycle parts including Paioli forks and suspension, four-piston calliper Brembo brakes and Antera rims. With pin-sharp handling and staggering performance – potentially the fastest production bike at the time – it was two-thirds more expensive than the Yamaha FZR1000 Thunderace. Its superb build quality extended from the alloy beam frame to the one-piece body-fairing and carbon fibre mudguards, although the Bimota rider had to cope with small idiosyncrasies such as the foot pegs being set far back, making motorway riding uncomfortable. On fast, twisting roads, the YB10 delivered awe-inspiring power.

Engine: 1002cc liquid-cooled two-cylinder four-stroke 20v
Power: 131bhp
Gearbox: foot change
Final drive: chain
Weight: 183kg (403lb)
Top speed: 282kph (175mph)

BLACKBURNE

ENGLAND 1913–22

Not a Blackburne but a Cotton modified for sprint work, showing off its special frame construction and fitted with a 500cc Blackburne engine.

BLACKBURN (WITHOUT THE 'E'), entered the market in early 1913 as the De Havilland, and was built privately before public sales began in 1911. Its engine had an overhead-inlet-valve whose pushrod ran through a tube set in the inlet tract, an outside flywheel and belt final drive.

The flywheel carried over onto the Blackburn. Built by Burney & Blackburne in Hertfordshire, this had a 499cc side-valve engine with a one-piece crankshaft. This, along with the large flywheel, made it one of the smoothest running engines of the time. It had belt final drive, Saxon forks and a bottle-shaped neat silencer.

By late 1913, the firm had moved to Tongham in Surrey and

extended their name to Blackburne. The single model had transmission improvements and Druid forks, while a single-speed TT model was also listed. Both continued until 1916.

After World War I, OEC of Gosport, Hampshire manufactured the marque and produced three models for 1919, one a three-speed single, the others a two-and-three-quarters horsepower two-speed single and an 8hp V-twin combination. This and the larger single lasted to 1921, and the twin

was the company's sole model in 1922. The two company names were combined from 1923 as OEC Blackburne up to 1925, building engines for other manufacturers, before finally shutting down in the 1930s.

A typical Blackburne engine as used by many firms between the wars, in this case an upright 348cc overhead-valve single with magneto and external oil pump.

BLACK PRINCE

ENGLAND 1919–20

DESIGNED BY E.W. CAMERON, based in Doncaster, Yorkshire, this advanced machine used a 292cc Union engine, or a 396cc flat-twin two-stroke engine with a single spark plug. The plug was installed in a tube which connected the two combustion chambers. This tube also contained an automatic poppet valve which controlled the passage of the mixture from the common crankcase to the pistons. The rest of the engine was more conventional and was mounted along the frame. It drove a clutch and two-speed gear which in turn drove a bevel pair for a shaft to the rear wheel.

Although it never went into production, the rest of the machine was equally unusual. The pressed-steel frame comprised two sides that joined at the headstock and extended to fully enclose the mechanics and form the rear

mudguard, with the fuel tank set in the top. Suspension was by bottom-link forks at the front and pivoted-fork, controlled by spring units, at the rear.

The Black Prince was remarkable and the engine did run. However, it was considered too specialist to make it to the showroom. In 1920, Cameron

committed suicide, and with him went the future prospects of the motorcycle and a new three-wheeler, Black Prince Runabout.

Full enclosure was not the only unusual feature of the abortive Black Prince; it could also boast a flat-twin, two-stroke engine and had shaft final drive.

BMW

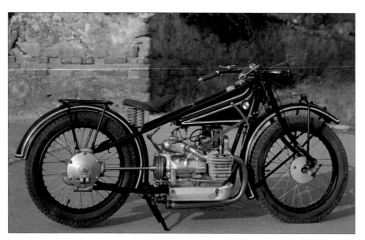

THE BAYERISCHE MOTOREN WERKE has seldom produced fashionable best sellers, and there have been times when the motorcycle line has been close to extinction; but BMW has always set its own agenda, and as a consequence, has produced some of the finest all-rounder motorcycles ever built.

The design philosophy is simple: the company does not

Above: The R42 of 1926 delivered over 40 per cent more power than the original R32, despite being powered by a side-valve engine of identical capacity.

build one-dimensional machines. Despite its success in breaking world speed records in the 1930s, as well as winning races, the firm has never made the fastest road-

going motorcycles in the world, though equally, its fastest machines have never been slouches. Its motorcycles are never the lightest and most precise on the road, but again, their handling frequently surprises those who dismiss them as suitable only for the staid and elderly. As touring machines, they can be ridden for very long distances, very fast, on

Above: The R11 (1929–33) introduced the pressed-steel 'star' frame, and had a 745cc motor delivering 18bhp – well over twice the power of the original R32.

Below: The R12 (1935) was a slightly updated R11, still with the 18bhp 745cc engine. It was replaced in 1937 by the R6, with the same power from only 600cc.

The R20 was the smallest BMW single, just 192cc, but delivered almost as much power as the 1924 flat twin: 8bhp instead of 8½.

any reasonable mixture of roads, with or without corners: with the possible exception of the American-orientated RT tourers, they are not huge, heavy, unwieldy and vulgar. From an engineering point of view, they are neither horrendously complicated, nor simple to the point of tractor-like crudeness. BMW is, of course, mostly associated with the transverse flat twin. This was the company's first successful design, and their customers refuse to let them discontinue it.

The company was formed by the amalgamation, in 1918, of the Bayerische Flugzeugwerke (Aeroplane Works) and the Gustav Otto Flugmaschinesfabrik (Flying Machine Factory). When demand for their original products fell rapidly after World War I, manufacturing motorcycles looked like a good idea. After two false starts – the two-stroke single Flink and the M2B15 flat-twin, designed for in-line installation – Max Friz, one of the founders of the Flugzeugwerke, designed the transverse flat-twin R32.

Even though restrictions on aero-engine manufacture were greatly relaxed in 1924, the R32 sold well enough to justify further development. Progress was extraordinarily rapid. First, the engine grew overhead valves in 1925 to become the R37, with almost twice the horsepower from

Steib's bullet-nosed sidecars were the classic accompaniment to BMWs – and Earles forks, as on this R60, were the classic accompaniment to Steib side-cars.

BEZDEZ
Czechoslovakia 1923–26: This firm manufactured auxiliary cycle-motors, and motorcycles with their own 145cc side-valve four-stroke engines.

BFG
France 1978–83: BFG (Boccardo, Favrio and Grange) built small numbers of a 1299cc Citroen car-engined Superbike, using a five-speed gearbox.

BH
Spain 1956–60: This company made two-stroke 49cc mopeds.

B & H
England 1923: This company specialised primarily in engine building, but made a few complete 996cc side-valve motorcycles.

BICHRONE
France (Paris) 1902–07: Made complete V-twin two-strokes of two-and-a-quarter to two-and-three-quarters bhp, as well as supplying engines to other makers.

BIKOTOR
England 1951: This auxiliary cycle motor was a 47cc two-stroke which weighed 5kg (11lb).

Above: The R90S, introduced in 1973 – a 1975 model is pictured – was BMW's first 'superbike', powerful and stylish with a unique airbrushed paint job.

Right: BMW first went to 1000cc (actually 980cc) in 1976: this 1978 racer has the old-style rounded rocker-boxes and 'bikini' fairing introduced on the R90S.

the same displacement, 16bhp at 4000rpm. Only 175 of these fast 134kg (295lb) twins were built before it and the R32 were replaced in 1926 by the R42 and R47. Both were still 68mm square, the former with side-valves and 12bhp, the latter, overhead-valves, with 18bhp.

Bigger engines followed, with yet more power, and the 1930s became BMW's record-breaking, race-winning era. In 1932, for example, Ernst Henne increased the world speed record for two-wheelers to 244.4kph (151.9mph), and the blown 500cc racers of 1939 delivered around 70bhp, about the same as the R100RS 27 years later, in a machine that weighed only 139kg (306lb).

During World War II, BMW reverted to making aero engines for the Luftwaffe and the amazing R75 for the army. Postwar restrictions meant that the singles (originally introduced in 1925) had to be the mainstay of the company for a while, after which there ensued a long period of dormancy when it looked as though BMW might even leave the motorcycle business.

However, the company's fortunes were revived by the new 'stroke' series, with their

Like most other bike manufacturers, BMW had to adapt to the 'motorcycle-as-toy' market. This Cruiser from 1997 is an example.

The F650 – a 1994 model is pictured here – was built by Aprilia and had a Rotax single-cylinder engine, which horrified true BMW aficionados.

completely redesigned engines, and by two landmarks in quick succession, the R90S and the R100RS. Then came the 'Brick'. This was an in-line, longitudinally mounted, liquid-cooled straight-four that BMW imagined would replace the seemingly immortal 'boxer'. There was also a K75, or three-quarter-brick, which was really the 1000cc engine with one cylinder removed to give 750cc.

But the boxer wouldn't die, and in 1992 came the new generation of overhead-valve, four-valve-per-cylinder boxers, which soon diversified more interestingly than the brick series, even though the bricks rose to 1200cc to preserve their power advantage.

To extend the BMW marque, the company also brought out the 650cc Funduro and the 125cc C1

scooter, but these are widely ignored by BMW aficionados, the former because it has chain drive quite apart from the fact that it was built by Aprilia with a Rotax engine. The latter doesn't qualify as a serious motorcycle.

The bottom line, however, appears to be this. No matter who attacks BMW, or how, they still manage to sell enough of their machines to remain profitable and competitive.

The 125cc C1 was BMW's rethink of the scooter – just when Lambrettas and Vespas were becoming fashionable again.

BIM
Japan (Tokyo) 1956–61: This Japanese firm made BMW copies with engines of 250, 350, 500 and 650cc.

BIMA
France 1952–unknown: Initially making an auxiliary cycle motor, this firm then manufactured 49cc mopeds with horizontal cylinders. A Peugeot trademark.

BIMM
Italy (Montemurlo) 1968–79: This firm, which became Bimotor in 1979, made two-stroke trials and motocross bikes with 49 and 123cc Minarelli engines.

BIMOFA
Germany 1922–25: Hansa side-valve engines propelled these Gustav Kunstmann-designed machines.

BIMOTOR
Italy 1979–unknown: BIMM (q.v.) changed its name to Bimotor in 1979 and made the same two-stroke trials and motocross bikes as before.

BINKS
England (Nottingham) 1903–06: One of the first straight-fours, and probably the first transverse four. The 385cc side-valve four-stroke was fitted in both orientations. However, Binks was later well known as a carburettor manufacturer.

BMW R32   1923

The old saying tells us that 'what looks right, is right', and BMW proved it with the handsome R32. The brakes are primitive, of course, and everything is more exposed than we are used to today, such as the Kardan shaft and the speedo drive. Saddle tanks were

The Ancestor: 68mm square for 494cc, and only 8½ bhp at 3200rpm, but still a shaft drive flat twin – still recognizably a BMW.

already in use elsewhere, but this machine has one of the cleanest flat-tank designs of all time, and

the immaculate standard of manufacture and finish reflected BMW's aero-engine ancestry.

The R32 soon evolved into the R37 and then the R42 and R47, setting a standard of incomprehensibility in model numbering that remained until the appearance of the 'stroke' series in 1969. The twins also developed from the R39 single in 1925, literally half a boxer, still 68mm square, but with overhead-valves. En route to the models with the 'star' frame, described below, BMW introduced the R52 and R57 in 1927, with incremental improvements on the R42 and R47, and then the side-valve R52, which was the first to vary the bore and stroke: it had a long-stroke 63x78mm engine for extra flexibility, still with 12bhp, while the R57 had 18bhp.

Then, in 1928, BMW brought out two further models with big

engines. The side-valve R62 used the 78mm long-stroke crankshaft and a square 78mm bore, for 745cc and 18bhp (with lots of torque) at 3400rpm. The sportier overhead-valve R63 had the old 68mm stroke with a heavily over-square 83mm bore, for 734cc and 24bhp at 4000rpm.

In only five years, BMW had produced an extraordinary number of variations on a theme. Their most powerful model now had three times the power of the original, and the single, thanks to its lighter weight, delivered almost the same performance as the R32 original twin.

Engine: 494cc sv transverse flat twin, 68mm 'square', air-cooled
Power: 8.5bhp at 3300rpm
Gearbox: 3-speed hand change
Final drive: Kardan shaft
Weight: 120kg (264lb)
Top speed: 90kph (56mph)

BMW R17   1935

The R17 was the most developed of the slightly strange-looking 'star' frame BMWs, and had telescopic forks, four-speed gearbox, and a significantly more powerful version of the over-square 83x68mm engine. Twin Amal carburettors helped to boost the power output to 33bhp.

The telescopic forks permitted wheels of the same size front and rear, which were made interchangeable. This remained a BMW feature until 1969.

The pressed-steel 'star' frame had first appeared in 1929 with the R11 and R16. The R11 used the 745cc side-valve, delivering the same 18bhp as before, while the R16 had the overhead-valve 734cc, now with 25bhp. At the same time that the R17 replaced the R16, the R12 replaced the R11: the same old 18bhp side-valve and a single carburettor.

When BMW returned to using conventional frames in 1936 with the R5, they also redesigned the

engine, with twin cams, to allow shorter, stiffer and lighter push-rods; this permitted higher engine speeds: 24bhp at 5800rpm.

At 165kg (363lb), with its new tubular frame, the R5 was 18kg (40lb) lighter than the pressed-steel R17, so it was only a little slower and a lot more precise on the road. Fitting a positive-stop

foot change also made it easier to ride at speed than the R5.

The R6 of 1937 was a side-valve derivative of the R5 with 70mm bore and 78mm stroke,

With an impressive 33bhp, the R17 was the fastest of the 'star' frame BMWs, though the weight of the frame told against it.

delivering the same 18bhp as the R11 and R12, but from a 600 instead of 734cc engine. The R51 and R61 of 1938 were essentially similar to the R5 and R6, but with rear suspension, and, in the case of the R61, slightly slower, thanks to a lower compression ratio and and extra 11kg (24lb), in weight.

Sports enthusiasts cheered the R66 of the same year, 69.8x78mm, 597cc, and 30bhp at 5300rpm in a bike weighing 187kg (411lb) for a top speed of about 145kph (90mph). Also in 1938 was the R71, the 745cc side-valve, but now with 22bhp at 4600rpm thanks to the twin cams and twin carbs, the first 745cc side-valve to use these components.

Engine: 494cc sv transverse flat twin, 83x68mm, air-cooled
Power: 33bhp at 5000rpm
Gearbox: 4-speed hand change
Final drive: Kardan shaft
Weight: 183kg (403lb)
Top speed: 140kph (87mph)

BMW R75   1941

The R75 is one of the most gloriously improbable outfits of all time. It was designed from the start as an outfit, with a power take-off

(with lockable differential) to drive the side-car wheel, with a machine-gun mounted on the side car. Despite the Wehrmacht's need

for a slogger that could operate equally well in the sands of the North African desert or the snows of the Russian front, it was an

overhead-valve design, not a side-valve; In fact, BMW were never again to make a side-valve after the R71. Lowering the

compression ratio to around 5.6:1 to 5.8:1 meant that it delivered only 26bhp. However, it did this extraordinarily tractably, though a gearbox which offered four speeds and reverse, and a two-ratio transfer box, so that it had in total eight forward and two reverse gears.

Unfortunately, it was very difficult to drive. A truly skilled rider could (and still can) traverse the most extraordinary and difficult of terrains, but to get the most out of the machine, the sidecar passenger really needed to help the driver with the gear-changing.

The R75 outfit was completely impractical compared to the American Jeep, but Russian and Ukrainian derivatives were still in production 60 years later.

At 420kg (924lb) it was heavy, too, and even the hydraulic brakes could struggle to stop it. The Jeep favoured by the Allies was a vastly superior vehicle in every practical sense, though reputedly, Harley-Davidson's fabled XA flat twin was the result of American admiration for the R75.

Engine: 745cc ohv transverse flat twin, 78x78mm, air-cooled
Power: 26bhp at 4000rpm
Gearbox: 8-speed plus reverse hand change
Final drive: Kardan shaft
Weight: 420kg (924lb)
Top Speed: 95kph (59mph)

BMW R24 — 1949

When BMW went back to motorcycle manufacture after World War II, engine size was initially limited to 250cc, so the firm had to rely on a single, the R24. Although the singles are far less well-known than the twins and never very fast, they have a devoted following of their own. All exhibited the very high degree of refinement and finish that charac-terised the twins of the same era, and to a considerable extent, they were simply half a twin turned through 90 degrees, complete with shaft drive.

The first BMW single, the R39, was made from 1925 to 1927, with the 68x68mm 'square' layout of the original twin, giving 247cc. Like all BMW singles, it was overhead-valve. Power output was six-and-a-half horsepower. Then came a series of swings in

Traditional BMW singles were built to the same standards as the twins: when BMW re-entered the singles market in the 1990s, they bought in a cheaper machine.

capacity, and a model numbering system that was incomprehensible: the R2 (198cc, 6hp, 63x64mm, 1931–36), R4 (398cc, 12hp, 78x84mm, 1932–38), R3 (305cc, 11hp, 68x84mm, 1936), R35 (340cc, 14hp, 72x84mm, 1937–40) and R20 (192cc, 8hp 60x68mm, 1937–38).

Subsequent singles reverted to 68x68mm, and unusually logical numbering: R23 (10hp, 1938–41),

R24 (12hp, 1949), R25 (12–13hp, three models, 1950–55), R26 (15hp, 1955–60), and the last, the R27 (18bhp, 1960–67).

Engine: 247 cc ohv vertical single, 68mm square, air-cooled
Power: 12bhp at 5600rpm
Gearbox: 4-speed foot change
Final drive: Kardan shaft
Weight: 130kg (286lb)
Top speed: 95kph (59mph)

BMW R69S — 1960

The R69S was the fastest production road-going BMW of the pre-'stroke' era, and the last machine that die-hard traditional-ists accept as being a true BMW. It was without doubt beautifully made and finished, significantly

better than later machines, but equally, it was not as well designed. In effect, it looked both backwards, to BMW's days as a manufacturer of fast tourers, and forwards, to the forthcoming R90S and R100RS.

It was the ultimate development of a lineage that began in 1951, the year that BMW resumed production of twins with the R51/2: 68mm square, overhead-valve, and 24bhp at 5800rpm. In 1951 came the very similar R51/3

7000rpm could just reach a top speed of 161kph (100mph).

In 1955, BMW adopted the distinctive Earles forks, which still attract devotees among side-car riders today but are generally regarded with mixed feelings by others. Otherwise the long-lived 494cc R50 was pretty much an R51/2 with another couple of horsepower, and remained in production until 1969. The R60 had 28bhp from the 590cc engine, while the Earles-fork version of the sporty R67/3 was the R69, again with 35bhp, this time at 6800rpm.

The R69 metamorphosed into the R69S, and the R50 into the R50S of 1960–62, this time with 35bhp from the 68mm 'square' engine, and 160kph (100mph) top speed, though the R50 continued in production and outlived the R50S.

Engine: 590cc ohv transverse flat twin, 72x73mm, air-cooled
Power: 42bhp at 7000rpm.
Gearbox: 4-speed foot change
Final drive: Kardan shaft
Weight: 202kg (444lb)
Top speed: 175kph (109mph)

and the R67, the latter a 72x73mm, 590cc machine with slightly more power (26bhp) despite a 5.6:1 compression ratio.

The R67/2 (1952–54) offered 28bhp instead of 26; the R67/3 was similar again; and the sporting R68 (1952–54) with 35bhp at

The R69S (this is a 1960 model) is regarded by many as the apotheosis of the classic Earles-fork BMW.

BMW R90S

1973

The R90S was the super-sports version of the /6 series, BMW's first high-performance 'superbike'. Forsaking Bings for Dell'Ortos helped wring a little more power out of the high-compression, big-bore engine, and 67bhp was enough to reach the magic 200kph (124mph) marker, with the rider crouched well behind the (mainly cosmetic) bikini fairing.

The performance was, however, only half the story. What really sold the bike was its looks, the near-miraculous airbrushed paint job on the tank and fairing that made it look very fast even when it was standing still.

In fact, the performance was deceptive, and at maximum speed, there was some high-speed weave that marred the top end performance of the /5 series as well. In practice, though, few riders regularly exceeded 161kph (100mph) in the USA, a very important market, so this didn't really matter. Even so, the /7 series addressed the problem with considerable success.

The other bikes in the /6 line-up were the R90/6, the R75/6 and the

R60/6. Unforgivably, the unfaired R90/6 was supplied with only a single front disk brake, even though the optional second brake was all but essential. In fact, it was needed on the R75/6, as well.

The /6 machines were the logical successors to the original 'stroke' series, the four-speed, drum-braked /5 models of 1969. From them they inherited the new engine with a one-piece crankshaft (instead of built up), a common

70.6mm bore, and a single camshaft mounted above the crankshaft. The 498cc R50/5 was under-square with a 67mm bore; the 599cc R60/5, over-square at 73.5mm; and the 745cc R75/5 well over square at 82mm. Power

The R90S (this is a 1975 model) was most popular in 'Bol d'Or' orange-on-yellow; today, models in this colour sell for much more than the grey-on-grey alternative.

outputs were 32, 40 and 50bhp respectively, allowing top speeds of 157kph (97mph), 167kph (104mph) and 175kph (109mph).

When the /7 series came out, the lack of a small-capacity machine was remedied with the R45 and R65, without a 'stroke' designation because they were not of the same series. The R45 was particularly interesting because it actually had a 473cc engine and could equally well have been called an R50 – an unusual example of understatement by a manufacturer. It was made in both 27bhp and 35bhp versions, partly for tax and insurance reasons and partly because some organisations had no need for a bike with more power. The R45 and R65 were good small bikes but were never a great success with private buyers.

Engine: 898 cc ohv transverse flat twin, 90x70.6mm, air-cooled
Power: 67bhp at 7000rpm
Gearbox: 5-speed foot change
Final drive: Kardan shaft
Weight: 205kg (451lb)
Top speed: 200kph (124mph)

BMW R100RS

1976

For many, the first series R100RS was the ultimate boxer, and arguably the greatest sports-tourer ever built. There have been faster sports-tourers, but none that could be ridden as fast, as far. The 24-litre (five-and-a-quarter-Imperial gallon, six-and-a-half US gallon) tank allowed a range of anything from 280km (175 miles) for really hard riding two-up, to well over 440km (275 miles) when ridden gently. The usable cruising speed was at least 185kph (115mph) and with the rider crouched behind the screen, speeds of well over 209kph (130mph) were readily attainable.

The engine was the most powerful development of the stroke-series pushrod flat twin in a road-going motorcycle – when the R100RS was reintroduced later, it dropped to 60bhp – and its fairing was wind-tunnel designed to give a high top-speed along with good protection from weather and buffeting. And, of course, it looked (and still looks) stunning.

The other bikes in the /7 line-up were the R100/7, the 'naked' version; the R100S, the successor to the R90S; the R100RT, with the

The R100RS (this is a 1977 model) was the Boxer that wouldn't die; dropped when the Brick came out, it was re-introduced in response to public demand.

barn-door fairing, suitable for slow cruising on wide roads; and the R75/7, later the R80/7 (also made as the R80RT) for those who could live without the extra power. Later

still came the mighty R80GS and R100GS off-road bikes, as detailed below.

Engine: 980cc ohv transverse flat twin, 94x70.6mm, air-cooled
Power: 70bhp at 7250rpm
Gearbox: 5-speed foot change
Final drive: Kardan shaft
Weight: 210kg (462lb)
Top speed: 200kph (124mph)

BMW R80GS

1980

No one could readily forget their first sight of an R80GS. Quite apart from its size and the huge fuel tank, the single-sided rear suspension was a big surprise. An off-road motorcycle of this size might seem at first to have limited

appeal; it is, after all, very big and heavy, and has rather more power than is generally needed on dirt. But the R80GS and the later R100GS were superb desert racers, doing very well in the Paris-Dakar races.

Without anything to compare it to, the R80GS looks quite modest. Only when you get on it do you realize how big it is.

Perhaps more importantly, they were also remarkably good town bikes, with power on tap, good suspension, and enough bulk to be a presence on the road.

For these reasons, the GS was, for a considerable period, the motorcycle for looking good on. Its only real drawback was that it really only suited tall riders.

Remarkably, even when the overhead-cam 'new' boxers came out, there were still GS versions: the R1100GS boasted 80bhp, an increase of 60 per cent over the original R80GS and 10bhp more than the original R100RS.

Engine: 798cc ohv transverse flat twin, 85x70.6mm, air-cooled
Power: 50bhp at 6500rpm
Gearbox: 5-speed foot change
Final drive: Kardan shaft
Weight: n/a
Top speed: 185kph (115mph)

BMW K1
1989

The K1 was as far from the BMWs of 1960 as could be imagined: very fast, and very eye-catching with its blue bodywork and vivid yellow graphics. It was decried by some as too big and too heavy to be a true sports bike; it is doubtful whether its detractors could have ridden it to its limit.

It was derived from the original 'brick' of 1983, which had 90bhp from the same capacity. The longitudinally mounted straight four was unusual enough. The designers fitted the engine on its side, with the crankshaft on one side and the overhead-cams on the other. This was a master-stroke, though the decision to do this may have been influenced as much by the desire to have a layout that was unique to BMW as to any other practical consideration.

The 'brick' was made in plain unfaired guise (K100), with a touring fairing (K100RT) and with a sports fairing (K100RS). The latter could top 225kph (140mph), and the unfaired K100 was at least as fast as the R100RS. In 1985, a 741cc triple was introduced, naked

like the K75 or with a miniature fairing like the K75S. With 74bhp and balance shafts to disguise the inevitable vibration that resulted from sawing off one cylinder, it was a nice bike but never really caught on and was eventually dropped.

The full-sized 'brick' was steadily improved, as it needed to

be. Early models smoked heavily when started, and the petrol tank could get too hot to touch as a result of heat transfer from the cooling system. The four-into-one exhaust was justly decried as ugly, and yellowed with use. There were, however, many excellent features; the sight glass to check oil levels was one.

The 1989 K1 was the go-faster version of the original 1983 Brick, with power voluntarily limited to 100bhp. A vivid paint job highlighted its angular lines.

The 1987 K100LT was a 'loaded' tourer with ABS brakes; in 1992, the K1100RT and RS appeared with 1092cc; and the 1997 K1200RS (actually 1171cc, 70.5x75mm) decided to disregard the voluntary 100bhp limit that every other manufacturer was ignoring, too. It boasted 130bhp, a six-speed gearbox, and a top speed that few had the nerve to explore. In many ways, it was a more practical version of the K1, though (as so often with BMWs) there were already faster motorcycles on the road. The K1200LT was the five-speed, 98bhp tourer.

Engine: 987cc dohc 16-valve in-line longitudinal four, 67x70mm, liquid-cooled
Power: 100bhp at 8000rpm
Gearbox: 5-speed foot change
Final drive: Kardan shaft
Weight: 234kg (515lb)
Top speed: 233kph (145mph)

BMW R1100S
1998

The R1100S was the super-sports version of the four-valve-per-cylinder, fuel-injected boxers that first appeared in 1992. Although Krauser had made four-valve heads for the older boxers, they were not well regarded. The new bikes not only had factory-installed four-valve heads, but also a single, chain-driven overhead-cam per cylinder.

In common with the makers of a number of other big twins, BMW decided not to take the conventional liquid-cooled route, but to take advantage of the cooling properties of the lubricating oil instead. Whereas oil-coolers (and deep, high-capacity sumps) were popular accessories for the old boxers (to help cooling at high speeds on hot days) oil cooling was an integral part of the new boxers right from the beginning.

Like Harley-Davidson, BMW were stuck with an engine format. Unlike Harley-Davidson with their V-twin, BMW made a real attempt to redesign their flat twin.

The most radical departure was not, however, the engine design, but the patented front suspension, the 'telelever' which effectively eliminated dive on braking and twist under any conditions. It can be seen most clearly on the unfaired models, looking at first glance like a mudguard that has unaccountably extended back to the engine. A monoshock behind the headstock provides the springing and damping. Of course it worked very well, but at least as importantly in a very conservative market, it didn't look too unusual.

Side-on, the R1100S looks neat and compact, despite its large engine. It is not until the bike faces you from the front that you realise how far the cylinders stick out.

The rather higher-set cylinders did, however, look a little odd to those used to 'classic' BMWs, and although they may have reassured new riders who feared grounding the 'pots' on the corners, the truth was that a lot of other things touched down before the rocker-box covers on the earlier bikes; crash bars, for one, were always a dubious idea, because they actually did get in the way of even moderately-spirited riding.

The new boxer line-up soon showed more variation (and popular appeal) than the 'bricks': an off-road R1100GS (with 'only' 80bhp) and an R850R (69bhp) in 1994, and an R1100R and R1100RT tourer in 1995. Then in 1996 came an R1200C cruiser, with an 1170cc version of the big

twin, delivering a mere 61bhp for very relaxed power delivery, even if traditional motorcyclists thought it looked strange. Interestingly, despite its impressive performance, the R1100S only has an 18 litre (four UK, five US gallons) fuel tank, the smallest of the Rs; the biggest, the R1100RT, boasts 26 litres (five UK, six US gallons). The motorcycle-as-toy has established itself very clearly, even among BMW's big twins.

Engine: 1085cc ohv 8volt four-stroke transverse flat twin, 99x70.5mm, air/oil-cooled
Power: 98bhp at 7500rpm
Gearbox: 5-speed foot change
Final drive: Kardan shaft
Weight: 229kg (504lb)
Top speed: 225kph (140mph)

BOAR

USA 1990s

BOAR MOTORCYCLES OF NAPLES, Florida, is one of many assemblers making Harley-Davidson lookalikes from proprietary components. Main parts include Kenny Boyce frames, RC components, Elite series brakes and wheels, and Sputhe motors. The base option is 1550cc (95cid), but 1700cc (104cid) is available and the machine can also be ordered with bigger engines such as the enormous 2179cc (133cid) Total Performance Prepared Motor.

More emphasis is placed on the number of polished components and the extensive use of stainless steel than on performance, such as the (stainless steel) brake rotors, although many BMW twins owners switched to aftermarket cast iron for better braking.

The tank is light alloy and the wheels are a very traditional 48cm (19ins) at the front and 46cm (18ins) at the back. The Connolly leather seats can withstand light rain only.

As ever with big American cruisers, there is a curious mix of ancient and modern, including 'maintenance-free self-diagnosing wiring' and a digital display that is, according to the reviews, not too good in bright sunlight but very dramatic in the evenings.

At 245kg (540lb) for the base model, Boars could be suitable for heavy solo touring or for light touring, two-up. For heavier touring two-up, there is the Classic, 268kg (590lb) dry.

BLEHA
Germany (Neiheim-Ruhr) 1923–26: This company used 247cc DKW two-strokes and its own 247cc side-valve four-strokes in its own motorbike frames.

BLERIOT
France 1920–23: Parallel twins of 498cc, in side-valve and overhead-valve guises, came from the aircraft manufacturer.

BLOTTO
France (Dijon) 1951–55: This company took the role of assembler and used 123 to 348cc proprietary two-strokes.

BLUMFIELD
England (Birmingham) 1908–14: These were short-lived machines, but nevertheless they were big enough to compete in TT races. Some engines were water-cooled.

BM
France 1954: Powered by its own 250cc flat twin, this may not have entered commercial production.

BM
Italy 1928–31: Side-valve and overhead-valve 490cc JAP engines powered these rare three-speed Italian motorcycles.

BM
Italy 1950–early 1980s: A bewildering range of mopeds, minibikes, lightweights, scooters and motorcycles up to 250cc with engines from Ilo, NSU, Minarelli and possibly others, as well as their own overheah-cam singles, came from this manufacturer.

BOHMERLAND

CZECHOSLOVAKIA 1925–39

BOHMERLAND, SOLD AS CECHIE in German-speaking areas, made some of the unlikeliest motorcycles ever constructed. Several are preserved in the National Technical Museum in Prague.

All but the last few were four-stroke singles: a 598cc overhead-valve engine with open pushrods and valve gear clattered away just in front of the rider's groin, because the top of the engine was rather above the top of the seat, which was in turn below the level of the top of the tyres. When introduced, the engine delivered 16bhp at 4000rpm, though later, it was persuaded to yield 25bhp at the lower speed of 3600rpm. Transmission was three-speed, hand change, with chain final drive, and unexpectedly, performance could be quite sprightly.

The enormously long frame of the Touring version (top speed 121kph, (75mph)) permitted two pillion seats behind the rider, and

the small front petrol tank was supplemented by two more torpedo-shaped tanks either side of the rear wheel. The Jubilee version (129kph, (80mph)) had a somewhat shorter frame and a more conventional tank, and the

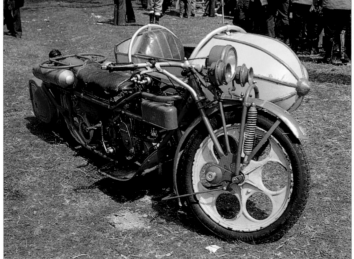

Racer variant of the Jubilee (148kph, (92mph)) enjoyed some success in hill climbs.

By contrast with the curious frame and the very old-fashioned engine, the wheels were cast alloy and look very modern. However,

Surprisingly few Bohmerlands were made, but surprisingly many have survived in museums and private collections.

they drew attention to the leading-arm front suspension (there was no rear suspension at all), a highly unusual design. All sales were direct from the factory, with no dealer network, and Albin Liebisch, the designer, was apparently keen to personalise the motorcycles for each customer.

In 1938, a 350cc Bohmerland was announced, apparently an overhead-valve four-stroke though one source reports a two-stroke. Very few of these machines were made before World War II spelled the end of all production and of an independent Czechoslovakia.

When you consider that many Bohmerlands were designed to carry three people, adding a side-car meant they had more seats than many small cars.

BOMBARDIER

CANADA 1978–87

THE BOMBARDIER SNOWMOBILE Group of Canada not only built the first snowmobile, but were involved with other forms of transport as well. For a while, they built motorcycles under their own

name, and also under the name, Can-Am. In both cases, they used Austrian Rotax engines, since the Group owned Rotax.

They also used the company name to rebadge various 50cc

mopeds and motorcycles that came from Puch, another Austrian firm, and these were sold through their existing sales outlets.

In 1978, the Group sought to increase sales by adapting one of

their dirt bikes for military use. They chose their 247cc enduro machine for this purpose. The bike had a single-cylinder, disc-valve, air-cooled engine with its carburettor fitted behind the cylinder to keep the width of the whole unit down. It was attached to a long inlet passage cast as part of the main castings which also carried the mixture along to the disc-valve and crankcase. The exhaust gases went into a high-level system that ran over the top of the engine and terminated with a spark arrestor. The engine drove a five-speed gearbox built in unit and final drive was by an exposed chain, not perhaps the best feature for a military model.

The frame and suspension were typical of the period for an off-road machine, with plenty of ground clearance under the duplex tubes. These ran close under the engine unit and into the sub-frame, while the rear fork was controlled by twin spring-and-damper units. Telescopic forks provided front suspension, with a 53cm (21-ins) wheel at the front and an 45cm (18-ins) wheel at the back. Both wheels used drum brakes and the machine came with full road equipment. A rear rack, panniers and extra rear-light were added to this package and the whole machine was finished in khaki. Despite its intended use and customer, the competition side

Right: This machine was produced in Canada and supplied to the British Army. Its design was based on the firm's off-road models.

plates were retained on each side.

The Bombardier was sold in small numbers to the Canadian Armed Forces and successfully tested by the US Marine Corps in 1981. Across the Atlantic, the machine was adopted by the British Armed Forces and built for them by the remains of the BSA Group, using several British components. This version was little altered from the Canadian one and was also used by Belgian forces.

Below: The rear quarter of the Bombardier shows its off-road roots and totally practical design for tough riding conditions.

BOND

ENGLAND 1950–53 AND 1958–62

BEST KNOWN FOR SMALL three-wheeled cars, Lawrence Bond produced many other designs including both motorcycles and scooters. His first motorcycle was a strange machine which appeared in 1950. This had an unusual all-alloy frame, made from sheet metal rolled into a large, tapered, oval-section tube, which was cut away at the rear for a massive mudguard to stiffen it. The whole frame was then riveted together. The front mudguard was equally large and both enclosed most of each wheel.

Neither wheel had any suspension; the 10-cm (4-ins) tyres

on 40-cm (16-ins) wheels with split rims had to iron out bumps. The 99cc Villiers 1F engine was hung from the main beam and flanked by large legshields which had built-in footboards. During 1950, the early tube forks were replaced by telescopic ones and a 125cc JAP two-stroke engine was briefly offered in 1951, with a three-speed, in-unit gearbox. The same year, manufacturing was taken over by Ellis of Leeds, Yorkshire, where production continued until 1953.

Meanwhile, Bond went on to design the more conventional BAC, powered by the 99cc Villiers or 125cc JAP two-stroke engines. These models appeared in 1951 and in 1952 were joined by the Gazelle scooter, which used a 122cc Villiers 10D engine with three-speed gearbox. While its line was typical of a scooter, it differed in that the engine was enclosed by a grille of steel bars. The fuel tank went on top of the rear mudguard behind the saddle; the front wheel had telescopic forks. In 1953, only

the Gazelle was listed, with the choice of 10D or 1F engines, but by the end of the year it had disappeared.

In 1955, Bond designed another scooter, the Sherpa, using a 99cc Villiers 1F engine under glass-fibre bodywork. It was launched in the car park of the Earls Court Exhibition Centre in London, but only one prototype was ever built.

The Bond name continued to appear on the three-wheelers. The

The side aspect of the Bond Minibyke shows its beam frame and vast mudguards. Usually powered by a Villiers engine this machine has a 125cc JAP unit.

firm moved to Preston, Lancashire, before producing another scooter in 1958. Although typical of its type, the glass-fibre body styling was heavy. Powered by a 148cc Villiers 31C engine with three speeds, it used a Siba electric starter. This, and a later model with a 197cc Villiers 9E engine and four speeds, had a revised styling for 1960, and they were made until 1962, when Bond concentrated on making cars.

The Minibyke had disc wheels and was just one of many vehicles designed by Lawrence Bond. His three-wheeled cars are probably the best known.

BORDONE

ITALY 1935–65

BORDONE OF MILAN BEGAN as a manufacturer of three-wheeled delivery vehicles in 1935, using 250 and 350cc engines and tubular frames. After 1936, the company improved the engines and switched to a pressed-steel frame.

The Model NB, which was their only real motorcycle, was named after the founder, Nicola Bordone, and was designed in the years immediately preceding World War II. The 500cc overhead-valve four-stroke single-cylinder engine was

a modern-looking design and drove the rear wheel by chain through a four-speed gearbox; the frame had suspension both at front and rear, with trapezoidal front forks and a conventional swinging-arm.

Production seems to have been limited to the first year of the war, though others were possibly built afterwards. As late as 1957, Bordone introduced a new three-wheeled delivery wagon with an overhead-valve 650cc motor.

BOSS HOSS

USA 1990–

IN THE AMERICAN MARKET, there has never been any substitute for cubes on wheels as big distances between destinations called for large-capacity engines working for hours without stress. For some, stock machines were not enough and so appeared the custom model built to the owner's specifications. One result of this trend was using a car engine for power, combined with a car's transmission and two rear wheels to create a tricycle.

Boss Hoss came from that background but differed by being a production model and a solo motorcycle. The company used an

enormous 5.7-litre (1.2 UK, 1.5 US gallon) Chevrolet V8 with its automatic transmission coupled to a belt final drive. This all fitted into a massive tubular cradle frame with telescopic front and pivoted-rear forks. Cast-alloy wheels carried fat front and extremely fat rear tyres with disc brakes to bring the bike's considerable weight to a halt.

The notion of using a large capacity V8 car engine for power was usually a custom trend but Boss Hoss are a fully-fledged, successful firm.

It sold well and was later offered with a smaller V6 engine or a larger 8.2-litre (1.8 UK, 2.1 US gallon)V8 offering 500bhp to drive its two-speed and reverse automatic transmission. Wild though the specification was, some owners added twin rear wheels, which made it easier to ride, or with major engine changes to boost the power even further.

Another example of the Boss Hoss, this one with a 4.3-litre V6 Chevrolet engine. Customers can specify their own special paint finish.

BRADBURY

ENGLAND 1901–24

LOCATED AT THE WELLINGTON WORKS in Oldham, Lancashire, this firm began as many others did by fitting a Minerva engine to the downtube of a standard bicycle frame. Late in 1902, the company began to offer machines built to the Birch design, where the crankcase was cast around two of the main frame tubes. In other respects, Bradbury's machines followed the lines of the new Werner and were typical primitives with direct belt drive, pedals and braced forks.

The main model, with a two-and-a-half horsepower engine, was listed as the Peerless, but there was also a lightweight that had its Clement-Garrard engine inclined above the downtube. From there it powered a chain-driven countershaft mounted ahead of the bottom bracket. This turned the rear wheel, also chain-driven. The rest of the machine was little more than a heavy-duty bicycle.

Over the next few years, the design of the main model saw the crankcase cast to the frame. Several power outputs were listed

An early Bradbury that was typical of many marques of the time, with cycle frame, simple girder forks and belt drive.

along with a tandem backseat frame, essentially a pillion seat with handlebars, and a forecar with a 4hp water-cooled engine, two speeds and chain drive.

In 1909, the firm produced a three-and-a-half horsepower model, still of the same construction but now with sprung forks. Later came transmission options and, in 1914, a 6hp V-twin with a three-speed gearbox, all-chain drive and a drum rear brake.

Late in 1913, these two machines were joined by a three-and-a-half horsepower flat-twin model whose engine had its magneto mounted on top of the crankcase, a chain-driven, three-speed gearbox and the choice of

A detail of a 1912 Bradbury with the crankcase of its 554cc side-valve engine cast onto the seat and down tubes of the frame.

chain or belt final drive. This model also had the drum rear brake and continued until 1915 along with the others.

Only the single, with various transmission options, and the V-twin were on sale until 1916, but both remained in production throughout World War I for service use. This line continued until 1919 and a two-and-three-quarters horespower single with two speeds and a chain-and-belt drive was added. For 1920, there were just three models, the two-and-three-quarter and 4hp singles and 6hp V-twin with three speeds and all-chain drive. In 1922, the smallest had transmission options but by 1923 was only sold with three speeds and chain drive.

For 1924, the two models were both redesigned and enlarged, the single to 572cc and the V-twin to 872cc. The firm also made a racing model with a 348cc overhead-valve Blackburne engine. In 1924, they went bankrupt and production ceased.

BRIDGESTONE

TODAY, BRIDGESTONE IS A NAME more closely associated with tyres than complete motorcycles, but despite never accounting for more than 10 per cent of revenue, two-wheelers played a vital part in establishing the company's post-war manufacturing reputation. Their range began with a simple 49cc two-stroke moped, later including 98, 175 and 250cc singles. But their finest and best-remembered model was their last: the 350GTR twin.

Intended mainly for the US market (a mere 33 were imported to the UK), the 350GTR was a revelation when introduced in 1966. Never had any two-stroke featured such a level of specification, not to mention acceleration, capable of humbling many 650 twins. Although broadly similar in layout to the Suzuki Super Six which appeared at about the same time, the Bridgestone was awash with even more advanced touches. Like the Suzuki, the Bridgestone's crankcases split horizontally to reveal a six-speed transmission.

Where the GTR differed most was in its use of disc-valve induction. A 'normal' two-stroke uses the rise and fall of the piston to control the flow of incoming and exhaust gases through ports in the cylinder walls. Because this inevitably gives symmetrical port timing, in highly tuned engines this can lead to poor running and spitting back through the

carburettor, particularly at lower engine speeds.

By offering asymmetric timing, rotary disc valves – basically cutaway discs mounted on the crankshaft – overcame this problem. The system was perfected by MZ's race engineer, Walter Kaaden, before the technology was used by Suzuki in

In 1968, Bridgestone stopped bike production to concentrate on tyres, which it now supplies to Grand Prix car and motorcycle teams.

1961. The GTR wears two such disc valves – one per cylinder – keyed to each end of the crankshaft. A 26mm Mikuni carburettor sits outboard of each of these.

Since side-mounted carburettors make the engine quite wide, the alternator was mounted in a 'piggy-back' fashion to keep width within acceptable limits - a feature adopted by Japanese four-stroke multis 16 years later. The cylinder bores are hard chrome, rather than iron, allowing tighter piston clearances. A dry, racing-style clutch is fitted. Not new, but welcome, was 'Jet Lube' positive oiling (driven by a pump under the right-hand carburettor), a version of the system first introduced on Yamaha's YA6 in 1964. The 2.5 litre oil tank features an inspection window, with another allowing riders to check gearbox oil level, both commonplace later, but big refinements at the time.

The GTR even accommodated a preference for right- or left-sided gearchange, since both the gear pedal and rear brake pedals could be swapped. It could even be kick-started in gear. Thanks to its rubber-mounted engine, the GTR was also the smoothest in its class. 37bhp offered searing acceleration with that exhilarating rush typical of high-performance two-strokes.

With its disc-valve induction, six speed transmission, 'Jet-lube' oiling and coated bores, the GTR was the most advanced two-stroke roadster of its era.

It handled well on suspension that was more supple than most, and the drum brakes were equally impressive. The GTR's build quality also earned high marks.

Inevitably, such a box of tricks attracted over-inflated performance claims of anything up to 177kph (110mph). The reality was around 150kph (93mph), yet at the time, this was probably still the fastest two-stroke roadster ever built.

Unfortunately, the GTR's price was also inflated. In 1968, it retailed at £340, about £60 more than a Super Six and only £29 less than a 650cc Triumph Bonneville. This, and doubts about the durability of such 'buzz boxes', severely restricted sales. Bridgestone abruptly ceased motorcycle production in late 1968 to concentrate on its core tyre-making business.

Engine: 345cc two-stroke parallel twin, 61x59 mm, liquid-cooled
Power: 37bhp at 7500rpm
Gearbox: 6-speed foot change
Final drive: chain
Weight: 150kg (330lb)
Top speed: 153kph (95mph)

BRITTEN

NEW ZEALAND 1992–99

BRITTEN ILLUSTRATES THAT, even today, the barriers to designing and building a complete, successful motorcycle – even a race-winner – are small. 'Backyard specials' built from existing components are not unusual, but the Britten not only featured its own carbon-fibre cycle parts but also its own unique, powerful engine. Although very few were built, the Britten was an intriguing machine, and is about as far from a Harley-Davidson clone as can be imagined.

The only motorcycle model that ever entered production was the V1000, though at the time of writing, the firm was working on at least one new model and on other non-motorcycle projects, despite the death of the company's founder, John Britten, in 1996.

Of the 10 V1000 machines built, some are in private collections and museums and have never been raced, some are in use and one, the last to be built, is in Las Vegas, still in its crate, where its purchaser is apparently wondering whether to leave it there as a time capsule. The machines have strayed as far afield as Alabama and Michigan in the USA, Milan in Italy, and the Netherlands.

Stripped naked, the awesome high-tech complexity of the eight-valve twin, with its tuned exhaust tracts, is clear for everyone to see.

The heavily oversquare 999cc (98.9x65mm) liquid-cooled V-twin engine featured two belt-driven cams and four valves per cylinder, a compression ratio of 11.3:1, titanium con-rods and valves (40mm inlet, 33mm exhaust), and (intriguingly) the option of either cast-iron wet liners or silicon carbide-lined alloy sleeves. Lubrication was wet-sump, with feeds to the big ends, gudgeon pins, camshaft lobes and gearbox shafts. Fuel supply was sequential injection, two injectors per cylinder, with programmable engine management and a history facility to read how the engine behaved in use. The standard gearbox was five-speed, though there was a six-speed option.

The engine was a stressed chassis member, with much of the chassis – the upper part, the girder and the swing-arm – made of a carbon fibre and Kevlar composite. Even the wheels 43cm (17ins) front and rear, were a carbon fibre composite, built in house, but the brake disks were twin 320mm (12.6in) cast-iron rotors at the front and a single 210mm (8.3in) rotor at the back; cast iron affords better stopping power, and better heat dissipation, than stainless steel. The ducted radiator was mounted under the seat.

The machine produced 166bhp at 11,800rpm with a limit of 12,500rpm, which was a

With 166bhp at 12,500rpm, the Britten V1000 was probably the most powerful 1000cc V-twin ever built, with or without forced induction.

staggering engine speed for a big V-twin. This is also about twice the brake horsepower of a standard Hesketh with a superficially similar engine. This was sufficient to power the 138kg (304lb) machine to about 303kph (188mph).

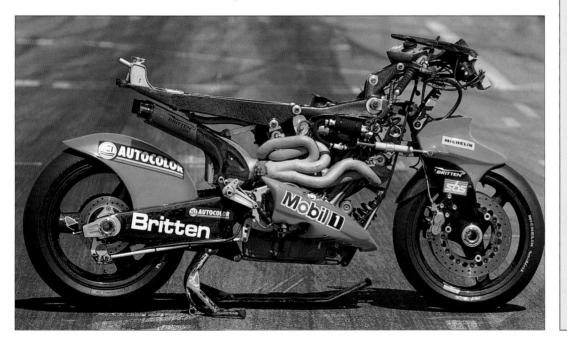

BOND
India 1990s: This Indian firm made Morini-engined sports mopeds, similar to BSA India. The 'Bond' was from 'Brooke Bond', the tea company.

BONZI & MARCHI
Italy (Milan) 1913–14: The original belt-drive model had a 3hp 330cc engine from Moser and weighed just 50kg (110lb); the second had chain drive, with a two-and-three-quarters horsepower Moser; and there were also two V-twins.

BOOTH
England (London) 1901–03: This short-lived company initially used Minerva and De Dion Bouton proprietary engines, then their own of two-and-three-quarter horsepower, three-and-a-half horsepower and 4hp motors.

BORD
England (London) 1902–06: Built lightweights with their own singles, variously described as one-and-a-half and one-and-three-quarter horsepower.

BORGHI
Italy (Milan) 1951–63: This firm assembled mopeds and lightweights with 38cc (Mosquito), 49cc (Cucciolo) and 123cc (BSA Bantam) two-stroke motors. There may also have been a 175cc Bantam-based bike. All were sold as 'Olympia'.

BORGO
Italy 1906–26: Confusingly, there were two Borgo factories, founded by three brothers. One, founded by A.B. Borgo and C. Borgo built four-stroke singles, initially, in 1906, a 497cc inlet-over-exhaust, then later 453, 493, 693 and 827cc, while the other, founded by E.M. Borgo, started in 1915 with a belt-drive 996cc V-twin. In 1921 came a race-winning eight-valve 477cc V-twin capable of 6000rpm, followed by a 496cc overhead-valve with a two-speed unit-construction gearbox. Borgo is now better known as a piston maker.

BROUGH

ENGLAND 1898–1925

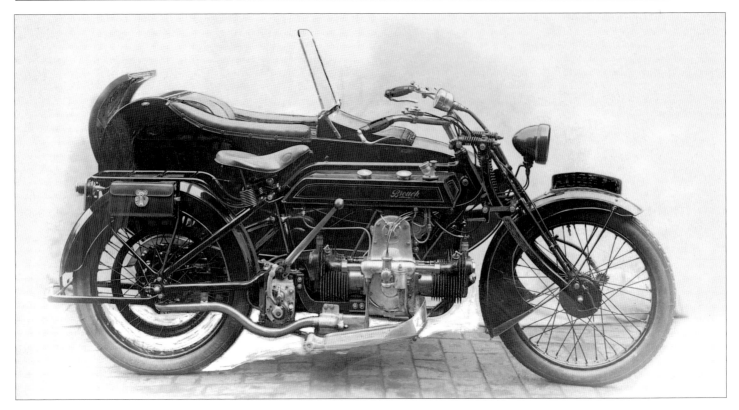

WILLIAM BROUGH NEVER BECAME as famous as his son George, but he began the Brough legend that became associated with the Superior. In 1898, he built a small car but in 1902, Brough's first motorcycle appeared with its engine hung from the downtube, belt drive and braced forks. Based at Basford, Nottingham, he had greatly improved the design by 1906 and the 1908 model had a vertically-mounted three-and-a-half horsepower engine and sprung forks. This machine was soon joined by a two-and-a-half

horsepower model and a 5hp V-twin, all made by the firm.

During 1910, Brough built an advanced experimental engine with a rotary valve above the cylinder and a sleeve-valve that shielded the sparking plug except when it fired. These were driven by bevel, shaft and spur gears. The engine was hung in a slave frame with the magneto on the front. The bike also had belt drive and sprung forks but it was never produced.

In 1911, Brough moved on to build a flat-twin engine, with good balance and minimal vibration,

The largest flat-twin Brough engine was 810cc and well able to haul a sidecar, as seen here in typical flat-tank style.

and returned to this theme once it was further developed. A larger 6hp V-twin appeared for 1912, available for touring or racing, while the three-and-a-half horsepower single was enlarged and a two-speed countershaft gearbox added. There was also an 8hp V-twin engine for the Brough Monocar and a three-and-a-half horsepower ladies model.

George Brough entered the 1913 Senior Isle of Man TT on a model with a flat-twin engine, but used an ABC twin. Later that year the firm announced a three-and-a-half horsepower, 497cc flat-twin model with overhead-valves with exposed pushrods and rockers, the U.H. magneto clamped to the top of crankcase and the two-speed gearbox attached to the underside. By 1915, only the flat twin was listed, joined by a larger version in 1916. In 1923, a larger 810cc model appeared, made until 1925.

BROUGH SUPERIOR

ENGLAND 1919–40

ACCORDING TO HIS OWN reminiscences, George Brough (1890-1970) was about 10 years old when he first rode his first motorcycle, an original Werner. Later, in his teens, he became a well-known racer using the flat twins, the original Broughs, his father built. He then went into partnership with his father to continue making them.

His father's motorcycles were, however, neither luxurious enough nor fast enough for his taste. In

1919, he founded his own motorcycle company in Nottingham, and in 1921 he built the first machine to bear the Brough-Superior name which was the suggestion of a friend, it seems, to distinguish the new marque from the old.

Despite the mystique that surrounds the name, Brough-Superior was in many ways no different to numerous other manufacturers that used bought-in engines and components. There

were, however, two ways in which the new company was very different indeed. Firstly, George's intention was always to build motorcycles in small numbers, finished to the very highest standards both mechanically and cosmetically, and to charge a commensurately high price for them. Although his engines were bought in, he paid for extra finishing and quality control on the top-of-the-line designs from JAP, MAG, Matchless and others.

Secondly, Brough was a consummate showman as his choice of company name might indicate. This was manifested both in the appearance of his machines, and in how he promoted them. The standard of finish was exceptional – enough for Rolls Royce to tacitly approve of the slogan, 'the Rolls-Royce of motorcycles', which apparently originated in a review in *The Motor Cycle*. It seems that a couple of Rolls Royce representatives who

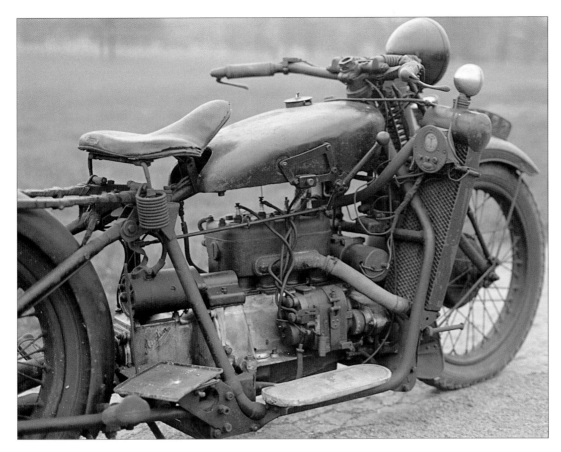

As well as the V-twins for which he is best known, George Brough also built a wide range of other machines, especially water-cooled fours.

subsequently visited the Brough works in Nottingham were impressed to see a man in white gloves paying great attention to the finish of a petrol tank, and concluded that indeed, Broughs were built to the same standard as Rolls Royces. It was not revealed to them that the tank was destined for a show model.

Apart from the looks and the finish, they were popular (and successful) racing machines, in the hands of Brough himself and also of Eric Fernihough, Freddie Dixon, E.C.E. Baragwanath, Bert Le Vack, and many more. What is more, they were the chosen machines of a number of famous personalities, none more so than T.E. Lawrence, or Lawrence of Arabia, who owned seven Brough-Superiors over the years (six of them SS100 models) and was indeed killed while riding one; he had an eighth on order.

Although V-twins made and sustained the machines' reputation, George Brough also kept his name in the spotlight by means of

prototypes and show specials, often with exotic engines such as air-cooled fours. In fact, the only four that ever made it into production was the water-cooled Brough-Austin.

The earliest machines were fitted with 986cc JAP engines, but because Broughs were bespoke motorcycles, a variety of engines was available either by special order or from the catalogue: side-valves, push-rod and overhead-cams, including four-cams, and eight-valves. Over the years, other capacities included 680, 750, a short lived 500, and the big side-valve 1096cc, intended for relaxed touring,

Although the 1000cc models are 'les imortelles', Brough also embraced many other capacities such as this 1920 Mk II with a 750cc engine.

preferably with a side car. The Austin four mentioned above was 800cc.

The extent to which the engines and other components (Sturmey-Archer gearboxes, Castle forks, Enfield cush-drives and Draper frames) were modified or specially built solely to George Brough's

specification is disputable. Most of these makers built engines or other parts for 'specials' and racers, and the work that Brough required (apart from having his name cast into some of the metalwork) cannot, in most cases, have been unique.

By 1923, when the company had been making motorcycles for

The SS80 does not command the respect (or the prices) of the SS100 but it is still a superb machine to this day and astonishingly easy to ride.

only a couple of years, he launched the SS80 with a written guarantee that it had been timed at 129kph (80mph) over 400m (0.25

mile). In 1924, the written guarantee was extended to 161kph (100mph) with the SS100. According to Brough's own advertising, testing was on 'a Private Road, one-and-three-quarter miles [2.8km] long', and not Brooklands, as often reported.

The SS100 remained the flagship model, with ever more

powerful engines and ever greater refinement, until motorcycle production ceased in 1940 with the outbreak of World War II. During the conflict, the Brough-Superior was engaged in all sorts of war work, but when hostilities were ended, production was not resumed. This was alleged to be because George Brough was not confident that he could buy engines of the quality that he needed.

While this story suits the legend of Brough Superior, it is not hard to challenge. He must have recognised that the day of the assembler was over, except at the bottom end of the market. Fully integrated designs such as the Vincent-HRD Series A Rapide showed greater promise than lots of bought-in components, no matter how expensive the components and how impressive the assembly.

The Series A Rapide 'plumber's nightmare' was road-tested at

By the time this machine was built in 1934, Brough Superiors were widely acknowledged as the finest motorcycles in the world – as well as the fastest.

177kph (110mph) in 1939 by *Motor Cycling*, a figure that the Matchless-engined SS100 of the time would have struggled to match.

There is also an often-repeated suggestion that World War II killed the Brough-Superior Dream (or Golden Dream), which resembled two BMW flat twins stacked one atop the other, with geared crankshafts like a Square Four. It is true that a handful were built (maybe five) but reliability was poor and one suspects that it was, like most of his other 'specials', a show-stealer that was never actually intended for series production.

Perhaps the most fascinating thing about Brough-Superiors is that a machine made in such tiny numbers, for just 18 years, should still be a legend today. About 4000 Broughs were built, of which about 10 per cent were SS100 models. And yet, if you asked the average lover of old motorcycles which three bikes he or she would most like to own, the SS100 would almost certainly be on the list.

The quality of the finish on all Brough Superiors was superb, as demonstrated by this immaculate 1927 saddle tank.

BROUGH SUPERIOR 1921

REPUTEDLY, THE SADDLE TANK on the original Brough Superior was the first on any production motorcycle; this is disputable. The immaculate paintwork of the tank, and the twin tommy-barred fillers (one for oil, one for petrol) are the first details to catch the eye on a Brough-Superior, after you have gasped at the magnificence of the whole machine.

Although 35bhp may not seem like much today, it had over four times the power of the first BMW flat twin, and a lot more power than many contemporary small cars.

The engine was a '90 bore' JAP unit. It featured total-loss lubrication via both hand-pump and foot-pump (both were fitted to all machines), and had a single cam and single valve springs. Pistons were light-alloy with two compression rings and a scraper ring. This was the machine that was to evolve into the SS80, with twin cams and double valve springs.

By 1927, the SS80 had 25bhp in standard form (L122:10s:0d) or 30bhp in special form (L130:0s:0d). As well as the original overhead-valve Brough-Superior, there was a side-valve JAP version (988cc, 85.5x85mm) and a so-called Mark II with a 72x90mm MAG inlet-over-exhaust engine. So there was no shortage of choice, particularly when these three were joined by a 999cc (86mm square) Barr and Stroud sleeve-valve engine.

Engine: 986cc ohv in-line V-twin, 90x77.5mm, air-cooled
Power: 35bhp approx.
Gearbox: 3-speed hand change
Final drive: chain
Weight: 190kg (418lb)
Top speed: 121kph (75mph) approx

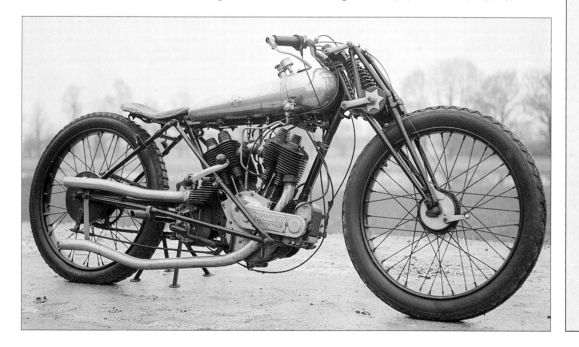

ORIGINAL SS100   1924

Oil consumption for the SS100 was claimed at 1450mpg, an alarming one litre every 500km (one pint every 180 miles). Suddenly the big oil filler cap makes sense!

Fuel consumption ranged from around 4 litres per 100km (50mpg) when driven hard, to 5.6 litres per 100km (70mpg) or better when driven normally. Today, when the normal route to increasing the power-to-weight ratio is to add on more power, these figures are a reminder that lower weight should not be neglected. The lightness of the SS100 was surprising.

The SS100 captured the public imagination and development continued. For 1926, Brough introduced the Alpine GS with an 80x99mm (995cc) JAP engine with triple valve springs and more power than the 'cooking' version. He also introduced the Pendine, which was guaranteed to have been tested at no less than 177kph (110mph), and was named after Pendine Sands, a popular place for record-breaking in Britain before people could easily cross the Atlantic to the USA to use the Bonneville salt flats.

The SS100 was essentially a refinement of the twin-cam, double-valve-spring SS80, and was offered late in 1924 as a 1925 model. The usual 'tweaks' to carburation and so on were

Lawrence, Shaw, Ross, Aurens... Call Lawrence of Arabia what you will, this most romantic of heroes will always be linked with the most romantic of machines, the SS100. This was his.

apparent, but a good deal of the extra pace came from lightening the valve gear to permit higher engine speeds. Unexpectedly, some power was also sapped by the fitting of a mechanical oil pump.

Engine: 988cc ohv in-line V-twin, 85.5x86mm, air-cooled
Power: 45bhp at 5000rpm
Gear box: 3-speed hand change
Final drive: chain
Weight: 180kg (396lb)
Top speed: 160kph (100mph)

BROUGH SUPERIOR 500   1931

The smallest Brough ever made is often described as an attempt to make a smaller, cheaper machine in response to the Depression. If this was the case, it was a strange way of going about it. The side-valve versions of the 680, below, have a much stronger claim to the oxymoronic distinction of being poor men's Brough Superiors.

The 500 was sold as a fast but docile 19bhp tourer that could easily be converted to a 31bhp racer by removing the lights and

the compression plates under the cylinders, in which guise it was capable of more than 145kph (90mph). Replace the lights and the compression plates, and the top speed dropped to about 137kph (85mph) but the whole machine was more tractable and entirely road legal. Another argument against the 500 being an economy model is the provision of a four-speed gearbox instead of three.

Prior to this machine, the Overhead 680 (introduced 1926)

had been the smallest at 70x88mm for 674cc and 25bhp, still enough to top 128kph (80mph) as the bike was relatively light. This was the basis of the Black Alpine 680, with its eggshell black finish and its Draper spring frame, a very fine middleweight tourer.

The success of the Overhead 680 prompted the introduction of a side-valve 680 in 1927, again from JAP (it had been in their catalogue for some time), and its economy derivative, the 5-15. Although the

side-valve 680 delivered only 17.5 bhp, this was still adequate for 128kph (80mph), about the same output as a modern Enfield Bullet 350. There was also a side-valve 750, with softer power delivery.

Engine: 498cc overhead-valve in-line V-twin, 62.5x80mm, air-cooled
Power: 19 to 31bhp
Gearbox: 4-speed
Final drive: chain
Weight: n/a
Top Speed: 145kph (90mph)

BROUGH-AUSTIN   1932

The humble Austin Seven provided the engine on which the Brough-Austin was based, a water-cooled 750cc unit that was stretched to

800cc for motorcycle use principally, one might suspect, in order to distance itself from its proletarian ancestry. The most

remarkable feature of the Brough-Austin was not the rather prominent radiator, well placed for hand-warming, but the highly

improbable twin rear wheel with the drive up the middle. Perhaps, needless to say, the machine was intended for side-car use, though

Despite its reputation, with only 23bhp and an outfit weight of 356kg (783lb), the 800cc Austin-engined Brough Superior was very slow.

there are reports of at least one being ridden solo, which must have been an interesting experience. It is perhaps equally remarkable that the Brough-Austin was made at all. Only about 10 were, over half of which are known to have survived.

Engine: 800cc sv in-line straight four, 57.9x76mm, liquid-cooled
Power: 23bhp at 4600rpm
Gearbox: 3-speed + reverse
Final drive: Shaft
Weight: 356kg (783lb) outfit
Top speed: 97kph (60mph) approx

NEW SS100   1933

Development of the SS100 continued from 1925 until it disappeared in 1940. The New SS100 of 1933 for the 1934 season was beyond belief. Even if the 74bhp claimed for the 50-degree JAP V-twin was an exaggeration, this performance would still have been impressive 50 years later.

The engine had twin carburetters, twin magnetos (one a magdyno for lighting) and an 8:1 compression ratio (when 6:1 was more usual) though 12:1 was apparently available for racing. It was known as the 'two of everything'; only eight were built.

Earlier 1928 versions of the SS100 had already offered optional rear suspension (rigid rear

ends were prized by traditionalists, because they were simpler, lighter and controlled the rear wheel better) and the year after the New SS100 came out, positive-stop foot change replaced the hand change. Another year on, a Norton four-speed gearbox replaced the old Sturmey-Archer three-speed.

From 1935 (for the 1936 season) the 50-degree, 990cc (85.5mm/sq) Matchless was used for the about 100 of the SS100s,

The New SS100 of 1933 looked very like this 1932 model but with 74bhp, which offered performance that would have been impressive in 1973, never mind 1933.

with hairpin valve springs instead of the coil springs of the JAP. It was more reliable, but less powerful, attaining only just 161kph (100mph).

The last SS100 was built in about 1940, except for Brough's 1944 prototype with a 90-degree V-twin, mounted conventionally (symmetrically about the vertical axis). This allowed a low seat height without extending the wheelbase.

Engine: 996cc ohv in-line V-twin, 80x99mm, air-cooled
Power: 74bhp at 6200rpm
Gearbox: 3-speed hand change
Final drive: chain
Weight : n/a
Top speed: 200kph (125mph) approx

BRAAK
Germany 1923–25: Used 129 and 198cc Heilo and Namapo engines in bought-in frames from Gruhn of Berlin.

BRAECKMANN
France (Nanterre) 1946: A rotary valve gear was built into the head of this light-alloy 11cc four-stroke machine. Larger versions were promised but they seem never to have actually materialised.

BRAND
Germany (Berlin) 1925–30: Horizontal two-stroke Bekamo-licence singles of 123, 147 and 173cc capacity powered these machines.

BRAVIS
Germany 1924–26: As well as their own 175 and 297cc two-stroke singles, Bravis also used a 293cc Bosch-Douglas flat twin.

BREDA
Italy 1946–51: These were autocycles with a 65cc two-stroke engine from the former aircraft factory.

BREE
Austria (Vienna) 1902–04: This was an early manufacturer of two-stroke one-and-a-half horsepower engines, whic where all fitted in a lightweight but sturdy frame.

BRENNABOR
(Brandenburg am Havel) Germany 1902–40: From 1902–12, this company built motorcycles with engines of their own manufacture as well as Zedel, Fafnir, Peugeot, Minerva and others. From 1933–40, they produced autocycles with 73 and 98cc Sachs and Ilo engines. They also built cars until 1933.

BSA

WHAT BECAME THE UK'S, and for a time the world's, largest manufacturer of motorcycles began life in 1854 as an association of 14 gunsmiths formed to supply arms to British forces in the Crimean War. Even today, three stacked rifles remains the famous logo of the inheritor of the company title, BSA Regal.

A year after its foundation, BSA moved into the Small Heath factory alongside the old Great Western Railway which was to be its home for the next 110 years. In 1861 it became a publicly-listed company, Birmingham Small Arms. Highly automated by the standards of the time, the company began making bicycle components in the 1880s, before producing its

first Minerva-powered two-wheeler in 1903. The first all-BSA model, a 499cc (3½hp) side-valve single, followed seven years later, already in the green and cream livery which would characterise Small Heath machines. This was followed in 1913 by the two-speed, all-chain drive side-valve Model H and the three-speed Model K.

The Olympia Show in London in 1919 introduced the first of a notable series of V-twins, the 770cc Model E, intended mainly for genteel sidecar use. Like many manufacturers, BSA also produced sidecars for hitching to their machines.

If the V-twin was the typical BSA of the 1920s, the 1930s were

characterised by single-cylinder machines such as the 500cc Sloper and the race-like Empire Star and its derivatives. Although less well-known than Morgan and Raleigh, the firm also produced a successful range of three-wheelers powered by two-and four-cylinder engines.

Perhaps not surprisingly, given its roots, diversification was always a BSA hallmark. During World War II, when they produced 126,000 military side-valve M20 motorcycles, the group owned 67 factories engaged in a bewildering array of industrial activities. Even during World War I, BSA was already a huge industrial conglomerate, building Daimler cars and supplying no less than

During the 1950s, the sturdy old side-valve BSA M21 and box sidecar, and the AA man's cheery salute, were an integral part of British motoring.

one-and-a-half million rifles to the military. A special factory, known as 'the 1915 building' was erected to cater for this demand, and it was from this same building that generations of 'Beezer' motorcycles would later emerge.

By the mid-1950s, BSA had acquired Triumph, Ariel, Sunbeam and many other marques and were the largest motorcycle company in the world. Yet their best-selling model, the humble two-stroke Bantam, was essentially a pre-war German DKW design. Ironically

DKW had themselves briefly been 'world's biggest' during the 1920s.

At the time, the rest of the BSA range centred around B- and C-series overhead-valve singles, and a range of overhead-valve parallel twins inspired by Triumph's success with the pre-war Speed Twin. Of the singles, many were humble runarounds although the most potent, the Gold Star, became a legend both on road and track. The twins series, meanwhile, began in 1946 with Val Page's 500cc A7, which later grew to become the 650cc A10. In 1962, these 7/10-series twins, of which the finest was probably the 185kph (115mph) Rocket Gold Star, gave way to the unit construction A50 and A65 twins, the latter remaining in production until BSA's demise.

In 1960, the company reported profits in excess of nine million pounds, and there were no clouds on BSA's horizon. Yet during the following decade, the company was negligently slow to respond to the influx of technically advanced, cheap new motorcycles from Japan. It is part of motorcycling's myth that the British industry was starved of good research and development facilities at the time, yet during this same period, BSA boasted a highly sophisticated development department at 'space age' Umberslade Hall (nickname 'Slumberland' by cynics), and perhaps the most automated motorcycle production line outside Japan.

Yet for all this potential, the company failed to find consistent policy or direction, producing a succession of failures in search of a replacement for the venerable Bantam. These included the Dandy

and Beagle commuter bikes, a 250cc scooter and the catastrophic Ariel-3 tricycle (an independently-designed model which crashed whilst demonstrating its prowess to BSA directors who, nonetheless, bought it. By the early 1970s, the group's losses were almost as great as their profits had been a decade before. Although the Rocket-3/Triumph Trident offered a glimmer of hope, the effort of attempting to compete with the Japanese eventually crippled the company. Its final effort was the ill-starred BSA Fury/Triumph Bandit. By 1972 the firm were broke.

Manganese Bronze, by then the owners of Norton, acquired the BSA Group, mainly for its remaining profitable car body and sintered products divisions. A proposed motorcycle rescue plan was thwarted by a determined workers' sit-in at Meriden, from which emerged the government-backed Triumph Cooperative.

The B40 was an ohv single of 343cc, derived from the earlier B31. This is the 'trialised' military version, on which a generation of British soldiers learned to ride.

After the BSA collapse, Norton Villiers Triumph took over the remaining motorcycle operations, now at Shenstone, north-east of Birmingham, whilst the BSA Small Heath factory and Norton's Wolverhampton plant were closed. From this emerged Norton Motors (the rotary-engined project), which passed through a succession of owners before ending up by default in the hands of the Canadian Aquilini family (along with the UK rights to the BSA motorcycle name).

Two other parts of the original NVT stake, BSA Co and Andover Norton, were later disposed of in management buy-outs. Bill Colquhuon's BSA Co produced Rotax-engined military bikes, plus Yamaha-based 'Bushman' machines for Third World markets. Mike Jackson's Andover Norton turned out Commando spares and AP Lockheed and other products. In 1991, the two merged to become a new BSA Group. Taken over by Southampton-based interests to become BSA Regal in 1994, the group has diverse light engineering interests, and in 1996 unveiled a new BSA model, the Gold SR. This had a Yamaha SR400 engine in an Gold Star-styled chassis.

By 1972, when these 650cc Lightning twins were produced, the BSA Group was in deep financial trouble, losing out to Honda and its CB750-4.

BREUIL
France 1903–08: This firm built singles and V-twins with their own engines as well as those of Peugeot, Aster, Zurcher and others.

BRIBAN
France 1950s: This company began with a 50cc auxiliary cycle-motor, then 98 and 123, and later a fan-cooled 123cc for scooters.

BRIGGS & STRATTON
USA 1919–20: The well-known manufacturer of stationary engines built the Briggs and Stratton Flyer auxiliary cycle motor. One model drove the rear wheel; another was built into an interchangeable front wheel.

BRILANT-ALCYON
Czechoslovakia (Zuckmantel) 1932: The Fuchs factory built a few Alcyon-licensed 98cc two-stroke machines which were named 'people's motorcycles'.

BRITISH-RADIAL
England (London) 1920–22: A radial side-valve triple with a 120-degree Redrup engine; the frames were bought-in from Chater-Lea. However, few were made.

BRITISH-STANDARD
England (Birmingham) 1919–23: This Birmingham company were assemblers who used a wide range of bought-in engines, such as Villiers, TDC, JAP, Bradshaw, Blackburne and Barr and Stroud and produced them in an equally wide range of capacities, from 147 to 548cc.

BSA SIDEVALVE V-TWINS

1919–39

The range of BSA V-twins which began in 1919 with the 770cc Model E was an enduring one. In fact, it lasted until the outbreak of World War II. And, despite a run of 20 years, there was relatively little to distinguish the last from the first. One of the last variants was the 986cc G14 of 1938. Like the rest, this was of side-valve layout, with the cylinders splayed at 50 degrees. This was a figure which offered a compact design at the expense of plenty of vibration and a hot-running rear cylinder.

Lubrication remained total-loss, fed from a 2.3 litre (half gallon) tank, from which a hand-pump fed oil to the cylinders and crankshaft. Unburned oil then collected in the

Big side-valve V-twins were at the heart of BSA's early reputation. Although often hitched to sidecars, this 1919 model stays solo. Note the puny front brake.

crankcase before passing through a valve to lubricate the primary chain and – eventually – the road. As well as this pump, the rider had to contend with two twistgrips. The one on the right was a conventional throttle, whilst the one on the left controlled ignition advance.

With a puny 4.4:1 compression ratio, power was modest but tractability immense. This was ideal for the attachment of a sidecar. The chassis, based round a massive forged steel backbone, was equally robust.

Despite its crudeness, such large V-twins were considered as luxury vehicles, not least because attaching a sidecar raised the price of the vehicle to that of a small car.

Engine: 986cc sv V-twin, 80x98mm, air-cooled
Power: 25bhp at 3800rpm
Gearbox: 4-speed hand change
Final drive: chain
Weight: 191kg (420lb)
Top speed: 121kph (75mph)

BSA SLOPER

1926–35

Launched in August 1926 as the Model S, the Sloper was the epitome of British pre-war thumpers. So called because of its forward slanted engine, the Sloper was good looking, dependable, quiet and relatively brisk. Displacing 493cc, the long-stroke engine offered enclosed pushrods and rockers (although the valve

springs were exposed), above large, sturdy crankcases containing a gear-type oil pump.

The long stroke motor developed easy, long-legged power, while massive flywheels smoothed the singles power pulses. The duplex frame carried girder front forks, while the rear end was unsprung.

Left: Note the hand gearchange on this Sloper, typical of the period. In 1932, four-speed transmission replaced the original three-speed gearbox.

No less than six different Sloper models were made, and these were in capacities ranging from 349 to 595cc, including two side-valve and four overhead-valve versions. In standard trim the overhead-valve 500 was good for speeds of over 112kph (70mph). For most of the models' life, BSA also offered a 'race kit', which comprised of a high compression piston and special spark plug, valves and springs, although the bike's stolid image was scarcely in keeping with such tuning.

In 1932, the original three-speed gearbox gave way to four-speed transmission.

Engine: 493cc ohv single, 80x98mm, air-cooled
Power: up to 25bhp at 4800rpm
Gearbox: 3-, later 4-speed hand change
Final drive: chain
Weight: n/a
Top speed: 116kph (72mph)

Reminiscent of later Panthers, the Sloper was one of the most fondly-regarded of British pre-War singles. It remained in production from 1926 until 1935.

BSA EMPIRE STAR/GOLD STAR 1936

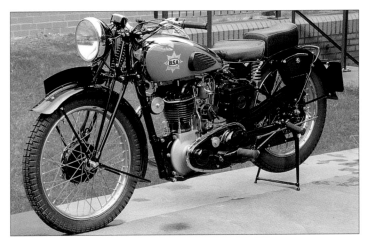

BSA, like Triumph, was never very competition-minded, a policy which was reinforced whenever they did take to the track. In 1913, six factory machines contested the Isle of Man TT, with only one finishing, in a dispiriting seventh place.

Eight years later, another six competed, with even worse results. It was perhaps surprising, then, that two of the company's most celebrated models made their reputations on the track.

One of these was, of course, the postwar Gold Star. However, during the 1930s another, quite different, machine enjoyed the same name, and similar success. It was based on Herbert Perkins' 1931 500cc Blue Star, and the model was further developed by D.W. Munro to become the Empire Star of 1936. In this trim it covered 805km (500 miles) at Brooklands circuit at an impressive average speed of 118kph (73.3mph).

The original Gold Star was a pre-war sports bike derived from the Empire Star. The racing Gold Star could achieve 160kph (100mph).

Even the BSA board's confidence was high, and engine development continued under Val Page. The result boasted new port design and ignition, and fully enclosed valvegear in a style typical of BSA's postwar singles. With ultra-high compression, it produced no less than 34bhp. Its racing debut came with the great Wal Handley at Brooklands in June 1937, producing victory at an average speed of over 164kph (102mph). The reward was a Brooklands gold star medal, hence the model's name when the 148kph (92mph) road version (called the M24) appeared in catalogues for 1938.

Engine: 496cc ohv single, 82x94mm, air-cooled
Power: n/a
Gearbox: 4-speed foot change
Final drive: chain
Weight: 159kg (350lb)
Top speed: 129kph (80mph)

BSA BANTAM D1 1946

Engine: 123cc single-cylinder two-stroke, 52x58mm, air-cooled
Power: 4.5bhp at 5000rpm
Gearbox: 3-speed foot change
Final drive: chain
Weight: 102kg (225lb)
Top speed: 89kph (55mph)

During the 1950s, the humble but hugely successful Bantam became one of the most ubiquitous of all British motorcycles, used by

policemen, postmen, commuters and even Australian sheep farmers. In competition, too, it proved its worth, becoming a popular lightweight trials and scrambles mount, as well as fostering its own class of track racing machines.

The Bantam's engine was essentially a German DKW RT125, a simple but dependable piston-ported two-stroke single.

The Bantam, such as this 1949 D1 model became the best-selling and most profitable model in BSA history.

Introduced as the 123cc D1 in June 1946 (initially for export only) to an economy desperate for cheap transport, the £76 Bantam was an instant hit, becoming the best-selling model in BSA's

history. At the time, understandably, little mention was made of the fact that it was essentially a pre-war German DKW RT125, the design of which passed to the victorious Allies by way of war reparations. Harley-Davidson's first two-stroke and the first Yamaha model were based on this same design.

More sophisticated and better-looking than contemporary Villiers-engined machines, the first Bantam sported a 123cc piston-ported engine with three-speed transmission in unit, telescopic forks and a rigid rear end. Plunger rear suspension soon followed, giving way to full swing-arm rear in 1955. A 148 version was also offered, along with a 172cc stablemate from 1960. The last Bantam produced was the 172cc Model D14 Super of 1968.

BSA GOLD STAR DBD34

1957–63

The 'Goldie', as it was affectionately known, was both the ultimate clubman's production racer and the hottest single-cylinder street racer of the 1950s. BSA's best-loved name was inherited from the pre-war M24 Gold Star, although post-war versions were in essence little more than hop-upped overhead-valve B31/32 and B33/34 roadsters. But what a bike!

The 350 Goldie first appeared in 1947 as the B32GS and was available in varying states of tune to suit different sporting activities, whether scrambles (motocross), trials or road racing. The plunger-framed 500cc version followed in September 1949. Model designations changed from B to ZB (1949–52), BB (1953), CB (1953–55), DB (1955–56) to DBD (1957–63). In all cases, Gold Star engine numbers ended with the letters GS.

The 500s first hit the headlines in winning 11 gold medals at the 1949 ISDT. In 1950, it acquired swing-arm rear suspension, and in a few short years had achieved such utter domination of the Clubmans TT races that the races themselves were threatened. The Goldie was becoming too fast for

Probably the most desirable, and certainly the most raucous of all British sporting singles: the immortal DBD34 Gold Star.

its own good. Of 68 entries in 1955, for instance, no less than 63 were Gold Stars.

Although produced in many specifications, the most popular DBD34 Goldie had a huge Amal GP carburettor, no tickover, no air-cleaner and a penchant for fouling spark plugs. In road trim it produced around 38bhp at 7000rpm, perhaps 5bhp more in race trim, compared to 25bhp for the 350.

Gold Star production ceased in 1963 after BSA declared their highly-strung hooligan single uneconomic to produce. They developed a 250cc single, the C15, for trials and scrambles. It grew to 250, 440 and 500cc, giving Jeff Smith two world motocross titles.

Engine: 499cc ohv single, 85x88mm, air-cooled
Power: 38bhp at 7000rpm
Gearbox: 4-speed foot change
Final drive: chain
Weight: 191kg (420lb)
Top speed: 177kph (110mph)

BSA A7 STAR TWIN

1950–61

BSA unveiled their first postwar big twin, the 495cc Model A7, at the 1946 Paris Motorcycle Show. Although greeted enthusiastically, the machine was not a success. Performance proved to be disappointing, with a tendency to 'run-on' through self-ignition when worked hard, partly due to the use of cast iron for the cylinder and head.

The man charged with improving the model was Bert Hopwood, one of the most creative spirits in postwar British motorcycle design and the man

Full headlamp and instrument nacelles were very fashionable when this Shooting Star was built in 1956.

also responsible for Norton's enduring Dominator. For 1950, Hopwood redesigned the 495cc BSA twin into the 646cc A10 Golden Flash. Although outwardly similar to the old A7, the use of light alloys and numerous internal changes made this a far better machine. These lessons were transferred to a revised A7, the Star Twin. In 1952, this was joined by a modestly tuned stablemate, the A7SS Shooting Star, although neither could rival the performance of contemporary Triumph twins.

In the same year, the Star Twin made one of the most impressive attempts on the Maudes Trophy, awarded for feats of exceptional motorcycle endurance. Three Star

Twins were ridden 1609km (1000 miles) to the ISDT (International Six Day Trial, now known as the ISDE) in Austria, competed with distinction, then continued until each machine had completed 7885km (4900 miles). This remarkable feat earned BSA the coveted trophy, and also gave the Star a reputation for mechanical strength which was shared by almost every subsequent BSA twin.

Engine: 495cc ohv parallel twin, 62x82mm, air-cooled
Power: 26bhp at 5750rpm
Gearbox: 4-speed foot change
Final drive: chain
Weight: 170kg (375lb)
Top speed: 137kph (85mph)

The Shooting Star, designated A7SS, was BSA's answer to Triumph's Thunderbird, although it lacked the Thunderbird's glamour and didn't sell as well.

BSA A65 SPITFIRE 1965–68

Prompted by Triumph's similar move, the unit construction BSA A50/A65 series followed the non-unit A7/A10 early in 1962. In addition, the new Small Heath twins had better electrics, weighed some 14kg (30lb) less than their predecessors, and were significantly less expensive than their Triumph competitors. They had clean, neat lines, perhaps too neat, because many considered the styling bland. But the first A65 claimed only 38bhp, and there was soon some concern about main bearing and oil pump failures.

In terms of performance, the bike to beat at the time was Triumph's T120 Bonneville, while Norton set the yardstick for handling. BSA twins, on the other hand, were ideal sidecar hacks with a reputation for robustness rather than sparkling looks or performance.

BSA had nonetheless created some worthy contenders, notably the A10RGS Rocket Gold Star twin. But these were specialised machines produced in relatively small numbers. It was not until 1965 and the arrival of the Spitfire that BSA truly entered the sports twin fray. A development of the

The Spitfire – this is a 1966 example – was perhaps the finest incarnation of the unit construction 650cc BSA parallel twin.

twin-carburettor A65L Lightning, this sported vibrant red paintwork, alloy wheel rims, close-ratio gears, high-compression pistons and substantially less weight.

The first Spitfire, with racing-style Amal GP carburettors and hot camshafts, claimed a potent 55bhp at the expense of fairly savage engine vibration. Later examples were slightly de-tuned, if less raucous, with Amal Concentric carburettors and slightly lower compression pistons. The chassis, on the other hand, was only slightly different from 'cooking'

BSA twins. The last of the Spitfires was the MkIV of 1968, with a twin leading shoe front brake and boastful 240kph (150mph) speedometer. Although a revised range of twins with oil-bearing frames appeared in 1970, these were dated and sold poorly.

Engine: 654cc ohv parallel twin, 75x74mm, air-cooled
Power: up to 56bhp at 7250rpm
Gearbox: 4-speed foot change
Final drive: chain
Weight: 193kg (425lb)
Top speed: 177kph (110mph)

BRUNEAU
France (Tours) 1903–10: After a couple of years of using Zedel engines, M. Bruneau put to use his own pioneering 500cc parallel twins.

B & S
Germany (Berlin) 1925–30: Bekamo-licensed two-strokes powered these machines from B & S, which stood for Brand und Sohne.

BSA
India c.1980–89: This company made Morini-engined sports mopeds which were sold under the BSA name.

BSM
Germany 1926: This firm was a short-lived, small, German assembler.

BSU
Italy 1923: Ugo Siniscalchi built a small number of Blackburn-engined 350cc machines.

BUBI
Germany 1921–24: This company was a bicycle manufacturer that strengthened its frames to fit a one-and-a-half horsepower two-stroke engine.

BUCHER
Italy 1911–20: This firm was successful for almost a decade with in-house overhead-valve singles and V-twins of 342, 499, 568cc. It was also known as Bucher-Zeda.

BSA ROCKET-3 (A75)

1968

When the BSA/Triumph triple was launched in 1968, the advertising insisted that 'After today, the motorcycle world will never be the same.' It wasn't, but it was Honda, rather than BSA/Triumph, which prospered. The triple was in some ways a better machine than the shattering CB750 launched one year later. It certainly handled far better. Yet somehow it never quite cut it against the sophistication and sheer flamboyance of the four.

Originally the BSA Group (which had acquired Triumph/Ariel in 1951) produced two versions, the Triumph Trident T150 and the BSA Rocket-3. The latter used forward-inclined cylinders in a tubular twin cradle, compared to the Triumph's upright powerplant in a single downtube 650-type frame. The BSA, too, employed a twin downtube frame compared with the Triumph's single tube chassis.

Imposing as it was, the powerplant was little more than a stop-gap measure, proposed by two of the more forward-thinking stalwarts in the British industry at the time. Designers Bert Hopwood and Doug Hele had proposed such an engine, essentially 1½ Triumph Tigers on a common crankcase, some years earlier. In the longer term, Hopwood favoured a modular engine system, not unlike that which would be adopted by

the Bloor/Triumph company 20 years later.

In the meantime, the overhead-valve three would have to suffice against the multis known to be coming from Japan, and it did so fairly well. A good one was at least as fast as the Honda. The first press test Trident, possibly a 'special', recorded almost 210kph (130mph), whilst others struggled to reach 190kph (118mph). And the handling, although certainly better than the Honda's, was compromised by the sheer mass of the machine.

Based on an engine design dating back to 1937, the three was less than state-of-the-art. Pushrods opened the valves,

Essentially 1½ Daytona twins on a common crankcase, the BSA Rocket-3 was distinguished from the Triumph triple by its forward-slanted cylinders.

at a time when overhead camshafts were becoming commonplace. The crankcases split vertically, like the twin's, and primary drive was by chain. A diaphragm clutch was more up-to-date, but the original four-speed gearbox was not. Overall, despite Ogle Design's styling (with 'Ray-gun' silencers and 'Bread-bin' fuel tank), the bike was more a child of the 1960s than the imminent 1970s.

On early versions the running gear, too, was less than advanced, particularly a feeble twin-leading shoe-drum front brake, which struggled to slow the 209kg (460lb) triple. Starting, unlike the Honda's, was by kick. Ironically, BSA bought an early Honda CB750 for evaluation. When its drive chain broke after less than 160km (100 miles), they dismissed the entire machine as 'no threat'. Despite a higher selling price, the triple simply wasn't as refined as the Honda.

By the time significant improvements came, BSA was in a state of collapse and only Meriden-built Triumph triples benefited. A Lockheed front disc brake appeared in 1973, but by then the triple was already five years old. Also in 1973, attempts to improve sales resulted in the Triumph X-75 Hurricane (the

Although designed as a road bike, the BSA and Triumph triples excelled on the race track where Rob North-framed models such as this one beat all comers.

prototypes for which were in fact badged as BSAs), one of the most eye-catching roadsters ever produced. However, despite its appearance, it flopped. Two years later still, the Triumph T160 electric start version appeared, now with more power from an engine leaning forward in the old Rocket-3 manner.

The track was where the triple scored its biggest success and anyone who has ever heard it still shivers from its haunting wail. For British race fans of the 1970s, the Rob North-framed triple was the 'feel-good' factor on two wheels; there were first, second and third positions at Daytona in 1971, countless other short-circuit victories and a succession of production TT wins for the legendary 'Slippery Sam'.

Engine: 740cc ohv transverse triple, 67x70mm, air-cooled
Power: 58bhp at 7250rpm
Gearbox: 4-speed foot change
Final drive: chain
Weight: 209kg (460lb)
Top speed: 190kph (118mph)

BSA FURY

1970

By the end of the 1960s, Japanese machines were completely dominant in the lightweight and middleweight classes and it was clear to BSA that something more sophisticated that overhead-valve singles and twins was needed if they were to compete.

First unveiled to the media in November 1970, the Fury was designed by the same Edward Turner who had created the seminal Triumph Speed Twin 33 years before. The 350cc twin was to be the first British roadster to feature double overhead-cams, and

Failure to bring the ohc 350cc BSA Fury and near-identical Triumph Bandit into production effectively spelled the end for the BSA Group.

was claimed to produce 34bhp at 9000rpm. With chain cam-drive, the design was in many ways Japanese-inspired. However, the crankcases were dry sump and continued to split vertically in the usual British tradition.

The Fury – and its sister, the Triumph Bandit – would be offered for sale at £380, with an electric start version adding another £21. But there was one problem. Although orders were accepted, development was incomplete and the factory was not ready for production. It was an embarrassing and costly disaster which took the BSA Group one step closer to bankruptcy.

Engine: 349cc dohc parallel twin, 63x56mm, air-cooled
Power: 34bhp at 9000rpm
Gearbox: 5-speed foot change
Final drive: chain
Weight: n/a
Top speed: n/a

BUCHET

FRANCE 1900–11

BUCHET WERE A PIONEER FIRM who, in its early days, built engines for cars, motorcycles and aircraft, as well as a small number of complete machines with two or three wheels. The firm's machines took part in inter-town races as early as 1900 and in that year Marcellin rode a 6hp Buchet to

first place in the motorcycle class of the Circuit du Sud Ouest held in February at Pau. By the time the Paris-Toulouse-Paris event took place in July that year his machine had a more powerful 8hp engine but he was not among the finishers.

These machines also took part in events held on banked cycle

tracks where they were also used to pace the pedal cyclists. One outcome of this involvement was a special machine built for Maurice

An early Buchet from 1903 built for cycle pacing work, hence the extended handlebars and low rear saddle position.

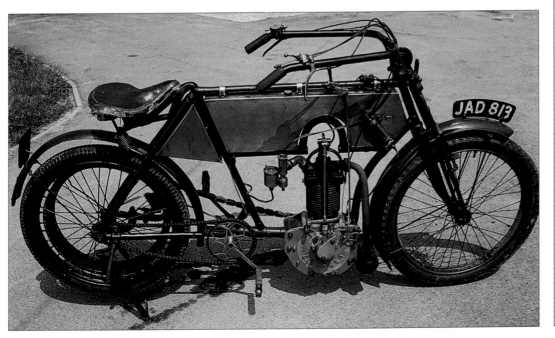

BUCKER

Germany (Oberursel im Taunus) 1922–58: This company was an assembler which, before World War II, made mostly four-strokes from (among others) Bark, Blackburne, Cockerell, Columbus, JAP, MAG and Rinne, in capacities of 98 to 996cc. Postwar, they used Ilo or Sachs two-strokes. The last models to come from them were a 197cc single and a 244cc twin, both Ilo-engined.

BUGRE

Brazil (Sao Paulo) 1954: This Brazilian firm began with a 48cc auxiliary cycle motor, and then went on to make the first South American motorcycle engine, a 124cc two-stroke single, which later went on to be enlarged to 175cc.

BULLDOG

England 1920: This company was an assembler which used the 269cc Villers engine.

BULLERI

Italy (Pisa) 1931: This firm made a horizontal two-stroke twin, apparently of extremely limited production.

BULLO

Germany (Bremen) 1924–26: This was an electric motorcycle with a 120Amp-hour battery and a 0.7hp engine. Very few of these particular machines were made.

BULOW

Germany 1923–25: These machines were lightweights with their own two-stroke engines of two, two-and-a-half and three horsepower.

Fournier. This had an enormous vertical-twin engine and, from the dimensions given in a contemporary report, the capacity was 2340cc, or 142.8cid. This motor had the carburettor behind the engine feeding front automatic inlet valves, the exhausts being stubs at the rear. It had direct drive to the rear wheel by chain with a form of clutch in the engine sprocket to aid starting and getting underway. The engine went into a loop frame that had the top tube bent up to clear it and a Truffault fork was fitted.

By 1903, it was clear that efficiency rather than size was the key to success when Bucquet,

riding a three-and-a-half horsepower Werner, won the motorcycle class in the ill-fated Paris-Madrid race. The event had to be stopped at Bordeaux due to the many crashes among the cars, which had grown too large and too dangerous. The over-large machine continued for a while and Fournier used it with success.

However, its capacity was dwarfed by that of a 1904 tricycle with a similar vertical-twin engine on the rear axle of around 4.5 litres (1 UK, 0.9 US gallon) with direct drive. It was known at the time as the 'Bête de Vitesse', but few riders were prepared to try the machine, much less race it.

These enormous engines were duly superseded by smaller and much more efficient ones. The style of the cycle pacer continued, though, with the rider sitting bolt upright right at the back of the machine to give the best protection to the cyclist.

Buchet continued to build motorcycles in a small way for some years but then moved on to the more lucrative car market in 1910. Motorcycle production ceased the following year.

A close up of the 1903 Buchet engine showing how the tank was formed to clear the exhaust valve rocker; the inlet was automatic.

BUELL

USA 1983–

NOW A PART OF THE Harley-Davidson empire, the Milwaukee-based company was started by the former racer, Erik Buell, who began building an idio-syncratic line of racing specials in 1983. The first of these, the RW750, had a four-cylinder 750cc two-stroke engine and was capable of almost 290kph (180mph). When this was outlawed by a change in racing regulations, Buell began his first Harley-Davidson-engined project, the RR1000 Battletwin.

All Buell's machines displayed an innovative approach to chassis design, particularly when compared to the conservative Harley-Davidsons. From the outset, the machines employed lightweight monoshock chassis with advanced suspension and braking components.

Some of 50 Buell-Harleys were produced with overhead-valve XR-1000 engines between 1987 and 1988, before the focus switched to the new Sportster 1200cc

Evolution powerplant with the RR1200 model. Tuned versions of the same 1200cc V-twin have powered all Buell models since.

Following the modest success of the RR1200, of which 65 were built, 1989 brought the first two-seater Buell, the RS1200. A single-seat sports variant, the RSS1200, evolved two years later. By this time, inverted telescopic forks and large, efficient disc brakes had become the norm for a marque which was at last gaining some credibility in the wider motorcycle community. By the end of 1992, Buell had built almost 450 motorcycles and brought its founder a solid reputation for engineering and design.

Aside from using Harley-Davidson engines, Erik Buell had

With panniers, taller windscreen and more comfortable seat, the S3T Thunderbolt is the touring model in the Buell range of motorbikes.

The RS1200 and single-seat RR1200 were the first Buells to employ the Harley-Davidson Sportster Evo engines, which have powered all Buells since.

other links with the big Milwaukee-based company. Buell had been collaborating with Harley-Davidson on design as early as the late 1970s when he contributed to the original belt-drive model, the Sturgis.

In February 1993 Harley-Davidson bought a 49 per cent stake in the Buell company. The merger gave Buell access to development funds and Harley-Davidson expertise, whilst offering Harley-Davidson a broader model range and a direct line into Buell's creative engineering. Since the merger, Buells have been marketed in parallel with mainstream Harley machines, using engines made at the 'small powertrains' plant on Milwaukee's Capitol Drive.

The current generation of Cyclone, Thunderbolt and Lightning Buell models was first launched in the USA in 1994 and have gradually been developing a good reputation, despite an embarrassing series of recalls in 1998–99. A 492cc single cylinder model, the Blast, was added in 2000. Buell have also taken yet another leaf out of the Harley-Davidson book by founding their own owner's club, which is named BRAG (Buell Riders Adventure Group).

Despite their similar engines, Buells could scarcely be more different in style from Harleys. Buell does not build cruisers, nor customs, nor tourers in the ElectraGlide sense. Buells are sports bikes, sports tourers or streetfighter machines: Harleys with attitude. This recipe has been very successful: the 25,000th Buell, a Cyclone M2, rolled off the production line during 2000.

BUELL M2 CYCLONE   1996

Unlike conventional Harley-Davidsons, Buells such as this M2 Cyclone make excellent 'wheelie' machines.

The base model of the Buell range when launched in late 1996, the Cyclone is powered by a tuned 1200cc Sportster V-twin engine. Claimed power is a heady 86bhp, more than even the biggest conventional Harleys. A wickedly broad torque band peaks at 79lb/ft at 5400rpm. The big twin engine is fitted using Buell's patented Uniplanar mountings, using tie-rods to reduce the effects of vibration. Final drive is by a Kevlar reinforced toothed belt,

similar to the one used on the mainstream Harley range, a set-up which, fittingly, Erik Buell first helped design.

The Cyclone runs on slightly less exotic chassis components than its siblings, notably conventional Showa telescopic forks, rather than the inverted forks of contemporary S1 Lightning and S3 Thunderbolt models. At the rear, in common with other models, a single White Power shock absorber is located

under the engine. The frame is the perimeter type, fabricated from high-grade chrome-molybdenum steel, and clothed in deliberately minimal bodywork. Although bestowed with only a single front disc, this offers an enormous friction area swept by a huge six-piston caliper. Both wheels are cast aluminium, of lightweight three-spoke design.

With a frame weighing a mere 12kg (26lb), the Cyclone is fully 35kg (77lb) lighter and over 10bhp more powerful than even the latest Milwaukee-built 1200S Sportster. Cornering clearance, handling, top speed and acceleration are equally un-Harley-like.

Engine: 1203cc ohv longitudinal 45-degree V-twin, 88.9x96.5mm, air-cooled
Power: 86bhp at 6000rpm
Gearbox: 5-speed foot change
Final drive: toothed belt
Weight: 197kg (435lb)
Top speed: 202kph (125mph)

BUELL X1 LIGHTNING   1999

When launched in 1999, the X1 Lightning replaced the S-series Lightning at the top of the Buell range. Sharing a name with a 4800kph (3000mph) experimental rocket plane, this is a muscular, 'streetfighter'-style sports machine, whose power and handling are vastly improved compared to more traditional Harley machines.

Powering the X1 is a tuned 'Thunderstorm' version of the familiar 1203cc Sportster V-twin, with higher compression pistons, larger valves and ports re-profiled for improved gas flow. Lighter flywheels improve both gear selection and quicken engine response. Most striking of all is the X1's Dynamic Digital fuel injection which employs sophisticated computer control to ensure that the big V-twin delivers its best under all conditions. The result is one of the crispest 'Harley's' ever built, and perhaps the most powerful. Fuel economy and exhaust emissions are also improved.

Like all Harley twins, the engine is hugely flexible but potent, too. Top speed is reached at around 220kph (135mph), although this varies since some markets normally receive models with raised gearing to help meet local noise limits.

The chassis is a tubular steel trellis, with a cast-aluminium alloy rear subframe and high-quality Japanese Showa suspension components at both ends. The

The X1 Lightning sits at the top of the Buell range. Now partly owned by Harley-Davidson, Buell represents the sporting end of the Milwaukee range.

Engine: 1203cc ohv longitudinal V-twin, 88.9x96.5mm, air-cooled
Power: 95bhp at 6000rpm
Gearbox: 5-speed foot change
Final drive: toothed belt
Weight: 199kg (439lb)
Top speed: 217kph (135mph)

BUMBLEBEE
England c.1920: Granville Bradshaw designed this improbable 90-degree, 100cc V-twin delivering three-and-a-half bhp at 5000rpm. Like many of his designs, it seems not to have taken off.

BURFORD
England (London) 1914–15: The inscrutably-named Consolidated Alliance Ltd. made a few side-valve 496cc singles with direct belt drive, to sell at 29 guineas, before World War I intevened and stopped production. There may also have been a 296cc Villiers two-stroke version.

BURGERS-ENR
The Netherlands (Deventer) 1897–24: This company began producing with their own technically advanced engines; then later switched to a 680cc JAP V-twin and a Blackburne 497cc engine. In 1922, they used a two-stroke Vitesse, but they closed down in 1924. Some sources show them continuing to 1961 but this seems unlikely.

BURKHARDTIA
Germany (Magdeburg) 1904–08: Hans Grade designed the early two-strokes which were a 165cc single and a 244cc twin that powered these pioneering machines.

BURNEY
England 1923–25: This English firm built mostly a 497cc single with external flywheel, plus a few 680cc V-twins. The full name of the company was Burney, Baldwin & Co, Burney being Cecil Burney, late of Burney & Blackburne, and Baldwin being the racing rider O.M. Baldwin.

inverted front forks are adjustable for pre-load, compression and rebound damping, as is the single underslung rear shock absorber. The front disc brake boasts a

340mm rotor gripped by a huge six-piston 'Performance Machine' caliper. A simple single piston caliper and 230mm disc adorn the rear.

With a wheelbase of only 1410mm (55.5in) and just 89mm (3.5in) of trail, the X1 turns quickly by Harley standards, yet stability is also surprisingly good.

The thinly-padded seat and overall ergonomics fall a long way short of ElectraGlide territory, but the sort of owners the X1 is aimed at will not mind that.

BUELL BLAST

2000

Added to the Buell range in 2000, the Blast is an entry-level machine aimed at newcomers to motorcycling, an area Harley-Davidson had always found difficult, the nearest previous 'starter' model being the Milwaukee-built 883cc Sportster. Power comes from a 492cc two-valve engine producing 206.8kPa

(30lb/ft) of torque at a modest 3500rpm, ideal for novice riders. Like its bigger brothers, a five-speed transmission and toothed belt final drive is retained, along with vibration-damping Uniplanar engine mounting.

The Showa suspension comprises conventional front forks

and a single rear shock absorber, offering 101mm (4ins) of travel at each end. Each five-spoke cast wheel has a single hydraulic disc brake, 320mm diamter at the front, 220mm at the rear.

The frame itself is a steel backbone with integral engine oil reservoir.

Engine: 492cc ohv single, 88.9x79.4mm, air-cooled
Power: 34bhp at 6500rpm
Gearbox: 5-speed foot change
Final drive: toothed belt
Weight: 163.3kg (360lb)
Top speed: 167kph (104mph)

BULTACO

SPAIN 1958–81

The man who gave his name to one of Spain's most famous makes was Francisco Bulto, who was the founder of the company which was set up in 1958 and situated near Barcelona. Butlo had recently parted company with Montesa– a firm which he had jointly founded – because of its reluctance to race its motorbikes.

Bulto's new firm, therefore, produced a series of small-capacity two-stroke racers throughout the following decade, which were quick enough to perform very well during this time in several Grand Prix events.

Among Bultaco's roadsters was the swift 250cc Metralla, which

Right: A well-used Bultaco trialler in its natural habitat. Among the stars that excelled on these machines were Sammy Miller and Yjrio Vesterinen.

boasted a top speed in excess of 160kph (100mph). But equally as celebrated were Bultaco's trials machines and when Sammy Miller won the 1965 Scottish Six Days Trial, the Bultaco two-stroke was well on its way to taking a dominant position in off-road trialling.

The Bultaco two-stroke took over as 250cc-class leader from Swedish make Husqvarna, and by the time the inaugural trials world

Left: The 350cc Frontera of 1977 was typical of Bultaco's trial bikes, its high-mounted mudguards emphasising the machine's long suspension travel.

championship was established in 1975, Bultaco was reigning supreme. In fact, it was to become the winning marque for five successive years afterwards. Ironically, once this happened, Bulto's old company, Montessa, promptly started building competition machines like the 172 and 250 Cota.

On the road-racing front, Angel Nieto and Ricardo Tormo won no less than a total of four 50cc world titles, all on Bultacos, up to 1981.

However, industrial strikes proved to be Bultaco's undoing. Its days were sadly numbered, and production of the state-of-the-art competition bikes came to an end soon after these victories.

BULTACO ALPINA
1970s

Bultaco's reputation was already well-established when interest in off-road motorcycling took off in the early 1970s, and the firm was ideally placed to offer a range of trials and motocross machines. Indeed, Bultaco's motorcycles had a hand in popularising the dirt-bike boom.

Capitalising on the burgeoning movement, Bultaco brought out

Bultaco's Alpina was a well-specified mid-1970s model that suited amateur trials competitors rather than serious enduro riders.

the Alpina, aimed at the amateur rider who wanted to get a taste of competition. It was more of a trail bike than an enduro machine, but by any standards, it was still a good off-roader.

The specification included high-level alloy mudguard, a silencing system, rear dampers, alloy brake hub, leading-shoe front drum brake, and rearward mounted footpegs.

Engine: single-cylinder 244cc
Power: 19bhp
Gearbox: 5-speed foot change
Weight:109kg (240lb)
Top speed: n/a

BULTACO SHERPA
1964

The Bultaco Sherpa was developed by leading trials exponent Sammy Miller and introduced in late 1964. As the name implied, the Sherpa led the rest of the field and proved to be almost invincible on dirt, and at a stroke rendered most other trials machines obsolete.

The Sherpa contrived to provide a hitherto unsurpassed combination of throttle response, low-down torque and all-terrain ability. Minimal and lightweight, the Sherpa used a number of components from the Bultaco parts bin, including its 18bhp 244cc two-stroke engine, wheels and forks, plus lightweight aluminium mudguards and alloy brake hub, with a bash plate to protect the

The Sherpa was developed by trials expert Sammy Miller in 1964 and represented the trials machine at its most basic.

underside of the machine on rocky ground.

The bike was so basic and purposeful that a claimed 12-day gestation period from prototype to production may not have been an exaggeration.

Engine: 398cc ohv flat twin, 68.5x54mm, air-cooled
Power: n/a
Gearbox: unit 4-speed hand change
Final drive: chain
Weight: 110kg (243lb)
Top speed: 100kph (60mph)

BURNOR
Argentina 1960s: This company was an assembler who made machines using 150cc two-stroke engines.

BUSI
Italy (Bologna) 1950–53: Starting in the 1940s as a frame manufacturer, Athos Busi also built sporting two-strokes of various capacities, from 125 to 200cc.

BUSSE
Germany 1923–26: This was a small German assembler, who initially used Grade motors, and later DKW two-strokes of 175 and 206cc.

BUYDENS
Belgium 1950–55: This company built 125cc lightweights, first with Ydral, then Sachs, engines.

BV
Czechoslovakia (Prostejov) 1923–30: Karel Balzer (B) and Jaroslav Vemola (V) built machines with their own engines: a 173cc two-stroke, 346cc side-valve single, 496cc overhead-valve (and overhead-cam for racing) single, and 746cc side-valve V-twin.

BVR
England 1985–91
BVR (Brian Valentine Racing), builder of limited production five-valve single-engined machines for competition or fast road use.

BYVAN
England 1949: These were fully enclosed machines of extremely unconventional design. The horizontal 148cc two-stroke was rubber-mounted on the front fork, with the drive divided two ways, having a chain drive to the rear wheel.

BULTACO METRALLA

1960s

The Metralla was a classy sports bike of the mid-1960s, and unlike the equivalent sophisticated 250cc Japanese sports machinery, the lightweight Spanish sports roadster was basically a motocross engine attached to a race-bred chassis and cycle parts. The formula was to prove highly successful when Bultaco Metrallas occupied the first three places in the 250cc production class at the 1967 Isle of Man TT races.

Although the Metralla was based on a road-going frame and cycle parts fitted with a motocross engine, it proved to be effective in tarmac competition.

The simple piston-port oil-and-petrol-fuelled two-stroke engine was devoid of performance aids like reed- or rotary-valves. A six-speed gearbox, expansion-chamber exhaust, enclosed final drive chain, and a twin leading-shoe front drum brake complete with an air scoop fulfilled the specification of this well-developed machine, which was in production for more than a decade.

Engine: 244cc single-cylinder two-stroke
Power: 25bhp
Gearbox: 5-speed, foot change
Final drive: chain
Weight: 123kg (271lb)
Top speed: 137kph (85mph)

BUTLER

ENGLAND 1884–97

IN 1884, ENGLISHMAN EDWARD BUTLER patented the world's first petrol-engined vehicle, a tricycle, a year ahead of that built by Karl Benz and the motorcycle constructed by Gottlieb Daimler in Germany. The Butler design had two front wheels on stub axles steered by levers with a single seat between them and a single rear wheel. It has to be remembered that at that time, the safety bicycle had not yet evolved but the forecar layout had appeared as a tricycle.

The engine had two horizontal cylinders, one on each side of the rear wheel, and it operated on the Clerk two-stroke cycle with pump compression. The piston rods ran in guides at the cylinder ends and extended to the front with a curved connecting rod run over each cylinder to the rear crank. Initial compression took place in the front section of the cylinder with the mixture then fed to a reservoir

The original Butler design of 1884 was a year ahead of his German contemporaries and well-advanced but for its direct drive.

below the cylinder and on to the combustion chamber.

Surprisingly advanced, the engine was water-cooled, with the rear mudguard formed as a tank to act as a container and a radiator, had electric ignition rather than hot tube, used rotary valves chain-driven from the driving wheel to let the mixture into, and exhaust out of, the cylinders, and a float chamber to supply the carburettor. Two small wheels were used to raise the rear wheel prior to starting the engine, after which it was lowered. Butler also designed a machine with an engine that used vertical cylinders but this was not built.

Three years later, Butler patented a machine, similar to the

original, as a 'Petrol-Cycle' and one was built in 1888. In this instance the engine operated as a four-stroke, used a spray carburettor and an epicyclic reduction gear was incorporated in the drive to allow the engine to run at a higher speed.

The Butler was a brilliant design and successful demonstrations were carried out but circumstances conspired against it. The highly restrictive British legislation made trials hard to conduct, except on private land, and this caused the backers to withdraw. The patents were bought by Harry Lawson but lapsed when his ventures collapsed so were not exploited.

The machine ran again in 1896, when some of the British legislative restrictions were abolished, but was

then scrapped. Much of Butler's early work was forgotten, but some material was found many years later and the potential of his ideas and lack of support from his financial backers became much clearer. With more help, his work could have been developed and this clever man would have received the credit due to him. Butler died in 1940 aged 93.

By 1888 Butler had revised his first design and is seen here with his Petrol-Cycle, as it was named, from the previous year.

CAGIVA

ITALY 1978–

ESTABLISHED IN SEPTEMBER 1978, the Cagiva firm has grown rapidly to become a major force in the European motorcycle industry, but it has not been without its problems.

The Castiglioni family purchased the old lakeside Varese plant, the former home of Aermacchi, from Harley-Davidson, and gave it the Cagiva name, which is an amalgam of CA from CAstiglioni, GI from Giovanni, the father of the brothers Claudio and Gianfranco who now control the organisation, and VA from VArese.

When asked why the family had acquired the plant, Gianfranco Castiglioni was reported to have replied simply: 'Because we love motorcycles, of course!' Certainly no one could have accused the Castiglionis of a lack of interest in motorcycles, because the Cagiva name had already been seen on the heavily modified Suzuki RG500s of Franco Bonera and Marco Lucchinelli, which were sponsored by the brothers, before they became a motorcycle manufacturer in their own right. This enthusiasm was to soak up a vast amount of their money until the early 1990s. Indeed, from the late 1970s until their final withdrawal at the end of the 1992 season, Cagiva tried all they knew to win the 500cc world racing title but, even though they had riders such as Randy Mamola and Eddie Lawson, the dream was to remain just that.

However, Cagiva did have the satisfaction of winning the world 125cc motocross title on more than

New machines come off the Cagiva production line. Since its creation in 1978, the company has grown to become one of the most important Italian manufacturers.

one occasion. In this sector of bike sport in the autumn of 1978, it authorised development of a liquid-cooled machine. Called the WMXX 125, this 56x50.6mm 124.6cc featured reed-valve induction, air- and water-cooling, six-speeds, magnesium outer engine covers, amongst other technical features. But what really set it apart was the liquid-cooled engine – the first production motocrosser to feature this innovation – and one soon copied by the Japanese. The rest of the Cagiva range for the initial two years consisted of updated designs

previously sold under the Harley-Davidson name. All were two-stroke singles, including 250 motocross and enduro mounts.

During its early years, there is no doubt that Cagiva had the advantage of being able to capitalise on the vast stock of spares and former Aermacchi/HD designs that existed at the time of the takeover. And one of these, the SST125, became the best-selling motorcycle on the Italian market in the all-important 125cc sector between 1979 and 1982. By giving it cast-alloy wheels, better switchgear and finally, in 1982, electronic ignition, Cagiva was able to sell large numbers of these 56x50mm 123cc piston-parted, five-speed street bikes on their home market.

But Cagiva didn't simply sit still. Unlike much of the Italian industry during the early 1980s, which seemed locked in a time warp, the Varese factory brought out a succession of new models from the end of 1981 onwards, both two- and four-stroke. To illustrate the great success of this approach, Cagiva built 6000 bikes in 1979, 13,000 in 1980 and by 1982 production had tripled to 40,000. This was also evident in its number of staff; 130 workers in 1978 increased to 300, of which

A rugged 1986 Cagiva 125 WMX motocross machine. This bike used reed-valve induction, had a two-stroke engine and six-speeds.

Above: The super stylish Planet was a fast and sure machine, thanks to its Mito mechanics.

Below: The V-Raptor (nearest) and Raptor both use Suzuki's TL1000 V-twin engine.

The Cagiva Gran Canyon of 1998 used a fuel injected Ducati 900SS engine, giving more than enough power for the sort of tricks necessary out on the trail.

They dreamed of a product line stretching from the smallest moped to the most powerful superbike. For this to become a reality they needed larger capacity, multi-cylinder models which, if developed from scratch, would have taken many years to reach fruition and billions of lira. Instead, the Castiglionis scoured Europe in search of a partnership deal that would speed the process and therefore not only broaden the range, but cost a lot less.

A partner was eventually found in the shape of Bologna-based Ducati and in June 1983 executives from both companies called a joint press conference. They announced that Ducati would supply Cagiva with engines for seven years. In fact, less than two years later Cagiva took over Ducati.

The next target was North America, but here Cagiva, and even Ducati, had problems: Cagiva's lack of reputation and, in Ducati's case, no efficient dealer network. The Castiglionis solved this by purchasing the world-renowned Swedish Husqvarna concern in 1986. All their motorcycles would now be Cagiva-developed machines, badged Husqvarna, and built in Italy.

The following year, 1987, Cagiva purchased yet another marque to add to their growing portfolio: Moto Morini.

At the 50th Milan Show, in November 1987, the four marques, Ducati, Husqvarna, Moto Morini and, of course, Cagiva dominated with a massive stand and a prime position. The Cagiva range was impressive in its own right. It included a 50cc Cocis named after a legendary American chief and a 125cc Tamanaco. Both of these used a hi-tech liquid-cooled, reed-valve single-cylinder motor with Paris-Dakar styling, twin headlamps, disc brake front and rear, monoshock rear suspension, and a striking multi-colour paint job. Then came the Cruiser, Blues and Freccia. They all used the same basic 56x50.6mm 124.6cc engine from the Tamanaco, but differed in purpose and level of tuning. The Cruiser was a trail bike, the Blues a custom cruiser and the Freccia a sportster with styling based on the Ducati Paso, with all-enveloping plastic bodywork.

Then came a quartet of trail bikes with either 343 or 452cc four-valve single-cylinder engines which where developed from the earlier two-valve Ala Rossa. Two Ducati-powered V-twins, the 350 Elefant and 750 Lucky Explorer, completed the street-bike line-up.

Finally, there was a pair of full-blown motocrossers, the WMX125 and WMX250, the latter now

50 were employed in research and development, by the beginning of 1982.

In 1981 the first foreign factory opened in Venezuela, which began producing Cavigas for the South American market from kits produced in Varese, followed by several other overseas projects, including talks with the Soviet government into the feasibility of supplying Cagiva expertise to the USSR in the same way as Fiat in the four-wheel sector.

At the 1981 Milan Show the company displayed its first 'own breed' four-stroke, the Ala Rossa, a 82x65mm 343cc single-cylinder trail bike with chain-driven single overhead-cam There was also a liquid-cooled 250, actually 67x54mm 190cc, motocrosser as well as an all-new 125 trail machine.

However, the Castiglioni brothers had even grander ideas.

fitted with a 70x64.8mm 247cc engine.

Strangely, after the end of the 1980s, which had seen the world's first production roadster – the Freccia – to sport seven gears, Cagiva seemed to lose its way, even though it sometimes produced an ace, such as the Mito Sportster in 1991 and the Gran Canyon 900 trail bike in the late 1990s. The reasons were many and varied, and ranged from the success enjoyed by Ducati to huge losses encountered in its non-biking generations.

A factory brochure for the 1987 Cagiva WMX 125 and 259 motocross bikes.

WMX125 MOTOCROSS
1980

Notable as the world's first liquid-cooled production motocross bike, the WMX Water-cooled Moto Cross appeared in prototype form during 1978, entering production in April the following year. There is little doubt that then it was the most competitive dirt racer in its class anywhere in the world, but equally it was the least known. Furthermore, the WMX125 owed absolutely nothing to what Cagiva had inherited when it purchased the factory from Harley-Davidson in the summer of 1978; it was all Cagiva's own work.

Its single-cylinder 56x50.6mm 124.63cc engine, which was both air- and water-cooled, made use of magnesium for the outer engine covers and carburettor body. Other notable features included reed-valve induction, a six-speed gearbox and a 34mm Dell'Orto carburettor. The aluminium cylinder had a nikisel bore, which was much more robust than the cheaper chrome system then widely in use. Ignition was a Japanese Nippon Denso electronic unit. Power output was a class-leading 30bhp-plus. It was good enough, in fact, for a Dutch rider to utilise the WMX engine to break the 125cc world speed record in 1981.

The frame employed chrome-moly tubing, while the suspension was taken care of by 35mm, soon replaced by 38mm Marzocchi leading axle forks with magnesium sliders. At the rear were a pair of Corte Cosso gas shock absorbers.

A super-lightweight aluminium radiator, and extremely robust American-made dural swinging-arm were further examples of the quality, yet robust, nature of the design.

From mid-1981, the finning of the head and barrel gave way to the more traditional liquid-cooled 'bald' castings, while from the 1983 model year Cagiva finally bowed to the inevitable and fitted a single shock rear end to the bike, which was marketed as the 'Soft Damp' system. By now, with the 35bhp and a larger 36mm carburettor size, the Cagiva was truly world class, and, by 1983, the factory had begun to take a serious interest in the world

championship series. In 1985 Caviga won the 125 world title for the first time and in the process scored a major publicity coup.

For 1986 a production version named 'World Champion Replica' appeared. Unlike many efforts, this was exactly what it said it was and, apart from the original bore-and-stroke dimensions, the engine was virtually the world champion of the previous year.

After this Cagiva purchased Husqvarna and the WMX125 became a Husky rather than a Cagiva.

Engine: 124.6cc Reed valve ts single, 56 x 50.6mm, water-cooled
Power: 37.5bhp at 11,500rpm
Gearbox: 6-speed foot change
Final drive: Chain
Weight: 88kg (194lb)
Top speed: 128kph (80mph)

The 1983 version of the trend-setting liquid-cooled WMX125 motocrosser. In 1986, Cagiva made a production version of the bike – for once, a real replica.

500GP C9
1983

The Castiglioni brothers, Claudio and Gianfranco, spent a decade and a half trying to win the 500cc road-racing world championship title. In the end this feat eluded them, but they did have the satisfaction of seeing their rider, Eddie Lawson, victorious for the first time during the 1992 Hungarian Grand Prix. One Grand Prix victory didn't automatically mean that Cagiva would have reached the goal, but by the time they quit the following year, they were on

The 1983 Cagiva C9 500cc Grand Prix racer piloted by Virginio Ferrari. Cagiva spent 15 years trying to win the 500cc World Championship without success.

the verge of greatness. Then the money ran out!

The first Cagiva 500GP bike was actually a modified Suzuki RG500 square four, which was raced in 1978 by Marco Lucchinelli, before the brothers took over the Varese factory that

summer. The first 'real' challenger was raced in 1980 as a full-blown Cagiva.

Behind the scenes, men like engine supremo Ezio Mascheroni and former Aermacchi works rider Gilberto Milani were key members of the Cagiva 500cc race development squad.

Recruiting the 1979 world championship runner-up, Virginio Ferrari, was Cagiva's first move in 1980 and the bike debuted at the German Grand Prix. The across-

the-frame four was housed in a Nico Bakker chassis. But for 1981 a completely new engine was designed and built, and it was the first 100 per cent in-house creation. Again it was an across-the-frame four, but its rotary-valves were located behind the cylinders and driven by a combination of bevel gears and toothed belts. It was not until the San Marino Grand Prix at Imola at the end of the season that their rider Ferrari finally qualified, but at last Cagiva had raced in a 500cc Grand Prix, and finished!

That winter the development team produced a completely new bike, more in the mainstream of Grand Prix design, with a rotary-valve square-four engine, featuring contra-rotating crankshafts. Measuring 56x50.6mm as on all Cagiva's 500 Grand Prix machines over the years, this bike delivered 124bhp at 11,600 rpm.

By 1983 the square-four specification was coming together. With Ferrari back in the squad (he didn't ride in 1982), the basis for a more serious Cagiva challenge in future years was mapped out.

Engine: 498.4cc 2s square four, 56 x 50.6mm, liquid-cooled
Power: 125 bhp at 11,200 rpm
Gearbox: 6-speed foot change
Final drive: chain
Weight: 120kg (245lb)
Top speed: 290kph (180mph)

ELEFANT 900
1992

The Elefant – not Elephant – was the most successful of the Cagiva models with Ducati-engines, both in terms of its sales and the fact that it remained in production for more than a decade. It was built in 350, 650, and also 750cc sizes.

The first versions – which were 350 and 650cc – arrived in late 1984, the 350 being aimed mainly at the Italian home market, and the 650, which would be replaced by the 750 from 1987 onwards.

To many, the 750 was the best-balanced version, although the definitive 900, with its dual front discs and inverted front forks, was both the best looking and the most powerful.

The Elefant was also highly successful in events such as the Paris-Dakar Rally, winning this

most gruelling of long-distance classics on more than one occasion, thanks to a combination of V-twin engine, sure-footed handling, reliability and, not least, the riding skills of Edi Orioli. The Elefant's last taste of competition success came in the 1994 Paris-Dakar event, with a famous first- and second-place result by Orioli and team mate, Franco Meoni.

One of the Cagiva team's main sponsors was the Lucky Strike cigarette brand, and for several years the standard production Elefant 750 and 900cc models were available in that company's

The Elefant was Cagiva's most successful Ducati-engined model. A winner of the Paris-Dakar rally, this is a 900 production version.

colour scheme, complete with the colourful Lucky Strike logo. In its final days the Cagiva Elefant racing team had 'Camper' as its main sponsor, with a bright-red paint job.

Eventually, in late 1997, the Elefant was superseded by the lighter and more modern Gran Canyon, which had the latest fuel-injected engine from the 900SS Ducati, instead of the twin Mikuni carburettors which were in the Elefant series.

Engine: 904cc desmo 2v V-twin, 92x68mm, air-cooled
Power: 68bhp at 8,000rpm
Gearbox: 5-speed foot change
Final drive: Chain
Weight: 204kg (449lb)
Top speed: 190kph (118mph)

MITO EVO 1994

Cagiva's Mito has the distinction of being the first production roadster to be fitted with a seven-speed – yes seven! – gearbox in history. Introduced in 1991, the Mito, together with Aprilia's Extrema subsequently renamed RS125 became the ultimate street-legal 125 sports motorcycle of the 1990s, offering a combination of racer-like handling, braking and style, with a 160kph (100mph) speed potential. Both of these bikes were more than capable of besting the Japanese opposition, including Suzuki's RGV and Yamaha's TZR models.

The Mito's liquid-cooled 56x50.6mm 124.6cc reed-valve two-stroke engine was a development of the one used in the Freccia, which had been in production during the late 1980s, and it came with many modern two-stroke features, such as an exhaust valve and pump lubrication. Starting was by press button, while the ignition was of the electronic capacitive type.

The early Mito series which ran until mid-1994 can be identified by the twin round headlamps, conventional front forks and different styling to the definitive

The Mito Evo was created by Massimo Tamburini, former Bimota boss, and designer of the Ducati 916 and MV Agusta F4.

Mito, the EVO (Evolution) which debuted in mid-1994.

The Evo was created by Massimo Tamburini, former part-owner of Bimota, and designer of Ducati 916 series and the new MV Agusta F4. In fact, the Mito Evo shared a very similar styling job with the 916: 'letter-box' headlamp, inverted forks and all. The only disappointment for buyers and onlookers was that

The Mito Evo (Evolution) was introduced in 1994. It could top 160kph (100mph) using only 125cc and sported seven gears.

when the engine was started, instead of the booming four-stroke V-twin Ducati sound there was a 'ring-ting' two-stroke noise. But if you could forget about having a small capacity, single-cylinder 'stroker', instead of a big vee, the rest of the bike was a sheer delight. And in SP guise the Mito could win straight out of the crate, as Dean Johnson was to prove on his Mick Walker Racing Mito SP in the 1995 British Super Teen championship series.

Engine: 124.6cc ts single, 56x50.6mm, liquid-cooled
Power: 30 bhp at 10,000 rpm
Gearbox: 7-speed foot change
Final drive: chain
Weight: 117kg (258lb)
Top speed: 164kph (102mph)

CALIFORNIA CUSTOMS

USA 1990s–

IT MAY SEEM THAT THERE were as many assemblers in the United States in the 1990s as there were in Germany in the 1920s. However, the big difference was that the modern companies had websites, and most of them stayed in business longer.

As with so many custom companies, some of the model names from California Customs of Mountain View, California were quite sad. Surely no one of normal sensibility would buy a motorcycle called a Violator? Those who were genuinely at home with such mayhem might reasonably be expected to steal their machines instead of buying them at high prices.

The others in the 2000 model year line-up were Nomad, Dominator – which is permanently associated with Norton to anyone who knows anything at all about motorcycles – Eliminator, Intimidator and Terminator. The motorcycles were powered by the usual S & S engines with a nominal 96cu in displacement. The actual dimensions were 92mm bore and 117.5mm stroke for a

swept volume of 1562cc, and carburation was also by S & S.

Frames were rigid, or imitations of the Harley-Davidson Softail, or conventional; some were rubber mounted, others not. Transmission was assembled by California Customs from Delkron cases with Jims gears, with both primary and final drive by belt.

A single, albeit four-piston, polished stainless-steel brake disc

The Nomad was fairly typical of the California Customs line-up, distinguished principally by a name that would offend far fewer people than most of the others.

at the front argued that these were not machines that were designed to be ridden hard and fast, though the Corbin seats that were fitted as standard are normally very comfortable. Long distances at low

speeds should therefore have been feasible within the limits imposed by the 18 litre (4 UK, 5 US gallons) tank, the wide bars and the forward controls. 'Slash' unsilenced pipes further assisted the riders to feel as anti-social as they liked, in a milk-and-water sort of way.

Characteristically, the manufacturers' specifications gave all kinds of information, such as front-fork diameter, but omitted those figures so precious to most motorcyclists, namely, weights, power outputs and acceleration and top-speed figures, which shows clearly the market that they had in mind.

Perhaps the most interesting model was the Nomad. This spectacular-looking tourer designed in association with Corbin was fitted with fully integrated, specially made Corbin lockable hard-side panniers. Even then, the manufacturers were at pains to point out that the panniers and the small handlebar fairing could be removed in five minutes to reveal a custom boulevard cruiser underneath.

CALTHORPE

ENGLAND 1909–47

BUILT BY THE Minstrel & Rea Cycle Co. of Birmingham, this make was already well known for its cars when it made its motorcycle debut at the late-1909 Stanley Show. Like the cars, the motorcycles were fitted with a White & Poppe engine of three-and-a-half horsepower, and this had a chain-driven Simms magneto, Amac carburettor, belt drive and Druid forks.

For 1911, they used Precision engines and began to add further models, including a lightweight. Later came one with water cooling and for 1914 the Calthorpe Minor with a one-and-a-quarter horsepower engine that had its two-speed gearbox in the crankcase. In 1915, there was also a two-stroke model, which continued for 1916.

From then on, two-and-three-quarters horsepower four-stroke and two-and-a-half horsepower two-stroke models, both with Enfield two-speed gears, were

built and these continued after World War 1. In 1922, these were joined by a 350cc two-stroke with a three-speed Burman gearbox,

and the following year, a version of this came complete with a sidecar. At the same time, the four-stroke changed to a 249cc side-

In the middle of 1939, Calthorpe introduced three models using Matchless single-cylinder engines, this the 500.

valve Blackburne engine and adopted two-speeds. There were three speeds for the 245cc two-stroke in 1924 when the 350cc version was dropped and JAP engines were used along with a 147cc Villiers.

In the main, these models continued with gradual improvements but all-new for 1925 was the Sports model with Calthorpe's own 348cc engine, a

Calthorpe sold a simple lightweight for many years and post-World War I it gained a two-speed gearbox but kept the belt drive.

three-speed Burman gearbox, light frame and Druid forks. A Super Sports version was added for 1926 but the new model for 1927 was a 498cc overhead-cam single of their own design.

The firm only used their own engines for 1928 with the 348cc in its two forms but the camshaft model was then dropped and in 1929 there came the best known of their models, the Ivory Calthorpe. For this they took the 348cc overhead-valve model, moved the magneto to behind the cylinder, revised the frame and cycle parts, added a saddle tank and finished the tank and mudguards in off-white. The

older model stayed in the lists for one more year to hedge bets and clear stocks but for 1930 it was a single-model range.

The 1930 machine differed in having an inclined cylinder – the trend of the time – and was listed as Ivory the Second. It then became Ivory III, being joined by the 494cc Ivory IV for 1932, along with the 247cc two-stroke Ivory Minor for one year only. For 1933, only the 494cc model was listed as the Major, but was joined by a 247cc version for 1944. Next came one of 348cc and competition versions, all running on through the decade.

In 1937, the marque was sold exclusively by Pride & Clarke of London. For this it had a change of colour to become the Red Calthorpe but sales failed to revive so the firm went into liquidation. Bruce Douglas of the Bristol firm of the same name bought the firm and moved the plant to Bristol. In 1939 he announced a three-model, Matchless-engined range but few were built before the plant was turned over to war work during World War II. In 1947, the name reappeared as the Calthorpe-DMW using a 122cc Villiers engine. This led to the DMW range in 1950.

CAN-AM

CANADA 1973–87

THIS WAS A BRANCH of the Bombardier Snowmobile Group that originated the snowmobile and was also involved with other transport forms. The group also owned Rotax in Austria, which built both two- and four-stroke engines in several sizes for them and many other firms in countries in Europe and elsewhere.

The Can-Am range comprised off-road trail and enduro machines at first, later joined by pure motocross models. The early bikes had a 175 or 250cc single-cylinder, disc-valve, two-stroke engine built in unit with a five-speed gearbox. Normally such a type would have the carburettor protruding out from the engine, which would be far too wide for off-road work, so Can-Am mounted the instrument behind the

cylinder on a long inlet passage, which fed the mixture to the disc valve to keep the engine narrow. This engine unit went into a tubular frame with long-travel suspension by telescopic front forks and twin rear shocks, wire

wheels, drum brakes and off-road tyres. The machine came street-legal with a spark arrestor on the end of the high-level exhaust system that curled over the top of the engine, speedometer, lights, a mirror and turn signals, but also

The Can-Am 250cc Qualifier was built as a serious enduro model, developed from earlier trail bikes. It led to a series of motocross machines.

carried competition plates on each side to show what it could do.

For 1978, the two models were joined by a larger 366cc version that differed in having a reed-valve engine with petroil lubrication in place of the oil injection used by the smaller engines. The range took on a much more serious line with laid-down rear shocks, Marzocchi front forks, more wheel movement and six speeds for the 175 and 250 models, although the 370 kept to the five. In this form they had become pure enduro models and were listed as the Qualifier. With the enduro line came a two-model motocross series sold as the 250 MX-5 and 370 MX-5 with engines of those capacities. These had more power, extended wheel travel and no concessions to anything other than fast lap times in competition –

thanks to all the special detail work incorporated in them.

The range extended for 1980 to include a 125cc motocross model, while the Qualifier came in 175, 250, 350 and 400 forms; in fact, the 350 was actually a 250 bored out to 277cc and fitted into the 400 chassis. By the 1980s, the emission legislation in the US began to bite further so Can-Am turned to Rotax to use the big four-stroke, single-cylinder engine with its overhead camshaft and four valves. During the 1980s, the firm found itself too busy with snowmobiles to work at keeping their motorcycles competitive, so production ended in 1987.

A motocross Can-Am model built purely for competition racing featuring the extended suspension necessary for success.

CANNONDALE

USA 1998–

THE PHENOMENON OF BICYCLE manufacturers taking up motorcycle manufacture was not unusual in the late-nineteeth and early-twentieth centuries; but by the late 1990s, it was very unusual indeed. Nevertheless, mountain-bike manufacturers Cannondale started to make an off-road motorcycle that made its racing debut early in 1999.

Cannondale hired outside talent early on. The result was a machine

that proved remarkably competitive from day one.

The engine that powered both the motorcycle line-up and later the quad bike was a 432cc, double overhead-camshaft, four-valve, liquid-cooled single driving though a five-speed gearbox. Bore and stroke were 95x61mm and heavily over square. Extremely unconventionally, the engine actually breathed through the frame, thanks to a unique design

of steering-head bearing. Not only did this allow cleaner air, it was also cooler, and therefore denser, which translates directly into more fuel-air mixture going into the cylinder. The long inlet tract was also advertised as improving low-

'Out of the box' thinking characterised motorcycles from mountain-bike maker Cannondale, with their own unique liquid-cooled 432cc singles.

speed throttle response, which seems entirely believable.

Still more unconventionally, the cylinder head was mounted 'backwards' with the inlet at the front and the exhaust at the back. The exhaust-valve cooling problem with such machines was apparently solved by the adoption of liquid-cooling overall and wind-tunnel testing of the ducted cooling design during development. Further advantages of the reversed head were claimed to be the opportunity to reposition the cylinder, thereby lowering the centre of gravity, shortening the exhaust pipe by nearly 30.5cm (12ins), creating a wider power band and rendering the exhaust pipe less susceptible to damage in an accident, and the rider less susceptible to burns from the exhaust pipe in the event of a spill. It is often said that everyone knows that reversed heads are bad news, but as technology advances, it is often a good idea to challenge what everyone knows.

Fuel was supplied via electronic fuel injection, and some idea of the degree of development that went into what is, after all, a limited-production motorcycle can be gleaned from the fact that during development, frame flex was actually measured via numerous tiny strain gauges. Depending on the state of trim, the bikes weighed 110–113kg

Unlike most American manufacturers who bikes have carried the Stars and Stripes flag, the Cannondale was not an overweight Harley-Davidson clone. In fact, its machines, like its bicycles, were genuinely innovative and competitive.

(242–249lb), with the heavier version being fully equipped with lights and instruments. Of the two lighter versions, one had no provision for lights, while the other could be fitted with a lighting coil for off-road racing. Tall, skinny tyres, in the usual off-road mould, made steering more precise, as did a modest degree of rake and a short wheelbase.

The fascination of the Cannondale lies in its contrariness. Most new American manufacturers made competent copies of Harley-Davidson V-twins, but Cannondale broke the mould with a genuinely original and competitive motorcycle.

CARABELA

MEXICO 1964–85

THE MEXICAN COMPANY Acer Mex created the Carabela marque in 1964, with technical help from the Italian Minerelli organisation which also supplied technicians in the early days of the project.

However, the Mexicans were not content to simply import foreign components and, over the years, followed a policy of gradually manufacturing more and more parts in their own factories.

By the mid-1970s there was a full range of models ranging from 60–450cc, with two and three wheels. Engines still came from overseas, including Minerelli and Jawa, and carburettors from Mikuni in Japan.

Initially the Carabela motorcycle line was designed and built primarily for commuter transport. However, during the early 1970s great effort was made to extend the company's activities into the field of motorcycle sport, with the introduction of off-road models for motocross and enduro

competition. These were powered by 125 and 200cc two-stroke engines, the former developing around 20bhp.

These two newcomers were also responsible for Carabela's attempts to export, notably to the US market; by 1974, a brand new 250cc motocrosser had been

The Carabella 100 Marquesa MK2, made in the late 1970s. The firm was eventually taken over by the Japanese giant, Yamaha, in the mid-1980s.

added. This bike had 100 per cent Mexican contact, including the engine. Dubbed the MX5 Moto Cross five-speed, it featured a duplex cradle frame, with steeply inclined twin shock rear-suspension units. Power output was 34bhp at 8500 rpm. This was exported to the US, with a 60cc mini-racer, complete with fairing and cast-alloy wheels, which was used by Carabela to promote a one-model race series in Mexico.

Carabela was taken over by Yamaha in 1985.

The Mexican Carabella marque began in 1964, but the mid-1970's it was building bikes such as this 350cc 3.5 Sport, which it exported to the US.

CARNIELLI

ITALY 1931–75

THIS MANUFACTURER HAD originally been a bicycle firm that moved into producing powered transport. This came into effect at the start of the 1930s, under the owner, Teodoro Carnielli.

His machines were also sold as the Vittoria, named after the town in Veneto where the company was based. They used imported engines, the smallest being a 100cc two-stroke German Sachs for a velomoteur, since at that time, nearly all Italian motorcycle firms offered this most basic of machines on their lists.

Carnielli also bought four-stroke engines from the British JAP and Rudge firms. These engines ranged from the essential 175cc for a lightweight, to 250 and 350cc models, up to a 500cc machine. Typical of the era, they had a separate gearbox, all-chain drive, rigid frame and girder forks. Rear

suspension came in time, since by 1939 few Italian makes did not feature this in one form or another, most opting for the pivoted-fork type.

After World War II had come to an end, the firm built lightweights, as well as a scooter. These were constructed using various small engines which were supplied by such companies as Sachs, Ilo, Victoria and NSU, and they were unusual in that they fitted German engines rather than buying Italian engines or making their own. They used the 98cc NSU overhead-valve engine, which was also uncommon because few of that size were four-strokes.

In later years, they introduced a folding moped which was sold under the Graziella name, and had a 50cc Sachs engine, single speed and automatic clutch. This folding moped rode on 20-cm (8-in)

wheels, and the company was able to sing its praises as compact, easy to store and easy to carry; they promoted it as the motorcycle in the boot.

The fold-away Graziella moped, powered by a 50cc engine. This tiny machine was promoted as a motorcycle that was easy to carry and store.

CASAL

PORTUGAL 1964–1990s

THIS WAS ONE OF THE FEW Portuguese motorcycle firms, and perhaps the most important, since they eventually supplied their engine units to other companies. In the beginning, however, they used Zundapp engines and their machines were in the style of the German marque, with a range comprising 50cc mopeds and motorcycles. In due course, they produced their own engines with two or four speeds while at the same time, retaining the Zundapp line.

By the early 1970s, the range had grown to include 75 and 125cc models with five speeds. Some of these models were built for off-road use. All were much in keeping with the style of the period, with front and rear suspension on even the most basic moped, with its single speed

The stylish Casal Magnum showing off its beam frame, cast-alloy wheels and modern line. Its single-cylinder two-stroke engine is in unit with the gearbox.

automatic transmission. There were two- and four-speed sports mopeds with spine frames, an off-road version, and a five-speed sports moped. The last two had duplex frames.

Over the years, this type of machine was the basis of their production because it suited their home market and that of their neighbour, Spain, since small motorcycles were a way of life in both countries.

A water-cooled model appeared in 1982 and combined 50cc with

six speeds and a road-racing style using cast-alloy wheels. Casal continued with the other models, and its style was revised to keep up with trends. A moped in a step-through format was later offered by the firm and in this way, they continued into the late-1990s, but no further.

A typical small-capacity Casal with spine frame, a 50cc two-stroke engine built in unit with gearbox, wire wheels and drum brakes.

CCM

ENGLAND 1971–80 AND 1987–

THE INITIALS CCM stand for Clews Competition Machines, a firm founded by Alan Clews at premises in Bolton, Lancashire. He had a background of success in scrambles and in 1971 bought a van-load of parts from the BSA competition shop when it closed. These formed the basis of the first batch of machines, then called the Clews Stroka.

The Stroka worked well; there was soon a demand from other riders and in May 1972 the first CCM machines were produced, based on the BSA B50 single-cylinder engine unit. These were either 499cc, or enlarged to 608cc, had a cylinder with the fins part cut away and many other changes. These big four-strokes were successful right through the 1970s and late in that decade were joined by a 345cc trials model that used an engine based on and developed from the BSA B40. Later came two-stroke scramblers using Italian Hiro engine units of 125 and 250cc.

Financial pressures caused CCM to be taken over by Armstrong in 1980 and, while the machines kept the CCM name for 1981, by the next year they were labelled Armstrong CCM. During that year the engine unit was changed to the

Austrian Rotax four-stroke single because Armstrong had links with that firm, and the model continued in this form for some years.

However, in 1987 Alan Clews was able to buy his old firm back and over the next two years built it up by selling spares and Armstrong machines against outstanding orders. CCM returned to the competition field in 1989 with the range still based on Rotax engines. For trials, there was a two-stroke engine but the motocross models used the big four-stroke single with a choice of 500, 560 or 590cc.

In this way, they continued into the new decade and for 1997 added a super moto for use on the road. Based on the motocross machine, it used the metric 598cc Rotax four-valve engine in a modern package to offer an excellent, if expensive, model. At the same time, the motocross model was available either in Enduro or Rallye Raid trim, all with the 560cc Rotax, so all the CCM machines had a common base.

Detail of the new CCM with its twin exhaust pipes from the single cylinder feeding into a single system.

A modern CCM with a Rotax engine, rising-rate rear suspension and enduro format, all modified for road use.

Plans for the future include a massive V-twin trail model using a 934cc Folan engine made in Sweden with double overhead-cams, water-cooling and a high-tech specification. Six speeds, a tubular frame, modern suspension and wire wheels with disc brakes all add up to a spectacular package with further development heralded. However, the initial thrust of the firm for the future lies with the well-established singles, for both road and off-road use.

CECCATO

Mondial, and finally, Ducati in April 1954. At Ceccato, he created a one-off double overhead-camshaft cylinder head, but this was shelved once he left in 1952.

Besides its excellent range of 4-stroke singles, which also included cheaper models with overhead-valve engines, Ceccato also built, in 1952, a 200cc two-stroke twin with horizontal cylinders.

By the early 1960s, motorcycle sales in Italy fell, so Ceccato ceased production to concentrate on its engineering activities.

BASED IN BOLOGNA, CECCATO is a high-class engineering company. During the immediate post-World War II period, it also designed, built and sold an impressive array of small-capacity motorcycles.

Most famous were the 75 and 100cc sport models, powered by a single overhead-cam unit-construction engine, with the drive to the camshaft by a train of gears

Above: The 75cc Ceccato stream-lined record breaker of the mid 1950s.

up the finned cylinder's offside. The 75cc was particularly successful in postwar long-distance road events, such as the Giro d'Italia (Tour of Italy). Powered by a 45x47mm 74.75cc engine, it won its class of the 1956

Right: Ceccato's single cylinder dohc engine was built in both 75 and 100cc displacements.

Milano-Taranto, with Vittorio Zito, while the larger-engined 98cc version challenged both Ducati and Laverda in the 100cc category.

Ducati's world-famous designer, Ing. Fabio Taglioni, worked for Ceccato before joining F.B.

CEMEC

THIS FIRM WAS FOUNDED after World War II as Centre de Montage et de Réparation, or CMR, and took the BMW flat-twin as its role model, building their machines using new and spare parts. They chose to produce two types, the R12 and R71, both using essentially the same 745cc, flat-twin, side-valve engine built in unit with a four-speed gearbox with shaft drive to the rear wheel. This engine was in the form used by BMW with a barrel crankcase in which the two cylinders were spigoted with separate heads, a gear train at the front to drive the camshaft and electrics, the valves

Based on the BMW side-valve flat-twin, but French built, the Cemec served both civilian riders and then mainly the police forces.

on the upper side of the cylinders and a single carburettor.

It was in the chassis that the two models differed because the R12, which dated from 1935, retained the old-fashioned pressed-steel frame without rear suspension. It was one of the first BMWs to have

telescopic front forks but these kept the pressed-steel style and paint lining of the past; the hand gear change also incorporated into

the right knee-grip on the side of the tank. In contrast, the R71, first seen in 1938, had the later tubular frame, telescopic forks in a more modern style, plunger rear suspension and a saddle tank in place of one set between the pressed-frame members.

During 1948, the name of the firm was changed to Cemec but the machines stayed much the same, although as the years went by, more and more parts were being manufactured in France. Meanwhile, BMW struggled back onto its feet, but were restricted to small motorcycles at first. A 60cc single was followed by a 125cc flat-twin and then by a 250cc single, before the first postwar twin came in 1950, all of which affected Cemec and their supply of parts.

Year by year, the Cemec became more French and, in due course, they also built machines on the lines of the R51 with its overhead-valve, metric 494cc engine in the existing cycle parts with telescopic front and plunger rear suspension.

Very French in style, a dancer pictured laughing with a gendarme and his Cemec flat-twin in June 1954. Hardly approved riding gear, but...

In addition, they built a similar model based on the 736cc overhead-valve engine of the R17 but without that model's rigid frame, so effectively it was a combination of the R51 with the R71 unit fitted with the R75 top halves.

Cemec supplied many of their flat-twins to the French police at local and national level but their work for the French Army was only to recondition other makes. Since these included

the Gnome et Rhone flat-twin, this was a useful exercise. This took the firm on to 1955 when the name changed to Ratier.

CHAISE

FRANCE 1920–39

THIS FIRM WAS an engine supplier to many French motorcycle manufacturers, much as JAP and Villiers were in Britain. The name cropped up on many marques while its range of engines included a four, overhead-camshafts and unit construction. The company was certainly enterprising and technically advanced. It was also able to supply the more ordinary engines to customers who required these.

The main range was based on four-stroke singles of 250, 350 and 500cc but extended at times to include two-strokes of 175 and 250cc as well as tiny 100cc units. The 350 and 500cc engines were built with overhead-valves as well as a single overhead-camshaft, and the latter had the camshaft driven by shaft and helical bevels. The magneto, dynamo and speedometer were all gear driven

The Chaise four appeared late in 1930 at the Paris Show, the engine a narrow-angle 750cc V-four with shaft final drive.

and the engine was built in unit with a three-speed gearbox with gear primary drive. The oil was carried in a wet sump, so the unit was fully self-contained, which made it easier for users to mount it in their own cycle parts.

Chaise also produced a 100cc two-stroke single for velomoteur use that had a detachable cylinder head, the decompressor in the top and the sparking plug inserted from the rear. A stub for the carburettor was cast to the cylinder's right side and the major part of the left crankcase was extended back as the inner primary case. The crankcase was closed by a door on the right side that included a main bearing. The primary drive was by gears on the left to a countershaft that drove the magneto, flange-mounted to the back of the inner case, while the shaft carried the final-drive pulley.

The Chaise four appeared late in 1930, along with another French

marque, Train, at the Paris Show and, despite the hard times of the Depression, other fours from Ariel and Matchless would make their debut a month later at the London Show.

The Chaise engine was a very narrow-angle 750cc V-four with its built-up crankshaft having the throws offset against the cylinder angle to give even running. It had a camshaft on each side for the overhead-valves with a line of pushrods running up the sides of the engine to the rockers, all the valve gear being exposed.

The magneto and its distributor went on the side of the crankcase, driven from the front of the crankshaft along with a centrifugal cooling fan with a cowl to direct

air over the engine. The exhausts combined into a single rear exit and the engine drove a three-speed gearbox.

Chaise supplied much of the French industry with motorcycle engines up until 1939.

A French Dollar machine from 1929 fitted with a 350cc overhead-camshaft Chaise engine built in unit with its three-speed gearbox.

CHATER-LEA

ENGLAND 1900–36

BASED IN GOLDEN LANE, London, and later at Banner Street, this firm was founded by William Chater-Lea in 1890. It began as a component supplier of lugs, castings and machined parts to the trade. Their first motorcycles appeared in 1900, essentially built to order using a variety of engines but in a few years they had one main model that was intended for sidecar use. This was of robust construction, powered by a 6hp JAP V-twin engine, had a two-speed gearbox, all-chain drive and leading-link front forks. There was also a two-and-a-half horsepower solo with JAP engine and belt drive.

By 1909, they were using a three-speed gearbox and crankshaft-mounted clutch on the sidecar outfit, then added alternative V-twin engines and further solos. For 1913, they reverted to one model, the 8hp

twin sidecar, but added a 269cc two-stroke with two-speed gearbox and belt final drive, these two continuing for 1916.

The company returned after World War I in 1920 with the 269cc two-stroke but added a 976cc JAP V-twin for 1921 and a 488cc side-valve single of their own design for 1922. More models were added for the next year with 246cc overhead-valve and 346cc side-valve engines, while 1924 brought 348cc side-valve and overhead-valve Blackburne engines, their own enlarged to 545cc, while the big V-twin entered its final year. It was also the year in which the firm began

Dougal Marchant at Brooklands in 1924 with his Chater-Lea fitted with a Blackburne engine, modified to overhead camshaft. This machine was a record breaker.

A Chater-Lea from the mid-1920s that had been altered, stripped and tuned for vintage racing, something it was well equipped to do.

to fit saddle tanks to their models. During this period, they made a name at Brooklands, where Dougal Marchant broke records; in 1924 he was the first to exceed 160kph (100mph) on a 350, using a Blackburne engine modified to overhead-cam.

For 1925, only three singles were listed but 1926 brought a new 348cc overhead-cam model of the face-cam type. This had a vertical shaft driven by bevel gears from the crankshaft with the camtracks mounted at its top, and

rockers that followed the cams to lift the valves. There were also two other sports models of 348cc using Blackburne or JAP engines, and the 545cc side-valve model.

Only the models using the Chater-Lea 348 and 545cc engines remained for 1927, until 1928 when the firm moved to Letchworth Garden City, Hertfordshire. A 247cc Villiers-powered lightweight was added for 1929, along with a Dirt Track machine, but only the three road models saw in the 1930s. The two-stroke was dropped; for 1931 there was just the Camshaft and Side-Valve models until the Camshaft ended in 1935 and the Side Valve a year later. After that, the firm returned to general engineering.

CIMATTI

ITALY 1937–84

FOUNDED BY MARCO CIMATTI, an Olympic gold medalist in cycle racing in 1932, the Cimatti marque began bicycle production in 1937, at the small provincial town of Porta Lame. But although it prospered as a bicycle manufacturer, the factory was destroyed during World War II. However, undaunted, Marco Cimatti restarted production and in 1949 branched out into powered two-wheelers. This was during an era when the supplier was king, virtually any type of motorcycle could find willing buyers.

Even so, Cimatti concentrated its efforts on smaller, cheaper designs, including mopeds. This policy was to pay dividends in the 1950s when many rival marques offering larger, more expensive

The Italian marque Cimatti, founded by a champion cyclist, concentrated on 50cc two-stroke machines such as this 1977 Kaiman Cross.

machinery began to suffer serious financial problems. By contrast, Marco Cimatti saw his company expand and prosper.

In 1960 the factory was relocated to Pioppe di Salvaro in the Apennines. In the 1960s the Cimatti works constructed a vast array of humble ride-to-work mopeds and also won the Italian national 50cc trials championship three years running in 1966, 1967 and 1968.

Cimatti also introduced some larger-engined models, with the 100 and 175cc Sport Lusso for street use and the Kaiman Cross Competizione for motocross racing.

At the beginning of the 1970s, a new 125cc motocrosser made its

Small-wheeled motorcycles were popular with Italian buyers in the 1970's; this 50cc machine was Cimatti's product for that market.

CHRISTOPHE
France (Neuilly s/Seine) 1920–30: Christophe produced two-stroke lightweights and 350 and 500cc four-strokes in 1920, as well as an overhead-cam 498cc which had twin exhaust valves.

CICALA
Italy 1952: This big-wheeled, fully-enclosed scooter with 49cc two-stroke power was built by Costruzioni Meccanice G. Vivani.

CICCA
France 1949: A 50cc Veloreve motor drove the rear wheel of this scooter via a friction roller.

CIE
Belgium (Herstal) 1900–05: The Compagnie International d'Eléctricité made this belt-drive, magneto-ignition single that claimed a top speed of 84kph (50mph). The machine was also constructed in London between 1904 and 1905.

CIMA
Italy 1924–27: Sporting machines with side-valve and overhead-valve Blackburne engines of 247 and 347cc.

CITA
Belgium (Liege) 1922–25: This company was a short-lived maker of 175, 200 and 350cc machines.

CITO
Germany (Suhl) 1905–27: This firm began with Fafnir singles and V-twins and after c.1923, produced their own 346cc two-stroke.

CITYFIX
Germany (Osnabruck) 1949–53: This was a scooter with a Sachs engine, initially 48, later 98cc. Another source reports the scooter as being fitted with 58cc Lutz engines.

debut sporting a five-speed gearbox; a roadster version was also sold. However, all Cimatti's machines used proprietary two-stroke engines bought in from Minerelli and Franco Morini.

An export drive was established under the direction of the founder's son, Enrico Cimatti, the principal markets being the US, France, Norway and Tunisia. By 1977, production was up to around 50,000 units per year. Cimatti was also reducing the workforce through the wide use of automation. This, combined with a policy of cutting its range to concentrate purely on the 50cc sector, seemed to have paid off for the company.

Then came the recession of the early 1980s and demand fell alarmingly. Cimatti was wound up in 1984.

CLÉMENT & CLÉMENT-GLADIATOR FRANCE 1898–1935

The Clément model Berceuses of 1928–32, also sold as a Gladiator, featured monoshock rear suspension and was usually fitted a JAP engine.

and sprung forks. These were typical of the time, some with belt drive and others with chain, dummy rim rear brake and flat tank, but as late as 1914 they still lacked a dropped frame, the top tube extended straight back to carry the saddle. They continued in competition, one notable success being victory at the 350cc class of the 1913 French Grand Prix.

Further confusion with the name arose in 1919 with the appearance of the Louis Clement marque with an interesting model that had a V-twin engine with shaft drive to both the overhead-camshaft and the magneto, unit construction, disc wheels and enclosed rear chain.

Clément themselves continued with a good range, some fitted with British JAP engines, both side- and overhead-valve types being used, and a small model with an 87cc four-stroke engine with two speeds, chain drive and pedals for starting. By the late 1920s, one of the Clément-Gladiator models was fitted with

The 4hp V-twin Clément with all-chain drive but dummy rim rear brake and without a dropped frame, hence the backward saddle location.

ADOLPHE CLÉMENT MADE his fortune in the bicycle industry before floating Clément-Gladiator-Humber in 1896 to produce both cars and motorcycles. The Humber connection soon went but the other names carried on, either singly or combined.

The first Clément was a tricycle built in 1898 with a De Dion engine. However, by 1901 the company was producing a machine powered by a Clément-built 142cc, four-stroke engine with overhead-valves, the inlet automatic, mounted inclined to the downtube of a bicycle with belt drive over a jockey pulley to the rear wheel. Known as the Autocyclette, its 1hp output gave it a speed of around 48kph (30mph).

Clément's interest in machines led him to the competition side of the trade. Since the existing trend

was to increase engine size to get more power, this lead to monster racing machines that were also used to pace bicycles on the banked tracks of the times. He decided that he would enter these races with a machine that would outpace all others. The outcome appeared in 1903 fitted with a V-four engine of around 1200cc. It was possibly the world's first racing four, was installed in a long frame fitted with heavy forks and drove the rear wheel by a notched belt from a countershaft. Braking was by a disc type on the front wheel.

Later on in 1903, the machine reappeared with a new and longer frame, chain drive and rear brake only, but by September a lighter machine with twin-cylinder engine was in use which showed the way of the future. However, the four

was used a year later by Marius Thé to win the 1904 world track championship, which that year was held in Paris.

The road machines were more conventional, with a range of singles and V-twins with side-valve engines, magneto ignition, two- and three-speed gearboxes

pivoted-fork rear suspension operating in the monoshock manner. Also sold as a Gladiator, this machine was known as the 'Berceuse', or lullaby, and while the move to rear suspension was good, it did result in an untidy layout of the frame tubes. The report of the Paris Show also commented that the Sturmey-Archer gearbox was installed upside down with the oil filler hole on the underside, while the

battery went under the gearbox, very close to the ground.

By 1931, all their models had the rear suspension on the same lines as before, while JAP engines provided the power. A velomoteur with a French engine was one model that did not fit the pattern but no firm could avoid listing one of these popular types.

As with most firms at that time, Clément were restricted by the Depression as to what they could

do to improve their models; depressed sales and reduced prices made it increasingly difficult to introduce any major changes or new ideas. However, French flair and style made up for much of this by minor changes and alterations to colour schemes to highlight different features from one year to the next, in a similar way that manufacturers would experiment with graphics many decades afterwards.

CLÉMENT-GARRARD ENGLAND 1902–5

IN 1902 CHARLES GARRARD OF Birmingham imported the French Clément clip-on engine unit to fit to a standard bicycle. It was of 143cc with an overhead exhaust-valve, small crankcase and large, external flywheel. Thus it could be fitted inclined to the downtube, inside the frame, driving the rear wheel by belt over a jockey pulley.

Norton frames were used for the new model. For 1903, a 3hp narrow-angle V-twin model joined the single, its engine in the same position, intended for tandems, but Garrard used it in competition.

A new design was offered for 1904 with the engine vertically mounted just behind the front wheel, its weight hung from the downtube and braced to the bottom bracket. Most of the frame was occupied by the tank and its compartments. However, suspended forks of the leading-link type and a two-speed gear with chain drive were also advertised. The V-twin was in a similar format with the frame revised to suit the engine. In 1904, after announcing a new forecar as a Garrard, the name faded from sight.

Above: The 1902 Clément-Garrard had its engine fitted high in the frame, direct belt drive and a frame supplied by the Norton firm.

Below: A long transmission line from the V-twin engine to rear wheel was a feature of this 1903 Clément-Garrard. Note the second set of pedals.

CL
Germany 1951: This was a producer of a mini-scooter with a 34cc engine.

CLAES
Germany 1904–08: Fafnir engines of three-and-a-half horsepower and 5hp in frames from a well-established bicycle company. These were also sold under the Pfeil name.

CLAEYS FLANDRIA
Belgium 1955–unknown: This firm produced mopeds (1955), a scooter (1956) and a lightweight motorcycle (1957), all powered by Ilo two-strokes.

CLARENDON
England (Coventry) 1901–11: This English company built bicycles, cars and motorcycles, the latter with a 3hp side-valve single. Engines were made in-house or bought-in from a variety of makers.

CLAUDE DELAGE
France (Clichy s/Seine) 1925: This firm assembled tiny numbers of cars and motorcycles in the few months of its existence. It was no relation to Delage cars.

CLESS & PLESSING
Austria (Graz) 1903–6: Their own two-and-a-half horsepower engine powered these pioneer machines, initially with shaft drive, then with belt drive. Later engines included a three-and-a-half horsepower single and a 5hp V-twin. They were also sold as Noricum.

CLEVELAND
England (Middlesborough) 1911–14: These sporting machines were fitted with Precision engines, and possibly others.

CLUA
Spain (Barcelona) 1954–64: Four-speed gearboxes and up-to-date suspension graced these 125 and 175cc two-strokes from the beginning. Later came a 49cc moped.

CLEVELAND

IN 1915, THE CLEVELAND Motorcycle Manufacturing Company began producing 222cc two-stroke single-cylinder machines, which featured in-line crankshafts and chain drive. The engine capacity was subsequently raised to 269cc, and these bikes proved to be very popular.

The Cleveland Lightweight was made between 1915 and 1927, and although in appearance it bore considerable similarity to its bicycle ancestors, it ranks as possibly the most successful two-stroke machine to be produced in the USA. Cubic capacity of the single-cylinder engine rose from an initial 222 to 269cc in 1919, and the crankshaft was mounted longitudinally with the final drive turned through 90 degrees by a worm and pinion gear. There was a two-speed gearbox, operated by a hand lever, and it was chain-driven with identically sized

Above: The 600cc four cylinder Cleveland. This 1925 model was not a success, and the Depression forced the company to close.

sprockets. The specification also included horizontally sprung pivoting front forks.

In 1922, Cleveland was able to buy out the Reading Standard Company and two years later it came out with a 350cc side-valve single-cylinder machine. Although it had a similar frame design to its predecessor, it did not sell as well.

Cleveland's first four-cylinder model was unveiled in 1925. Its engine was based on the Fowler Four, a design originating from L.E. Fowler. In sales terms it was not a success, however, and so to improve their outlook, in 1926, Cleveland brought out a replacement using a 737cc engine designed by Everitt DeLong.

Introduced in 1929, the Tornado model was endowed with a 1000cc motor, which featured the inlet-over-exhaust design, in which the exhaust valve was mounted to the side of the engine with the mechanically operated inlet valve located above the exhaust. The

A 1919 269cc lightweight bike, which became possibly the most successful two stroke machine ever built in the USA.

Tornado's vast wet-sump engine featured a horizontally split crankcase and was fitted with alloy pistons to save weight, and bigger valves to improve performance. It used a three-speed gearbox with chain final drive and had leading-link forks, and the stand pivoted off the end of the rigid frame that supported the rear mudguard.

However, the Tornado was as unsuccessful as Cleveland's 1925 four-cycliner model, despite being built to a high standard. The reason was that the Tornado failed to match the performance of the larger-capacity four-cylinder offerings which were coming from Ace and Henderson during that period. Cleveland's response was to raise its capacity by degrees, first to 737cc and then to a full 1000cc in 1926.

Unfortunately, like so many other American manufacturers, the company was unable to weather the economic crisis of the Depression and it was forced to close down after the Wall Street Crash in 1929.

There was no connection between the US Cleveland and the English Cleveland make that operated from 1911 to 1924, making three-and-a-half bhp single-cylinder machines with Precision engines.

CLYNO

ENGLAND 1909–23

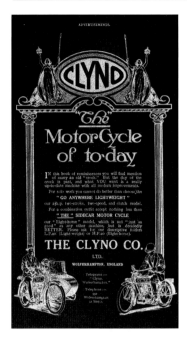

FRANK AND AILWYN SMITH were cousins who produced an adjustable engine pulley for motor-cycles, and then moved on to produce motorcycles. They were based at Thrapston, Northampton-shire and first exhibited at the late-1909 Stanley Show with two models, a 3hp single and a 6hp V-twin, both fitted with Stevens engines, belt drive, their own adjustable pulley and sprung forks.

Two Clyno models were featured in this advertisement, a 2½hp, two-stroke lightweight single and an 8hp V-twin for sidecar work.

Late in 1910, Clyno production moved to the Stevens' former Pelham Street factory in Wolverhampton for mutual benefit. For 1911, the twin had the option of two speeds and chain drive, which was upped to four speeds in 1912 using twin primary chains. There was only the V-twin for 1913, with three speeds and chain drive, but this was joined in the next year by a 269cc two-stroke lightweight with two speeds.

A larger two-stroke made a brief appearance in 1915 when a second version of the V-twin was added as a combination for army use to carry a heavy machine-gun and ammunition. This alone continued for 1916 and some were sent to Russia, followed by a later batch fitted with an 8hp JAP engine.

After World War I, they appeared at the 1919 Olympia Show with the two-stroke and a new 925cc V-twin model with leaf-spring rear suspension intended for sidecar use but a financial reorganisation delayed its appearance until 1922. At the end of the following year, motorcycle production ceased in order to make space for their car lines.

Detail of a 1912 6hp V-twin Clyno model with three speeds and all-chain drive, a model designed for, and well-suited to, sidecar work.

CM

ITALY 1930–57

THE CM MARQUE WAS based in Bologna and was the brainchild of the famous rider and engineer, Mario Cavedagna. He was assisted by Oreste Drusiani, brother of Alfonso, creator of the 1950s 125cc FB Mondial championship-winning Grand Prix racers.

Cavedagna sold out in the mid-1930s. The new owners continued to produce the overhead-cam models in capacities of 173 to 496cc and a brand new 496cc overhead-valve single. There was also a competitive 348cc overhead-camshaft racer which, ridden by Guglielmo Sandri, was particularly successful.

After World War II, only the 500 overhead-valve single and a massive-looking 250 single with chain-driven overhead-cam continued. From 1944 onwards,

there was a new range of two-stroke singles of 123 to 173cc.

At the Milan Show in 1952, CM exhibited an entirely new 248cc two-stroke parallel twin with slightly inclined cylinders. In sports form it was a very capable machine with a maximum speed of over 128kph (80mph), very swift for a legal road-going 250.

A specially tuned version for events

At the 1949 Milan show, CM had a bewildering array of motorcycles – a much wider variety than would be expected today from a small firm.

such as the Milano-Taranto and Giro d'Italia was produced in small numbers and even kitted out as a pukka racer for short-circuit events. During the 1956 Milano-Taranto, a CM finished sixth overall, also winning the 125 and 250cc production categories.

CLYDE
England (Leicester) 1898–1912: This firm fitted carburetters built under a Simms licence to early engines of their own manufacture: . These engines were two-and-three-quarters horsepower, six-and-a-half horsepower, 7hp and 8hp V-twins, later with JAP engines. They were tehcnically advanced, and used water-cooling as early as 1903.

CMK
Italy 1950s: This was a surprisingly advanced four-speed scooter with 50cc two-stroke, having a chromium-plated bore and delivering 4.2bhp at 6700rpm.

CMM
England (Coventry) 1919–21: The initials CMM stand for Coventry Motor Mart. The company made a few machines with the inevitable 292cc two-stroke motor, even though they were bought-in from Union, and not Villiers.

CMP
Italy (Padua) 1953–56: This firm was the producer of machines that initially used two-stroke Ceccato engines of 75, 100 and 125cc; then 49cc Sachs and, finally, a 125cc four-stroke Ceccato.

CMR
France 1945–48: These French-built BMW copies were made with many R12 and R71 parts, probably to get around the non-availability of new BMWs. 'Montee en Sarre' Leica cameras were built for the same reason

COCYMO
France late 1950s: This firm produced first the Cocynette moped, then later produced a 125cc two-stroke lightweight.

CODRIDEX
France (Lyon) 1952–56: This French company built two-stroke mopeds with 49cc and 65cc engines.

COFERSA
Spain (Madrid) 1953–60: This firm was a producer of basic 100–175cc two strokes, which were latterly powered by Hispano-Villiers engines.

COBRA

USA 1990s–

COBRA'S OWN PUBLICITY material summed their machines up well: 'The first and only motocross bike ever built in the USA. Our parts are 98 per cent American made, we have won the Amateur National Championships since 1994 and the engine is designed and manufactured in our own shop.'

The market chosen by the New Middletown, Ohio, firm was a very small niche indeed – junior motocross, or children's racing – but they attacked it with enthusiasm, originality and skill and ended up with considerable success. If other manufacturers had applied Cobra's vision and diligence instead of turning out overweight Harley-Davidson clones, American motorcycles might have regained the pre-eminent position they briefly enjoyed before World War I.

The company's success rested on two similar models, the air-cooled CM50 for children aged four to six, and the liquid-cooled King Cobra for seven and eight year olds. Both were very much 'real' motorcycles, with TIG-welded chromemoly tubular frames, kick-starts, and in-house parts such as hydraulic front forks, 140mm (5.5ins) travel on the CM50, 230mm (9ins) travel on the King Cobra, remote-reservoir shock absobers, and more.

Although Cobras were expensive 'toys' at $2775 for the CM50 and $3350 for the King Cobra 2000 prices, and although rider skill must always count for at least as much as the machine itself, there is no doubt that a motorcycle-loving child could receive few, if any, more desirable gifts.

COCKERELL

GERMANY 1919–24

COMPARED TO HIS unorthodox Megola motorcycle with its five-cylinder rotary engine built into the front wheel, Fritz Cockerell was quite conventional with the machines that bore his own name. Produced in Munich for a few years, he used small two-stroke, single-cylinder engines of 110, 145

The Cockerell machines had their two-stroke engines set horizontally so they could be almost completely concealed as on a scooter while retaining the motorcycle form.

Above: The four-cylinder, water-cooled Cockerell prototype of 1927 with chain drive and leading-link forks; one of many designs by the talented Fritz Cockerell.

and 170cc, all with the cylinder laid horizontal to the ground. They had the simple three-port layout but were constructed on sound engineering lines, unlike some others of that era.

The engines sat low down in a cradle frame with light girder forks and a simple transmission carrying a pulley for the belt final drive. Light and well made, they were successful in German competitions for which the engines were often water-cooled. Cockerell sold the firm to Abako of Nuremberg in 1924 but continued to design many types of two-stroke engines, ranging from a small bicycle attachment to a water-cooled four. This had the cylinders in line along the frame and chain final drive, a dummy-belt rim for the rear brake but a drum and leading-link forks at the front. Its capacity was around 750cc and it was built in 1927. There were also diesel and car engines, while during its time, Cockerell's firm had supplied engines to other manufacturers: they appreciated their merits of power, low fuel consumption and reliability.

COMET

ITALY 1952–57

ALTHOUGH THE MARQUE lasted less than five years, this Bologna-based company was one of the most innovative of its era. 'One of the most interesting models on view', was how *Motor Cycling* described the 175cc Moto Comet in their Milan Show issue of 1952. Designed by the legendary FB Mondial engineer Ing. Alfonso Drusiani, it was of considerable technical interest.

The engine was a vertical twin, with light-alloy cylinders and heads, the overhead-camshaft being driven by a chain located between the cylinders. It used overhung cranks, with gear primary and chain camshaft. In unit with the engine, a four-speed gearbox drove an in-built distributor being located in the fuel tank cutaway. Telescopic forks and hydraulically damped rear shock absorbers for the swinging-arm completed an exceptionally neat engineering and styling package.

A sports version was presented at the Milan Show in 1953, and there, in 1954, the company displayed an experimental larger-capacity Comet model. Alfonso Drusiani's 250 four-stroke used the slide-valve principle. The barrel had three bores in line, a main cylinder between two smaller ones. Three crankshaft assemblies were geared together, with the 'valve cylinder' pistons at half engine speed.

There was also a new 250cc Comet vertical twin, and a racing 175 single with overhead-cam and outside flywheel.

At the 1954 Milan show, Comet displayed this 175cc ohc single cylinder MT (Milano-Taranto) sports model, designed by Alfonso Drusiani.

COLELLA
Italy (Rome) 1981–unknown: This was a 'mini-moped' of just 1100mm (43ins) in length which weighed 37kg (81lb) and was powered by a 49.9cc two-stroke motor of the company's own design.

COLIBRI
Austria 1952–54: This Austrian scooter was fitted with a 123cc DKW motor.

COLIBRI
Germany (Munich) c.1950s: This firm was the producer of a cycle motor with the name Colibri, which means humming bird.

COLIBRI
Sweden 1920: This was an obscure make powered by a four-stroke 96cc engine of the company's own design.

COLOMB
France 1950–54: This firm was a small-scale assembler of mopeds and lightweights.

COLONIAL
England (Nuneaton) 1911–13: This firm built a few machines fitted with their own 450cc two-stroke single.

COLUMBIA
USA 1900–05: This US firm installed Pope single and V-twin motors in diamond cycle-type frames.

COLUMBIA
France 1922–26: This was an early producer of side-valve singles of 198 and 250cc capacity.

COLUMBUS
Germany (Oberursel — Frankfurt/Main) 1923–24: This German firm produced overhead-valve 250cc singles as well as 600 and 800cc twins. They also offered an overhead-valve 49cc cycle motor. The company was renamed Horex when it was bought out by the Kleeman factory.

CONDOR

SWITZERLAND 1901–1970s

TOGETHER WITH MOTOSACOHE and Universal, Condor was a major player in the Swiss motorcycle industry for the first half of the twentieth century.

When Condor built its first motorcycle in 1901, the company, based in Courfaivre, had already become an established brand in the pedal cycle world. Its first powered two-wheeler was a one-and-a-half horsepower lightweight motorcycle. This and other early models employed machines using bought-in engines. At first these were of Zedal manufacture, but later Condor fitted single-cylinder and V-twin two-stroke engines in its bikes.

During World War II, Condor, like all of the Swiss motorcycle industry, continued largely undisturbed by the conflict raging outside its borders in the rest of Europe. It even benefited as German, Italian, French and British imports were discontinued during wartime.

In 1947, Condor built the EC580, the first motorcycle to use an engine entirely of Condor's own design and manufacture. It was a 597cc side-valve horizontally opposed twin with shaft final drive. The capacity was subsequently increased to nearer 750cc and as well as the original

civilian prototype, military versions were constructed and sold.

In 1950, Condor debuted a 349cc twin cylinder two-stroke, and in 1956 a prototype 248cc model with an overhead-camshaft single-cylinder Italian Masserati engine. The A250, an overhead-cam single with shaft drive, arrived in 1959.

Later still, using imported Ducati engines, the company built a 340cc overhead-cam model which was used by the Swiss armed forces for the next 20 years.

The Swiss Condor concern built its first motorcycle in 1901. They then went on to produce a wide range of machines for both civilian and military use.

CONFEDERATE MOTORCYCLES USA 1990s–

SOMEWHAT IMPROBABLY, the logo of Confederate Motorcycles of New Orleans, Louisiana, was in Fraktur, the German black-letter script much favoured by the Nazis. The names of some of the colours for the 1999 model year – Rebel Black, Combat Grey, Blood Red – were thrown into the realms of bathos by the option of Candy Blue, and one can only conjecture that Officer Yellow was a Vietnam-era joke. Further colour options were added for 2000, including multi-coated metallics. Frames were powder-coated, matched to the paint job, and had a fairly typical wheelbase of 165cm (65ins) with a rake of 30 degrees.

As usual, the standard motor was from S & S, this time in the 113cid, two-valve-per-cylinder,

pushrod guise, with no power output given. With an actual bore and stroke of 101.6x114.3mm, the true swept volume was 1853cc. The engine is described as 'hand-built, blueprinted and balanced', and given some of the other features on the machine, this seems not unlikely.

A 'high output' engine option was promised for 2000 but with no quoted power outputs, it is not possible to make comparisons. At a rough guess, an engine of this size and configuration should deliver 80–90bhp. What is seldom realised, however, is that when they are tested on the dynamometer, it is common for big, relatively simple engines like this to deliver power that varies by as much as 10 per cent from

Confederate machines – this is a Grey Ghost – tend to have a distinctive look which sets them apart from many lesser Harley-Davidson-inspired motorcycles.

engine to engine. These variations are influenced significantly by air temperature and humidity.

Primary drive to the five-speed Andrews gear set was by belt; the inverted front shocks came from Paioli; and even though there was only one front disc, it was 320mm (12.6ins) in diameter with a braking surface of ductile iron, with a six-piston calliper. Fasteners were all nickel-plated hard steel or aircraft-grade stainless steel. For the 2000 model year, the fuel tank was changed from light alloy to carbon fibre.

Marchesini 43-cm (17-ins) wheels front and rear and Pirelli radial tyres, a two-into-one

silencer with an expansion chamber, and a ground clearance of 16.6cm (6.5ins), further argued that Confederate motorcycles were, unlike some of their competitors, designed to be ridden, although, the small size of the fuel tank – 14.5 litres (3.2 UK or 4 US gallons) – suggested, not far.

The two models, the NBF Hellcat and the REL America GT, were distinguished principally by the GT's pillion seat. Both weighed 227kg (500lb) dry with a maximum permitted gross vehicle weight of exactly twice that. The Confederate, it seems, looked like an impressive example of a 'Harley-Davidson clone'.

The single seat Hellcat blends retro looks with a good deal of decently modern engineering, especially in the forks, brakes and other areas affecting handling.

CORGI

ENGLAND 1948–54

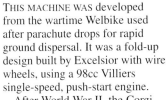

A line drawing of the Corgi that was based on the wartime Welbike but used an Excelsior engine in place of the Villiers, both of 98cc.

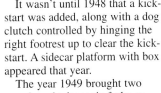

It wasn't until 1948 that a kick-start was added, along with a dog clutch controlled by hinging the right footrest up to clear the kick-start. A sidecar platform with box appeared that year.

The year 1949 brought two speeds and telescopic forks as options, these becoming standard for 1952. The Corgi did a useful job in its early days, but standards were improving. It was built until 1954, when it gave way to the mopeds coming on the scene.

THIS MACHINE WAS developed from the wartime Welbike used after parachute drops for rapid ground dispersal. It was a fold-up design built by Excelsior with wire wheels, using a 98cc Villiers single-speed, push-start engine.

After World War II, the Corgi differed in that it used a 98cc Excelsior Spryt engine. First announced in 1946, it reached the public in 1948 with its engine mounted in a low duplex frame with rigid forks and chain drive. It had a small fuel tank, disc wheels, foldable handlebars, seat and footrests.

The Corgi offered crude but adequate transport in its day, until times improved and the moped arrived.

COSSACK

USSR 1974–77

THE COSSACK NAME WAS applied to a range of Soviet-made motor-cycles that came from several factories and was marketed in Great Britain by the Satra Belarus company from its Byfleet, Surrey headquarters.

The three models offered, in what was a major attempt to break into the lucrative British market, were the Voskod, a 175cc twin port two-stroke single; the Jupiter,

The Cossack name was used to market Soviet motorcycles in the West during the 1970s. A model called the Ural, with a sidecar, is illustrated.

COLUMBUS
USA 1960: From this firm came the Rocket, which was a small scooter fitted with a two-and-a-half horsepower single-cylinder engine.

COM
Italy 1926–28: This company produced lightweights with 123 and 173cc engines.

COMERY
England (Nottingham) 1919–22: This was an English assembler that used Villiers and Blackburne engines.

COMESA
Spain 1957: The Comesa was a licence-built FB-Mondial machine.

COMET
England (London) 1902–07: Minerva engines and BSA-based frames are characteristic of these pioneers.

COMFORT
Italy (Milan) 1923–27: This up-market assembler used overhead-valve motors bought-in from Bradshaw (later Barr & Stroud), with Sturmey Archer gears.

COMMANDER
England 1952–53: The General Steel and Iron Company built the Commander, a remarkably ugly 1930s-style machine. It was fitted with a chrome-plated cage to conceal its 99–123cc Villiers engine.

of IZH manufacture, a 350cc twin cylinder two-stroke, and the Ural, an overhead-valve horizontally opposed twin, based on an obsolete BMW design.

Headed by former Lambretta UK sales manager Alan Kimber, Satra Belarus certainly tried hard enough. They spent a considerable amout of money on an advertising campaign with full-page advertisements in all the most important motorcycle magazines in the UK.

But Satra faced two major problems. The first was that, as with the Russian Lada car, the technology was at least two decades out of date. The second was that, for increasingly overcrowded British traffic conditions, the braking

performance of all these machines was vastly inferior to the mainstream Japanese and European bikes being sold at that time. In an attempt to improve matters, each motorcycle had its brake linings (all models featured drum brakes) upgraded by exchanging the originals with British-made Ferodo components. Even so, braking remained a major problem.

As for the dated technology, this was only a positive feature in the Russian home market because not only were Russian roads of inferior quality to Western ones, but it was also important that mechanical transport could be serviced by the owner at the side of the road if necessary.

When Satra went out of

business, a new company, Neval, continued to market Soviet bikes in the UK.

The Ural used a development of the pre-war BMW flat twin ohv engine. Popular as a sidecar tug.

COTTON

THE COTTON FIRM was located in Gloucester. Between the wars, Cotton models were noted for their triangulated frame that had been devised by Francis Willoughby Cotton as a straight-tube design. This was first seen around 1913.

As a trained lawyer, Cotton was able to prevent any attempts by rival manufacturers to copy the design that gave the machines such good handling. The frame was based on four straight tubes running from headstock to rear

wheel, a layout that enabled most engines to be accommodated and gave Cotton plenty of choice.

The engines ranged from a 269cc Villiers two-stroke to large four-strokes, with a variety of transmissions using two or three

speeds and chain or belt final drive.

It was on a 348cc Cotton that Stanley Woods made his TT debut and finished fifth, even after many problems.

In 1923, the range expanded with a 247cc two-stroke and models with side-valve and overhead-valve, all with Burman two- or three-speed gearboxes. Fame came that year when Stanley Woods won his first TT on a Cotton. In the next two years, Cotton machines won various competition places, and to top it all, they were in the first three places in the 1926 Lightweight.

With the marque name now well established, the range continued to be both large and varied, improving over the years and following the trends as they came along. Engines continued to come from JAP and Blackburne in the main, but Villiers, Sturmey-Archer and Rudge were also in use. A saddle tank went on the overhead-valve models in 1930 and then on all models from 1932, the year that two 150cc machines with Villiers and JAP engines were added.

Maintaining a long list of machines, with something for everyone, served the company well through the difficult times of

Derek Huxley takes off on a 250cc Cotton during the 1978 Formula III race held in the Isle of Man. The machine featured a Rotax engine.

the 1930s. By 1937 all bikes, bar one, used JAP engines and these took the firm to the end of the decade, along with a 122cc Villiers lightweight. After World War II, the marque remained nominally available, and was largely unchanged with girder forks as late as 1952. Few machines were built in this period which ended when, in 1954, Pat Onions and Monty Denley took over and changed to two-stroke power.

This range used a variety of Villiers engines to power it, as well as two British Anzani twins, and had names such as Vulcan, Cotanza, Trials, Herald and Messenger, with sizes running from 197 to 324cc. By 1959, some machines had a degree of rear enclosure and all fitted Armstrong leading-link forks. In the 1960s came 246cc Villiers singles and names such as Scrambles and Double Gloucester, while in 1963 there was the Villiers Starmaker engine for the scrambles Cobra and the road-racing Telstar models. The accent was firmly on sports and competition but new variations failed to halt a decline in sales until 1968 when Villiers ceased to produce engines.

A 350cc Cotton from the mid-1920s showing the triangulated frame construction that gave the bike such good handling, regardless of what engine was fitted.

Cotton then turned to the 170cc Minarelli engine, offering a range of competition models, but also used a Villiers-type engine made by DMW. They became involved with CCM and Armstrong, which led to the Cotton-EMC road racer of 1979 that used a Rotax engine and motocross machines, but

eventually, these all became Armstrongs and the Cotton came to an end.

In 1991 it was revived by Fluff Brown and since then replicas of Cottons of the 1960s have been built by AJS Motorcycles of Andover, Hampshire. These machines were the Cobra and Telstar with the Starmaker engine, and the Trials Special with the same unit or the 37A. Strong demand for these continued, thanks to the nostalgia boom of the 1990s.

COVENTRY EAGLE   ENGLAND 1899–1940

BASED IN COVENTRY, this firm had its roots in bicycles before turning to tricycles at the end of the nineteenth century. Its products were usually an assembly of bought-in parts but these were selected to go together well and the result given a good finish. The machines were well received in the market and this enabled the firm to survive longer than most. The early range included a model with an MMC engine hung from the downtube and for the early part of the twentieth century there was a range of singles in loop frames with sprung forks and belt final drive.

Little more was reported on the marque for some time but by 1914 there was a small range using Villiers, JAP and Abingdon engines of various sizes. This continued after World War I with

During the 1930s, Coventry Eagle produced a series of Silent Superb models using a range of Villiers engines fitted with large and stylish exhaust systems.

CONDOR
England (Coventry) 1907–14: This firm built a large 96x112mm (810cc) single.

CONDOR
Germany (Braunschweig) 1953–54: This German firm produced scooters and lightweights with 50cc two-stroke engines.

CONNAUGHT
England (Birmingham) 1910–27: Bordesley Engineering began with a 293cc two-stroke engine, which was later enlarged to 347cc. In 1925, the firm then switched to 350cc Blackburne side-valve and Bradshaw overhead-valve motors.

CONSUL
England (Norwich) 1916–22: The inevitable Villiers 269cc two-stroke powered this machine from Burton & Theobald Ltd. There may also have been a 247cc model.

COOPER
Mexico 1972–73: Made in Mexico but sold principally in America, these were 246cc two-stroke singles in both trials (enduro) and moto-cross form.

COPPI
Italy 1958: This firm was the builders of mopeds which were with 48cc two-stroke motors.

CORAH
England (Birmingham) 1905–14: This was a company which initially made machines with bought-in JAP motors. They went on later to manufacture machines using their own overhead-valve 498cc singles and 746cc twins.

CORONA
England (Maidenhead) 1901–04: Corona was the name of this assembler which used Minerva, Clement and possibly other engines.

many changes in the range that included singles, twins and sidecar outfits, although without two-strokes after 1925.

The best-known model from this postwar period was listed as the Flying Eight. It was developed from the 1923 V-twin with a 976cc JAP engine. In its various forms, this sporting twin would become one of the best remembered motorcycles and was available with side-valve or overhead-valve JAP engines. With the latter and a Jardine gearbox, it was the second most expensive machine on its market.

The 'four-stroke only' policy came to an end with the 1928 range when Villiers engines in 147, 172 and 172cc twin-port, super sports forms appeared in a set of pressed-steel cycle parts, the result of 12 months of intensive development by the firm. Frames and forks pressed from sheet steel were not uncommon in Europe at that time, but Coventry Eagle were the first major producers in Britain to adopt this practice and it was one that they turned into a great success over the next ten years.

Minor frame changes came for 1929 along with 196cc Villiers and 197cc JAP side-valve engines to give a five-model range of the

From the early 1920s, the top of the Coventry Eagle range was their Flying Eight. This 1928 modle had a 976cc overhead-valve JAP V-twin engine.

type. While the Flying Eights continued their stately progress, a similar name style was conferred upon models using 344 and 490cc

two-port overhead-valve JAP engines, which became the Flying 350 and Flying 500. Both had a new cradle frame and the tubular Webb girder forks that had been fitted to all the four-strokes by 1929.

Most of the range continued on for 1930 when new models were added using dry-sump Sturmey-Archer inclined engines of 348 and 495cc in conventional tubular frames. After 1931, the twins were dropped to leave only the two-strokes. These continued for some years, although they were often

very distinctive. The Silent Superb series had a massive and stylish exhaust system. The most basic of these two-strokes was the 98cc Marvel. Other names were Wonder and Eclipse, and most were in the pressed-steel frame.

Although JAP-powered four-strokes returned for a season or two, the next sensation from the firm was the Pullman series of 1936. This had a new type of pressed-steel frame, which offered considerable enclosure of the mechanics and the rear wheel, while the rear suspension was controlled by leaf springs running along the frame sides.

In 1937, the company saw a return to four-stroke singles using Matchless engines in three sizes. These, with a variety of two-strokes from an autocycle to the Pullman, carried on until the end of the decade.

A curtailed range was listed for 1940. However, few machines were built before production ceased, and it was not to start again after World War II.

A side-valve engine was used for some Coventry Eagle Flying Eight models. This is a 1925 example with a two-into-one exhaust system.

CRESCENT

SWEDEN 1937–74

Crescent were for many years associated with NV, before becoming part of the MCB (Monark Crescent Bolagen) group in 1960. This 50cc F50 GLX model is from 1964.

FOR MANY YEARS CRESCENT was associated with another Swedish marque, NV. During that time, NVs were often badged Crescent. Then in 1960, rivals Monark purchased NV and Crescent to form the MCB Monark Crescent Bolagen group. It would be true to compare the British AMC Associated Motor Cycles AJS and Matchless group as a similar operation because both groups produced different motorcycle brands in the same factory. In MCB's case this was based in the Swedish town of Varberg, on the west coast of the country.

The most famous, glamorous Crescent was the 500 of 1967, a three-cylinder two-stroke. The 60x58.8mm 498cc engine was Cresent's own design and manufacture and was intended for marine use in the company's outboard division, one of the first attempts to use a boat engine in a racing motorcycle, and an idea taken up by Konig of Berlin.

In racing tune, the Crescent outboard engine had a power output of 64bhp at 7500rpm. The pistons were slightly domed and there were three transfer ports per cylinder. The water pump was belt-driven from the crankshaft, outboard of the triple contact breaker assembly.

Swiss sidecar star Rudi Kurth and his English female passenger Dane were successful with the Cat-Crescent outfit, and their best finish was fourth in the 1973 Finnish Grand Prix.

The MCB group ceased their two-wheel and three-wheel involvement at the end of 1974.

CROCKER

USA 1934–41

THIS MAKE WAS BUILT in Los Angeles by Al Crocker who, after years of running Indian agencies, began to build speedway frames for Indian engines in 1931; this led to the introduction of a complete machine, late in 1933, built on British lines with a 500cc overhead-valve engine. It worked well until the JAP engine dominated, so Crocker tried the overhead-cam layout, but this was not suitable for speedway, and his machines were only built for two years.

Crocker then turned to road machines and early in 1936 launched a V-twin aimed at the top of the market in all aspects, effectively hand-built to specification. For this he used an overhead-valve, 45-degree engine with gear drive to the three-speed gearbox, a tubular frame, girder

The valve gear of the Crocker V-twin engine was exposed but was then concealed to appear as a camshaft drive. This improved its appearance.

CORONA
Germany (Brandenburg) 1902–24: Until 1907, Fahrradwerk & Metallindustrie produced unremarkable machines with Zedel and Fafnir singles and V-twins of 2 and two-and-a-half horsepower, but they were also known for a special tandem model. The later series (1922–24) had 346cc side-valve singles of uncertain provenance, as well as offering BMW 493cc flat twins.

CORONA-JUNIOR
England 1919–23: A long stroke of 100mm characterised this company's 450cc two-stroke single.

CORRE
France (Neuilly) 1901–10: This firm fitted Zuercher, Peugeot and Zedel proprietary motors to their machines. They were better known for automobiles.

CORYDON
England (Croydon) 1904–08: Bradbury Brothers built a two-and-a-half horsepower single and 3 and three-and-a-half horsepower V-twins.

COSMOS
Switzerland 1904–07: This firm constructed bicycle-type frames which were fitted with Zedel and Fafnir engines.

COTTEREAU
France (Dijon) 1903–09: Cottereau was actually better known for building automobiles, but they also constructed motorcycles with engines of their own make, as well as with those bought-in from Minerva and Peugeot.

COULSON
(London, later Birmingham) England 1919–24: Also known as Coulson-B, this firm initially made machines with 347 and 497cc Blackburne engines. They later 497cc overhead-valve JAP-powered twins, and last of all, an oil-cooled Bradshaw 346cc.

forks, wire wheels and drum brakes. The tanks were aluminium and cast in the firm's own foundry along with many other parts used on the machine.

Crocker's market lead was short-lived as the Harley-Davidson Knucklehead appeared that year and offered much the same but with four speeds, at a much lower price. Crocker still had some sales points; one was an option on engine capacity by boring and stroking to run from the original 61cid up to 84cid. Production

was minimal due to the high price and all lost money. It ended in 1941 after their final machine, the Scootabout; production of this was also limited.

CSA

USA 2000–

IT IS DEBATABLE whether CSA should be regarded as a separate brand from Confederate Motorcycles, but it was conceived as a 'second string' for Confederate, of equal quality, but with price in mind.

There were just the two models, with starting prices at $19,800. The intended production run for the 2000 model year was 500 machines. Both models came in the proverbial 'any colour you like, as long as it's [Rebel] black'.

The engine was from S & S, of similar specification to the Confederate machines but only of 100 cubic inches instead of 113. The 101.6-mm (4-ins) 'square' engine had an actual swept volume of 1647cc. Many other components were similar to those on the original machines: Paioli upside-down forks, five-speed Andrews gear-sets, and so on.

The weight of the PLC Wildcat dropped a useful 13.6kg (30lb) to

214kg (470lb), while retaining a 227kg (500lb) load-carrying capacity. This was still no lightweight by European standards, but not bad for a machine with such a big engine. The other model, the JPB Confederado, stayed the same weight as the earlier machines at 227kg (500lb) but the load-carrying capacity was upgraded to an impressive 318kg (700lb). To handle the braking, twin 220mm

(8.7ins) ductile-iron disks with four-piston callipers were fitted at the front. Instead of the 43cm (17ins) Marchinesi wheels and Pirelli tyres on the Confederates and Wildcats, the Confederado came with spoked wheels with stainless spokes and light-alloy rims, and Avon bias-belted tyres, 40cm (16ins) at the front and 38 (15ins) at the back. The fuel tank held a modest 15 litres (3.3 UK or 4.2 US gallons).

CURTISS

USA 1902–12

BASED IN HAMMONDSPORT, New York, this make was designed by Glen Curtiss, later famous as an aviation pioneer, who built machines with one, two, three and even eight-cylinder engines, the last an experimental aircraft unit. The company began with singles constructed in the primitive form with direct belt drive, braced forks and automatic inlet valve. These early machines were Indian's only real racing opposition. In 1904, the singles were joined by a 60-degree V-twin of 42cid. A racing version of this model was ridden by Curtiss to set a 16km (10 mile) record at over 107kph (67mph) on Ormond Beach, Florida. His machines that year

Right: A close-up of the amazing Curtiss V-8 unit. The bike had to be towed to 64kph (40mph) to even start the engine.

had twistgrip controls, a first ahead of Indian.

For 1905, Curtiss had a 21cid single set upright in a diamond frame and a 42cid V-twin that went into a loop frame, both engines with overhead-inlet and side-exhaust valves. In 1907, he ran a tuned version of the twin at 124kph (77mph) but more

Below: The famous Curtiss V-8 with direct shaft drive, which was claimed to run at 220kph (136mph) in 1907.

sensational was the V-8 that had the engine installed along the frame to drive the rear wheel by

shaft and exposed bevel gears. It had automatic inlet valves, twin carburettors, battery ignition and was towed up to 64kph (40mph) to start it. Over the mile it was claimed to be timed at 219kph (136mph) but this was never recognised as a record since the machine only ran in one direction. On another attempt, a universal joint broke and the engine power twisted the frame.

The F-head layout continued on the Curtiss and the V-twin was unusual in that the camshafts were located outboard of the cylinders so one was ahead of the front cylinder and the other behind the rear one. This engine, and much of the machine, also appeared as the Geer, a firm who applied their transfer to other makes with little else altered. In 1909, Curtiss built a triple with a massive capacity in excess of 100cid, the centre cylinder vertical and the others inclined to front and rear. A 144kph (90mph) top speed was claimed from this belt-driven monster with its rigid frame and braced forks.

From 1910, the road models were also sold as the Marvel from the same New York town, their advertisements making great play on the use of the Curtiss engine. In 1912, the Curtiss marque dropped from the motorcycle market as Glen turned his attention to the aviation field where he had already become world famous.

CUSHMAN

USA 1936–65

PRIOR TO 1937, this Lincoln, Nebraska-based firm's main sphere of activity was the production of the side-valve Husky engine for industrial applications. The notion of scooters as a more civilised means of two-wheeled transport was taking shape in the US at the time and so Cushman entered the field using the Husky engine. Its Auto-Glide models were in production until after World War II and during the war these machines were supplied to the military and used in action by paratroops. The postwar scooter boom in the US saw Cushman prosper, but like many other Western makers, it proved impossible for Cushman to compete with mass-produced, mass-market Japanese rivals such as the big-wheeled Honda 50 Cub. Instead, it turned its hand to producing golf buggies thereafter.

While Vespas from the early 1960s probably represent the most elegant and stylish classic scooters, Cushman's early offerings from the late 1930s were bizarrely comical, if not downright austere in appearance. Production of these proto-scooters started in 1937. The basic Auto-Glide frame was made of channel-section steel, while the engine was a simple industrial side-valve Husky power unit, and it lacked the benefits of either suspension or a gearbox. As became customary, the throttle was controlled by a twist-grip, while the clutch and back brake were foot operated. The engine was exposed in the side of the bodywork with protruding kick-

Cushman's Eagle of 1958 represented a variation on the American scooter craze of the mid-1950s, sporting motorcycle styling but running on tiny scooter wheels.

COVENTRY-B & D
England (Coventry) 1923–25: Barbary and Downs (B & D) catalogued JAP-engined machines in various capacities, from 350 to 1000cc, and also made the Coventry B & S with a Barr and Stroud 350cc motor.

COVENTRY-CHALLENGE
England (Coventry) 1903–11: Bicycle dealer Edward O'Brian assembled machines with Fafnir and Minerva engines.

COVENTRY-MASCOT
England (Coventry) 1922–24: This firm made 350cc singles with Barr & Stroud sleeve-valves and oil-cooled Bradshaws.

COVENTRY-MOTETTE
England (Coventry) 1899–1903: After starting with three-wheelers, this company introduced a Ladies' Model in 1901 with the engine fitted behind the pedals. A Miss De Veille became famous for riding one of these all the way from Coventry to London.

COVENTRY-STAR
England (Coventry) 1919–21: This was a firm of assemblers that used Coventry and Liberty engines in the machines.

COVENTRY-VICTOR
England (Coventry) 1919–36: A leading maker of flat-twin engines, which were also supplied to other manufacturers.

CPC
France 1931–37: This firm built lightweights with 100cc two-stroke motors.

CP-ROLEO
France (Paris) 1924–39: This company fitted JAP, Voisin, Chaise and MMC engines into pressed-steel frames, which incorporated the petrol tank.

start, and there was no front brake included.

Cushman's scooter production continued throughout World War II, and a quantity of machines were supplied to the US military, while the bulk of production entered the civilian market. The 30 series came out in 1942, followed by the 32 in 1945. This model had a sprung front fork and was fitted with Floating Drive, which consisted of an automatic clutch and transmission system. Although it was still an extremely rudimentary machine, its re-styled bodywork incorporated a luggage compartment, and front and rear lighting equipment was standard. The 32 Auto-Glide's 244cc engine was concealed behind a louvred panel, and capacity was subsequently upped to 246cc, which gave a commensurately higher performance. Then in 1946 the 50 series replaced the 30 range.

It used to be fashionable amongst the British mod fraternity of the early 1960s to strip down the popular Italian makes as a reaction against the chromium-plated baubles with which they were previously bedecked and, in fact, they then resembled nothing so much as the Cushman Highlander. Cushman had supplied a stripped-down version of its

Auto-Glide model to the US military during World War II for use by paratroopers following airborne invasions and, when peace returned, Cushman continued to produce these machines for sale to the public. They were based on the regular Auto-Glide but without the bodywork, and the seat and fuel tank were mounted on a simple tubular structure. From 1949, it was known as the Highlander, and subsequently it was fitted with a rather unusual leading-link front-fork layout.

Among the crazes that swept the US during the 1950s was that of small-wheeled motorcycles. These machines combined the small wheels and power units of scooters with chopper-esque styling cues. The main proponents of this fad were the Mustang and the Powell A-V-8, while Cushman's somewhat homemade affair was called the Eagle. This was first released in 1949 and, astonishingly perhaps, did well enough for production of this utterly basic contraption to continue right up to 1965.

The Cushman Eagle was powered by a 319cc 8hp single with two-speed transmission, and this utterly basic machine remained in production from 1949 to 1965.

CWS

THE CWS M III IS one of the great might-have-beens of history that was destroyed by the Nazi invasion of Eastern Europe.

The impetus for the design came from the army, who offered a prize of 4200 zloty for a practical, on- and off-road machine, also suitable

for use in a sidecar outfit. The M III designation was apparently a slight exaggeration – the original was a fairly indifferent prototype,

as was the second version – but it would have been an ideal machine for a rapidly industrialising, recently independent country.

The 45-degree V-twin had a total swept volume of 995.4 cc with a compression ratio of only 5:1, so it would very nearly run on cough syrup. The engine, the heavy steel tubular frame, and most of the cycle parts were home-grown Polish, though a few components such as the Bosch electrics were bought in to begin with, and later, the motorcycle was apparently all-Polish. The engine delivered something between 20 and 22bhp at 4000 rpm, but the flat power-curve meant that 18bhp was available, even at 3000rpm.

This 1929 M55 seems to have been one of the prototypes that preceded the M III mentioned above, but the big V-twin seems to have been similar.

Starting was designed with the cruel Polish winters in mind; apparently, it was comparatively easy, even at –39°C (–39°F). How anyone rides a motorbike at that temperature is another matter.

From the limited information available, the controls appear to have been Indian-style, with the throttle on the left and a manual ignition advance/retard on the right. Mechanical drum brakes were provided to all wheels, including the sidecar wheel on the outfits. There was also a parking brake. The factory finish was black with gold and cream, or khaki with gold trim lines, though the army who bought most of the

bikes apparently repainted many in camouflage colours.

Primary drive was geared and immensely strong, with a multiple-plate clutch, five steel plates, six copper/asbestos, operated by a footpedal on the left, and a right-hand three-speed gear change. Final drive was by chain. The solo machine weighed a fairly spectacular 270kg (594lb), while the outfit was 375 kg (825lb), that is, about 10 per cent lighter than the fabled BMW R75 outfit, but also with about 10 per cent less power. The comparison is particularly useful because, from 1938 onwards, there were experiments with a powered side-

car wheel, though the prototypes never made it through to production. Top speed was about 100kph (56mph), a little higher than the BMW outfit.

The Polish Army reckoned that it was actually superior to the American machines that they had been using until the CWS entered service, and from independent reports, their opinion does not appear to have been entirely due to patriotism. Approximately 3400 machines were built between 1933 and 1939, but inevitably when the Germans and Russians destroyed most of Polish industry during World War II, the CWS M III was a casualty.

CYCLEMASTER ENGLAND 1950–60

THIS CYCLE ATTACHMENT was sold as a complete rear wheel to be exchanged for the normal bicycle one. It was manufactured by EMI at Hayes in Middlesex to a Dutch design and comprised a large hub, the whole assembly was fitted within this.

The engine was a 25cc disc-valve two-stroke, and drove a countershaft carrying a clutch by chain with a further chain drive to the hub. The petrol tank went above and behind the engine and it amounted to a neat and successful package.

For 1952, the capacity was increased to 32cc and, in the next

year, the firm offered a complete machine called the Roundsman. This was intended to be used as a delivery bicycle and featured a large carrier hung over a small front wheel.

In 1955, the company moved to Chertsey in Surrey. At their new location, they went one step further; the Cyclemate was created in the image of the moped by mounting the engine ahead of the bottom bracket of a Norman bicycle. Despite becoming dated, the engine unit was popular and sold up to 1958. The Cyclemate was also popular, and was bought until two years later, up to 1960.

Before then, in 1956, the firm introduced the Piatti scooter. This had a 124cc two-stroke engine and three speeds, built as a unit with the rear wheel, with the whole assembly pivoted to provide the rear suspension. The frame was in pressed-steel and of inverted-bath form to conceal the works. For maintenance, the machine was laid on its side. However, it didn't sell well and was only listed to 1958.

The Cyclemaster wheel that replaced an existing bicycle one to provide drive from a 25cc, later 32cc, two-stroke engine via a clutch and two chains.

CYCLONE

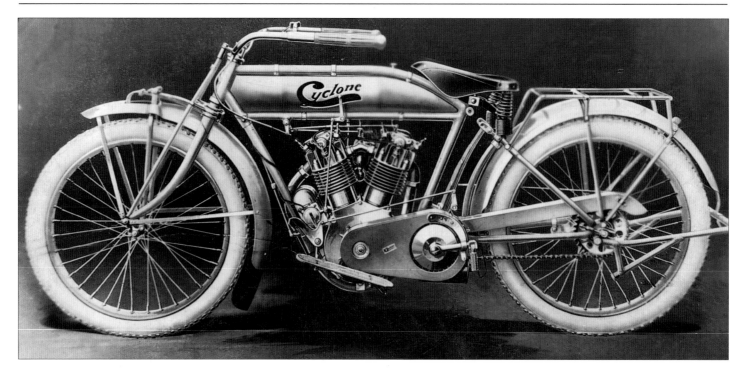

ALWAYS FINISHED IN yellow, the Cyclone was only built for three years but was one of the most advanced machines of its time. Its engine construction used techniques not common for many years, while the road models had pivoted-fork rear suspension controlled by a monoshock leaf spring. A 61cid V-twin engine with overhead camshafts driven by shaft and bevels that also drove the magneto provided the power – this was in an era of F-head motors – and was built to high standards. Ball and roller bearings, forged flywheels, spigoted heads and barrels were only a few of the advanced technology features of this machine.

A loop frame with trailing-link forks housed the engine, which

A 1914 Cyclone. This machine was powered by a 996cc motor. The firm was initially successful on the race track, but lost out as bigger marques entered the market.

Drive side of the advanced Cyclone with its large V-twin, overhead-camshaft engine, all-chain drive, loop frame and suspension front and rear.

drove a countershaft and thence the rear wheel by chain, so it was a single-speed machine. For board or dirt track racing there was no suspension and the drive was direct to the rear wheel. The track racers were extremely fast motorcycles, able to run 177kph (110mph) laps of the steeply banked board circuits in 1914 and, even on the dirt track ovals, around 144kph (90mph).

Such a complex design tended to suffer minor problems which limited its success, but these bikes were able perform on a par with the best on occasion.

Production ceased after 1915 and the assets were moved around more than once but no further machines were built, despite postwar attempts.

CZ

THIS FIRM WAS FOUNDED in 1922 at Strakonice in Bohemia after World War I to produce armaments and took the initials of its name, Cesk-Zbrojovka, which meant

Czech arms. However, it was not until 1932 that the company began to produce motorcycles and after 1945 it and the Jawa firm were nationalised and linked together,

although both marques continued with their own badges.

The first CZ was little more than a clip-on because it was based on a heavy-duty bicycle

with a metric 60cc two-stroke engine fitted to the front forks, with direct drive to the wheel, much as some postwar cyclemotors. It was soon

superseded by a larger 76cc model with the engine installed in a modified bicycle frame with chain drive, pedalling gear for starting and a light leading-link front fork. To help on the hills, the capacity was then increased to metric 98cc and later came three speeds.

In 1934, CZ moved on to a 175cc model using a single-cylinder, two-stroke engine driving a three-speed gearbox, with a pressed-steel frame and girder forks. In this they founded the bedrock of their road machines, since such simple models would continue to sell well and be their main product for many years to come.

The one model was soon expanded into a range, first with a 250cc single and then a 175cc twin with four speeds and footchange. These were followed by a 350 single and sidecars were then added to go with this larger model, taking the firm on to the end of the 1940s.

The factory was badly damaged during World War II but repairs were made and, in 1946, CZ production took up where it had

Part of the CZ range for the 1970s was this 250cc two-stroke twin, which was much the same as the 175cc single, with unit construction and modern suspension.

The early CZ had a small engine housed in a modified bicycle frame with light forks and simple transmission. This kind of machine offered cheap, basic transport.

left off with the prewar 175 and 250cc models, as well as a new 125 of modern design. The new machine had equal bore and stroke, aluminium cylinder head, unit construction of gearbox and flywheel magneto. Twin exhaust pipes were used and the gearchange pedal and kick-start went on concentric shafts on the left.

The firm began to make their mark in competition soon after, and a team on 125s took the runner-up Vase in the 1947 ISDT, with the Trophy going to a Czech team riding Jawas. CZ took the Vase again in 1949 and several times during the 1950s, which led to their serious entry into motocross, where they won several World Championships in both 250 and 500cc classes during the 1960s.

CZ was not unknown in road racing either, with a series of single-cylinder four-strokes with one or two camshafts first seen in the late-1930s and run in the 1950s and 1960s, although these failed to achieve the same level of success, most being on the lines of Italian machines of that time. They did run a 125cc twin and a 350cc single but their most complex motor was a metric 350cc V-four with twin-overhead camshafts and 16 valves. Despite the effort put into this, it was never really on the pace for a factory machine and

CSEPEL
Hungary (Csepel) 1932–51: Own-make 98, 123 and 146cc two-strokes gave power to these machines which came from the Manfred Weiss steelworks. In 1951, the name Csepel was dropped from the models and the same bikes were branded Pannonia and Danuvia.

CUB
USA 1950s: A small two-speed automatic scooter that was hard-pressed to reach a speed of 40kph (25mph).

CUDELL
Germany 1898–1905: These pioneering machines were powered by De Dion Bouton engines of 402 and 510cc.

CURWY (CURSY)
Germany (Frankfurt a. d. Oder) 1923–31: This was a series of unremarkable 350 and 498cc side-valve and overhead-valve singles, as well as a (rare) 348cc overhead-cam. The name was changed to Cursy in 1927.

CYC-AUTO
England (London) 1934–56: An autocycle that had a Scott 98cc two-stroke engine. The 1956 Bantamoto was a 38cc two-stroke cycle motor.

CYCLE-SCOOT
USA (New Jersey) 1953–55: This was a scooter which had a two-and-a-half horsepower four-stroke engine.

CYCLE-STAR
Netherlands (Rotterdam) 1952: This moped was fitted with a 38cc two-stroke engine mounted under the pedals and friction drive to the rear wheel.

Over the years, CZ listed a range of motocross models, from 125 to 400cc. The company drew on its extensive experience in this field, where it had won world titles.

was retired in 1972.

In the meantime, the firm continued to build its range of simple road models, all two-strokes of 175 or 250cc, a 350cc twin, and later a 125. They kept to the form of the early postwar machines with unit construction, telescopic forks and, in time, pivoted-fork rear suspension. One quirk was the adoption of a single pedal for both starting and gear changing. For the former, it was swung up to the usual operating position; for the latter, it reverted to the normal horizontal. In addition, operation of the gear lever also lifted the clutch, so the hand lever was not needed when changing gear. All this took some getting used to by riders not

familiar with it, while the combined use made the pedal rather heavy for gear change, although satisfactory for kick-start.

A scooter was first built in 1946 and the early versions were joined

by the Cezeta in 1958, which used the 175cc engine. During the 1970s, motocross and enduro versions of the road machines were added to the range and these benefited greatly from the firm's

experience of such events and the ISDT. From this came trail models and there were also mopeds.

The basic line of 125, 175 and 250cc singles ran on and on as the years went by, with their lines becoming seen as more traditional because they did not really change. With them ran the 350cc twin but eventually much of the range adopted the Jawa badge and were no longer built in the CZ form, although the firm kept its Jawa-CZ title.

CZ machines were never noted as scintillating road models, but they were invariably ordinary, basic, worthy, useful. Although they were hardly exciting, however, in competition the reverse was true, and they enjoyed

Cagiva took over CZ in 1993 and one outcome was this model. It was effectively a Cagiva machine taken from the company's extensive range, with CZ badges.

considerable off-road success and innovative designs for the racetrack. During 1993, the Italian Cagiva group bought a controlling interest in CZ and continued to produce the 125 and a larger 180cc single for a number of years, but production finally stopped altogether.

During the 1930s, CZ turned to pressed-steel frames and forks in common with other European firms, this a 350cc model from 1939.

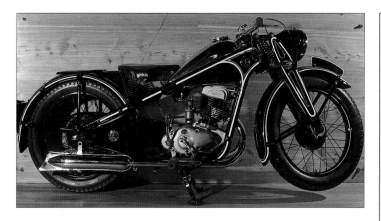

CZ175 1976

This basic model had a very long production life since its origins dated back to prewar days. Its modern form appeared initially in 1946 as a 125 and this soon changed, first to a 150, and then to 175 and larger. As a 175, it was also available in trail and enduro forms.

The 175 single had a simple two-stroke engine built in unit

For many years, the basic CZ model was this 175 (a 1980s model is pictured), also offered with a 125cc engine. It was good at providing low-cost transport.

with its four-speed gearbox with its multi-task gear lever. It kept the same bore and stroke throughout its life and had a cast-iron cylinder with light-alloy head. In due course, it went over to a pump lubrication system. The carburettor sat behind the barrel with an air cleaner to feed it and the exhaust ran down to a long silencer on the left.

The engine unit went into a tubular frame with telescopic front and pivoted-rear forks for suspension, with wire wheels, drum brakes in full-width hubs and alloy wheel rims in some

years. One of its assets was the fitment of a full case for the final-drive chain so that this was protected from the weather.

By the 1970s, the CZ175 was fitted with turn signals as well as the full electric equipment. It served as a basic machine for domestic use.

Engine: 172cc two-stroke, vertical single, 58x65mm, air-cooled
Power: 15bhp at 5600rpm
Gearbox: unit 4-speed foot change
Final drive: enclosed chain
Weight: 112kg (247lb)
Top speed: 115kph (70mph)

DAELIM

JAPAN WAS FAR FROM being the only country in Asia to produce motorcycles in the postwar era, although they usually were the prime mover and supplied the technology. Sub-assembly work for Japan went on all over Southeast Asia and the offshoot was often a home market make based on Japanese machines.

One such company was Daelim, which produced their own machines, all lightweights and most with single-cylinder, two-stroke engines built in unit with their gearbox. They were sold locally, and served a domestic need, but were unknown elsewhere.

In the late 1970s, the firm established a more formal link with Honda and that gave them a range of small machines to build.

The scooterettes appeared along with models using the same overhead-camshaft engines as a motorcycle. Most featured a spine frame, simple suspension front and

A Daelim Liberty moped, typical of the products of this South Korean firm and based on an older Honda, in this case with two-speed automatic transmission.

rear, drum brakes and wire wheels with a period style they kept for a decade or two. There was no point in constant updates in that market, because all that was required was a cheap, reliable method of transport.

Two-stroke singles were built as well, all essentially in the original Honda image, so some had a five-speed gearbox and others a disc front brake.

Nowadays, these serve as something of a reminder of how far design has moved on. Old, basic transport it may be, but it is also well tried and just what is needed for that market.

The VS125 Daelim lightweight motorcycle showing its clear origins from the Honda CB125 single, a most suitable choice for its home market.

DALIFOL

THE EARLIEST EXAMPLES OF self-propelled transport were steam powered using the technology of external combustion. It was not until the mid-1880s that an internal combustion engine appeared but steam continued to rival it beyond the turn of the century. There were steam motorcycles from Michaux-Perraux, Parkyns-Bateman and Copeland in France, Britain and the US, all built on the lines of contemporary bicycles. The Dalifol came later and was based on the safety bicycle.

The engine was a double-acting, single cylinder with a slide valve and connected directly to a crank formed with the rear hub, since there was no need for clutch, gears or reduction ratio with steam

power. Its great advantage was maximum torque at zero rpm but, while basically simple, it requires many ancillaries, is slow to start and needs a good supply of fresh water.

The flash-boiler was a round, steel drum located with a coke furnace beneath it, fed by hopper from a tank mounted within the frame. The boiler water was carried in a 22-litre (5 UK, 6 US gallons) tank formed as a rear mudguard and its supply by a feed pump controlled the power output,

Steam power was high-technology during the 19th century and was used by both cars and motorcycles in the earliest days, although the Dalifol came a little later.

which was varied by the adjustment of a valve.

It is believed that a Dalifol took part in the 1896 London to

Brighton Emancipation Run; a French steam bicycle was listed among the starters, and one was timed at 40kph (25mph) in 1895.

DARDO

THIS TURIN MAKE debuted at a time when unit construction was gaining ground in Italy, long before it became at all common in other countries. One reason for this was that Italian manufacturers had to operate in a relatively small market and therefore had to use innovation to tempt buyers to purchase their machines. Dardo chose to do this and attracted attention by offering machines powered by small two-stroke engines that had the cylinder in a horizontal position. Capacities of 125 and 175cc were built to suit two of the main classes of the Italian market and both of them had two speeds.

The remainder of the well-built machines was much as others of the period, with a simple rigid frame, girder forks and the lines of the decade. Once established in this small way, Dardo continued for a few years and extended the range to add a four-stroke model. This had a 175cc engine with overhead-valves but it was, as with the two-strokes, located with a horizontal cylinder. In this it followed the route taken earlier by the much better known firm Moto Guzzi and also later by Aermacchi.

As with so many small firms in all countries, Dardo found that building and selling motorcycles were fraught with problems, both technical and commercial. Sensibly, they left the market at the right time, just before the Depression.

DAX

IN 1932 PIERRE DE FONT-RÉAULX and Robert Dahan formed Dax and showed their first model at the Paris Show that year. It had a compact, unit-construction 350cc engine with overhead-valves closed by hairpin springs, rear-mounted magneto, oil carried in the sump, gear primary drive, and cross-over gearbox. This well-styled and well-built unit was in a conventional rigid frame with girder forks, drum brakes and a saddle tank.

The 350 was joined by a 500 in 1935 (the Rafale) and by the Baby, a velomoteur with a unique specification. Nothing on the Baby was skimped, starting with the 100cc twin-port, four-stroke, all-alloy, unit-construction engine with overhead-valves closed by hairpin springs and ignition by flywheel magneto. It had gear

primary drive and the gearbox had a choice of two or three speeds, the unit fitted into a rigid frame with girder forks. Ingeniously, the footrests could be locked to become the pedalling gear. On the road, it was much faster than the average velomoteur.

Above: A typical Dax, the 350cc single for 1934 with its ohv engine, and unit construction.

Below: The Dax Baby model was a velomoteur with a 100cc four-stroke engine and quality build, better than others its class.

DAK
Germany (Pinneberg) 1923–25: These were lightweight deflector-piston two-stroke engines of 117 and 147cc capacity and they were bought in from Ilo. The new enterprise was started in 1923 by an association of several German car dealers.

DALESMAN
England 1969–74: These were lightweight, successful competition machines, several of which were fitted with 98 and 123cc engines from Puch. Other machines were fitted with 123cc engines from Sachs.

DALL'OGLIO
Italy c.1926: Guido Dall'Oglio, founder of GD (reference below), bestowed his name upon a horizontal single 125cc engine with a bronze cylinder head. This Italian engine was equipped with a two-speed transmission.

DALTON
England (Manchester) 1920–22: This company was a small assembler of machines with 348 and 498cc singles from Blackburne and the 688cc flat twin from Coventry Victor. Some machines were fitted with solid (disk) wheels.

DANE
England 1919–20: This was an English firm of assemblers who had on offer two-stroke and four-strokes in a variety of capacities – 350 to 1000cc – with engines bought in from Precision, JAP and others. These included overhead-valve engines. However, which of the motors were eventually built and sold has been much open to conjecture.

DAYTON

USA 1911–17

A SHORT-LIVED MARQUE in the American style, Dayton was an assembler whose engine and other parts were shared by several firms with almost identical products.

The Davis Sewing Machine Co. of Dayton, Ohio, marketed the machine that started out with a conventional F-head V-twin engine, single speed and sturdy frame and forks. This changed in 1913 when they turned to the Spacke De Luxe V-twin built in Indianapolis, Indiana, which went into a loop frame with trailing-link forks but kept the single speed.

For 1914, they used a rocking fork and two-speed gearbox. The fork was revised for 1915 when electric start became an option. In this unusual Spacke engine, the overhead inlet and side-exhaust valves were lifted by face cams machined on a skew-gear-driven shaft that ran along the engine with the follower a small rocker. Skew gears also drove the magneto set across the engine.

In addition to its odd valve gear, the Spacke had a master connecting rod for the rear cylinder with the front rod the slave. Late engines were built in unit with a two-speed gearbox but none of this offered any real advantage over convention.

The Dayton had several major changes in its short life with three forms of front suspension and two engines.

DE DION-BOUTON

FRANCE 1895–1910, 1926–30 AND 1955–66

ONE OF THE CORNERSTONES of the motor industry, De Dion-Bouton, was founded in 1895 by Count Albert de Dion and Georges Bouton. Prior to making motor vehicles, the company built steam engines and launches, and created their first petrol engine in 1889. This was followed by trials with Michelin tyres in 1892. By 1894 the De Dion axle that separated driving components from suspension – and which is still employed today – was in use, and

the following year, the company's first tricycle was on sale. Although inherently more difficult to control than a regular two-wheeler, the tricycle layout had obvious advantages for mounting an engine and a transmission system, because there was a platform between the rear wheels. It also negated the risk of side-slipping to which early motorcycles were prone. The 1895 DeDion-Bouton used the company's own 211cc atmospheric/automatic inlet valve

Left: Motoring pioneers Albert De Dion and Georges Bouton (on the right).

Right: The De Dion-Bouton tricycle of 1893. This early pioneering machine had its engine mounted low between the back wheels. The company was a major innovator.

engine, an early system where the inlet valve was kept closed by a weak spring and opened by atmospheric pressure as the falling piston created a vacuum in the cylinder barrel. The engine was mounted vertically behind the rear axle, and the trike had braced front forks. The machine had conventional bicycle pedals and chain, and the fuel tanks were mounted within the triangulations of the tubular frame. It was perceived as

The De Dion-Bouton tricycle was well-equipped and robust. The low engine position gave the machine a low centre of gravity, and the fuel tank was behind the rider.

a high-quality vehicle and was widely copied, with and without authorisation.

At the same time, Count De Dion founded the Automobile Club de France and, shortly afterwards, the Baron Van Zuylen invested some FF400,000 to sustain the company. After a fire in 1899, frames were sourced from Clément, but in 1901 tricycles were phased out as De Dion-Bouton went over to producing four-wheeled vehicles.

It was at this stage that it was also beginning to phase out steam-powered vehicles, and had experimented with electric power. Some 15,000 three-wheelers had

been made, and De-Dion-Bouton continued to supply engines to a large number of fledgling motor manufacturers. In 1909 it started making bicycles, but this phase lasted for only five years.

The second incarnation of De Dion-Bouton from 1926 to 1930 had no actual connection with the original company, but was involved in the production of motorcycles with engines of 173cc and over. Following a brief revival of the car concern after World War II, the firm of A. Chichery used the De Dion-Bouton name to identify a range of scooters, mopeds and bicycles between 1955 and 1966.

DANUBIUS
Germany (Ratibor) 1923–24: Ganz were the German firm who were responsible for making this conventional 198cc side-valve machine.

DANUVIA
Hungary 1955–63: This model was a two-stroke 123cc lightweight and was manufactured by the Hungarian firm Csepel (reference above).

DARLAN
Spain (Zarauz) 1958–60: These lightweights were manufactured with in-house 94cc two-stroke engines.

DARLING
Switzerland (Bern) 1924–26: This company built small numbers of machines powered by an in-house 250cc two-stroke three-port single engine.

DART
England (Coventry) 1923–24: This was a rare overhead-cam machine of 74x81mm (348cc). It was designed by A.A. Sidney and delivered a very creditable seventeen-and-a-half bhp. It deserved to do better, but few machines were actually manufactured.

DART
England (Kingston) 1901–06: Built by Frank Baker (not the same Baker as Precision engines and motorcycles), these two-and-a-half horsepower machines were fitted with Minerva and MMC engines. It seemed that they were largely unremarkable. However, on closer inspection, the Roubeau carburetter inside the engine was a fairly advanced design compared to other carburettors being produced at that time.

DEI

ITALY 1906–14 AND 1934–66

MANY OF THOSE WHO founded motorcycle firms, especially in the early days, had their roots in making and selling bicycles. Umberto Dei was no exception. He entered the powered market with a machine powered by a four-stroke, single-cylinder engine mounted in a heavy-duty cycle frame with belt drive to the rear wheel. As was common, production ceased at the outbreak of World War I.

The name Dei did not return until the 1930s when it appeared on lightweights fitted with 75 and

100cc Sachs engines for the velomoteur class. As the decade progressed and as the tax on larger models was removed, these were augmented by larger models fitted with 250cc Villiers two-stroke and 500cc JAP four-stroke engines. However, this advantage was counter-balanced by the steep rise in import tariffs. All were in the style and form of the period, but the larger four-strokes had a separate gearbox and rear suspension, as was then common for Italian machines.

Just before World War II, the firm added a motorcycle using the 100cc Sachs engine and a smaller 60cc velomoteur. After the war, a link with Garelli was established and their fine 38cc Mosquito engine unit was used as an attachment for bicycles and later to power a moped.

The Sachs connection remained to power motorcycles up to 150cc, all using two-stroke engines, all with the lines and specifications which were common to other motocycles of the era.

DELLA FERRERA

THIS FIRM WAS FOUNDED in 1909 in Turin by Federico Della Ferrera and his brothers who used quality materials to build fine machines. In the early years, it soon became one of the best organised Italian firms, producing machines with single-cylinder 350 or 500cc engines with side- or overhead-valves.

Not all Della Ferrera models had unit construction, as demonstrated on this earlier machine, which featured a side-valve engine and flat tank.

In common with most Italian firms, Della Ferrera soon became involved in competitions. This led to a 500cc V-twin, overhead-valve engine and a four-valve overhead valve single in 1914. These had their successes in Italian events, while the road models benefited from the lessons learnt there. By 1914, the typical single had the engine with magneto ignition driving a countershaft carrying a variable-ratio pulley for the belt drive to the rear wheel, installed in a diamond frame with girder forks.

Italian firms were quick to use unit construction of engine and gearbox – this Della Ferrera ohv single of the 1930s was based on a decade of experience.

After World War I, the company listed singles and 45-degree V-twins, the singles of 498cc with overhead-valves, or 636cc with side-valves. The larger ones had a four-speed gearbox and both had all-chain drive. The V-twins eventually included 494, 598, 746 and 1004cc engines, the smallest

with overhead-valves, the others with side-valves. The largest twin had a four-speed gearbox built in unit with the engine; some models had rear suspension, while all had girder forks.

In 1921, Federico took the 494cc V-twin as the basis of a machine for records, hill climbs and racing. For this purpose, an overhead-camshaft and rockers were fitted to the top of each cylinder head, the valves well splayed out to give a hemispherical combustion chamber in the cylinder head. The camshafts were driven by chain directly from the right end of the crankshaft, a third sprocket at that location driving the magneto fitted on the front of the crankcase. The required reduction ratio was done simply by the sprocket sizes in one step, and none of the chains was enclosed. The primary drive chain was also open and ran from the left crankshaft end round a jockey sprocket to a three-speed gearbox. The engine and gearbox went into a rigid frame fitted with leading-link forks and the complete machine set records at 140kph (87mph) and was successful in many 1920s Italian events.

The range of singles and twins ran on through the decade with improvements each year. Unit construction was used for many models, as were both side- and

Detail of a flat-tank Della Ferrera showing the fine script of the tank transfer and the front forks that allowed rocking and upwards movement.

overhead-valves, depending on the model type and its intended purpose. The gearbox had three or four speeds and was of the cross-over type to put the final-drive chain on the right side of the machine. Girder forks continued at the front and pivoted-fork rear suspension was used on several models, not a common feature at that time. Drum brakes went on both wheels and increased in size over the years, while a saddle tank was added near the end of the decade. The lines of machine and engine unit remained Italian and gave their origins away at a glance.

At the start of the 1930s, which was a difficult decade for industry in many countries, Italy's problems were reflected in its motorcycles and their tax structure. Early on, the 175cc class was popular but as the tax was removed from larger capacities, so the 250cc models replaced and took over, noticeably around 1934. At the same time, import duties

A Della Ferrera from the 1920s featuring a separate gearbox, all-chain drive and the special front forks with rocking action. There is no rear suspension.

By the late 1930s, the Della Ferrera had pivoted-fork rear suspension as seen on this 1935 Turismo with its 499cc side-valve, unit construction engine.

increased so that sales of other European makes suffered. This was even more obvious in 1935 when, to protect the Italian industry, the tariff rates leapt upwards to such a degree that firms that used imported engines and other components from Britain for their Italian motorcycles turned

to home producers or began to make these items themselves.

This continued through the decade and it was reflected in the number of major foreign makes at the annual Milan Show until there were just two British and two German in 1939. By then, Della Ferrera had been reduced to the status of a minor manufacturer with only three models. The smallest of these had a 174cc, overhead-valve engine built in unit with a three-speed gearbox and mounted vertically in a rigid frame. The other overhead-valve model was of 348cc with the engine inclined in the frame and driving a four-speed gearbox in unit with it, the machine having front and rear suspension, the latter by pivoted-fork. These two were listed as SSL models. The third and largest model, listed as the Turismo, was similar but had a 499cc side-valve engine.

The firm had to turn to war work during WWII, but could not return to the motorcycle business afterwards and went bankrupt.

DELLA FERRERA RECORD MODEL   1921

The record-breaking V-twin was based on a road model so its engine had the cylinders set at a 45-degree angle. It was of conventional construction but did have the bore and stroke equal at 68mm, which was rather unusual in an era when longer strokes were more common. The dimensions gave a 94cc capacity and the crankcase was split vertically with a main bearing in each half.

The cylinders were offset to suit the big ends side by side on the crankpin and mounted to the crankcase on four studs. Four

further studs were used to locate the cylinder heads and fitted with long holding down nuts that extended up to carry the rocker spindle plates and camshaft bearings. The inclined valves had coil springs while each head had stubs for both inlet and exhaust ports. All four of the chains were exposed, but this was not a concern with a machine built for record attempts. The machine rode on 6x66-cm (2.5x26-ins) tyres. It was ridden by Della Ferrera himself in the record attempt that set a claimed world speed figure

close to 145kph (90mph), a first for an Italian make. However, an Indian had run at over 165kph (103mph) in 1920 at Daytona and this had been recognised, and accepted, as the record. For all that, the Della Ferrera was fast.

Engine: 494cc ohv V-twin, 68x68mm, air-cooled
Power: 20bhp at 5300rpm
Gearbox: 3-speed hand change
Final drive: chain
Weight: n/a
Top speed: 140kph (85mph)

DELTA-GNOM

THIS FIRM STARTED UP after World War I to meet the demand for transport, beginning with a clip-on two-stroke for a bicycle. It soon enlarged the engine for a light-weight of simple specification, light frame and belt drive. By 1925 they were using their own 250cc two-stroke engine.

The next year brought their first four-stroke models using JAP side- and overhead-valve single and V-twin engines. The cycle parts were conventional with hand change for the gearbox, a diamond frame, girder forks,

Right: The 1929 Delta-Gnom with the Hans Pitzek-designed 498cc overhead-valve engine used briefly in place of the usual JAP.

Left: Delta-Gnom began with two-stroke engines and had their own 250cc unit by 1925. This is a 1929 model.

chain drive and wire wheels with drum brakes. They built their own 500cc overhead-valve engine for 1927 but production stopped after 1928.

It recommenced in 1932 with the line much as before, using JAP engines, but the machines now sported saddle tanks, larger brakes and improved electrics; footchange followed. In 1938 production of components and assemblies was rationalised, having fallen under German control and was used to support the German industry.

The Delta-Gnom make returned after the war but it was only to produce a range of small two-strokes using bought-in engines from Ilo, Puch or Rotax.

DEMM

ALTHOUGH USUALLY ASSOCIATED with mopeds during its final years, the Milan-based Demm concern, which was owned by Daldi and Matteucci, actually manufactured a wide range of lightweight motor-cycles over almost three decades.

For example, in the mid-1950s, they offered a superbly crafted 175, the TL Turismo Lusso and the TL Turismo Lusso which featured an overhead-camshaft driven by shaft and bevels, which ran up the offside of the cylinder and was almost out of sight within the engine's finning.

Power output from the 60x61mm bore and stroke engine was 10.5bhp for the TV and 9bhp for the TL, at 7000rpm. Primary drive was by helical gear. The gearbox was a four-speeder, with a heel-and-toe gear lever on the offside of the unit-construction powerplant.

Also offered during the same period were a pair of 125s: the two-stroke Normale Lusso and overhead camshaft Turismo. Both shared essentially the same rolling chassis to keep costs down. Demm offered a range of Motocarris three-wheeled trucks but, strangely, these were powered by a totally different engine, a 175 two-stroke with fan cooling.

In 1956 at the Monza Autodrome, with Fausto Pasini and Franco Mauri, Demm broke

24 world records in the 50, 75 and 100cc classes, powered by a 49cc two-stroke motor. Demm also supplied engines to rival marques, notably Testi, with whom they maintained a close association for many years.

During the 1970s, imports of Demm machines were handled by the Suzuki importers, the Heron Corporation. Only one model, the Dove, was marketed. Previously, in the late 1950s, Demm products had been imported by the London-based Nannucci organization, at that time they listed a 49cc two-racer for £125.

Demm finally hit the financial rocks in the early 1980s recession.

Demm built a wide range of mopeds (like this 1960's machine) and lightweight motorcycles from 1953 until 1982, breaking 24 world records in the mid-1950s.

DERBI

SPAIN 1949–

As with many other motorcycle firms, Derbi had its roots in the bicycle trade from back in 1922 and continued in a modest way for many years. Founded by Simeón Rabasa Singla at Mollet near Barcelona, it became a company during 1944, being renamed Nacional Motor, S.A. late in 1950.

The firm entered the powered transport market in 1949 using the initials of the of the founder, SRS, for a 49cc two-stroke model having two speeds and a basic specification. In 1950 they launched their first true motorcycle using the Derbi name that came from DERivados de BIcicletus, Spanish for 'derivative of bicycle'. The machine had a 250cc single-cylinder, twin-port, two-stroke engine of Jawa design built in unit with a four-speed gearbox. This went into a cradle frame which had telescopic forks and plunger rear suspension in a

The Derbi Senda series was built for enduro racing to a high standard using the best of technology in all areas – a feature of this company.

style that was advanced for its time.

The 250 was soon followed by other models, all two-strokes with unit construction and ranging from 90 to 100 and, later, 125cc, this last with pivoted-fork rear suspension. A scooter was added in 1953 with a 98cc engine, three speeds and plunger rear suspension, being joined by a

Derbi listed race-replica models during the 1990s using their extensive experience, the result being machines with top class specifications.

125cc version in 1955, both continuing to 1957. For that year their largest model was added, a 350cc twin with four speeds and the specification and style that had

DAX
France (Clichy) 1932–39: This firm built well-made machines of original design with 100 and 175cc two-stroke engines. They also produced overhead-valve four-strokes which were available in a variety of capacities: 125, 175, 250, 350 and 500cc. They were early users of foot-change gearboxes.

DAY-LEEDS
England (Leeds) 1912–14: Job Day and Sons made an inlet-over-exhaust 500cc single engine. Some sources suggest that the Leeds company might have continued producing this model until as late as 1917.

DAYTON
England (London) 1913–20: Charles Day used the Dayton name for auxiliary cycle motors of 162cc. He then went on to do the same for a 269cc Villiers-powered lightweight.

DAYTON
England (London) 1954–60: This was a scooter, initially powered by 198cc Villiers engines – which were later to become 175 and 259cc engines.

DECA
Italy 1954–57: This firm initially produced a 48cc four-stroke moped. From these rather ordinary beginnings, they went on to produce a 100cc lightweight that could top 90kph (55mph). They were also responsible for manufacturing 48cc cycle motors. However, the firm was to disappear, despite their announcement of new 100 and 125cc machines in 1958. Their name is also occasionally found with a variant spelling, under the reference DE-CA.

A lightweight Derbi from the 1970s, the 50cc Antorcha Tricampeona. The machine was available with three or four speeds.

built a 125cc V-twin with the cylinders one above the other at a narrow angle, geared crankshafts and disc valves, but this was never competitive. The 50cc models were a different story with close battles between Derbi, Suzuki and Kreidler and places in Grand Prix events for the Spanish firm in 1967 and 1968, the year when Barry Smith won the TT for them.

Real glory came in 1969 when Angel Nieto took the 50cc world title, repeating this in 1970 when they also ran a new, water-cooled 125cc twin. It won first time out, finished second in the title race and went on to take the title in 1971 with Nieto aboard. He repeated this feat in 1972 when he also won the 50cc title for the third time. They also ran a 250 in some 1971 events but with limited success, although it did win the 1972 Austrian race.

The firm withdrew from racing at the end of 1972 when they celebrated half a century of business with a plan to build a new factory. In 1973 they offered an Angel Nieto 50cc Replica but while it had the style, it was well down on performance.

Mopeds continued to be the main output and were offered in many forms but 1976 brought a new twin, at first of 187cc, but

become associated with the marque.

This took them up to the 1960s when they dropped the larger models to concentrate on those from 50 to 125cc, especially the smaller which were in great demand. To advertise the marque they had developed an involvement in competition on the race circuits and off-road in motocross and endurance events with some success. At that point, unknown outside Spain, they moved onto the world stage in 1962 with an entry in the first 50cc World Championship race held in Spain on the tight Montjuich Park circuit in Barcelona. For this they fielded José Busquets on a Derbi with disc-valve inlet and eight speeds and after a race-long duel he finished less than a second behind the winning Kreidler, and well ahead of the works Hondas.

They also had considerable success in off-road events and did well in Spanish and French national road races. At world championship level they were always competitive in the 50cc class although they did not contest many rounds. In 1964 one of their machines was ridden by Angel Nieto who was destined to become

For off-road trail riding Derbi listed the 50cc Diablo, based on the road machine with changes to wheels and other items to suit its purpose.

second only to Agostini in both race wins and world titles.

An offshoot of the race programme was the appearance of a 50cc racer in the range, a simple air-cooled two-stroke with five speeds but competitive at local levels. It led on to two sports road models of 50 and 75cc, which had the engine hung from a spine frame, four speeds, good performance and a fine style, set off by a seat with race tail. Race kits became available for both models and enabled many young

Spaniards to try their hand at road racing.

Moped production continued apace thanks to changes in the Spanish legislation which allowed younger riders to use them. Alongside them came a 75cc trial model for the avid off-road enthusiasts; this proved a great success. Derbi was now a major producer and became the largest in Spain with the bulk of the machines being simple, reliable, cheap and well made.

On the road-racing side they

Style as well as performance is everything in the smaller classes and Derbi had both in this 1991 race replica model with its modern specification.

converter. It sat on 25-cm (10-ins) wheels, and the firm would continue to offer scooters of various sizes from then on.

They returned to the Grand Prix scene in 1984, running in the very competitive 80cc class which had by now superseded the 50cc class. In 1986 their rider, Jorge Martinez, took the title, with Manuel Herreros second and this was repeated in 1987. Martinez won again in 1988 when he also took the 125cc title and in 1989 Herreros won the final 80cc title. That was the last year for the class, and it made a total of 10 titles for the firm.

Derbi continue to build their range of small capacity two-stroke machines that suit their market so well.

later bored out to 199cc. It had six speeds, a conventional specification and good style, being stretched to 217cc during the

1980s. In 1982 the firm returned to the scooter market with an 80cc reed-valve engine mounted near to horizontal and driving a torque

DERBI CROSS

1975

THE 50CC CLASS was a Derbi stronghold for many years; they produced models for road, trail, motocross and road racing. The Derbi Cross had a 48.8cc air-

cooled, two-stroke engine with an alloy cylinder head built-in unit and the gearbox was driven by helical gears. Its had slimline telescopic front forks and a

The Derbi Cross engine unit was based on that of the road machines but installed in a tubular spine frame with an upswept exhaust and more suitable suspension.

DECLARET
England (Stevenage) 1962: This English firm, based in Kent, southern England, were responsible for the production of several mopeds.

DE-DE
France (Courveboie) 1923–29: This French firm were shortlived. They underwent a limited production of, initially, 100, 125 and 175cc models. They later were responsible for the production of more machines, including several 250, 350 and 500cc JAP-powered models.

DEFA
Germany 1921–24: This was a firm of frame builders who were also responsible for manufacturing a complete 198cc side-valve motorcycle.

DEFY-ALL
England 1921–22: These unusual spring frames from this English firm housed the usual motors. These motors were bought-in from Villiers with 269cc, and also bought-in from Blackburne with 350 and 500cc.

DELAPLACE
France 1951–53: This company was responsible for the installation of 173 and 247cc engines from Ydral and fitting them into several Delaplace frames.

DELIN
Belgium (Leuven) 1899–1901: This Belgian firm was responsible for building De Dion-Bouton machines under licence. Later in its shortlived production span, the company was to switch to the use of Fafnir engines.

pivoted-fork rear suspension controlled by twin spring units. The wire-spoke wheels were fitted with Akron aluminium-alloy rims and had drum brakes front and rear. The machine had braced handlebars, high-level exhaust, good ground clearance, and flexible mudguards well clear of the trail tyres for off-road use.

The Cross was strongly linked to other 50cc models in the Derbi range, such as the Tricampeona, although that had a pressed-steel spine frame, low exhaust system, three or four speeds and full road equipment. In either case, their models offered good performance and style and sold well thanks to the firm's racing successes.

Engine: 48.8cc, 2s vertical single, 38x43mm, air-cooled
Power: 4bhp at 5700rpm
Gearbox: unit 4-speed foot change
Final drive: chain
Weight: 52kg (115lb)
Top speed: 76kph (46mph)

DERBI WORKS 125
1970

COMPETITIVE AT WORLD championship level in the 50cc class from its outset in 1962, the first Derbi works racer had an air-cooled, disc-valve engine and eight speeds. It finished a close second in the opening round. Two years later, Angel Nieto began to ride for

Angle Nieto brought five world titles to Derbi in the 50 and 125cc classes and is seen here in characteristic style on the larger model.

the firm and went on to win five of his 13 world titles on Derbi machines: three 50cc in 1969, 1970 and 1972 and two 125 titles in 1971 and 1972.

The 125cc machines all had twin-cylinder engines with the water-cooled cylinders well inclined to reduce overall height. A disc valve went on each side with the drive to the six-speed gearbox built in unit with the engine on the right. Expansion chamber exhausts ran under the unit which was mounted in a tubular frame with conventional suspension, wire wheels and twin-leading-shoe drum brakes front and rear.

First seen at the 1970 Belgian Grand Prix, halfway through the season, it won there and three more times that year to finish second in the championship. It was ridden by Nieto who went on to win the title for the next two years against strong opposition. By then, the original 34bhp power output was up to a claimed 40 which helped, but at the end of the year, the firm withdrew from racing until the 1980s.

Engine: 123.97cc 2s inclined parallel twin, 43.4x41.9mm, water-cooled
Power: 34bhp at 14,500rpm
Gearbox: unit 6-speed foot change
Final drive: chain
Weight: 85kg (187lb)
Top speed: 225kph (135mph)

DERNY
FRANCE 1939–58

THIS FIRM BUILT SOME unusual machines, which were very much in the French style and first seen in 1939 as early forms of cyclomoteur in both solo and tandem forms. In either case, the small engine was fitted to the downtube and its fuel carried in a cylindrical tank mounted on the headstock. The engine inclination varied with the solo model being close to upright and the tandem well angled. The frame tubing was designed and manufactured to run around the motor.

The transmission for both models began with a chain that ran to a countershaft fixed above the front bottom-bracket with a second chain to the rear wheel of the solo. For the tandem, the second chain ran to a second countershaft above the rear bottom-bracket and thence by chain to the wheel. A bicycle frame and forks with drum brakes were used, the frames with extra bracing to suit the added loads. Postwar, these two models were listed as the Bordeaux-Paris and the Cyclotandem, the engines coming from Zürcher.

The firm showed an unorthodox scooter at the 1952 Paris Show, which had a 125cc two-stroke, fan-cooled engine mounted to the left of the front wheel. This drove a three-speed gearbox fixed just behind the wheel by exposed chain and a further chain drove a roller pressed against the tyre. All this weight must have had a major effect on the steering and it all went under a large bonnet that had a headlight mounted at each outer corner. The rear of the machine, including the wheel, was enclosed and the seat was mounted on top of the enclosure. Less usual were stabiliser wheels on each side. Thereafter, little more was heard of this scooter.

For 1956, the firm introduced the Taon motorcycle with a choice of engine units: the 70cc Lavalette with a three-speed preselector gearbox, or the 125cc French AMC two-stroke with horizontal cylinder, built in unit with a three-speed gearbox. In either case, this

hung from a simple rigid frame with twin tubes from the headstock to the rear wheel spindle and loops under the engine. Leading-link forks with rubber band suspension served at the front, and the fuel tank extended forward in a fine sweep to enclose the steering head and to carry the headlamp.

In 1957 the Taon only came

with the AMC engine and the Standard was joined by a Sports version having long leading-link front and pivoted-fork rear suspension. The Sports style changed the saddle for a dual seat that blended well with the tank and rear mudguard to enhance the line. However, despite the innovation, the marque came to an end in 1958.

DEVIL MOTO   ITALY 1953–57

THE CAREER OF DEVIL MOTO was brief but bright. They began in 1953 with two-stroke lightweights of 125 and 160cc, along with the three-wheeler, 250cc delivery vehicle, an almost mandatory product in the Italian wheeled industry at the time, which could carry up to 500kg (0.5 ton). This pleasant but less than over-whelming line-up was little changed for 1954 but in 1955 Devil started to expand the range in a big way.

The 48cc Develino moped was unremarkable, even if it was made in both sporting and standard

versions, but a 175cc four-stroke single arrived alongside the 160cc two-stroke which was improved for the 1956 season and re-launched in Sport form. Not to be outshone, the 175cc four-stroke was upgraded to Sports status that year, with double overhead-cams, 15bhp at 7800 rpm, and a top speed of well over a claimed 135kph (80mph). This would have

The 160cc two-stroke Sport Extra boasted 7 1/2 hp and was good for around 110kph (almost 70mph) – performance that was not at all bad for the mid-1950s.

This strange logo used a 'V' for the 'devil's' horns which made it hard not to read the beard of the marque's 'devil' as a 'W'.

been a good performance for a 175cc two or three decades later, and was comparable with many 350cc singles.

The double overhead-camshaft Sport bike was, in turn, developed into a 175cc racing version with no less than 20bhp at 11,000 rpm, a five-speed gearbox, and a top speed of more than a claimed 180kph (110mph). However, there were no major successes, and the firm failed to make an impact on the market; little was heard of the promising Devil Moto after 1957.

DIAMANT   GERMANY 1903–08 AND 1926–40

DIAMANT HAD A BRIEF early history producing motorcycles and forecars that were typical of the 1910s, at first using Fafnir engines and later their own singles and V-twins. Production ceased for nearly two decades but restarted in 1926 with a conventional range powered mainly by Kühne engines: at first they produced a 346cc with overhead-valves which was followed by a 496cc, side- and overhead-valves with JAP engines were an option. All went into a conventional frame with a separate

gearbox, all-chain drive, girder forks and drum-braked wire wheels.

Diamant merged with the Elite car firm in 1927 and both became associated with Opel during the following year, which led in time to the EO motorcycle. From 1928 the Diamant factory produced Opel machines, but only for two or three years.

The EO, with its light-alloy frame on Opel lines, was built from 1930 for two years and powered by 348 and 498cc overhead-camshaft Küchen

engines, the camshaft driven by shaft and bevels.

Production then ceased again but restarted in 1937 with a range of lightweight models fitted with Sachs two-stroke engines from 75 to 125cc. All were conventional in form with two or three speeds, simple frame and forks, drum brakes and direct lighting similar to a number of other German makes built for that market. These machines continued until 1940 but did not appear again after World War II.

DIAMOND

THE DIAMOND BICYCLE was built by D.H. & S. Engineering at works in Wolverhampton, but when they announced a four-model motorcycle range in mid-1908, they became Dorsett, Ford & Mee, or D.F. & M., which was handled by the Victoria Trading Co. of London. All four motorcycles were powered by Belgian FN engines but did not have the shaft drive normally associated with that firm. There were two singles, of two-and-a-half and three-and-a-half horsepower, and three-and-a-half and five horsepower V-twins with vertically positioned rear cylinder All had a Bosch magneto and FN carburettor. The models were long and low for the time and all except the smallest had sprung forks. Direct belt drive was employed and the finish was in French grey. These were typical primitives, and production was limited.

Late in 1912, the firm announced a far more advanced and interesting two-and-three quarters horsepower model. Both

From 1919, Diamond used a variety of bought-in engines and this 1921 model had a 2½hp side-valve JAP driving a two-speed gear by an enclosed chain.

THE 2¾ h.p. DIAMOND MOTOR CYCLE

THE SENSATION OF THE M.C.C. LONDON-EXETER-LONDON TRIAL.

Only one 2¾ h.p. Diamond Motor Cycle entered, and *that* with sidecar and passenger (total weight of driver and passenger, 22½ stone). This machine successfully finished the course and easily climbed all hills including the notorious **Trow Hill, Chard, and Lyme Regis.** And adds another **Silver Medal** to its long list of laurels.

A 2¾ h.p. machine that will take a sidecar and passenger over this most severe route, up such atrocious hills, against such wind, rain, and awful road surfaces, will do anything, and go anywhere.

The Ideal All-Weather Machine.

LET US MAIL YOU OUR LATEST CATALOG of

THE MACHINE WITH SO MANY ADVANTAGES.

AGENTS WANTED.

PARTICULARS of THE MAKERS :— **The D. F. & M. ENGINEERING Co., Ltd., Sedgley St., Wolverhampton.**

the valve gear and the transmission differed markedly from the norm and the valve gear had an overhead inlet above a side exhaust, both at the front of the engine. Their camshaft ran forward along the right engine side and was driven by a bevel gear on the end of the crankshaft. It extended on to the magneto at the front of the crankcase and was fully enclosed.

The crankshaft bevel also drove a second shaft that ran back via a cone clutch to a housing in which went two sets of bevel gear pairs

to provide both a two-speed gearbox and a means of turning the drive. Final drive was by an enclosed chain. The cycle side was more conventional although the rear chainstays ran straight forward to pass either side of the crankcase just below the cylinder and thence to the downtube. Druid forks were fitted.

Early in 1913, the magneto was turned to fit across the frame and this introduced a further bevel pair. Otherwise the model went on to 1915 when a new model joined it, with a 269cc Villiers two-stroke

The interesting 2¾hp Diamond was introduced late in 1912 with unusual drives for the camshaft, magneto and two-speed gearbox, all well enclosed.

engine with two-speed gearbox. This had belt final drive and in 1916 was joined by one using a two-and-a-half horsepower JAP engine.

Postwar, the firm moved premises, although they were still based in Wolverhampton, and continued with these two models, entering the TT for several years, but without success. The range expanded with further Villiers, Blackburne and JAP engines, as well as a Barr & Stroud and then an oil-cooled Bradshaw. By 1927 the company was back to two-strokes only and after 1928 production stopped for a while.

The make returned in 1930 with a single 247cc two-stroke which was soon joined by others, including two fitted with overhead-valve JAP engines.

This continued for a couple of years but by 1933 there was just one model with a 148cc Villiers engine. After that the firm turned to manufacturing trailers and milk-floats.

DKW

GERMANY 1919–66

IN MANY RESPECTS DKW ranks equally with BMW and NSU as a giant of German motorcycle manufacturing. For many years, the company was world leader in two-stroke design, using technology it had largely developed itself.

The story of DKW really began with the birth on 30 July 1898 of Jorgen Stafte Rasmussen in Nakskow, Denmark. The young Rasmussen moved to Dusseldorf, Germany in 1904 and then in 1907 to Zschopau, 20km (12 miles) south of Chemnitz in Saxony. Here, Rasmussen held a number of engineering posts and in 1919, formed his own company, J.S. Rasmussen.

The saga of how the company came to adopt the famous DKW initials is quite a tale. In 1963, at his 85th birthday celebration, Rasmussen put forward three explanations. The first was *Dampf Kraft Wagen*, which came from his first engine, a steam-powered unit for cars. The initials stuck and when, between the wars, the company's racing machines were cleaning up at Berlin's Avus circuit, the second slogan was coined: *Der Knabishe Wunsche*

DKW's SM (Steel Model) of 1925 was powered by a 175cc two-stroke engine and was extremely popular. The machine featured some pioneering design.

(the schoolboy's dream). As if that wasn't enough, the introduction of a small car in 1928 brought the third twist: *Das Kleine Wunder* (the little miracle), this version being the most widely accepted.

The fledgling company's first full year of trading was 1920 and it was very much one of development and research. A major milestone came in 1921 with the introduction of the Hugo Ruppe-designed 122cc auxiliary engine. This could be mounted to a conventional pedal cycle, driving the rear wheel by means of a leather belt. By mid-1922, some 25,000 of the miniature engines had been sold, with the two-stroke motor gaining an excellent reputation for reliability.

This success was quickly followed by the scooter-like 122cc

The 142cc Lamos scooter was an advanced design when it made its debut in 1922, but unfortunately for the marque, it was to prove a sales failure.

Golem 1921 and 142cc Lamos 1922 models. Although both offered 'armchair' comfort, they were poor sellers. But unphased by these setbacks, Rasmussen and Ruppe came up with a series of top sellers. The first of these, the advanced SM (Steel Model) highlighted the pioneering type of design work of which DKW was capable. The 173cc single cylinder SM was a trendsetter due to its use of a pressed-steel frame. Even though this was soon copied by other manufacturers, DKW was able to stay ahead of the pack. By 1927 it had absorbed 16 other

companies and employed a workforce of 15,000.

Three years later, with even more rapid expansion, DKW could truthfully claim to be the world's largest motorcycle manufacturer. However, this level of growth was to cause side-effects, the main one being high losses and massive bank debts. Rasmussen was able to solve this problem with a business method that would characterise the motor industry in the latter half of the twentieth century. This was the grouping of companies through mergers and takeovers.

In DKW's case this happened in 1932 when it was merged with Horch, Audi and Wanderer to become Auto Union AG, headed by Carl Hahn. The new combine took as its trademark four silver interlinked circles which, almost 70 years later, are still to be found on Audi cars. But, unlike today, this amalgamation of four companies was not purely a badge-engineering exercise: the other three concentrated upon four wheels while DKW continued to be a bike builder, and a good one at that.

Above: This 1928 model was made at a time of rapid expansion for DKW. By 1930, the firm could claim to be the largest motorcycle manufacturer in the world.

Below, left: A 1929 DKW 500 Sport. The machine boasted 18bhp, weighed 170kg (374lb) and was capable of an impressive 120kph (75mph).

achieved this with angled inlet ports. These allowed the mixture taken in during the induction stroke to proceed up the cylinder, across the combustion chamber and down the other side of the cylinder, taking the course of escaping exhaust gas through its conventional control port. Considerable experimentation ensued before the optimum shape and positioning of the ports was finalised.

During the late 1930s, DKW was almost unbeatable in Grand Prix racing with its howling 250 and 350cc machines, which were also successful at record-breaking. Besides racing, DKW did well in International Six Days Trials-type

events, winning gold medals galore.

DKW's all-round success was reflected at the 1938 Berlin Show. This was the biggest yet, with sales reaching record levels and DKW playing a major part in Germany's overall prosperity. The future looked bright, even though the same could not be said about the political situation.

Then in 1939 with the outbreak of war, DKW, like the majority of other motorcycle plants, was forced to turn over its production to the war effort. Between 1939 and 1945 it built a number of military bikes, including the NZ250 and 350. But of all the motorcycles that the war brought

A 250cc DKW with a twin-port single engine, dating from 1938. This period was one of great success for the company, both on road and track.

Once the Great Depression showed signs of starting to clear, DKW were ideally placed to take full advantage of the upturn in both domestic and export markets.

Production of DKW engines had been greatly helped by the introduction in 1929 of the loop scavenge system devised by Ing. Schnuerle. This was a major step forward for the two-stroke, which had been hampered by breathing problems. It was for this reason that DKW had earlier revived the ancient Bichrome layout, using a

separate cylinder acting as a charging pump. This could deliver the mixture with a degree of supercharging at normal atmospheric pressure. However, the Schnuerle system with its flat top pistons soon proved far more effective than either this system or the earlier designs incorporating a piston with a crown in the centre that formed an asymmetric deflector.

Schnuerle's principle offered superior power, improved flexibility and more even firing. It

into being, DKW's smallest model would have the most enormous significance for postwar development. This was the Hermann Webber-designed RT125. It was to be, in the immediate postwar period, the most copied motorcycle in history.

As for DKW, their Zschopau works were in the Eastern Communist section when Germany was partitioned at the end of the war. Consequently, DKW had to set up a new factory from scratch in the West, at Ingolstadt on the River Danube in Upper Bavaria.

After resuming production, the first particular bike, an RT125, was built in 1949. The 'new' DKW factory had got a racing version on the circuit as early as 1947, together with a prewar supercharged 250.

But the really big DKW racing news of the era was the introduction of a brand new 350 three-cylinder, which arrived in 1952. This model was campaigned until the company quit competition at the end of 1956.

Like all DKWs, this 1938 350 GS is a two-stroke machine. It was specially constructed for long distance tials such as the famous ISDT event.

The street-bike line of the 1950s included the RT125, RT175, RT200, RT250 and RT350. All were two-stroke singles, except the 350, which was a twin.

In October 1954, the 250,000th DKW motorcycle to be made since the end of the war left the Ingolstadt plant. During the same period, 122,000 cars, also two-strokes, were built in the same factory.

For DKW, like the majority of the West German motorcycle industry, 1956 was a black year. Although a new moped, the Hummel (bumble bee) had been launched in July, things were becoming difficult at Ingolstadt.

DKW also had great success during the 1930s racing super-charged bikes – two-strokes of course, the trademark of the firm. This is a 1939 350cc model.

The four-wheel side of the business kept the company afloat. In November 1958, financial problems resulted in Express, Victoria and DKW joining forces to form the Zweirad Union; a plan masterminded by Franz Flick, owner of Daimler Benz, who had acquired 88 per cent of Auto Union shares.

After this amalgamation in 1958, DKW's name was used as a badge-engineering exercise only.

DE TOGNI

Italy (Milan) 1932–40s: This was effectively an armchair on a motorcycle frame. It was fitted with outrigger wheels and enjoyed the brute power of a 175cc DKW motor, which must have really felt the need for its three-speed gearbox. After the end of the hostilities of World War II, De Togni switched to light delivery vehicles and fitted them with Sachs engines.

DETROIT

USA c.1903: An upper frame tube was the oil tank, and a lower frame tube the silencer, in these early machines. One version of the bike was started by magneto ignition, while the other version was started by coil ignition.

DFB

Germany 1922–25: The 159cc engine manufactured by this company was sold both as an auxiliary cycle motor and on complete machines.

DFR

France (Neuilly) 1921–33: Desert et De Font Reault began by building motorcycles with Train two-stroke engines and Bradshaw oil-cooled four-stroke engines, with chain primary drive and belt secondary. Then in 1925, or thereabouts, they moved on to produce a pump-charged 250cc two-stroke single engine and then on to 350cc MAG engines. Following that, they progressed to 175 and 250cc two strokes, overhead-valve 350cc four-strokes, and other machines. They raced a supercharged machine with an engine from Bradshaw with some success between 1925 and 1927. The company was eventually taken over by Dresch a few years later, in about 1930.

SS250 RACER

1935

The Berlin Show of 1935 saw DKW debut an 'over-the-counter' racer known as the SS250. This was based on the all-conquering works machinery and used the same basic split-single, water-cooled power unit.

There is not a four-wheel racing fan worth his salt who does not know of the legendary achievements of the Auto Union 'Silver Arrows' racing team of the mid- to late-1930s. On two-wheels, DKW was almost as successful, both in Germany and abroad, during the same period.

In 1925, DKW entered the racing fray with 175 and 250cc bikes using, of course, two-stroke engines, but with intercooling and the Bichrome system of supercharging. However, it was not until 1931, when the Hermann Webber-designed split-single layout appeared, that the marque enjoyed any real success.

August Prussing, who worked in the DKW racing department alongside Weber, was also involved with the successful development. During the next few years, just about every one of Germany's top riders raced the

An SS250 racer of 1935, a very rapid split-single two-stroke. This was an over-the-counter racer, based on the works machines which were enjoying great success.

'Deeks', including Fleischmann, Klein, Muller, Ley, Rosemayer, Wunsche, Kluge and Winkler.

The first of the new generation of split-singles was a quarter-litre

machine in which the supercharging piston operated in the front of the crankcase. Models based on this design went on to achieve a truly amazing number of victories and lap records throughout what were for DKW the golden 1930s.

Before long DKW's track reputation had spread outside the German borders and in their day

these machines were often winning in faster times than the 350s. DKW even ventured to that bastion of British motorcycling, the Isle of Man TT.

In 1938, Ewold Kluge who had led the 1937 TT, only to retire from the race, became the first German to win a TT when he took his 250 DKW to victory.

The following year, in 1939, DKW not only had the largest racing department in the world, with around 150 engineers, but also some extremely competitive bikes. These included the 250US, a supercharged, double-piston twin that pumped out an impressive 40bhp at 7000 rpm, and a similar 350 producing 48bhp. These machines also had the dubious honour of producing the world's most ear-splitting sound, the exhaust noise drowning out every other machine on the circuit!

Engine: 248.4cc 2s twin split-single, liquid-cooled
Power: 30bhp at 7000 rpm
Gearbox: 4-speed foot change
Final drive: chain
Weight: n/a
Top speed: 170kph (106mph)

RT125

1939

Throughout the 1930s, DKW had expanded rapidly until, on the very eve of the World War II, the company was the acknowledged world leader in the field of the two-stroke engine, for both road and circuit.

From the mid-1930s, DKW was building extraordinarily fast 250cc racing motorcycles with supercharged, double-piston, twin-cylinder engines. By 1939 the Zschopau (Saxony) factory

employed some 150 technicians in their racing department, the largest in the world. All this technical expertise, and its experimentation and developments, had a knock-on effect for the bread-and-butter production machines.

The original DKW RT125, designed by Herman Meier, made its debut in 1939. This is a 1950 model, almost unchanged from the original.

The prime example of this was DKW's most famous and influential model, the RT125. Designed by Hermann Weber, this lightweight motorcycle was powered by an all-new 122cc piston-port, two-stroke with unit construction, and a three-speed, foot-change gearbox; bore and stroke dimensions were 52x58mm (2x2.3ins).

The RT125 immediately found a buyer in the *Wehrmacht* (German Army), who used the lightweight newcomer for a variety of tasks. The centrepiece of the machine was its engine, with a light-alloy head and cylinder barrel in cast iron.

The German motorcycle industry was rationalised late in 1938 by Colonel Oberst (later General) von Schell, who was granted complete control in a way that is only possible under a totalitarian regime. Together with other types of vehicles, the number of powered two-wheeler types was slashed from 150 to 30.

But the RT125 was such an excellent design, it was ordered into production as soon as its test programme had been completed. Its lightness, excellent performance and durability ensured that it was built in large numbers for the German armed forces throughout the war.

After the end of the conflict, it went on to become the most copied motorcycle in history. The British BSA Bantam, American Harley-Davidson Hummer, the Soviet Moska, the Italian Morini and even the original Yamaha YAI (Reg Dragon) all showed DKW design influences.

The RT125's designer, Hermann Weber, was destined to die in a Soviet prisoner-of-war camp.

Engine: 122.2cc 2s single, 52x58mm, air-cooled
Power: Four-and-three-quarters bhp, 5000rpm
Gearbox: 3-speed foot change
Final drive: chain
Weight: 68kg (150lb)
Top speed: 76kph (47mph)

RT250   1952

BESIDES ROAD RACING, DKW also took part in long-distance trials, both before and after World War II.

The RT250 debuted in the 1952 ISDT International Six Days Trials. It was based on the piston-port, three-speed unit construction design of the RT200, which had been introduced into production the previous year, but with the capacity increased to 70x64mm (244cc). Running on a compression ratio of 6.3:1, the 250 produced 11bhp at 4000rpm. The carburettor was a Bing type AJ2/26/15. Other details of the machine's specification included 48-cm (19-ins) tyres, oil-damped telescopic front forks, plunger rear suspension and, unlike earlier DKWs, the final drive chain was totally enclosed. Maximum speed was a shade over 96kph (60mph).

With the RT250, DKW could now offer three roadster singles, the others being the latest RT125 and the earlier RT200. And even though the RT125 remained the top seller, the two larger-engined machines both sold well and, perhaps most important of all, proved both reliable and long lasting in service.

For the 1954 model year, two more RT models were placed in production: the RT175 single and the factory's first postwar roadster twin, the RT350. The RT250 was

The RT250 arrived in 1952. It not only proved an excellent street bike, but it won gold medals in the ISDT. This was another period of growth for the company.

updated to include more power – 12bhp at 4650rpm – a larger-capacity fuel tank, wider tyres with an extra 4.8kph (3mph) maximum speed but the four-speed gearbox from the new RT350.

As for the new twin, this was, like the RT250, a handsome machine, with an air of quality, clean styling and an excellent finish.

An interesting technical feature of the RT350 was its hydraulically

operated rear brake, the master cylinder of which was housed in the offside toolbox. Just as the RT350 was entering production, so DKW returned to cars, initially with a 900cc three-cylinder two-stroke engine. By 1954, the workforce had more than doubled since 1950. This growth funded a return to Grand Prix racing.

Engine: 244cc 2s single, 70x64mm, air-cooled
Power: 11bhp at 4000rpm
Gearbox: 3-speed from 1954 model year 4-speed foot change
Final drive: chain
Weight: 134kg (195lb)
Top speed: 100kph (62.5mph)

350 THREE-CYLINDER RACER   1955

In the 1930s, DKW had shown the world that its two-strokes could lead the world on the race circuit. Then, after World War II, and relocated at Ingolstadt in the West,

Originally created in 1952, the three-cylinder air-cooled DKW Grand Prix machine came of age for the 1955 season. The triple relaunched the DKW marque.

DKW tried to repeat its past glories.

Its first efforts were centred on specially tuned versions of its RT125 roadster, followed in the early 1950s by brand new twin and three-cylinder models. It was to be with the triple that the re-born DKW marque was to achieve its greatest success.

The debut of the 250 twin came at Hockenheim in April 1952, while the 350 triple arrived a month later. At that time, the DKW racing effort was in the hands of the young engineer Erich Wolf, who had previously tuned Austrian Puch and earlier types of DKW engines, prior to joining the famous two-stroke specialists.

Over the next couple of seasons Wolf was not entirely successful, resulting in the racing design work being handed to another engineer,

Hellmut Georg. At the same time, Robert Eberan von Eberhorst, a former assistant to the legendary Ferdinand Porsche was placed in overall control of DKW's racing division.

Together, Georg and von Eberhorst turned the 53x52.8mm 349.4cc three-cylinder racer into a world-class entry. At the start they kept Wolf's original design for the machine and the basic layout of two vertical cylinders and one

horizontal one was left alone. However, in Wolf's 1952 creation everything had been done to reduce weight, and the result was to make the bike unreliable. So Georg upgraded not only the engine components but also the chassis, brakes and suspension. This resulted in more power and far greater durability.

Another important feature of the Georg update was the revised exhaust system, which, for the first

time, made use of expansion chambers.

For two seasons, 1955 and 1956, the revised three-cylinder DKW made a serious bid for the 350cc World Championship, and although in the end it was beaten by the single cylinder Moto Guzzi, it was a very close-run affair.

At the end of 1956, DKW's management decided to call a halt to the firm's Grand Prix challenge. However, their top rider, August

Hobl, gave fans something dramatic to remember when he gained runner-up position in the 350cc World Championship series.

Engine: 348.48cc 2s triple 53x52.8mm, air-cooled
Power: 46bhp at 9700rpm
Gearbox: 5-speed foot change
Final drive: chain
Weight: 145kg (320lb) with streamlining
Top speed: 225kph (140mph)

DMW

ENGLAND 1950–67

DAWSON'S MOTORS OF Wolverhampton DMW were in the motorcycle business prewar and briefly linked to the Calthorpe name postwar. However, their motorcycle production did not start until 1950 when their Valley Road Works was located in Sedgley, Worcestershire. Over the years, Villiers engines were used for nearly all their machines and their first range had the choice of 99cc 1F, 122cc 10D or 197cc 6E units. All had MP telescopic forks, another product of the firm, and the larger pair had the option of plunger rear suspension.

In 1951, two De Luxe models with frames made from square-section tubing were added, while the 99cc model was dropped after that year and a 197cc Competition model was added for 1952. From

Above: DMW listed an extensive range of road and competition models. This was the 1962 Mk15, using a 246cc Villiers 32A engine.

Below: This 1953 DMW had a Villiers 197cc engine, plunger rear suspension and square-section tubing for the frame.

then on, they would use both round and square tubing for their frames along with some sheet steel in later years.

DMW sprang a surprise in 1953 when they introduced models using 125 and 170cc overhead-valve engines from AMC (this being the French Ateliers de Mécanique du Centre), instead of using engines from the British firm at Plumstead. This link brought two further models, one with a 249cc overhead-camshaft engine and the other a 125cc double overhead-camshaft racing machine called the Hornet.

This liaison did not last long and DMW were soon back with their range of two-strokes that included trials and scrambles models, as well as the road bikes. To these was added the Leda with 147cc 29C engine and the Cortina with the 224cc 1H, while the competition models became more built for purpose and less related to the road bikes.

In 1957, the Bambi scooter appeared fitted with the 99cc 4F engine under a monocoque frame that was also the body. The Dolomite joined the road models and used the 249cc 2T twin engine, this unit also going into a scrambles model for 1958. More sensible was the 1959 use of the 246cc 32A engine for trials and the 33A for scrambles, while a 324cc 3T version of the Dolomite was also added.

In the 1960s the Bambi was dropped but 1961 saw a new concept, the Deemster. This combined the merits of scooter and motorcycle in order to offer weather protection and good handling, but was powered by the 249cc 2T engine. The rest of the range continued with improvements and late in 1962

The DMW Hornet was only listed for 1954–55, used a French 125cc double overhead cam AMC engine, and was built purely for road racing.

DMW took over Ambassador, which resulted in some rationalisation. The following year brought a new competition model, the Hornet road racer with its

247cc Starmaker engine in a form which was very popular at that time. Later on, the firm built a 500cc twin using two of these engines, but this was strictly for themselves to run.

The range shrank in 1966 when the Deemster was built using a 247cc Velocette flat-twin, two-stroke engine. as well as the usual 2T. However, only the Hornet racer and the Highland Trials model using a Cotton frame and a 37A engine continued on until 1967.

In 1967, the firm effectively ceased making motorcycles, although they continued to make parts and the occasional trials machine. In the late-1970s, they did produce some Villiers-type 246cc engines which they supplied to Cotton and Dot but this did not last long.

DOT

ENGLAND 1907–78

THIS FIRM WAS FOUNDED by Harry Reed and located in Hulme, Manchester, and was still there some 90 years later, albeit no longer producing motorcycles.The name Dot was said to mean 'Devoid Of Trouble' and the first Dot bike had a three-and-a-half horsepower V-twin Peugeot engine and belt drive. Its fuel tank was torpedo shaped and helped to give a low line to the machine.

Reed took part in competitive events around the country to promote his firm with considerable

success. The highlight of those early years came in 1908 when he won the twin-cylinder class of the TT. He continued to race for many years and as late as 1924 was placed second in the Sidecar TT.

The road range was typical of the era, with a variety of engines from Peugeot, JAP and Precision, singles and V-twins, and gradual improvements to the transmission. By 1915, this had settled down to JAP engines only and Albion or Jardine gearboxes with two, three or four speeds.

During its long history Dot used the 348cc oil-cooled Bradshaw engine for some years. This model is from 1928 and follows the style of the period.

A small range reappeared postwar comprising a single and two twins but this expanded for 1923 when the JAP-powered models were joined by one using the 348cc oil-cooled overhead-valve Bradshaw engine. This latter, along with the same size of Blackburne engine, expanded the

DIESELLA
Denmark 1954: This Danish machine was a moped with a 50cc two-stroke motor. The motor was mounted under the pedals. In later versions, the motor was fitted behind the saddle, with friction drive to the rear wheel.

DIETERLE-DESSAU
Germany 1921–25: This company made 350cc two-stroke engines but suffered in the harsh financial climate of the interwar Weimar Republic. The firm was eventually wiped out by inflation, in the same way that many others were at that time.

DIFRA
Germany (Frankfurt a.d. Oder) 1923–25: These lightweights were produced with 198cc Namapo motors.

DIHL
Germany (Berlin) 1923–24: This German firm initially made a partially enclosed machine with 269cc two-stroke motor. They went on later to manufacture lightweights which were fitted with 125 and 150cc engines.

DIK-DIK
Italy 1950: Vanzango built this 43cc auxiliary cycle motor with friction drive to the rear wheel. The petrol tank sat atop the rear mudguard, with the engine more or less hanging below, on the right, with a tiny silencer. It allowed a top speed of up to 35–40kph (22–25mph).

DILECTA
France 1920–39: This was a firm of assemblers who used motors bought-in from numerous sources. These sources included Soyer, Aubier-Dunne, Chaise, and JAP, as well as Villiers.

1924 range in which a model with an overhead-valve JAP V-twin engine and another with a similar Anzani were introduced.

The range then reduced to three 350s for 1925 and there was little more for the next year when Harry Reed left the firm which had passed to new hands. The new owners extended the range further and included a 172cc two-stroke, adding 147 and 247cc bikes the next year. These continued along with the various 350cc four-strokes but then came the Depression and the range quickly shrank with manufacture ending after 1932. The company changed hands again.

However, this was not the end of the Dot motorcycle, for just after World War II the firm began to produce a three-wheeled motorcycle truck powered by a 122cc Villiers engine. In 1949, this led to a single road model with a 197cc Villiers engine unit and from this sprang a new series of mainly competition machines. Road models did appear and one such came in 1951 that differed in using the 248cc Brockhouse single-valve engine. The Mancunian in 1956 utilised

Above: Vintage Dot machines are still raced today at historic meetings. This one had a 350cc JAP ohv engine and three speeds in its gearbox.

Below: Competition again for a vintage Dot with 350cc JAP engine. These events are very popular and well supported by riders and spectators.

Villiers 9E power and yet another, for 1959, used the 349cc RCA twin two-stroke but these were soon dropped.

The range became trials and scrambles machines with various combinations of front suspension, lights and exhaust systems. At first, the 197cc Villiers engine was used alone, but in 1953 a 246cc version in its various forms and the Villiers Starmaker unit were used.

To augment their range, the firm added the Dot-Vivi mopeds from 1957 but these were all imports using Victoria engines. From 1959, there were the Dot-Guazzoni two-stroke machines from Italy in 98, 125 and 175cc sizes, but all were dropped by 1962. The line was reduced in the 1960s as trading conditions worsened and, after 1968, machines were only available in kit-form to suit a tax loophole. In addition, the supply of Villiers engines dried up and they had to turn elsewhere, so the firm used the Italian 170cc Minarelli for their closing years. This combination was built in small numbers up to 1977, after which they used a Villiers-type 246cc engine built by DMW, but this effort came to nothing in the face of the Spanish trials machines then available. Thereafter, the firm continued in business, producing shock absorbers for cars and motorcycles.

DOUGLAS

ENGLAND 1907–57

DOUGLAS WAS A many-splendoured company that made TT racers, and had side-car and solo victories. It held a number of world records at various times. It made one of the most famous despatch bikes of World War I. His Majesty King George VI bought one when he was still Prince Albert, so they gained the coveted 'By Appointment' endorsement. For years, the ultimate dirt-trackers were 'Douggies'. A Douglas bike was the first 500cc machine to exceed 160kph (100mph) on British soil in March 1922. The later 350s were among the fastest, possibly even the fastest, of that capacity on the market. These bare facts convey only the glory. Unfortunately, there is another set of bare facts that tell the story of the company's 50 rollercoaster years producing motorcycles.

William Douglas of Greenock, who had set up in the foundry business in Bristol in 1882, began motorcycle production in 1907 in an attempt to revive his financially overstretched company. It nearly went under in 1925 after a massive tax demand, was threatened by a fire in 1927, was sold as a result of family feuds, in 1931, to become Douglas Motors 1932 Ltd, then

The Brooklands model was a 733 derivative of the highly successful dirt-track series: its ancestry is clear in the wheel sizes and handlebars.

went broke in 1933 and was reconstituted as William Douglas Bristol Ltd. It was on the point of failure when it was bought out by the British Aircraft Company in 1936 and became Aero Engines Ltd. After World War II, under a new name – Douglas Kingswood Ltd – adopted in 1946, it ran out of money and went into receivership, before being rescued by Charterhouse Investment Trust

in 1948 as Douglas Sales and Service. This was taken over in 1956 by Westinghouse Brake and Signal, with the result that all motorcycle production ceased in 1957. Remarkably perhaps, Douglas went on as a successful importer of scooters afterwards but that is another story.

The original begetter of the Douglas was the Fee or Fairy, an indifferent in-line flat-twin

The in-line flat twin of this 1911 Douglas was clearly derived from John Joseph Barter's 1905 Fée, which was not, itself, a successful machine.

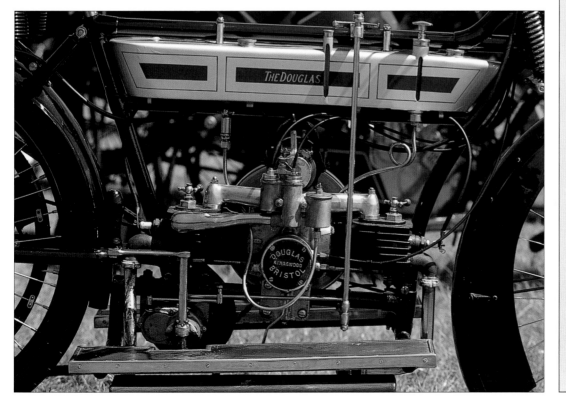

designed by Bristolian John Joseph Barter and built for him by Douglas. It didn't sell, so when Barter's Light Motors Ltd. founded in 1905, went under, Barter – who must have been a smooth-talking fellow – persuaded Douglas to take him on as works manager of a new motorcycle division. The new machine would be a similar but enlarged 340cc instead of 200cc in-line flat twin.

This 1949 T35 Mk 3 was a surprisingly advanced motorcycle, but very overpriced and not blessed with great reliability – two common Douglas failings.

This was right in the middle of the first ever slump in the infant business, in 1907, when annual sales industry-wide were down about 25 per cent. About two dozen machines were sold that year, and fewer than 100 in 1908. Not until 1910, with the adoption of a two-speed gearbox, did Douglas sales really begin to take off.

Even then, the machines were increasingly old-fashioned, with automatic inlet valves until 1912, when the 'free engine' or clutch was also introduced, albeit only as an option, although final drive by belt was to survive for years

longer. The 1914 model gives some idea of the sort of machines that were used as despatch bikes, and helped consolidate the position of the manufacturer.

The early 1920s were perhaps the glory years of the company. In 1921, the 494cc S1 was 'square' at 68mm, while the 733cc S2 was a long-stroke model with the same bore but an 83mm stroke. Then, in 1923, came the overhead-valve RA, one of the most successful Douggies of them all.

In the late 1920s and early 1930s, a craze for dirt-track racing swept Britain. As a result, Douglases were extremely successful, thanks to their low centre of gravity and good ground clearance (although the shorter, nimbler Rudge singles would eventually supplant them). As so often happened, however, they were a day late and short of money, and they went bust again.

The adoption of transverse engine location in the 500cc Endeavour of 1935 rekindled interest. However, it failed to rekindle sales and, after yet another financial reorganisation, there was few new developments

Douglas machines were extremely successful in speedway racing, because of their low centre of gravity and good ground clearance.

on the motorcycle front until the very promising T35, which was announced in 1946 for the 1947 season.

But this was the beginning of the end. Subsequent Douggies were variations on the T35 theme, but by this time, building Vespas under licence attracted the company more, and the production of actual motorcycles withered and died.

DOUGLAS DESPATCH RIDER BIKE 1914

FOR THE 1914 MODEL YEAR, Douglas had finally abandoned the use of pedals. By now, the comapny had shed all of their most primitive roots, sometimes doing so reluctantly. However, they produced machines which featured a chain-cum-belt drive.

The 350cc machine illustrated above was produced in large numbers over 25,000 for the armed forces in World War I. With a 'free engine' clutch and two-speed gearbox, it lacked the mud-plugging power of the 550cc Triumph singles that were also

By the end of the World War I, Douglases were respected despatch rider machines, light, manoeuvrable and reliable. This is a 2³⁄₄hp twin of 1918.

widely used, and the low-mounted sparking plugs were, of course, susceptible to shorting out in deep puddles. However, on dry terrain, grass or any reasonably solid ground, it was well regarded by those who had to use it. It also made a good deal of money for the company who were responsible for manufacturing it.

As well as the 350cc, there was a big-bore 74.5x68mm, 593cc model for side-car use, introduced in 1916, which was particularly interesting for its adoption of what would later be called 'squish' heads.

Engine: 348cc sv longitudinally mounted flat twin, 60.8x60mm, air-cooled
Power: n/a
Gearbox: 2-speed hand change
Final drive: belt
Weight: n/a
Top speed: 80kph (50mph) approx

DOUGLAS RA 1923

The overhead-valve RA, developed by Les Bayley from the existing model, was a modernisation of the previous twins. The engine sat lower in the frame, for a lower centre of gravity and better stability, and considerable use was made of light alloys to reduce weight. The 'RA' name was apparently derived from a new brake design developed at the British Research Association – a rare concern, in an era when most manufacturers paid far more attention to going than to stopping. Even the 500cc version weighed only 116kg (257lb), so a combination of this early disk brake fitted front and rear and the light weight of the machine made it very quick to start and stop, at least by the standards of the day.

Lessons learned from the RA were remembered in designing the side-valve EW of late 1925 for the

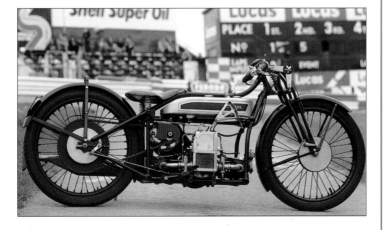

The RA had overhead valves, a low engine position and better brakes – an impressive combination.

1926 season. It suffered at first from reliability problems as it was lightly built in order to comply with British tax regulations.

Engine: 348cc sv longitudinally mounted flat twin, 60.8x60mm, air-cooled
Power: n/a
Gearbox: 3-speed hand change
Final drive: chain
Weight: n/a
Top speed: n/a

DOUGLAS D31   1931

The D31 for the 1931 model year was an updated S6 sports-tourer; the corresponding standard 600 was the E31. In 500cc guise it was the C31, while the A31 and B31 were substantially similar 350cc models, the A31 below the government's (91kg) 200lb tax limit, the B31 above it.

This machine was very much in the mould of the traditional Douglas, even down to being technically fairly primitive despite its good handling. The big external 'bacon slicer' flywheel meant that it was smooth and torquey, though these attributes were of more interest to the sidecar user than to the sporting motorcyclist, hence the E31. At least it had dry-sump lubrication; this had been added to the specification in 1929.

From a modern perspective, it is hard to understand quite what people saw in this increasingly dated range of motorcycles, as it was a long way from the firm's TT heritage, which in turn was increasingly rooted in the past. This may well have been one of the reasons why William Douglas sold the company to a group of investors to create Douglas Motors Ltd, 1932. Then, two years later, when the new consortium failed, having sold some of the company's machine tools in an attempt to raise money, he bought the company back and created William Douglas Bristol Ltd.

Engine: 596cc sv in-line flat twin, 68x82mm, air cooled
Power: n/a
Gearbox: 3-speed hand change
Final drive: chain
Weight: n/a
Top speed: n/a

DOUGLAS ENDEAVOUR   1934

THE ENDEAVOUR, the first transverse twin from Douglas, looked very handsome and frankly BMW-like, right down to its car-type clutch and shaft drive. However, it never achieved the same degree of success as the German machine as a result of the financial instability of the company, and because of the Douglas reputation for dubious reliability (although this had been dramatically improved over the previous few years). Principally, it was unsuccessful because it was simply too expensive at £72. In the depths of the Depression, such a price did nothing for sales, so the conventionally mounted in-line twins continued to be the bread and butter of the company.

Left: The transverse engine was much better cooled than the in-line version (especially the rear cylinder of the in-line version) and the engine/gearbox unit was neat.

The variety of machines made in the 1930s was remarkable, with in-line side-valve twins of 350, 500, 600, 750 and even 1000cc, various overhead-valve models, a range of Villiers-engined single-cylinder two-strokes, including a 150cc Bantam long before BSA borrowed the name and, of course, the transverse-engined Endeavour, which was based on a 250cc prototype called the Golden Star.

This could have been another Golden Age, with new models, improved reliability, and William

Above: The 1934 Endeavour 500cc was the first transverse twin from Douglas, but it still had classic Douglas characteristics: it was costly, and not very reliable.

Douglas back in charge between 1933 and 1935 but, as ever, lack of capital was the firm's downfall. Gordon England of the British Aircraft Company took the company over and scrapped motorcycle production, eventually profiting from the war.

Engine: 498cc transverse flat twin
Power: n/a
Gearbox: 3-speed hand change
Final drive: chain
Weight: n/a
Top speed: 97kph (60mph) est.

DOUGLAS 80 PLUS   1949

An 80 Plus that delivered 24.8 hp might be slightly slower than a 90 Plus that delivered 25.2 bhp, but with a well-adjusted chain, it could be faster.

The 80 plus was the descendant of the original, all-new postwar T35 transverse twin with torsion-bar suspension, and was noted for its progressive design and fracture-prone frame. It was in Mark III guise that the T35 became the fastest production 350, and in 1949 for the 1950 season this was formalised as the 80 Plus and 90 Plus, with their alloy rims, twin carbs, big-fin heads and other go-faster goodies, though the Mark series would continue even unto the Mark V. The twin cams were mounted high in the block, to keep

the push-rods as short, stiff and light as possible, permitting very high revs: note that maximum power was delivered at a claimed 7500 rpm.

Reputedly, all engines were tested after completion, and if the dynamometer showed over 25bhp, a new-built motor was stamped '90', and if below, '80'. These referred, of course, to the likely top speeds of the machines to which they would be fitted, which were the metallic gold 90 Plus or the maroon 80 Plus. The 90 plus was available in full racing specification at no extra cost. The brakes were a part of that racing legacy, in that they were very large for the period and the weight of the motorcycle, with a 22-cm

(9-in) drum at the front and 17.7cm (7in) at the back, although the front was still only a single leading-shoe, despite being ribbed and ventilated.

An oddly high and large Feridax dual seat was standard, but spring saddles were also fitted and looked a lot better, and the Radiadraulic leading-link forks were apparently a second choice after torsion bar, which was used at the rear, totally undamped. Handling was very precise, except in the occasional, unexpected, but far from unknown case when a series of bumps coincided with the frequency of the torsion bars at rear end and it started to hop like a bunny.

The 80 Plus and its relatives mixed no-expense-spared engineering such as cast-alloy side-boxes with mechanical disasters, like sharing its oil with the rest of the world, and it was overpriced, costing more than a Triumph 500cc twin.

Engine: 348cc ohv transverse flat twin, 60.8x60mm, air-cooled
Power: 25bhp approx. at 7500rpm
Gearbox: 4-speed foot change
Final drive: chain
Weight: 179kg (393lb)
Top speed: 137kph (85mph) approx

DOUGLAS DRAGONFLY   1955

The Dragonfly – known in prototype as the Dart – was Douglas's last machine. As ever, they managed to shoot themselves in the foot by whipping up a fair amount of interest at the 1955 Earl's Court Show, then taking nine months to put the machine into production. By this time, they were expending most of their time and money on building Vespa scooters under licence, so that the motorcycle side of the business was neglected.

Apart from the engine and transmission, most Dragonfly components were bought in, which was not a bad idea, given the reputation of the Mark V frame. Paradoxically, the overall design looked more integrated than the in-house Plus machines. A single carburetter kept the power down, but the bike itself was sweet, nimble and overpriced; on the whole, it was a fairly typical Douggie.

This 1957 Dragonfly was the last series-production machine to be made by the company and is widely sought after by collectors to this day. Chain drive was an odd choice for a transverse flat twin.

Engine: 348cc ohv transverse flat twin 60.8x68mm, air-cooled
Power: 17bhp at 6000rpm
Gearbox: 4-speed foot change
Final drive: chain
Weight: 178kg (392lb)
Top speed: 116kph (72mph)

DRESCH

HENRI DRESCH PRODUCED a fine range of models over the years ranging from a 100cc velomoteur to a 750cc machine. Some were fitted with proprietary engines from firms such as Chaise, JAP or MAG, while others were made by the firm. In the smallest class, they kept to direct belt-drive for some time with the tiny two-stroke engine lost in the frame and a tubular fuel tank. Later, the top tube became the tank and the downtube the silencer, but the belt drive remained via a countershaft.

Innovation came in 1930 with a model having a 500cc, in-line, tandem-twin, four-stroke engine with side-valves. Unusually, the output was taken from the camshaft that carried the clutch to drive a three-speed, hand-change gearbox with shaft drive to the

The innovative Dresch tandem-twin model with its direct drive from the camshaft, three speeds, shaft final drive and pressed-steel frame.

rear wheel, all in a pressed-steel frame with girder forks.

The tandem-twin model was also built using a 250cc single-cylinder engine. In 1933, a twin with an overhead-valve engine was added.

Alongside such machines ran the more prosaic, with 250, 350 and 500cc single-cylinder engines and conventional lines. However, these were enlivened by the use of styling features and the French flair.

The 1930s was a decade that saw the motorcycle industry contract and move away from the

production of larger-capacity models. Most companies employed the same bought-in engine for many different

marques. As with many other similar manufacturers, Henri failed to rejoin the motorcycle business after World War II.

DRYSDALE

Gigantic brakes – twin-disk on the front, of course – mark out the Drysdale as a machine for serious riding, rather than for posing on the boulevards.

Drysdale was able to take a number of short cuts without unnecessarily imperilling the integrity of his design. Inevitably, the decision to use parts from other machines meant that there were some interesting problems, such as the 1mm (one twenty-fifth inch) between the caps of the eight Keihin flat-slide carburetters. Like Philip Vincent, Ian Drysdale was concerned with reparability and wanted his buyers to be able to run their motorcycles and buy new parts, for as long as possible, even if his company left the business. However, the Keihins were due to be replaced with fuel injection, for a vastly lighter throttle action and considerably greater ease in setting up.

Yamaha FZR 400 heads, a Kawasaki ZZR 250 alternator, Yamaha-Kawasaki gearbox components, Suzuki/Yamaha clutch, Honda CB 1000 oil circulation and a water pump from a Kawasaki ZZR 1100 were all accommodated using custom cast light-alloy crankcases and a machined-from-the-solid

THE DRYSDALE 750-V8 was an unlikely capacity – the one-litre class, or still larger, would have been a more obvious choice for a 'superbike' – in an unusual cylinder configuration. Although it came from a country that has

generally been more noteworthy for its enthusiasm than for its original contributions to motorcycle construction – and it's true to say that Dandenong does not have quite the same reputation for motorcycle building as, say,

Coventry, Birmingham, or even Stevenage – Australia can boast of Phil Irving of Melbourne and later of Stevenage, who was one of the greatest designers of all time.

By 'borrowing' parts from a number of motorcycles, Ian

crankshaft. Underseat radiators on the original proved entirely inadequate for cooling, so they were replaced with two conventionally mounted radiators, one high, one low, in parallel, and these proved capable of cooling the machine even in the very high temperatures of a hot Australian summer.

Drysdale also opted for a single-plane crankshaft, thereby ensuring

The 750cc V8 Drysdale may have relied heavily on bought-in components, but it was still a magnificent, fascinating and very fast machine.

the famous V8 'burble', and the whole plot was quoted as good for 120kW, 161bhp, with a blood-line at 17,000rpm for street bikes and 19,000rpm for racers. Compare this with the 166bhp extracted from an engine nearly one-third bigger in the V-twin Britten, and the advantages of the V8 layout become clear although, of course, there are frictional and other losses that are greater in the V8.

A 20-litre tank (4.4 UK gallons, rather over 5 US gallons) was scarcely suitable for long-distance touring, but it could hold enough fuel to provide the bike with a reasonable range.

This 2002 GP Racer well illustrates the interesting blend of ultra-dramatic styling with serious technical innovation that always characterises Drysdales.

The intention of the Drysdale V8 was to build a road-legal, race-quality motorcycle, which was inspired on the one hand by the passion of the fastest Italian motorcycles – Moto Guzzi, obviously, as a trailblazer in V8s, but also Bimota and Ducati – and on the other, by the 'household appliance' reliability of Japanese machines, as this is an area in which the Italians are not unknown to fall short. The V8 would combine the best of both worlds. Its design makes an MV Agusta look modest, both in concept and execution but, at the time of writing, it was not possible to determine whether the machine was a success, or merely a brilliant idea.

Quite apart from producing the V8, however, Ian Drysdale was a pioneer in two-wheel-drive and even two-wheel-steering motorcycles using hydraulic drive. His firm 'Ausdale Engineering' has also been involved in such projects as converting all-terrain vehicles for disabled drivers, building movie-making equipment, camera cranes and tracking systems, and more.

DOMINISSIMI
Italy (Pordenone) 1924–28: The Dominissimi brothers made four models in the four years they were in business during the 1920s. They fitted the machines with 172 and 248cc engines, which they bought in from DKW.

DONISELLI
Italy (Milan) 1951–73: This manufacturer of delivery bicycles moved into the production of auxiliary cycle motors and light delivery vehicles, before starting the production of mopeds. After that, it began to produce 50cc scooters. All machines which left this firm's assembly line were fitted with proprietary motors bought-in from companies such as Ilo and Alpino.

DOPPER
The Netherlands 1904: An early overhead-valve engine of 269cc gave power to this pioneering machine.

DORION
France (Boulogne) 1932–36: This French assembler used 123cc Aubier-Dunne two-stroke motors.

DORMAN
Hungary 1920–37: This was an assembler who used proprietary engines from such companies as Villiers, MAG and also JAP. However, the company ultimately made few machines.

DORNIER
Germany 1949–57: This famous aviation company manufactured the Pearle moped with an aluminium frame. The firm also produced three-wheelers but it returned to its roots, recommencing aircraft production in the late 1950s.

DUCATI

DUCATI BEGAN MANUFACTURING electrical equipment in the 1920s. Their first contact with two-wheels came in 1945 when they concluded a licence agreement to make the Cucciolo (little puppy dog) auxiliary 48cc four-stroke engine.

After Cucciolo sales boomed, Ducati's first complete motorcycle, using a 60cc development of the Cucciolo arrived in 1950.

In May 1954, Ing. Fabio Taglioni joined the firm as chief designer. His first effort was the 49x52mm 98cc overhead-camshaft Gran Sport single, nicknamed Marianna. Sturdily constructed, it offered potential owners a competitive mount for long-distance road events such as the Milano-Taranto and Giro d'Italia (Tour of Italy). Capable of around 136kph (85mph), the Marianna packed its class leader-board in its debut outing, the 1955 Giro.

The ST2 (Sport Touring 2-Valve) Ducati V-twin made its debut in 1997. The machine gave Ducati an even wider appeal.

A larger version was achieved by simply boring the cylinder to 55.5mm, giving a displacement of 124.5cc. Features of the engine design – which were to remain in succeeding models – included unit construction, an overhead-camshaft driven by shafts and bevels, gear primary drive and wet-sump lubrication.

The 125cc GS was developed into the Formula 3 model, with

Following Mike Hailwood's famous 1978 TT victory, Ducati built the Hailwood Replica from 1979 until 1985.

more power and featuring enclosed valve gear, while a new 125cc double overhead-camshaft engine was constructed for a batch of special Grand Prix machines, which debuted in spring 1956.

However, it was to be the desmodromic version, with its positive-valve closing and opening mechanism that really put the Ducati name on the racing map. Ing. Taglioni worked on this design throughout the spring and early summer of 1956, before factory rider Gianni Degli Antoni gave the prototype a victorious debut at the Swedish Grand Prix in July.

On the production front, the 175 – 62x57.8mm 174cc – was the first street model to employ Taglioni's bevel overhead-cam single layout. It debuted at the Milan Show in November 1956.

During 1958, not only did more versions of the production roadsters enter production, including the 125 and a new 200 – 67x57.8mm 203cc – but Ducati rider Alberto Gandossi finished runner-up in the 125cc world road-racing championships.

The following year, 1959, Mike Hailwood won his first Grand Prix, riding one of Taglioni's 125 Desmo singles. But at the end of

DOTTA

Italy (Turin) 1924–26: These lightweights and delivery vehicles which were produced in the Italian city of Turin were fitted with 125cc two-stroke motors bought in from Piazza.

DOUE

France 1903–10: This French firm was responsible for the installation of one-and-three-quarter horsepower motors into strengthened bicycle frames.

D-RAD

Germany (Spandau) 1921–33: Deutsche Industriewerk AG began life as a weapons factory, and in 1923 introduced a 393cc side-valve flat twin motorcycle. They followed this three years later in 1926 with a 500cc side-valve single engine which had been designed by Christiansen and then had undergone refinements under the direction of Martin Stolle. Overhead-valves were to appear in the R10 model. This was introduced for 1929, which was just prior to the union with NSU. The last machines were fitted with two-stroke engines which came from Bark. The D-Rad name would continue in production right up until 1933.

The 1974 Desmo was the ultimate development of the Taglioni-designed bevel single cylinder line.

that year the factory struck the first of its many financial problems.

In the spring of 1961, the first full-size 250 single, 74x57.8mm 248cc, entered production. Versions of this machine were to dominate Ducati's production for most of that decade, culminating in the high performance Mach 1 1964 and Mark 3D 1968.

Mach 1 is generally regarded as the world's first series production 250 capable of doing 160kph (100mph), while the Mark 3D was to achieve fame as the world's first desmodromic roadster. Other notable achievements of the 1960s included the 350, 6x75mm 340cc, and the 450, 86x75mm 436cc, as well as the arrival of the 'widecase' singles engine in 1968.

But this, together with race victories such as the prestigious Barcelona 24 Hours, couldn't stave off another bout of financial problems, which came to a head in

1969, resulting in the long-serving Dr Montano's removal from office and a large cash injection from the Italian Government.

In 1970, with new government-appointed management of Arnaldo Milvio and Feredmano Spairani in place, Ing. Taglioni was given the green light to design a brand new 80x74.4mm 748cc 'L-shape' V-twin.

Using the same formula as the singles, including bevel-driven cams, the first production model, the GT, entered production in 1971.

In April 1972 came one of Ducati's biggest ever triumphs when Paul Smart and Bruno Spaggiari caused a sensation by winning the inaugural Imola 200 against the cream of the racing world, including Agostini and MV.

A year later came a victorious debut for the newer, larger 860, 86x74.4mm 864cc, when the Spanish pairing of Benjamin Grau and Salvador Canellas won the Barcelona 24 Hours at record speed. The first road-going version, the 860 GT, arrived at the end of 1974.

DREADNOUGHT

England (Birmingham) 1915–39 [alternatively dates are given elsewhere as between 1915 and 1925]: Despite the splendid, awe-inspiring name, these machines had a rather tedious specification, which was something of an anti-climax: they were powered by the ubiquitous Villiers 269cc two-stroke. They were built by Williams Lloyd Cycle, who was also responsible for making Quadrant and LMC machines.

Debuting in 1993, the Monster has proved a massive hit. This example is a 1998 600 Monster Dark.

After an ill-starred attempt by management to broaden its range with a series of what were to prove sales flops, the factory got back on track during the late 1970s with machines like the Darmah, Super Sport and MHR.

The latter came about as a result of Mike Hailwood's famous comeback Isle of Man TT victory in 1978, when he raced an 860, to gain Ducati's first world title.

Four more world titles came in the early 1980s, each with

A 2000 model 748R being put through its paces.

Englishman Tony Rutter at the controls. His mount was the TTF2 version of the Taglioni-designed Pantah with belt-driven cams,

which had entered production in 1979, in the shape of the 500SL model of 74x58mm 499cc.

Soon, larger-engined Pantahs including the TTF2 racers arrived. The first, the 600SL of 80x58mm 583cc went on sale in 1981, followed by a 350 of 66x51mm 349cc in 1983 and a 650 of 82x61.5mm 649.5cc the same year.

In 1983, Ducati agreed to supply engines to their rival Cagiva and, following more financial problems, Cagiva purchased Ducati on 1 May 1985. This heralded a new era of progress and also saw Massimo Bordi replace Fabio Taglioni as the factory's design chief. Cagiva also brought in Massimo Tamburini as its main stylist.

A new belt 750 of 88x61.5mm 748cc, the F1, debuted just before the Cagiva takeover and was joined by the new 750 Paso sport and Indiana custom models at the beginning of 1986. The Paso displacement was later increased to 92x68mm 904cc, and this latter displacement was also used on the

A 1996 916 Senna. 916cc Desmo V-twin; 105 bhp at 9000 rpm.

new 900 Supersport, which arrived for the 1990 model year.

Meanwhile, 1986 had seen the debut of the first four-valves-per-cylinder, double overhead-camshaft, liquid-cooled, fuel-injected superbike. Still a 90-degree V-twin, the first versions arrived in 1988 as the 851.

The 1990s saw an explosion of activity. Ducati won no less than eight of the 10 WSB (World Super Bike) titles: Carl Fogarty won four, Doug Polen two, and Raymond Roche and Troy Corser

The 1985 750 F1, with its 748cc belt-driven 90-degree V-twin engine, was the final design of Ducati's legendary Fabio Taglioni.

one each. There is no doubt this track glory helped Ducati achieve record sales during this era.

The most significant models of the 1990s were the SS series, the four-valve models 851, 888, 916 and 996, and the Monster range.

The new SS range arrived in 1991 and eventually comprised 350, 400, 600, 750 and 900cc

versions. Originally, these had inverted forks, single shock rear suspension and Mikuni carburettors but, from 1998, the larger machine featured fuel injection and new styling.

The top-of-the-range four-valvers were at the very forefront of the performance league, offering not only state-of-the-art technical development and stunning looks but blistering performance that could usually match the best Japan had to offer.

The Monster was the work of Migual Angel Galluzi and with its successful combination of practicality and street-fighter looks was responsible for bringing a new type of owner into the Ducati fold. The engine range mirrored that of the SS series.

In 1996, the ST2 Sport Touring two-valve made its debut. The appearance of this new model gave Ducati an even wider appeal than it had enjoyed before, with a four-valve version added in 1998.

The American investment house TPG (Texas Pacific Group) bought a 51 per cent share of Ducati in 1996, gaining the rest two years later. In March 1999, Ducati was launched as a public company on the stock market.

DUCATI 175 — 1957

Originally displayed at the Milan Show in November 1956, the 175 was the first Ducati production model to be offered with the single overhead-camshaft, bevel-driven engine. This engine was directly developed from Fabio Taglioni's original Ducati design, the racing-only 98cc Gran Sport Marianna of 1955.

Ultimately, the 175, at 62x57.8mm (174.5cc) was offered in a wide variety of guises. These included: S (Sport), T (Turismo), Americano (Custom), Formula 3 (Racer) and Motocross (Dirt Bike).

But by far the most popular model in the series was the Sport which, with a maximum speed of 84mph, was faster than many 500cc bikes that were available in the same era. Fuel consumption was also truly impressive, in that almost 2.78L/100km (100mpg) was possible with a light throttle hand.

Complementing this was a whip-free chassis that provided racer-like handling which, combined with a dry weight of

A 1958 Ducati 175 TS (Turismo Sport). The machine was the first series production Ducati bevel single.

only 103kg (a shade over 200lb) and large full-width aluminium brake hubs, made up a bike that went, handled and stopped better than anything in its class.

Engine: 174.5cc sohc 2v single 62x 57.8mm, air-cooled
Power: T - 11bhp at 7500rpm
S - 14bhp at 8000rpm
F - 316bhp at 9000rpm
Gearbox: 4-speed foot change
Final drive: chain
Weight: n/a
Top speed: T - 121kph (75mph), S - 135kph (84mph), F - 161kph (100mph)

DREVON
France 1946–53: These were French lightweights which had been fitted with engines bought in from Ydral and Aubier-Dunne.

DRS
Italy 1967: This 125cc Grand Prix racer was produced in relatively small numbers and bought only by privateers. The macine was a horizontal single two-stroke and featured a water-cooled cylinder and an air-cooled head. It was recorded as delivering 22bhp at 19,800rpm.

DS
Sweden (Hedemora) 1924–28: This short-lived 742cc V-twin was fitted with an engine from MAG. In its conception, it was aimed primarliy at buyers from the Swedish military market. Over the years, the Swedish military market has been responsible for sponsoring a number of unusual vehicles on two and four wheels.

DSH
Austria 1924–32: Three Austrian men, Herren Doller, Seildl und Hauler, lent their initials to the name of this firm. The company went on from 1924 to build unremarkable road machines. These machines were powered by imported British engines from firms such as Villiers and JAP, and then later on from MAG. The firm enjoyed some competition success with their racers. However, the tragic death of Rupert Karner on a 350cc DSH at the Hungarian TT in 1928 brought things to an abrupt halt, marking the beginning of a gap in production. It would not get going again until Franz Doller decided to instigate a revival of the marque a year later in 1929.

DUCATI MACH 1

1964

In the war of the 160kph (100mph) series production 250s, it was a straight fight between Japan and Italy, which meant in practice that it was between two motorcycles: Suzuki's Super Six and Ducati's Mach 1.

The Italian model debuted first, in 1964 in Britain on the eve of London's Earls Court Show and caused an instant sensation. It was clearly based around the 248cc Diana, which had been launched at the 1961 Bologna Motor Show

The 1964 250 Mach 1 was the world's first 160kph (100mph) two-fifty street bike.

and which featured the company's well-tried overhead-cam single cylinder, with unit construction of the engine and gearbox, bevel-driven camshaft and wet-sump lubrication.

In comparison with its forerunner, the Mach 1 featured five-speeds, a three-ring Borgo high compression forged piston, larger valves, stronger springs, a massive 29mm Dell'Orto SS1 racing-type carburettor, rear set footrests, distinctive red and silver paint, and an optional white face Veglia racing tachometer.

Testing a Mach 1 in *Motorcycle News*, Pat Braithwaite wrote: 'In a Lightning jet fighter Mach 1 plus a

bit takes you through the sound barrier. The new-for-1965 Ducati Mach 1 takes you through the 'ton barrier'. And it's only a 250.' This was very much a racer-for-the-road as the following comments reveal: 'A fast corner looms up. The gear ratios are as close as a racer's … change down twice and keel over to sample steering and roadholding second-to-none!'

Many Mach 1s found their way on to the race circuit. The cost in 1966 of the racer was around £350.

Engine: 248cc oc single, with vertical cylinder, air-cooled
Gearbox: unit 5-speed
Final drive: chain
Weight: 128kg (282lb)
Top speed: 161kph (100mph)

DUCATI 750 IMOLA

1972

V-twin engines have been around for many years but rarely have they been seen in the L-shape configuration chosen by Ducati's design chief, Fabio Taglioni, when he created the 750 GT prototype in 1970. Despite the layout's advantages, including the 90-degree vee of the cylinder which promoted smooth running, excellent cooling and a low centre of gravity, the need to accommodate the horizontal cylinder within the frame could lead to an over-long wheelbase and poor handling.

However, Moto Guzzi and Aermacchi had already demonstrated that a horizontal engine albeit of the single cylinder variety need be no disadvantage, and Taglioni partly solved the problem of length by sticking the front cylinder between the two front downtubes of the frame. The

result was a package that handled extraordinarily well. A bike that set out to capture the grand touring market quickly became a sportster and racer par excellence.

In April 1972, with a Desmo version of Ducati's 750 V-twin,

Ducati riders Paul Smart and Bruno Spaggiari beat the cream of the racing world – Honda, Triumph, BSA, Moto Guzzi and world champions, MV Agusta and star rider Giacomo Agostini – to win the inaugural Imola 200.

A 750 Imola with Desmo cylinder heads of the type used by Smart and Spaggiari to score a famous one–two at Imola in April 1972.

Except for its Desmo heads, larger 40mm carburettors and triple disc brakes, the Imola racer was remarkably similar to the 750 GT tourer, sharing its 748cc engine displacement and 80x74.4mm bore and stroke.

Ducati later offered a replica of the Imola model for sale: the 750 SS. Although it was street-legal, it was still a pure-bred racer at heart.

Engine: 748cc sohc, Desmo, 2v, V-twin, 80x74.4mm, air-cooled
Power: 70bhp at 9000 rpm
Gearbox: 5-speed foot change
Final drive: chain
Weight: n/a
Top speed: 233 kph (145 mph)

DUCATI NCR 900

1978

ESTABLISHED DURING 1967, its name taken from the initials of its founder's surnames (Nepoti, Caracchi and Rizzi), NCR was involved with Ducati on an official basis from 1972. This lasted until the retirement of Giorgio Nepoti and Rino Caracchi in 1995, the third founder, Rizzi, having left shortly after the partnership was founded.

During these years NCR, in co-operation with Taglioni, Farne and the rest of Ducati's experimental department, were responsible for the preparation of many of Ducati's most successful exploits, including the legendary comeback of Mike Hailwood in the Isle of Man TT in 1978.

Signed up by the Manchester-based Sports Motorcycles director,

Steve Wynne, Hailwood's machine was one of a small batch built by NCR in 1978. Although based around the existing bevel 900 SS, these bikes had several differences over the standard production street roadsters.

Items such as the sand-cast crankcases and dry clutch assemblies came from the NCR endurance racers. There were also

special bigger bore Malossi-modified Dell'Orto carburettors, while the frame was specially fabricated by the Bologna-based Daspa concern. Although similar to the production version, this bike was considerably lighter. The rear suspension units were of British Girling origin.

On 2 June 1978, Mike Hailwood lined up at the start against some

100 other riders, including the seven-times World Champion Phil Read, to compete on a works four-cylinder Honda. When the gruelling race was finally over, Hailwood and Ducati had become the new Formula 1 World

A 1978 NCR 900 bevel V-twin racer similar to the one ridden by Mike Hailwood.

Champions. This was, in fact, Ducati's first title after many attempts.

Engine: 863.9cc sohc, Desmo, 2v, V-twin, 86x74.4mm, air-cooled
Power: 90bhp at 8000rpm
Gearbox: 5-speed foot change
Final drive: chain
Weight: n/a
Top speed: 241kph (150mph)

DUCATI PANTAH   1979

During the mid-1970s, the Ducati management decided it needed a middleweight parallel twin with which to take on the Japanese. Chief designer Fabio Taglioni was against the idea from the start, wanting instead to build a smaller version of his L-shaped 90-degree V-twin.

Just as Taglioni had foreseen, the parallel twin proved a massive sales flop, and the result was that at last he was given the green light for his smaller displacement vee project. The product of his work was the Pantah – the originator of all of today's Ducati family of models – with its belt-driven Desmo top end.

First seen in prototype form in 1977, the Pantah entered production during 1979. The 1979 bike was the 500 SL, which featured bore and stroke dimensions of 74x58mm respectively. Ducati sources claimed 50bhp at 9050rpm. Other details of the machine's specification included electric starting, a five-speed gearbox, 45-cm (18-ins) cast-alloy wheels, triple Brembo cast-iron discs with

The 499cc Pantah 500SL arrived in 1979. It was the first production Ducati with belt driven camshafts and was the work of Fabio Taglioni.

two-piston callipers and a racing riding position. A half fairing came as standard equipment, as did a single/dual converter seat.

Incidentally, the 500 SL was not imported to Britain until 1980 and a 'Mark II' version debuted in 1981.

Also in 1981, the 500 was joined by a 600, still coded SL. This was the first Ducati production model to feature a hydraulic clutch.

By 1983, a 350 SL had been added. Also new that year was the touring-bias 350 XL and 600 TL models. Finally, also in 1983, came the 650 SL, the last of the line. Production ceased in 1986.

The other Pantah was the 600 TT F2 racer. This version sported a special Verlicchi-made frame, with monoshock rear suspension. The English rider, Tony Rutter won no fewer than four world championship titles during the early 1980s on the TT F2 racer, making it Ducati's most successful racing model until the advent of World Super Bike racing in the 1990s.

Engine: 498.9cc sohc, Desmo, 2v, V-twin, 94x58mm, air-cooled
Power: 45bhp at 9500 rpm
Gearbox: 5-speed foot change
Final drive: chain
Weight: n/a
Top speed: 193kph (120mph)

DS-MALTERRE
France (Paris) 1920–58: Before the war, Deblades et Sigran made 500cc overhead-valve bikes that seemed as if they were quite advanced when introduced in 1920. However, these bikes were to look distinctly less advanced when compared to other makes at the outbreak of World War II in 1939. In the postwar years, the company made lightweights with overhead-valve AMC engines (124 and 246cc) and 123 and 247cc Ydral two-strokes.

DUCATI (MOTOTRANS)
see **MOTOTRANS** (below).

DUCSON
Spain 1956–early 1970s: These Spanish machines of fairly enduring success were two-stroke 50cc engined mopeds.

DUMO
Germany 1924–25: This shortlived German model was in fact a sports version of the two-stroke 198cc Autinag. '

DUNJO
Spain (Barcelona) 1952: Although this was an interesting 32cc two-stroke diesel with variable compression ratio, apparently it failed to emerge from the drawing board to make it into series production.

DUNKLEY
England (Birmingham) 1913–20 and 1957–?60: The first series from this company began life fitted with motors of 199, 499, 750 and 988cc from Precision, before moving on to singles and twins from 300 to 700cc from JAP. A 350cc two-stroke engine was also available. After a long absence from the motorcycle market, the company returned and introduced the Whippet line of lightweights and scooters.

DUCATI 851

An 851 KI, of which 200 examples were built in 1988.

street and Kit supersport variants, with a total of 500 examples, named the Tricolore after the green, red and white colour scheme, being sold that year.

In 1988, Marco Lucchinelli won the first-ever round of the World Super Bike WSB on a racing version of the 851 at Donington Park, England. Shortly after, the factory built a racer for the general public, the first machines going on sale in 1990. Like Lucchinelli's works' machine, they displaced 94x64mm 888cc. Frenchman Raymond Roche aboard another factory-entered machine won Ducati's first WSB title in 1990. The 851 series was finally discontinued at the end of 1993 and it was replaced by the new 916.

Engine: 851cc dohc, Desmo, 4v, V-twin, 92x64mm, liquid-cooled
Power: Strada - 88bhp at 9250rpm Kit - 100bhp at 10,500rpm Racing 888cc 120bhp at 11,500rpm
Gearbox: 6-speed foot change
Final drive: chain
Weight: n/a
Top speed: Strada - 241 kph (150mph) Kit - 254kph (158mph) Racing - 273kph (170mph)

For some three decades, chief designer Fabio Taglioni's talent had set Ducati on its way. He was responsible for a truly vast array of bikes: singles, twins and even occasionally four-cylinder machines for both road and track. But the maestro chose largely to ignore the development potential inherent in four-valve cylinder heads. However, this omission was more than rectified by Taglioni's successor, Massimo Bordi.

The first prototype of Ducati's liquid-cooled, double overhead-camshaft, fuel-injected, four-valves-per-cylinder V-twin, made its debut at the 1986 French Bol d'Or 24-hour endurance race.

The Castiglioni brothers, who took over Ducati in May 1985, brought with them much-needed funding, which made it possible to develop a new family of bikes. The production model of the 92x64mm 851cc Superbike was unveiled to the public at the Milan Show in November 1987. The Superbikes went on sale early the following year in both Strada

DUCATI SUPERMONO

Almost two decades after the last of the bevel-drive singles had rolled off the Bologna factory's production lines, in the summer of 1993 a brand-new single was born, the racing-only Supermono.

Much of the engine design followed 851/888 V-twin practice, including the four-valves-per-cylinder, Weber/Marelli electronic fuel injection, six-speeds, dry clutch and Desmo valve system.

Ing. Massimo Bordi, who had replaced Fabio Taglioni as mechanical design chief, first tested his doppia bielletta (double conrod) Supermono engine on the bench in the winter of 1990. This prototype had a displacement of

The first series of hand-built Supermono racing-only machines appeared in 1992, using technology from the 888cc V-twin. The engine displaced 549cc.

95.6x66mm 487cc with tests revealing 62.5bhp. Next came a 95.6x70mm 502cc version, with power rising to 70bhp, before Bordi and his team finally settled on 100x70mm 549cc as the definitive layout. The power was now up to 75bhp measured at the gearbox output shaft. The second conrod was, in fact, in place of a conventional balance shaft.

If the engine was Bordi's domain, the chassis was very much the work of Claudio Domenicalli. The tubular steel frame was manufactured at the Cagiva works in Varese from a new high-resistance material

coded ALS 500 which provided the same stiffness as the more familiar 25 Cr M4 chrome-moly steel but at a lower cost.

The Bologna-based Verlicchi firm built the aluminium swinging arm, which pivoted on the crankcases like the belt-drive V-twins. The Swedish suspension specialists, Ohlins, were responsible for both the inverted front forks and single rear shock.

The third man in the creation of the Supermono was the South African Pierre Terreblanche, who drew out the bike's beautifully sculptured lines.

A Series 2 Supermono was built

A Series 2 Supermono racer. These had a larger 102mm cylinder bore size, giving a new engine displacement of 572cc. The Supermono was styled by Pierre Terblanche.

from late 1994 and was known as the 102. This was in reference to its 102mm bore size, which gave a new engine capacity of 572cc.

Engine: 549cc dohc, Desmo single, 4V, 100x74mm, liquid-cooled
Power: 75 bhp at 11,000rpm
Gearbox: 6-speed foot change
Final drive: chain
Weight: 123.5kg 272lb
Top speed: 241km/h 150mph

DUCATI 916   1994

FOR ALMOST THREE DECADES, Fabio Taglioni's design talents had set Ducati on its course. He had been responsible for creating the singles and later the V-twins that had made the Company a household name. But he had chosen largely to ignore the development potential of four-valve technology. This was left to his successor, Massimo Bordi.

The first of the Bordi four-valve-per-cylinder models made its debut at the 1986 Bol d'Or. Although it subsequently retired after eight of the 24 hours, it

The Ducati 916, designed by Massimo Tamburini, was perhaps the most exciting motorcycle of the 1990s.

showed great potential. The Cagiva takeover of Ducati in 1985

provided the funding for the project and the initial production

DUNSTALL
England 1967–unknown: This company was essentially a frame builder, which was responsible for making 'beefed up' frames. These frames were used to enclose high-output derivatives of engines from various manufacturers. Dunstall also made frames for engines where the manufacturer's standard frame was not able to withstand the power of its motor, and needed to be enclosed by something more durable.

DURAND
France 1920–23: This French firm was an assembler who used two types of engine – side-valve and ovehead-valve – which were supplied by Zurcher.

DURANDAL
France (Dijon) 1925–32: These machines – which were self-proclaimed as 'The Indestructible Motorcycle' – had a pressed-steel frame. They were fitted with engines from JAP, Zurcher and Chaise. There was also a works racer which was fitted with a Velocette KTT 348cc to give the 'Indestructable Motorcycle' its power.

DURYEA
USA 1897: Charles E. Duryea was well-known in the USA during the last decade of the twentieth century as a pioneer in the automobile trade. However, in 1897, he entered the new field of motorcycles and patented a design of one of these vehicles. It left the production line complete with a flat twin in the front wheel.

DUVAL
Belgium 1950–55: This company was an assembler who used mostly 123cc two-stroke engines from Royal Enfield.

A 2001 996R with a 998cc (100x63.5mm) fuel injected V-twin engine. It was the latest development in the 916 family series.

But the really big news was the arrival of the ground-breaking 916 street bike with its engine size matching its code number, achieved by increasing the stroke of the 888 from 64 to 66mm. Not only was the maximum power of almost 110bhp bigger than the 888, but engine torque was much improved.

But it was the balance of Massimo Tamborini's design that really set the 961 apart. There was a ram-air system (originally developed for Cagiva's 500 Grand Prix racer), a single-sided swinging-arm, patented adjustable steering, and if all that was not enough, a styling job that knocked the opposition for six!

Engine: 916cc dohc 90-degree V-twin, 4 valves per cylinder, liquid-cooled
Power: 110bph at 9000rpm
Final drive: chain
Gearbox: 6-speed
Weight : 19 kg (429lb)
Top speed : 259kph (161mph)

model, the 851, arrived in 1988, the same year as Marco Lucchinelli won the first ever WSB World Super Bike race at Donnington Park.

Compared to the stock 92x64mm 851cc, Lucchinelli's machine had 94x64mm 888cc.

Ducati then made many street, supersport and racing four-valvers,

including the SP (Sport Production). The 851 was discontinued in 1993, and in 1994 the Corsa Racing model was increased to 926cc.

DUNELT

ENGLAND 1919–35 AND 1957

THIS FIRM WAS AN offshoot of Dunford & Elliott, a Sheffield steel producer, but was based in Birmingham. A Dunelt bike was first seen at the Olympia Show in 1919 but was not put into production for a year. Its engine differed from others in being a 499cc two-stroke single with a double-diameter piston and cylinder, iimproving the crankcase compression at the expense of increasing the length and weight of the piston. Assembly was tricky.

The rest of the engine followed standard design, was inclined in the frame and drove a three-speed gearbox with belt final drive, soon replaced by chain. Thanks to the engine design and a massive external flywheel, the Dunelt could pull like a steam engine from very low speeds but acceleration was gradual. Thus this bike was ideal for sidecar work and it was offered as a complete outfit in various guises.

Three other versions were added for 1923 and no less than eight for the following year, including

Dunelt adopted Villiers two-stroke engines in the 1930s and this example was a 1932 V2 model fitted with the 346cc engine and three-speed gearbox.

outfits of commercial van, truck and box carrier types. By 1925, all models had chain drive and mechanical lubrication via a Pilgrim pump. The year also brought fire engine and milk truck variants, with what appeared to be a saddle tank, but was two tanks with a centre join and an oil tank built into one.

This long list of 499cc models was

joined by one of 249cc for 1926, which followed the same lines for its engine. Its performance matched that of the larger model and a sports version was added for 1927. A de luxe model came in the next year for the 499cc model. There were just three versions of the 249cc two-stroke for 1929 but they were joined by the first Dunelt four-stroke with a 348cc Sturmey-Archer overhead-valve engine.

In 1929 the firm won the prestigious Maudes Trophy using the overhead-valve 350. They repeated this success the following year with a new 495cc overhead-valve model. The 1930s saw the end for the 249cc two-stroke, but in 1930 they listed a model with a 249cc overhead camshaft engine of the face-cam type.

The overhead camshaft engine proved too noisy to be a success so the 1931 range comprised machines with 297 and 598cc side-valve plus 348 and 495cc overhead-valve Sturmey-Archer engines, along with one using a

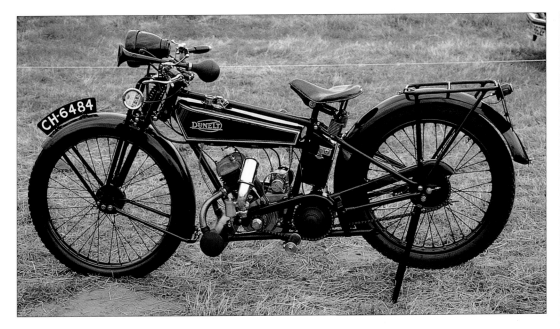

A double-diameter piston was a feature of Dunelt two-stroke engines up to 1930. This model is an earlier machine from the vintage years.

346cc Villiers. All were given bird names such as Cygnet, Drake or Heron. Late in 1931, manufacture was transferred from Birmingham to Sheffield and the machines were given the name of Sheffield-Dunelt for a year or two.

With much the same range, it was back to model codes for 1932, with the addition of a 148cc Villiers lightweight. For 1933, 249cc Villiers and 248cc overhead-valve Python models were added, while for 1934, there were 148 and 249cc Villiers plus 248 and 495cc overhead-valve Python engines. But time was running out for Dunelt. Their range down to the two Villiers models and 245 and 490cc overhead-valve JAP machines, in 1935, they closed down. The name reappeared briefly in 1957, when it was revived for a 50cc moped.

DURKOPP

GERMANY 1901–1960

BEST REMEMBERED FOR the contribution to the postwar scooter boom, the Durkopp marque was one of the true pioneers of German motorcycling. Founded in Bielefeld in 1867 by Nikolaus Durkopp, the company made bicycles from 1989 and motorcycles as early as 1901. By 1905 it made not only singles and V-twins, but also an air-cooled in-line four-cylinder model.

Durkopp ceased motorcycle production just prior to the outbreak of World War I, but resumed in the 1930s with bicycles powered by auxiliary 'clip-on' engines of 60, 75 and 98cc capacities. 'Real' bikes were not offered again until 1949 when models powered by 98cc Sachs and 123cc Ardie and Ilo engines appeared.

In 1951 the Bielefeld marque debuted a new 150cc machine fitted with a Durkopp-made engine, quickly followed by similar 175 and 200cc models. From then on no further proprietary engines were

Almost 25,000 Diana scooters were built by the Bielefeld-based Durkopp marque between 1954 until two-wheeled production ceased in 1960.

employed. In 1954 Durkopp introduced the 194cc Diana scooter. This was an exceptionally high-quality product offering a stylish and fast performance and good handling to equal any scooter on the road. The Diana was the cornerstone to Durkopp's two-wheel business during the mid-1950s boom and helped it to weather the depression that followed when most of its other models were taken out of production. But unlike many other

bike builders, Durkopp was a flourishing general engineering concern and was not wholly reliant on motorcycle business.

Production of the various Diana models ceased in 1960, by which time 24,963 had been manufactured.

EADIE

LONG BEFORE ALBERT EADIE produced a motorcycle he was well known for his bicycle coaster hub with back-pedalling brake. In due course, he set up a factory to make sewing machines and rifle parts as well as bicycles. One of his brand names was Royal Enfield, adopted after winning an arms contract, which eventually led to the motorcycle firm of that name. In 1898, Eadie produced a tricycle, which was a virtual copy of the De Dion design, using the engine from that firm located behind the rear axle, so it lacked the even weight distribution of others.

Eadie motorcycles soon followed using a heavy-duty bicycle frame in the format of the time. Various engines from firms such as De Dion, MMC and Minerva were fitted; the last usually hung from the frame downtube. Rigid or braced forks were the norm, as was direct belt drive with options of an adjustable engine pulley and hub gears for the rear wheel. As a parts supplier, Eadie was in the best position to note engineering trends, reflected in his own machines. He could also learn from others' mistakes.

The Eadie machines soon left the market as the Royal Enfield marque became dominant.

However, Albert continued to be a prominent figure in the motorcycle world. Early in 1907, his company amalgamated with BSA and he joined the main board of that firm, becoming involved with the design of their first motorcycle of 1910.

EGLI

THE SWISS RACER and engineer Fritz Egli leapt to international fame in the 1960s with the Egli-Vincent, the classic V-twin engine in a modern, racing frame that offered significantly better handling than the original Vincent chassis. Despite the fact that the only engines available to him were already at least 12 years old, the Egli-Vincent was a competitive racing machine and remained so for some years.

Egli's secret then, and in subsequent machines, lay to a considerable extent in keeping

Left: An Egli-Kawasaki, fitted with a tuned Kawasaki 900 engine mounted in a light, sweet-handling frame.

Below left: Switzerland's answer to Buell: a familiar looking V-twin but in a frame actually designed to stop, go and turn corners.

Below: The purist's Egli – the lovely Egli-Vincent. Arguably the most beautiful V-twin of all time in one of the finest frames of its era.

weight to the minimum through the use of light-alloys and ingenious design, a salutary reminder that there are two sides to the power-to-weight equation. In addition to this, Egli's tuning skills were (and are) legendary, so he could extract the maximum possible power from any given engine. His Honda Red Baron sported the transverse six-cylinder taken out to 1200cc, yet it weighed only 215kg (473lb), not exactly a lightweight you might say, until you consider the capacity. The later Egli-Kawasaki Bonneville was taken out to 1200cc again, and weighed in at even less at 205kg (451lb).

An early user of Kevlar-reinforced composites, Egli also experimented with forced induction: a Kawasaki-based four-cylinder, taken out to 1425cc, delivered 300bhp at the rear wheel. His experience with very high power outputs led to Pirelli commissions for tyre research.

At the time of writing, Egli was still working his magic on a wide range of machines, as disparate as the mighty V-Max and the lowly Enfield Bullet. His work does not come cheap, but there are few, if any, with more experience and know-how.

ELMECA-GILERA

ITALY 1960–80

AFTER IT PULLED THE PLUG on Grand Prix racing at the end of the 1950s, the famous Gilera marque used trials as an effective means of generating publicity.

Following the Piaggio takeover of Gilera in 1969, interest in dirt bikes continued, with much of the development being done in conjunction with the Cafesse (near Turin) Elmeca concern. This company was an established off-road specialist that had also been involved with Gilera before the Piaggio buy-out. In fact, customer-versions of the trials bikes were sold under the Elmeca-Gilera brand name.

Gilera withdrew at the end of 1974 and thereafter Elmeca built a number of Gilera-inspired designs under licence, until Gilera took control again in 1980. But until that year, Elmeca made a big impact in off-road sport. This was made not only in the home market of Italy, but also on the European stage.

Elmeca were able to make use of the excellent rotary-valve two-stroke engine which had been introduced by Gilera in 1968. Various versions were eventually built by the company, including 100, 125 and 175cc.

An updated 54x54mm (123.5cc) engine was ready for the 1973 season. Success was soon forthcoming, with victory in that year's European two-day enduro championship series. Elmeca-Gilera machines were also used that year by the Italian national squad in the Silver Vase Trophy at the ISDT (International Six-Days Trial).

For 1974, a new 175 was developed, which featured new 61x59.5mm bore and stroke dimensions. Like its smaller brother, it had rotary-valve induction and six-speeds.

For two decades the Elmeca concern had close connections with the Gilera factory, building specialised dirt bikes like this 1976 125 Regolarita model.

Production versions of these machines were to remain competitive until they were outpaced by a new breed of enduro bike, such as SWM and KTM, which arrived on the scene from 1977 onwards.

An Elmeca-Gilera 125 motocross bike was built from 1976 until 1979, which utilised a tuned version of the Elmeca-Gilera enduro engine. It differed from the original works Gilera models in that it had a shorter stroke of 53.6mm, instead of 54mm. This shorter stroke gave an engine size of 122.7cc. Producing 24bhp and ridden by Dario Nani, the Elmeca-Gilera dirt racer won the 1978 Italian Motocross title.

EAGLE
USA 1910–15: These machines had Spacke 4hp singles and 7hp V-twins.

EBE
Sweden (Amal) 1919–30: In 1925 this firm were making 172 and 598cc overhead-valve singles and their 173cc auxiliary cycle motor.

EBER
Germany (Einbau-Ebersach) 1924–28: This firm assembled a range of 350- and 500cc-engined machines.

EBO
England (Leicester) 1910–15: Edward Boulter used Precision engines and some JAP V-twins.

EBS
Germany (Berlin) 1924–30: This firm built side-valve and overhead-valve machines, using their own singles of 198 to 496cc, and a 796cc V-twin.

EBU-STAR
Japan 1952–55: These 250cc V-twins were unusual; one cylinder pointed forward, the other up.

ECHO
Japan (Tokyo) late 1950s–early 1960s: Echo made 123 and 148cc two-stroke lightweights and a scooter, the Pandra.

ECONOMIC
England 1921–23: The Economic's 165cc flat twin was mounted in line in early machines, and transide-valversely in later ones.

EDETA
Spain (Barcelona) 1951–60: These were two-stroke 173cc lightweights.

EDMONTON
England 1903–c.1910: This pioneer assembler used Minerva and Fafnir engines.

EDMUND
England (Chester) 1907–24: This firm installed engines from various manufacturers — Barr & Stroud, Blackburne, Fafnir, JAP and MAG — in their own well-made frames, some of which were sprung.

EFA
Netherlands 1950s: This 34cc auxiliary cycle motor weighed 6kg (13lb) and gave three-quarters horsepower at 4000rpm, and a speed of 24kph (15mph).

EMC

JOSEF EHRLICH CAME to the UK from Austria in 1937 and by 1939 he was testing a 240cc engine of his own making in an old Francis-Barnett machine at the Brooklands racetrack. He adopted the split-single, two-stroke type of design with a side inlet and rear exhaust.

Ehrlich launched a 345cc EMC in 1947 with the same split-single engine whose block had unusual rectangular fins of alternating depth. Petroil lubrication was used for the tourer and a Pilgrim pump for the sports, while both had magneto ignition. The engine drove a four-speed gearbox and this went into a rigid duplex frame with Dowty Oleomatic forks. Ehrlich claimed over 2.75L/100km

(100mpg), but owners found it closer to 5.5L/100km (50mpg). The 345s were expensive but continued until 1953.

In 1951, Ehrlich built a 125cc road-racing model with an Austrian Puch split-single engine, while 1952 saw a road model with a 125cc JAP two-stroke engine on show at Earls Court in London.

The firm was wound up in 1953 but Ehrlich, while remaining involved with racing for many years, in 1982 became involved

Below: The 1947 EMC with its 345cc split-single, two-stroke engine and four-speed Burman gearbox installed in a duplex, rigid frame with telescopic forks.

Above: The engine of the EMC with its two bores in tandem, inlet into the rear one, and oil pump driven from the chain sprocket for the magneto drive.

with the Waddon, which became an EMC in 1983, still with the Rotax tandem-twin, two-stroke engine unit. It won the Junior 250cc TT in 1983, 1984 and 1987.

ERCOLI CAVALLONE

THE V-TWIN ENGINE layout became popular when it was realised that it was easy to add a second cylinder to a single and the result fitted so neatly into the diamond frame. Since then, it has always been with us.

The angle between the cylinders has varied over the years, although some firms, such as Harley-

Davidson, have stuck to their first choice. The angle used has an effect on engine balance and while 90 degrees has considerable advantages, angles between 45 and 120 degrees have been used. Other major sales assets include the fact that twin carburettors are desirable and the beat of the exhaust due to the uneven firing of the V-twin.

Nearly all V-twins are four-strokes but a very few have been two-strokes and Ercoli Cavallone was one of the few. The detailed design of the engine followed conventional two-stroke practice with induction controlled by the piston into the crankcase, transfer via ports to the cylinder and exhaust from the cylinder side.

The engine was built in-unit with the gearbox but other than that and the use of the two-stroke cycle, the machine was conventional and much as others of the era.

As with other attempts to be different at that time, few were sold and the machine consequently failed to make any real impact on the market.

ESO

THE ESO (ACE) STORY began in 1949, when two Czechs, Vaclav Stanislav and Jaroslav Simandl, veteran competitors from pre-war

days, returned home from riding in the ISDT in England. There they had also been hunting parts for JAP speedway engine spares. At

this time, if you wanted to go speedway racing your only option was the famous JAP 500 overhead-valve single.

Stanislav had managed to purchase a con-rod for his JAP engine but he still needed a camshaft, so his friend Simandl offered to make it. When Stanislav poured scorn on this, Simandl went one better and declared he could build a complete engine, adding that it would be better than the JAP! In fact, due to demand, he actually built not one, but eight engines, four of which were for spare parts.

As far as designer Simandl was concerned, that was the end of the story, but official interest from both the Czech Sports Commission and Motokov resulted in the project being developed further. One of the first real commercial decisions was to

display the new engine in Sweden later in 1949. The original Eso (499cc) engine was based on the JAP, which by then was over 20 years old. Its success led not only to more orders but to participation in road racing, and track events.

During the early 1950s, Eso grew rapidly, resulting in a new short-stroke engine. Coded S-45 (because tests soon proved 45bhp), its 88x81.7mm (497cc) dimensions proved ideal on the long sand tracks of Europe where top end speed was all-important.

In 1954, Jaroslav Cervinka took over as chief designer; he was

later to win fame as the creator of the four-valve Jawa speedway engine.

The next step was that Eso merged with Jawa, although it was not until January 1964 that Eso was to lose its own identity.

The Jawa speedway engine (read Eso) went on to world-domination of the shale sport over the following decades.

The Eso marque was founded by Valav Stanislav and Jaroslav Simandl in 1949. This S45 speedway bike dates from 1959; it used a 499cc ohv engine.

EXCELSIOR USA 1907–31

THE EXCELSIOR MOTOR Manufacturing & Supply Company of Chicago, Illinois, was a major player on the US motorcycle scene for many years and had no connection with an obscure firm of the same name and town that built the De Luxe machines under several labels. Nor did it have any connection with the older British Excelsior firm and, to avoid confusion, machines sold in the UK were badged as the American-X. In 1925, they took the name Super-X and used this both at home and abroad.

The early Excelsior was typical of the time with a 30cid, F-head, single-cylinder engine with automatic inlet valve mounted upright in a diamond frame with leading-link front forks and direct

belt drive. The cycle parts were period and included pedalling gear.

A 50cid V-twin appeared in 1910, its cylinders set at the usual 45-degree angle and with

By 1915 the Excelsior 61cid V-twin had three speeds and all-chain drive in line with its main American rivals. It continued to use the F-head engine type.

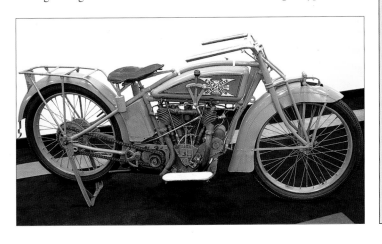

A trailing-link front fork controlled by a leaf spring became an Excelsior feature in 1914 along with two speeds, but pedalling gear remained.

version, both of which adopted a new trailing-link front fork and the dark-blue finish of the Henderson four after Schwinn had bought that company in 1917. Production of the four then took precedence, since it was the better one to sell in that capacity market against the Harley and Indian twins.

The twin continued as an F-head with the carburettor between the cylinders and the magneto on the front of the crankcase. The three-speed gearbox continued as before but the trailing-link forks connected to a single, enclosed spring fitted in front of the headstock and both brakes went into the rear-wheel hub. The Excelsior big twins continued in this form until 1925 but were then replaced by the Super-X.

Hitherto in 1920, the firm's interest in racing had led them to build some factory team machines with V-twin engines having overhead-camshafts. These were on the lines of the Cyclone with shaft and bevel drive to each camshaft and the front-mounted magneto but they weren't copies. Sadly, a team rider was killed in practice at their first outing, the team withdrew, interest and development flagged and the potential of the design was never fully realised.

Excelsior introduced a new model in 1925, the Super-X that featured unit construction of its 45cid V-twin engine and three-speed gearbox. Primary drive was by a train of three helical gears so the engine continued to turn in its

mechanical inlet valves. It was joined by a 61cid version for the following year when Ignaz Schwinn took over the company. From 1913, only the V-twin was listed, but in 1914 all-chain drive and two speeds came along with leaf-spring, trailing-link front forks. In 1915, the transmission moved on to a cross-over, three-speed gearbox, primary drive was on the left, along with the kick-start, and the final drive on the right.

A lightweight model joined the twin in 1914 but this was really the British Triumph Junior model built under licence. It had a 225cc two-stroke engine with large external flywheel built in-unit with a chain-driven, two-speed gearbox with belt final drive. This had magneto ignition, no clutch or kick-start, and went into a loop frame with rocking forks. It was only built for a few years.

The V-twins took Excelsior into contention with Indian in competition from 1911 and in the following year one of their machines was timed at 160kph (100mph) on a board track near Los Angeles, California. Other successes followed, still with the F-head engines against the Indian eight-valve types, and these machines were based on stock ones with tuned engines, open exhausts and stripped of all non-

Above: A close-up of the 1914 Excelsior 61cid engine, with the cylinders at 45 degrees and magneto out in front, mounted in a substantial frame.

Right: By 1914, the Excelsior badge had taken this form, in part to distinguish it from the UK marque, and later continued for the Super-X models.

essentials. By 1915, they were listed as 'Big Valve' racers due to the considerable size of both inlet and exhaust valves.

After World War I, the 61cid twin was joined by a 74cid

normal direction, which was important for the lubrication of its internals. The gears were enclosed by a cast-aluminium oil bath case and the gearbox continued to be the cross-over type so the final drive remained on the right but the kick-start pedal was moved over to the same, more usual, side.

The last year of the earlier Excelsior with separate gearbox was 1924 but the pedals indicate an older machine.

The Super-X engine also kept to the F-head valve layout, front-mounted magneto and single carburettor between the cylinders.

The whole unit went into a duplex frame and a return was made to leading-link front forks. It made for a handsome machine and the stock model was soon followed by a factory racing version with an overhead-valve engine for 1926, which had some successes before the firm turned more to hill climbs.

Revisions to style came in 1929 for the Super-X when the fuel tanks adopted a more streamlined shape and the saddle tank form already popular in Europe. This gave the machine a good style for the new decade but early in 1931 Ignaz Schwinn brought all Excelsior and Henderson motorcycle production to a halt. He clearly saw that the market for such machines would shrink more during the Depression so turned to his many other business interests, which included the Schwinn bicycle.

Years later, in 1998, an attempt was made to revive the name, with production a possibility in the new century. However, it is as a firm that took on Harley-Davidson and Indian at their own game that Excelsior and the Super-X are best remembered.

EXCELSIOR SUPER-X   1925

The Excelsior was first sold in the UK as American-X from 1921 to distinguish the make from the British firm of the same name.

The new model of 1925 continued with the Super-X name. It enabled the firm to enter the 750cc class and although it introduced unit construction, it kept the F-head engine type. Thus, as with earlier engines, there was a single rocker on each cylinder head with these having the inlet manifold plus carburettor between them. The exhausts ran down to a single pipe.

Thanks to the unit construction, the primary drive was by a train of gears enclosed by the engine unit castings, making a much neater and cleaner arrangement. The final-drive chain went on the right and the whole engine unit was housed in a sturdy duplex frame with single top tube carrying the twin tanks, the left for petrol and oil, the right for petrol only, resulting in three tank caps. The hand gear-change lever went on the left side of the nicely styled tanks, which had an instrument

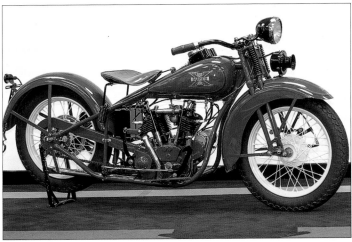

A 1931 version of the Super-X Excelsior introduced in 1925 with its unit construction, gear primary drive, leading-link forks and F-head engine.

panel mounted on top in the American style of the era.

The Super-X was also available on the market in a Super Sport version with a higher compression ratio and the model performed well on board and dirt tracks before turning more to hill climbs, which brought even further success.

Engine: 746cc ioe V-twin, 76.2x81.75mm, air-cooled
Power: n/a
Gearbox: unit 3-speed hand change
Final drive: chain
Weight: 150kg (330lb)
Top speed: n/a

EXCELSIOR

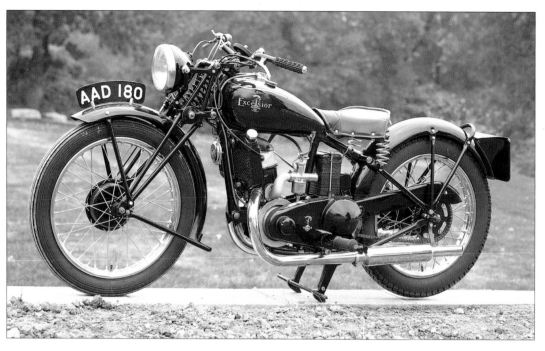

WHAT IS GENERALLY regarded as the UK's oldest motorcycle manufacturer began life as Bayliss, Thomas and Company, building bicycles in Coventry, the capital of British pedal power and a focal point for the emerging motorcycle industry. In around 1896, they became possibly the first British manufacturer of powered two-wheelers, initially using 1¼hp single-cylinder motors by Minerva.

By 1902, engines supplied by MMC were favoured. Potential customers were offered free tests on these machines, the start of a forward-thinking and, later, competition-oriented policy with which the company would always be associated. In 1903, Harry Martin became the first man to break the mile-a-minute barrier when he covered 1.6km (1 mile) at Dublin's Phoenix Park in 59.8 seconds, riding a Bayliss Thomas.

In 1910, by which time motorcycle production was well established, the name Excelsior Motor Company Ltd. was adopted. The Excelsior logo, depicting a mountaineer holding a banner, appeared on the company's bicycles in 1874. However, with German and American companies sharing the same name, British Excelsiors sold in Europe retained the Bayliss Thomas name into the 1930s. During the 1920s, cars were also built under the name.

After World War I, control passed to R. Walker and Sons and motorcycle production moved to Tyseley, Birmingham, in England. The Walkers – Reginald and son Eric — built up a broad range of models from 98 to 1000cc, most with bought-in Blackburne, JAP and Villiers engines. Most were singles, including a monstrous, 850cc Condor-engined model, although a few Blackburne-engined V-twins were built. Road

Generally considered to be Britain's first manufacturer of motorcycles, Excelsior produced powered two-wheelers for almost 70 years. The logo dates from 1874.

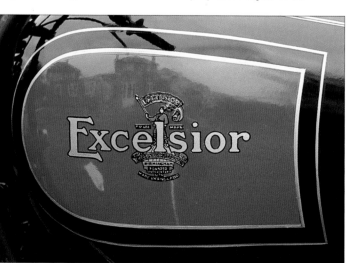

Excelsior made well-designed machines. Road racing was high on the company's agenda, but success on the track did not translate into sales.

racing was invariably high on the agenda, with JAP-engined machines of 173 and 248cc. The factory's first major success came with victory in the 1929 Lightweight TT, with Leslie Crabtree riding. A road-going 'replica' of Crabtree's machine, the B14, was quickly created for an eager public, and became Excelsior's premier model.

Like New Imperial, Excelsior had the misfortune to reach their heyday in the depths of the

Depression. Two years later, at Tat in Hungary, the company came close to capturing the world speed record when their Silver Comet recorded 262kph (163mph). This astounding device was powered by a supercharged 1000cc JAP V-twin, running at 15 psi boost and producing 100bhp at 5400rpm.

More successful was the legendary Blackburne-engined 'Mechanical Marvel' developed by Ike Hatch, on which Syd Gleave won the 1933 Lightweight TT with a fastest lap of 116.87kph (72.62mph). So-called because of its complexity, this 250cc single had twin carburettors, twin camshafts and a pushrod-operated four-valve radial cylinder head.

Unfortunately, these successes failed to reap their reward in sales since they coincided with the global economic slump following the Wall Street Crash in the USA. Equally, the Mechanical Marvel's complexity ensured that there would be no replicas. Instead, Excelsior set about creating a new range of overhead-camshaft models that would become the Manxman series. Also striking in its way was a series of 249cc single-cylinder, liquid-cooled two-stroke models, launched in 1933 and culminating in the D9 Viking.

Despite these fine machines, commercial success was moderate and the firm's bread and butter were humbler two-strokes. Having launched the 98cc Villiers-engined Autobyke, a forerunner of the commuter moped in 1937, they continued in similarly low-key manner when peace returned after World War II.

Incidentally, Excelsior also built a 98cc two-stroke model, the Sprite, for the Corgi company, and the 'Welbike' for military use in World War II.

The 98cc Consort, which initially sold well despite its crudeness, employed a mere two speeds, 2.8bhp and little by way of suspension. The Talisman, however, was out of a completely different mould, yet still failed to prosper. In the early 1960s, the 148cc Monarch, which was an attempt to cash in on the scooter boom, was no more successful and Excelsior folded in 1965. The factory was sold to the Britax concern.

EXCELSIOR MANXMAN 250 ROADSTER   1936

– devised a simpler and more elegant overhead-camshaft single, which used a conventional bevel-driven overhead-cam.

The Manxman was first unveiled in 248cc form at London's Olympia Motorcycle Show of 1934. In 1936, a racing four-valve version was built and placed second in the Lightweight TTs of 1936 and 1937.

Engine: 246cc ohc single, 63x79mm, air-cooled
Power: 16bhp at 5000rpm
Gearbox: 4-speed foot change
Final drive: chain
Weight: 135kg (297lb)
Top speed: 121kph (75mph)

Above: A modernised, sprung-framed 348cc Excelsior Manxman, being raced at England's Cadwell Park circuit.

Right: The Manxman in standard, rigid-frame trim. The four-valve single was solidly engineered and built in 250, 350 and 500cc sizes.

This machine came about because its creators – Hatch and Walker – were horrified at the prospect of putting anything so complex as the Mechanical Marvel into private hands. Instead, Hatch – Blackburne's chief engine designer

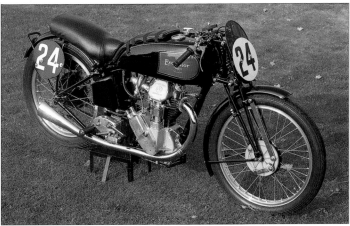

EXCELSIOR TALISMAN   1949

Although always a disappointing seller, the Talisman, unveiled late in 1949, was a far more sophisticated machine than most other two-stroke models of the era. The twin-cylinder engine featured a built-up 180 degree crankshaft; a layout which would become standard on the all-conquering Japanese machines 20 years later. However, unit construction was not used. Instead, a four-speed Albion gearbox bolted to the rear of the engine.

From the outset, the Talisman featured telescopic front suspension with a plunger rear end. In 1953, the Talisman Sport arrived, with a true swing-arm rear end, twin Amal carburettors and greater cylinder-head finning for improved cooling. In 1959 capacity increased to 328cc for the Special Talisman, with the fashionable enclosed rear bodywork.

Engine: 244cc two-stroke parallel twin, 50x62mm, air-cooled
Power: 12bhp at 4000rpm
Gearbox: 4-speed foot change
Final drive: chain
Weight: 113kg (250lb)
Top speed: 105kph (65mph)

Despite a relatively advanced specification, the Talisman two-stroke twin was not a sales success. This is an early, 244cc spring-hub example.

EXCELSIOR-HENDERSON

USA 1999–

AT FIRST GLANCE, the Excelsior-Henderson of Belle Plaine, Minnesota, was just another Harley-Davidson clone. Upon closer examination, it turned out to be about as far from the Milwaukee machine as a big V-twin aimed at the American market could be. There was also the enormous difference that Excelsior-Henderson was intended from the first to be a volume producer, making 20,000 machines a year, rather than a specialist manufacturing a few machines on a custom basis. At the time of writing, in fact, they were operating at considerably less than capacity and were having the usual financing problems that can beset start-ups which, to some extent, was the result of casting their financial net too wide at the initial offering, with no fewer than 17,000 initial investors. All (including the founders) lost their entire equity stake in the financial reorganisation, which happened on 24 May 2000.

From an engineering viewpoint, however, the basic difference between an Excelsior-Henderson and just about any other 'clone' was the engine. Instead of the 'knife-and-fork' type, the 50-degree, 93x102mm (1386cc) air-cooled V-twin was a modern, offset design with the two con rods (with removable caps and bearings) running side by side on a forged crankshaft. Both the offset and the increased cylinder angle (5 degrees greater than Harley-Davidson), allowed significantly better cooling.

Better still, each cylinder head had twin, chain-driven camshafts

Is the revived Excelsior-Henderson a misguided attempt to modernise an outdated design, or a clever update of a classic design? Or perhaps both? You decide!

and four valves, although unexpectedly for an overhead-camshaft design, actual valve operation was reportedly hydraulic. Fuel injection was designed in from the start. This was once again made easier by that small increase in cylinder angle. Given these specifications, the actual power output — reported as 'in the sixties' [brake horsepower] — is surprisingly low since 45-50bhp/litre had been achieved on plenty of road-going bikes, even big V-twins, by the end of the 1920s.

There are numerous other mechanical innovations, some that are technically interesting, some that are imposed by the styling requirements of the American 'big cruiser' market, and some that are both. For instance, the cam chains are concealed within the oversized cylinder outline, which looks very clean but is of dubious merit from an engineering viewpoint: it is an invitation to distortion if the machine is ridden very hard, although given the low power output of the engine, this is perhaps not a machine to be ridden very hard. Also, test reports indicate bad vibration periods at around 2200rpm and again after 3500rpm, all the way up to the point where the rev-limiter comes in and cuts the spark to one cylinder at 5500 rpm.

Another unusual feature is an hydraulic clutch, which reduces maintenance and potentially makes clutch operation easier but, of course, it costs more, weighs more and is more difficult to service on those rare occasions when it does need anything doing to it. To pass the Californian emission regulations the Excelsior-Henderson had only to add an evaporative emission canister, two valves and some extra hoses.

The styling, too, was unique. The aim was to re-create the look of the old Excelsiors, right down to the (apparently) rigid rear end, although, of course, it is a sprung monoshock. They even re-created the way in which the forks went through the front mudguard, something that was rather more successful in the 1930s, when forks and tyres were much skinnier.

Many other features were strictly conventional. The five-speed foot-change gearbox drives the rear wheel by belt; there are footboards in the American cruiser style, which were reportedly all too easy to ground, and the machine was, to European eyes, grossly overweight at 314kg (690lb). A single 29cm (11.5ins) front disk (with four-pot callipers) was typically American: elsewhere in the world, twin, smaller disks might be more usual. Unexpectedly, the rear brake is the same size as the front brake.

The top speed of this machine is not stated and this is perhaps academic anyway because of the vibration problems.

Despite (or perhaps because of) its technical innovations, the new V-twin is vast, creating the impression of an engine with a motorcycle attached.

EXPRESS

GERMANY 1903–58

EXPRESS-WERKE AG was founded in Neumarkt, Nurnberg in 1882 for the purpose of manufacturing pedal cycles. Then, in 1903, it became one of the early pioneers of the German motorcycle industry by adding a bought-in Fafnir engine to offer its first powered two-wheeler. Over the next 55 years, the company was to forge ahead and run a profitable business but it never became a really big name in the domestic industry as did BMW, DKW or NSU.

In 1904, Express built their first racing model; this was a V-twin with, for the time, the mighty power output of 8bhp!

After World War I Express reverted to its pedal cycle business but in 1933 it tried to break into the motorcycle sector again, with a range of two-stroke lightweights. With the coming of war it returned to bicycles and was the major supplier of these to the German armed forces throughout World War II.

Postwar, Express made a comeback and by 1950 it was making large numbers of pedal cycles. It also manufactured a new range of lightweight motorcycles powered by Fichtel and Sachs engines.

EXPRESS RADEX 255

EXPRESSWERKE AKTIENGESELLSCHAFT NEUMARKT (OPF.) BEI NÜRNBERG

Through the first half of the decade, the Express works was at full stretch, even working round-the-clock in an attempt to meet demand from a transport-starved German population. This led Express to develop a host of sophisticated new models up to 250cc.

During the recession of 1956 and 1957, Express managed to sell its products, whereas many other famous names struggled.

Founded in 1882, Express produced its first motorcycle in 1903. This 1954 Radex 255, with a Sachs two-stroke engine, featured unusual trailing-link front forks.

At the beginning of 1958, there was little to suggest an upset, with the company having just celebrated its 75th year, but in November it merged with DKW and Victoria to form Zweirad Union.

EYSINK

NETHERLANDS 1899–LATE 1970s

EYSINK LASTED FOR AROUND 75 years without ever setting the world alight; they are almost ignored by motorcycle historians.

D.H. Eysink founded the company in 1886 and had become interested in automobiles and motorcycles by the turn of the century. By World War I, their 365

and 425cc singles were widely used by the Dutch Army; there were also 366 and 409cc singles, and a 774cc in-house V-twin.

In 1921 came a 702cc flat twin, but their 1926 range used a variety of bought-in engines of between 147and 1150cc. After the war, Villiers engines were mostly used.

Eysink was the only Dutch motorcycle marque to compete in road racing before and after World War II, and to compete in a pre-war Isle of Man TT race in 1934. After the war, they built a series of small capacity two-strokes.

In 1948, the 125cc class was introduced at the annual Dutch TT, and a local Eysink emerged victorious. In 1949 an official world series was introduced, including the 125cc class, but Eysink machines fared badly. In 1955, their racing days ended.

The company produced 98 and 250cc scooters and, until the late 1970s, offered tandem bicycles and sports mopeds.

The Dutch Eysink concern lasted for more than 75 years. During this time it built a wide range of road and competition bikes. This is one of their earliest efforts.

FAFNIR

IN THE ERA BEFORE World War I, Fafnir was a major supplier of engines to other firms and also manufactured complete machines under its name for a short time. The company came early into the field in 1900 with engines and later acquired a licence from Werner to build engines in their form.

Made by the Aix-la-Chapelle Steel Works, Fafnir engines were typical of their day, with cylinder and head in one, automatic inlet valve, side exhaust valve, vertically split crankcase and a Fafnir spray carburettor. For 1903, two sizes were listed, the two-and-a-quarter horsepower of 289cc and the 3hp of 353cc, both designed to run at 1800–2000rpm.

These machines were typical of the era, with adjustable pulleys, hub gears and direct belt drive, but by 1905 they were fitted with a countershaft gearbox. At around the same time, the automatic inlet valves were modified to positive opening by adding camshaft, pushrod and rocker.

The firm soon stopped manufacturing the motorcycles, preferring to concentrate on engines alone. They supplied these to many home market companies

The Fafnir was typical of its time with belt drive from an adjustable pulley with clutch. The engine had overhead inlet valves.

and exported them to other European firms. In this way, they could devote their time and energies to improving the one unit rather than having to develop a complete machine.

Singles and twins continued to be listed in a range of capacities and both air- and water-cooling

Fafnir only built complete machines for a few years, afterwards concentrating on supplying engines to other firms.

were used, the latter more common for the twins. The firm continued to operate in this manner until 1914.

FANTIC

FOUNDED IN 1968 by Henry Keppel Hasselink, a Dutch-Italian, Fantic Motor have rapidly expanded to become one of Italy's most successful small manufacturers, with an emphasis on off-road machinery, especially in the trials field. Their first model was a small child's bike, the Bronco TXI, powered by a four-stroke Aspera

engine. At the same time came a prototype tricycle with the same engine. These were followed by a succession of models, including the Caballero (enduro), Chopper

This strange machine is a Fantic Koala, with a two-stroke engine, plastic bodywork and balloon tyres, from the 1990s.

(custom) and Super Six GT (roadster). On the dirt, the 125 RC enduro won countless awards and medals for works and private riders during the 1970s. After this success, Fantic built a motocross version of this air-cooled, twin shock two-stroke flier. In the world

Since the late 1970s, Fantic have made highly successful trial bikes; typical is this 307 model of 1991.

of one-day trials the Bargazo Como factory really make its mark. During the late 1970s and onwards Fantic machines have often dominated this branch of motorcycle sport and have gained a whole string of world and national championship titles along the way.

In the early 1990s, Fantic absorbed the Garelli marque; in the 1920s and 1930s, the latter had been one of the top five Italian bike manufacturers (along with Benelli, Bianchi, Gilera and Moto Guzzi) and, even as late as 1987, Garelli had been the winner of the 125cc world road-racing championship title.

FÉE

ENGLAND 1905–07

THIS MAKE WAS THE predecessor of the famous Douglas motorcycle, and it established the tradition of using a flat-twin engine. Built by Joseph Barter of Bristol, whose first machine came in 1902 under his own name, it had a single-cylinder engine of his design that mounted the belt drive pulley on the camshaft, enabling it to be much larger than usual, thus reducing belt slip.

Barter was impressed by the lack of vibration of Lanchester car engines, which led him to the flat-twin type. This work brought him in contact with the Douglas firm who supplied castings. His flat-twin engine was of 269cc with automatic inlet and side exhaust valves, a surface carburettor at first, and a trembler coil plus distributor for ignition. A massive external flywheel went on the left end of the crankshaft and accounted for 2.7kg (6lb) of the 6kg (13.5lb) engine weight. The engine was mounted high in a standard bicycle frame that had braced forks and it drove a countershaft mounted under the downtube by chain. This incorporated a small clutch, while final drive was by belt, with cycle brakes for stopping.

A 1905 report told of quiet running with little vibration and a performance that suited short town journeys. By the end of 1905, Light Motors was formed and the model renamed Fairy. Douglas later took over the design.

FERRARI

ITALY 1951–59

ALTHOUGH BASED IN the same province as Marenello, near Modena, the Ferrari motorcycle concern was not connected to its far more illustrious four-wheel cousin. What linked the two, besides the name, was the high level of mechanical engineering which the two Ferraris shared.

Ferrari Moto built both four- and two-stroke models. The Milan Show of 1952 saw the firm exhibit a chain-driven overhead camshaft parallel twin. The engine assembly was of particularly clean design, featuring wet-sump lubrication. The four-speed foot-operated gearbox, together with the clutch, was in unit. Displacing 199cc, this was capable of around 14bhp and was mounted in a modern swinging-arm frame with oil-damped telescopic front forks.

The 200 Ferrari was joined by a smaller capacity 175cc version in 1953, but as far as sales were concerned, it was the marque's two-stroke models (the firm's livelihood) which were the most important. Using piston-port induction these all employed only a single cylinder and were built in 98, 124 and 148cc engine sizes. Even though endowed with a

No relation to the famous car company, Ferrari Moto built high-quality motorcycles during the 1950s. A 1955 148cc single-cylinder two-stroke is shown here.

famous name and usually painted bright red, the two-wheel Ferraris never sold in any numbers. Prices were invariably higher than comparative rivals, and the expense, together with a lack of any real dealer network, sealed Ferrari's fate. After the rapid decline in sales of powered two-wheelers at the end of the 1950s, Ferrari Moto closed in 1959.

FABULA
Germany (Bielefeld) 1922–1924: This firm made a 246cc two-stroke engine with shaft drive.

FAGAN
Ireland (Dublin) 1935–37: Fagan used a 123cc Villiers single in this machine.

FAGGI
Italy (Milan) 1950–53: Two-strokes from Ilo (125 and 175cc) and Villiers (125 and 198cc) powered these motorcycles and delivery vehicles.

FAINI
Italy 1923–27: This 1925 light motorcycle was a 198cc side-valve.

FAIRBANKS-MORSE
USA 1956: This three-wheeled machine reached 7kph (4mph).

FAIRFIELD
England (Warrington) 1914–15: Alfred Forster built this 269cc two-stroke before World War I struck.

FAKA
Germany (Salzgitter-Bad) 1952–57: Kannenberg's scooters had 147, 174 and 197cc Ilo two-stroke engines.

FALCO
Italy (Vercelli) 1950–53: Erminio di Giovanni used Fichtel and Sachs two-stroke engines of 98 and 147cc.

FALKE
Germany 1923–25: This assembler used 142cc Grade and 145cc DKW deflector-piston engines.

FALTER
Germany (Bielefeld) 1952– : This firm's scooter (1954–1959) had a 49cc Fichtel & Sachs engine; mopeds had 49cc Sachs, Ilo and Zundapp engines.

FAM
Italy 1951–69: Benelli built 115cc singles and 195cc flat twins.

FAMA
Germany 1923–25: This firm built in-house singles of 190 and 420cc.

FAMA
Netherlands (Utrecht) 1938: This lightweight had a 125cc Villiers motor.

FAMAG
Germany (Schweinfurt) 1923–25: This was a 420cc side-valve, then a 197cc side-valve with belt drive.

FAMO
Germany 1923–26: These had 127cc two-strokes and triangular frames.

FAR
Austria 1924–27: FAR fitted machines with 346 and 496cc JAP and Blackburne singles.

FEW PARAMOUNT

THE PRE-WAR FIRM of F.E. Waller produced valve spring covers under the FEW trade name, so this was used in 1920 when they entered the motorcycle market. Late that year, they announced a model with a 6hp JAP V-twin engine, direct belt drive, a low sports frame and Saxon forks. A

The Paramount Duo took the full enclosure concept as its theme to hide the engine and lower the seat height. It failed to catch on, as did others using this format.

friction gear was mentioned but no details given. However, although a prototype was built to show to potential makers, none came forward.

The name returned late in 1926 with a novel model that took the car-on-two-wheels format with the engine and transmission out of sight under metal panels. The rider was seated low in a bucket seat. Power came from side-valve JAP engines, either a 976cc V-twin or a 600cc single being offered, and driving a three-speed gearbox.

Three versions were listed as available: the Paramount Special with single seat, the Paramount Duo with a second bucket seat, and the latter with the single engine. All featured a low frame with the headstock supported by tubes that ran up to it and its girder forks. The panels extended down to cast-alloy footboards, forward to act as legshields and back over the rear wheel for luggage.

Little changed during 1927 but later on that year the models were

Few Paramount's first attempt to enter the motorcycle market was this 1920 machine with a 6hp V-twin JAP engine and direct belt drive. It didn't sell.

confirmed for the following year. The single would be renamed the Paramount Popular and was to be fitted with a 499cc single valve Blackburne engine.

As was so often the case with such designs during that era, few were actually made and even fewer were sold.

FIGINI

LUIGI FIGINI WAS a pioneer who set up in Milan with Lazzati. They operated as a single firm, while each produced machines using his own name. Lazzati fitted De Dion engines into heavy-duty bicycle frames with braced forks; Figini took a different route.

The first Figini model arrived before the Werner brothers had moved their engine from the headstock to within the frame, differing from that layout in that the engine was installed to act as the lower part of the seat tube running down from the saddle and normally to the bottom bracket. It

Right from the start, the Figini was constructed with its engine acting as part of the seat tube. The unit was later lowered and the pedals moved to accommodate it.

pre-dated the more famous Indian make of 1901 from America. The Indian engine sat above the bottom bracket, whereas the Figini motor was lower and acted as the link to the downtube. Its crankcase was sufficiently low-set that the pedal shaft ran across its top front. In other ways, it was a bicycle with an engine. Lazzati went in 1904; Figini, at the end of that decade.

FN

FN, OR LA FABRIQUE Nationale d'Armes de Guerre, was formed in 1889 when the Herstal-based company was set up to rival Sarotea in arms manufacture. Like their rivals, they turned to pedal cycles, before in 1901 turning their attention to motorised bicycles.

The standard FN bicycle was equipped with a slender fuel tank beneath its crossbar and provided with an engine displacing 133cc featuring belt final drive and a massive 'bacon slicer' outside flywheel. Development continued on this model over the next three

years, but in 1904 it was eclipsed when FN introduced their Paul Kelecom-designed 363cc in-line four-cylinder model to massive public acclaim. The Kelecom-designed four-cylinder range was produced over the next two decades in a variety of engine

sizes, but after their creator left FN in 1926, only twins and singles were offered.

Certainly the FN single-cylinder models formed the backbone of production for most of FN's life, and it wasn't just the fours which benefited from shaft final drive.

F. N. 250 CC 2 TEMPS, LUXE-CARÉN

FN

back at Monza's autodrome speed bowl for the ultimate prize, a new 24-hour world record which they duly set, covering 2526km (1500 miles) at an average speed of just over 105kph (65mph).

This was just the beginning of FN's record-breaking achievements. Englishman Wal Handley, riding a more highly tuned 350 FN single, set a new flying start record for the 5km (3 miles) distance (average speed over 177kph (110mph)). Later still in 1931 Milhoux and Tacheny annexed many of the established 500cc-class world endurance records. Then finally in 1935 Milhoux and Charlier set new records for the 500, 750 and 1000cc categories in one last FN-sponsored record-breaking spree.

The Isle of Man TT was regarded then as the premier racing event, but after R.O. Clarks magnificent third in the Twin Cylinder class of the 1908 event on an FN four, the Belgian company's participation was less glamorous. In 1909 a single machine retired, then in 1914 FN's finished 33rd and 36th in the Senior race. Finally, in 1931, their only entry (again in the Senior) ended in retirement.

Below: During the 1950s, FN produced a range of four-stroke singles with either side or overhead valve engines, as this period brochure shows.

Above: FN began making armaments in 1889, then bicycles, before turning to motorcycles in 1901. This Ilo-powered model dates from the mid-1950s.

For example, a new 249cc inlet-over-exhaust single with this luxury debuted in 1909, featuring the same twin-support tube frame as the four, with the crankshaft mounted lengthways in the frame. Later this design was enlarged to 293cc and was still being built in the early 1920s. A distinctive feature was the use of a multi-plate clutch and two-speed gearbox. Leading-link forks were very similar to the Kelecom four-cylinder range. The 283cc version weighed in at 80kg (176lb) and had a maximum speed of 85kph (53mph).

Another well-known early FN single-cylinder model was the speed record breaker of 1926. This used a 342cc (74x80.5mm) overhead-valve engine and was

derived from the standard production FN of the mid-1920s, ugly in the extreme but very robust in service. This latter trait ensured that FN's 350 single was able withstand not only abuse, but the tuning which was necessary to turn it into a record breaker. Three riders, Flintermann, Lowinfosse and Sbaiz, took the FN overhead-valve single to Monza, Italy where, on 2 August 1926, they set several new world speed and endurance records. Eight days later the Belgian team was

FARNELL
England (Birmingham) 1901–05: Farnell used Minerva engines in strengthened bicycle frames.

FAVOR
France (Clermont-Ferrand) 1919–59: This firm used JAP 350cc singles, then 100 to 250cc two-strokes and, post 1945, Aubier-Dunne two-strokes and AMC four-strokes to 250cc.

FAVORIT
Germany (Berlin) 1933–38: Favorit began with a 996cc side-valve JAP V-twin but then used 100 and 125cc two-strokes.

FB
England (Birmingham) 1913–22: Fowler and Bingham built 206, 269 and 411cc two-strokes.

FB
Germany (Breslau) 1923-25: FB began with 269cc two-strokes, then used a 250cc two-stroke and 348 and 496cc JAP and Blackburne singles.

FB-MONDIAL:
See Mondial (below).

FEDERATION
England (Birmingham) 1919–37: (also Federal) These had either Villiers two-strokes (147 to 250cc) or JAP four-strokes (250 to 500cc).

FEILBACH LIMITED
USA (Milwaukee) 1912–15: Singles (550cc) and V-twins (990 and 1130cc) characterised this make.

FERBEDO
Germany (Nurnberg-Doos) 1954: Betthauser built this basic scooter with a 49cc Zundapp motor.

FERRARIS
Italy (Milan) 1903: This strengthened bicycle frame had a Peugeot engine.

FHG
Germany 1927–29: AJS importer Pleus sold the FHG 173cc two-stroke.

FIAM
Italy 1923–25: This was an auxiliary cycle motor of 110cc.

FIAMC
Italy (Parma) 1952–53: This firm made a 125cc two stroke for a motorcycle and scooter.

FIDUCIA
Switzerland 1902–5: In-house 450cc motors ran these Swiss pioneers.

FIMER
Italy 1952–57: This was a 125cc two-stroke scooter, later in a 'Luxus' version and a lightweight motorcycle of the same capacity.

This four cylinder model dates from 1908. Its 498cc engine produced nine horsepower, enough to power the white-tyred machine to 45kph (28mph).

models such as the M13, used a series of side- or overhead-valve single-cylinder engines, featuring chain final drive and unit construction with wet-sump lubrication. Many employed a front fork design of the trailing-link type, where near-horizontal springs were tensioned by the upward movement of the front wheel. From 1953 conventional oil-damped telescopic forks were fitted to the FN range. The FN four-stroke single made a big impact in the early days (early to mid-1950s) of motocross, but from 1956 FN had largely switched to lightweights with two-stroke engines for their production roadsters. A moped was introduced before production ceased in the mid-1960s.

Below: The Belgian rider Auguste Mingles rode a 500cc FN to become European Motocross Champion two years running, in 1953 and 1954.

Just before World War II, FN, with rivals Gillet-Herstal and Sarotea, designed and built a number of specialised military motorcycles, most notably a 1000cc-class flat twin of mammoth proportions. FN also built a tri-car using the flat twin M12 as a basis, like the Italian motocarri (motorcycle truck), combining a motorcycle's front end (including the engine and drive assemblies) with a car-type rear structure. In FN's case this

Above: For almost seven decades FN built a huge array of models including singles, twins (shown) and fours. Four-stroke and two-stroke engines were both used.

consisted of an open body with two rows of seats, and four-speed gearbox with a reverse. Postwar, it offered the same device, suitably modified as a delivery truck.

Other FN models used by the military included the M11, M71 and M86. All these, like postwar

FN Four Cylinder   1904

FN WAS A PIONEER in the birth of the four-cylinder motorcycle. However, they were by no means the first of the type, this honour going to the English Holden design in 1897. Even so, the Belgian company gained much fame and glory through their use of this engine type.

The FN four-cylinder series came about due to the brilliance of the company's chief designer, Paul Kelecom who, in 1904, was responsible for conceiving an all-new 363cc (45x47mm) in-line four. This was air-cooled and featured what would have been then the great luxury of shaft final drive.

Other details of Kelecom's outstanding design included magneto ignition, automatic inlet valves and a hand-operated oil pump. The maximum speed was

FN was a pioneer in the birth of the four-cylinder motorcycle. The great English rider, R.O. Clark, used an FN four in both road racing and trials with great success.

just over 64kph (40mph), but the four-cylinder FN's big advantage – and selling point – was the virtually vibration-free nature of its engine.

In order to publicise the new design, FN organised a grand tour, taking the four to all the major European cities, including London and Paris. It finally arrived at the latter destination towards the end of 1904, just in time for a major sales drive in advance of the 1905 season.

The four-cylinder engine was enlarged over the next few years and by 1907 it had grown to 493cc (and 498cc for the American market). By this point, it had gained a clutch, gearbox and internal enclosed brakes. It also now featured improved spring forks.

On the racing front, Englishman R.O. Clark took one of the FN fours to a rostrum (third) position in the 1908 multi-cylinder category in the Isle of Man TT. Clark covered 255km (158.5 miles) in four hours and 11

minutes, travelling at an average speed of just over 58kph (36mph). It is also interesting to relate the fact that the FN was the most economical bike in the event, as it averaged no less than 32km/l (90mpg), which was pretty impressive.

R.O. Clark was a great all-rounder and also used the same FN for other branches of motorcycle competition, including long-distance trials such as the MCC (Motor Cycling Club) London-Edinburgh-London run, winning a Gold medal in 1908, as well as racing successfully over the world's first purpose-built circuit at Brooklands in Surrey.

Designer Paul Kelecom left FN in 1926 and production of his four ceased shortly thereafter.

Engine: 363cc ioe in-line V4, 45x47mm, air-cooled
Power: n/a
Gearbox: single-speed
Final drive: shaft
Weight: n/a
Top speed: 68kph (42mph)

FRANCIS-BARNETT

ENGLAND 1919–64

Not to be confused with the successful Cruiser of the 1930s, the version pictured left was the 250cc Cruiser 84 introduced in the late 1950s.

Motorcycle Show in late 1923. During 1926 and 1927, in publicity stunts 172cc versions of these machines reached the summits of Snowdon and Ben Nevis in 22 minutes and 120 minutes respectively. One machine averaging 69km/litre (196mpg) was dubbed in company publicity as 'cheaper than shoe leather'.

Two of the best-known models of the 1930s – the two-stroke Cruiser and four-stroke Stag — employed more conventional welded-up frames rather than Fanny-B 'bridges'. From its debut in 1933 until 1940, the Bill King-designed Cruiser was a huge success, partly through the sheer practicality of its scooter-like layout, making it one of very few 'full enclosure' British machines ever to prosper. The year 1938 saw the introduction of the unit construction 125cc Snipe and a pedal-assisted 98cc moped, the Powerbike.

Given such a model range, and Gordon Francis' army background, the company might have been expected to make a serious contribution to Britain's war effort. Indeed, the design for a military version of the Snipe was well advanced. However, in 1940, the factory was obliterated in the same bombing raid that destroyed nearby Triumph. Some production

'FANNY-B', AS IT QUICKLY became known, was founded by Gordon Francis, the son of Graham, co-founder of the Lea-Francis motorcycle concern. In 1919, with his father-in-law, Arthur Barnett, he founded Francis and Barnett Ltd (Graham Francis provided some of the necessary capital, for which he was granted a seat on the board). Shortly afterwards, when production of Excelsior machines moved to the Monarch factory in Birmingham, the new company moved into the abandoned Excelsior premises at Lower Ford Street, Coventry. In March 1920, the company's first model was a 292cc JAP-engined side valve machine with two speeds and belt final drive. A similar model of 346cc soon followed. Further four-strokes singles came after, both side-valves and overhead-valve, in capacities up to 350cc.

This early Francis-Barnett model from the 1920s used a JAP single cylinder engine as its power unit. Eventually available in capacities up to 350cc, it had belt final drive.

However, it is for two-strokes that the company is best remembered, the move to which was prompted by the end of the motorcycle boom of the early 1920s. All were Villiers-powered, and most were singles, although a 344cc parallel twin, the Pullman, caused a stir in 1927 but it was doomed by overheating problems.

Unused chassis were instead employed in a 250cc single, the Empire model.

The need to cut costs also brought about the introduction of Fanny-B's unique bolted-together frames. The first of these – a nickel-plated example with a 147cc Villiers engine – was unveiled at London's Olympia

was possible from premises at Earlsdon; but it was not until the Lower Ford Street factory re-opened in 1945 that motorcycle manufacture resumed.

After the war, the range became entirely two-stroke, with Villiers engines now ranging in capacity from 98 to 248cc. In June 1947, the company joined James in the AMC empire. A decade late, it abandoned the Villiers connection in favour of in-house two-strokes from British-based Italian Vincente Piatti. Partly due to poor assembly, the venture failed and Fanny-B looked yet again to the Villiers power which, for all its shortcomings, was enjoying considerable success in trials and scrambles. Other than colour (Francis-Barnetts were red, James were green), the two marques were practically indistinguishable and, along with Matchless, sank together in 1964. The last Fanny-B model, the futuristic-looking 150cc Sports Fulmer 90, with pressed steel leading-link forks and streamlined bodywork, proved to be the last production motorcycle built in Coventry.

'Fanny-B' was how the marque was known. Although its first models were four-stroke, in later years, the factory was associated with budget two-strokes.

FMT
Italy (Treviso) 1929: This firm built a two-stroke lightweight of 132cc with two- and three-speed gearboxes.

FOCESI
Italy 1952–55: This firm made Gloria mopeds and lightweights; 49 and 160cc two-strokes, and 98cc overhead-valves, Touring and Sport.

FOCHJ
Italy 1954–57: This firm used a wide range of NSU four-stroke engines, from mopeds to the 250cc Max.

FOLLIS
France (Lyon) 1903–60: This firm used bought-in engines (JAP, Python, Blackburne, Ydral and AMC).

FORELLE
Germany (Bad Wildungen) 1955–58: These mopeds had 49cc Ilo and Sachs engines.

FORONI
Italy (Modena) 1975: These mopeds and mini-scooters had 48cc Morini engines.

FORSTER
Switzerland (Zurich) 1921–32: This firm made two-stroke singles of 140, 200 and 250cc.

FORTUNA
Germany (Nurnberg) 1921–28: These were three-port two-strokes of 150, 175 and 200cc, with external flywheels.

FORWARD
England 1909–15: These were small capacity V-twins (350 and 500cc) in very light frames.

FOX
France 1931–late 1940s: This was a 100cc lightweight.

FRANCAIS DIAMANT
France 1931–35: This small manufacturer made two- and four-strokes of 100 to 500cc.

FRANCE
France 1931–35: These two-stroke lightweights had in-house 98 to 245cc engines.

FRANCHI
Italy (Milan) 1950–58: Franchi made lightweight motorcycles from 1950 with Sachs 98 and 150cc engines, in 1954 a Sachs-engined 49cc moped, and a 125 and a 175cc Gran Sport.

FRANZANI
Germany (Nurnberg) 1923–32: This firm used a 283cc two-stroke engine, then JAP engines of 198 to 490cc, and 497cc Kuchen engines.

FRANCIS-BARNETT BLACK HAWK
1930s

DESPITE THE MODESTY of their products, Francis-Barnett had a fondness for naming their bikes after birds of prey. For all its predatory pretensions, the Black Hawk was typical of the company's pre-war fare: an immensely strong frame mated to a simple 196cc Villiers single-cylinder engine of considerable economy, if unimpressive performance. An optional four-speed gearbox was available.

These frames, fully triangulated from straight tube and jointed by pins, were advertised as being 'Built like a Bridge'. They were both rigid and relatively light for the time, and easy to assemble (for factory fitters, at least. Some advertising suggested that the

frames could be dismantled and fitted in a golf bag, but only an optimist would try). The earliest triangulated frames employed leaf-spring front forks but by the time of the Hawk, conventional coil-spring girders were standard. The idea for this design had come to Gordon Francis during World War I when, as an officer, he had been

appalled by the fragility of more conventional frames.

Engine: 196cc 2s single, 61x67mm air-cooled
Power: n/a
Gearbox: 3-speed hand change
Final drive: chain
Weight: n/a
Top speed: 77kph (48mph)

The Black Hawk was powered by a 196cc Villiers engine. More important, however, was the fully triangulated frame, bolted together from straight tube.

FRANCIS-BARNETT STAG

1935

A FOUR-STROKE FANNY-B came as a surprise in 1935 when the 250cc Stag was introduced. The engine was an overhead-valve single, built by Blackburne, designed by Harry Hatch and mated to a non-unit Albion gearbox. Francis-Barnett's built-up frame was replaced by a welded one, the rear tubular and the front downtube of forged, H-section steel. A sturdy, popular machine, it offered reasonable performance and good economy.

When first unveiled in 1935, the Stag surprised everyone by being four-stroke powered. The ohv Blackburne engine was yet another Harry Hatch design.

Engine: 248cc ohv single, 68x68mm air-cooled
Power: n/a
Gearbox: 4-speed foot change
Final drive: chain
Weight: 113kg (250lb)
Top speed: 97kph (60mph)

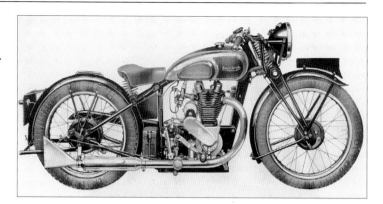

FRANCIS-BARNETT MERLIN

1948

Although a well-designed and competent commuter model, sales of the 122cc Villiers-engined Merlin suffered at the hands of BSA's all-conquering Bantam, the UK's best-ever selling machine.

Engine: 122cc 2s single, 50x62mm air-cooled
Power: 3.2bhp at 4400rpm
Gearbox: 3-speed foot change
Final drive: chain
Weight: 79kg (175lb)
Top speed: 71kph (44mph)

LAUNCHED IN THE LATE 1940s, the 122cc Merlin was typical of Fanny B's postwar fare. Compared with the contemporary BSA D1 Bantam, it was neat and well made, if old-fashioned. Power came from a 1930s Villiers '9D' twin port two-stroke engine, employing flat-topped pistons and Schnurle loop cylinder scavenging. Top speed was well below 80kph (50mph). A neat touch was the addition of an emergency tank for two-stroke oil.

FRERA

ITALY 1906–36 AND 1949–60

FOUNDED BY LEONARDO FRERA at Tradate, Varese, this firm became one of the largest in Italy until the start of the Depression in 1930, the firm having been taken over by Emilo Fossio in 1929. Production ceased in 1936 but in 1931 Leonard Frera, son of the founder, set up his own company, which was short-lived, but the original name survived to return after World War II.

The first Frera had a 500cc engine, with automatic inlet valve, mounted inclined to the line of the downtube in a simple loop frame. It had a gear-driven magneto fixed to the crankcase behind the cylinder, belt drive, pedalling gear and sprung forks. The make was soon involved successfully in competitions in Italy and its range expanded to add machines from 300cc to a massive 1140cc V-twin.

A 1909 Frera, typical of the earlier models of this marque. Its designs continued for many years in many different types and sizes.

this last with overhead inlet valves. Transmissions moved on from direct belt drive to a separate three-speed gearbox and all-chain drive, the chains fully enclosed in cases. The front forks continued sprung but with a rocking motion pivoted about the lower crown, while the frame remained rigid. Many Frera machines served in World War I in both solo and sidecar forms, the latter often as an ambulance.

After the war, the firm listed 500 and 600cc singles, plus the 1140cc V-twin, all with three speeds and sprung forks. These three were joined by a 269cc two-stroke model, which also came with three speeds. All models were built in considerable numbers.

On the competition front, there were four-valve engines of 350 and 500cc as well as a 750cc V-twin, all of which were successful in the famous Milan-Napoli races of 1919 to 1925 that preceded the Milan-Taranto events of later years. This took the firm up to the end of the decade and new ownership but they then lost much of their market to the competition, namely Moto Guzzi.

Production of the Frera ceased in 1936 despite a fine 1935 model with a 500cc high-camshaft, overhead-valve engine with hairpin valve springs and overhead-camshaft looks.

The name returned in 1949 when it became another Italian firm offering a range of small-capacity two-stroke models. There were many such in Italy at that time, most using bought-in engine units, although some made their own. Frera followed both courses.

The engine size ran from 50cc for a moped to 150cc with the gearbox built in-unit with the engine. Frame, forks and brakes followed the contemporary fashions of Italy, so telescopic-front and pivoted-rear forks were the usual fitment, while the wheels soon moved to full-width hubs, ample drum brakes and light-alloy rims. The sweep of the rear frame from the fork pivot up to the top of the suspension units was typical of the time and similar to that found on many Italian lightweights, regardless of their engine type or their degree of tune.

Commonly, the 125 and 150cc models, and some larger, were listed by the firms in several forms such as Turismo, Lusso, Sport, Rapido and Competition for Formula racing, all being based on one basic model.

As the market declined, so the smaller firms fell by the wayside and Frera was just one example of such a firm.

FUSI
ITALY 1932–58

ACHILLE FUSI DID NOT begin to use his own name for his machines until 1936, until when they were known as the RAS, although they were still built in Milan. In due course, he bought the CF firm and it was then that his name appeared on the fuel tank.

As with the RAS, Fusi used JAP engines imported from Britain ranging in size from 175 to 500cc. All were singles and most had overhead-valves, being installed in conventional frames in the style of the time.

From 1936, he used the Fusi name and produced the 250cc face-cam engine taken over from CF, while the rest of the line

One of the machines from the 1939 Fusi range with a inclined, ohv engine installed in cycle parts. The bike was well designed and looked good, too.

continued as before with JAP engines built under licence in Italy. Rear suspension appeared, the 175cc model was dropped and by 1939 a four-model range appeared, three of these with 247cc engines, all inclined in the frame. Of these, two had equal bore and stroke, overhead-valves, four speeds and rear suspension but the third had a

A Fusi with a 250cc face-cam engine fitted in a late-prewar frame with pivoted-fork rear suspension of typical Italian form.

long-stroke, side-valve engine, three speeds and a rigid frame. The fourth machine had a 499cc overhead-valve engine set upright in the frame, four speeds and rear suspension.

After World War II, the firm continued with production of the 250cc face-cam engine for a while and added a line of small two-strokes which were fitted with Garelli engine units. These came in various sizes with unit construction of the gearbox and went into frames with front and rear suspension. They were modelled in the typical style and line of their era.

GALBUSERA

ITALY 1934–55

GALBUSERA BEGAN BY using engines built by the Italian Miller firm under licence from Rudge in Britain, who employed the Python name for the engines in these transactions. Galbusera used 175, 250, 350 and 500cc engines, all with four-valve cylinder heads, the smallest Miller built especially for the Italian market, and the rest similar to others in Italy at that time.

At the 1938 Milan Show the firm created a sensation with two machines with unconventional two-stroke engines made by Marama-Toya. Both were multis with the cylinders set in a 90-degree V. The smaller 250cc unit had no less than four cylinders, while the larger 500cc engine was a V-eight, with two V-fours coupled in line. Both had a

centrifugal supercharger fitted to the front of the crankshaft, where it was fed by a single downdraught carburettor. A four-speed gearbox was built in unit with the engine, final drive was by chain and the engine unit hung from the frame. Neither multi was produced, but they stole the limelight at Milan.

An early Galbusera fitted with a four valve, ohv engine built by Miller in Italy under licence from Rudge in Britain. It came in a variety of capacities.

A prosaic side-valve single-cylinder model from the Galbusera range of the 1930s, a far cry from the sensational V4 and V8 two-strokes built in 1938.

The conventional models took the firm on to the end of the decade. After World War II, they turned to lightweights, using mainly Sachs engines from 75 to 175cc, but also some four-strokes left over from their past. The machines followed Italian style for the period, but failed to survive.

GALLONI

ITALY 1920–31

MOST FIRMS START with single-cylinder engines and move on to twins later, but Alberto Galloni of Borgomanero did it the other way round, appearing on the market after World War II with a line of V-twins. Galloni built these in 494 and 744cc capacities with side

A 1922 Galloni V-twin with three speeds, sprung forks, rigid frame and minimal brakes. It was a typical Italian machine, hence the open exhaust pipes.

valves and magneto ignition with both sizes available in Turismo and Sport forms. All had a three-speed gearbox and all-chain drive in a conventional format with girder forks, and so were similar to many others of that period, except that they employed a patented rear suspension method.

The V-twins were soon joined by a range of singles of 250, 350 and 500cc with side- or overhead-valves. These had similar cycle parts to the twins, with the

separate three-speed gearbox and all-chain drive, but used a rigid frame. Singles and twins together made up a good range that covered the market needs well, and for a few years Galloni were one of the leading firms.

During the 1920s their machines followed the trends of style and specification, but towards the end of the decade, other companies began to take the leading role from

Galloni built V-twin engines right from the start, entering the market with this 494cc model and a larger version built in the same design.

them and, as trading conditions worsened when the Depression began to bite, Galloni struggled on, using their own engines plus others imported from Britain. In 1931 they closed their doors.

GARABELLO

ITALY 1906–29

FRANCESCO GARABELLO WAS a pioneer of motorcycle development in the early days of the Italian industry. Inspired by the aim to improve the design of the bike, he encountered problems and found solutions to these problems which would later benefit others. Garabello, like so many other innovators, did not himself make great financial gains from his endeavours but he was driven by the idea of progress, and profit seems to have been a secondary consideration to him. His first motorcycles had single-cylinder engines of various sizes with belt drive to the rear wheel. The clever engineer decided that this crude arrangement, with its bicycle-style frame and forks, needed considerable improvement. After World War I, he set out to incorporate this improvement into his new designs.

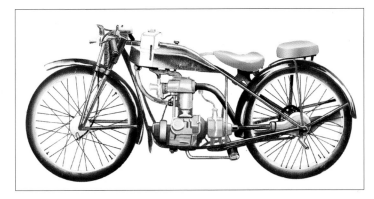

An innovative Garabello water-cooled 175 single with shaft drive to the rotary valve in the cylinder head. It also had shaft final drive.

His new model for the 1920s was totally different and powered by an in-line, four-cylinder, water-cooled engine of 1-litre capacity

with side-valves. It drove back to a gearbox and from there by shaft to the rear wheel, and this substantial assembly went into a suitably sturdy frame with girder forks and fixtures to suit.

The four was too expensive for the Italian market so few were sold but, undaunted, Garabello produced an even more innovative design later in the decade. This had a 175cc single-cylinder engine with a shaft-driven rotary valve in the cylinder head, water-cooling and shaft final drive. This too was a costly exercise and its failure contributed to the firm's downfall.

The in-line, four-cylinder Garabello of the early 1920s had water cooling, side valves and a one litre capacity, plus shaft final drive.

The Italian flair for design was not particularly evident in this 1927 Garanzini, which still retained a flat tank two or three years after saddle tanks became the norm.

GARANZINI

ITALY 1921–31

ORESTE GARANZINI RACED motorcycles – he was the Italian 350cc champion in 1921 – and was the importer of the English Verus (below) renamed Veros for the Italian market. He was also a motorcycle designer in his own right. The first machine to bear his name was a 349cc side-valve single, which was sold both as a two-speed Sport and as a three-speed Luxus with bigger wheels and an oil-bath for the chain final drive. In 1922, he started calling his motorcycles Garanzini-JAP,

and even JAP-Garanzini, using a side-valve JAP of 350cc; later he offered Blackburne four-strokes of varying sizes and Villiers two-strokes of 147cc to 248cc.

He continued to race and at Monza in 1923, he rode a 350cc

JAP-engined machine with a four-valve head and three-speed gearbox. As ever, racing improved the breed, and success influenced his road bikes. For the 1925 season he had a 250cc overhead-valve single, a 350cc side-valve single, three 350cc singles (two side-valve, one overhead-valve) and 500cc and 615cc twins. All models had his patented fork.

In 1926, new Standard, Sport and Super-Sport models were introduced from 250cc to 680cc. The 250 CTO had a shaft-driven overhead-cam in an oil-cooled cylinder head, delivering 12bhp at 7000rpm. At Monza in the same year Garanzini presented a 175cc overhead-cam lightweight. The

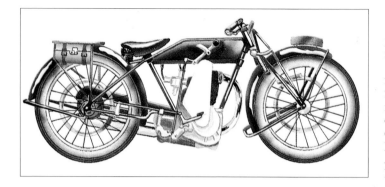

This Garanzini model dates from 1926. Although this machine was powered by a 250cc motor, the range was available up to 680cc.

following year saw two revised 250s, a side-valve 350 with a modified JAP, side-valve or overhead-valve 500s and a JAP 680, the latter also appearing as a Brough Superior. Villiers two-strokes and JAP four-strokes came in 1929. Production stopped in 1931.

GARELLI

ITALY 1919–

ADALBERTO GARELLI WAS BORN in Turin during 1886. In 1908, at the age of 22, he gained a degree in engineering and from 1909 dedicated his work to the study and perfection of the first two-stroke engine produced by the giant Fiat concern. But Fiat did not share Garelli's enthusiasm for two-strokes, and he left their employment in 1911. He then built his prototype motorcycle (a 350cc split-single) before joining Bianchi in 1914 as head of its motorcycle division. His next stop was at Stucchi, another important motorcycle works of the period. He remained with them for three years (1915–1918) during which time he won a competition organised by the Italian Army for a military motorcycle with a special

version of his 350 split-single. Finally, with World War I at an end, in 1919 he was able to realise a personal dream and set up his own factory at Sesto San Giovanni, near Milan.

From then until 1926, the Garelli 350 split-single made a major impact in both series production and in racing, helping to establish the company. From 1927 onwards Garelli became less and less active in the motorcycle field and by 1928 had switched a large percentage of production over to the manufacture of military equipment, to such an extent that by 1936 the marque no longer appeared on the annual list of Italian motorcycle factories.

It was not until after World War II had passed, and with it the

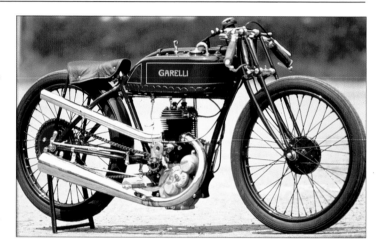

Below: During the late 1970s and early 1980s one of Garelli's best-selling models was the small-wheeled two-stroke Katia moped.

Above: During the early 1920s, the Garelli 350cc split-single two-stroke made a major impact in both series production and racing.

demand for military equipment, that the name reappeared, initially with an engine called the Mosquito, made for fitment to conventional pedal cycles. This proved such a success that Garelli returned to the production of complete powered two-wheelers during the mid-1950s.

In the late 1950s came the first contacts with the Agrati organisation. This led in 1961 to a merging of Agrati and Garelli, with the formation of the Agrati-Garelli group. This merger not only strengthened both companies, but also allowed Garelli to return to its sporting origins, at first through record-breaking. This was helped by the development of a 50cc sports model known as the Junior. Two specially built examples were constructed by Ing. William Soncini for record attempts at Monza, in both the 50 and 75cc categories. The two fully streamlined machines were ridden by a team of riders in atrocious

Above: The 1978 Cross 5V used a five-speed, two-stroke, single cylinder engine. Aluminium was used for both the head and barrel.

Below: Garelli entered the trials arena in 1982 with the model 323. This sported a 321cc engine with a bore and stroke of 80x64mm.

Bottom: The 1985 GTA 124 sports roadster came with a liquid-cooled, single-cylinder, two-stroke engine and monoshock rear suspension.

weather conditions in November 1963. Garelli came away the holders of several records, of which the 24-hour 50cc record is still intact, despite numerous attempts to break it since.

The 1970s saw Garelli at the very forefront of moped developments, with such well-known models as the Rekord, Tiger Cross and Katia, to name but three. Towards the end of the 1970s, a new, younger management team was put in place, the result being a higher profile – including new models, extra publicity and a return to GP racing. From 1982 until the end of 1987 Garelli was the 125cc road-racing world-title holder. Also during the mid-1980s, a new 250cc V-twin racer was constructed, together with a 320cc trials bike. This latter machine was placed in limited production. Named the 323, it had an exact displacement of 321.53cc (80x64mm).

Even though the Milan Show of 1985 saw a wave of new models, including a pair of brand new trail bikes and a reborn Mosquito auxiliary engine, Garelli's financial fortunes were starting to slide. With powered two-wheeler registrations falling, the Agrati

group had to rely more and more on their Torpedo bicycles. The long-established British arm, Agrati Sales of Nottingham, also closed down during this period. By the time the 50th Milan Show came around in November 1987 it was evident that Garelli was in serious trouble and a major management reshuffle saw the Agrati family leave. Even this did not improve matters; by the eve of the Milan Show in 1991 Garelli had been taken over by the much smaller Fantic, although the Garelli brand-name survived.

GARELLI 350 SPLIT-SINGLE   1919

Founded by Adalberto Garelli, the famous Garelli factory quickly established itself and became well known in the 1920s for its excellent 350cc split-single two-strokes. There were production and racing versions based on Garelli's original which he constructed in 1913, but by the time production commenced in 1919, many details of design had been improved.

Garelli first had the idea for a split-single during 1912. It consisted of two cylinders cast in a single block with a common combustion chamber, the two pistons working in parallel, both connected by a long gudgeon pin and single connecting-rod. Each piston had a capacity of 174.6cc, making a total of 349cc. To prove his design in 1914, Adalberto Garelli became the first person to ascend the Moncenisio Pass in northern Italy on the prototype machine.

But it was as a racing machine that the split-single made its real mark; even its debut outing in the Milano-Napoli road race ended in victory. Besides this win many other race successes were

recorded, amongst these the Circuit of Lario in 1921, the international Grand Prix at Monza in 1922 and the first victory by an Italian motorcycle abroad at the Strasbourg circuit in 1922. The first national racing champion of Italy was Ernesto Gnesa, who won his title aboard one of the Garellis at Monza in 1922.

Apart from racing, the split-single was also actively involved in attempting to break world records. On 7 September 1922 Visioli and Fergnani broke eight world records. Following this, a second attempt was made in the autumn of 1923 with Gnesa, Sbaitz, Fergnani and Maghetti. They were extraordinarily successful with no less than 76 world records broken, some over long distances and times up to 12 hours. Speeds recorded included an average of over 106kph (66mph). The final attempt was in 1926 when three bikes were ridden by no less than 14 riders, alternating with each other. The result this time was an incredible 138 hours, with speeds up to 131kph (81.5mph).

Company founder Adalberto Garelli is seen here astride one of his 350cc split-single, two-stroke machines. It was this model type which established his reputation.

A 350 Garelli was the first in the world to be equipped with an oil tank for separate lubrication, oil being mixed automatically with the fuel. Another milestone in two-stroke technology was the use of

an expansion chamber-type exhaust. The final 1926 model reached 30bhp at 4500rpm with a top speed of 141kph (87.5mph).

Engine: 349cc 2s vertical split-single (2 x 174.6cc), air-cooled
Power: 20bhp at 4500rpm
Gearbox: 2-speed hand change
Final drive: belt or chain
Weight: 97kg (213lb)
Top speed: 141kph (87.5mph)

GARELLI MOSQUITO   1950

Garelli's first postwar product of note was the Mosquito, an engine which could be 'clipped-on' to a conventional pedal cycle. Designed by Adalberto Garelli with assistance from Ing. Gilardi, the Mosquito was, like the earlier 350 split-single, an instant success. In fact, this is an understatement. During its life-span over, two million of these machines were sold to countries all around the world.

In its original form, the Mosquito had a displacement of 38.5cc with an external flywheel, roller drive, four-fifths brake horsepower output, a 5.5:1 compression ratio and a maximum speed of 32kph (20mph). As was to be expected, it was a two-stroke, but with a horizontal cylinder layout, weighing just over 4kg (9lb) and able to run for 64km (40 miles) on one litre of fuel. It

Another Garelli milestone was the Mosquito; its engine could be clipped to a conventional bicycle.

was easily fitted to a conventional bicycle and power was transmitted to the rear wheel by means of a friction roller.

In 1952 over 400,000 Mosquito engines were manufactured. The following year, the original version was replaced by the new 35 B and 1955 saw the most substantial change when the engine size was upped to 49cc and the use of a Centrimatic clutch

was adopted. In principle, this type of clutch was the forerunner of all the centrifugal clutches used on fully automatic mopeds and scooters of today.

This continued success with the engine led Garelli to develop both the Velomosquito (a complete machine, and one of the very first real moped designs) in 1955, and the following year the 315, a three-speed variant of the Mosquito. The Mosquito also spurred Garelli back into production with a full range of moped scooters and ultra-lightweight motorcycles.

Engine: 49cc 2s single, 40x39mm, air-cooled
Power: one-and-a-half bhp at 5000rpm
Gearbox: single-speed
Final drive: chain
Weight: 40kg (90lb)
Top speed: 52kph (32mph)

GARELLI 125CC TWIN GP RACER
1982

In 1982 Garelli made a triumphant return to road racing. The results was the company's first world championship titles. Garelli entered both the 50 and 125cc classes, but it was the latter in which they were ultimately successful. In fact, Angel Nieto and Eugenio Lazzarini not only finished first and second in the championship title stakes, but Garelli took the constructors championship as well.

For many years the 125s had been limited by the FIM, the sports governing body, to a twin-cylinder, six-speed formula. So if one compares the Yamaha 125 V-four of 1968, and one of the world's most exotic GP bikes of all time, the Garelli's 47bhp from a twin-cylinder layout is all the more amazing.

The 124.7cc (44x41mm) liquid-cooled disc-valve engine had first been conceived by the well known two-stroke engineer, Jorge Moller, for the Minerelli company, under whose banner it won its first Grand Prix in 1978, ridden by Pier-Paolo Bianchi. By the time Garelli used the design, it featured six transfer and one exhaust port per cylinder. There was a pair of 39mm (1.5in) Dell 'Orto magnesium-bodied carburettors.

Other features of the 1982 Garelli 125 GP twin included a

Debuting in 1982, the Garelli 125cc GP racer won no less than five world championship titles. The disc valve twin cylinder engine produced 49bhp at 12,000rpm.

duralumin monocoque frame with conventional twin Bitubo gas-filled rear shock absorbers, an aluminium swinging-arm, 32mm (1.2in) Marzocchi front forks with magnesium sliders and a mechanical anti-drive system. The ultra-low dry weight of only 78kg (172lb) was helped by the magnesium Campagnolo wheels and tiny dimensions of the bike, including the narrow-section 44cm (17ins) tyres.

The success of the 125 GP twin cannot be understated as, following Nieto's 1982 success, it went on to win the world title another four times – until the FIM changed to a single-cylinder formula from the 1988 season onwards. Garelli did build a single but it was never to repeat the glories of its older twin-cylinder brother.

Engine: 124.7cc disc-valve 2s parallel twin, 44x41mm, liquid-cooled
Power: 47bhp at 12,000rpm
Gearbox: six-speed foot change
Final drive: chain
Weight: 78kg (172lb)
Top speed: 233kph (145mph)

GAS GAS
SPAIN 1992–

The Gas Gas Endurocross 250 is here piloted by Petteri Silvan through the kind of terrain for which it was designed.

SPAIN SEEMS TO HAVE a curious affinity for off-road motorcycles, and the Gas Gas line-up was one of the later twentieth-century marques in a long and successful tradition.

Most were suitable only for off-road use, as they were not really fitted with saddles. The Trials series made no pretence whatsoever – it did not even have a strip of nominal padding – as they were designed to be ridden standing up, and the Enduro series was not a lot better. Only the Pampera had what could decently be described as a proper saddle.

By the same token, not all models were fitted with lights. In fact, some of the models could not be fitted with lights at all. It was this one-dimensionality that made these machines so successful, with

The Pampera police bike. You have to admire the kind of thinking that equips the police with seriously competitive off-road motorcycles.

GAZZI
Italy (Milan) 1929–1932: This firm made an advanced 175cc overhead-valve single of their own design.

GB
England 1905–1907: Minerva engines of three-and-a-half, four-and-a-half and five-and-a-half horsepower moved these pioneers, noted for their long wheelbase.

GECO-HERSTAL
France (Jeumont) 1924–1928: Etablissements Gerkinet & Co – GECO – built their own 175 and 350cc side-valve singles, as well as building Belgian Gillet machines under contract.

GEER
USA (St Louis, Minnesota) 1905–1909: The Harry R. Geer company put their own singles and V-twins into strengthened bicycle frames.

GEHA
Germany 1920–1924: These were two-stroke lightweights with their own one-and-a-half horsepower engines.

GEIER
Germany (Lengerich) 1934–early 1960s: This bicycle manufacturer dabbled in Ilo- and Sachs-engined autocycles and lightweights.

GEKA
Germany 1924–1925: These lightweights had 173cc DKW engines.

GE-MA-HI
Germany (Magdeburg) 1924–1927: These interesting-looking machines were powered by 131 to 175cc two-strokes from a variety of suppliers: Esbe, Bekamo, Grade, DKW and Villiers.

GEMINI
Taiwan 1970– : These were Yamaha two-strokes, built under licence.

GEMS
Italy (Milan) 1921–1923: Galazzi & Moroni built a 269cc two-stroke vertical single.

(seven-and-half ins to 10ins) depending on model, with four-piston callipers; at the back, 130 to 220mm (5 to eight-and-a-half ins), again four-piston. Given that the biggest, heaviest machine, the Pampera, weighed a mere 95kg (209lb), stopping was clearly not a problem.

Power outputs were not given for all engines. To give a representative sample: the Enduro EC200 was quoted as 38bhp at 9000rpm; the EC250, 49.84bhp at 8669rpm; and the EC300, 50.6bhp at 7340rpm. The meaninglessly

high precision of the figures for the latter two engines, both for power and for engine speeds, leads to the suspicion that the firm were having a joke on those of their customers who insisted on knowing data that is less important than the answer to a simple question: do they win races? And they did.

This 1999 model exhibits the classic Gas Gas flair for combining strikingly modern good looks with race-winning performance.

both class- and overall world championships.

The range of engine sizes, all two-strokes, was bewildering and changed frequently as they re-designed the machines to make them even more competitive. How many manufacturers have ever offered both air-cooled and liquid-cooled engines of the same capacity? Their standard engine, however, despite this variety of choices, was liquid-cooling.

The nominal and actual swept volumes for the 2000 model year were 125 (124.6cc), 200 (162.7cc for Trials and 199.4cc for Enduro),

Above: Both liquid cooling and air cooling have their advantages, and their adherents, so Gas Gas offered both. This is a Contact trials bike with liquid cooling.

249 (247.7cc), 250 (249.3cc), 280 (272.2cc), 300 (294.7cc), 321 (327.7cc) and 370 (333cc). Bores are easily varied but strokes include 50.4mm, 50.6mm, 60mm, 61mm, 65mm and 72mm.

Five- and six-speed gearboxes were used, always with chain drive, and protected discs, front and rear, took care of the stopping: at the front, 185 to 260mm

GD

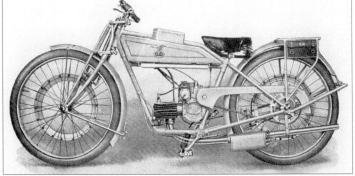

GUIDO DALL'OGLIO LENT his initials to this company, which later was known as GD-Ghirardi when he went into association with Ghirardi. Dall'Oglio also built a machine under his surname in 1926 (see above). The machine that made the company's name was a 125cc horizontal single two-stroke, which enjoyed considerable racing success, winning the Monza GP and being ridden by numerous famous racers of the day: Alfonso Drusiani, Frederico Castellani, Gugliemo Sandri and Amilcare

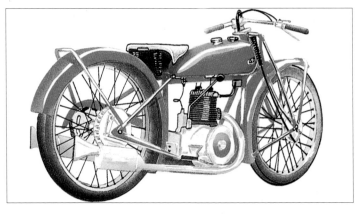

Above, left and right: The difference between the 1931 saddle-tank, ohc four-stroke (left), and the 1929 flat-tank machine (right) could hardly be greater. The former is almost a modern motorcycle, the latter is little more than a pioneer machine. And yet, it was the latter, a 125cc flat-single, that made the company's name.

Left: This 250cc two-stroke twin was light and powerful: a characteristic of most of Guido Dall'Oglio's machines.

Rosetti. Surprisingly, it had only a two-speed gearbox. In 1928, a four-speed 250cc parallel twin, still two-stroke, joined the line-up, to be followed by 175 and 350cc overhead-cam four-strokes, and a year after these, a 100cc two-stroke. The firm's glory days were over, however, and the 1930s were a period of decline. The firm probably ceased production in 1939; one source suggests 1943.

GEELY MOTORCYCLES CHINA 1997–

ALSO KNOWN AS CHINA GEELY Motorcycles, this company is one of the biggest manufacturers that most people have never heard of. Based in the city of Taizhou in Zhejiang province, between Shanghai and Hangzhou, they have benefited from China's immense internal market.

Geely attempted to satisfy this vast demand for transport by manufacturing a bewildering array of scooters and motorcycles of 50, 80, 90, 100, 125, 150 and 250cc; this numbered over 60 models in all. It is hard to believe that it could be cost-effective for the company to produce such an immense range of sizes and models, but some idea of the ways in which Geely managed to be both prolific and profitable at the same time can be gleaned from looking at the figures in the following examples.

The flagship model in the year 2000 at the time of writing was the JL250T-3 scooter, with its 250cc engine delivering a claimed 18bhp at 9500rpm. This gave a maximum speed of around about 85kph (60mph). Weighing 130kg (286lb),

The 100T was no racer – it was hard pushed to reach more than 49kph (25mph) – but it could carry almost one-and-a-half times its own weight.

Although superficially more 'show' than 'go', the JL150 offered a creditable 12bhp and the ability to carry very nearly its own weight.

the JL250T-3 could carry rather more than its own weight of 140kg (308lb).

At the other end of the scale, the JL50QT was powered by a 50cc engine delivering a mere three-and-a-quarter brake horsepower at 7500rpm. It weighed 98kg (215lb) and was able to transport only 80kg (176lb) at up to speeds of just below 40kph (25mph). The JL50QT-27 had an even less

powerful engine (3bhp at 6000rpm) but at only 65kg (143lb) it was allegedly good for speeds of up to almost 50kph (30mph). It was however quoted (once again) as having a 'Max Loadage' of 80kg (176lb).

In between these two capacities, by way of example, the 100cc engine in the JL100T and JL100T-7 offered just over 8bhp at 7500rpm; the machine weighed 98kg (216lb) and it could reputedly transport 140kg (308lb) while offering (presumably when not fully laden) speeds of just below some 70kph (40mph) top whack.

Among the motorcycles, the JL150 had, predictably, a 150cc engine delivering 12bhp at 8500rpm for a top speed of just under 90kph (55mph). Weighing in at 146kg (321lb) meant that it could carry slightly less than its own weight, the usual 140kg (308lb).

As well as this myriad of two-wheelers, China Geely (almost unbelievably) also offered for sale a range of four-wheelers. Again, a broad spectrum of machines were available, ranging from 'domestic use economical automobiles' to mini-trucks, and even light buses and travel buses. As if this were not enough, the company also made decorative fascia materials and provided an education facility.

GEROSA

THIS FIRM WAS LOCATED in Brescia and produced a range of machines of typical Italian form, style and line for over two decades. At first they made their own engines of 125 and 175cc capacity with overhead-valves and built in unit with the gearbox. A tubular frame carried the engine unit with telescopic front and pivoted rear forks. The wire wheels had full-width hubs with drum brakes, and alloy rims were fitted on to the more sporting versions.

The Italian style was to produce several types of one basic model, with Turismo, Lusso and Rapido machines commonly produced by many firms. This served the market well, as it kept costs down and allowed buyers to choose the machine that suited their needs,

more importantly keeping it within their price range.

Eventually Gerosa found that producing their own engines made

their machines too expensive for the Italian market and they turned to Minarelli for these engines. This lowered costs but it did lose them

As with many Italian firms, Gerosa used Minarelli engine units for their later models as their own became too expensive for their market.

some of their individual style. The machines consequently became more similar to many other small firms that sold a lightweight line in Italy.

The new range remained much the same but engines were two-stroke powered and extended down to 50cc for both mopeds and motorcycles.

Like many other small firms, Gerosa found it increasingly difficult to compete with the larger firms, despite being protected by tariffs from the effects of imports, and they were eventually forced to close down.

GILERA

GIUSEPPE GILERA WAS BORN in a village just outside Milan on 21 December 1887. From an early age he was fascinated by any form of mechanical transport. At only 15, the young Gilera entered employment with the Bianchi factory in Milan where he gained practical experience. He then moved to the Moto-Reve works and later to the famous engineering firm of Bucher and Zeda, quickly building up a large store of knowledge which was to prove vital in future years.

By now the ambitious young engineer had also taken up road racing, gaining recognition for his

excellent showing in hill-climb events. However, the speed events always came second to his burning desire to become a motorcycle manufacturer in his own right. By 1909, at the age of 22, he was ready to take the plunge. His first model was a 317cc (67x90mm) four-stroke. With both the inlet and exhaust valves being operated mechanically, it was quite a rare layout for the time. Next came a V-twin and thereafter the first of a famous line of 500 singles.

After World War I the demand for motorcycles accelerated and Giuseppe Gilera decided to establish a new factory at Arcore,

Left: The LTE military model was built from 1936 to 1944. It was fitted with a 49cc (84x90mm) side-valve single-cylinder engine and Gilera's own rear suspension unit.

Above: Gilera's first motorcycle was a 317cc (67x90mm) four-stroke single, with vertical cylinder and belt final drive; it was made in 1909.

between Milan and Lecco (only a few kilometres from Monza Park where the famous autodrome was to be constructed). His first product was the three-and-a-half horsepower Turismo of 1920 with a 498.76cc (84x90mm) inlet-over-exhaust single-cylinder engine. From 1925 a 346.3cc (70x90mm) engine was also offered and sport versions of both were available. In 1929 all the models were replaced

by a new overhead-valve version of the same basic engine, the Gran Sport, which was manufactured until the end of 1931.

Throughout the 1920s and early 1930s Gilera not only grew into one of the country's largest factories, but gained considerable success in events such as trials and long-distance races. Gilera's brother, Luigi, also played an important part in the factory's

Top: Piero Taruffi pictured in the twin-boom Gilera Tarf record-breaking machine in October 1954. It was powered by a 500cc Gilera four-cylinder GP engine.

Above: The Saturno, with its 500cc ohv single-cylinder engine, was probably Gilera's most famous model. This one is from 1953.

fortunes and was particularly successful on three-wheelers, using Gilera-powered sidecars in trials and racing for many years.

However, Gilera's ultimate goal was the International Grand Prix racing scene and, at the beginning of 1936, the chance to acquire the futuristic four-cylinder Rondine racing design was heaven-sent. First appearing back in the early 1920s as an air-cooled single overhead-cam, and named GRB (Gianini Remor Bonmartini), the design was later developed into a double overhead-cam with liquid-

This 1977 TGI roadster featured a 122.5cc (54x48mm) single-cylinder engine with piston-port induction and a five-speed gearbox.

cooling. Within a year the machine had been totally updated by the team of Piero Remor, Piero Taruffi and Giuseppe Gilera himself. Its original rigid, pressed-steel frame was superseded by a tubular device with swinging-arm rear suspension.

From then until the outbreak of World War II, the supercharged 492.7cc (52x58mm) four-cylinder Gilera went on to break world-speed records and win Grand Prix races, to become one of the most

GERRARD
England 1914–1915: Probably a misprint for Gerard (see above) or an abbreviation cum misspelling of Clement-Garrard (see above).

GERVO
Germany 1924–1925: This firm produced lightweights with 173cc DKW two-strokes as well as unspecified 198cc lightweights.

GH
Czechoslovakia 1924–1925: Gustav Heinz fitted 172cc Villiers engines to his machines.

GHIARONI
Italy 1970s– : Efrem Ghiaroni founded a bicycle factory in 1966 and went on to build mopeds such as the Bimbo Bip Bip and the Camel with Morini motors.

GIACOMASSO
Italy (Vignola) 1926–1935: This firm produced initially a 175cc two-stroke, later (1927) an overhead-valve Moser of the same capacity, then (1933) 489 and 595cc overhead-valve twins with shaft drive using Felice Giacomasso's own engines.

GIANOGLIO
Italy 1932: This firm made 70cc autocycles.

GIANT
Japan 1924: Murato Iron Works built the first post-World War I Japanese motorcycle.

GIGANT
Austria (Vienna) 1936–1938: Side-valve and overhead-valve JAP engines powered roadgoing Gigants of 500, 600 and 750cc. Racers used JAP and Husqvarna.

GIGUET
France (St Denis) 1903: This was a pioneer with Minerva and De Dion Bouton engines.

GIMA
France (Puy de Dome) 1947–1956: These were lightweights of 108 to 250cc fitted with a variety of bought-in engines.

feared motorcycle contenders in Europe. By this time, together with Moto Guzzi, Gilera had become the largest motorcycle manufacturer in Italy. Besides its highly successful overhead-valve singles, ranging from the 175 Siro through to the best selling V-series of 500s, Gilera also built the moto carri (motorcycle truck), which appeared in 1936 and was to continue until 1963.

During the war, Gilera followed in the footsteps of its great British racing rival, Norton: just as the Bracebridge Street, Birmingham, marque raced the superb double overhead-cam single – yet went to war with its plodding 16H side-valver – Gilera produced the equally gutless LTE model for the war. But the Italian company went on to build the much superior Marte (Mars) which, despite being in sidecar form, had a much better performance, as well as shaft final drive. It was unique amongst wartime motorcycles as it provided drive for both the rear wheel and the sidecar at the same time as offering rear suspension.

Postwar, Gilera soon got back in its stride by offering the 498.77cc Saturno and the smaller 247cc (68x68mm) Nettuno models. The larger machine, first designed in 1939 by Ing. Giuseppe Salmaggi, became one of their all-time greats.

Also during 1939, Gilera had sanctioned a smaller four, a 250. Development spread into June 1940 when Italy joined the war; although the engine was completed and test run, its fate

The Nordwest 600 arrived in 1991 and was highly acclaimed. Some examples were even raced in single cylinder events.

was sealed by the combination of the conflict and the subsequent FIM ban on supercharging in postwar racing. However, the 350 four played a vital role in the development of a new four-cylinder 500 racer which Ing. Remor designed in the immediate postwar era.

Completed during 1947, this new 496.7cc (52x58mm) was not wheeled out for action until 1948. The newcomer was entirely different from the pre-war design, with the exception of the unaltered across-the-frame layout of the cylinders. Normally aspirated and air-cooled, the engine (in 1948) put out 48bhp at 8500rpm; maximum speed was 200kph (125mph).

In 1949, the first year of the new FIM World Championship series, the first ever 500cc title holder was AJS-mounted Les Graham; Gilera's Nello Pagani was runner-up. Controversy came when Gilera's chief designer Ing. Remor left to join arch rivals MV Agusta. When rider Arciso Artesiani and chief mechanic Arturo Magni made the same move, Gilera rallied by re-engaging Taruffi, this time as team manager. Giuseppe Gilera also promoted Remor's former assistants, Columbo and Passoni, to joint heads of the technical department. The revised design

Above: The advanced 1992 125 GFR SP could reach 160kph (100mph) and was a serious challenger to Aprilia and Cagiva.

Below left: Gilera launched the futuristic 125 CX in 1991 at the Milan Show. It had single-sided front and rear forks.

team was obviously pressed for time to carry out its task, but even so, the re-organised squad struck gold, winning the 1950 500cc world title with Umberto Masetti, who had been signed to replace the departed Artesiani. The four-cylinder Gilera's finest hour was yet to come and this was with the signing of Englishman Geoff Duke at the beginning of 1953.

Gilera also eventually took part in other classes besides the Blue Ribbon 500cc categories, having works entries at various times in the 125, 350 and 500cc classes. At the end of the 1957 season, Gilera quit the Grand Prix through cost reasons, together with FB Mondial and Moto Guzzi.

Although Gilera did return to the GP scene during the mid-1960s – via the Scuderia Duke effort (1963), the success of the

Argentinian Benedicto Caldarella (1964), plus sidecar achievements with the Swiss star Florion Camathias (1964) – it was never to reach the level of the success it garnered in the golden days of the 1950s. Instead, it concentrated on trials and later, motocross, as a way of publicity, and was then caught up in the general sales recession which hit the Italian motorcycle industry of the 1960s.

Besides its range of overhead-valve parallel valve unit-construction singles (which ranged from 98 to 202cc), Gilera also had its 305.3cc 300 twin, all of which were basically 1950s designs, the Saturno/Nettuno series having been discontinued at the end of that decade.

Gilera also attempted to introduce new models, including a moped, a couple of scooters and a quartet of larger capacity four-strokes: the B50 500 overhead-valve twin (prototype only); the 350/500cc double overhead-cam twins (again only in prototype guise); and a 750cc triple with styling akin to the original Honda CB750 four.

However, all these innovations were to no avail and, finally, in November 1968, a receiver was appointed at the Arcore plant where 280 of the 550 workers were already working on short time.

A few months later the giant Piaggio organisation gained control. As for Giuseppe Gilera, his retirement was to be relatively

With scooter sales booming in the 1990s, Gilera introduced several new models, including this 1998 50cc Stalker, which featured automatic transmission.

short-lived, and on 21 November 1971, just before his 82nd birthday, this great figure of Italian motorcycling passed away.

Under Piaggio stewardship, the Gilera marque was reborn in the 1970s and once more became a powerhouse of activity, both on the production front with a raft of new models (both two- and four-stroke) and in the sporting world with ISDT gold medals and participation in the world motocross championships.

During the 1980s Gilera was in the very vanguard of Italian motorcycle industry developments with an entirely new range of small capacity two-strokes (up to 350cc) and also some exciting four-strokes, beginning with the new 348.9cc (80x69.4mm) Dakota trail bike which debuted at the Milan Show in November 1985. This was followed by a whole family of models including the Nuovo Saturno and the Nordwest. Two-strokes were not forgotten either, with the GFR 250 (GP racer), Crono (racer replica) and the futuristic CX 125. However, just before the opening of the Milan Show in late 1993, Piaggio announced that it was ending motorcycle production at the Arcore factory. Most observers thought this was the end, but it was not. Gilera has survived and today looks set for a major return, backed up by a range of new four-cylinder superbikes.

Gilera built a small number of the Piuma racing-only version of its Saturno Nuovo from 1991 to 1993. These were campaigned in the European Supermono race series.

GILERA SATURNO

1946

The original Saturno is probably Gilera's most well-known series production model and was the work of Ing. Giuseppe Salmaggi who returned from Belgium where he had worked for Sarolea who, together with FN, represented that country's two premier motorcycle manufacturing concerns.

The Saturno gained its name from Gilera's astronomical theme which produced other models with names such as Nettuno (Neptune) and Marte (Mars). Making its debut in the spring of 1940 in competition guise, it won two races in the Italian Junior Championship series at Palermo and Modena, ridden by the diminutive Massimo Masserini, on both occasions beating a pack of Moto Guzzi Condors in the process.

Then came the war and no more civilian production until late 1945. The year 1946 saw three distinct Saturno models: Sport, Turismo and Competition. The three versions were virtually identical except for sate of engine tune, with the same basic overhead-

Designed by Giuseppe Salmaggi, the Saturno, with its ohv single cylinder engine, was built in three versions: Sport, Turismo and competition. This is a 1952 Sport.

valve 498.7cc (84x90mm) engine size employed on the earlier V-series in pre-war days. However, apart from this, the engine of the Saturno was considerably different. The more specialised

San Remo racer made its debut in 1947 and produced 35bhp at 6000rpm.

The first really major update for the Saturno range came at the end of 1950 with telescopic forks, full-width alloy front-brake hub and a restyling exercise. A year later, the rear suspension was changed in favour of vertically mounted twin shock absorbers. The racing model with these changes was renamed

Corsa and built between 1951 and 1956. There was also the Franco Passoni-designed twin cam racing Saturno – only two machines with the engine were built (1952–1953). Another facet of the Saturno was the Cross (motocross) model, which was built between 1952 and 1956.

As for the roadster, this continued in production from 1952 onwards, and featured developments such as telescopic fork, twin short swinging-arm and alloy front hub. The final two Saturnos (Sport roadsters) were sold in 1960, although they had been built the previous year. In total, some 6450 examples of all Saturnos were manufactured; 170 of these were racers.

Engine: 498.76cc ohv 2v vertical single, 84x90mm, air-cooled
Power: 18bhp at 4500rpm, Sport model: 22bhp at 5000rpm
Gearbox: 4-speed foot change
Final drive: chain
Weight: 168kg (370lb)
Top speed: 120kph (75mph), Sport model: 130kph (81mph)

GILERA B300 TWIN

1954

The B300 twin was the sensation of the 31st Milan Show held at the end of 1953. Its 305.3cc (60x54mm) seems an unusual choice of engine size. However, this was because Gilera had refused to allow themselves to be confined to arbitrary capacity limits and had chosen instead to design according to the requirements of the job in hand. In any case, this had the added advantage of ensuring they were able to employ several mechanical components from the well-developed 150 (introduced a year before in Turismo and Sport guises, including the same 152.68cc and 60x54mm bore and stroke measurements).

In its general appearance the twin followed the smaller models with its telescopic forks, twin shocks, swinging-arm rear suspension and full-width polished-alloy brake hubs. The wheel rims were of light alloy and so too were the Gilera-made silencers. Although lacking any real power (12bhp at 5800rpm on the first series), the B300 did have

The B300 ohv twin made its debut at the 1953 Milan Show, and remained in production until 1969. The picture shows a Series 2 machine, built in the early 1960s.

the advantage of being exceptionally smooth, easy to start, with decent flexibility. When *Motor Cycling* magazine tested an example in December 1954 they recorded a maximum speed of only 113kph (70mph), but this was a tourer, not a sportster.

Much of the engine also followed features pioneered on the 125/150 overhead-valve single; such as parallel valves, coil valve springs, wet multi-plate clutch, built-up crankshaft, four-ring piston and dynamo lighting. The cylinders were inclined forwards 10 degrees from the vertical.

The 300 Extra (and also a smaller 250 Export) were launched at the Milan Show in November 1955, and they went on sale early in 1956. The most notable change compared to the original series was the fitment of a dual saddle to replace the single spring seat.

Later the Extra gained Silentium-made chromed steel silencers in place of Gilera's own alloy-bodied type.

Besides mainland Europe (the small twin was not imported into the UK), Gilera's B300 was sold in the USA during the early to mid-1960s. Production finally ceased in 1966.

Engine: 305.3cc ohv 2v parallel twin, 30x54mm, air-cooled
Power: 15bhp at 6800rpm
Gearbox: four-speed foot change
Final drive: chain
Weight: 150kg (330lb)
Top speed: 125kph (77.5mph)

GILERA 500 GP FOUR
1954

The arrival of Geoff Duke in 1953 heralded a fresh bout of development for Gilera. Following his arrival, the Gilera engineering team began intensive development and testing, incorporating some of his suggestions. The 'nortonised' model was the result, looking like the Norton Featherbed; the engine specification was unchanged.

This was rectified for 1954. Ing. Franco Passoni, responsible for Gilera's race development, focussed on the power unit. The

A 500cc four-cylinder Gilera Grand Prix bike of the type raced by factory riders, including World Champion Geoff Duke, during the mid-1950s.

stroke was increased from 58 to 58.8mm, giving a displacement of 499.504cc. A modified sump placed the engine lower in the frame, yet ground clearance was increased by tucking the exhaust pipes closer to the engine. The valve angle was widened and the valve diameter changed.

Passoni used built-up crankshafts and the gearbox was given an extra ratio, making five in all. The Lucas rotating-magnet magneto was fitted. The 500 four-cylinder Grand Prix Gilera had reached its definitive form. A smaller 350 (349.66cc, 46x52.6mm) four arrived in 1956. Between 1949 and 1963, Gilera won 38 solo and eight sidecar GPs with its four-cylinder models, and six world championships, all 500cc.

Engine: 499.49cc dohc 2v straight 4, 52x58.8mm, air-cooled
Power: 70bhp at 10,500rpm
Gearbox: 5-speed foot change
Final drive: chain
Weight: 150kg (330lb)
Top speed: 260kph (161.5mph)

GILERA CI CROSS
1981

Thanks to the success garnered by the Elmeca-Gileras (see separate marque section), Piaggio authorised Gilera to build batches of off-road models, and also to enter works-supported riders.

To achieve this, the services of the Dutch two-stroke specialist Jan Witteveen were acquired. He took charge in 1980, which resulted in a new 125 with water-cooling. His expertise was applied to the existing Gilera engine (used by Elmeca-Gilera to win the 1978 Italian Motocross title in air-cooled form) making it more efficient, rather than having to create a completely new unit. Thus the 54x53.6mm bore and stroke dimensions of the Elmeca-developed engine were retained.

One of the Witteveen water-cooled 125 motocross machines was campaigned in the 1981 and 1982 Italian and World Championships by factory rider

The C1 Cross and the C1 Enduro (the latter illustrated) were essentially the same bike with detail changes and were the work of Dutchman Jan Wittereen.

Michele Rinaldi with some success. The works model, raced by Rinaldi, had Marzocchi single shock rear suspension. The customer version, the CI Competizione Cross, differed by its twin rear shocks (Corte Cosso), but still used the liquid-cooled motor. An enduro version of the production bike, the EI, was also offered. For 1983, the customer motocrosser became the C2 with revised styling and the single

shock rear suspension, as pioneered on the works model.

Gilera also built a 125 twin motocrosser in 1981, which gave a class-leading 36bhp at 12,000rpm.

Engine: 122.75cc 2s reed vertical single, 54x53.6mm, liquid-cooled
Power: 32bhp at 10,000rpm
Gearbox: 6-speed foot change
Final drive: chain
Weight: 85kg (187lb)
Top speed: 140kph (89mph)

GLORIA
England 1924–1925: Campion built the frames, and Train supplied the two-stroke engines for these machines.

GLORIA
England 1931–1933: This was a Villiers-engined 98cc lightweight.

GLORIA
Italy 1948–1955: Focesi built mopeds and a 123cc lightweight.

GN
Italy 1920–1925: Giuseppe Navone assembled 346cc two-strokes from mainly English components.

GNADIG
Germany 1925–1926: Franz Gnadig built a 500cc overhead-valve machine with shaft drive; the power unit reputedly formed the basis of the first Kuhne proprietary engines.

GNOM
Germany 1921–1923: This was an auxiliary 63cc cycle motor.

GODIER GENOUD
France 1980s: This firm produced racers and high-performance sports machines with Kawasaki and Honda motors up to 1300cc: the 1135 R delivered 120bhp at 8500rpm, weighed 241kg (530lb) and could top 260kph (160mph).

GOEBEL
Germany (Bielefeld) 1951–1979: These mopeds were fitted with 49cc Sachs engines.

GOETZ
Germany 1925–1935: These were in limited production (79 machines in total, mostly built to order) with a wide variety of engines.

GOGGO
Germany (Dingolfing) 1951–1954: Ilo two-strokes of 123, 147 and 173cc powered scooters from Hans Glas, better known for his later Goggomobil micro-cars.

GO-KART
USA 1959: Tiny, light (25kg/55lb) mini-bike, the Big Bear Scramble.

GOLD-RAD
Germany (Cologne) 1952–1981: These mopeds were fitted with 49cc proprietary engines.

GILERA DAKOTA 350

1986

The first the world saw of Gilera's new 1980s breed of four-stroke, designed by Ing. Lucio Masut, was at the Milan Show in November 1985. Not only did the famous old factory have one of the biggest and most impressive stands at the exhibition, they also had an exciting newcomer in the shape of the 350 Dakota trailster, with the added promise of a larger version in the pipeline.

The Dakota 348cc (80x69mm) single employed every trick in the book, including liquid-cooling, four-valve cylinder head, twin exhaust ports, twin 25mm (1in) Dell 'Orto carbs, double overhead-cam driven by toothed belt, a balancer shaft (gear-driven directly off the crankshaft) multi-plate hydraulically operated clutch, five-speed gearbox and Japanese-made electronic ignition and electric starter. There was also a forged piston and one-piece crankshaft which ran on anti-vibration ring bearings. With all this technology, it was something of a shock to realise that this hi-tech engine only

put out 33bhp at 7500rpm. Gilera had, for sales reasons, built a dual-purpose on-off-roader rather than a street bike because, at the time, sales of machines like Yamaha's Tenere were riding high in mainland Europe, if not in Britain.

To counter the machine's biggest failing (lack of power) Gilera introduced a 500 (492cc, 92x74mm) variant in 1987. At the same time, an ER version of the 350 was offered. This featured a smaller tank, and the twin

Designed by Lucio Masut, the 348cc (80x69mm) Dakota made its debut in November 1985. It featured liquid-cooling, four valves and belt-driven cams.

radiators were now shrouded by abbreviated plastic panels. These two changes enabled the rider to sit further forward and thus in a more comfortable position.

With a dry weight of 147kg (324lb) for both engine sizes, the Dakota was one of the heaviest machines in its class. However, the basic engine was very strong and the square-type enduro-based chassis was fully capable of taking more development.

The result was the XRT 600 and this machine debuted at the end of 1987.

Engine: 348.89cc dohc 4v vertical single, 80x69.4mm, liquid-cooled
Power: 39bhp (crank)
Gearbox: 5-speed foot change
Final drive: chain
Weight: 148kg (326lb)
Top speed: 145kph (90mph)

GILERA NUOVO SATURNO

1988

The Nuovo (New) Saturno, first displayed to the general public at the 1987 Milan Show, was a classic sports roadster using modern technology. Very much a joint Italian-Japanese project, it was initially commissioned by the Japanese trading company, C. Itoh. After Milan, the prototype was displayed by Itoh at the Mega Show in Tokyo in December 1987.

The Gilera-built machine was the work of Arcore engineer Sandro Colombo, and the Japanese technician N Hagi Wara. Re-inventing the classic Saturno big single in a modern, user-friendly guise, the duo used the 492cc Dakota engine to create a compact café racer. Weighting in at 135kg (296lb), the Nuovo Saturno had a purpose-built trellis steel-tube frame and an aluminium swinging-arm with eccentric adjustment for the final drive chain. The components were best quality: the footrests, rear brake and gear-change levers were in aluminium, as was the kick-start lever. The 40mm (one-and-two-thirds ins) front forks had 120mm (four-and-a-half ins) of travel and were of

The Nuovo (New) Saturno was an Italian-Japanese joint venture. Using the 492cc Dakota engine it was built as a modern-day café racer.

conventional layout. The rear end was taken care of by an adjustable racing-type single shock absorber, with 130mm (5ins) of travel.

Other details of the specification included a half-fairing, clip-ons, rear-set foot controls, a single race-type saddle and a hi-level black exhaust system which exited into a single silencer. The engine literally hung in the frame and was readily accessible. Producing 45bhp (crank) and thirty-six-and-a-half brake horsepower (rear wheel), the Gilera single could achieve 178.5kph (111mph). It was sold in other markets besides Japan and Italy, including Great Britain.

Engine: 492cc dohc 4v vertical single, 92x74mm, liquid-cooled
Power: 45bhp (crank)
Gearbox: 5-speed foot change
Final drive: chain
Weight: 140kg (308lb)
Top speed: 178.5kph (111mph)

GILERA GFR 250 GP RACER 1992

In 1991 Piaggio (Gilera's owners) had set up a racing division to promote their motorcycle marque (like the Honda Racing Corporation), especially to design and build racing prototypes. It was

The hi-tech GFR 250 racer of 1992 was built to challenge the Japanese dominance of the 250cc racing class. It produced 85bhp and could reach 265kph (165mph).

headed by former Bimota design chief Frederico Martini.

At the Milan Show in 1991 it was announced that Gilera would be contesting the 1992 250cc World Road Racing Championship series, with riders Carlos Lavado (winner of 19 GPs in the 250cc class) and Jean Phillipe Ruggia, on a brand new 75-degree V-twin two-stroke, very similar to its two main rivals, Honda and Yamaha. A

more detailed appraisal of the machine revealed twin Mikuni or Dell 'Orto carburettors (fuel injection was also tested), reed-valve induction (designed by the Austrian engineer Harold Bartol) with electronically timed exhaust valves, a six-speed gearbox, balancer shaft and magnesium engine casings. A single crankshaft was used to prevent possible flexing at ultra-high engine revolutions. The chassis was of Delta-box aluminium with Kyaba suspension front and rear. Inverted front forks featured an adjustable steering head rake.

But Gilera and Martini couldn't quite succeed with the GFR, even though its power output (85bhp) was identical to Honda's championship winning NSR.

Engine: 249cc reed 2s V-Twin, 56x50.7mm, liquid-cooled
Power: 85bhp at 13,000rpm
Gearbox: 6-speed foot change
Final drive: chain
Weight: 95kg (209lb)
Top speed: 266kph (165mph)

GILERA RUNNER SCOOTER 1998

For those countless enthusiasts around the world who believed the Gilera name had been lost at the end of 1993, there was good news. Since then, Gilera has risen from the ashes by building an entirely new range of machines, heading the class-leading range of liquid-cooled Runner scooters. Scooter might not be a word many would have associated with Gilera, but at the dawn of the twenty-first-century, scooter sales are actually booming.

Gilera publicity material announces that the Runner series (available in three engine sizes: 50, 123.5 and 175.8cc) are 'combining for the first time, the practicality and ease of use of a scooter, with rigidity, and handling of a fully-fledged motorcycle'. Several machines from the past have already attempted to bridge the gap between scooter and motorcycle (such as the Moto Guzzi Galletto), so this remains to be seen.

But what sets the new Gilera apart from the earlier efforts of the 1950s is the advantages of modern technology. The Runner's

The Runner Scooter is built in three engine sizes; 50, 125 and 180cc. The latter is capable of 120kph (75mph). All feature automatic transmission.

specification includes features such as super-rigid frame construction, inverted front forks, alloy wheels with low-profile tyres, a powerful hydraulically operated disc front brake and a sleek fairing with flowing lines.

The largest Runner – coded the 180 – is capable of 120kph (75mph). All three employ liquid-cooled, single-cylinder engines with automatic oil pumps, electronic capacitive ignition (CDI) with variable advance and a choice of kick- or push-button electric, and 12volt batteries.

Since 1999 the Runner 50 and 125 scooters have provided the base for the Gilera Runner Trophy, an international one-model race series which involves more than 200 riders from all over Europe. The series is organised in two engine sizes (70 and 180cc) in collaboration with engine tuning specialists Malossi.

Engine: 175.8cc 2s horizontal single, 65.6x50mm, liquid-cooled
Power: 21bhp at 8000rpm
Gearbox: automatic CVT variator with torque convertor
Final drive: gears
Weight: 115kg (254lb)
Top speed: 120kph (75mph)

GILLET-HERSTAL

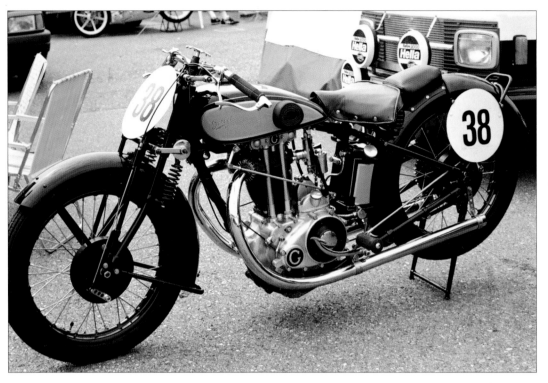

FOUNDED BY LÉON GILLET, this was one of the major firms in Belgium. Their first motorcycle was designed by Fernand Laguesse and went into production during 1920. It had a 301cc two-stroke engine built in unit with a two-speed gearbox which sat ahead of the crankcase to place the final drive belt pulley as far from the rear wheel as possible. This was positioned here in order to reduce slip. Other features included a front-mounted magneto, rear exhaust port, loop frame and girder forks.

Later in the year the company added a model for sidecar work, using a 750cc MAG V-twin engine, and in 1922 this was joined by one of 996cc. By then, the two-stroke engine had been bored out to 347cc and the firm was much involved in competitions of various types. In 1924 this led Laguesse to design a water-cooled, two-stroke engine with opposed pistons in a common bore and a single crankshaft. One piston was attached in the normal manner, and the other was attached by a pair of extended rods.

Another design was a 347cc two-stroke engine, with a rotary valve built into one mainshaft and

Gillet-Herstal built engines featuring unit construction from the start, first making two-strokes, then four-strokes, such as this 1930 ohv model of 499cc.

three primary gears on the other for the gearbox ratios, that had a very compact crankcase to boost primary compression. On two of these machines, François Andrieux and Robert Sexé rode round the world during 1926 to bring fame to the firm and a new model, the Tour du Monde. By this time, the compact engine had become reversed in the frame to put the magneto at the rear, the exhaust at the front and the gearbox output shaft better placed for chain drive.

In 1926 a 499cc overhead-valve engine made its debut and kept the unit construction typical of the marque. It was installed vertically in a conventional frame and would progress over the years to follow the trends to saddle tank, better forks, foot change and larger brakes. During 1928 Van Oirbeek was recruited from FN to design racing engines, resulting in a trio of overhead-camshaft unit-construction singles of 348, 499 and 582cc, the camshaft driven by vertical shaft and bevels, the magneto at the rear. With these

and the overhead-valve engines, the firm won races and set records in both solo and sidecar classes.

There were new models for 1930, the start of a new decade, using 398 and 499cc side-valve plus 346cc overhead-valve engines, all inclined but still of unit construction. These were joined by a side-valve of 547cc in 1932 which was stretched to 600cc

A Gillet-Herstal from the 1930s with the unit-construction, ohv engine it used for many years. This type of engine also appeared in several capacities.

for the next year, but with the engine back to vertical, and later joined by an overhead-valve 600. The hard times of the Depression years brought a simple lightweight to the range powered by a 166cc two-stroke engine with three speeds. It was later joined by a 100cc vélomoteur and a smaller 123cc lightweight and these small machines, plus the single-cylinder four-strokes, formed the basis of the range up to 1939.

By the mid-1930s, the firm was supplying machines to the army and this culminated in the 720 model that was built solely for them in sidecar form. It had a 708cc twin-cylinder two-stroke engine built in unit with a four-speed and reverse gearbox with chain drive to the rear wheel and by shaft from that to the sidecar wheel.

After the war the firm continued with some of the four-strokes, now with telescopic front forks, and late in 1946 announced the Superconfort model with a 239cc two-stroke engine in a modern style with rear suspension. It was later joined by others in the same form, while the rear suspension soon went on the whole range. The two-strokes ranged in size from 125cc upwards and in 1953 a scooter was added, but this was a Bernardet built under licence.

In 1955 Gillet merged with FN and Saroléa in an attempt to survive in a contracting market and 1956 saw them offer a moped, but this was common to the group and made under licence. Gradually, production wound down and finally ceased in 1960.

GITAN

ITALY 1950–85

THE GITAN MARQUE WAS an amalgam of GI from the name Gino, and TAN from the name Tansini, the company's founder. The company's factory was located in the Italian principality of San Marino and its first products included a DKW RT125-like single-cylinder two-stroke with piston-port induction and a l60cc four-stroke powered by an overhead-valve unit construction single-cylinder engine.

The two-stroke was the more popular of the two machines, and employed blade-type front forks and plunger rear suspension. Later, a more modern version with telescopic forks and a swinging-arm frame was introduced by the company.

A 175cc four-stroke single, again with pushrod operated valves and unit construction of the engine and gearbox arrived in 1955.

Then, in the late 1950s, Gitan became something of a pioneer within the Italian motorcycle industry; the company manufactured the Grillo (Cricket), this machine being of a very similar design concept to Honda's best-selling C50 Cub model, with its pressed-steel step-through frame.

During the 1960s, Gitan hung on. This was a time when many

Located in the principality of San Marino, Gitan offered various machines, including this DKW RT125-like single-cylinder two-stroke from the mid-1950s.

smaller Italian marques went to the wall but the Gitan marque managed to stay alive by concentrating its production on 50cc-class machines. Notable amongst these were the utilitarian commuter models, with the occasional sports ultra-lightweight motorcycle thrown in to keep the Gitan name alive and in the media spotlight. This trend continued throughout the 1970s, even though by this time many other companies

had returned to full-size motorcycles powered by engines of – at least – 125cc.

In the end, this refusal to design and build machines larger than 50cc models was to be Gitan's undoing. The 1980s arrived, and brought with them a recession from which Gitan couldn't recover, as by this time capital to reinvest in new models didn't exist. The company was consequently wound up in 1985.

The Gitan 125 Sport featured a 123cc piston-port induction engine, blade-type girder front forks and plunger rear suspension. Top speed was 100kph (62mph).

GRAPHIC
England (Wolverhampton) 1903–1906: This assembler used Minerva, MMC and Sarolea engines.

GRASETTI
Italy 1952–1965: These were two-strokes with in-house 123 and 148cc motors.

GRATIEUX
France 1919–1921: These two-stroke radials came from a firm better known for aircraft engines.

GRAVES
England (Sheffield) 1914–1915: The Graves Speed King was an 'own-brand' machine built for Graves by Omega at Wolverhampton with 293cc JAP side-valve.

GREEN
England (London, later Bexhill) 1919–1923: This firm built water-cooled engines, mostly singles; and later converted air-cooled engines to water-cooling.

GREYHOUND
USA (Buffalo, New York) 1907–1914: These singles were rated at four-and-a-half horsepower and built by Thor.

GREYHOUND
England 1905–1907: Fafnir, Minerva and MMC engines powered the machines from this small assembler.

GRG
Italy (Turin) 1926–1927: Two 175cc Della Ferrera singles were coupled together to give a 350cc twin. The firm also made auxiliary cycle motors.

GRI
England 1921–1922: G.R. Inshaw designed these 350 and 500cc machines, built by MacRae & Dick.

GRIGG
England 1920–1925: After beginning with a 200cc two-stroke scooter, Grigg built a great variety of machines up to 1000cc with proprietary engines, both two- and four-stroke.

GRIMPEUR
see LE GRIMPEUR

GRIMSHAW
England (Sunderland) 1908: This monster 2596cc V-twin rated at 20hp; the whole bike weighed only 150kg (330lb).

GORI

FOUNDED BY GIANCARLO GORI, this marque was known for its excellent dirt bikes; motocross, enduro and trials. Gori also produced children's models and a couple of ultra-sporting 125s: a pukka racer and a super sports roadster.

The racer, using a specially tuned German Sachs two-stroke engine with six-speed gearbox, was successful in hill-climb events; Guido Valli became the Italian national champion in both 1974 and 1975 on his Sachs-powered 125 Gori. Following this, Gori offered a customer version of the same machine. Its specification included: 123.6cc (54x54mm), 13:1 compression ratio, 34mm (one-and-a-third ins) Bing carb, Motoplat ignition, Marzocchi suspension, 170mm (6.7ins) Fontana double-sided drum front brake and a low-slung expansion chamber exhaust. Producing over 24bhp at 11,600rpm, the Gori hill-climber had a maximum speed of almost 185kph (115mph).

The street version, named the 125 Sport Valli Replica, used the same (slightly detuned) Sachs unit, but with a full fairing, twin front discs, cast-alloy wheels and sharp styling. Barely road legal, it was the quickest production 125cc street bike in Italy, with a claimed maximum of 148kph (92mph).

This 1978 Gori 250 enduro bike was powered by a bought-in Hiro two-stroke engine. The spec also included long travel forks.

By 1980 Gori offered motocross and enduro models of 125 and 250cc, using Hiro-built two-stroke engines. The 125 RG (enduro) featured a six-speed transmission, Sachs Hydra cross rear shocks, Dell 'Orto 30mm (1in) carburettor with fully sealed air filter, long-travel front forks, Metzeler tyres, Megura levers and unbreakable plastic for the mudguards, tank and side panels. The motocross version had lighting equipment and a more highly tuned motor.

SWM acquired Gori in 1980. The new firm, Go-Motor, collapsed in 1985 with SWM, both being badly hit by early 1980s recession.

Above: On a works-support Gori 125, Guido Valli became Italian National Hillclimb Champion in 1974 and 1975.

Below: By 1980, when this 250cc trials model was built, Gori was concentrating its efforts in the off-road market.

GNOME & RHÔNE

FRANCE 1919–59

GNOME & RHÔNE, well known as an aircraft producer, began motorcycle manufacturing with the British Bradshaw-designed ABC flat-twin machine under licence in 1919. In 1923 it began constructing its own range of singles, from 300 to 350 and 500cc, considered to be very high quality products. From 1931 it made flat-twin machines in the BMW shaft-drive idiom, with a 250cc single-cylinder bike, and in 1935, turned its attentions to the production of the 724cc overhead-valve Type X. In 1939, as war clouds loomed, it came out with an 800cc side-valve twin exclusively for use by the French Army.

Gnome & Rhône's postwar output centred on top class 125 and 200cc two-stroke motorcycles, but production ended in 1959.

In the same way as BMW, this prestigious French company had a history of making bikes powered by flat-twin engines. During the 1930s, it made its own flat-twin machines; the overhead-valve

Type X of 1935 was one of the largest and most prestigious bikes produced in France. It developed 30bhp at 5500rpm, and proved to be an excellent workhorse for hauling sidecars. It had a four-speed gearbox with shaft drive transmission and a pressed-steel frame with girder front forks.

Above: The company's post-war production focused on quality two-strokes, having abandoned its flat twin machines in 1939.

Below: During the 1930s, the company was noted for robust ohv flat-twin bikes, such as this 499cc CV2 from 1934.

GREEVES

ENGLAND 1953–77

THE ESSEX-BASED COMPANY Greeves was founded by draughtsman and engineer Bert Greeves and his cousin Derry Preston-Cobb. The latter was disabled, so they set up as Invacar

to make invalid carriages powered by Villiers engines. As experienced motorcyclists, Greeves and works manager Frank Byford came up with a prototype motorbike in 1950 as a means of evaluating a

weatherproof rubber suspension set-up, giving 128mm (5ins) of travel at the front and 103mm (4ins) at the rear. Power for the productionised motorcycles of 1953 came from 197cc Villiers

won the European 250cc Championship in 1962 and 1963. The following year Greeves and Stonebridge came up with their own 246cc engine for the Challenger, an all-new scrambles bike producing 30bhp at 7500rpm.

These machines were sturdy, with knobbly tyres fitted both front and rear and, latterly, capacious plastic mudguards. However, Greeves was a casualty of the influx of Spanish Bultaco and Montessa rivals, and it lost its prime slot in the off-roaders market.

When Villiers' engine production ended in 1968, the 197cc single – the East Coaster twin and Challenger trials model – had no readily available source for their engines. In the early 1970s, Greeves listed only the Griffon, using a 380cc motor. When the founders retired in 1977, the company ended production.

Below: Greeves offered telescopic forks for the first time in 1967, and its scrambles machines, like this 380cc Griffon, helped keep the company going until 1977.

engines, and Greeves proved to be a great success in trialling and scrambles. Unusually, they were built up on a cast-alloy H-section beam frame, and the rubber suspension persisted until the mid-1950s, when regular spring/damper units came in. Up front, hydraulic dampers were superseded by telescopic forks as late as 1968, and a more conventional tubular frame was also available.

Greeves were exported in large numbers during the 1950s, and larger 250cc Villiers and two-cylinder British Anzani engines were sold as roadster models, some bought by police forces.

Above: One of the marque's greatest successes was its victory in the 1969 Scottish Six Days Trial, using a 250cc Villiers-powered Anglian similar to this one.

The Hawkstone was a 197cc scrambles bike named after the venue. Development engineer Brian Stonebridge took on the challenge of the best of the scrambling fraternity and beat the top names on the little Greeves in the 350cc event and came second in the 500cc challenge. So often success breeds success, and he was followed by Dave Bickers, who became Greeves' work's rider and

GRIFFON

FRANCE 1901–55

THEIR FIRST MOTORCYCLE was a heavy-duty bicycle with braced forks, a Clément engine with belt drive and the fuel tank mounted on the headstock. From this small beginning the firm was soon involved with a range powered by single or V-twin Swiss Zedel

An early Griffon with a 220cc engine with automatic inlet valve and reduction gear to the belt pulley. This helped improve the belt contact and reduced slip.

engines. The twins were used for racing, and in 1904 they represented France in the International Cup with Demester the winner, although the race was declared void.

The road models remained a single and a V-twin, both with automatic inlet valves and, when the twin had the optional magneto, it went high above the engine, driven by a long shaft and bevels, the fuel tank recessed for it. Belt drive remained, while leading-link

front forks disappeared. By 1909 the single was listed with a 220cc engine with a reduction gear built in unit to allow the use of a much smaller rear-wheel pulley. Zedel engines, as well as some from Anzani, continued in use after World War I.

Singles and V-twins continued for the 1920s with magneto ignition, separate gearbox, girder forks and drum brakes. There were also lightweights with two-stroke engines and the simplest specification. Style was chic, but later in the 1920s the firm became part of the Peugeot group and so throughout the 1930s and postwar, the Griffon was simply a Peugeot with a change of badge.

GRINDLAY-PEERLESS

ENGLAND 1923–34

LOCATED IN SHAKLETON ROAD, Coventry, this firm was known for its excellent sidecars prior to entering the motorcycle lists in

1923. With their background, it was hardly surprising that they scorned the usual lightweights that most started with, instead offering

a model powered by the massive 999cc sleeve-valve Barr & Stroud V-twin engine. This machine drove a three-speed Sturmey-Archer

gearbox with chain final drive and was well finished. It was a fine sight, especially when coupled to a Grindlay-Peerless sports sidecar.

The V-twin was joined by a single with a 488cc overhead-valve JAP engine for 1924. The next year saw this replaced by a 499cc sleeve-valve Barr & Stroud. These two were joined by three smaller singles, one with a 348cc sleeve-valve engine and the other two with 344 and 346cc overhead-valve JAP engines. The 488cc JAP returned for 1926 and that year the marque was noticed at Brooklands.

This was thanks to Bill Lacey, who became famous for his tuning and riding abilities, and also for the immaculate, clean appearance of his machines. He began to win using a 344cc JAP-powered Grindlay-Peerless in 1926; two years later he set the 500cc one-hour record to 166km (103.3 miles), increasing this to 169km (105.25 miles) in 1929.

The sleeve-valve models were dropped for 1927 to leave the 344, 346 and 488cc JAP engines. The larger was revised to 490cc for the next year when the range was extended to add models with 677cc side-valve JAP V-twin and 172cc Villiers two-stroke engines. All went forward for 1929 with a

Grindlay-Peerless were well known for breaking records at Brooklands, usually with singles, but this 1929 machine used a 996cc, ohv JAP engine.

490cc overhead-valve single, and 674cc overhead-valve and 750cc side-valve JAP V-twins for the close of the decade and 1930. The new decade added 196 and 247cc Villiers two-strokes, a 245cc (and more versions of the 490cc) overhead-valve JAP.

For 1931 the firm shortened their long list, dropping the

Villiers and JAP V-twin engines. They kept some JAP singles for that year alone and turned to the Rudge Python engine – using this in 348 and 499cc sizes, including the Ulster – but the range for 1932 was three models with Python engines; the 248cc overhead-valve Tiger Cub, and the 499cc overhead-valve Tiger and Tiger Chief, this last with the Ulster engine. More variants were added for the next year, with 248 and 499cc Speed Chief models plus the R500 for racing. In 1935 the firm turned to other products.

GUAZZONI

ITALY 1949–79

FORMERLY WITH MOTO MORINI, Aldo Guazzoni set up his own factory at Via Alta Guardia 6, Milan, quickly building up a reputation for innovation and quality.

Besides the staple diet of small capacity two-strokes, Guazzoni found time to create a very smart 200 (actually 191cc) overhead-camshaft model in 1954. This came equipped with telescopic front forks, swinging-arm rear

suspension and a full duplex frame. A tuned version which produced 13bhp took part in the long-distance events so popular at the time, such as the Milano-Taranto.

November 1959 brought the news that the newly released Guazzoni 175 horizontal two-stroke single-cylinder model was to be imported in Britain by the Manchester-based DOT concern. This was followed in June 1960 by

another model, the 125 Sport, which featured an upright cylinder. There was also a 98 Sport, essentially the 125, but with a smaller engine displacement. Despite being an attractively styled on-off roader, the 125/150 Modernly was not imported.

Later Guazzoni built some interesting disc-valve models, notably a 60cc (45x41mm) racer in 1966, to be followed in 1969 by a 50cc version which took the Italian Senior Championship that year. This success brought about an exciting twin-cylinder 125 for GP events. But although it produced 32bhp at 12,500rpm, it could not match machines such as the Spanish Derbi, Japanese Suzuki or German MZ and was soon withdrawn.

During the 1970s, Guazzoni concentrated its efforts on mopeds and 50cc motorcycles, before finally closing later that decade.

In 1966, Guazzoni built a 60cc disc valve racer. This was followed in 1969 by the 50cc version which won the Italian Senior Championship that year.

GS MOTORI
Italy c.1950: The Gioello two-stroke cycle motor was also sold complete with a bicycle.

GSD
England (Coventry) 1921–1923: R.E.D. Grant built two shaft-drive models: one with a White and Poppe 350cc two-stroke, the other with a transverse-mounted Bradshaw 496cc flat-twin.

GUARALDI
Italy 1905–1916: This firm began with a 4hp Fafnir, and later used other engines as well (possibly Sarolea) from two-and-three-quarters to 4hp.

GUIA
Italy (Milan) 1950–1954: Ettore Buralli put small two-strokes (98 to 147cc) in both conventional tubular frames and pressed-steel frames.

GUIGNARD
France (Lyon) 1933–1938: These were lightweight two-strokes of 100 and 125cc.

GUILLER
France 1950–late 1950s: These were mopeds and lightweights, both two-stroke and four-stroke, up to 250cc, with engines from AMC, Aubier-Dunne, Junior, Vap and Ydral.

GUIZZARDI
Italy (Turin) 1926–1932: These lightweights had 125 and 175cc overhead-valve machines, including an overhead-cam model.

GUIZZO
Italy (Bologna) 1955–1962: Palmieri & Gulinelli made a 48cc moped and a 150cc scooter.

GULDNER
Germany 1925: Guldner built 350 and 50cc singles that were sufficiently similar to contemporary Nortons to allow interchange of many parts.

GUSTLOFF
Germany (Suhl) 1937–1940: These mopeds werer designed by Martin Stolle with 98cc engines.

G&W
England (Liverpool) 1902–1906: Guy and Wheeler used Fafnir, Minerva and Peugeot engines.

GYS
England early 1950s: These were mopeds and auxiliary cycle motors of 49cc.

HAGG TANDEM

ENGLAND 1920–24

THIS WAS ANOTHER ATTEMPT to offer both weather protection and enclosure of the works. Built by Arthur Hagg near St Albans, Hertfordshire, England it appeared at the 1921 Olympia Show as the Hagg Tandem.

It had a 349cc Precision two-stroke engine, two-speed Burman gearbox, belt final drive, and a long hand lever for starting, while the frame had a large diameter sloping top tube with angle steel members to carry the works and front and rear suspension.

The mechanics were concealed by side panels that hinged down to provide access for servicing.

Right: Weather protection, a two-stroke engine and rear suspension failed to entice many buyers for the Hagg Tandem. A sleeve-valve engine did no better.

Left: The Hagg Tandem used Biflex forks for its front suspension and had a saddle tank fitted over the large frame top tube.

Above went the cylindrical saddle tank and saddle, while below were footboards that ran forward to deep legshields. Aft of the panels was further enclosure and this rose up to support a bucket seat with sides for the pillion rider before continuing on to the rear number plate. This rear section had sides that shielded part of the rear wheel.

Despite reductions in engine noise, adding a conventional model, and changing the names in 1923 to the HT Tandem and HT Sports, sales were always low. Production ceased after 1924.

HARLEY-DAVIDSON

USA 1903–

THERE ARE FEW MACHINES which look or sound as much like motorcycles as a Harley-Davidson, and most of those are long out of production. The Harley is justly a legend and, like another legend, the Porsche, is a magnificent demonstration of how a primitive design can be refined until it stands comparison with many, much more advanced, machines.

The first ancestor of today's machines was a one-off, built in 1903 by three young men: Bill Harley designed it; Arthur Harley made the patterns; and Walter Davidson built it. They made two more the following year and sold them. Aunt Janet Davidson did the pin-striping and created the logo. Then in 1905 came eight more. In 1906, this was 50; in 1907, 100. Time to quit the day job. The next year, 1908, saw 450 machines, and the first V-twin – the design with which Harley-Davidson is inseparably linked – came in 1909.

Although the company continued to grow rapidly, it was not at first in the same class as its main rival Indian, whose machines were more technically advanced and (above all) faster. In the three or four years before World War I, competition between the two led to rapid technical improvements, including the adoption of the 'free engine', then gearboxes.

World War I was kind to the company for two reasons: first, they sold a lot of motorcycles to the government for the war effort and, because of better financial control, they made a lot more money out of them than Indian did. Second, they reserved almost half of their production for the civilian market, taking great care to steal as many Indian customers and dealers as possible. They also built up the famous Wrecking Crew racing team, and from 1914 until 1921 achieved an ever-more dominant position in the admittedly specialised world of American racing. When the war was over, Harley-Davidson was much better placed financially and in the marketplace than Indian. This lead grew until Indian went under.

The famous 'Wrecking Crew' racing team on a wood-block speedway. It is hard to convey what a terrifyingly slippery surface wood is to race on.

However, it was not all plain sailing for Harley-Davidson, either. As early as 1920, the low-cost automobile – bought second-hand if necessary – was increasingly affordable in the United States, a country with immense natural resources and few inhabitants, so the attractions of a motorcycle as everyday transport diminished accordingly. The company stopped official support for racing in 1921 and, although their export markets remained reasonably strong through the 1920s, they still declined: the 67 countries in which there were Harley-Davidson dealers in 1921 was never to be exceeded.

They still did well in countries like Australia, where there were vast distances and terrible roads to rival America's own, but they were increasingly out of the mainstream, and they looked increasingly old-fashioned. By the mid-1930s, foot clutches and hand changes were passé, principally because they were only suitable for bouncing along in straight lines: for nimble work on fast, twisting road, a hand clutch and positive-stop foot change were essential.

New models were introduced sparingly by modern standards, and often the first year's production was dogged by serious faults: the 1930 VL was one of the worst, with frame breakages, an undersized clutch, silencers that rapidly bunged up with soot, and more. When they got it right, as they did in 1929 with the 737cc (45cid) Flathead, they kept it in production for a very long time: the engine was used in road bikes until 1951, and in the three-wheeler Servi-Car until 1974.

Long before either of those, there had been the short-lived and gutless flat twin of 1919–22: its 584cc engine could just pull it along at 80kph (50mph) on a good day. The 1200cc (74cid) Superpowered Twin of 1922 delivered a claimed 18bhp, which is not impressive when compared with a contemporary Brough Superior, which probably had twice the power from a JAP engine of five-sixths the capacity.

The 165cc Hummer two-stroke is not the sort of machine usually associated with Harley-Davidson, but to this day, the bike has its own fan club.

The 350cc (21cid) side-valve single of 1926–35 was more of a success overseas than in the United States, and in Peashooter overhead-valve guise, it formed the basis of a well-known racer. Another single was the 500cc (30.5cid) of 1929–36; this did better overseas than at home.

The substantially disastrous VL has already been mentioned, and the overhead-valve Knucklehead of 1936 was a much better machine once they had sorted out the inadequate lubrication in the first model year. Indeed, this is the lineal ancestor of the 1999 Twin Cam 88, via the 1948–65 Panhead, the 1966–85 Shovelhead and the 1984–99 Evolution (or Blockhead).

This represents a total of only five new engines in two-thirds of a century, and to anyone other than a Harley-Davidson fan, the changes were not particularly great. Until the Twin Cam, nothing was done

The '61 inch' twin of 1917 was one of the finest machines of its era – but one wonders why they chose a metric capacity (one litre) but still gave the capacity in cubic inches.

to address the issue of poor cooling and bad vibration, and even then these problems were not properly addressed. Any major re-design would have changed the appearance of the engine, and to H-D buyers, looks matter more than performance. The volumetric efficiency of the 'all-new' 1998 Twin Cam, at 45bhp/litre, was more characteristic of the early 1950s than of the late 1990s, and was inferior to the more powerful JAP engines of the early 1930s.

There was however a separate line of evolution that Harley-Davidson themselves trace back to the 737cc (45cid) Flathead K of 1952–56, and thence via the Ironhead Sportster of 1957–86 and

The Topper scooter, made in the early 1960s, was one of Harley-Davidson's less successful attempts to broaden their market.

the Evo Sportster introduced in 1986, although if they are going to include the Flathead K (again plagued with problems in its first year) there seems no reason not to include the original Flathead 45. Alas, the KL, a 60-degree machine with offset con-rods instead of a 'knife-and-fork', never made it into existence; the K was a poor substitute for a more advanced engine, to any but the most rabid traditionalist. But Harley riders were more and more inclined to be strong traditionalists.

In reality, the Harley-Davidson buyer has long demanded a machine that looks good, feeds his or her fantasy of being a biker and is extremely reliable, even when it is seldom ridden and poorly serviced. As long as it starts first time and makes that wonderful V-twin noise, speed and handling are secondary considerations.

When the company has forgotten this, its market share has fallen, even threatening the existence of the firm. When it has prospered, it has done so by making the machines more reliable (in particular, stopping them leaking oil), and by paying ever more attention to looks.

Harley-Davidson really are masters of niche marketing through cosmetic changes. There have been big wide 'Fat Boy' tanks, preferably with a speedometer in them and tiny 'peanut' tanks. There have been wire wheels and solid wheels. There have been skinny mudguards and huge, flowing ones. Handlebars have ranged from flat 'racer' style ones to Easy Rider 'ape hangers'. Forks ranged from sensible, to 'overs', for the chopper look. But there has not been that much variation in the engines, or indeed, in the frames.

In 1980, for example, there were 16 models (not counting the sidecar and non-sidecar variants of the FLHC, but counting the Police models of the FLH-80 and the FLH-1200 as different from their civilian counterparts), with just two basic engines: full-size V-twins and slightly smaller Sportster V-twins. There were variations in capacity and tune, but the two series of engines could trace their ancestry back to the Knucklehead and the Flathead 45 without any interruption.

Intriguingly, because the big 1200 and 1340cc (74cid and 80cid) engines typically deliver under 50bhp per litre, while the smaller 883 and 1000cc (55cid and 61cid) engines typically deliver over 50bhp per litre, the actual power outputs are not always all that different, and some of the smaller engines actually delivered more brake horsepower than many of the big ones, although, of course, they had less torque.

Quite apart from all the V-twins, there was also the Model B Hummer deal, the copy of a wartime DKW that was made too

The American Dream: a big, heavy motorcycle, lots of accessories and trim, and a laid back riding position that is just perfect for leisurely cruising.

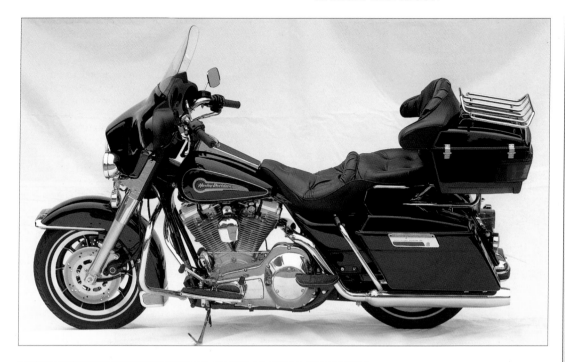

HAKO
Germany 1924–25: These were German motorbikes which had JAP 350 and 500cc engines as their powerbase. These engines were fitted into a close copy of contemporary HRD machines. The company name came from the first two initials of the name Hans Korn.

HALUMO
Germany 1923–26: In-house engines, which were initially a 147cc two-stroke, later 146 and 198cc overhead-valve, provided the source of power for these German machines from the Weimar Republic era.

HAM
The Netherlands 1902–06: These machines from the first decade of the twentieth century were pioneer singles which had been fitted with 2hp Altena motors to provide their power.

HAMILTON
England 1901–07: This firm was known as an engine-maker, and was responsible for manufacturing singles of two-and-a-quarter horsepower to 4hp as well as manufacturing V-twins of four-and-a-half horsepower. The company also made complete machines.

HAMPTON
England (Birmingham) 1912–14: Cross 500cc engines were fitted into these machines as the powerbase. These machines were unusual in that they were some of the earliest users of the foot-change gearbox.

HANFLAND
Germany (Berlin) 1920–25: The in-house 147cc two-stroke engine which was fitted to power these machines was supplied to the company by Flink.

Above: The SS125 was a two-stroke that was about as far from a big four-stroke V-twin as can readily be imagined.

Above: The Electra-Glide was a Duo-Glide with electric start; a Duo-Glide was a Hydra-Glide (hydraulic front forks) with rear suspension.

late in 1959 and 1960; the Topper scooter of 1960–65; the 175cc Bobcat, Ranger, Pacer and Scat of 1962–66, which were rather ordinary two-strokes; and the production between 1961 and 1978 of Aermacchi Harley-Davidsons, which is covered in the Aermacchi section.

The only other topic to cover is the organisational side of the company. Incorporated in 1907, it remained a family-dominated business until it went public in a big way in 1965; in fact, with 326 private shareholders, it must have

seemed like the only way out for them.

Going public culminated in 1968 with the takeover by American Machine and Foundry (AMF), who were willing to invest large sums in the company but unfortunately didn't seem to understand the motorcycle business: insofar, of course, as anyone understands it.

The result of the AMF takeover was falling market shares and rising losses, until a management buyout – which happened between 1981 and 1982 – brought about a revival of the company's fortunes.

This 1972 XR750TT may belong more to the early 1960s than to the 1970s, but it was still a decade ahead of most of the other bikes Harley-Davidson was making at the time.

HARLEY-DAVIDSON SILENT GRAY FELLOW

1906

The original singles were finished in black, but in 1906 a Renault grey, with carmine pin-striping, was offered as an option. The name Silent Gray Fellow reflected both the paint job and the unusually effective silencer (muffler).

The exact swept volume varied. According to the official company history, the very first single was 405cc (24.7cid) but late in 1906 this was increased to 565cc nominal (35cid). Other sources refer to a 500cc (30.5cid) intermediate version and give a different time-scale. In 565cc (35cid) guise, albeit with improvements to the valve gear (from automatic inlet to mechanical inlet) the engine continued in production until the year 1918.

The first machine had a bicycle-type frame but this was soon changed to the loop frame illustrated and, during production,

This 1914 model is typical of the early singles made during this period, although, as noted in the text, there was a programme of continual improvement, which included making the pedals redundant.

final drive seems also to have been changed to chain. From the start ignition was electric via three dry cells. A choice of engine pulleys was available: 114mm (4.5ins), 133mm (5.25ins) and 150mm (6ins). Fuel consumption was advertised as approximately 2.5 to 3.5 litres per 100km (65 to 100 miles per US gallon), and lubrication was by gravity-feed.

Engine: 405cc aise vertical single, air-cooled
Power: n/a
Gearbox: direct drive
Final drive: belt
Weight: n/a
Top speed: 80kph (50mph)

HARLEY-DAVIDSON FLATHEAD 45

1929

The Flathead 45 was introduced in three versions: the low-compression D, standard-compression DL and high-compression DLD, hence the range of top speeds given below, although the power output quoted is for the standard version. The earliest models had twin headlights, and pre-1936 bikes (the R model, as distinct from the post-1936 W model) had slightly more rake to their steering, making them more stable on the appalling roads of the day.

Alloy pistons (instead of cast-iron ones) were fitted after 1930, and the high-compression version

The single headlamp marks this machine as a 1930 model or later (in fact it was made in 1930). 'Chairs' were still popular in those days, even in the USA.

disappeared after a couple of years. The only other significant change over the very long life of this engine was the adoption in 1936 of the recirculating oil system designed for the Knucklehead.

These heavy, slow bikes enjoyed considerable racing success in the USA, principally because of the rules that favoured American machines. Even after production of motorcycles with the Flathead 45 ceased in 1951, the engine continued in production until 1974 for the Servi-Car.

Engine: 743cc sv in-line V-twin, 70x97mm, air-cooled
Power: 23bhp at 4600rpm
Gearbox: 3-speed hand change
Final drive: chain
Weight: n/a
Top speed: 105-120kph (65-75mph)

HARLEY-DAVIDSON KNUCKLEHEAD

1936

The Knucklehead was Harley-Davidson's first standard, roadgoing overhead-valve model, and was introduced in both 999cc (61cid) nominal (actually 988cc/60.32cid) and 1200cc (74cid) guises with a choice of compression ratios. The name, of

course, came from the knuckle-like protrusions on the heads.

Although the Knucklehead was powerful, with lots of torque, it is easy to see the difference of emphasis between it and the lighter, more powerful Vincent Series A Rapide of a couple of

years later. The Harley was still designed to cover immense distances on poor roads at relatively low speeds, while the Vincent, at 59kg (130lb) lighter with rather over 10 per cent more power and an extra 32kph (20mph) at the top end, was

designed to cover the same distances, a lot faster, on much better roads.

In the same year that the Knucklehead came out, there was also a massive 1310cc (80cid) side-valve: the size was of course nominal, the actual dimensions

being 1281cc (78.2cid) from the 87x108mm twin. Apart from early problems with the new four-speed transmission, this was an excellent machine, although it ceased production during the war and did not reappear afterwards.

Less is more? No: with Harley-Davidson, more is more – though this 1938 model is actually the 'baby' version of the Knucklehead, powered by a relatively small 61-inch (988cc) engine.

Engine: 988 cc ohv in-line V-twin, 84x90mm, air-cooled
Power: 40bhp at 4800rpm
Gearbox: 4-speed hand change
Final drive: chain
Weight: 256kg (565lb)
Top speed: 145kph (90mph) approx.

HARLEY-DAVIDSON WLA   1941

Essentially, this is a civilian WL with a number of modifications to make it suitable for the army: a heavy-duty luggage rack, a rifle scabbard, blackout lights front and rear and a 'bash plate' below the crankcase. It also supplied a good deal of reading matter on a specifications and maintenance plate on the tank. The actual top speed was higher than the 105kph (65mph) figure given below, but this was the Army recommendation.

Given that the standard procedure for taking cover involved laying the bike on its side and stepping off, and that many of its riders had never been on a motorcycle before, it is as well that the thing was virtually indestructible. The WLC (Canadian) version had a hand clutch and foot change instead of foot clutch and hand change – some 20,000 WLCs were made, and 68,000 WLAs – and another variant was the very rare 44-U Navy outfit, of which 130 battleship-grey models were delivered.

Original wartime-spec WLAs and WLCs are now much sought after: most versions were 'civilianised' to make them more saleable.

Because the armed forces insisted on immense quantities of spares, Flathead 45s remain readily reparable to this day.

Engine: 745cc sv in-line V-twin, 69.85x96.84mm, air-cooled
Power: 25bhp at 4000rpm
Gearbox: 3-speed hand change
Final drive: chain
Weight: 245kg (540lb)
Top speed: 105kph (65mph)

HANSA
Germany (Bielefeld) 1922–26: This make was characterised by a side-valve engine of 197cc capacity and an overhead-valve of 298cc capacity.

HANSAN
England 1920–22: This was an English firm of assemblers who were known for using Arden two-strokes and Blackburne 346cc side-valve engines to fit into their machines. The company is also found listed in some sources (probably incorrectly) under the name Hansa.

HAPAMEE
Germany 1925–26: These German-built machines were fitted with in-house deflector-piston engines of 198 and 246cc capacity as their powerplants.

HARDING–JAP
France (St Cyr) 1912–14: Englishman H.J. Harding went to live in France, where he built English-style motorcycles from English components. In particular, this expatriate was well known for using the 500cc JAP V-twin engine to power his machines.

HAREWOOD
England 1920: Two-stroke engines from Villiers and side-valve motors from Precision, which were of 269 and 346cc capacity respectively, powered these machines which were assembled by this English firm.

HARLETTE
Austria 1925–28: Puch built these split-single two-strokes of 125 and 175cc capacity. These machines were also sold under the name Harlette-Geco when they were assembled at Jeumont in France by Gerkinet & Co.

HARLEY-DAVIDSON PANHEAD

1948

Engine: 1207cc ohv in-line V-twin,
87x100mm, air-cooled
Power: 50bhp approx
Gearbox: 4-speed hand change
Final drive: chain
Weight: 255kg (560lb)
Top speed: 153kph (95mph) est.

The Panhead was an all-new
overhead-valve engine, with
hydraulic valve actuation instead
of pushrods, light-alloy cylinder
heads instead of cast-iron, and a
distinctly culinary look about the
valve-covers. The theory was that
the head would lose heat better
than cast-iron, while the hydraulics
would eliminate tappet noise.
Lubrication was also better than on
the Knucklehead, with 25 per cent
greater flow to the overhead-valve
gear at one bar pressure. It came in
both 1200cc (74cid) versions and
988cc (61cid).
   Surprisingly, power output was
about equal to the 1200cc (74cid)
engines, although in the following
year (1949) they managed to find
about 10bhp more lurking in the
inlet and exhaust tracts. At the
same time, they introduced

Hydraglide front forks; even so,
they still had a rigid rear end and
hand change (at least 15 years out
of date). Foot change and hand
clutch were optional in 1952, but

rear suspension appeared on the
big twins with the Duo-Glide of
1958, which became the electric-
start Electra-Glide in 1965, just
before the new Shovelhead of 1966.

**The culinary associations of the
valve covers is clear in this shot of
a 1949 Panhead Hydra-Glide
(hydraulic front forks, still rigid
at the rear).**

HARLEY-DAVIDSON XL

1957

In 1957, 40bhp from a reliable
motorcycle of under 900cc – the
883cc capacity equates to a
nominal 55 cubic inches – was
quite impressive. Admittedly, it is

2bhp less than the contemporary
BSA DBD34 Goldie, which was
only a little over half the capacity
and weighed 68kg (150lb) less.
However, the XL was a much

**The XL Sportster could be turned
into a real sporting machine by the
standards of its day; this 1957
model would be better with flatter
handlebars and a bigger tank.**

better behaved and more tractable
machine. A year later, the XL
acquired more power through
higher compression (domed
pistons), bigger valves and a
lighter valve train.
   In 1959, the cams were made a
little more aggressive, and by
1962, the XL Sportster was one of
the best and fastest Harley-
Davidsons of any era. It was also
one of the few road-going bikes
that genuinely echoed the early
sporting days of the Harley-
Davidson company.
   By 1968, the company was
claiming 58bhp at 6800rpm for its
machine, and in 1972 both the
bore and stroke were increased to
give a 1000cc variant.
   This motor was used to
excellent effect in the XLCR
(below).

Engine: 883cc ohv in-line V-twin,
76.2x96.8mm, air-cooled
Power: 40bhp at 5500rpm
Gearbox: 4-speed foot change
Final drive: chain
Weight: 230kg (500lb) approx
Top speed: 170kph (105mph) approx

HARLEY-DAVIDSON FLH SHOVELHEAD — 1966

Engine: 1207cc ohv in-line V-twin, 87x100mm, air-cooled
Power: 60bhp
Gearbox: 4-speed foot change
Final drive: chain
Weight: n/a
Top speed: 180kph (110mph) approx.

Lest we forget, the 74cid Shovelhead was still available in 1972 in a 'super sport' hand shift FLH guise. The idea of a hand gear-change in 1972 is all but unbelievable; that anyone could call such a machine 'super sport' shows how far the United States' vision of a motorcycle had drifted from the vision embraced by the rest of the world.

The original 1966 FLH was essentially an Electra-Glide with a new carburetter, higher compression, and a different look to the rocker-box covers: it had 60bhp, while the less highly tuned FL had a mere 54bhp, 45bhp per litre. In 1971, the FLH gave rise to the Super Glide FX, which was 32kg (70lb) lighter, owing something to the (relatively)

lightweight Sportster series, and the traditional heavyweight models. This was arguably the first 'factory custom', later spawning the FXS Low Rider with its 68cm (27ins) seat height and 'fat bob' (twin, split) tank in 1977.

Then, in 1980, came four new models, with the same engine and, at last, five-speed gearboxes (though in fairness, a huge, 'soft' engine with a broad torque range has far less need of extra gears than a small, high-revving one). They were the Tour Glide, a heavyweight tourer with a full fairing; the Sturgis, a belt drive cruiser; the Wide Glide and the Fat Bob.

The Shovelhead marks the beginning of the end of Harley-Davidson's attempts to build anything other than big, heavy motorcycles.

HARLEY-DAVIDSON XLCR — 1977

Fewer than 3000 XLCRs – CR for Cafe Racer – were made, and were not a commercial success at the time, although they are highly sought-after today.

The company's attempts to build genuine sports bikes were seldom successful, though the XLCR is arguably the finest machine it has made in the last 25 years.

They illustrate how Harley-Davidson is constrained by its own success. The vast majority of buyers seem to be traditionalists who want big, heavy, tractor-like machines, and when the firm offers something else, it sells neither to the traditionalist nor to those who dismiss all Harleys as big, heavy and tractor-like. Willie G. Davidson and his two sons regarded the XLCR as one of the greatest bikes they ever made. The 999cc (61cid) nominal engine was derived from the 1957 XL engine, 883cc and 40bhp at 5500rpm.

Engine: 997cc ohv in-line V-twin, air-cooled
Power: 61bhp at 6200rpm
Gearbox: 4-speed foot change
Final drive: chain
Weight: n/a
Top speed: 200kph (125mph)

HARLEY-DAVIDSON SOFTAIL EVO — 1984

The 'Evo' (for 'Evolution') engine of 1983 was as big an advance over the preceding Shovelhead as the Shovelhead had been over the

Panhead: in other words, very significant in Harley-Davidson terms, but barely noticeable to non-Harley riders. Essentially, it

was an alloy-barrel version of the Shovelhead, with a lighter valve train and better breathing. It weighed a welcome 9kg (20lb) less than the preceding all-iron engine. It reportedly delivered 10 per cent more power, but changing ways of calculating power outputs, plus federal and state emission controls, meant that all stated power outputs were suspect.

The idea behind the Evo was to produce an engine that was more reliable and more oil-tight than its predecessor: it was successful in this ambition. Perhaps more important was the Softail frame, a bogus hard-tail with the suspension disguised so that the machine looked like a pre-Duo Glide big Harley. So successful was this strategy that the Heritage Softail (1986) wrapped its (Showa) forks in huge shrouds for

The 'Evo' is sometimes known as the 'Blockhead', though for some reason, this name never really caught on. This is an '80 inch' machine from the 1980s.

a 1940s Hydra-Glide look. Such cosmetic exercises added to the weight and gave no advantages in handling, but well illustrated the Harley-Davidson ethos.

Engine: 1340cc ohv in-line V-twin 87.3x100.8mm, air cooled
Power: 60bhp approx.
Gearbox: 5-speed foot change
Final drive: belt
Weight: 273kg (600lb) depending on model
Top Speed: 170kph (105mph) approx

HARLEY-DAVIDSON TWIN CAM
1998

The Twin Cam was the latest engine at the time of writing, but contrary to the expectations raised by the name, it was not an overhead-cam design. Rather, it was a bigger and (probably) better

version of the preceding Evo V-twin, albeit still with the same primitive knife-and-fork bottom end.

All sources consulted were extraordinarily reticent about

confirming what horsepower was measured at the crankshaft, although one source measured 52bhp at the rear wheel, rather less, they reckoned, than most Evo-engined bikes could deliver. It

was built in two versions, one for rubber mounting and the other with balance shafts for rigid mounting and three per cent less power.

The rationale behind the under-square engine appears to have been offering bigger and bigger displacements as factory options – 1550cc (95cid) was initially bandied about – while taking the opportunity to address shortcomings in the previous engine.

Initial reactions, as ever, ranged from the predictable slavish admiration of anything Harley-Davidson chooses to do, to the equally predictable condemnation from traditionalists who regarded all change, for any reason, as always being for the worse.

Engine: 1450cc ohv in-line V-twin, 95x102mm, air/oil-cooled
Power: 65bhp est.
Gearbox: 5-speed foot change
Final drive: belt
Weight: 278kg (612lb)
Top speed: 177kph (110mph) est.

The Twin Cam engine pursued (as ever) the twin goals of developing more power along with a smaller propensity to lose its lubricants.

HAZLEWOOD
ENGLAND 1911–24

INTRODUCED LATE IN 1911, this machine was built at West Orchard, Coventry, England, by a firm established in 1876. It used a

two-and-three-quarters horsepower JAP engine with belt drive to a three-speed Armstrong rear hub. Druid forks were fitted, the brake

gear was well executed and the pedals retained.

By 1912 Hazlewood had a Colonial model for South Africa

and for 1913 added a twin with a three-and-a-half horsepower or 5hp JAP engine. The smaller twin kept to the hub gear of the single,

A 1914 Hazlewood sidecar outfit seen during the Banbury run in England. Its 5hp JAP engine would be quite adequate for the hills along the route.

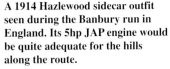

but the larger fitted the hub as a countershaft gearbox driven by chain, while keeping the belt final drive. This line continued during 1914 but the next year saw the single with a three-and-a-half horsepower JAP engine driving the

countershaft gearbox. All ran on until 1916.

Postwar, Hazlewood returned to the listings for 1920 with just the 5–6hp, 654cc V-twin fitted with their own three-speed gearbox with chain-cum-belt drive, but the following year the range was extended by a larger 976cc V-twin and the option of all-chain drive for both. Only chain drive was used in 1922 when the twins were joined by 292 and 488cc side-

The Hazlewood at rest shows off the details of the engine and transmission, though the most obvious feature is the period wickerwork sidecar body.

valve singles with JAP engines. The range was down to the 292cc single and 654cc twin for 1923, the latter with the choice of transmissions, and just a 678cc V-twin for the final 1924 year, still with the final-drive choice.

HECKER

GERMANY 1922–57

FOUNDED BY HANS HECKER in August 1922, the firm became a major factory in the years between World War I and World War II. Production included 245cc two-strokes, later 346cc overhead-valve singles, both with engines of Hecker's own design. Following this came a range of machines powered by British JAP engines and a 746cc V-twin with inlet-over-exhaust valve operation manufactured by MAG. During the 1930s Hecker built a pair of light-weight models with square-tube frames and either 73 or 98cc Sachs two-stroke power units.

Halted during World War II, production recommenced in 1948. Initially it was purely a one-model range: the K125 powered by a 123cc Ilo two-stroke single. Then during 1950, the V200 made its debut, featuring a British 197cc Villiers engine. Also available were the K175 (1951–54), K175V (1954–56), K200 (1953–56) and the K250 (1953–56). All these latter bikes used single-cylinder Ilo power.

In the sporting world, Heckers, like many other German marques of the period, participated in long-distance trials, including the famous ISDT (International Six Days Trial). Hecker riders won several gold medals during the early 1950s, the highlight coming in the 1954 ISDT when Best, a member of the German Trophy Team, struck gold riding a 248cc Hecker in Wales.

Then came the great German motorcycle sales collapse of the mid-1950s. Hecker, like countless

others, were totally unprepared and thus helpless to stave off the financial turmoil that this caused. The factory finally ceased trading after 35 years in the industry on 2 May 1957, although no complete motorcycles had been manufactured since the end of the previous year.

This 1931 Hecker was powered by a 199cc, ohv JAP engine. The company was successful later in its history in the ISDT trials, but folded in 1957.

HAWKER
England (Kingston–on-Thames) 1920–23: Harry Hawker, the aviation pioneer, used 348 and 548cc side-valve engines from Blackburne, as well as his own 293cc two-stroke engine, to provide the powerbase for these machines.

HAXEL-JAP
England 1911–13: This was an English assembler who admitted his debt in its name to the 293cc engine that had been fitted to power his machines.

HAZEL
England (London) 1906–11: Cripps Cycle and Motor Co. from London, England, began manufacturing their machines in the first decade of the twentieth century with singles and V-twins which came from Peugot, before moving on to engines which had been bought in from JAP.

HB
England (Wolverhampton) 1919–24: The Hill Brothers used 350 and 500cc side-valve and overhead-valve Blackburne engines to act as the powerbase for their motorcycles.

HEC
England 1922–23: Two-stroke engines bought in from Villiers with a capacity of 250cc powered these machines. Despite the reliability of the engines, the machines had a shortlived career in the early 1920s.

HEC
England 1939–55: These were autocycles manufactured in England which had been fitted with 80cc Levis two-stroke engines in order to provide the powerbase.

HEINKEL

TOGETHER WITH CLAUDIUS DORNIER and Hugo Junkers, Ernst Heinkel became virtually synonymous with the resurgence of German aircraft between the wars. He began his company in 1922 and, with the importance placed on aviation by the Nazis after their rise to power in the early 1930s, the firm developed many innovative designs. Inevitably, it was not long before several of these were stretching the production facilities to the utmost for the war effort.

The cessation of hostilities after World War II brought a ban on the manufacture of aircraft and associated products, which meant Heinkel had to find another outlet. It chose to produce mopeds, scooters and micro-cars.

After a slow start, development began in 1951. Their first product, the 149cc overhead-valve Tourist scooter, was launched onto the market with a fanfare of publicity in January 1953, followed in 1954

Heinkel's most successful two-wheeler was the Tourist scooter series. Built from 1953 until 1965, production topped 100,000 machines.

by the alloy-framed 49cc Perle (pearl) moped. Remarkably this model was designed and placed in production in the ultra-short time span of six weeks. But although technically advanced, its high cost stunted sales.

The Tourist's engine size was upped to 174cc, then in 1956

Heinkel launched the Kabinen (cabin scooter) with car-type steering and independent suspension powered by either the 174cc Tourist engine, or a specially developed 198cc version. Like the later BMW Isetta, access was gained by a single outward-folding front door.

In 1957 Heinkel launched the Roller 112, an unsuccessful 125cc-class scooter. The following year Ernst Heinkel died and micro-car production began in southern Ireland. These vehicles were later imported from Ireland into Britain under the Trojan name in the early 1960s.

In 1960 the Tourist was updated (and became known after that year as the MK2) and in 1962 a new scooter was introduced, named the 150. Both scooters were discontinued in 1965 as aircraft production returned to a healthy level, by which time Tourist production had topped 100,000 units.

HENDERSON

HENDERSON WENT THROUGH several distinct phases both with regard to its organisation and its products. It was founded in 1912

in Detroit by Tom and William Henderson: Tom brought experience he gad gained at Winton cars and William was the

designer. In 1917 they sold the firm to Ignaz Schwinn who added the marque to his Excelsior line. The brothers remained with the

group until 1919 when they left to create the Ace.

All Henderson motorcycles had an in-line four-cylinder engine set along the frame, and chain final drive. What set the first design apart from later ones was the lengthy wheelbase and the frame that extended ahead of the engine; this was to such an extent that the pillion seat went in front of the rider and pillion footrests were provided to each side of the front wheel. A further feature was a cylindrical fuel tank with rounded ends that was set between the upper and lower frame top tubes and which ran from the headstock to well behind the saddle.

The first engines had a capacity of 965cc, overhead-inlet and side-exhaust valves, separate cylinders mounted on a horizontally split crankcase and the timing gears at the front. The forged crankshaft ran in three main bearings with

The early Henderson fours had an extended frame, available up to 1915, but a shorter version was also sold. Only in 1912 did the rider sit in front of the passenger.

HECKER
Germany (Nurnberg) 1921–56:
This German firm followed a
common path of that period,
beginning manufacturing machines
with their own two-stroke engines
of 245cc. They went on to produce
their own 350cc overhead-valve
engines; then used four-stroke
singles from JAP and MAG and V-
twins up to 750cc. They fitted
Sachs two-strokes engines into
their smaller machines. After World
War II had come to an end, the
company fitted their machines with
Sachs and Ilo engines of various
capacities, ranging from 100 to
250cc.

HEDLUND
Sweden 1963: This Swedish model
manufactured during 1963 seems to
have been shortlived. It was a long-
stroke (80x99mm) double
overhead-cam 499cc motocross
machine.

HEIDEMANN
Germany (Hanover) 1949–52: This
German company produced
lightweights which were fitted with
engines from Fichtel & Sachs to
provide their powerbase. These
engines were of 98cc – and
possibly also a 123cc, according to
some sources – capacity.

HEILO
Germany 1924–25: This German
firm were responsible for the
manufacture of machines which
were fitted with in-house two-
stroke engines. These engines were
produced in capacities of 120 and
150cc.

HELI
Germany 1923–25: This German
product was fitted with an in-house
water-cooled 246cc two-stroke
engine, which was equipped with
belt drive.

splash lubrication, and ignition
was by a Bosch magneto on the
left side. A hand crank on the right
side made starting easy and a free
engine clutch went at the rear of
the crankcase with bevel gears to
turn the drive. The frame was
tubular with leading-link forks, the
space ahead of the engine was
filled by a cast-aluminium
footboard and above this went two
pedals to left and right. Either of
the pedals served to operate the
rear brake.

Long-distance work was the
strength of the Henderson and this
was highlighted when a 1912
model circled the globe in 1913: it
was the first time this had been
done on two wheels. The next year
saw the capacity increased to
1064cc, the fuel-tank shape altered
to flat sides and the pillion seat
moved behind the rider, while
1914 brought the option of a two-
speed Thor rear hub. A second,
shorter version appeared in 1915
without the front footboard,
separate ones on each side, a much

reduced wheelbase which gave
improved handling and their own
two-speed rear hub.

The engine was revised and
given pump lubrication for 1916,
when only the short wheelbase
was listed, while 1917 brought a
three-speed gearbox and new
trailing-link front forks. In this
form it proved popular and was
frequently used for long-distance
record attempts. That year the firm
passed to Schwinn but only small
changes were made to the
machines.

**From 1920, the Henderson four
had a side-valve engine and three-
speed gearbox but retained the
chain final drive, all mounted on a
heavier frame and forks.**

A new engine was introduced
for the 1920 Model K, which had
side-valves, but the general layout
stayed much the same, although
both frame and forks were heavier.
Right through the 1920s the
Henderson was improved
according to trends and continued
to make its mark in sales and

**A Henderson from the 1913–15
period, with front footboard ahead
of the in-line, four-cylinder, F-head
engine and slab fuel tank, which
was used after 1912.**

competition. By 1928 they were back to leading-link forks, but 1929 brought the final major change: the engine reverted to the older side exhaust and overhead-inlet valve layout but had a five-bearing crankshaft. A large number of improvements were made and the result was the KJ and KL standard and super sports variants. The styling was changed enormously and was far ahead of the competition which did not match it until the late 1930s.

Sadly, by then the Henderson had disappeared from the lists as Schwinn had realised that the Depression would run for some years, sales of top-level motorcycles would fade away and it would be selling at a loss. So in 1931, production stopped and the firm reverted to bicycle manufacture with great success.

HERCULES

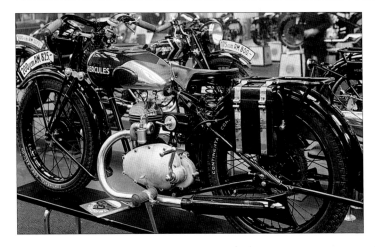

HERCULES WAS FORMED in April 1886 by Carl Marschutz. In common with many other German motorcycle marques, production began when an inlet-over-exhaust engine was mounted according to the fashion of the time in a frame which can be best described as that of a heavyweight bicycle. Transmission was by direct belt drive to the rear wheel, and the bicycle pedals and chain were retained on the model for assistance on steep hills.

In the years that followed, Hercules employed a variety of proprietary engines, including Bark, Columbus, Fafnir, JAP, Ilo, Kuchen, Moser, Sachs, Sturmey-Archer and Villiers. By the 1930s, it was manufacturing a wide range of motorcycles from 73 to 498cc, the latter featuring an overhead-valve, single-cylinder British JAP engine. Using a specially tuned version of this bike, together with a 248 JAP-powered single, Hercules achieved considerable competition success. Hans Kahrmann was the company's star rider.

Hercules also fared well in the long-distance trials of that time, with Carlchen Geffers and Rudi Grenz shining. As the war clouds loomed, such events began to die out, but the company's success was finally snuffed out with the beginning of World War II in September 1939.

A 200cc Hercules twin-port two-stroke single on display at the company stand at the Berlin Show 1933. Specification included girder forks and rigid frame.

During early 1945, the Hercules factories were badly damaged by Allied bombing. Repairs and reconstruction were not completed until 1948, with the result that motorcycle production was delayed until 1950.

The first two of Hercules' postwar machines, models 212 and 312, were displayed at the Frankfurt Show in March 1950. Like all postwar Hercules efforts, bar one, these had two-stroke engines. The 212 was an extremely primitive, ultra-lightweight commuter, with a 98cc (48x52mm) Sachs engine and two-speed gearbox. Its unsprung frame was equipped with a pair of blade-type forks.

The more advanced 312 was much more interesting, with a specification that included telescopic front forks. It used a 123cc (52x58mm) Ilo engine, with a three-speed, foot-change gearbox. It also featured twin exhaust ports, like many contemporary German engines, and there were separate exhaust systems running down each side of the bike. Its maximum power of just over 5bhp gave a road speed of 76kph (47mph).

Even though neither model would seem too exciting today, in a transport-starved Germany, they were like manna from heaven;

strong sales meant that Hercules was able to forge ahead with the development of further new models.

Three more arrived in 1951. These were a pair of Sachs-powered machines with 98 and 147cc power units, and an Ilo 174cc. Both of the larger-engined offerings sported four-speed gearboxes, telescopic forks and plunger rear suspension. The plungers were made for Hercules by Jurisch, and were thus of the same design found on many other German lightweights.

Continued success saw a whole string of ever-more luxurious and more powerful bikes and soon Hercules was selling its products throughout Continental Europe. Holland, Belgium and Switzerland were its best export markets.

With such a large range, many pundits thought it would be

A typical Hercules moped from the 1970s, this M5 model used a Sachs engine with horizontal cylinder and front and rear suspension. Top speed was 45kph (30mph).

During the late 1970s, Hercules, now owned by Sachs and GKN, built a series of excellent enduro models, including this 1977 GS125 ISDT bike.

difficult for Hercules to make an impact at the second postwar Frankfurt Show in 1953. But it did, with a luxury 247cc (65x75mm) twin, with Ilo-made engine.

Although many new models had been introduced in rapid succession, Hercules then stuck with the same range until 1956. This proved a wise decision. Despite the sudden fall in sales that hit the German market in the mid-1950s, the Nurnburg factory was considerably less vulnerable than others because it was not committed to either an expansion programme or to the costly development of new models during this critical period.

So Hercules stayed afloat while many others sank without trace. At the beginning of the 1960s, the company was one of the few survivors of Germany's industrial collapse of the previous decade. Indeed, Hercules had even absorbed the ailing Rabeneick in 1958. The policy was to concentrate mainly on a range of machines powered by engines of less than 100cc – although the D175 (introduced during the late 1950s) was still listed and used as

the basis of Hercules' highly successful ISDT entries.

In 1966, Hercules joined the Zweirad Union (originally a combination of the DKW, Express and Victoria companies) but this meant that Hercules, along with the others, was swallowed up by the huge Fichtel Sachs industrial empire when the latter acquired Zweirad Union in 1969.

But even within the corporate giant, Hercules was destined to survive, being the only marque of the Zweirad Union to maintain its own identity throughout many management changes and mergers.

Fichtel Sachs backing also allowed Hercules to launch the world's first production Wankel-engined motorcycle in 1974.

Other important Hercules models included the K125BW military bike and the GS range of enduro machines. Another was the K125T roadster, with air-cooled, six-speed Sachs engine.

Sachs itself was taken over by GKN (Guest, Keen and Nettlefold) in 1976. During the late 1970s and early 1980s, Hercules developed a range of roadsters with liquid-cooled Sachs engines, including 50, 80 and a 350cc prototype-only twin. Today, it almost exclusively builds 50cc-class machines.

For many years Hercules supplied the German Army with specialised military bikes. This is a K175 BW model from 1992, with a hi-level exhaust and enclosed chain.

HELIOS
Germany 1921–22: This shortlived and unsuccessful machine was fortunate enough to be powered by the original 500cc BMW M2B15 flat-twin engine, which was mounted longitudinally on the frame.

HELLA
Germany (Munich) 1921–24: This south German company produced horizontal two-stroke single engines of capacities of 147 and 183cc.

HELLER
Germany 1923–26: This firm began manufacturing machines which were fitted with the 500cc BMW M2B15 flat-twin, like the Helios. After 1924, the company switched to using the similar, but larger, 750cc MJ side-valve engine to power their vehicles.

HELO
Germany 1923–25: This was a two-stroke with a pumping cylinder in its crankcase, and was of a 149cc capacity.

HELVETIA
Switzerland 1928: Universal AG from Switzerland built this 170cc lightweight machine.

HELYETT
France (Sully-sur-Loire) 1926–55: Before World War II, this company were responsible for the manufacture of a good range. Capacities were from 100cc upwards, and their machines included interesting V-twins (some of which were mounted transversely) of up to 750cc, as well as racers. After World War II and its commerical and logistical constraints had come to an end, the firm manufactured various mopeds and lightweights.

HERCULES W2000

1970s

Engine: 294cc Wankel single chamber, air-cooled
Power: 27bhp at 6500rpm
Gearbox: 6-speed foot change
Final drive: chain
Weight: n/a
Top speed: 148kph (92mph)

Hercules built a machine in 1974 which emerged as the world's first Wankel-engined production motorcycle. In a Wankel unit there is an epitrochoidal chamber, and within this chamber revolves a rotor (piston) shaped like a curved-sided equilateral triangle. This is connected to a gear attached to one of the side housings and supported on an eccentric bearing, which allows it to rotate while keeping its three tips in contact with the chamber.

To prevent gas leakage through the gaps between the rotor and chamber at the tips of the triangle, there were special strips, a feature which gave much initial trouble but by the time the production W2000 model appeared, the rotor seals benefited from the advantages of ceramic technology.

The Sachs licence with NSU (see NSU section) was limited to a power output of 30bhp, and this was to prove a major stumbling block to Hercules and the W2000 project. Because of this displacement, it was limited to 294cc, so when the first models rolled off the production, it was soon found that 27bhp at 6500rpm was uninspiring, even though the machine sported a six-speed gearbox.

Nevertheless, as the first production Wankel-engined motorcycle, the W2000 has been assured its place in the history of motorcycles.

In 1974, the Hercules W2000 made history, by becoming the first Wankel-engined motorcycle to enter production. This is the original 1970 prototype machine.

HESKETH

ENGLAND 1982–

THE HESKETH IS THE ANSWER to the question, 'What would happen if someone built a Vincent or a Brough Superior today, with the same classic looks and the same very high quality, but with modern technology?'

Producing racing motorcycles in small numbers, at correspondingly high prices, is relatively commonplace, and the Hesketh is, in effect, a road-going motorcycle

The finish on a Hesketh, as exemplified by the tank badge, was always outstanding. Vincent, Sunbeam, Brough Superior – the Hesketh rivals them all.

produced in a racing shop. In 2000, actual production (at about 10 a year) was by Broom Development Engineering, which also does all kinds of prototype and development work for major automotive firms, including racing developments.

The original Hesketh operation was founded in 1982, at an inauspicious time, and soon ran out of money. But a skeleton organisation continued to exist in order to service machines already sold, and to build limited numbers of new machines. This organisation was headed by Mick Broom. In due course, he took over the whole operation, which was still based at Easton Neston, the ancestral seat of Lord Hesketh,

whose idea it was to build a new British motorcycle. Hesketh grand prix cars were world beaters, and the Hesketh motorcycle drew on much of the same expertise.

The mainstay of the operation was and is the V1000, an unfaired machine of classic looks and impeccable finish. About 200 were built in the first 18 years of production. The Vampire is the faired version, somewhat rarer; about 50 were built in the same time. Listed, but not yet in production at the time of writing, is the Vortan, a long-stroke but still well oversquare 1100cc version (95x78mm) with a racing-style frame and 27kg (60lb)

lighter. The original engine was entirely air-cooled, but later versions incorporated oil-cooling for the rear cylinder, along with programmable electronic ignition.

To a very large extent, the Hesketh is a bespoke motorcycle. For example, it is possible to customise the seat and suspension to suit a rider who is 152cm (5ft 2ins) tall; anyone who is more than about 170cm (5ft 7ins) should be able to handle the standard seat.

The V1000 – this is a 1984 model – had changed relatively little between its introduction and the time of writing, and was a grievously underrated machine.

HILDEBRAND & WOLFMÜLLER GERMANY 1894–97

THIS WAS THE FIRST EVER series-production motorcycle; estimates vary widely on numbers sold between 800 to 2000. Almost equally importantly, it was the first machine to bear the title of Motorrad (motorcycle). Heinrich Hildebrand and Alois Wolfmüller were credited as the manufacturers, but Hans Geisenhof was responsible for some of the design, although Heinrich Hildebrand had, in 1889 at the age of 34, built a steam auxiliary motor for a motorcycle with the help of his brother Wilhelm. The machine also seems to have been manufactured under licence.

Technologically, it was a dead end, and a failure to develop more modern and (above all) faster running engines contributed to the firm's early demise. Direct drive was taken to its logical conclusion, with the connecting rods on each of two water-cooled cylinders, one on either side of the frame and parallel with the ground, acting directly on the rear wheel, which also acted as a rather light flywheel; rubber straps further assisted the return of the pistons on the compression stroke.

The fuel/air mixture was supplied via a surface vaporiser, and ignition was by hot tube. Bore

This is one of only six Hildebrand & Wolfmüllers known to exist, out of 1000 made. Although technologically a dead-end, it was the first ever series-production motorcycle.

and stroke of the automatic inlet valve four-stroke engine were 90x117mm, for a swept volume of 1488cc, and power delivery was two-and-half horsepower at 240rpm. The rear mudguard incorporated the cooling radiator.

The frame was made from steel tubing, in a sort of elbow box section. The machine weighed about 55kg (120lb) and was good for about 40kph (25mph).

HINDE NETHERLANDS C.1900 AND 1936–38

THIS FIRM WAS ORIGINALLY a bicycle manufacturer in Amsterdam but at the turn of the twentieth century became briefly involved with powered transport. Their motorcycle was similar to many others with a 2hp De Dion engine with automatic inlet valve, crude carburettor and coil ignition mounted in a heavy-duty bicycle frame with rigid forks and belt drive. The pedalling gear remained, as did the cycle brakes, and the firm soon found that they did better business selling bicycles without an engine.

The name was revived in 1936 by another firm located in Amsterdam, who built a small range of light machines using German Ilo engines that were simple, well made and installed with the cylinder either horizontally or inclined. Flywheel magneto ignition was used and units of 61, 98 and 118cc with either one or two speeds were employed, the smallest a very popular Ilo engine.

The Hinde was only produced for three years and was typical of the era with a basic specification:

the frame was rigid; suspension was supplied by lightweight girders; lighting direct with an optional battery system; braking was achieved through small drums in wire wheels; and the fuel consumption of the machine was very modest.

There were many similar types to the Hinde on the market and so it had only a short production run, which was possibly shortened even further by the rationalisation within the German industry in 1938, which may have cut off the supply of the Ilo engines.

HEMY
France 1946: These were auxiliary cycle motors, which initially came in a capacity of 34cc, and later, in 48cc capacity.

HENKEL
Germany 1927–32: This company took over responsiblity for the production of the 500cc Krieger Gnadig (KG) machines after they had been dropped by Allright. Allright bought Cito, who in turn purchased the rights to manufacture the KG from the designers. After 1929, a 198cc side-valve single engine which had been bought in from Blackburne was used as a powerbase for the Henkels.

HENLEY
England (Birmingham, then Oldham) 1920–29: The early machines which came from this company were fitted with 269cc two-strokes from Villiers and 497cc side-valves from Blackburne for their powerbase. They were then fitted with side-valve and overhead-valve JAPs and Blackburnes of various capacities – such as those of 248, 293 and 346cc – or, if the customer so wished, MAG engines could be fitted to order. The company name eventually changed to become New Henley in 1927, two years before production ended.

HERBI
Germany (Bad Liebwerde) 1928–32: This company, which was based in Bad Liebwerde, Germany, offered potential customers a choice. They could either have their machine fitted with the 198cc side-valve engine bought in from Blackburne, or could have it fitted with the 498cc overhead-cam three-valve engine which had been bought in from Kuhne.

HOBART

ENGLAND 1901–24

THIS MARQUE WAS PRODUCED by suppliers Hobart Bird of Coventry, England, who built a primitive machine, but by 1903 they had an advanced model with its engine placed upright in a loop frame fitted with braced forks. This continued to be built for several years, although there was a lapse in production between 1906 and 1910. The new Hobart was a two-and-a-half horsepower lightweight with an adjustable pulley for the belt drive and Druid forks. The next year brought a three-and-a-half horsepower twin and a ladies'

An advertisement for the 'Handy Hobart', emphasising the record it set at Brooklands in late 1910 when the machine averaged 53.26km (32.85mph) for 100 miles.

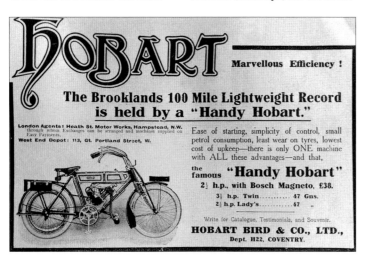

model with an open frame, lower engine mounting and enclosure. Villiers two-stroke and JAP single and V-twin engines were then used as well as their own.

Postwar, Hobart offered the two-stroke, with or without rear suspension, plus a 292cc JAP side-valve for 1920. More versions were added but there was no spring frame after 1921. For 1922 there were new machines with 348cc Blackburne and 346cc JAP side-valve engines, in solo and sidecar forms. The next year saw the 269cc Villiers replaced by a 170cc Hobart two-stroke engine driving a two-speed gearbox, and the 292cc JAP by a 249cc side-valve Blackburne. All the four-strokes had a good range of transmission options with two or three speeds

An early Hobart with its engine clamped into a loop frame, its cooling fins aligned with the ground and its magneto attached to the crankcase.

and final drive by belt or chain. The range went down to the 170cc two-stroke and 346cc JAP for 1924, plus the 292cc JAP, but after this the marque was not listed. Hobart engines were supplied to other firms for some years.

HODAKA

JAPAN 1964–78

HODAKA ENTERED THE motorcycle world by supplying engines to the Yamaguchi marque in 1962. When Yamaguchi collapsed in 1963, Hodaka began building bikes. Unlike other Japanese companies, Hodaka only sold to the USA. It was very much a joint American-Japanese operation, with the development and marketing done in co-operation with the Pacific Basin Trading Co (Pabatco).

The mainstay of Hodaka production were excellent 100 and 125cc enduro style two-stroke singles with excellent specification and an equally excellent build quality. This meant many orders and personal recommendations. Thus a company without the

Above: Built for schoolboy motocross events, the 1978 Hodaka Dirt Squirt 80 was a proper dirt racer in miniature. It was a race winner in the right hands.

Left: Built in Japan, Hodaka bikes were not for sale in their home market, only in the USA. This is a 1972 125cc Wombat trials bike with a single cylinder engine.

resources and competition successes of the major Japanese marques survived for many years in the world's most demanding market. For over 15 years they mounted a pretty successful challenge in the on-off road sector.

Hodaka's 'street scramblers' of the 1960s were renamed 'trail bikes' as the 1970s dawned. But in the mid-1970s, the market became more specialised. In 1978, Hodaka's demise meant the end of a unique trading partnership.

HOLDEN

ENGLAND 1897–1902

THE FIRST MOTORCYCLE with a four-cylinder engine was built in Britain in 1897 by Colonel Holden and was a flat-four with two cylinders set side by side along the frame. Each had a single, double-ended piston with a gudgeon pin at its centre that connected to a crank on the rear-wheel axle. This gave a direct drive at a fixed ratio dependent on the wheel diameter. With no rotating parts, a chain drive was taken from the rear wheel to drive the camshaft and distributor.

This first engine was air-cooled and the mixture was supplied by a surface vaporiser and controlled by a lever mounted on the handlebars. The engine was installed in a frame with rigid front forks, a pillar saddle and a tray for the battery behind the rider. The front wheel was not

The world's first four-cylinder motorcycle, the Holden, was built as a flat-four with direct drive to the rear wheel but only remained in production for five years.

only larger than the rear but was also fitted with pedals to assist starting. Its hub was of the crypto type with epicyclic gearing inside it to gear up the turns of the pedals to the wheel axle as first used by bicycles some 10 years earlier.

The early machine had a top speed of some 39kph (24mph) and it was succeeded by a model with

a water-cooled engine in 1899. This was said to produce 3hp at 420rpm, and it was so well made that it went into production in this form.

However, the limits of the small rear wheel soon made the Holden technically obsolete and, unfortunately, 1902 was its last year of production.

HONDA

JAPAN 1947–

JUST AS A NUMBER OF German companies prospered in the wake of the devastation of World War II, so the Japanese motorcycle industry spawned over 100 manufacturers after 1945, who grasped the opportunity of providing sorely needed cheap personal transport in a ravaged domestic economy. They also enjoyed the protection of substantial tariffs on imported products.

Among them was the Honda Motor Company, founded by Soichiro Honda, who was a self-taught engineer and built his first powered two-wheeler in 1947. Born in Komyo near Hamamatsu in 1906, Soichiro Honda's father was the village blacksmith. He left school aged 16 and became an apprentice car mechanic in Tokyo, setting up his own repair shop back in Hamamatsu in 1922. As

The 1961 125cc Benly Super Sport CB92 was a simple yet reliable bike, paving the way for Honda's consolidation in the market place during the rest of the decade.

the business prospered, Soichiro took up motor racing, and entered a car in the 1936 All-Japan Speed Rally, setting an average speed that lasted for 20 years. He was later sidelined by a serious accident. Another facet of his company's success was its talent for high-volume production. Soichiro studied metallurgy at his

local technical college, and after experimenting with various alloys, he moved into the mass-production of piston rings, operating as Tokai Seiki Heavy Industries. This was the company's principal endeavour until the factory was flattened by an earthquake in 1945, which finished off what the Allied bombers had

started the previous year. Soichiro sold off any remaining plant, and set up the Honda Technical Research Institute in October 1946. The basis of his operation was the acquisition of 500 army surplus two-stroke engines and, going back to first principles, these were attached to standard bicycle frames with belt-drive transmission to the rear wheel. Thus were the first Honda motorcycles born, and they ran on a cocktail of petrol and turpentine. When this stock of engines was used up, Honda began manufacturing its own copies, designated the A-type, producing a humble 1bhp from 50cc at 5000rpm. Ancillaries included a slide carburettor, a crankcase valve to aid induction, and a flywheel magneto.

Before long, Honda graduated to a purpose-built frame. Like the very first motorcycles and contemporary mopeds, the bikes were still equipped with pedals, and fitted with sprung front forks. Evolutions followed quickly. In 1948, Honda introduced the B-type model, which was a three-wheeler with a load-carrying cargo deck. Engine capacity rose to 89cc and, predictably, this larger power-unit was applied to the next two-wheel machine known as the C-type. This bike retained the belt-drive transmission, but in 1949, Honda came out with the D-type, or Dream, which was the company's

Phil Read gets the 888cc Honda Britain-entered four-cylinder machine airborne at Ballaugh Bridge during the 1978 Isle of Man TT.

The powerhouse of the 1969 CB750 was its 736cc air-cooled transverse four, which at a stroke brought motorcycling into the modern era.

first true motorcycle. It was based on Honda's channel steel frame, powered by a 98cc two-stroke engine allied to a two-speed gearbox and chain drive. At the time it was one of the best machines to be had in Japan, and Honda's accountant Takeo Fujisawa set up a national dealer network. Many of these operators

were merely small bicycle shops that enjoyed at best a transitory and impecunious existence, but the seeds of a successful sales and spares network were sown. Soichiro Honda was thus free to concentrate on product design, and by 1950 the company was much the largest motorcycle producer in Japan, accounting for almost half the national output at a time when the industry had embarked on a price war with heavy discounting.

Two new models came out in 1952. The more technically advanced of the two was the E-

In the mid-1960s, Honda was racing glorious-sounding five-cylinder 125cc and six-cylinder 250cc machines. Here, the squad is pictured at Daytona in 1965.

model Dream, which was based on the frame and cycle parts of the D-model, and powered by Honda's first four-stroke engine. This was a 146cc single-cylinder motor equipped with twin carburettors and three valves per cylinder – two inlets and one exhaust – developing five-and-a-half brake horsepower at 5000rpm and

The 105bhp six-cylinder CBX1000 of 1968 was characterised by its magnificent set of exhaust manifolds emanating from its in-line engine.

driving through a two-speed gearbox. The downside was indifferent handling and a thirst for oil. For more less affluent riders, Honda introduced the F-model Cub. This was nothing more than a bicycle with a lightweight 50cc two-stroke engine mounted low on the left-hand side of the rear wheel. Developing a minimal 1bhp at 3000rpm, it weighed only 6kg (13lb) and was a huge success, soon accounting for nearly three-quarters of Honda's output.

'Stack them high and sell them cheap' may not have been a Japanese expression, but it summed up Honda's position in the early 1950s as prodigious production volumes enabled Honda to undercut and outsell the competition. To further his expansion, Soichiro Honda visited Europe and the USA in 1952 and ordered over one million dollars worth of machine tools and, ironically, his investment almost brought the company down. It coincided with a downturn in the Japanese economy, but Honda's bankers were sufficiently far sighted to maintain their support.

Honda's first modern machine was the J-model that appeared in 1953, using a pressed-steel frame with telescopic forks and torsion-bar rear suspension, and powered by an 89cc overhead-valve engine and three-speed gearbox with foot-operated change. The following year, Soichiro Honda attended the Isle of Man TT races, and

absorbed many details of the state-of-the-art European machinery, which were subsequently applied to his own products.

Honda's first overhead-camshaft engine was the Dream SA, launched in 1955 with a 246cc

Honda's CX500 Turbo of 1981 started a short-lived fad for turbocharging; the capacity of the shaft-drive, transverse V-twin was increased to 650cc in 1983.

unit-construction engine, and this was followed by the 344cc SB version. These models evolved into the M-series having been fitted with new forks in 1957. It was about this time that the Japanese market leader began to explore the export market, and its principal offering was the step-through, a cross between a moped and a scooter. The 90cc Super Cub C100 was released in August 1958, and made a huge impact economically and socially as well, bringing modest yet respectable mobility to millions world-wide.

Honda's RVF dominated Formula 1 and endurance events during the mid-1980s, spawning the road-going RC30 (VFR750R). It was powered by a 112bhp motor.

The Gold Wing GL1500 flagship tourer of 1991 ran a water-cooled flat-six and differed sharply from the lean original of 1975. This was an enormous machine.

Not only was it economical, but also practical, due to its faired-in mechanicals and weather protection allied to motorcycle wheels, centrally mounted engine and automatic clutch. The formula must have been right, as the C100 and its derivatives are the best selling motorcycles in the world.

Meanwhile, with the Japanese market at saturation point, Honda set up its US concession in 1959, with European and south-east Asian operations following soon afterwards. With Honda's promotional material deliberately targeting non-riders, a new two-wheeled boom took off, with US sales skyrocketing. In the wake of the C100 came a raft of step-through bikes, which all were

eventually fitted with chain-drive overhead-cam engines. First to get one was the single-cylinder 8bhp CS90 in 1964, which had head and barrel in light alloy.

Honda's first road-going twin was the 247cc C70, which came out in 1957, and owed much to the NSU overhead-cam twins that Soichiro had seen at the TT three years earlier. The engine was in aluminium, developing 18bhp at 7400rpm, with 8.2:1 compression ratio, 360-degree crankshaft that meant the pistons rose and fell in unison, with the camshaft driven by a central chain. Transmission was via a four-speed gearbox and chain. The C70 retained leading-link forks rather than telescopic ones.

The air-cooled single-cylinder NX650 Dominator was a long-lived trailie-styled machine that handled well in most situations, but was slightly cumbersome off-road.

The four-stroke, V-four VFR750F was mounted in an alloy beam frame. The bike was the world's best all-rounder for more than a decade after its launch in 1986.

There was an inexorable move towards the creation of a civilised motorcycle, and in 1958 the C71 model was equipped with an electric start, making kick-starting redundant. The 20bhp RC70 scramble bike came out the same year, which had a tubular frame instead of pressed-steel. New engine capacities included the C90, which was a scaled-down eleven-and-a-half brake horsepower 125cc version of the C70, also available as the sporting CB90. The range-topping 305cc C75 and CS76 were based on the bored-out 250 engine, and their relatively exotic overhead-cam and aluminium spec mechanicals, coupled with reliability and modest pricing, raised many eyebrows when they appeared in US and European markets.

The sporting 250cc CB72 of 1960 featured wet-sump lubrication, 180-degree crankshaft, twin carburettors and 9.5:1 compression, now with telescopic forks and a tubular frame. Before long, the rest of the range followed suit, heralding Honda's entry into modern styling. The CL72 was the trailie derivative of the CB72, and introduced a new generation to the delights of off-road riding. Much of the company's success was derived from racing, making high-revving, high-performance four-stroke twins the norm for road use. Honda first competed on the international stage at the 1959 TT, entering five riders and nine machines for the 125cc event,

although they were no match for the NSUs. In 1960 four-cylinder Honda 250 finished fourth in the 250cc TT, and then in the absence of MV Agusta in 1961, Honda dominated the 125 and 250cc classes during the season as a 21-year-old Mike Hailwood won the Championship. It was a similar picture in 1962 and 1963, with Jim Redman lifting the 250cc crown for Honda, and the marque ousted MV Agusta for the 500cc Manufacturers' title in 1964. It was a period that saw the appearance of exotic machinery such as the five-cylinder 125 and 250 six, and it was Hailwood's turn in 1967 to clinch the 250 and 350 titles for Honda, which had by then notched up 136 Grands Prix victories.

Meanwhile the company was matching its ventures into the bigger engined racing classes with higher capacity road bikes. The first Japanese machine to mount a serious challenge to the British and European manufacturers was the CB 450 Dream, released in 1965. It featured a new 445cc twin-cam engine with torsion bar valve-springs and twin carburettors, mounted in a conventional cradle frame that differed from Honda's typical tubular frames in which the engine was suspended from the spine. Nicknamed the Black Bomber, it brought 161kph (100mph) to a market accustomed to realising this sort of speed from a traditional 650 twin, and paved the way for similar performance machines from rival Suzuki, Yamaha and Kawasaki concerns.

There were always going to be less frenetic versions of the sporting bikes, and in 1967 Honda

Above: The NSR500 used a V-four, two-stroke engine in an alloy beam frame and could top 320kph (200mph). Mick Doohan dominated the 500cc series from 1994.

came out with the CD 175 twin, aimed at riders graduating from a 125. It used a single carburettor and four-speed gearbox while sporting models in the range like the CB 175 were getting twin carburettors and five-speed boxes. A new high-revving CB250 model appeared, producing 30bhp at 10,000rpm, but this too was matched by more prosaic CD and CL trailie versions. By 1970, all were equipped with front disc brakes and the rounded styling cues were in place for much of the decade, rendered obsolete by the new look ushered in by the Superdream in 1977. By now the CB450 Black Bomber had evolved into the CB500T, albeit with long-stroke engine and lower compression ratio.

As the 1960s rolled into the 1970s, Honda was busy diversifying in both directions of cubic capacity. Among its small singles was the screaming SS50 sports moped, which could develop 6bhp at 11,000rpm, and the more pedestrian PC50 moped that used the familiar overhead-cam engine fitted in a basic step-through frame. Trail bikes included the SL and XL series, which would eventually embrace a

range of capacities including 125, 185, 250 and 500cc. Most basic of all was the pushrod CG125, a machine so basic that it survived in production in Brazil into the late 1990s.

At the other end of the scale, the CB750 created a different kind of impact on the motorcycling establishment. While the C100 forged a path into totally new markets, the big four-cylinder machine set new standards for the performance sector, and was highly instrumental in taking sales away from traditional marques like BSA and Triumph. The thing was, the specification of the mass-produced CB750 contained features that had previously been considered a luxury, like five

The XRV750 Africa Twin was the definitive giant trailie of the mid-1990s. Like most machines in this class, it could be difficult to handle off-road.

gears, front disc brake and electric start, and the bikes were available from local dealers at competitive prices. Moreover, it was reliable, delivering an unstressed 67bhp at 8000rpm, taking it to 201kph (125mph) maximum. It was fed by four carburettors and used Honda's tried and tested two-valves-per-cylinder layout, with single chain-driven overhead-cam.

The CB750 was followed in 1971 by the four-cylinder 50bhp CB500 and the CB350 in 1972. Two years on, the latter evolved into 400 four, and went on to become one of Honda's best sellers, and it was a capacity size that prospered due to licensing perameters. The 500 was also increased to 544cc and identified as the CB550.

In 1975 Honda came out with its top tourer, the 1000cc shaft-drive Gold Wing. It was powered by a flat-four water-cooled engine fed by four carburettors, developing 80bhp at 7000rpm. Due to ancillaries like the water radiator, it was a relative heavyweight at 295kg (650lb), although the horizontal engine kept the centre of gravity low. The fuel tank was under the seat, and the dummy tank contained the electrics. The emphasis was on comfortable high-speed cruising, and the Gold Wing evolved to 1085cc in 1980, to 1182cc in 1984, and by 1989 it had become the six-cylinder 100bhp GL1500. Windscreens, fairings and luggage were de rigeur, and in a bid to outdo Harley-Davidson, all creature comforts were present, even down to reverse gear.

The rival Kawasaki's response to the CB750 had been the Z1, and to match that, Honda took a leaf out of Benelli's book and came up with the CBX. This six-cylinder machine was launched in 1978, a year after the Benelli Sei, but the CBX motor ran with 24 valves, developed 105bhp and enabled a 217kph (135mph) top speed. Indifferent sales meant that for 1981, the CBX was reinvented as an equally short-lived sports tourer with a half-fairing and de-tuned engine.

If the archetypal V-twin is the Moto Guzzi, Honda came up with a similarly configured machine

that won the steely hearts and minds of an army of despatch riders, won over by its low maintenance and reliability. The CX500 didn't enjoy an auspicious debut in 1978, when it was dubbed the Plastic Maggot on account of its somewhat rotund appearance. It was powered by a liquid-cooled transverse-mounted 499cc V-twin, with four pushrod-operated valves per cylinder. Its 50bhp was transmitted via shaft drive which contributed to the modest maintenance schedule. The CX650 came out in 1984, followed by the Turbo version, which boasted 82bhp but was hampered by weight and the very complexity that the unblown CX was unfettered by. In the event, motorcycles had such a good power-to-weight ratio in standard

The CBR600F was the sports all-rounder every other manufacturer aspired to. Launched in 1987, regular developments kept it well ahead of the opposition.

When unfaired bikes became popular in the late 1990s, Honda took the panels off the CBR600F and offered the naked Hornet for almost £2000 (US$3200) less.

format that turbocharging became an irrelevance.

The CX was followed by a series of sports-orientated longitudinally mounted V-twins and V-fours using chain-drive transmission. There was something of an advantage in the balance of the bike, as well as smoother running, in employing this configuration. This is immediately evident if an in-line four and a V-four are ridden back to back. First of these V-fours was the liquid-cooled VF750, launched in 1983, followed by 400 and 500cc variants. In 1984 there was also a liquid-cooled V-twin VT250 and VT500. Due to valve-gear problems with the slimline VF750, Honda replaced the VF with the VFR750 in 1986. This standard bearer for the sports touring

market used gear-driven camshafts to overcome the VF's failings. The VFR750 was so good that it was only superseded after 12 years by the fuel-injected 100bhp VFR800.

The Honda V-fours were at the forefront of an explosion in race-replica machines that blossomed in the late 1980s and lasted well into the following decade, fuelled by the rise of 'grey imports'. The VFR series of 400cc machines was epitomised by the brilliant little NC30, featuring racing colour schemes on its fairings and single-sided swing-arm suspension. The RC30 of 1988 and the RC45 were closely related to the RVF racer. Possibly the most radical was the NR750, Honda's road-going machine fitted with similar oval-pistons to the racing NR500 of almost a decade previously. The NR750 had eight valves per cylinder and developed 125bhp at 14,000rpm, yet proved to be no quicker than more mundane 750s.

The longitudinal V-twins included the big off-road XRV750 Africa Twin and the XL600V Transalp, which was a medium-sized 583cc trailie, both of which occupied a central position in a fashionable market niche. Similarly, the road-orientated 996cc Varadero V-twin released in 1999 reflected in the glory of Honda's success in the Dakar Rally.

Similar power units graced the shaft drive NTV650, marketed as the Revere, and with chain drive as the Bros in 400 and 650 format.

Like its Japanese counterparts, Honda took on Harley-Davidson and produced the retro VT1100 Shadow. This 1993 bike looked right, but lacked charisma.

These machines were also excellent workhorses and took over where the CX left off. The NT650V Deauville of 1998 was a fully-equipped touring bike fitted with fairing, panniers and shaft-drive. Contrast was provided by the VT750 Shadow, a classic custom V-twin model. Finally, and not to be confused with that house-on-wheels the Gold Wing, Honda brought out the ST100 Pan European as the ultimate touring sportster in 1990. It was powered by an 1100 V-four engine delivering 100bhp, which made it capable of 210kph (125mph), and with its comprehensive fairing, it was a success with the police, paramedics and rescue services, and even as a taxi.

The motorcycle that was to become the Honda standard bearer was introduced in 1987: the CBR600. It made this category of sports machine almost its own. Clad in fully-faired bodywork, it was as good an all-rounder as the

Eleven-times TT winner Steve Hislop corners an RVF at Donington, England, in 1994. The road-going derivative was the RC45, released the same year.

VFR, but was powered by an in-line 599cc liquid-cooled four-cylinder twin-cam, developing 85bhp. It accounted for 100,000 sales in its first eight years in production, which made it the best-selling motorcycle in the world. Its chief attributes were its easy handling and power delivery, and it remains the acknowledged benchmark Japanese sportsbike in a heavily contested arena.

As had become traditional practice, Honda introduced two

The 1084cc ST1100 V-four Pan European was beloved of long-haul tourers and emergency services riders, for whom time in the saddle was no object.

other similarly styled machines in the CBR range along with the 600, although they paled into insignificance beside it. The CBR 750 was only available on the grey import market, and the 130bhp CBR1000 that was a competent long-distance sports tourer. At the

the fastest production bike in the world. Top speed was a dazzling 266kph (165mph), placing it in the realms of the supercar. Not only that, but it had handling to match. The recipe for its success was the 123bhp produced by its 893cc in-line four, coupled with light weight – its 185kg (407lb) was comparable with the average 600 middleweight – based on its aluminium-beam frame.

During the 1990s the race was on to create the fastest road bike, and Honda's next contribution was the CBR1100 Blackbird which went on sale in 1997. It was classified as a sports tourer, and didn't have the visual appeal of the FireBlade. However, at 285kph (177mph), it could with justification claim the top velocity accolade. Other contenders were the 303kph (188mph) Suzuki 1300cc Hayabusa and Yamaha R1. Contemporary with these models was Honda's VTR1000 Firestorm, powered by a 996cc V-twin engine and aimed fair and square at Ducati.

Not forgetting its roots in the commuter market, Honda's 250cc Foresight 'super scooter' played a starring role.

other end of the scale, the CBR400 was a lively race replica bike, although again this model was more prolific on the grey import front. This in-line four made an eloquent comparison with the VFR 400 V-four.

In 1992, the motorcycling world was buzzing with news of the CBR 900 FireBlade RR, hailed as

The machine that brought sports capability to the common man, the CBR900RR Fireblade possessed awesome performance and was annually refined from 1992.

HONDA C50 SUPER CUB
1958

Sometimes vehicles emerge that help bring about radical change in transportation, like the Model T-Ford or the Mini. Honda's step-through range falls neatly into that category. Most basic was the 49cc four-stroke powered single, the ubiquitous Honda 50, which could manage 64kph (40mph), sufficient to cope with urban traffic certainly, and many rural situations. The 50cc Super Cub from August 1958 brought motor-cycling mobility to the masses, not just in the industrialised nations but in third world environments where metalled roads were few. The step-through configuration of these machines meant they were practical, easy to mount, with an enclosed chain, and scooteresque fairings and plastic legshields offered a certain amount of weather protection. Typically of Hondas, they were well made and proved reliable, a vital asset in a third world environment. No fewer than 24,000 units were sold in the first five months of production, and the floodgates to mobility were opened.

The first new model to receive the chain drive overhead-cam engine was the all-alloy single-cylinder 8bhp CS90 from 1964, in which the barrel was close to the horizontal and the cam ran directly into the head. Variations included the overhead-cam C50 of 1967, while the C70 and C90 gave a bit more performance. The C110 was a motorcycle-style version, with the C100's engine suspended from a pressed-steel frame, while the diminutive CZ100 Monkey Bike from 1960 had the C100 engine and transmission, with 128mm (5ins) wheels in a rigid frame and forks.

From 1960, Honda sold half a million step-through bikes a year, and by 1983, 15 million had been built. Today, the step-through is still selling well all over the world; it is the most successful powered two-wheeler of all time.

It may not look like a wild beast, but the C50 Super Cub certainly caused a revolution. Convenience and reliability brought motorised mobility to the masses.

HONDA CB750 1969

At the other end of the scale, the CB750 created a different kind of impact on the motorcycling establishment. While the C100 forged a path into totally new markets, the big four-cylinder machine set new standards for the performance sector, and was highly instrumental in taking sales away from traditional marques like BSA and Triumph. The thing was, the specification of the mass-produced CB750 contained features previously considered a luxury. Discrepancies in performance and handling were outweighed by the CB750's plus points. It was reliable, clean and civilised, as well as docile at low speed. Far from being over-tuned, it was actually quite mild, and its 76bhp at 8000rpm was well within the new four's limits.

The new engine was relatively simple and based on well-proven features that Honda had been using for over a decade. It had just two valves per cylinder, and the single overhead-cam was driven by a central chain. There were four carburettors and four exhaust pipes. The frame was a conventional tubular cradle with

Introduced in 1969, the CB750 was Honda's first attempt at a big bike, and it was so successful that it completely transformed the market for large machines.

gaitered telescopic front forks. A five-speed gearbox, electric start and a front disc brake completed the specification. The flexible engine and big comfortable seat made it practical for touring, yet this was a 201kph (125mph)

motorcycle which did not need constant attention. In fact, so successful was Honda's concept of a big, affordable in-line four, that all the Japanese manufacturers later built one.

The automatic transmission version of the 750cc, de-tuned to 47bhp at 7500rpm and with a torque converter replacing the clutch, was less successful and only sold in small numbers. By 1979, the original single-camshaft 750 was outclassed by the opposition, so Honda produced a double overhead-cam 16-valve replacement with 77bhp on tap. Alongside this came the 95bhp CB900 that could reach 217kph (135mph). This developed into the CB1100R, with a half-fairing and improved handling. Over 30 years on, the CB750 is still in production.

Engine: 736cc transverse-mounted in-line four, 61x63mm
Power: 67bhp at 8000rpm
Gearbox: 5-speed, foot change
Final drive: chain
Weight: 220kg (485lb)
Top speed: 200kph (124mph)

HONDA GOLD WING 1975

Launched in 1975 with just a 1000cc four-cylinder motor, the Gold Wing rose to 1200cc and was re-designated the GL1500 in 1988, and reigned supreme as the proverbial house on wheels.

In fully dressed format, it metamorphosed through Interstate and Aspencade incarnations in 1980 and 1982. The Gold Wing was built in Ohio, USA, and offered the most lavish

specification of seating, equipment and storage for the touring rider and pillion, and only the top Harley-Davidsons could match what the Gold Wing had to offer.

A foot pedal controlled both front and rear brakes, while accessories included cruise control, a digital clock and radio-casette player. The water-cooled 1.5-litre flat-six engine made long-distance cruising simply effortless,

The original Gold Wing of 1975 was an ordinary-looking bike, intended to compete with the Kawasaki K1. It gave no hint of the creature comforts to come.

and in certain markets with large land-expanses where its abilities could be fully appreciated – like the USA – it too acquired cult status.

In more congested environments like the UK, the ST1100 Pan European with its shaft-drive transverse-mounted V-four was a more appropriate size. Honda also produced a naked cruiser version of the GL1500 Gold Wing called the Valkyrie or F6C, which was powered by the same six-into-six flat six 1520cc engine.

Engine: 1520cc flat-6, water-cooled
Power: 100bhp at 5200rpm
Gearbox: 5-speed, including reverse, foot change
Final drive: shaft
Weight: 368kg (811lb)
Top speed: 187kph (116mph)

HM
Sweden late 1960s: Sven Hakanson designed this extremely unusual water-cooled 500cc (69.4x54mm) V-twin, of about 60 degrees, with the lower cylinder pointing straight forward.

HMK
Austria 1937–38: This pre-World War II Austrian company was the manufacturer of English-style JAP-engined machines. They came in a range of capacities, of 250cc and, possibly, even larger.

HMW
Germany 1923–28: This German firm was responsible for the manufacture of side-valve singles which had been fitted with in-house engines.

HMW
Austria 1946–64: The Halleiner Motorenwerk of Austria began their production career with 49cc auxiliary cycle motors. They later moved on to producing mopeds, lightweights and even a scooter (the 75cc Bambi-Roller). All were fitted with two-stroke engines.

HOCHLAND
Germany 1926–27: This German product was a 496cc overhead-valve flat-twin. It was a shortlived machine, and was made in only small numbers.

HOCKLEY
England (Birmingham) 1914–16: These English machines, produced in Birmingham, were two-strokes which were fitted with 269cc engines bought in from Liberty and Villiers.

HOCO
Germany (Minden) 1924-28: These wood-framed machines were manufactured in a factory which normally produced furniture. They were fitted either with two-stroke motors of 150 and 250cc from Villiers, or side-valves of 300 and 350cc from JAP.

HONDA CBR600F
1987

From its introduction in 1987, the CBR600F quickly established itself as the bike for all seasons. Riders used it for commuting, touring and scratching, which it could do with aplomb. On the race circuit it was equally competent, racking up more Supersport 600 titles by 2000 than any middleweight rival. It struck the right balance for most riders

The original CBR600F's dumpy looks were streamlined in a 1991 facelift and power was boosted from 95 to 100bhp. An all-new bike was listed for 1999.

between speed, comfort and practicality, with enough performance boosts over the years from 83bhp with the H-model up to 108bhp and 258kph (160mph) to retain a sporting edge. This ranking was called into question in 2000 by Yamaha's R6 and Triumph's T955.

The styling of the innovative fairings altered as the bike matured, although the colour scheme that altered almost annually was always focussed on Japanese race-replica imagery. One major change in chassis design came in 1991 when a smaller twin-spar steel frame was

provided, along with other refinements including a four-into-one exhaust system. For 1999, a lightweight twin-spar aluminium-beam frame was introduced to enclose the engine, and the swinging-arm pivoted directly on the engine casings. The result was a stronger, lighter

Above: Every year, the colour scheme of the CBR600F was changed to another distinctive set of hues, this version being one of the patterns available for 1997.

chassis that rewarded the rider with masses of feedback. The engine was also 3kg (6lb 9oz) lighter and power was up too. New machines that year also got a re-designed direct air induction system that fed the 36.5mm (one-and-two-fifths ins) flat-side carburettors.

Its very competence made the CBR600F something of a target for theft, so from 1999, security included an electronically coded ignition system that could only be operated by the bike's originally encoded keys.

Engine: 599cc dohc in-line transverse four, water-cooled
Power: 99bhp at 12,000rpm
Gearbox: 6-speed, foot change
Final drive: chain
Weight: 185kg (408lb)
Top speed: 258kph (160mph)

HONDA CBR900 RR FIREBLADE
1992

At its launch in 1992, the Honda CBR900 RR FireBlade took the superbike category higher and on to new levels, and apart from challengers like the Ducati 916 and Triumph T595 Daytona, the CBR900 RR would continue to wear that crown throughout the 1990s.

It was only in 1998, when Yamaha's R1 was released, that the FireBlade seemed to be seriously threatened. Originally of 893cc, improvements to the

FireBlade's 123bhp 16-valve transverse four extracted yet more performance and capacity was lifted to 918cc, while the lightweight aluminium twin-beam chassis and racy steering geometry was tweaked to make the bike rather more docile than the tearaway original.

FireBlades won the Production TT on three successive occasions in the mid-1990s and dominated the 1998 British Production Powerbike Championship.

Released in 1992, the FireBlade immediately dominated the supersports category, and its raw edges were gradually eroded by modifications to frame and steering geometry.

Engine: 893cc 16v dohc transverse straight-4
Power: 123bhp at 12,000rpm
Gearbox: 6-speed foot change
Final drive: chain
Weight: 185kg (407lb)
Top speed: 266kph (165mph)

HONDA RC45

1994

Honda's ultimate V-four production bike was the RC45, created in 1994 to replace the previous RC30 World Superbike contender. Powerplant was the 749cc water-cooled V-four engine allied to a six-speed gearbox, mounted in a twin-spar aluminium frame with single-sided swinging-arm. To a great extent the RC45's componentry evolved from the work's racing RVF machines, with mighty four-pot calliper front disc brakes, although the RC45 had a completely

Engine: 749cc ohv V-four, water-cooled
Power: 118bhp at 12,000rpm
Gearbox: 6-speed, foot change
Final drive: chain
Weight: 189kg (417lb)
Top speed: 282kph (175mph) depending on gearing

new engine in which the camshafts' gear drive was taken off the end of the crankshaft. Electronic fuel injection superseded the previous model's carburettors on the customer model, and performance could be upped to 150bhp by fitting Honda's aftermarket race kit,

Launched in 1994, the RC45 – or RVF750 – was developed from the work's fuel-injected V-four race bikes into a sophisticated supersports road machine.

thereby doubling the price of what was already an extremely exclusive machine.

HONDA FES PANTHEON 125

2000

Powerful, comfortable and effortless to ride, the Honda Pantheon 125 cost £2825 new in the UK in 2000, and was the cream of the crop of the trendy new scooters flooding the market. It was the smaller sibling of the FES250 Foresight of 1998. Although one of the heaviest scooters of its type, it carried its weight in the right places, making it more stable than some competitors. Compared with a traditional-looking machine like the Aprilia Habana Custom 125, the Honda wasn't a thing of beauty. But the seat was relatively low and allowed for a good range of positions for the rider's feet. It ran with a two-stroke engine – the Active Radical Combustion motor – that supplied power smoothly from low revs to provide better acceleration than serious rivals from Peugeot or Yamaha. The Pantheon was equipped with the Combined Braking System (CBS), borrowed from Honda's sports bikes, in which either lever applied a proportion of its pressure to the other brake. This facility was not

universally popular with bikers who preferred to make their own choice about which brake to apply, but Honda's market research evidently showed that commuters weren't so fussy. For those two-up dashes to the office or a weekend away, the Pantheon's broad pillion seat was a few inches higher than the driver's and rated as one of the most comfortable, although the grab handles were sharp-edged.

Honda embraced the burgeoning scooter market of the late 20th century with a range of practical machines like the Pantheon FES125 and FES250 Foresight.

Engine: 125cc ohv 2s single, liquid-cooled
Power: 15bhp
Gearbox: V-matic
Final drive: chain
Weight: 145kg (319lb)
Top speed: 113kph (70mph)

HOENSON
The Netherlands 1953–55: This company was one of hundreds of firms based in the Netherlands which had originally been a bicycle factory and which took on a side-line in motorcycles. These motorcycles were powered by 147cc singles bought in from Sachs and 198cc singles bought in from Ilo, as well as a 248cc twin from Ilo.

HONE
Germany 1950s: This German product was an auxiliary two-stroke cycle motor of 48cc capacity.

HOFFMANN
Germany (Düsseldorf) 1949–54: This German company began manufacturing machines which were fitted with Fichtel & Sachs and Villiers two-stroke engines. After they had moved on to using Ilo 250cc engines, they were briefly responsible for making 250 and 350cc overhead-valve flat-twins with shaft drive, which were very similar to the miniature BMWs. The firm eventually ended up making Vespas under licence before they were forced to close their doors in 1954.

HOLLEY
USA (Bradford, Pennsylvania) 1902–late 1910s: These American machines from Pennsylvania featured belt-driven single engines with a rear-leaning cylinder. These engines were fitted by the company into a bicycle frame which had been strengthened.

HOLROYD
England 1922: This shortlived English company produced sporting machines, with JAP 250 and 350cc machines. The firm was built under the impetus of Jack Holroyd, the well-known racing motorcyclist.

HONGDU

CHINA IS NOW A MAJOR producer of motorcycles; manufacture has increased greatly in the last two decades. Hongdu started by building Japanese models under licence and were one of the first Chinese motorcycle firms.

Hongdu worked with Yamaha and their first model was the YG1, one of the most successful of the early Yamaha two-strokes. It had an 73cc capacity with the cast-iron

cylinder inclined forward and topped by a light-alloy head. A rotary inlet valve controlled the mixture intake, it was ignited by a flywheel magneto and kick-started into life. The engine was built in unit with a four-speed gearbox and hung from a spine frame with telescopic front and pivoted-rear forks, wire wheels and drum brakes.

This set the pattern for the firm and in time the 80 was replaced by

Left: For the lightweight road market, Hongdu offered this JH90 during the 1990s, another model based on an older, but highly successful, Yamaha.

Above: Typical of the Hongdu range, this 1995 JH125L was a trail machine based on the older Yamaha DT series, which was very popular.

a 100 and later a 125. All followed the same lines but progressed technically through the years. Rotary valves gave way to reeds for the inlet, electronic ignition replaced points, and electric start was added to assist the kick. More speeds went into the gearbox,

tubular frames took over from the spine type for some models, and disc brakes made their appearance.

The range ran from 50 to 125cc for most years and included mopeds, scooterettes, small motorcycles and scooters in various forms.

HOREX

FRIEDRICH KLEEMAN WAS the head of the Horex marque which he ran together with his son Fritz. Kleeman was involved in several business ventures in the early 1920s. They owned a company in Bad Homburg which manufactured Rex patent containers, and Friedrich Kleeman was also the main shareholder of the Columbus Motorenwerke of Oberusel, which built auxiliary engines for bicycles and larger units for motorcycles.

In 1923 the father-and-son team founded another company, this time with the intention of manufacturing complete motorcycles. Its Horex name came from taking the first two letters of

A 1938 596cc Horex, with a single cylinder four-stroke Columbus engine. Horex was owned by the father-and-son team of Friedrich and Fritz Kleeman.

Homburg and adding them to the Rex brand name. One year later the first Horex motorcycle appeared.

Perhaps it was only to be expected, but the newly set up Horex chose a Columbus engine; a 248cc overhead-valve single, with a hand-operated three-speed gearbox. Final drive was by chain, whilst the frame was the typical basic steel tubular device of the period, with a flat tank and spring saddle following standard pre-1930 design fashion. The front fork employed a rocker arm which was suspended on a central spring and incorporated a single friction shock absorber.

Soon Horex was fitting ever larger engines as demands for its products grew, having drawn attention to themselves by participation in both racing and trials. By 1930 Horex was firmly established and the production tempo had increased to such an extent that some engines had to be made under a Sturmey-Archer licence. In addition, Columbus power units were being used in increasing numbers by several other leading German marques, including AWD, Tornax and Victoria. Eventually Horex and Columbus merged their interests by moving engine production from Oberusel to Bad Homburg, but not before another commercial success was achieved with the Ghom, a 63cc engine with 'clip-on' attachments for any ordinary bicycle.

The 1930s heralded even more success for Bad Homburg, when Horex took on the gifted designer

Below: Factory Horex rider Friedl Schon gets to grips with the new 497cc (65x75mm) dohc twin racer at the Dieburger circuit, 6 April 1952.

Above: A 1951 Horex single seat sidecar. Because of good low-down torque, Horex models were popular with the three-wheel enthusiasts.

Hermann Reeb, who created a succession of interesting and innovative designs: first 498 and 596cc side-valve and overhead-valve singles; then 198, 298 and 346cc models, all with overhead-valve. Reeb created a major coup in 1932 when he designed a pair of large-capacity vertical twins of 598 and 796cc with chain-driven overhead-cam. The drive to the overhead-cam was on the offside of the engine, enclosed in a large alloy casting which dominated that side of the power unit. This led to the design's only serious drawback: the spark plug for the timing side was obscured by this vast housing. There had been vertical twins before, of course, but not like this. Although Triumph and Edward Turner are

HOOCK
Germany (Cologne) 1926–28: As well as importing engines from Villiers for distribution, this company from Cologne in Germany were responsible for the installation of some of these engines into their own motorcycle frames.

HORAK
Czechoslovakia 1969: This shortlived Czechoslovakian company of the late 1960s were responsible for the manufacture of machines for motocross use. These machines were fitted with 250cc desmodromic singles. The company also built a desmodromic four.

HORSY
France 1952–53: This machine from France was one of many scooters being produced at that time. The scooter would have been fitted with motor of 85cc capacity.

HOSK
Japan 1955–57: The Japanese firm Nikon Kososu Kikan were responsible for the manufacture of the 235cc Hosk SS and the 143cc Hosk BC-CA. Both these machines were equipped with three-speed gearboxes and both featured full suspension.

HOSKISON
England 1919–22: This company had a history of three years, were responsible for the manufacture of three models, and used engines which had been bought in from three different engine-makers. These engines were, namely, a 269cc from Villiers and 292cc two-strokes from Union, and Blackburne 497cc side-valves. All were fitted in conventional open frames, which was standard fare at that time.

A 1953 Regina Sport model with a single port ohv engine. It offered owners a superior performance to the standard model, with 20bhp and a 125kph (78mph) top speed.

today universally credited with the conception of the modern vertical twin, Horex and Hermann Reeb could argue they got there first.

Both in the showroom and on the race circuit, Horex was doing well in the mid-1930s. For example, not only did it have new four-valve singles in 500 and 600cc engine sizes, but Reeb's overhead-cam parallel twin had been increased in size to 980cc. But it was an overhead-valve model, the 348cc S35 using a Sturmey-Archer engine, which was the top seller. Further new models would have appeared, had not the war intervened. After 1945, Horex was one of the first German motorcycle builders to get back into production, thanks, some said, to the Kleeman family's close association with the Americans.

As related elsewhere, Horex's seller in the immediate postwar era was the 350 Regina, and in the spring of 1950 a racing version of the overhead-valve single made its track debut. This closely followed the lines of the production roadster, but with a suitably modified engine, British Amal TT racing carburettor and a Bosch

magneto which replaced the standard production model's battery/coil ignition system. The racing Regina produced 25bhp and was capable of around 161kph (100mph). However, it soon became evident that, ranged against the overhead-cam Norton and AJS production racers, let alone the factory-entered machinery, the pushrod Horex simply wasn't quick enough.

Horex also built a series of racing twins often using the Imperator (Emperor or General)

name. These should not be confused with the entirely different production roadster of the same name. The first of the new twins debuted in early 1951, and compared to Reeb's pre-war parallel twin, the 1951 racer (497cc, 65x75mm) was considerably wider. The drive to the overhead-cam was again by chain, but this time running between the two vertical cylinders. Also, when compared to the earlier Horex design, the new engine's symmetry of layout had the

advantage of offering more equal cooling for each cylinder and allowing the designer to fit spark plugs in the conventional position. The central camshaft drive also allowed the cam itself to be shorter, thus avoiding the possibility of flexing with its obvious effect upon valve timing.

The chassis also displayed several innovations compared to normal Horex practice. Rather than relying on the engine assembly as a stressed member, the frame was a full duplex cradle affair that enclosed the power unit. In place of the standard plunger rear suspension of the then-current Horex roadster line, the twin-cylinder racing prototype featured an entirely new swinging-arm system.

There was no oil tank as the engine used a wet-sump lubrication system. But the power output fell well short of expectations, resulting in a major re-design which was ready in time for the following year, its debut coming in May 1952 at Hockenheim with works rider Friedl Schon aboard. The new double overhead-cam engined machine (the 1951 was single overhead-cam) scored an impressive victory but such success was not to be repeated in the world championship series

The 350cc Resident ohv single was the replacement for the best-selling Regina model. Entering full production in 1955 it was never as successful as its older brother.

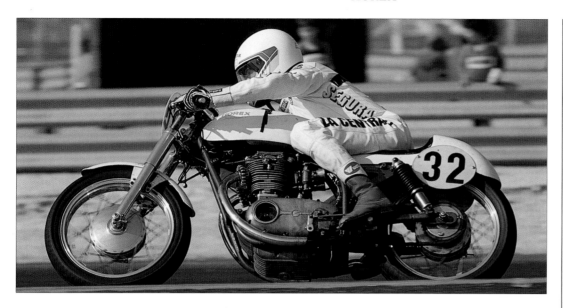

A race-converted 500 Imperator ohc twin-cylinder model, at a classic racing event during the late 1980s. Note the absence of megaphones on the exhaust pipes.

where the Horex twin retired more often than not. Fortunately, Horex had the gifted engineer/rider Roland Schnell to fall back on. Schnell, together with Hermann Gablenz, rode specially built double overhead-cam Horex singles in both 250 and 350cc classes. These semi-works singles were much more robust than the twins, and fast too, gaining many

successes between 1952 and 1954 at international meetings all over Europe. The final Horex racing project was another prototype double overhead-cam twin, again brand new, and was the work of the Austrian engineer Ludwig Apfelbeck, appearing briefly in 1954.

The main Horex production models of the early to mid-1950s were the Regina single and Imperator twin-cylinder models. The factory also built a number of Sachs-powered two-stroke lightweights, including the Rebell 100 and the abortive and costly

Rebell scooter, the latter powered by a horizontal 249cc overhead-cam single. Horex also built a new four-stroke single, the Resident, in both 350 and 250cc engine sizes.

Sales for 1955 dropped to less than 5000; this resulted in massive losses and the firm's closure by the beginning of 1958. Despite a brief revival in the 1980s, the name then disappeared for good.

Horex was reborn in the 1980s thanks to Fritz Roth. The new company built models with Minerelli or Rotax engines. This is a 1984 500 Rotax-powered single.

HOVY
Belgium 1954: These machines from Belgium were lightweights which were powered by engines bought in from Villiers. The engines came in a range of capacities, of 125 and 150cc, as well as 200cc.

HOWARD
England 1905–07: This English machine was a fairly typical two-and-a-half horsepower pioneer. Where it was not typical was in its early attempt to employ the method of fuel injection.

H&R (R&H)
England (Coventry) 1922–25: Messrs Hailstone & Ravenhall, based in Coventry, England, also went under the shorter name R&H. The company was responsible for the manufacture of a 147cc machine, which had a Villiers engine as its source of power.

H&R
Germany 1921–25: The German company Hartman & Richter of Heros were responsible for the manufacture of motorcycles which were fitted with in-house engines. These engines came in various capacities, namely, 155, 185 and 250cc.

HT
England 1920–22: This machine was an early, fully enclosed scooter. It was initially powered by a 292cc Union two-stroke engine, which later was to become a 350cc Barr & Stroud sleeve-valve.

HUC
Germany (Berlin) 1924–25: The usual DKW two-strokes of 145 and 172cc capacities powered these Max Hecker-designed machines from Germany.

HOREX REGINA 350

The Horex marque's best seller during the immediate post-World War II era was the Regina 350 overhead-valve single. In many ways, this was the most British of all German bikes of the late 1940s and early 1950s. Much of the Regina's appeal was down to its rugged reliability, frugal fuel economy and ease of servicing. At its heart was a long-stroke 342cc (69x91.5mm) semi-unit construction thumper. This turned out 15bhp at a lowly 3500rpm, but more importantly offered its rider vast amounts of torque.

Both pushrods were encased in a narrow external tube on the offside of the engine, giving it the appearance of an overhead-camshaft design with shaft and bevel gears. Inside was a three-ring 6.8:1 compression Mahle piston. Both the cylinder and head were of cast-iron, with a large one-piece rocker box in aluminium, displaying the marque's pre-war heritage, as did the twin exhaust ports and separate header pipes running down each side of the

The 342cc ohv twin-port Regina first appeared in the late 1940s and became the company's most successful model ever; this is a 1952 version.

machine. The crankshaft featured a roller bearing big-end and three ball-race mains. The valve gear was totally enclosed and tappet adjustment was by simple screw and locknut. Lubrication was taken care of by a dry-sump system, the oil pump housed under the timing cover on the offside of the engine. A four-speed foot-operated gearbox and duplex primary chain, together with a simplex rear chain, locked after the transmission.

If the Regina's engine could have said to be influenced by pre-war design, the same could not have been said about the chassis. Here, all the latest in motorcycle-design practice was employed, including oil-damped telescopic front forks, plunger rear suspension and the use of the engine, gearbox and clutch assembly as a stressed member of

the frame. The brakes, however, looked modern, with their full-width aluminium hub construction.

All in all, the Regina deserved to be a commercial success, which it was. Although the 350 was the most popular model, there were also 248cc (65x75mm) and 399cc (74.5x91.5mm) versions. Production of the Regina continued right up to the firm's closure at the beginning of 1958.

Engine: 342cc ohv vertical single, 69x91.5mm, air-cooled
Power: 15bhp at 3500rpm
Sport: 20bhp at 4500rpm
Gearbox: 4-speed foot change
Final drive: chain
Weight: 145.5kg (320lb)
Top speed: 122kph (76mph)
Sport: 126kph (78mph)

HOREX IMPERATOR 400

Presented very much by the company as its flagship model for 1954, the all-new Imperator shared nothing with the ill-fated double overhead-cam 497cc racing twin campaigned a couple of years earlier by Horex, in 1951 and 1952.

In fact, the only thing which the two designs had in common was the name, for the reason that the production roadster was an altogether superior machine. It is interesting to note that the Imperator was a 400 rather than the more obvious 500 – and this applied both to the largest Regina single as well as to the new twin – for the simple reason that road fund taxation and insurance premiums were the same for machines of 350 and 400cc capacity, whereas the cost was 25 per cent more with regards to a 500cc model.

With its 392cc (61.5x66mm) chain-driven single overhead-cam unit-construction engine and modern appearance, the Imperator would not have looked out of place two decades later when the Japanese produced and sold

„Imperator"

countless thousands of very similar middleweight twin-cylinder motorcycles.

In fact, the Imperator was probably the most modern series production model made by the German industry at that time, and deserved a far better fate than the one it was drawn.

Instead of being a large commercial success, this machine

Production of the 392cc ohc Imperator twin began in 1954. In many ways it was a forerunner of the Japanese middleweights which appeared two decades later.

never reached its full potential, thanks to the dramatic decline in sales suffered by the entire German motorcycle industry from the mid-1950s onwards.

With a maximum speed of 135kph (84mph) the Imperator produced a good performance for what was, after all, a sports/touring model. In addition to this was its specification which included the following: a full duplex tubular-steel frame with twin shock swinging-arm, rear suspension, oil damper, telescopic front forms (Schnell pivotted forks were available as an option), full-width aluminium brake hubs laced to 460mm (18ins) alloy rims, deeply valenced mudguarding (the rear could be hinged upwards to allow easy wheel removal) and a fully enclosed rear drive chain.

The Horex twin was also credited with being an extremely comfortable machine, thanks to its riding stance, flat touring handlebars and luxurious Denfeld dual seat.

Engine: 392cc sohc parallel twin, 61.5x66mm, air-cooled
Power: 26bhp at 6500rpm
Gearbox: 4-speed foot change
Final drive: chain
Weight: 180kg (396lb)
Top speed: 135kph (84mph)

HUMBER

ENGLAND 1896–1905 AND 1909–30

FOUNDED BY THOMAS HUMBER to produce bicycles, this firm moved into powered transport building tricars under licence. The eccentric Pennington was built in their works and in 1898 an electric tandem for cycle pacing appeared. They manufactured a Ladies Motor Safety with the engine behind the seat tube as well as the Olympia Tandem forecar based on the Pennington with the engine hung out behind the rear wheel but none of these early efforts ran past 1899.

Humber began producing motorcycles in 1902, offering two models, both successful. The smaller used a one-and-a-half horsepower engine hung from the downtube with belt drive; the larger was made under licence from Phelon & Rayner and had the engine fitted as the frame downtube with two-stage chain drive to the rear wheel. New models appeared for 1903, all with chain drive and offered in Beeston or the cheaper Coventry forms, this being Humber's bicycle practice. However, by 1905 the firm was concentrating on its car business so the motorcycles were dropped for a while.

The name returned in 1909 with just one three-and-a-half horsepower model of conventional form with belt drive and the option of a two-speed rear hub. Less usual was the silencer that formed

This 1903 Humber forecar had its Phelon & Moore engine, built under licence, fitted as part of the frame. There was also a two-stage chain transmission.

part of the frame downtube and the sprung front forks whose blades pivoted on a bearing in the lower crown against springs. For 1910 these were replaced by a normal silencer and Druid forks. The firm entered the TT and added a 2hp lightweight model during the year, also in ladies' form.

The TT races moved to the Mountain course in 1911 and Humber built a new two-and-three-quarters horsepower V-twin

model to run in the Junior event. Of 339cc, the engine was unusual in having a master connecting rod to which the second rod hinged. The Bosch magneto was gear-driven and clamped to the rear of the crankcase, the carburettor was a B&B, and Druid forks were used. The new model made a remarkably good debut in the TT, with all six entries finishing, one of them as a winner with P.J. Evans as the rider.

Early in the 1920s, Humber listed this prosaic 349cc side-valve single. The machine came after a series of flat-twin engines and one special triple.

For 1912 the three-and-a-half horsepower model was revised and a two-and-three-quarters horsepower V-twin introduced, while the 2hp machine ran on as it was. All models continued basically unchanged for the next two years, joined by a water-cooled version of the three-and-a-half horsepower model for 1914, intended for sidecar work.

However, late in 1913 Humber announced a new model with a horizontally opposed, three-cylinder engine. This unusual layout was achieved by having one 373cc cylinder facing forwards and two 185cc cylinders with a common combustion chamber facing aft. The crankshaft was formed to take the two rear rods either side of the front one, there was a large external flywheel and the magneto sat on top of the crankcase. This extraordinary engine drove a three-speed car-type gearbox by chain with chain final drive. Only one small batch of this model was made.

By 1915 only the three-and-a-half horsepower single remained in production, while the three was replaced by a conventional 6hp water-cooled flat-twin driving a

three-speed gearbox with chain final drive. In 1916 only flat-twins were built with the 6hp model joined by an air-cooled three-and-a-half horsepower one, also with three speeds and chain drive, but few of these were actually produced.

Postwar, the 6hp twin was dropped, while the three-and-a-half horsepower flat-twin was joined, then replaced by, a four-and-a-half horsepower version of 601cc. A sports model was added for 1921 and in 1923 the twins were joined by a 349cc side-valve single and then dropped. The two forms of single were joined by an overhead-valve model of the same capacity for 1927, and 1928 brought a neat overhead-cam version with shaft and bevel drive, rear magneto and the oil pump driven from the camshaft end. These three 349cc models continued as Humber's motorcycle range to 1930, after which the firm concentrated on its cars.

From 1928 to 1930, Humber offered this 349cc ohc engine. It also sold side- and overhead-valve models of the same size, mounted on similar frames and suspension.

HUSQVARNA

SWEDEN 1903–

THIS SWEDISH GEM NEVER lost its identity as the producer of some of the best off-road machines in the world, despite ownership being transferred in recent years to Italy. Husqvarna's origins lay in the production of bicycles and armaments, and its first powered machines were fitted with Moto-Rêve, NSU and FN engines. It

wasn't until 1920 that it produced its own engine, which was a 550cc side-valve V-twin, and even then it continued to import 250 and 500cc

Although it began making motorcycles in 1903, Husqvarna didn't produce its own engine until 1920, as used in this 500cc side-valve, V-twin machine.

single-cylinder units from Sturmey-Archer and JAP. Meanwhile, the Husqvarna V-twin increased to 992cc, producing 22bhp. The company's most famous model from 1932 was a racing bike powered by the new 498cc overhead-valve V-twin engine, designed by Folke Mannerstedt and Calle Heimdahl.

At the time it posed a serious threat to the dominant single-cylinder bikes, and it quickly evolved through 348cc and 36hp

One of the first bikes built after the Cagiva takeover was this 1993 CR250, which displayed all the hallmarks of a serious off-road machine.

and a weight reduction to 125kg (275lb). The V-twin won the Swedish Grand Prix on three successive occasions, and Stanley Woods broke the Manx lap record on his Husqvarna in the 1934 TT.

In 1935, the company built its first two-stroke, a 98cc two-speed machine, which set a precedent for its postwar production. Its two-strokes grew in capacity, while the only four-strokes it made were the Albin-engined motocross bikes. The focus of its attention was on off-road competition, and by 1960 Husqvarna had become a world-class contender. During the following decade, the marque captured no fewer than 10 World Motocross titles. The machine that provided the basis for these successes was the 22bhp 250 model, developed from the 175cc three-speed road-going model of the mid-1950s. By 1963 the so-called Husky was top motocross bike, and Torsten Hallman was almost completely invincible in 250cc World Championship events. The engine and four-speed gearbox was of unit construction and was used as a stressed member in the simple tubular frame, while a single large-

Compared with the CR250's exuberant tank logo, opposite, the crested 'H' on this 250cc WR Enduro shows how muted the firm's 1970s image was.

diameter tube connected the swinging-arm pivot to the headstock. It used light-alloy conical brake hubs, and Norton front forks were standard issue, with Ceriani forks optional. By 1979, the top model was the 390WR, a 384cc air-cooled single-cylinder two-stroke six-speed off-roader with a steel tubular frame, available in three versions for motocross, enduro and desert-racing specifications. The enduro, with its headlight, larger fuel tank, spark-arresting silencer and side-stand, was popular in the US.

Subsequent developments included water-cooling and

The dual-purpose TE610 came out in 1998, aimed at the market for supermoto machines, and was equipped with road-going tyres and electric starter.

automatic transmission. In the 1980s it revived the four-stroke off-road series. In 1986 the Cagiva group acquired their motorcycle division; a year later production was transferred to Italy, and a new product began to emerge. The TC610 of 1992 had a 577cc water-cooled four-valve double overhead-cam single, with a six-speed gearbox and top quality suspension.

HUMMEL
Germany 1951–54: This shortlived German company from the 1950s is best known as a manufacturer of scooters. Various sources differ about which engines the company used to provide power. They have been quoted as using anything from 58 to 149cc, which were apparently bought in from Ilo. They also were responsible for the manufacture of lightweights of capacities of up to 248cc.

HURIKAN
Czechoslovakia 1947–49: Jaroslav (one source cites the name Vladislav) Vlk of Czechoslovakia was responsible for the manufacture of a very nice overhead-cam 250cc machine. Other sources suggest that the company possibly also made machines of 350cc capacity.

HURRICANE
Japan late 1950s–61: A 350cc overhead-valve single was the biggest machine to come from this company. Their line-up included two-stroke lightweights of up to 250cc capacity, as well as the Rabbit scooter of both 90 and 125cc.

HURTU
France 1903–58: This French firm had a long history. It was initially was better-known for the production of lightweight cars. However, they also built lightweight motorcycles, like many before World War II. They went on to produce auxiliary cycle motors after the war.

HUSAR
Germany (Munich) 1923–25: Sources vary on the engine size used by this company: some quote either 300cc side-valve, or 350cc and 500cc. Whichever size was used, few of these particular machines, with their leaf rear-springs, were ever built.

HUSQVARNA V-TWIN RACER

1932

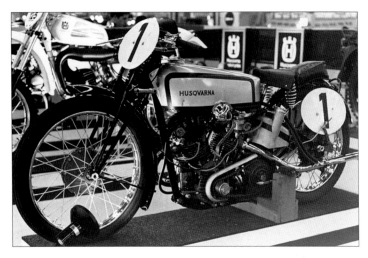

At the heart of the purposeful V-Twin race bike was its longitudinally mounted 498cc engine, occupying the whole of the frame and relegating the oil tank to the side of the rear wheel. Other

The 500cc V-twin racer was not a sophisticated machine, yet it could beat the highly-tuned singles. In 1934, Stanley Woods broke the Senior TT lap record on it.

features included hairpin valve springs and tuned exhaust pipes, which meant the rearmost pipe extended beyond the rear of the bike by at least 0.3m (1ft). The long fuel tank occupied the top run of the tubular perimeter frame, and the front girder forks featured a central spring connected to the headstock. At the back was a conical hub with an integral brake drum and sprocket carrier. The V-Twin's performance could have been better than its handling would allow, in spite of the use of alloy materials to minimise the weight.

Husqvarna unveiled the V-Twin in 1932 and developed it strenuously throughout its brief three-year stint in top flight competition.

The simple twin proved that the highly strung works singles could be beaten. Its successes included winning the Swedish GP three times. Had he not run out of fuel, the rider Stanley Woods could have won the 1934 Senior TT, instead of merely breaking the lap record.

Engine: 498cc longitudinally mounted V-twin
Power: 44bhp at 6800rpm
Gears: n/a
Final drive: chain
Weight: 127kg (280lb)
Top speed: 190kph (118mph)

HUSQVARNA TC610

1992

After the Husqvarna company's buyout by Cagiva in 1986 and subsequent move from Sweden to Italy, Husqvarna was in a position to start to address the burgeoning market of off-road competitions with a renewed vigour.

The outcome of their developmental work was the 50bhp TC610. This machine was introduced in 1992, and its tubular-steel cradle frame was powered by a state-of-the-art 577cc double overhead-cam four-valve water-cooled two-stroke single, which was allied to a six-speed gearbox.

Up front were massive upside-down telescopic forks, and an alloy swinging-arm linked to the rear monoshock.

Typical of the supermoto category, the single-cylinder TC610 was brash and unrefined, requiring a degree of physical acumen to haul it around in rough terrain.

The top half of the machine was clad in the typically sweeping fairings of that period which incorporated the seat, with the trim, high-rise exhausts emerging either side above the knobbly rear tyre.

Engine: 577cc dohc 4v 2s single, water-cooled
Power: 50bhp
Gearbox: 6-speed foot change
Final drive: chain drive
Weight: 117kg (258lb)
Top speed: dependent on gearing

HYOSUNG

KOREA 1978–

AFTER WORLD WAR II MUCH OF Europe was desperate for personal transport, yet unable to afford the level of car ownership that was common in other countries. This is still the case in many parts of the world today. Then, owing to modern manufacturing techniques and the inevitable replacement of labour with capital, many of the two-wheelers built to meet this demand were surprisingly sophisticated and even desirable vehicles. The Hyosung company were one

of the manufacturers which followed this principle and who are still suppliers of these machines today.

The smallest capacity Hyosungs are well represented by the 49cc Prima scooter: it weighed under 88kg (200lb), but was still provided with both electric- and kick-starters, automatic clutch and gearbox, suspension at both ends (telescopic forks at the front, coil springs at the rear) and with disk front- and drum back brakes.

The next level up provides the 99cc, 90kg (198lb) Zephyr city scooter, and a steady progression of vehicles follow thereafter, up to, and including, a 250cc V-twin. This diversity explains how Hyosung can export not only to China but also to Brazil and even to Germany, these three countries representing the biggest export markets from the 60 countries into which Hyosung sold in 2000.

The question is how long companies such as Hyosung can

stay in the motorcycle business, and whether they will move into other (and more interesting) areas of motorcycling. If two-wheeled transport is merely a transitional stage, they may be expected either to switch to cars, or to go out of business. But equally, it may be that the rules have changed, and that the sheer expense of cars (and of fuel to drive them) may mean that they do not flourish in those countries where their use is not already deep-rooted.

IFA

BEFORE WORLD WAR II the Saxony township of Zschopau was the home of the most advanced two-stroke motorcycles in the world. DKW had earned the respect of other, predominantly four-stroke, manufacturers for both its production roadsters and its Grand Prix winning racers in the years leading up to the outbreak of hostilities in September 1939. When the conflict was finally over, the DKW factory was nothing but rubble, and Zschopau found itself in Germany's eastern zone, under the occupation of the Soviet military. DKW therefore set up its postwar activities in Ingolstadt, in the western sector.

Meanwhile, from the ashes of the old plant in Zschopau arose a new addition to the ranks of the world's motorcycle manufacturers: IFA, or to give its full title Industrieverband-Farhzeugebau. Later this was to become known as MZ. Reconstruction on the works began in 1945, with the first production machines – essentially civilian RT125 two-strokes –

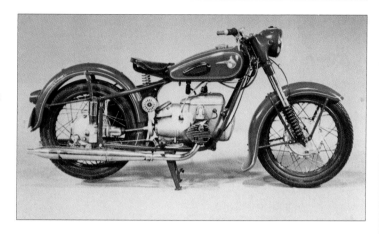

IFA's first brand new design was this 350cc flat-twin two-stroke with shaft final drive. It was introduced in 1954 and ran through to 1960.

emerging the following year. In those postwar days anything with an engine and wheels was in demand, so it didn't matter that the RT125, and other pre-war DKW models, were slavishly copied. But by the end of the 1940s, IFA was

beginning to develop its own ideas, first through racing. It was aided by a private Germany tuner, Daniel Zimmerman, who modified his own home-brewed IFA racer by means of a crankshaft-driven rotary disc-valve conversion, and later by the legendary engineer Walter Kaaden of MZ fame.

IFA's first brand new production design was a 350cc flat-twin two-stroke with shaft final drive, sold as MZs from the start of the 1960s.

IMME

FOR 50 YEARS, motorcycle design clung tenaciously to the diamond frame setup with forks supporting each side of the front- and rear-wheel spindles. In the late 1940s, the Imme, one of the most talked about, ultra-lightweight motorcycles of that era, broke with tradition. The machine's layout was ingenious; the 99cc single-cylinder two-stroke engine was egg-shaped and exceptionally clean. The Imme was created by Norbet Riedl and was built in the town of Immenstadt in Bavaria,

where visitors might have expected to hear the jangle of cow bells, rather than the sound of motorcycles.

Its 52mm bore and stroke dimensions ensured a high engine revolution. Mounted in a single steel tubular member, which acted both as an exhaust outlet and rear-fork support, the ultracompact unit

The ingenious Imme was created by Norbert Riedl. The 99cc two-stroke engine was egg-shaped and sat in an advanced chassis with single-sided forks fore and aft.

transmitted the final drive by chain to the rear wheel, which was of a conventional pattern, but could be detached quickly by removing three nuts. The three-speed twist-grip-controlled gearbox, shaft and spindle centres were equidistant from each other, which ensured that the chain tension remained constant. The front wheel was quickly detachable, thanks to its single-sided mounting.

The frame was sprung by a massive pivotal bearing in a lug between the rear and central frame members, and movement of this point was controlled by a barrel spring situated beneath the single seat. Auxiliary damping was provided by a rubber block, housed within this spring, and the rider could further control the degree of frame movement with an adjustable friction damper.

Although the machine won world-wide praise for innovative design, very few examples were actually sold. resulting in Riedel Motoren being forced to close its doors in 1951.

IMN

The IMN Rocket was one of the sensations of the 1956 Milan Show. As well as its horizontally-opposed ohv twin engine, its frame was of particularly advanced design.

BASED IN NAPLES, IMN (Industria Meccanica Neapolitana) manufactured torpedoes for the Italian Navy, but in 1945, it was decided to produce a range of two-stroke motorcycles from 49 to 248cc.

However, at the Milan Show in November 1956 IMN displayed the sensational Rocket. This was a horizontally opposed twin-cylinder (BMW-style) with a bore and stroke of 52x46.5mm, giving a displacement of 199cc. The engine featured pushrod-operated valves and with a compression ratio of 7:1, developed 11bhp at 6000rpm.

The frame was particularly noteworthy; not only was it of the tubular space variety, but the engine and gearbox were bolted up to form a unit and to the rear of the gearbox was bolted a substantial light-alloy fork, the nearside arm of which housed the final drive shaft. The entire engine/gearbox assembly pivoted with the rear wheel, and the pivot spindle, which passed through bushes in an extension of the top of the gearbox, was its only point of contact with the frame. So the front and rear wheels were connected only through a single 15mm (0.5in) diameter steel rod!

Unfortunately, the Rocket was not fully developed when it was put on sale in early 1957, and its unreliability, combined with high development costs, meant the end of IMN's motorcycle manufacturing.

INDIAN

INDIAN WAS FOUNDED well before Harley-Davidson, and rivalry between the two was what drove progress in that brief period in the early twentieth century when the United States led the world in motorcycle design and production. Surprisingly, ancient rivalry continues to this day, even among those who were born long after the last few Big Chiefs were built in 1955 for a (blatantly rigged) police contract: the actual production line ended in 1953. Today good machines are once more made under the Indian name; but after a hiatus of more than four decades, and numerous lawsuits, the current company has been given a separate entry elsewhere in this book.

George Hendee and Oscar Hedstrom met in January 1900, and founded the Hendee Manufacturing Company as a

Left: Indians were always popular with the various institutions, including the police and the army. The company's rivalry with Harley-Davidson was legendary.

Above: The 'backwards' layout of the engine – against the rear frame tube, instead of the front – was common among early American singles.

partnership to sell motorcycles under the Indian trademark. In 1901, they built about six motorcycles and sold three. By 1915, they were the biggest motorcycle manufacturer in the world, with a record 31,950 motorcycles built that year; not a bad rate of growth.

The earliest Indians were well-made, unremarkable 215cc singles with automatic inlet valves and fixed all-chain drive, but via astute publicity, mostly at bicycle shows and competitions, they soon had more orders than they could fill. Like any successful manufacturer in the earliest days, they kept up

The three-wheeled Dispatch-Tow was the inspiration (and sometimes the basis) for custom trikes. The front mudguard is almost a parody of Indian styling.

with the latest technical innovations, doubling up the single for the 1906 season to make a 42-degree V-twin, and offering mechanically operated overhead inlet valves as an option on the 633cc (69.85x82.55mm) 'improved twin' in 1908. By 1910, a new option was a two-speed gearbox with a 'free engine' or clutch, although the absence of either a kick-start or pedals meant that the only way to start the machine was still by pushing it.

In 1905, they had twist-grip controls, advance/retard on the right, although the throttle on the left, although the French Millet was probably the first with twist-grips in the 1890s. Wisely, they recognised that racing was excellent publicity, and at the fifth Isle of Man TT in 1911 they beat the British, coming in first, second and third.

Meanwhile, 1907 had seen the beginnings of Indian's long association with the police, when the Metropolitan Police Force of New York City bought two twins. The unusual left-hand twist-grip throttle is often attributed to police influence, as it would allow the officer to make signals and even to fire his revolver with his right hand. Anyone who has experience of both motorcycles and revolvers might wonder about the latter.

Their memory today rests principally on three models – the Scout, the Chief and the Four – but there were others. The original V-twin was upgraded steadily, most notably to the Powerplus of 1915: 1000cc (61cid), 16–17bhp on the dynamometer, 7hp SAE rating. This was the one that nearly broke the company: the first 20,000 machines that were supplied to the US Government at $187.50 were sold at a steadily mounting loss, not least because of very poor financial control and cost estimation at the factory, which was to be a recurrent factor for the rest of the company's life. These big twins went on well into the 1920s as the Standard, in both

The huge, curved, front-wheel mudguard became a trademark of Indian machines. Another feature was the face mounted on the front.

1000cc (61cid) and 1212cc (74cid) guises.

There were various catalogued and special racers, mostly V-twin but some singles, whether for road, endurance or board-track. The last were typically clutchless, brakeless, direct-drive brutes with a fixed wide open throttle; the only rider control was a kill switch. Some of the road-racers and record breakers were, however, very sophisticated, with eight-valve heads.

Although Indians are principally associated with V-twins and of course the Four, other engine layouts were not neglected. As well as the original single, and its 300cc successor of 1906, the underpowered two-stroke Model K Featherweight, 59kg (130lb) and 225cc, was introduced in 1914. It lasted less than three seasons, being discontinued in 1916.

Another lightweight, the 250cc in-line flat-twin Model O, was a Douglas copy that ran from 1917 to 1919; the Prince, a 350cc side-valve single (optional overhead-valve from 1926) ran from 1925 to 1929; and over 1000 transverse V-twin side-valve 750cc (45cid) machines, the Military Model 841, were built in 1943. Several hundred of the latter are reckoned still to exist. In the 1940s, Indian bought the Torque company for their (rather inferior) singles, which were never a success, and after production ceased, Royal Enfield singles were badged as Indians and sold until 1959.

In addition, Indian also produced the following: a 1931 three-wheeler delivery vehicle based on the Sport Scout, the Dispatch-Tow; outboard motors; an abortive light car project; and even aero engines.

IMPERIA
Germany 1923–25: JAP engines of 350 and 500cc powered this small assembler's products.

IMPERIA
Germany (Cologne) 1924–35: For their first decade or so, Imperia was a successful large-scale assembler using MAG V-twins of 500 to 1000cc, and various bought-in singles of 260, 350 and 500cc but import restrictions in Hitler's Germany meant that they had to develop their own engines. The strangest was a 348cc flat-twin (or two-piston single) with a single, central, common combustion chamber and a crankshaft at either end.

IMPERIA
Italy (Turin) 1932–mid-1950s: Enrico Torelli began by assembling English-style machines with JAP and then New Imperial engines, before coming out in 1939 with his own 500cc (86mm square) dry-sump single that made extensive use of light-alloys. A postwar (1954) overhead-cam version was distinguished by its generous cooling fins.

IMPERIAL
USA 1903–c.1910: This was a 450cc single of unusual obscurity.

IMPERIAL
England 1901–10: These belt-driven three-and-a-half horsepower 500cc Coronet-engined singles were remarkable for an early form of disk brake.

IMPRESE GENERALI MECCANICHE
Italy (Arcore) 1955: This firm's Bantam scooter had a 125cc two-stroke engine.

INDIAN SINGLE

1904

Early Indian singles clearly betray their bicycle ancestry, with the cylinder incorporated in the rear downtube of the diamond frame, unsprung front forks, and the 'camel back' petrol and oil tank in the position normally occupied by the carrier rack. Even so, it did incorporate some progressive features such as chain drive rather than belt and a carburettor instead of a surface vapouriser or wick. Lubrication was by drip feed with a sight glass, as was usual at the time.

The very earliest machines were painted deep blue instead of the red which would become synonymous with the name; Indian Red was introduced in 1904, the last year of the bicycle-style frame. The engine capacity also

varied: the earliest models were 225 rather than 288cc. Not until 1903 were frames numbered.

The engine was easy to start by pedaling, even without a clutch – an exhaust valve lifter meant that

The famous red paint, which became synonymous with the marque, was not introduced until 1904, two years after this distinctly bicycle-related single was made.

there was negligible engine compression to overcome – but with no front brakes, minimal rear brakes, and an engine that could not be disengaged, stopping turned out to be rather more difficult, especially if you were going downhill.

Engine: 288cc aise vertical single, air-cooled
Power: two-and-a-half bhp est.
Gearbox: fixed, via countershaft
Final drive: chain
Weight: 45kg (98lb)
Top speed: 50kph (30mph)

INDIAN POWERPLUS

1915

In one sense, the Powerplus was a retrograde step: both valves were side-mounted. In another, it was a

great leap forward: it delivered significantly more power than the previous Big Twin; it was much

This Powerplus dates from 1915, and was one of the fastest machines of the period.

easier to maintain; and it was the basis for most of Indian's subsequent successful engines. It was built with the same crankcase dimensions as the previous Hedstrom design and fitted into the same frames, even though it came with an improved gearbox and stronger clutch. Both spring and rigid frames were offered.

This was the engine that powered 'Cannonball' Baker's 1915 Three Flags run, from Vancouver to Tijuana, 2669km (1655 miles) in three days, nine hours, 15 minutes, with a three-hour nap in Fresno his only rest on the journey. Not only was it a lot more powerful than Indian's own previous offering, it also restored Indian's reputation with regard to Harley-Davidson and Excelsior, both of whom were getting ahead in the power stakes.

Despite this, the debut of the Powerplus coincided with the initial successes of Harley-Davidson's racing efforts. Consequently, by the time competition was suspended in November 1915, the Indian Powerplus was looking distinctly second-best.

Engine: 998cc sv in-line V-twin, air-cooled
Power: 17bhp
Gearbox: 3-speed hand change
Final drive: chain
Weight: n/a
Top speed: 100kph (60mph)

INDIAN SCOUT 1928

The Scout and its derivatives are probably the best known Indians of all. The Scout was introduced in 1921 with a 606cc (37cid) engine (actually 596cc/36.38cid, 69.9x77.8mm), delivering about 12bhp, and good for a top 90kph (55mph). The 750cc (45cid) machine, with bigger bore and stroke, was introduced in 1928, after which sales of the smaller engine declined; it was dropped from the 1931 catalogues.

The best Scout of all – for most Indian aficionados – was the 1928 101, introduced to compete with the then-new Excelsior of the same capacity. From then to the adoption of the new frame in 1932, it was, by American standards, light, easy to ride and powerful. Within months, someone had worked out that by fitting Chief flywheels (milled down slightly to fit into the Scout crankcase) it was possible to increase the stroke of the engine by 25 per cent to give 935cc (57cid). These stroker Scouts were the summit of the ambition of many American riders of the period, and their performance frightened Harley-Davidson badly.

Introduced in 1928, the famous Scout V-twin appeared in a variety of guises, and found its way into army use. This is a 741 model, from 1942.

Another variant was the 1932 Motoplane, a 101 Scout in a variation of the frame from the Prince single, with dry-sump lubrication, better cooling via bigger fins and better breathing with a bigger carburettor for more power. Afterwards came the Depression-special Junior (or Pony) Scout of 500cc (30.5cid), with the engine sleeved down to 63.3mm (2.5ins).

Engine: 745cc sv in-line 42-degree V-twin, 73x88.9mm, air-cooled
Power: 21bhp approx
Gearbox: 3-speed hand change
Final drive: chain
Weight: n/a
Top speed: 121kph (75mph)

INDIAN FOUR 1938

The Four began in 1912 as a Henderson, but the original under-capitalised Henderson company was bought out by Schwinn (who made Excelsiors) after which

William Henderson brought forth the Ace in 1920.

Unfortunately the Ace was sold at a loss, financial astuteness being a rare quality among motorcycle

The 'Collegiate Four'– of which this 1938 example is fairly late – gained its name when educational standards were better regarded than today.

manufacturers, and Ace folded in 1924. It was then bought by the Michigan Motors Corporation before ending up in the hands of Indian in 1927.

At first, the Indian Four, marketed as the Collegiate Four, was essentially a rebadged Ace, but as time went on, it grew more Indianised. The engine was always

a nominal 1261cc (77cid), actually 1265cc/77.21cid, but a five-bearing crankshaft replaced the original three-bearing in 1929. The new frame of 1932 has already been mentioned. In 1936, an unusual exhaust-over-inlet valve arrangement replaced the old inlet-over-exhaust layout, and then in 1938 the whole engine was re-

designed for greater reliability with better cooling and lubrication, again with inlet-over-exhaust.

In an age that prized flexibility, the Model 438 was a winner, with a top-gear range from a walking pace to 161kph (100mph). Predictably, it would overheat if driven fast (over 81kph/50mph) for any length of time. About

12,000 Indian Fours were made; production stopped in March 1942.

Engine: 1265cc ioe 4s in-line straight-4, 69.9x82.6mm, air-cooled
Power: n/a
Gearbox: 3-speed, hand change
Final drive: chain
Weight: 200kg (440lb) approx
Top speed: 160kph (100mph)

INDIAN MILITARY MODEL 841   1943

The Indian 841 was, like Harley-Davidson's XA, the result of a government contract during World War II. But whereas the Harley-Davidson was a copy of a pre-war BMW, Indian's bike was totally new and had the potential to be an excellent design in its own right. As well as state-of-the-art suspension front and rear, it had a four-speed, foot-change gearbox instead of the hand change still favoured by Harley-Davidson.

Transverse V-twins were nothing new; Clement Ader had built them as early as 1905, and others had followed, including Spring, Stylson, Finzi, Walter and P&M, but this one offered excellent cooling, a low centre of gravity and high spark plugs (important for wading). Moto Guzzi did very well out of this layout, and it is hard not to suspect that, if they had had the money, Indian could have done well with

a 'civilianised' overhead-valve version of the 841.

However, this was not to be. With Indian's usual mixture of bad luck and bad judgement, their 'war chest' for postwar development was all but wiped out when the US Government refused to pay for spares that Indian had believed to be covered by wartime contracts.

It is not unrealistic to say that Indian never recovered from its financial misfortunes from World

War I, and the financial misfortune which happened after World War II delivered something very close to the finishing stroke to the company.

Engine: 745cc sv transverse V-twin, 73x88.9mm, air-cooled
Power: n/a
Gearbox: 4-speed foot change
Final drive: shaft
Weight: n/a
Top speed: 113kph (70mph)

INDIAN CHIEF   1946

The Chief was effectively an enlarged Scout, introduced in 1921 with a 999cc (61cid) engine, actually 998cc/60.88cid, 79.4x100.8mm. Top speed was

well over 150kph (90mph), or 110kph (70mph) even with a side-car, in which form it was popular for booze-running during the Prohibition, but it still featured

total loss lubrication and side-valves. It was joined by the 1212cc (74cid) Big Chief (actually 1206cc/73.62cid, 82.6x112.7mm) for 1923. Like the Scout, the

Chiefs grew Ricardo-type heads in 1925, with still further improved breathing in 1926.

In 1929 these big, heavy, fast machines were fitted with a front brake for the first time, and thereafter there was remarkably little technical progress until World War II, during which period the Scout formed the basis of most of the machines which the company produced for the war effort.

After the war, the pre-war Big Chiefs were put back into production. Just before their demise in 1953, they grew to 1340cc (82cid), still without foot change or hydraulic forks.

Although changeless machines will always have an appeal to collectors and traditionalists, they seldom constitute a big enough market to keep an entire marque afloat, and while Harley-Davidsons were still primitive by European standards, they were more advanced than the machines from Indian. So died the marque that many reckon should have been the survivor in place of the Harley-Davidson.

This 1946 Chief was made less than a decade before Indian went out of business. The machine originally appeared in 1921, powered by a 999cc (61cid) engine.

There is a fine line between a 'classic' and a machine that is simply outdated – and the hand-change, rigid-frame, post-war Chief was, unfortunately, simply outdated.

Engine: 1206cc sv in-line V-twin, air-cooled
Power: 40bhp
Gearbox: 3-speed hand change
Final drive: chain
Weight: n/a
Top speed: 140kph (85mph)

INDIAN   USA 1998–

After the demise of the original Indian company, numerous attempts were made to revive the marque, from badge-engineering Royal Enfields and Velocettes to Ehler Industries. There was even a Vindian, a Vincent-engined Indian. The legal situation as to who had the rights to the name grew increasingly murky, and lawsuits flew in all directions. The situation at the time of writing was as follows: The Indian Motorcycle Company, headquartered in Gilroy, California, seemed to have full rights to the name, and planned the production of 11,000 machines a year: not a back-alley Harley-Davidson clone shop.

In order to come to market as quickly as possible, they did not begin with their own motor, but instead used the readily available S&S 1441cc (88cid) nominal

displacement V-twin, actually 1436cc, 108x92mm. The use of a proprietary engine was quite commonplace: Brough Superiors built their reputations on bought-in V-twins, initially JAP and later Matchless and the original Indian engines were built for them by Thor. The finished product was built to look as similar as possible to a 1953 Indian Chief, from the last year of full production. Deeply valanced mudguards, a fringed saddle and an Indian Head running light all meant that it looked the part.

It was, however, an assembled machine, not an all-Indian Indian, and a great deal turned upon the promised in-house engine, which was due to appear in 2000. Other parts were supplied by the following: Supertrapp, exhausts; Showa, front forks; Arlen Ness,

headlights; and Corbin, seat. At 295kg (650lb) dry weight, what might be called the homologation machine was as portly as it was handsome, with a tendency to ground the floorboards during anything other than the most sedate cornering; as the reviewers said, it would take time to sort out the handling as well as the looks.

As with so many American motorcycles, performance figures such as engine output and top speed were not normally quoted; looks, rather than anything else, are what sell big V-twins in the United States, and the Indians certainly had that.

The 'new' Indian concern seemed to be torn between making functional, reasonably modern V-twins like this 2001 Scout and pure nostalgia cruisers.

IPREM

ITALY 1977–81

BASED IN THE ADRIATIC coastal township of Pesaro, Iprem built only road racing machines. Its creator was Enzo Ridolfi, who chose at first to enter the 50cc category with a Kreidler-like 49.64cc (40x39.5mm) horizontal liquid-cooled single-cylinder model. This produced a very respectable 16bhp at 16,000rpm.

In 1977, ridden by Guido Mancini, it won the prestigious Italian Senior Championship, beating some far more well established marques, as well as several star name riders. By 1980 the Iprem 50 had been developed into a world-class bike, so much so that Iprem's latest signing, Eugenio Lazzarini was able to take the 50cc World Championship title with wins in Italy and Spain, a second at Spa Francorchamps in

The Iprem rider, Eugenio Lazzarini, astride his 124.68cc (44x41mm) horizontal disc-valve, two-stroke twin, prior to the start of the 1980 Italian GP at Misano.

Belgium (the fastest circuit in the calendar) and two thirds (in Holland and Yugoslavia).

Also in 1980 a 124.68cc (44x41mm) liquid-cooled horizontal twin, with disc-valve induction, made its debut. This latest creation was the work of the engineer Paolo Marcheselli, with assistance from Lazzarini. Its first Grand Prix finish came during the French round when Eugenio Lazzarini came home ninth. Then at the British GP (at Silverstone) the same rider finished an impressive fifth. But the Iprem team's best ever result with the

horizontal twin-cylinder model came in 1981 when Lazzarini was fourth in the 1981 Austrian Grand Prix at the Salzburgring.

However, Iprem could not sustain the costs of GP racing and Lazzarini left at the end of the year to join rivals Garelli.

ISO

ITALY 1948–64

FOUNDED BY RENZO RIVOLTA at Bresso in 1939, Isothermos (Iso) had just begun trading when World War II broke out. Reformed in 1948 as Iso Autotiveicoli SpA, Rivolta then began to build autocycles and scooters. With increasing sales Iso introduced the famous Isetta micro car, with its own 236 overhead-valve engine. Various licence agreements ensued, the most successful with the German BMW company. With production lasting well into the 1960s, many thousands were sold all around the world.

Next came a series of motorcycles and scooters, some of which used split-single two-stroke

engines. One of these units was fitted to a scooter-like machine, with 124.7cc displacement, featuring a pair of 38mm (1.4ins) pistons; the stroke was 55mm (2ins). From this, a family of models developed, both scooters and motorcycles, including the 125 Gran Turismo; a larger 150 version (with the dual bore increased to 41mm); a 250 class engine (236cc, 48x2x64mm); and a 200 (196cc, 44x2x64mm) featuring shaft final drive.

1957 saw the debut of the Milano scooter. Of much more modern appearance, it used a new 146cc (57x57mm) single-cylinder two-stroke engine and looked like

Left: This small-wheeled scooter-like machine is powered by a 123cc two-stroke engine and dates from the mid-1950s. Iso switched to making supercars in 1963.

a cross between a Vespa and Lambretta.

For 1961 the Milano was joined by new overhead-valve four-stroke motorcycles: two 125s and a 175. The latter gave eight-and-a-third brake horsepower at 6200rpm from its 172cc (60x61mm) four-speed unit-construction engine. A BMW-like 492cc overhead-valve flat-twin displayed at the Milan

Above: Founded by Renzo Rivolta, Iso built two-, three- and four-wheeled vehicles. This 1953 200cc motorcycle had a split-single two-stroke engine.

Samples Fair during April 1961 did not reach production, but featured a full duplex frame, electric starting, 22.6bhp and a claimed 145kph (90mph).

In 1963 all two-wheeled production came to an end; Iso concentrated on luxury cars. After several turbulent years, in 1975 Iso was declared bankrupt and in 1979, the last car was built.

ITALJET

ITALY 1966–

ITALJET RAPIDLY ACHIEVED cult status with its Formula and Dragster Supersport Scooter ranges in the late 1990s. However, the first Italjet machines were powered by CZ and Triumph engines when founder Leopoldo Tartarini set up the company in 1966. Italjet was also involved in the construction of the Indian Velocette, of which around 100 units were made between 1969 and 1970. This Anglo-Italian hybrid used the overhead-valve single-cylinder 500cc Velocette engine in a twin-loop frame with Marzocchi suspension. It was commissioned by former Californian Indian dealer Floyd Clymer who sought to revive two famous names in one go, but the project stalled with his death in 1970. Thereafter, Italjet concentrated on producing children's mini bikes such as the 47cc Moroni-powered M5B scrambler of 1973, a beautifully executed scaled-down replica of a full size bike. Then in 1977 Ducati launched its handsome 864cc Darmah model, which had been styled by Leopoldo Tartarini and

Founded in 1966 by Leopoldo Tartarini, Italjet built finely detailed, small-capacity mini-bikes from 1970, progressing to 350cc road bikes and trials machines.

featured a novel duck-tail rear end. Italjet's other work in the 1980s embraced 350cc road-going custom bikes and two- and four-stroke trials machines.

Italjet followed the scooter boom of the late 1990s and early 2000s with its Dragster range, including 50, 125 and 180cc machines. The Dragster 50 was capable of only 76kph (47mph), but it was a very purposeful machine, endowed with some of the most effective brakes in the industry. Based on a sparse Ducati-style trellis frame with a shock-absorber arrangement that wouldn't look out of place on a

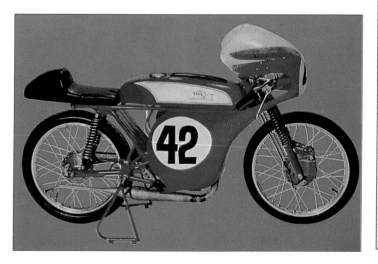

The Formula 50 was the starter model in Italjet's range of state-of-the-art scooters. Their sporting specification was matched by the best aesthetics in the marketplace.

Buell, the Dragster 50's 50cc motor delivered enough torque to allow rapid progress in town riding. The Italjet Formula F125LC of 1999 uses a 114cc liquid-cooled two-stroke twin pushing out just 12bhp but still capable of 129kph (80mph). Its weight – just 100kg (220lb) – helps here. At the other end of the scale, Italjet also produced a custom café racer.

ITALKART
Italy 1960s: This go-cart manufacturer briefly diversified into 50cc mini-bikes.

ITALMOTO
Italy (Bologna) 1952–54: This was a reasonably modern four-speed 160cc four-stroke.

ITAR
Czechoslovakia (Prague) 1921–29: J. Janatka & Spol began with a 750cc in-line flat-twin, primarily for the military market, and followed it up with an unsuccessful 350cc single of their own before switching to 350 and 500cc side-valve and overhead-valve JAPs.

ITO IMC
Japan 1951–60s: For most of the 1950s, this firm relied on a 247cc pushrod single; in 1960, on 246cc and 124 two-stroke twins.

IVEL
England (Biggleswade) 1902–05: These were the usual strengthened bicycle frames with a variety of bought-in motors, beginning with De Dion Bouton.

IVER-JOHNSON
USA (Fichtburg, Massachusetts) 1907–15: These were strong, reliable V-twins of up to 1090cc.

IVO LOLA RIBAR
Yugoslavia 1956–unknown: This firm made Vespa 125 scooters under licence.

IVY
England 1908–32: This firm offered a choice of JAP, Precision and Green-Precision 225cc two-strokes, the last water-cooled. They later made their own two-strokes – 225, 250, 300 and 350cc – and at the end of the 1920s, side-valve four-strokes of 250 and 300cc.

IXION
England 1901–03: The smaller, earlier Ixion concern was a bicycle-maker who used De Dion Bouton and MMC engines.

IXION
England (Birmingham) 1906–23: The bigger, later company used a wider variety of bigger engines: Abingdon, Precision, Peco and Villiers from 269 to 670cc.

ITOM

THE VERY FIRST ITOM was a cycle motor designed in 1944. Based in Turin, the company soon built up an excellent reputation for its 50 and later 65cc models, all of which were powered by a series of single-cylinder two-stroke engines, with piston-port induction.

During the late 1950s the marque became involved in the 50cc racing boom, which

During the 50cc racing boom of the late 1950s and early 1960s, the 49cc (40x39.5mm) Itom was a popular choice with privateers, even at world championship level.

ultimately led to the class being accepted for World Championship status in 1962. The early racing models had a three-speed gearbox, geared primary drive and a hand-operated twist-grip gear change. The Mark VII had four gears, and the Mark VIII four gears with foot change.

Although the factory itself never entered works machines, private Itom riders made up the majority of any 50cc race programme for several years (from the late 1950s until around 1963) before being totally outclassed by official production racers such as the double overhead-cam Honda CR110 and the various Kreidlers, let alone the top works bikes from Derbi, Kreidler, Suzuki, Honda and Tomos, amongst others.

In December 1965 *The Motor Cycle* put one of the 49cc (40x39.5mm) Competition models through its paces, being impressed enough to comment: 'It has disadvantages, true enough; but a remarkable, exceptionally smooth engine, allied with exemplary road-holding is compensation enough for any discomfort!' Costing the princely sum of £118, this fully road-legal sports 50 was imported by A.H. Tooley of London.

A few short months later, the factory was forced to close as the number of orders it was taking was constantly falling, and this was no doubt affected by its racing decline.

Brochure for the Itom Astor Super Sport. The Turin-based company had an excellent reputation for its series of 50 and 65cc two-strokes.

IZH

IZH (THE NAME TAKEN from the first three letters of the company's location, Izhevsk) has been one of the mainstays of Soviet and Russian motorcycle production, as well as a strong supporter of the two-stroke engine. Like the vast majority of Soviet motorcycle builders during the 1930s, 1940s and 1950s, much of the technology was copied from the West. In IZH's case, this was Germany and DKW.

Even before the war and the subsequent seizure of DKW's plant at Zschopau by the communist authorities, the Izhevsk factory had been copying German practice. Then, when Hitler launched Operation Barbarosa in June 1941, the Russians used captured examples of the DKW NZ350. This featured long-stroke dimensions of 72x85mm for its single-cylinder, twin-port engine.

A view of the IZH factory in 1947. In the foreground is one of the company's 350cc, two-stroke DKW-derived models, still with hand gear-change mechanism.

The four-speed transmission featured both hand- and foot-change, whilst the frame was constructed from channel sections of steel pressings with a rigid rear and had blade-type girder front forks. After the war, the NZ350-inspired IZH continued in production. In the immediate postwar period, racing versions used the same engine and cycle parts.

By the 1960s, IZH had begun to build specialised bikes for events such as the ISDT. These were often far removed from the obsolete offerings that were the company's bread and butter. The performance and handling of these dirt bikes was world class, bringing the Soviet teams gold medals.

In 1961, a twin-cylinder roadster model, the Jupiter, entered production. Later, a modern single, the Planeta, arrived. Both sold hugely in Eastern Bloc countries. Export to the West, including the UK, began in the mid-1970s and these designs remain IZH's main production models. New machines are rumoured to be in the pipeline.

JAMATHI

THE AMSTERDAM-BASED Jamathi-Nederhorst marque grew from the efforts of two men: Jan Thiel and Martin Mijwaart. Both exceptionally skilled engineers, their first machine was a racing special which debuted at the 1962 Dutch TT at Assen. The bike came home ninth, ridden by Mijwaart himself.

The following year a third man joined the team: this was leading Dutch lightweight rider Paul Lodewijkx. Lodewijkx soon proved his worth by gaining a number of important placings in both the Netherlands and in Belgium. The highlights were a sixth place in the domestic Grand Prix, followed by the same result a week later in the Belgian GP held over the ultra-quick Spa course in the Ardennes.

If anyone had thought the 1967 Jamathi racer was a fluke, the following year proved them wrong, as Lodewijkx came second in the 50cc world championship series, after only contesting three

of the five rounds. The 49.6cc single-cylinder engine was a liquid-cooled version of the original 1967 prototype, featuring a disc valve and a gearbox with no less than a nine speeds.

In 1969 Jamathi won three GPs,

During the late 1960s, Jamathi built a number of highly successful 50cc Grand Prix racing models. Specification included water-cooling, disc valves and nine speeds.

while the following year, with the former Van Veen rider Alt Toerson riding, Jamathi tied with Derbi in the championship. The title was awarded to the Spanish team because they had more victories.

Jamathi also built a series of street bikes, but with air-cooled engines. They proved quite popular on the home market, but Thiel and Mijwaart opted to work for the likes of Bultaco and Cagiva instead.

A 1970 Jamathi Trials model, with an Italian 172cc Minerelli piston-port two-stroke engine, 16bhp at 6000rpm, full-width aluminium hubs and full cradle frame.

JAMES

THE JAMES MARQUE WAS founded by the manager of a Birmingham engineering works, Harry James, when he was already well established and approaching his retirement. The James Cycle Company was a success, and in 1902 it emulated many of its contemporaries by fitting engines to its bicycles. The James motorcycle was equipped with a bought-in Belgian Minerva and FN engine that was clipped to the frame's front downtube, and was

belt-driven. Nothing out of the ordinary there, but in 1908, P.L. Renouf designed a motorcycle for James that was highly innovative. Most notably, both front and rear wheels were mounted on stub axles, and it aslo had hub-centre steering and internally expanding brakes, in which respect it was probably the pioneer. The 523cc single-cyliner engine had concentric inlet and exhaust valves, and the cylinder-head cooling fins were arranged in a

pineapple layout. However, the stub axles and hub-centre steering were soon dropped. In 1911, James came out with what was a state of the art all-chain transmission featuring a two-speed gearbox and multi-plate clutch. This was followed by a variety of new models in the next few years, ranging from a small two-stroke in 1913, to a 500cc side-valve V-twin and 599cc side-valve single in 1914. The 599cc machine was called the Perfect, and promoted as

---

JAC
Czechoslovakia (Horadzovice) 1929–32: J.A. Cvach built this interesting, unorthodox shaft-drive 500cc single with pressed-steel frame and petrol tank under the saddle.

JACKSON-ROTRAX
England 1949–66: These machines had JAP 500cc overhead-valve speedway engines in frames designed by speedway rider Alec Jackson.

JACK SPORT
France 1927–31: These machines had JAP Jack 350 and 500cc singles.

JAK
Germany 1922–25: DKW (119 to 173cc) and Bekamo 129cc engines powered these lightweights.

JALE
Germany (Munich) 1923–25: Motorradbau Jakob Lehner built 170cc deflector-piston machines with air- and water-cooling.

JANOIR
France c.1905–1920s: This was initially a 995cc flat–twin (in line with the frame) with three-speed gear. In 1921, it became a new, fully enclosed version.

JAVON
Germany (Nurnberg) 1929–32: J.A. Vogler was a small assembler who used 142cc two-strokes and JAP 200 and 500cc four-strokes in his own original frames.

J-BE
USA 1950s: Joe Berliner had motorcycles built in Europe, with Fichtel & Sachs engines of 100 and 125cc, for sale under this name. The name is also rendered Je-Be in some places.

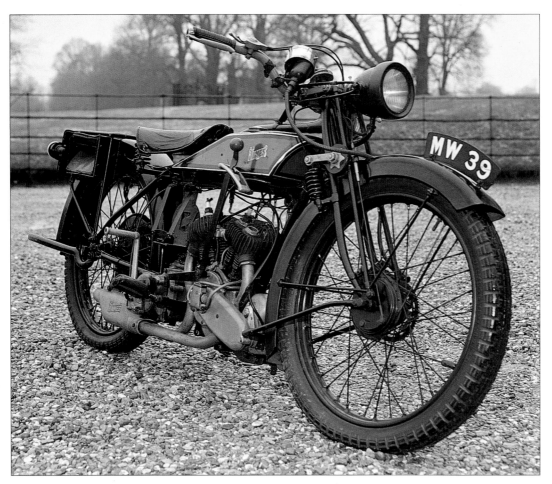

Above: The line-up for the late 1950s and early 1960s included the 250cc Commodore (pictured), the Villiers-powered Superswift twin and the Sports Captain.

Left: During the 1920s, James built its own engines, such as this 1925 500cc motor, but it was more economical to fit Villiers engines in the bigger capacity models.

a sidecar combination, available in 1914 for £77. The solo machine was available for £63, and featured an enclosed chain final drive, stirrup brakes and a foot-operated all-metal clutch, a device popular with speedway riders into the 1950s. By 1914, James had a base in Birmingham at 9, Broad Street Corner, and at Holborn Viaduct in London.

Postwar production included a small autocycle and overhead-valve 250, 500 and 750cc V-twins. Being self sufficient with engines proved expensive, and in the mid-1930s James followed the trend set

The 350cc single-cylinder model was in production in 1928, but by the mid-1930s, James had limited its output to 250cc machines, a trend set by other small marques.

by other small British manufacturers and bought in its powertrains from Villiers, restricting its output to just 250cc machines. James downscaled its product line yet again in 1938 with the Autocycle, a 98cc Villiers-powered motorised bicycle, partly prompted by the launch of the new engine, and partly recognising the need for economical personal

transport. Some 6000 units were sold as essential vehicles during World War II, and James also built the ML 125cc Military Lightweight motorcycle for the British Army as a dispatch rider's mount.

Civilian production got going again in 1946, and the Autocycle proved to be ideal for the prevailing climate of austerities and petrol-rationing. James also made a non-military version of the ML finished in maroon and grey, and as Villiers' postwar engine range grew larger, the James catalogue expanded to match. The James utility of 1949 was an ideal machine to haul a sidecar. However, in 1951 the company was taken over by Associated Motor Cycles, which also owned the Francis-Barnett marque, and was obliged to toe the corporate line and fit the in-house two-stroke engines in its Cadet, Cavalier and Commodore models. These bikes

The wedge-shaped tank and detailed coachwork used by James during the 1920s were very distinctive, though the sight-gauge was typical of the period.

were built on part pressed-steel frames. James also entered the scooter market that was to all intents and purposes sewn up by the Italians by the time that the British makers arrived on the scene. The 150cc James scooter had a low centre of gravity and ample luggage space, but was too heavy and lacked the elegance and panache of the Italians.

During the 1950s the James and Francis-Barnett models became more and more similar. James enjoyed a measure of success with off-roading machines and ran a factory team for many years. The

Commando trials bike and Cotswold scrambler were popular, while the road-going bikes included the 250cc Commodore single, the 250cc Villiers-powered Superswift twin with its faired-in rear quarters and the range-topping Sports Captain. These were adequate, but the invasion of Japanese lightweight machines in the mid-1960s meant that the majority of the British motorcycle industry was doomed; Associated Motor Cycles collapsed in 1966, and James went with them.

JAMES 600 PERFECT 1913

BY 1913, JAMES MOTORCYCLES had started to build its own engines, in both two- and four-stroke format.

The company's two main products were the 500cc side-valve V-twin and big 599cc side-valve single. The latter featured the distinctive pineapple-finned vertical cylinder, and the machine's appearance was still based on a cycle frame with fuel tank beneath the top tube and engine cradled in the bottom bracket. It featured stirrup brakes at the front, 666mm (26ins) wheels, an enclosed chain final drive, and a foot-operated all-metal clutch. Known as the Perfect, the 599cc machine was also available as a sidecar combination.

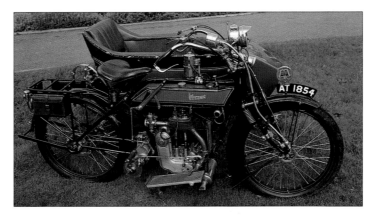

Engine: 599cc sv 4s single
Power: 7hp
Gears: 3-speed, hand change
Final drive: chain
Weight: 164kg (360lb)
Top Speed: 72kph (45mph)

The 599cc Perfect was a highly specified machine that was also available as a sidecar combination. This is a 1914 model with luxuriously padded chair.

JAP ENGLAND 1903–08

J.A. PRESTWICH FOUNDED this firm in Tottenham, London, to produce engines. He built motorcycles for a short while, but then concentrated on engines which ranged from a modest 175cc single to a massive 1000cc V-twin. His first engine was built in 1901 – a single-cylinder four-stroke – and in the next year he considered production for general sale.

The early engine was around 300cc with an automatic inlet valve in the top of the one-piece head and barrel that sat on a vertically split crankcase. His engine and complete machines were on display at the Stanley Show held late in 1903, By then the engine was of three-and-a-half horsepower. It had overhead valves and the design contrived to open both using a single pushrod and rocker arm. The arm spanned both vertical valves, and the cam had a track to both pull and push, this movement opening the appropriate valve.

The JAP motorcycle used a BSA frame and sprung forks to house the vertically mounted engine with belt final drive. A second machine used a two-and-a-

quarter horsepower inclined engine and was listed as a lightweight model. The motorcycles continued for 1905 as

The British JAP firm produced four-stroke engines in many sizes for many years both at home and abroad, with one or two cylinders, the latter V-twins.

a two-and-a-half and three-and-a-half horsepower, along with a car-like three-wheeler. In 1906 there was a three-and-a-half horsepower single, a 6hp V-twin and a forecar having an 8hp three-cylinder in-line engine.

By 1908 the firm was making engines and the motorcycles were dropped.

JB-LOUVET
France (Argenteuil) 1926–30: This was an assembler using two-stroke Aubier Dunne engines (175 and 250cc) and four-strokes from JAP (350 and 500cc).

JCM
France (Vesoul) 1980s: These were original trials bikes, such as the 303 (82x58mm) with the tank under the saddle, which used Italian TAU motors.

JD
England 1920–26: Equipped with both pedals and a clutch, this 116cc machine was made in both ladies' and gents' models. It may also have been sold as an auxiliary cycle motor.

JEAN THOMANN
France 1920–30: The smaller 100 and 250cc two-strokes were identical with Alcyon, and there was also a 500cc overhead-valve engine with external flywheel.

JE-BE
see **J-BE**

JEECY-VEA
Belgium 1923–27: King Albert of the Belgians favoured these in-line flat-twins with proprietary engines: Coventry Victor 498cc overhead-valve and 688cc side-valve, and Watelet 750cc side-valve.

JEHU
England 1901–c.1910: This firm offered normal pioneer fare with MMC, Minerva and possibly their own engines of two-and-a-quarter, two-and-a-half and 3hp.

JELINEK
Czechoslovakia (Prague) 1904-07: As well as the usual Minervas and Fafnirs, this firm also fitted Czech Orion engines.

JAWA

OF ALL THE ONCE GREAT Czech motorcycle marques, Jawa is the most well known. It originally began in 1929 when Frantisek Janecek of the National Arms Factory in Prague decided that his company should become involved in powered two-wheelers. He obtained a licence from the German Wanderer concern to manufacture one of its designs which, although troublesome, did coin a new name: Jawa (from the names JAnecek and WAnderer).

The next move came with the arrival of the leading British engineer George Patchett, who joined Jawa in 1930. It was Patchett who put the fledgling Czech firm on the map with a string of notable designs, such as a racer with a 500cc pushrod engine.

In 1932 Jawa introduced its first two-stroke, a modern-looking lightweight with a 173cc British Villiers deflector piston engine. A succession of production roadsters followed with two-stroke or side-valve power units. Apart from the Villiers and Wanderer engines made under licence agreements, these were all the work of Patchett himself. But with the onset of war in 1939, George Patchett returned to England.

During the conflict, the company managed to prepare for the postwar era by designing and developing, in secret, a new range of motorcycles. One of these was an ultra-modern 248cc two-stroke single, with unit construction, an automatic clutch (which was to remain a feature of Jawa's production roadsters for several

In 1932, Jawa introduced its first two-stroke, using a British Villiers engine. This 350cc model, dating from the mid-1930s, used an engine of Jawa's own design.

years thereafter), telescopic front forks and plunger rear suspension.

In 1947 Jawa swallowed up the rival Ogar factory and introduced a brand-new model, a 346cc two-stroke twin, which employed many cycle parts from the 248cc single. It was also during this era that the first postwar racers appeared. Designed by Vaclav Sklenar, these were 348 and 498cc double-overhead-cam vertical twins in supercharged and unsupercharged forms.

Jawa had been nationalised at the end of the war and a link was made with old rival CZ in 1949, when both companies came under communist control. At this time, Jawa was officially authorised to take an interest in sport. The firm began racing with a new set of parallel-twins, and competed in off-road events as well.

This marked the beginning of Jawa's ISDT glory years. Czechoslovakia won the Trophy contest in 1958, 1959 and 1962, and captured the prize seven times during the 1970s – in 1970, 1971, 1972, 1973, 1974, 1977 and 1978 – using 250, 350 and 360cc single-cylinder two-stroke Jawas.

In July 1954, this 498cc dohc twin, ridden by Jan Koster, appeared at Zandvoort, Holland and won first time out, beating noted British and Dutch riders.

Although Jawa was never quite as successful in tarmac racing as on the dirt, it nonetheless made a sustained bid for honours from the early 1950s until the mid-1970s mainly using four-strokes, usually double-overhead-cam parallel-twins in the 500, then 250 and 350cc classes

The new 350cc-class bike with which Jawa began the 1960s was developed from the smaller-engined model. But the 347.7cc (59x63.5mm) double-overhead-cam parallel-twin now had the vertical shaft relocated between the cylinders at the rear, and drove the inlet camshaft by means of bevels. A horizontal shaft, lying along the top of the engine, took the drive forward to the exhaust camshaft. Each cylinder barrel and head was a separate casting in light alloy, while steel liners were employed for the cylinder bores. The oil was now carried in a deeply finned wet sump, in place of the previous dry sump and separate oil tank. Later a four-

valves-per-cylinder engine was used, but this did not prove as reliable as the original two-valve unit.

During the mid-1960s Jawa took over the Eso concern and with it that firm's speedway engine. This powerplant was hugely successful, being raced throughout the world; the latest four-valve version is still used.

Although Jawa had built and sold a 350cc single-overhead-cam twin street bike in the 1950s, its postwar roadster production – except for a 500cc Rotax-powered machine in the mid-1980s – consisted exclusively of two-strokes, both singles and twins. Even today, Jawa concentrates on the manufacture of two-strokes for its bread-and-butter series-production models.

Following Jawa's takeover of Eso in the late 1960s, it has become the largest manufacturer of speedway motorcycles in the world. This is a 1994 model.

JAWA 500 OHC TWIN
1950s

The 488cc dohc Jawa roadster twin first took to the road in 1949; this is a later model (1955) with full-width brakes and dual seat.

IF JAWA'S 250/350 TWO-STROKES brought in a basic income for the Prague company, then its series of four-stroke twins created prestige during the early postwar years.

The first news of a twin-cylinder model with a double overhead-camshaft emerged in 1948. In early 1949 prototypes of this 488cc (65x73.6mm) machine first took to the road. The camshaft drive was by shafts and bevel gears. There was a single Jikov 24mm carburettor, together with a foot-operated four-speed gearbox.

It took a further three years before the model, coded 15/01, entered production in 1952. Lubrication was of the dry sump variety, with an oil pump and a separate oil tank with a capacity of 4.5litre (1 imp. gal). Its maximum power was 26bhp at 5500rpm. The frame, based on the 250 Jawa Springer (a twin-port two-stroke single), had been reinforced for the extra power and weight with oil-damped telescopic front forks and plunger rear suspension. With a dry weight of 155kg (344lb), Jawa claimed 140kph (87mph).

For the 1953 season Jawa released it as the updated model 15.02, with a more powerful engine (28bhp) and maximum speed of 146kph (91mph). In 1954 a dual seat was added, then massive full-width brakes.

Despite the air of prestige, sales were low. The company ended production in 1958.

Engine: 488cc dohc 2 parallel twin, 65x73.6mm, air-cooled
Power: 28bhp at 5500rpm
Gearbox: 4-speed foot change
Final drive: chain
Weight: 156kg (344lb)
Top speed: 91mph (146kph)

JAWA 350 GP V-FOUR
1969

THE FIRST PROTOTYPE of the GP V-four was finished in June 1967. The engine followed the vee layout of the Japanese Yamaha fours although, in fact, it had been designed independently. The two crankshafts were geared and used much of the technology employed on the 125 V-twin. Induction was again by disc-valve, which designer Zdenik Tichy thought necessary for ultimate performance. The 344.5cc (48x47.6mm) engine had a compression ratio of 16:1 and power of 9000–13,500rpm. Drive to the rear wheel was by chain, via a seven-speed gearbox.

Unlike the Yamaha, this engine's water-cooling was on the thermosyphon principle, and it was generally accepted that the appearance of the Czech engine was much neater than the Japanese fours.

Initially it was unreliable, but by mid-1968 the 350 V-four had finished a Grand Prix. With a top speed of 258kph (160mph), it was the only serious competitor to MV and Giacomo Agostini.

Designed by Zdenik Tichy, the 350 V-four racing Jawa featured disc-valves and water-cooling. Power output was 70bhp at 13,000rpm.

Eventually fitted with electronic ignition (before this, four sets of contact breakers had been used), the engine was producing 70bhp, giving it a performance equal to that of the previously unbeatable three-cylinder MV. As the Grand Prix circus entered the East German round at Sachsenring, many thought it possible that the Jawa, with Bill Ivy, could win.

Tragically, a practice run cost Ivy his life, and also ended dreams of glory for the Czech factory.

Engine: 344.5cc 2s rotary valve V-four, 48x47.6mm, water-cooled
Power: 70bhp at 13,000rpm
Gearbox: 7-speed foot change
Final drive: chain
Weight: 265lb (120kg)
Top speed: 258kph (165mph)

JAWA MODEL 6 SERIES ENDURO

1970s

The Jawa 653 was a 350cc single-cylinder, two-stroke enduro bike, which dominated its sport, including the famous ISDT, during the 1970s.

THE 1970S ENDURO SCENE belonged to Jawa. In 1968 a tubular duplex frame was tested and was found to be so good that it was used throughout the entire team's bikes at the 1969 International Six Day Trial. The layout of the new frame had two downtubes curved under the power unit and two top tubes extending rearwards from the steering head to meet the seating supporting tubing. To provide additional support, a third tube ran from the base of the steering head rearwards to join the other at the seat tube area.

Front forks and the brake assembly came from the CZ motocrosser, while the swinging-arm was controlled by conventional twin shocks. To provide maximum strength, the duralumin rear hub was forged, instead of cast.

Massively finned, the cylinder head (with twin plugs) was of light alloy, as was the cylinder, the latter with a cast-iron liner. Needle rollers were employed for both the small- and big-ends' assemblies. Crankshaft design was unusual in that it was virtually a one-piece electron casting, with a cover on the nearside for access. On the offside there was access to the five-speed in-unit gearbox. Apart from an inherent rigidity, the one-piece casting allowed the crankshaft and gears to be dismantled without removing the engine assembly from the frame.

Built for the 250, 350 and ultimately 500cc class sizes, the Jawa 652, 653 and 654 series of enduro machines dominated the 1970s ISDT series. They won the coveted Trophy team contest in 1970–1974, 1977 and 1978, and the Vase contest in 1970–1972, 1974, 1976, 1977 and 1979.

Engine: 344cc 2s single 78x72mm, air-cooled
Power: 36bhp at 6200rpm
Gearbox: 5-speed foot change
Final drive: chain
Weight: 158kg (347lb)
Top speed: 150kph (94mph)

JAWA SPEEDWAY MODEL 897

1986

THE FIRST JAWA SPEEDWAY engine was a development of the earlier Eso design, Jawa having absorbed that company during the late 1960s.

By the mid-1980s the Czech company had risen to be the largest producer in the world of both engines and complete motorcycles for speedway and long-track racing events and 95 per cent of this production was exported around the globe.

The engine was a 496cc (85x87mm) single-overhead-cam four-valve single with a vertical alloy cylinder barrel and head. A forged two-ring piston was supported by a duralumin alloy-forged connecting rod, with a pressed-in bronze bush for the gudgeon pin, and a hardened-steel ring for the big-end bearing. The flywheels themselves were specially hardened which permitted repeated crankpin replacement.

The camshaft was driven by a single row chain. Four different camshafts of different lifts were available to enable riders to choose the power curve best suited to their particular requirements.

Jawa's model 897 speedway bike of 1986 had a 496cc four-valve sohc air-cooled engine, which developed 69bhp at 8800rpm.

Ignition was courtesy of a PAL magneto with a Bosch ignition coil, while carburation was taken care of by an Italian 34mm (one-and-a-quarter ins) Dell 'Orto instrument, with a K & N air filter. The carburettor was mounted flexibly; this was to avoid vibration which could cause loss of performance.

Lubrication was via a dual pump, and the quantity of lubricant could be checked and adjusted. Oil (a castor-based oil was recommended) was stored in the frame's top tube and drawn down to lubricate the engine components. The used oil then fed to a waste oil tank and was drained after one or two races.

Engine: 496cc sohc V-four single, 85x87mm, air-cooled
Power: 69bhp at 8800rpm
Gearbox: none
Final drive: chain
Weight: 82kg (181lb)
Top speed: 129kph (80mph)

JEFFERSON

USA 1911–15

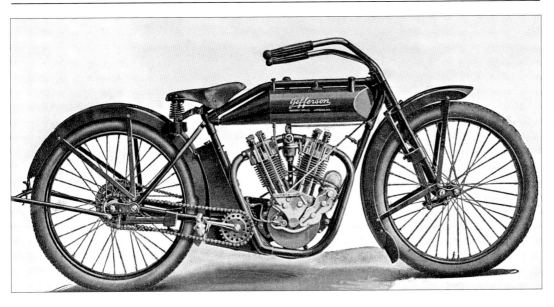

THIS MARQUE WAS INITIALLY sold as the Waverly, or sometimes even as the Kenzler-Waverly, while one 1912 model was called the P.E.M. in honour of Percy E. Mack who designed the Mack engine they used and also their spring frame and fork.

It was not until as late as 1913 that the Jefferson name appeared on the models; however, such confusion of names was fairly common on the American motorcycle scene, particularly before the outbreak of World War I.

All this arose because the machines were built by the Kenzler-Waverly Motorcycle Company of Cambridge and the Waverly Manufacturing Company of Jefferson, while Mack engines were built by the Universal Machinery Company of Milwaukee, all three of these towns being situated in the state of Wisconsin.

The Mack engines came with either 'Mack' or 'Waverly' cast into the crankcase, seemingly regardless of their final destination (this was another quirk of the

period) and all of these engines were of the overhead-valve type with parallel valves, in an era of F-head motors.

Both single and V-twin machines were manufactured, and both of these were based on a 491cc (30cid) cylinder size. In both cases, the head and barrel were held to the crankcase by long studs (good engine practice), and the pushrods were positioned on the right and were exposed. They ran up to the rockers that were located across the head. This was a layout which suited the parallel valves. Ignition was by a magneto which was fitted in front of the cylinder and was driven by a train of gears.

The loop frame and forks were further evidence of the clever design that went into the machine, with pivoted-fork rear suspension and leading-links at the front. The rear suspension was controlled by a leaf spring fixed to the seat tube and connected to the fork by a short link which ran to the top of the fork sub-frame. In this way, it was not unlike a modern monoshock. The front fork was

This machine was known by various names, but by 1914 it was called a Jefferson, an advanced model with front and rear suspension and a gearbox.

controlled by two leaf springs and these were each fixed to the back of a fork leg. They were connected to the links by further small members.

Wire wheels were used in these machines, and the brake was fitted in the rear one as, at that time, few riders in the USA would have a front brake due to the nature of the dirt roads outside most towns. Transmission for the road models was all-chain with clutch, countershaft and gearbox, but in competition form the machines had direct drive by chain, plus a cycle chain on the right to aid starting.

The road models were well able to perform with the best on the street. However, despite being fine machines, they failed to survive for long, partly due to their high price, and partly due to the emergence of the Ford model-T.

JONES

DURING 1936 THE PROTOTYPE of the autocycle made its debut as a new form of two-wheeled transport that came with pedals to both start it and assist the engine. Aimed at the bottom end of the market to offer local transport at minimal cost, it was based on the 98cc Villiers engine.

It was designed by G.H. Jones in conjunction with Villiers. The engine unit included a clutch. Construction was simple, with the one-piece cast-iron head and barrel laid horizontal, an overhung crankshaft, flywheel magneto and the main castings run back to enclose the chain-driven clutch on its own shaft. An expansion box under the cylinder was part of the unit.

The autocycle, made popular by the Jones company. Its simple construction and design meant it was copied by other firms, until the late 1950s.

The engine unit was mounted in a simple open frame with sprung forks, saddle, petrol tank and caliper brakes. The pedal shaft ran through the centre of the clutch shaft so the whole unit could be bolted in place to the special bottom bracket of the frame. This feature failed to reach production as the final engine (sold as the Villiers Junior) dispensed with it. Jones thought it might be uncomfortable when pedalling, Villiers that it could bend in a fall.

The design was soon taken up, first by Raynal in 1937, and then by others in the next year or two; most continued postwar.

The type continued in use up until the late-1950s; it was during this decade that the moped took over.

JONGHI

THIS MAKE WAS BUILT in France by two Italians, Giuseppe Remondini and Tito Jonghi. Their first model was of unit construction with a 346cc side-valve engine driving a three-speed gearbox and installed in a rigid frame with girder forks. The engine had a rear-mounted magneto with the one-piece crankcase and gearbox casting sealed by side plates. The external flywheel and primary-drive gears

went on the left and the final drive chain on the right. It was an advanced design for a first model; however, Remondini had worked for Negas & Ray in Italy where he designed a similar engine unit.

This model was quickly joined by an overhead-valve version, as had happened at Negas & Ray, with exposed hairpin-valve springs and similar cycle parts. It made its mark in competition by winning the 1932 European Grand Prix

A typical postwar Jonghi with an unusual ohc engine (rather than a two-stroke) and trailing-link front forks (rather than telescopics).

350cc race, held near Rome, from a field of British machines; quite an achievement. In 1933 the side-valve model demonstrated its potential by averaging over 116kph (72mph) for 24 hours at Montlhèry to secure 10 world

records, another fine demonstration of the speed and reliability of the marque. Later came an overhead-camshaft engine, at first for 350cc races, and in time reduced to enter 250 and 175cc events. The range was extended to add lightweights using small proprietary two-stroke engines.

In 1936 they joined up with the Prester firm and shared machines; their overhead-valve Flèche d'Or and Racing models were the Jonghi in all but tank badge. It was the same with their velomoteur, so the two lines ran side by side to the end of the decade. Postwar, the bulk of the range was still built with both names and comprised small two-strokes with unit construction, three speeds, rigid frame and girder forks; these were later replaced by trailing-links. Both 100 and 125cc models were built right from the start of the company's existence and a 250cc model was added later.

In 1947 Jonghi added a 125cc four-stroke with Italian lines intended for road and racing use. It had a unit-construction engine with the single overhead-camshaft driven by a train of gears that ran up inside the barrel and head on the right. Camshaft, rockers, valves and hairpin-valve springs were fully enclosed by a single cover. The magneto was driven by chain on the left while the gear primary drive to the four-speed gearbox went on the right with the gears in the timing chest.

The frame had pivoted-fork rear suspension in monoshock form with the spring unit under the saddle and the trailing-link front

forks. It was a fine machine that continued the sports model style of the marque and remained in their range until the end.

JUNAK

POLAND 1954–64

AFTER WORLD WAR II the Council for Mutual Economic Aid allocated production of different categories of goods to the various Communist Bloc countries. Czechoslovakia, the German Democratic Republic and the Soviet Union were among the countries in which motorcycles were produced. The only model of the Junak, the 350cc M10, was built in Poland.

The original specification had called for a 500cc heavyweight suitable for military use. Somehow, at the hands of designers Jan Ignatowicz and Stefan Porazinski, it metamorphosed into a 350cc overhead-valve design, which was first shown at Wroclaw in 1954, on the 10th anniversary of the Polish People's Republic. But a shortage of tools, workers and training meant that there was no actual production until 1956, when about 30 machines were built, largely by hand.

In 1957, this number rose to 253 (out of a planned 20,000 a year). It was not until 1958 that the Szeczin Motorcycle Factory (SFM) started production in earnest. By this time its faults were known and were working against it. One problem was the positioning of the hygroscopic magneto on the front of the engine where it picked up

A 350cc outfit may seem modest to today's recreation-oriented motorcyclist; but given a choice of 350cc or no family transport at all, it looks much better.

water from the front wheel; another problem – and a very basic one – was a feeble dynamo which produced only a very weak light.

The M10 sold in many countries: Bulgaria, Cuba, Hungary, Libya, Mongolia, Syria, Turkey, Uruguay, the United States

of America and Venezuela. But few of the bikes were noted for their motorcycling prowess or sophistication. At just under 23,000 zloty, it also lost sales to cheaper imports in its native Poland.

Many Junak owners have wished for some modifications to be carried out; for instance, an improved 12volt dynamo and coil ignition. A few changes were made, such as a 'casquette' style head lamp faired into the front forks, deeper mudguards, better brakes, enclosed chain and options such as side-car and a cross-country versions.

But despite these changes, production ceased in 1964. There was talk of a modern twin-cylinder 'Iskra' to replace it; however, this never went beyond prototype form.

Many sources also refer to a 250cc version of the same motor, but the few Polish sources consulted bear no evidence of this, and given the history of the machine and its intended markets, the existence of such a machine seems unlikely.

The clean, traditional lines of the Junak are clear from the picture, and with minimal improvements, it really could have been a classic machine.

KAWASAKI

KAWASAKI MOTORCYCLES IS actually part of a very large group with interests in shipping, aircraft, railways and much else. While it may not be the largest of the four Japanese motorcycle firms now dominating the market, its history and origins are very different from the rest. The firm came to two wheels later than and for reasons far removed from the others.

Kawasaki Heavy Industries is one of the world's largest industrial concerns and therefore their motorcycle business is something of a sideline in comparison to their other activities. However, this different setup has resulted in the production of machines that have been the performance leaders of their time, setting the bench mark for others.

Due to their late arrival on the motorcycle scene, Kawasaki missed most of the dramatic affairs of the 1950s when the Japanese industry grew from small to large, a few firms became many and then takeovers reduced the numbers again. That decade saw the build-up of a massive home market behind very high tariff walls and the start of expansion overseas to America and Europe.

Most of the Japanese firms of the early postwar era came into the transport business to provide some means of travel, as an alternative to walking or using crammed public transport, in a country desperate for anything that could provide mobility. The early results were often crude, but lessons were

soon learned and progress made. Once there was stability, then came production, and then competitions in which to advertise the product.

Kawasaki's background was as different as it could be from Honda, Suzuki or Yamaha, for their origins went back to a shipyard founded by Shozo Kawasaki in 1878. By the end of that century it had become a major

company and in 1901 diverted into railways and then civil engineering. By 1911 they were in marine transportation, then sheet steel and, later, aircraft and thus engines.

After World War II all but one of their divisions were kept busy with reconstruction. The aircraft factory that had skills, materials and machinery had, however, no product. So they turned to making motorcycle parts for other firms and then complete engine units. This activity kept them busy for much of the 1950s but by 1959 they were having serious doubts regarding whether or not to stay involved: their products were starting to slip behind those of other firms and there were alternative employments they could use the facilities for.

The deciding factor that prompted them to continue was image. Or rather; their lack of it. They might have been well known

Late 1972 saw the launch of the 903cc Z1 four, the machine destined to take over from the Honda CB750 as King of the Road.

The three Kawasaki 750cc triples that ran in the 1971 Daytona 200 with little success, ninth the best placing. They had better results elsewhere.

within the shipping, railways and aircraft industries, but were not a familiar name with the general public. Motorcycles could offer a remedy, and were a field in which they had some involvement already, so they went ahead. They had a link with the Meguro firm which dated back to pre-war days and they had been building complete machines under the Meihatsu label. Something better would be needed if the world was going to hear about Kawasaki and, as others had found before them, competition was to prove the key. However, as they were only committed to their home market, they declined to follow others to Europe and the expensive grand prix circuit.

Instead, they turned to the Japanese motocross championships where they tuned a stock machine, painted its fuel tank red, and took the first six places in the 125cc class. Quickly

they were known as the Red Tank Kawasaki and the firm now had good promotion material. They were not to forget that early lesson, for in the years to come they would adopt lime-green as their colour for the competition machines and these became known as the Green Meanies. This helped, but they still had to build up a reputation. They lacked the years of experience others firms had gained in their desperate struggle to keep going. And now the home market was becoming saturated and the need to look abroad and to export their product became more and more apparent.

Like many others, Kawasaki began with a small range of simple two-stroke singles using the same basic engines in a variety of guises. This enabled them to offer road and trial models, some in touring and others in sports form, and in time this was extended to mini machines and motocross models. The technical details were all similar, with the air-cooled engine having its cylinder inclined forward a little from the vertical. Induction was usually by a rotary disc on the side of the crankshaft, but sometimes by the piston. Lubrication was by a pump with throttle controlled output in nearly all cases and ignition by a crankshaft-mounted flywheel magneto that also charged the battery.

The engine drove a four- or five-speed gearbox built in unit with it by gear primary drive to a multi-plate clutch. The gearbox was of the cross-over type and the rear chain was either guarded or fully enclosed. This engine and gearbox unit was mounted in

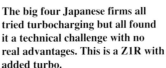

either a conventional tubular frame constructed of steel tubes welded together, or a spine frame built up from steel pressings. Virtually all models had telescopic front forks and pivoted-fork rear suspension, while wheels were wire-spoked and had drum brakes. The fixtures and fittings were suited to the intended purpose of the model; the road machines had a dualseat, lights, turn signals, a silencer and a horn. The trial machines differed little but had off-road tyres and more ground and mudguard to wheel clearance.

In this way Kawasaki built up a good range of models while using the same basic parts. Thus, their 90cc engine with its five-speed gearbox served no less than 14 different, but essentially similar, models before it was bored out to 100cc and continued on to modern times.

The big four Japanese firms all tried turbocharging but all found it a technical challenge with no real advantages. This is a Z1R with added turbo.

These small machines gave Kawasaki a good base for their motorcycle business and allowed them to gather some experience of off-road requirements along with the stock road needs. However, they were not going to get much publicity or attention as all the major firms offered similar models with equally long production lives. In addition, their early tentative ventures into the American market in 1964 had shown only too well that they did not have a product that was going to impact against the many offerings already on that market from Japan and Europe.

For the USA, something else was needed to grab public attention and for this, the firm returned to Meguro. First they tried a 250cc four-stroke single, but this had little impact in a land where capacity was everything and performance the king. Next they turned to the larger Meguro K2 twin of 500cc that had the lines of the English BSA twin although it was very different on the inside.

By 1966 this twin had been stretched out to become the 624cc W1 and was soon popular in Japan, becoming the best-selling machine of its size, the largest

After the frantic H1 came this H2 Mach IV triple that was listed up to 1975. Its 748cc engine was too powerful for its chassis, despite some improvements on the H1.

K
Germany (Baden-Baden) 1925: Schiele & Brucksaler built overhead-cam 350 and 500cc engines with fixed heads.

K125
Russia (Kovrovsk): This was a copy of the pre-war 125cc DKW two-stroke single.

K&K
Germany (Hanover) 1924–25: Kuhlmann & Konecke built 197cc side-valve machines.

KADI
Germany 1924–30: This firm's big bikes used the three-valve overhead-cam 498cc Kuchen single; their small machines used a 198cc side-valve.

KANNON
USA 1990s–: This company were responsible for the production of the monster V6 and V8 machines with Ford and Chevrolet V6 and V8 powerplants; they used their own patented automatic transmission.

KANTO
Japan 1957–60: This machine was a modest 124cc two-stroke.

KAPISCOOTER
Spain 1950s: This three–speed scooter was fitted with a pushrod 174cc engine.

KAPTEIN
The Netherlands 1938–51: Originally an importer of French machines, Kaptein later produced machines with 49, 125, and 175cc engines heavily based on Motobecane. They also produced mopeds.

KARU
Germany (Stockdorf) 1922–24: These flat-twins were fitted with licence-built Bosch-Douglas or BMW engines.

Smallest of the Kawasaki triples of the 1970s was the 250, first seen in 1971 as the S1 and listed as the KH250 from 1976. This version has a disc front brake.

model on sale in Japan, and also a favourite with the police in that country. Thus encouraged, Kawasaki launched it in the USA. However, it turned out to be a disaster: there it had to meet the competition head on and was soon found wanting. The word went round that the W1 could not stay with the big English twins and from that moment it died in the showrooms. The twins remained in production for some years, being built in touring and sports forms right up to 1975, but essentially as a home-market model.

Kawasaki thought hard about what the customer in the USA wanted and came to the conclusion that while speed was essential, it was acceleration that was the key. They realised that many of their potential customers had only a passing interest in long-distance cruising, economy or handling. What counted on the street was the stop-light race, quick to contest and easy to settle in a short time without the trauma of encountering corners. The existing large but heavy twins were never going to do this job, for they were slow from the line and took too long to reach their undeniably high top speed. Something quicker and much more exciting was needed if Kawasaki was to become known for performance. The firm therefore chose to take two very different routes to reach this accolade.

Kawasaki built an extensive range of small two-strokes in many forms. This is one of the 90cc trail machines that grew to 100cc and was made for many years.

As an interim measure they brought in a series of two-stroke twins, at first of 247 and later of 338cc. First seen in 1966, the smaller had an air-cooled engine with disc valves on each side, a five-speed gearbox built in unit

with it, a conventional frame and forks, drum brakes and all the expected features of the period. Most of all, it had excitement, for it could rocket away from the line, cover the standing 400m (one-quarter of a mile) in 15 seconds and reach around 161kph (100mph). Plenty of big four-stroke twins could exceed the last figure; few could match the former.

Within a few months there was a racing version and a street scrambler with its twin exhaust systems run high on the left in fine style. They were listed as the Samurai and early in 1967 were joined by a larger version, named the Avenger, and built in both the street scrambler and road forms. Produced up to 1971, the twins put Kawasaki at the performance head of their class, but their next move would elevate them to absolute leaders in the delivery of exciting machines.

In 1968 Kawasaki introduced the 499cc H1 that was also known as the Mach III. The policy seemed to be that if two cylinders were good, then three would be better, especially if they operated on the two-stroke cycle. For that was what the H1 was: a three-cylinder two-stroke with the

barrels in-line across the machine and fed by three carburettors mounted behind them, so piston-controlled induction replaced the discs of the twins. One stylish exhaust system ran along the left side of the machine and two went on the right to give a line easy to spot on the road, quite appropriate at a time when Agostini was master of the major grand prix, riding an MV Agusta three with a similar arrangement of megaphones. The rest of the H1 was typical of the time with pump lubrication, an early form of electronic ignition and a five-speed gearbox built in unit with the engine. The frame was tubular with telescopic front forks, rear suspension and drum brakes, and it was this, as much as the power from the engine, that made for the excitement the model could generate.

The Mach III was fast, really quick for a 500, with a claimed top speed close to 193kph (120mph) and 400m (one quarter of a mile) times under 13 seconds. This acceleration plus a short wheelbase meant that it was hard to avoid either a wheelie or smoking rear tyre away from the lights. But that problem was

A 250cc tandem twin racing model, first seen in 1975. It won eight world titles in both its 250 and 350cc forms between 1978 and 1982.

nothing compared to the difficulty encountered when going around a corner: violent acceleration was one thing, but the engine also had an abrupt kink in its power band so that when it was added to the already considerable power in use, it had a major effect on cornering. With a frame that was not really up to handling the 60bhp that the engine could put out, the short wheelbase, plus the light weight, a smooth throttle hand became essential.

This prodigious performance resulted in a corresponding thirst for petrol but at that time few worried about this, except when trying to locate the next filling station. Anything over 48km (30 miles) to a UK gallon indicated that the rider was not fully using the machine's performance. Few machines can have offered such ferociously fast acceleration, high speed and wild handling, and the H1 was soon joined by other triples, including a racing version, the H1R. In 1971 came the 748cc H2 with even more performance but an improved chassis, plus the 249cc S1 and 346cc S2 of more modest behaviour. In 1973 the latter became the 400cc S3 and in time the triples lost some of their raw edges and became more

civilised, while the escalation of fuel prices took the edge off the fun. After 1976 only the 250 and 400 were left to run to the end of the decade, but without the glamour and wild fever of the first Mach III.

Part of the reason for the taming of the triples was the alternative approach the firm took in their endeavour to become the performance king on the street. In total contrast to the two-strokes, this was to be achieved through sophistication, and a four-stroke four-cylinder machine of more than ample power was chosen to

reach this aim. Work began in 1967 before the triples were launched, but an unexpected setback came in 1968 just a month after the Mach III rode wickedly onto the scene.

As Kawasaki watched the reactions of the public to their outrageous offering in September, the ground was cut from under their feet in October when Honda

This KE100 trail model appeared in 1976, based on an earlier version, and continued to be listed until 1997. Most improvements were made to the suspension.

launched their fabled CB750 four at the Tokyo show. At a stroke, Kawasaki's intentions to build a 750cc four with performance, style and sophistication were brought to nought. But then reflection brought the realisation that all was far from lost. Let Honda test the market for a big four with its single-camshaft engine, electric start, disc brake and all the trimmings; meanwhile Kawasaki could plan to outdo them, now knowing what they were up against and had to improve upon.

The result was launched in September 1972 at the Cologne Show as the Z1 and out-specified Honda with a 903cc capacity, not one but two overhead-camshafts, the expected electric start, four exhaust systems, disc front brake and all the usual fixtures and fittings. It ran to 209kph (130mph) with a standing quarter time in the low twelves, and handled as well as any large and heavy machine at that time. This meant it was fine for fast touring, but less so for hard sports work.

The Z1 was soon King of the Road and was quickly being pressed into use for production racing, for it was fast, could be tuned and was strong. There was also a 750cc version known as the Z2 for the Japanese home market, as it was restricted to that capacity, and in 1976 the Z1 became the Z900 when it was joined by a

custom version known as the Z900 LTD.

In the mid-1970s the firm began to expand its range, especially the four-strokes, and to use a revised system for coding them in two forms. The first was the marketing code used to identify the machine and year for its specification and maintenance data. It comprised two or three letters followed by the basic capacity and a suffix letter and number, this last usually altered each year to reflect changes. The second code for the model was often the first code minus the suffix number but in time it became the code by which the machine was known and advertised by.

Two-stroke codes began with the letter K and four-strokes with Z except for some off-road models coded KL much as the two-strokes they copied in style. There were a few exceptions beginning with A in the two-strokes and B, E or V in the four-strokes, but the real difference for the latter was the use of series codes and names such as GPX, ZZ-R, LTD, Tengai, Eliminator or Ninja. There was a logic behind the system but it became more complex over the years as the range grew and new styles made their appearance on the market.

The expansion of the four-stroke range in 1976 introduced the Z900LTD, the first in a long series

A new form of 125cc machine appeared in 1983, called the AR125. It incorporated liquid-cooling, six speeds and Kawasaki's Uni-Trak rear suspension.

of custom models. The changes were small and comprised cast-alloy wheels, the rear a 41cm (16ins), twin front discs, twin megaphone-style silencers and a two-level seat. The type would become more radical over the years.

Also new for 1976 was the Z750B powered by a 745cc twin-cylinder double overhead-cam engine fitted with the balancer shafts already in use in the Z400 twin series, first seen in 1974 with

a 399cc overhead-cam engine. Both twins had five speeds and electric start along with the Japanese style, finish and good electrics of the period. Meanwhile, the two-stroke line was moving more towards off-road models: trail, enduro and motocross, plus mini machines for the younger rider and sometimes trials models. The basic road models, mainly in 90, 100 and 125cc sizes, ran on, the last, continuing today, little changed since its introduction.

All the two-strokes benefited from Kawasaki's involvement in motocross, for developments in that field soon filtered onto the enduro and then the trail models. Along with the technical improvements came the style, and buyers liked to see the motocross line and colour appear on their own trail machine.

In 1977 the big four was stretched out to 1016cc to create the Z1000 and Z1000LTD custom models. They were joined by a new four-cylinder model, the Z650B in the style of the Z1 and the same specification. With it came the Z650C with cast-alloy wheels, but hardly a custom style, as it retained the same 652cc double overhead-cam engine. At the other end of the scale was the Z200, a 198cc overhead-cam single, produced for commuting, in the company style. From it came the KL250 in 1978, a 246cc overhead-cam single introduced for the trail market with the engine unit based on the Z200 but the

The original Z1 was soon expanded to capacities of 1000cc or more and appeared in many forms. This is the 1988 ZX10 with an all-aluminium frame.

cycle side was modified to suit off-road use.

One version of the Z400 was given a six-speed gearbox for 1978 while another true custom model appeared as the Z650SR or Z650D with the expected features plus a cross-over pattern for the exhaust pipes. Another version of the big four was added as the Z1-R which had its own style with cockpit fairing, new tank, seat base, side panels and cast-alloy wheels.

In the two-stroke range the bulk continued in the established capacities with models coded KH for the road, KE for trail, KD at first for mini motocross and later for enduro, KDX for enduro and KX for motocross which ran up to

a 400. There was also a KV mini, KC economy, KM mini trail, KT trials and KR for a road model based on a racer. One of the KV series was the Agi model for farm work and this came with rack, protection bars and a large spade. The motocross models were at the top of technical innovation with a disc-valve engine for the KX125, but not the KX250 or KX400. The smaller machines had reed-valve induction for 1978; the largest had been dropped from the range by then.

More new four-strokes joined the ranged for 1979 with the trail single joined by the KLX250 that was to evolve into a street-legal enduro machine in time. In the 250cc road class, the Z250A

The appearance of larger four-stroke trail models led to this dual-purpose 1991 KLE. It had a twin-cylinder engine in a trail chassis, modified for urban riding.

appeared with a 249cc overhead-cam twin-cylinder engine, rather than the expected single, and it was listed as the Scorpion. Two 400 twins were added, one with a mild custom style, the other far more radical. Another four appeared; one was the 498cc double overhead-cam Z500B, a fine motorcycle in the Kawasaki style. There was also a Z750D four, but this was only sold in South Africa that year. The Z1000 had changes and improvements made to it, and was joined by a shaft-drive version that proved equally fast at 217kph (135mph).

The major four-stroke news for 1979 was the introduction of the Z1300, a massive model with a 1286cc six-cylinder double overhead-cam water-cooled engine driving a five-speed gearbox with shaft final drive. It was large and heavy, essentially a fast tourer rather than a sports model, as were the Honda CBX and Benelli Sei sixes.

In 1993, Scott Russell won the World Superbike title on his 750cc Kawasaki four, but had to give way to a Ducati twin the following year.

KENI
Germany (Berlin) 1921-23: This company produced two-stroke lightweights, fitted with engines of sizes given (variously) as 145, 158 and 164cc.

KENILWORTH
England 1919–24: This company produced a belt drive scooter/step-through fitted with engines reported variously as Norman 142cc overhead-valves, Villiers 269cc two-strokes and JAP 293cc side-valves. Kenilworth may also have made a conventional machine with the JAP motor.

KENZLER WAVERLEY
USA (Cambridge, Wisconsin) 1910–14: Early use of overhead-valve engines characterised these singles and V-twins, which were associated with Jefferson.

KERRY
England 1902–15 and c.1960: The first generation of these machines (1902–10) was reputedly made in Belgium with Kelecom (and possibly FN) engines for the East London Rubber Company. The next generation (1910–15) was built by Abingdon with 499cc singles and 670cc V-twins, and the third generation (late 1050s) were Italian-built 49cc mopeds.

KESTREL
England 1903–04: Minerva and (possibly) MMC engines of 211cc powered this short-lived brand.

KG
Germany (Suhl, then Cologne, then Mabendorf) 1919–32: The Krieger brothers and Franz Gnadig began with shaft-driven 503cc inlet-over-exhaust singles, then moved on to the 499cc overhead-valve of advanced design. These were built by the Cito works, and were followed in 1923 by a belt-drive flat-twin. Then in 1924 Cito had financial problems and were taken over by the Köln Linderthaler Metalwarenfabrik, giving rise to the Allright-KG. When production of this stopped, ex-Cito man Paul Henckel bought the machinery and rights and created the Cito-KG from 1927. Each new generation marked a decline in production and increasing obsolescence.

The Kawasaki fours of the 1990s proved very race competitive, at first as a stock super-sports model with race kit, later as a production racer.

A junior motocross KX80 was added to the two-strokes with the choice of 79 or 83cc capacity, and later also of a large or small front wheel. The KDX came in 1980 to introduce a true enduro type based on a combination of the existing trail KD175 and motocross technology. At the same time the rear suspension of the main KX models changed to a rising-rate type called Uni-Trak which had been developed on the works grand prix machines that won the firm several titles in the 250 and 350cc classes.

In 1980 Kawasaki listed no less than six 250cc road models, with three singles, two twins and one triple two-stroke, creating some confusion. This also applied to the

next size of machine; three Z400 twins were joined by four 444cc Z440 models in various forms, one with an important alteration: the use of a toothed-belt final drive. To further extend the range, the

Z400J four and two 554cc Z550 models were added while the Z750 four went onto general sale together with a custom version, common to all the models, and was joined by a Z750 custom twin.

Electronic fuel injection appeared on a Z1000, but with limited success, and a version of the Z1300 with fairing and full luggage equipment joined the stock model.

A pair of 50cc two-strokes joined the range for 1981 in road and trail formats, matched by 80cc versions and a further proliferation of four-strokes that included Z305 twins. More important was the Z550H, which became better known as the GPZ and introduced Uni-Trak to the road range, soon joined by a GPZ750. The other real change that year was made to the KX125; it turned to liquid-cooling for the engine, something that soon was adopted by the KX line and then the enduro line. An

The massive VN1500 V-twin of 1987 was joined by the smaller VN800 version in 1995. Both followed the same laid-back, Harley-Davidson cruiser style.

offshoot was the AR125 of 1983 with liquid-cooling and many features derived from road racing, including Uni-Trak. At the other end of the scale had come the Z1100 series in various forms from sports to touring.

An important new model arrived in 1984: the ZX900, better known as the GPZ900R and sold in the USA as the Ninja. There was also a 750 and both had liquid-cooled 16-valve engines to set new performance standards. Equally new, and moving into a new area, was the KL600 single with liquid-cooling, four valves and a package with enduro styling to emphasis its dual purpose nature. The firm also offered the Z750 Turbo, a route all the other Japanese firms tried but with no real success.

On the two-stroke front, the KR250 tandem twin was offered as a true race replica, for it was based on the disc-valve machines which had won eight world titles. It was later replaced by the KR-1, a parallel twin, but the day of the hot two-stroke was past and the firm instead concentrated on its motocross, enduro and trail models to leave just one road model: the KH125, for basic, low-cost transport.

The Kawasaki line of super sports, sports, touring and custom four-strokes ran on alongside the trail, enduro and off-road machines. Among the custom models the LTD450 appeared in 1985, using what was effectively half of the Ninja engine, with a

radical style. Smaller versions of the Ninja four appeared with a perimeter frame while the GT shaft drive fours became favourites with despatch riders.

A new custom style was introduced for 1985; the VN750 had a V-twin engine and was sold as the Vulcan. It had kept the best Kawasaki technology so there was liquid-cooling, double overhead-cam, eight valves, internal balance shafts and rubber mountings, along with shaft drive and the full custom style and trim. At

New for a new century, the Kawasaki ZX-12R with a 1199cc engine. It was able to contest the supersports class with the best of the rest.

Over the years, the Kawasaki motocross range grew to list machines from 60 to 500cc. This is a 1999 KX125 showing off its capabilities.

the same time, a fresh style of long and low machines, the muscle bike, appeared. The ZL900 Eliminator used some of the sports four plus custom parts. It was a new form of street creed to exploit.

All these styles continued to become ever-more sophisticated to meet demands for all types. One result was the VN15, a V-twin of 1471cc, and another a whole series of Eliminator models. At the end of the 1980s one further type made its debut: the retro that combined the new technology with the style of the past in acknowledgement of the classic machine revival then taking place.

Of the existing models, the KL types were given the name Tengai while track editions of the race-replica sports models began to appear with aluminium perimeter frames. For 1990 a new code was used for the super-sports line, the ZZ-R, and this ran through the line from 250 to 1100. At the same

KIEFT
England (Wolverhampton) 1955–57: These 150 and 200cc Sachs-engined two-stroke scooters were actually built by Hercules of Nurnberg. As a company, Kieft was better known for small, light sports and racing cars.

KILEAR
Czechoslovakia (Brno-Malomerice) 1924–26: These were largely unremarkable 250cc two-strokes.

KINETIC
India 1972– : This firm began production with licence-built Vespas and then moved on to their own-brand two-stroke mopeds, finally adding a licence-built Honda 100 in 1986.

KING
England 1901–07: This company used a wide range of engines in their machines: De Dion Bouton (shared with three wheelers, which they also made), Minerva, MMC, DAW, Antoine, Sarolea and maybe others.

KING FRAM
Sweden 1957–early 1960s: These mopeds were fitted with 49cc engines, all from a variety of sources.

KING-JAP
Germany (Augsburg) 1928–31: This was a German assembler which fitted JAP engines.

KINGSBURY
England 1919–23: This firm was a former aircraft engine works that briefly made motorcycles with their own two-stroke engines, variously described as 216 or 261 and 350cc. The company also made light cars and a scooter which resembled the Autoped.

KINGSWAY
England (Coventry) 1921–23: JAP 293cc side-valve engines powered these unremarkable machines.

The ZX-6R was a strong contender in the hot 600cc class for 2000, its 599cc capacity, six speeds and fine chassis combining to make to a highly-competitive machine.

time, the retro range expanded, while the ZXR line developed into a limited edition model for racing, but based on the road version.

An even earlier style was used for the 1992 Estrella model with a simple 249cc engine and lines from the 1950s, but it sold best on its home market. Two years later the original Ninja was replaced by a new version with many new attributes, but the original was brought back in 1996 by popular demand to sell alongside the new.

There were now fewer completely new models. Most were revised or were based on existing machines. Changes came and went for customs, cruisers, Ninjas and retros to use the latest technology, while graphics highlighted the year. Anti-lock brakes came as standard in 1996 for one model after some years of trials, while a new and simpler type of machine appeared in 1997 as the ER-5. This used the 499cc twin engine in an older style tubular frame, had no frills, a retro line and proved a best-seller as basic transport combined with good performance.

For 1998 Kawasaki listed their first 125cc four-stroke, again with a simple specification in an older style for first-time buyers. At the top of the scale, the big V-twin was used for a Classic Tourer, sold as the Vulcan Nomad in the USA. In 1999 it was joined by the Drifter, in two engine sizes, which in some

parts harked back to a pre-war style. That year, the retro range looked back to early days with the W650 bringing back memories of the W1 of 1966 with an engine with its overhead-camshaft driven by shaft and bevels, but with the eight valves of the modern models. Of the two-strokes there was only

one trail model left, but the enduro and motocross range was as competitive as ever.

The new century saw Kawasaki covering the market from end to end, as they had done for so long, emphasising that now, as from the beginning, their name stood for high performance.

KAWASAKI W1   1966

The Kawasaki W1 was based on the earlier Meguro K2 twin and, like this model, it bore more than a passing resemblance to the BSA

A7 twins in the line of the timing cover and general layout.

Internally it differed from the BSA A7 twins in that it had one-

The W1SS version of the 624cc twin Kawasaki first produced in the 1960s. The series was popular in Japan but failed in the American market.

piece connecting rods and a three-part crankshaft that was pressed together, but the valve gear and drives to magneto and dynamo were very similar. This close likeness continued for the separate gearbox, frame, suspension and wheels.

The W1 was a success in Kawasaki's home-market of Japan but it was to prove a disaster in the USA. There, it failed to perform to the level needed to meet the competition.

An attempt to improve matters resulted in the W2SS street scrambler of 1967. This was fitted with twin carburettors and enjoyed a change of style.

In 1968 came the similar W1SS and the W2TT with upswept exhaust systems on the left. None lasted beyond 1971, but the next year brought the W3 for the Japanese market and this ran on to 1975.

Engine: 624cc ohv parallel twin, 74x72.6mm, air-cooled
Power: 50bhp at 6500rpm
Gearbox: 4-speed foot change
Final drive: chain
Weight: 180kg (398lb)
Top speed: 175kph (105mph)

KAWASAKI SAMURAI A1   1966

The Samurai was Kawasaki's alternative for the US market for it offered the acceleration that was the key, even if it was not quite as

fast as the W1. It had a 247cc twin-cylinder two-stroke engine with disc inlet valves and a carburettor on each side. This was built in unit

with a five-speed gearbox and the whole was installed in a full cradle frame with suspension for both wire wheels and their drum brakes.

Fixtures and fittings were typical Japanese of the period, which meant that they were of a high quality.

The first Kawasaki performance bike was the 247cc A1 Samurai twin two-stroke. It was soon joined by the 338cc A7 Avenger.

The A1 was quickly joined by the A1R for road racing and in 1967 the A1SS street scrambler that had both exhaust systems mounted high on the left, braced handlebars and a sump plate. A larger twin was also introduced, the 338cc Avenger A7, which was faster and had better acceleration. Late in 1967 came the expected A7SS and a limited number of racing A7R twins. All the road twins went to the end of 1971, but were overtaken by other models well before then.

The result worked well and was soon leaving larger machines behind at the lights to establish the Kawasaki name for performance.

Engine: 247cc rotary 2s parallel twin, 53x56mm, air-cooled
Power: 31bhp at 8000rpm
Gearbox: 5-speed foot change
Final drive: chain
Weight: 145kg (319lb)
Top speed: 160kph (95mph)

KAWASAKI H1 — 1968

Late in 1968, Kawasaki moved the performance development on with the H1, sold as the 500-SS in Japan and the Mach III elsewhere. The H1's performance could exceed most other machines; powered by a 499cc three-cylinder two-stroke engine set across the frame, it had conventional porting and was built in unit with its five-speed gearbox, the rest in the form of Japanese

The ferocious H1 Mach III triple was introduced in 1968. It moved the whole performance concept on from the days of the two-stroke twins. Shame about the handling.

machines of that time. The engine gave 60bhp with a vicious kick in the power curve. This, plus a chassis barely adequate for the job, gave it instant excitement and reputation.

The Mach III was violent on the road with shattering acceleration and a top speed close to 193kph (120mph) and was able to run away from the opposition. In the curves, it could give odd handling and ride.

In time the H1 lost its violent edge and by 1976, its final year, it was fast but tamed. Before then, it had been joined by other triples, beginning with the racing H1R for 1970, then the 249cc S1, the 346cc

S2, and the 748cc H2 (following the format of the H1, offering plenty of power and a prodigious thirst). The largest was raced very successfully by Kawasaki. After 1975 the H2 had gone, but the smallest triple (with the 400cc S3 that replaced the S2 in 1973) ran to 1980, when its wail was no more.

Engine: 498.8cc 2s triple, 60x58.8mm, air-cooled
Power: 42bhp at 7000rpm
Gearbox: 5-speed foot change
Final drive: chain
Weight: 152kg (335lb)
Top speed: 196kph (118mph)

KITAGAWA
Japan 1955–unknown: The original four-speed overhead-valve twin shaft-drive TW 247 produced by this company was similar to a Sunbeam S7, but was a much smaller machine at 247cc. Kitagawa's 1956 Liner 250 was a 248cc overhead-valve single, again with shaft drive, and Earles forks; and the Liner Crown was a 125cc model.

KLOTZ
Germany (Stuttgart) 1923–26: These up-to-date two-strokes (variously reported as 200 and 246cc) were promoted by racing successes. However, despite receiving this attention, they never sold very well.

KM
Germany 1924–26: This German company produced two-stroke machines which were fitted with 142 and 159cc engines built in-house.

KMB
Germany (Cologne) 1923–26: The Kölner Motorradwerk Becker built motorcycles with their own 249cc two-stroke and 350 and 500cc JAP and Blackburne motors, although one source contradicts this and says that all motors were four-stroke, and all were in-house.

KMS
Germany 1922–24: Unusually, the in-house 196cc overhead-valve single which came from this company was the bigger machine, while a bought-in Grade 142cc two-stroke completed their range.

KOBO
Germany (Barmen-Hatzfeld) mid–1920s: Kohler and Bolenkamp were a well-known chain manufacturer who briefly made a machine which was powered by an in-house 276cc two-stroke engine.

KAWASAKI Z1   1972

In a complete contrast to the H1 came the refined 1972 Z1. This machine put the firm at the top of the performance tree.

Called King of the Road, the Z1 lived up to its name, setting the standards for the superbikes and establishing Kawasaki as a performance firm from then on. It followed the Honda CB750 format, which was launched in 1968, one month after the H1 triple.

The Z1 was launched in September 1972 and offered more. Its 903cc four-cylinder engine had twin overhead-camshafts, electric start and four carburettors. It was a very tough unit, ready for considerable tuning, with five speeds and all the fixtures and fittings needed to reach to 209kph (130mph) or to trickle through towns, quietly and refined.

For Japan there was the 746cc Z2, while for police work both sizes were available with suitable equipment. By 1976 the model had become the Z900 and was joined by a custom version. But this was their last year, for the Z1000 series replaced them for 1977.

Engine: 903cc dohc transverse four, 66x66mm, air-cooled
Power: 82bhp at 8500rpm
Gearbox: 5-speed foot change
Final drive: chain
Weight: 230kg (506lb)
Top speed: 220kph (130mph)

KAWASAKI Z1300   1979

By the late 1970s Kawasaki had new targets: to match – the Honda CBX and Benelli Sei, both with six-cylinder engines. Once again they went for sheer size but to some the result was too extreme. Their Z1300 had its 1286cc liquid-cooled six-cylinder engine set across the frame, twin overhead-camshafts, five speeds and shaft drive. It rode on cast-alloy wheels with disc brakes. The result was a massive machine for touring, a job it did extremely well.

The six had all the equipment that could be expected of such a

Having produced a four that was larger than Honda's CB750, Kawasaki had to repeat this with their six, the Z1300. This was of vast size and weight and was listed from 1979 for a decade.

comprehensive machine and therefore had relatively few changes made to it during its 10-year evolutionary life span.

It was joined by a version with touring panniers and top box in 1980 which was only to last for two years as buyers preferred to make their own choices with regard to extra equipment.

However, Kawasaki was undeterred and 1983 saw the launch of a similar tourer, the Voyager, which was built for the US market only. Its engine had digital fuel injection, which was fitted to all versions of the bike the following year. This took it on to its final year of production, 1989.

Engine: 1286cc dohc transverse six, 62x71mm, liquid-cooled
Power: 120bhp at 8000rpm
Gearbox: 5-speed foot change
Final drive: shaft
Weight: 295kg (650lb)
Top speed: 225kph (135mph)

KAWASAKI GPZ900R NINJA   1984

By 1984, it was time for a new version of the old GPZ series and a new name, Ninja for the US market. The result took over from the GPZ1100. A brand new engine design was used: the four cylinders set across the frame were liquid-cooled and closer together; the chain drive to the twin overhead-camshafts was taken from one end of the crankshaft; and the alternator was mounted behind the cylinders. There were 16 valves in the head and a balancer shaft in the crankcase as the engine unit with its six-speed gearbox was a stressed member of the spine frame. The latest forks at the front, Uni-Trak at the rear, it rode on cast-alloy wheels with disc brakes and had a fairing in the GPZ style.

Another Kawasaki classic, the GPZ900R Ninja was built for ten years, scrapped, but returned due to popular demand for its great abilities on the road.

The big Ninja was one of the most successful models built by the firm and was later joined by similar machines of other sizes. The original was replaced in 1993, only to return for 1996 and 1997 due to popular demand.

Engine: 908cc dohc 4v transverse four, 72.5x55mm, liquid-cooled
Power: 115bhp at 9500rpm
Gearbox: 6-speed foot change
Final drive: chain
Weight: 228kg (501lb)
Top speed: 270kph (160mph)

KAWASAKI ZXR750   1989

In 1989, when this ZXR750 was built, a race kit was offered for sale as well. Later it became easier to produce two versions, one for the track, one for the road.

suspension. A fairing was fitted with twin headlights and vents to feed cool air via two hoses to the airbox.

At first, the model was offered with an optional race kit so that owners could, if they wished, set it up for track work. However, by 1991 the differences had become such that the firm offered two distinct versions: one for the road and the other a limited production machine incorporating all the special parts for racing. This was the way to go and the firm continued in that direction.

The Kawasaki ZXR750 was the start of a line of models which was built more for racing than road use. The line was based on an existing sports machine. In fact, the first was derived from the factory endurance racer that had its origins in a road model, and the result was styled and finished to resemble the racer. This meant that it had a 748cc twin-cam liquid-cooled four-cylinder engine driving a six-speed gearbox and a chassis with their best, fully adjustable

Engine: 748cc dohc 4v transverse four, 70x48.6mm, liquid-cooled
Power: 92bhp at 10,000rpm
Gearbox: 6-speed foot change
Final drive: chain
Weight: 205kg (452lb)
Top speed: 275kph (165mph)

KAWASAKI KX250   1999

This motocross model had a long history dating back to 1974 when it replaced the 1968 models. The first KX250 bore little relation to the modern one for it had a piston-ported air-cooled engine, low-level exhaust and twin units for the rear suspension. In 1978 came a a reed valve for the engine and high-level exhaust plus improved suspension,

Steady development over many years resulted in this fine 1998 KX250. It had a liquid-cooled, reed-valve engine and sophisticated chassis and suspension.

KOCH
Czechoslovakia 1934–35: These machines were advanced 348cc overhead-cam singles which came from J.F. Koch, who had been formerly employed as chief designer at Praga (see also JFK).

KOEHLER–ESCOFFIER
France 1912–57: The first company to build overhead-cam V-twins in large numbers, with their own in-house 996cc, this French firm also made an in-house overhead-cam 500cc single and bought-in 350 and 500cc Chaise and MAG overhead-valve engines, a 300cc side-valve and 250cc Villiers two-strokes. After World War II they brought out Villiers-powered models of 100 or 125, 175 and 250cc.

KOFA
Germany 1923–25: This assembler used bought-in 283cc two-stroke engines.

KOHOUT
Czechoslovakia 1904–06: This company was the first Czech motorcycle maker, and used two-and-three-quarters horsepower Minerva and Fafnir engines to power its machines.

KOLIBRI
Germany 1923–30: The Kolibri (Hummingbird) was an auxiliary two-stroke cycle motor of 110cc, and was also available ready-built into a bicycle.

KOMAR
Poland c.1958–68: These Polish machines were 50cc mopeds.

KOMET
Germany 1902–05: This company was originally a bicycle manufacturer who branched out into motorcycles. Under licence, they were responsible for manufacturing Ixion two-stroke engines of 1hp to 4hp.

as the latter was always the key to success in motocross.

The rear suspension had a major change for 1980 when the Uni-Trak type appeared on both the KX250 and the smaller KX125, later to go onto many other models. Both adopted a disc front brake for 1982, the year the KX125 went over to liquid-cooling which the KX250 was given the next year. A much revised engine came in 1985, a disc rear brake in 1986, changed to a longer stroke for the engine in 1987, upside-down forks in 1989, a perimeter frame in 1990, an even longer stroke in 1992 and revised Uni-Trak in 1994. These additions, made to the other motocross models, kept them all at the front of the field.

Engine: 249cc reed 2s single, 66.4x72mm, liquid-cooled
Power: 54bhp at 8500rpm
Gearbox: 5-speed foot change
Final drive: chain
Weight: 97kg (213lb)
Top speed: n/a

KRAUSER

MIKE KRAUSER MADE his name producing high-quality motorcycle luggage for BMW flat twins, as he was also a BMW dealer. His interest in road racing led him to develop a four-valve cylinder head for the BMW Rennsport. From this work came a conversion for the 1-litre road engines.

The Krauser head for road models kept the qualities of the BMW flat-twin and furthermore enhanced these to such an extent that it raised the power. As well as that, the overall engine width was reduced by 35mm (one-and-three-quarter ins) thanks to the compact design.

In the early 1980s Krauser moved on to produce his MKM1000. This was a complete machine with a new tubular frame in trellis form, built up from many tubes welded into a rigid structure that carried the engine 25mm (1in) higher. To this was fitted the stock R100RS BMW engine, complete with its five-speed gearbox and shaft final drive. The wheelbase

The Krauser MKM1000 with its tubular trellis frame, stock BMW R100RS engine and special fixtures and fittings.

was increased with BMW telescopic front forks, cast-alloy wheels, and double-disc front and single-disc rear brakes.

To this assembly was added a 21 litre (5 UK gallon) fuel tank in aluminium under a body shell that ran back to carry the seat and form a tail, and a fairing, which was lower than the standard R100RS type. These were all finished in a matching style. Some 200 of these machines were built, either in kit

Mike Krauser was heavily involved in sidecar racing, making his own engines. This is a typical model, with the engine behind the driver.

form or complete, and Krauser continued his involvement in racing and special machines for road use.

KREIDLER

FOR MANY YEARS, KREIDLER'S claim to fame was as 'King of the Tiddlers', a reference to its concentration on 50cc machines for both production and competition use.

Based at Kornwestheim, north of Stuttgart, the Kreidler concern was famous for its 50cc models, like this 1956 R50 Scooterette, which produced 2.3bhp.

But in 1982, when the Austrian star Stefan Dorflinger piloted his Kreidler to the world title, the German marque's tally rose to six, a new record for racing's smallest class. With the 50cc division replaced by the 80cc category a few months later, that record looks set to stay forever.

The company's expertise was in specialised alloys, tubing and forgings, produced in a sprawling factory complex in the town of Kornwestheim, just north of Stuttgart. Kreidler began manufacturing motorcycles in 1951 as a sideline, with the firm's real profits earned supplying semi-finished metal to German industries. Its first model was the K50 moped, with a 49cc (38x44mm) piston-port two-stroke engine of excellent quality,

reflecting Kreidler's background in specialist metals. In all other respects, the bike followed conventional practice with a U-shaped 'step-through' frame, a motorcycle-type exhaust system, front and rear suspension and pedal starting.

Sales demands for the K50 soon led to the introduction of a de luxe version, the K51. Then, in 1955, the two original machines were joined by the R50 scooterette; this employed the same two-speed twist grip-controlled gearbox. Another innovation in the same year was the use of a light-alloy cylinder with hard-chrome bore.

In 1957 came Kreidler's most famous series-production model, the Florett (Foil). The racing version, the Renn Florett, was used in Kreidler's first circuit

From the late 1960s, much of Kreidler's racing programme was run by the Dutch Van Veen company. This Van Veen 50 GP bike dates from the mid-1970s.

efforts in 1959, and was little more than a standard Florett with the mudguards removed, low handlebars fitted and the engine tuned. The marque's most widely known rider was future Suzuki world champion Hans Georg Anscheidt, who joined the company in 1960 and worked in its research and development department. That same year, Anscheidt became a works-supported racer and won the Hockenheim Moto Cup for his factory. It was a prelude to Kreidler's full-blown competition entry the following year.

Kreidler's 1961 Renn Florett was remarkably similar to the standard production model, except for the use of a dolphin fairing and special engine preparation. Developing 8bhp at 12,000rpm, it could top 121kph (75mph). This proved good enough to win the

Coupe d'Europe (European Cup), with Anscheidt at the controls.

In 1962 Kriedler introduced a new bike, using disc-valves and twin carburettors, for the fledgling 50cc FIM World Championship. Anscheidt won the very first Grand Prix, in Spain, but eventually finished the season behind Suzuki's Ernst Degner.

An interesting technical feature of the new model was its four-speed foot-change gearbox, which

gave the rider no fewer than 12 ratios, thanks to an external three-speed overdrive controlled by a twist grip on the handlebars. Unlike the 1961 production-derived frame, the 1962 tubular component was manufactured with

A 1977 to 1978 Kreidler 50 GP machine. This bike was an evolution of the earlier, and highly regarded, 50cc GP machine of the 1960s.

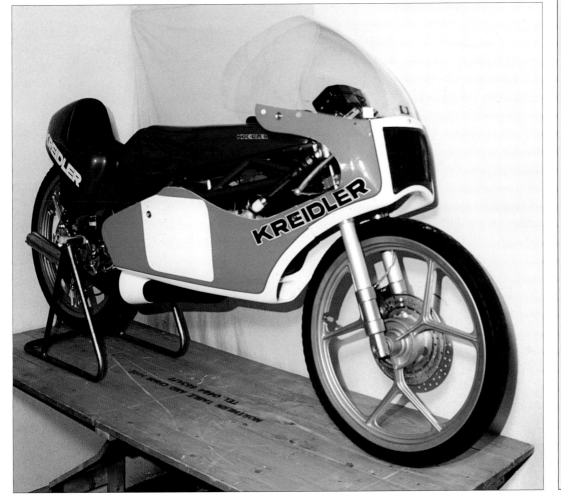

KOMET
Russia 1950s: These were racers with 500cc flat-twins and shaft drive. The Komet 2 was solo; Komet 3, chair.

KONDOR
Germany 1924–25: These machines were available with a choice of Ideal side-valve (3hp) engines or Simplex two-stroke (three-and-a-half horsepower) engines.

KOSTER (KS)
Germany (Schwerin) 1923–25: This was an odd looking machine with a hybrid tubular/pressed-steel frame, which was powered by 123cc Bekamo or 144cc Cockerell two-strokes.

KOVROVETZ
Russia (Kovrov) early 1960s: This had a hybrid tubular/ pressed-steel frame and two-stroke power: the 175cc engine gave 8bhp at 5000rpm. There was also a 125cc model.

KR
Germany (Munich) 1924–25: This company produced flat-twins with BMW engines, and an MAG 998cc V-twin. Sources suggest they were related to Karu.

KR
Germany (Munich) 1922–24 or 1930–33: Karl Ritzinger assembled limited numbers of machines. Sources differ both on the dates and on the motors. Once source says 150cc two-stroke, another, 200 and 250cc four-strokes.

KRAM-IT
Italy (Arcore) late 1970s–unknown: These were trials and similar machines with engines from Minarelli (50 and 80cc) and Rotax (125 and 250, and later 300cc). The firm later adopted the HRD name to make sporting machines.

aircraft-grade chrome-moly. The fairing took almost as much time to perfect as the rest of the machine: using a Stuttgart wind tunnel, Kreidler engineers put Anscheidt in the racing crouch and went to work, day after day. The rider later commented that those wind-tunnel sessions were harder than actually racing the bike!

The 1973 works Van Veen Kreidler engine developed 17½bhp at 16,000rpm. The liquid-cooled horizontal single could reach an amazing 200kph (125mph).

Over the next few years, Kreidler and Anscheidt often led the championship race, but never actually took the title. The marque even had a couple of successful

record-breaking sessions, to create a series of new top speeds in the 50, 75 and 100cc categories (all with the same 49cc engine).

The first liquid-cooled Kreidler racer appeared in 1969, although at that time it was only a prototype. In co-operation with the Dutch Van Veen team, Kreidler had a new machine for 1971. Developed by Jorg Moller, the bike had a brand-new frame and a water-cooled motor that produced 17.5bhp. The result was the German factory's first-ever world title, coming from Dutch rider Jan de Vries. From then on, Kreidler largely dominated the class, winning the championship in 1973, 1974, 1975, 1979, 1981 and 1982. There was yet more record-breaking when a Kreidler named 'Black Arrow' set a new world 50cc speed record of 228kph (141.7mph) in 1977, piloted by Henk Van Kessel and prepared by Piet Plompen.

At the Cologne Show in September 1978 Van Veen Sport, based in Duderstadt, displayed the Gelandesport. This 50cc enduro

bike developed 12bhp and employed a space frame. Another product of the same firm was the KVV 'schoolboy' motocrosser; both used Kreidler engines with one-off chassis.

As the 1980s dawned, Kreidler still featured strongly on the racing scene. Commercially the company was beginning to struggle and sales fell to an all-time low in 1981. In a last-ditch effort the factory introduced a string of new models, including the 24bhp three-speed Sport Mofa Flott (Fast Sport Moped), with a tubular spine frame, bolted-up Honda Comstar-type wheels and the familiar horizontal engine with revised square engine casings. There was also a range of 80cc (actually 79.8cc) lightweight motorcycles – the Florett 80, 80E and 80L – together with the Mustang 80 trail bike. Kreidler also built a concept bike styled by Target Design, the creators of Suzuki's famous Katana series. However, none of this action stopped the firm's slide. Kreidler finally went into liquidation in the summer of 1982.

KREIDLER FLORETT

1957

The Florett (Foil) was without doubt Kreidler's most famous street bike, although in many ways it should be described as a flyweight. Debuting in 1957, the heart of the machine was an entirely new, horizontal-cylinder 49cc (40x39.5mm) piston-ported three-speed engine. It was produced both with and without pedals, and could thus be sold both as a moped and as a motorcycle.

Not since the Imme of the early 1950s had a German manufacturer used an engine with a flat-single configuration. In common with other Kreidler models, the bore was hard-chrome plated directly onto the aluminium cylinder, while the gearbox was still operated by twist-grip control.

A notable feature was the Florett's pressed-steel frame which, together with the deeply valanced mudguards, fully enclosed chain and partly covered engine, gave the bike an entirely different style compared with other moped-cum-motorcycles of the era. Although the frame remained an open 'U' device, the fuel tank and saddle (either in single or dual form) had only a small gap between them. Completing the

specification was a full motorcycle-type suspension with Earles-pattern front forks and a swinging-arm at the rear, full-width alloy brake hubs, and fan-cooling for the engine.

In unrestricted motorcycle guise, the Florett could achieve 80kph (50mph) and was an exceptionally modern-looking design, and one

which was to prove so popular and long-lasting that the factory presented owners who had completed 100,000km (62,137 miles) with a solid gold tiepin bearing the Kreidler emblem.

With the Florett, Kreidler was able to exploit a virtually untapped market for a cheap and reliable 50cc machine that looked like a

Kreidler's most famous model was the Florett (Foil). Introduced in 1957, this 49cc ultra-lightweight was available either as an ultra-lightweight motorcycle or moped.

full-blown motorcycle but came at a fraction of the usual cost. Kreidler also had considerable success with the Florett in racing events and long-distance trials such as the ISDT (International Six Days' Trial).

The model proved hugely popular both in its home market and in the Netherlands, where 100,000 machines had been sold

by 1971. The Florett lasted, at least in name – with the introduction of a 79.8cc (46x48mm) ultra-lightweight motorcycle – until the closure of the Kriedler factory in the early 1980s.

Engine: 49cc two-stroke single, 40x39.5mm, air-cooled
Power: 3.5bhp at 6500rpm
Gearbox: 3-speed foot change
Final drive: chain
Weight: 84kg (185lb)
Top speed: 80.5kph (50mph)

KREIDLER 50 GRAND PRIX   1962

The first Kreidler 50 Grand Prix machine arrived in the first year of the 50cc world-championship class and was developed from Hans-Georg Anscheidt's Coupe d'Europe winning Renn (Racing) Florett of the previous year.

Although based on the production Florett engine, the 1961 winning bike had been modified to rotary-valve induction, twin Dell'Orto carburettors and a six-speed gearbox. With a claimed output of 8bhp, the ultra-lightweight 49cc (38x44mm) horizontal cylinder two-stroke single was capable of 129kph (80mph).

For 1962, and led by Johannes Hilber, the race team totally re-designed the engine for its step up

into world championship Grand Prix racing. It still employed a horizontal layout and, to gain the maximum possible displacement allowed under the rules, the engine size was increased to 49.9cc, with new bore-and-stroke sizes of 40x39.7mm respectively. The cylinder barrel was cast in aluminium and finished with a 'pin-pricked' hard chrome surface. The idea was that the tiny holes would retain oil for improved lubrication. In fact, Kreidler was the first German motorcycle manufacturer to use this system, which had been developed by Porsche for their high performance cars.

The Dell'Orto carburettors were replaced by a pair of specially

Hans Georg Ansheidt on his 50cc Kreidler during the 1964 Dutch TT. Although competitive, Kreidler had to wait until the late 1960s to win the world championship.

constructed Bing instruments (one for each rotary valve). The power was routed via a 12-speed gearbox; actually, there were only four speeds, the other ratios being obtained by means of an external, three-speed overdrive controlled by a twistgrip on the handlebars.

A new frame replaced the roadster-based 1961 version, and was manufactured from high-grade aircraft-quality tubing. The Earles-type front fork was retained, as was the swinging-arm, twin-shock, rear suspension.

KRASNY-OKTOBR
Russia 1930–34: Sold under this name, the Red October was heavily based on the contemporary DKW, with a 296cc engine. They were the first large-production machines in the history of Soviet motorcycles.

KRIEGER (ORIGINAL KRIEGER)
Germany 1925–26: The Krieger brothers of KG fame built various KG-like machines. These included their own shaft-drive 500 and a Blackburne 350. They were also known to have supplied frames to other manufacturers.

KROBOTH
Germany (Seestal-Lech) 1949–54: These were scooters with Sachs engines of 100 to 175cc and were built by Czech ex-racer Gustav Kroboth.

KRS
Germany (Berlin) 1921–26: This company was yet another small Berlin assembler among many at that time. Sources differ on exactly which proprietary engines were used by this firm.

KRUPP
Germany (Essen) 1919–21: This was an unsuccessful scooter, with 185 and 198cc engines mounted over the front wheel, from the company which was also known as the famous steel and weapons group.

KSB
Germany 1924–29: This was a firm of assemblers who installed a wide variety of engines (including DKW, Kuhne, Blackburne and JAP, of capacities from 150 to 500cc) in their own frames.

KUHNE
Germany 1928–29: This company produced overhead-valve 350 and 500cc engines, and then went on to produce a desmo.

Keeping the bike on the ground was one of the major problems of this machine with its dry weight of only 54kg (118lb), even though the diameter of the front brake had been increased to cope with the superior maximum speed of around 145kph (90mph). The fairing was also given much attention to improve penetration at higher speeds.

For 1963, a new duplex chassis, stronger (telescopic) front forks and an increase in power output to 12bhp helped Anscheidt retain his runner-up spot in the championship title race, the same position he had achieved in 1962.

Determined to win the world crown in 1964, Kreidler came up with almost a new bike. The engine sported many changes including a new cylinder, stronger air-cooled clutch and a new expansion chamber exhaust, while its 12 gears had been reduced to six in the engine, with a two-speed, cable-operated overdrive. There was also another new chassis (a latticework construction), new forks and more powerful brakes. With 14bhp on tap, the machine could now reach 160kph (100mph).

Unfortunately, all this was still not enough, as by this point, Suzuki and Honda also had produced even faster bikes. So Kreidler had to wait until the Japanese stopped racing in the late 1960s before, at long last, winning the world title for themselves.

Engine: 49.9cc disc valve to single, 40x39.7mm, air-cooled
Power: 14bhp at 11,500rpm
Gearbox: 6-speeds in engine, with 2-speed overdrive, foot-change
Final drive: chain
Weight: 58kg (128lb)
Top speed: 160kph (100mph)

KTM

AUSTRIA 1953–

THE INITIALS KTM stood for Kraftfahrzeuge Trunkenpolz Mattighofen in 1953, when KTM built its first motorcycle. In 1955, the K stood for Ernst Kronreif who joined the business as Hans Trunkenpolz's partner. They went on to become Austria's most successful motorcycle producers, next to Puch. The first KTMs were 98cc Rotax-powered machines, followed by mopeds, scooters and lightweight bikes using Puch, Sachs and Rotax two-stroke engines, typified by the Tarzan 125 of 1957. One of its early competition models featured a twin overhead-cam 125cc engine based on an MV Agusta four-stroke. KTM concentrated exclusively on manufacturing mopeds between 1960 and 1965, and in 1967 it built the 97cc Sachs-engined 100 four, resembling a Honda CB77 and sold

Below: In the late 1960s, KTM started building motocross bikes and a decade later, when this 250cc was made, had become synonymous with off-road bikes.

in the USA as a Hansa. Now developing motocross bikes powered by its own engines, the firm became synonymous with this category of motorcycle sport. In 1977 it won the 250cc Motocross Championship with Soviet rider Gennady Moisseyev. Experience always benefits the production machines; in this case, the result was water-cooling and rising-rate rear suspension.

The firm weathered an economic crisis in the early 1990s. Recovering, it built a wide range of off-road machines, including a 125cc two-stroke trailie and the more serious 193, 297, and 368cc two-stroke and 398, 539 and 625cc four-stroke Enduro and Supermoto

Above: Having survived an economic crisis in the early 1990s, KTM came out with a wide range of off-roading machines, including the 125cc two-stroke Sting.

categories. Invented in France, the latter segment consists basically of scramble and motocross bikes with road tyres; KTM's Duke fits the mould. The road-legal KTMs, like the LC4 Supermoto and 625cc Duke, were fitted with electric starters and road tyres. In 1998 KTM came under new management, and in 1999 a KTM rider training course opened at Mallory Park in Leicestershire, England. KTM was developing its own V-twin motor in 2000.

KTM 620 EGS-E ADVENTURE

1997

The KTM Adventure was introduced in 1997, and its potential ownership was instantly restricted to riders over 180cm (6ft) tall by virtue of its stratospheric 95cm (37ins) seat height.

Sharing its chassis and 609cc four-valve powertrain with its LC4 enduro and Duke siblings, the Adventure was a fun machine with excellent back-road potential, as well as superlative off-road capability. It was noted for its quick steering and fine handling, thanks to its long-travel WP suspension. It was fitted with screen and hand protectors, and a colossal fuel tank capacity – 28 litres (29 UK gallons) – which

Crazy graphics and very high seat position mark KTM's 620 EGS Adventure as one for the bold and brave. Although excellent off-road, it could prove uncomfortable over long distances.

gave great range for the long distance rider, but the downsides were an unyielding seat and relatively low-slung exhausts. The reason for these was so that the bike could be equipped with panniers for all-terrain touring; the paradox was that the Adventure was uncomfortable to ride for long distances without frequent breaks.

The bike also came with an electronic competition computer

trip master so the rider could calculate distances between comfort stops.

For riders of shorter stature, KTM's eight-valve four-stroke 400 LSE (Low Seat, Electric Start) was a better bet, and just as beautifully made, although this machine was constructed without the advantages of the Adventure's touring capabilities.

Engine: 609cc single, liquid-cooled
Power: 50bhp
Gearbox: 5-speed, foot change
Final drive: chain
Weight: 166kg (365lb)
Top speed: 153kph (95mph)

KTM 200 EGS

1999

The KTM 200 EGS was a roadable version of KTM's proper 200 EXC enduro.

The main difference between these two machines was that the EGS had a gear-driven oil pump and a bit more stuffing in the seat. The lightweight machine – which weighed in at just 98kg (216lb) –

was powered by a 193cc two-stroke single-cylinder engine. As such, the machine derived much of its agility and surefootedness from its in-house manufactured WP suspension.

Using top class componentry, KTM motorcycles were not cheap, but in a sense, this is typical of its

type, as specialised machinery is always expensive.

Engine: 193cc single, liquid-cooled
Power: 80bhp
Gearbox: 5-speed foot change
Final drive: chain
Weight: 98kg (216lb)
Top speed: 129kph (80mph)

KULI
Germany (Berlin) 1922–24: This German firm was a typical assembler of 150 and 200cc two-strokes.

KUMFURT
England (Rise) 1914–16: Villiers 269cc two-strokes and Precision singles and V-twins powered these Berkshire-built machines.

KURIER
Germany (Berlin) 1921–24: Unusually, this company built their own 150cc two-strokes and also supplied engines to assemblers (which was obviously a big market in 1920s Berlin).

KURRAS
Germany 1925–27: Bekamo 173cc two-strokes powered these slightly sporty machines.

KV
Germany 1924–27: In-house overhead-valve singles of 200 and 250cc powered these otherwise unremarkable machines.

KYNAST
Germany (Quackenbruk) c.1950s: These machines were robust mopeds with two-speed auto transmission.

KYNOCH
England (Birmingham) 1912–13: This company was better known as a manufacturer of ammunition. They may have used their own engines, but were more likely to have bought them in; these were namely singles (500cc) and V-twins (770cc).

KZ
Germany 1924–25: Franz Gnadig (KG, above) designed these machines with their bought-in 200cc side-valve engines from Alba and 348cc overhead-valve engines from Kuhne.

KTM Duke II

headlight was curiously insect-like, and the tail ran out into a pointed rear light, with a pair of high-rise mat-alloy silencers flanking either side. The Duke II also provided full instrumentation and lighting, with relatively comfortable seating. Suspension was by WP, set up to suit a variety of terrain, and overall styling and build quality meant the Duke II was top of its class.

Engine: 248cc single, air-cooled
Power: 50bhp
Gearbox: 5-speed, foot change
Final drive: chain
Weight: 145kg (319lb)
Top speed: 145kph (90mph)

As well as its obvious off-road potential, the original KTM Duke supermoto could also pose as urban warrior, with its aggressive looks.

The 620cc Duke of 1996 was KTM's first road-going version of its big Supermoto trailie, and the second incarnation appeared in 1999. Powered by the water-cooled 640cc LC4 engine, the Duke II used a chrome-molybdenum double cradle frame and was equipped with 12-spoke alloy wheels rather than the wire spokes

Above: The 2001 edition of KTM's Duke II featured contemporary styling cues, such as the vertical twin headlights.

traditionally fitted on off-road machines. Its styling was equally innovative in a niche where any bodywork is needfully minimalist. The front-fairing containing

Kymco

TAIWAN WAS A POPULAR manufacturing centre for the Japanese motorcycle industry for many years. It carried out sub-assembly work although the engine units were still put together in Japan. The firms would deal with chassis items such as hubs, wheels, electric wiring harnesses and handlebars, all of which helped to built up their experience, ability and technical knowledge, giving them an understanding of individual parts and how they went together, and of production techniques as well.

Eventually, Kymco began to produce complete machines and these were exported to Italy as well as sold on their home market. They opted for simplicity with 50cc two-stroke and 125 and 150cc four-stroke engines derived from Honda units in the main. These went into mopeds and small motorcycles, styled and finished to meet the demands of the period, plus a range of scooters, most with 50cc engines.

The scooters had modern lines and specifications with electronic ignition, automatic lubrication and electric start in many cases. Automatic transmission was usual while front suspension was either trailing-link or telescopic for the scooters and all had rear suspension. Small disc wheels with drum or disc brakes were used by the scooters, some with a mix of disc front and drum rear.

Names such as Dink, Filly, Heroism, Movie, Vivio, People, Sniper and Top Boy were used to sell this line in both the home market and abroad.

In common with most Kymco models, this Sector 125 was based on an earlier Honda single for the design of its four-stroke engine and five speeds.

LA MONDIALE

FIRST SEEN IN LATE 1923 and built in Brussels, this marque was noted for its use of the pressed-steel type of frame and fork. Their first machine had a 308cc two-stroke engine enclosed by the sides of the frame, which ran down from the headstock to the rear wheel. A bucket seat sat on a low-mounted fuel tank and behind this set-up was a deep rear mudguard which also formed a luggage platform. The front mudguard was equally deep while the forks were of the rocking type.

If the frame was unusual, the mechanics were equally so, with the engine inverted, the barrel inclined forward and the crankshaft in line with the frame but angled to run downwards. The large flywheel at the rear drove a cross-shaft using a friction disc. The disc could be moved across the flywheel face to offer a choice of five ratios. A transverse kick-starter pedal was fitted and final drive was by fully enclosed chain.

This unusual design was taken up by Fondu of Vilvorde at the end of 1925 which continued to make the machine in various styles with 350cc engines from Blackburne and JAP with side- or overhead-valves. A Sport version was added for 1926 and this had a new frame that used pressed-steel technology to form a tube frame. The conventional vertical engine and chain-driven gearbox were on view and the saddle was mounted on top of the frame.

The same frame was used for the Tourisme model of 1927 which used the rare 344cc Villiers in-line, two-stroke, twin-cylinder engine. This engine incorporated a clutch and worm wheel to drive the three-speed gearbox built in unit with it. The next year brought a 500cc Chaise engine and some competition successes for Jules Fondu. In 1929, the company showed a shaft-drive model at the Paris Show and also one with a nickel-plated frame, 350cc La Mondiale engine and five speeds. In 1930 and 1931 they contested the TT races but their only finish was 20th in the Junior race of the first year.

The company continued to innovate and a 1931 model had a 350cc two-stroke engine with the crankshaft set along the frame and the gearbox built in unit with the engine. The next year saw a model with a 148cc Villiers engine and another 350cc model which featured a saddle tank. These were joined by a range of four-stroke models with 350, 500 and 600cc side-valve engines, plus 350 and 500cc overhead-valve engines; all these power units came from Sturmey-Archer.

However, times were hard, especially for a firm that was prepared to risk its capital on continuous innovation. Pressed-steel frames were going out of fashion and prices for these machines were rising. Buyers looked and admired, but then bought the conventional.

Over the next year or two the La Mondiale range contracted and by 1934 it had run its course – the end for this interesting marque.

A 1931 model, with a 350cc two-stroke motor and gearbox built in unit with the engine. Note the distinctive frame, a feature of La Mondiale's bikes.

LAMAUDIERE

ONE OF THE MOST OBSCURE of the pioneering French firms, and sometimes also known as Lamaudiere et Labre, existed for a short while in the early days at the dawn of the twentieth century. At that time there was limited under-standing of the relatively new internal combustion engine and the effects of various factors on its power output. What was completely comprehended was that more power meant more speed, records, racing success and good business. But the way to this was anything but clear.

Engines still had an automatic inlet valve and a crude carburettor, troublesome ignition systems and were controlled by ignition timing more than anything else. One fact

---

L-300
Russia 1932–1940s: The Russian military were heavy users of these DKW-based 294 and 346cc two-strokes and 350cc four-strokes.

L&C
England (London) 1904–05: Engines from De Dion Bouton, Minerva and Antoine powered these assembled machines.

LABOR
France 1908–60: Initially a 350cc single, the name resurfaced with Alcyon, with two-stroke lightweights and a four-stroke moped and, in 1954, an overhead-cam 250.

LADETTO (LADETTO & BLATTO)
Italy (Turin) 1923–32: Emilio and Giovanni Ladetto began with 125cc two-strokes. After Angelo Blatto joined them in 1927, other engines were added, including a 175cc overhead-valve four-stroke and a 250cc side-valve. They enjoyed considerable racing success until Blatto left in 1930.

LADIES PACER
England (Guernsey) 1914: A Gloucester-built JES engine powered this open (ladies') frame machine.

LADY
Belgium (Sainte Mariaberg) 1925–38: These were conventional machines fitted with a wide variety of proprietary engines: Blackburne, JAP, MAG, Rudge Python and Villiers, from 175 to 500cc.

LAFOUR & NOUGIER
France (Nimes) 1927–36: This company's own frames had 100 to 500cc engines from Aubier-Dunne, JAP, Train, and Villiers.

LA FRANCAISE
France 1936–50s: Before World War II, this firm made lightweights and machines of 100 to 350cc, two- and four-stroke; afterwards, a 100cc lightweight; then (in 1948) a 49cc pushrod engine; four-stroke lightweights of 169 and 175cc (in 1949); and in 1953 a 250cc overhead-cam motorcycle.

LAG
Austria 1921–29: Liesinger Motorenfabrik AG began with 118 and 148cc auxiliary cycle motors, moved on briefly to a 250cc two-stroke motorcycle; and then made a 350cc two-stroke from 1927.

LA GALBAI
Italy 1921–25: All machines from this line were powered by in-house two strokes: 276, 301, 347cc singles and a 492cc V-twin.

was very clear, though: a larger engine capacity means more power. Engines grew in size despite tight weight limits in competition; only later was it realised that efficiency was the real key to success.

The Lamaudiere failed because it went for size alone in an era when racing motorcycles became monsters and ran on banked tracks in their own events and to pace bicycles.

Their machine had a large, crude engine mounted in a modified bicycle frame with rigid forks. It had direct belt drive, a saddle perched on a sub-frame to be directly over the rear wheel, and pedalling gear with a massive front sprocket to give it the high gearing needed for the speeds. By 1903 such types were already being overtaken and all were soon gone.

This 1902 Lamaudiere was built for the Paris-Madrid inter-city race so was less extreme than the type built for use on banked cycle tracks for races or pacing.

LAMBRETTA ITALY 1946–

FERDINANDO INNOCENTI established his own workshop at the age of only 18. In 1922, aged 31, he moved to Rome where he developed ways of improving the manufacture of steel tubing. Nine years later he moved once more, this time to the Milanese industrial suburb of Lambrate where he founded a steel company which was to be the basis of his future empire. But the Lambrate plant was almost totally destroyed during the war, so he was faced with the daunting task of not only rebuilding the works but also finding a profitable niche of the metal-finishing market in which to sell his wares. The result was to be one of the major success stories of the postwar two-wheel sphere: Lambretta. The idea of making scooters came with the realisation that Italy was devastated and that a simple, cheap form of transport was a leading priority, and also that there was already a proliferation of motorcycle manufacturers.

So Innocenti picked the motorised scooter and in 1946 introduced the first Lambretta, the model A. He also realised the importance of publicity for his two-wheel enterprise and authorised the construction of specialised record breakers, and of a 123cc (52x58mm) single-cylinder two-stroke racing motorcycle: the 2T. This debuted in 1949 and included piston-port induction, an offset Dell 'Orto carburettor, a four-speed close ratio gearbox and, most interestingly, shaft final drive to the rear wheel.

By 1950 production at the via Pitteri Milan factory was up to 300 scooters per day and two new models, the 125C and LC, had just

Above: Lambretta's first scooter, the model A, appeared in 1947. Compared to its Vespa rival, it had no bodywork on the engine.

Below: During the early 1950s, Lambretta created this superb 250cc dohc V-twin racing motorcycle, with shaft final drive.

been introduced. And the same year Lambretta took more records at Montlhery in France. Early the following year, arch rivals Vespa hit back, but then Lambretta retook these with a specially constructed, fully streamlined machine ridden by Romolo Ferri, with speeds of up to 195kph (121mph) – truly amazing for a 125cc scooter!

At the same time, an agreement was concluded with the German NSU company for the manufacture of the Lambretta scooter in that country. This lasted until 1956, when NSU began making its own Prima scooter. June 1951 revealed

Lambretta's 125cc F type was the company's last scooter to lack bodywork. Over 32,000 examples were sold between March 1954 and April 1955.

Above: The SX200 was the firm's most powerful scooter and was built between 1966 and 1969. It used a revised version of the 175 TV3's mechanical disc front brake.

Below: The LD series was built between 1954 and 1958, in 125 and 150cc engine sizes. Over 414,000 left the factory, making it second only to the Li series.

the firm's well kept secret: a new 250 V-twin racing motorcycle (see separate entry). At the 1954 Milan Show, Lambretta launched a 48cc two-speed moped with front and rear suspension. However, it never sold in the hoped-for quantities. After the LC came the LD, but perhaps the most important model of all was the Li series, which arrived in late 1958. These used a choice of either 124 or 148cc engines. Earlier that year the company had introduced the TV 175, a luxury model with a 170cc power unit and a top speed approaching 97kph (60mph).

After 1962, scooter sales declined rapidly. Even though Lambretta tried hard to combat this trend by launching a host of new models, including the Cento 100, GT200, SX200 and 122cc Starstream, the company could not single-handedly reverse this decline. This fall from grace by

the scooter did not matter too much, as from the mid-1950s Innocenti had three divisions: one building scooters; one making mainly tubing; and the third specialising in machinery, including presses and machine tools. Much of the other two divisions' products went to the car industry, including the majority of the

Lambrettas have been built in many countries including Italy, India and Spain. One of the latter models, a 1977 50cc motorcycle, is shown here.

Italian ones, as well as Ford and Volkswagen.

In 1961 Innocenti moved into car production itself, initially with licence-built British cars such as the Austin A40. At the height of its industrial success the group employed 7000 workers, but after the death of its founder in June 1966, it lacked leadership and by 1975 was in deep financial trouble. Innocenti went to the Italian Government and thence to a new private management under Alejandro de Tomaso. By the late 1970s at least one of Innocenti's production facilities in Milan was building Moto Guzzi V35/50 V-twin engines for another section of the de Tomaso empire (see Moto Guzzi). Lambretta scooters are made today, under licence agreements, in Spain and India.

LAMBRETTA 250 V-TWIN RACER

Of all the Italian racing motorcycles of the classic era, none has a stranger history than Lambretta's 250 V-twin. The story goes back to the late 1940s when scooter sales were beginning to explode in Italy and several Italian bike builders, including Moto Guzzi, were eyeing up the scooter market. Expecting strong competition, Lambretta decided to prove it could build motorcycles, as a direct warning to Guzzi and the other bike marques. The result was to be one of the most beautifully engineered small motorcycles of all time. First seen in public in June 1951, the Lambretta 250 V-twin was designed by Ing. Giuseppe Salmaggi (who had previously designed the Gilera Saturno).

Lambretta's V-twin had its crankshaft in line with the frame, whilst the cylinders were set at 90 degrees. Cast integral with each alloy cylinder head was a cam box enclosing the single overhead-camshaft and valve gear, which included two-valve-per-cylinder

Designed by Guiseppe Salmaggi, the Lambretta 250cc V-twin racer was built as a warning to bike manufacturers such as Moto Guzzi not to build scooters.

triple-coil valve springs and shim set tappets. Camshaft drive was a shaft and straight-cut bevel gears, supported by ball-race bearings. Each cam was supported by a roller bearing, with a ball-bearing at the drive and another at the outer end; roller bearings were provided for the rockers. Mounted on the forward end of the crankshaft was a flywheel magneto and above this the rev-counter drive. Lubrication was of the dry sump variety, with a finned oil container under the seat. Other sections of the bike's specification included a five-speed gearbox, shaft final drive, full-width drum brakes and telescopic front forks. The machine was tested with two types of suspension: torsion bar with friction shock absorbers and also orthodox rear hydraulic

shocks. One of the design's most interesting features was the 'backbone' frame which comprised a large-diameter single top tube running downwards to pressed-steel lugs which extended forward to form the main engine mounting. There were no front down members.

Although extensively tested (at Monza) Salmaggi's creation was

Engine: 247cc sohc transverse 90-degrees V-twin, 54x54mm, air-cooled
Power: 30bhp at 8000rpm
Gearbox: 5-speed foot change
Final drive: shaft
Weight: n/a
Top speed: 190kph (120mph)

never raced, even though it was proved to be quick enough to have worried the opposition.

LAMBRETTA TV 175 SERIES 3 SCOOTER

Although the 1957 Maserati 250cc motorcycle and the little-known American-made Midget Motors Autocycle of 1961 got there first, Lambretta's TV 175 Series 3 of 1962 was the first mass-produced powered two-wheeler in the world to be equipped with a disc front brake as standard equipment. The TV (Turismo Veloce – Touring Speed) was introduced in 1957 as the Series 1. The idea was to offer customers a faster, more luxurious machine to challenge Vespa's 150 Gran Sport. Unfortunately for Lambretta, although the concept and timing were fine, the TV Series 1 was underdeveloped and was plagued by poor reliability.

Innocenti moved quickly to replace the troublesome Series 1 with the Series 2, which debuted in January 1959, 16 months after the former had been introduced. The Series 2 had a new engine with bore and stroke dimensions of 62x58mm. Midway through the

Lambretta's TV 175 Series 3 scooter of 1962 created history by being the first mass produced powered two-wheeler to feature a disk front brake as standard.

Series 2 programme, its 23mm carburettor was replaced by a 21mm instrument to promote smoother running.

But it was to be the Series 3 which really defined the TV family and brought it attention. For starters, it wore the new go-fast Slimline Lambretta styling. There were front hydraulic dampers to provide a much smoother ride, and a 20mm Dell

'Orto replaced the late TV2's 21mm assembly. But it was the mechanically operated disc brake up front which really gave it an edge – at least in the PR stakes. This disc brake was the early use of a system which would be the industry norm from the mid-1970s onwards. However, Lambretta found that many potential owners were worried about complexity and reliability. Even so, it was a

bold move and one which was proved right by subsequent events in both the motorcycle and automotive industries.

Engine: 175cc 2s horizontal single, 62x58mm, fan-cooled
Power: 8.6bhp at 6750rpm
Gearbox: 4-speed, twistgrip change
Final drive: enclosed chain
Weight: n/a
Top speed: 99kph (62mph)

LAURIN & KLEMENT
AUSTRO-HUNGARIAN EMPIRE 1899–1908

IN THE MID-1890s mechanic Vaclav Laurin and bookseller Vaclav Klement began building bicycles at Mlada Bolesav in what was then part of the vast Austro-Hungarian Empire (now Czechoslovakia). They had a single rented room and five employees, but their Slavia cycles sold well and in 1898 a larger factory was acquired. The following year they began to make motorcycles, at first powered by Werner engines mounted over the front wheel and in 1903, replaced by singles and V-twins of Laurin & Klement's own design mounted conventionally within the frame. Sold as Slavias in the home market, the bikes were Republics elsewhere, except Germany where they were Germanias, built under licence by Seidel & Naumann. The first four-cylinder machine came out in 1905, when Laurin & Klement began producing cars. Aero engines and a wide range of commercial vehicles followed, and by 1909, motorcycle production had terminated. However, the company continued its expansion until after World War I, which saw the demise of the vast Austro-Hungarian Empire and its large market potential severely curtailed. In 1925 Skoda bought the firm, and used the Laurin & Klement badge until 1927. The partners died in 1930 and 1938, having stayed with Skoda to the end.

Top: Laurin and Klement built their first powered cycle in 1899. Soon after, the TB model appeared (pictured), with the engine cradled in the hooped frame.

Above: By 1903, the company was building V-twins of its own, like this CCR model from 1905, the same year the company went into car production.

LAVERDA
ITALY 1949–

LAVERDA CAN TRACE its commercial history back to 1873, when Pietro Laverda founded a company to manufacture farm machinery in the town of Breganze, in the mountainous north-east of Italy. In 1948 his

grandson, Francesco, decided to build his own lightweight motorcycle. Originally this was not intended for production but simply for personal use. Unlike the majority of small bikes in postwar Italy, Laverda's creation was a

four-stroke. This first effort featured a single-cylinder 74.75cc (46x45mm) overhead-valve unit-construction engine with a three-speed foot-change gearbox. It took Francesco Laverda a full year to create his prototype, and

LARDORI
Italy (Castellina) 1925: This firm assembled near Siena from Train 350cc motors, Ideal three-speed gearboxes, and Druid forks.

LATSCHA
France 1948–53: This firm fitted Aubier-Dunne two-strokes (98 and 123cc) or JAP four-strokes (350 and 500cc).

LAURENTI
Italy (Bologna) 1956–unknown: An overhead-cam 173cc engine of their own design powered their machines.

LAVALETTE
France 1952–unknown: This firm produced mopeds of 48 and 65cc, and 70cc scooters and lightweights, often with automatic transmission.

L'AVENIR
Belgium 1959– : These mopeds had HMW or Fichtel & Sachs engines.

LAZZATI
Italy (Milan) 1899–1904: Lazzati was one of the earliest Italian manufacturers, fitting De Dion Bouton engines into strengthened bicycle frames.

LDR
Germany 1922–25: This very basic 548cc side-valve had an external flywheel. It was chain/belt drive, then later all-chain.

LEA FRANCIS
England (Coventry) 1911–26: Until 1920, this firm used JAP and MAG V-twins, and after that, MAG only. Capacities ranged from 500 to 750cc. George Bernard Shaw rode a Leaf.

LEBELT
Germany 1924–25: In-house two-strokes and four-strokes of up to four-and-three-quarters horsepower powered these machines.

LECCE
Italy 1930–32: The head of Lecce, Otello Albanese, modified 173cc Moser engines with 'go-faster' cylinder heads and put them in his own sporting frames.

LE FRANCAISE-DIAMANT
France 1912–59: This firm was a part of Alcyon: 100 to 500cc models came before World War II, two-strokes up to 250cc after it.

LEGNANO
Italy (Milan) 1954–68: This firm initially made mopeds with Sachs, Minarelli and Mosquito motors, later (1967) supplementing them with a 175cc motocross machine.

The Husqvarna-engined Laverda 125 Enduro was launched at the Milan show in November 1977. There was also a 250cc version of the same motorcycle.

his efforts included casting the piston in the kitchen of his home!

When the machine made its first public outing, several of Laverda's friends, including the local priest, wanted replicas made. This led Laverda into the role of motorcycle manufacturer, and by 1951 some 500 examples had been constructed. In the same year, as a means of publicising the marque's existence on a national scale, Laverda prepared a bike for the prestigious Milano-Taranto long-distance road race. Although this was destined to retire, the factory entered a squad of four specially

prepared '75s' the next year. In the 1953 event Laverda struck gold, taking the first 14 places in its class. This was followed by an increase in displacement to 98cc, by which time Laverda's domination of the Milano-Taranto race had extended to the 100cc class as well.

However, by 1956 the company's racing days in both that event and the Giro d'Italia (Tour of Italy) were rapidly coming to an end. Although it built customer versions of the Milano-Taranto machines (coded MT), the Breganze marque quit sport to concentrate on its series-production models. Thanks to its diverse commercial interests, which included foundry work and the production of combine harvesters and caravans, Laverda

The 250 2TR enduro bike of 1977 used the same 249.9cc (68x68mm) piston port single-cylinder engine as the Chott. It was of Laverda's own design and manufacture.

was able to survive the Italian motorcycle industry recession of the mid-1960s. This sales decline, brought on by the arrival of cheap cars such as the Fiat 500, was to claim the scalps of firms such as Aero Caproni, Parilla and Rumi.

Laverda was also an early entry into the world of large-displacement machines. The original prototype of its famous big twin line was an overhead-cam 654cc (75x74mm) example displayed at London's Earls Court Show in November 1966. The engine featured a four-bearing 180-degree crankshaft, a duplex chain drive, a single overhead-camshaft with a triplex chain for the primary drive, a five-plate clutch and a five-speed gearbox. The aluminium cylinders were slightly inclined from the vertical and featured iron liners, while the cylinder head was a one-piece casting, with hemispherical combustion chambers.

A year after its debut, the Laverda twin had grown to 743.9cc, achieved by increasing the bore size to 80mm. Just as in previous years with its small singles, Laverda chose to publicise its new 750 twin by competing in long-distance events. In 1969 a Laverda 750S won the Oss 24 Hours, repeating the victory in 1970.

In 1971 the specialised (and expensive) 750 SFC was launched. The SFC was a truly hand-built motorcycle with the express purpose of winning sports-bike

races. Until production ceased in the mid-1970s, the model was to earn a fantastic reputation for staying the course, even though it didn't always win.

The first public sighting of any Laverda with more than two cylinders was late in 1969 at the Milan Show. The new machine, a triple, created a huge stir, but Laverda had been somewhat hasty and couldn't match production to potential customer expectation. This prototype was just that – a hand-built one-off machine. It was very much a 'parts bin' special, and in its original form was far too heavy and slow. The bore and stroke measured 75x74mm (the same as the 650 twin), giving 980.76cc, but except for the engine size, bore and stroke and the across-the-frame layout, much was to change before production began in 1973. In the interim, Laverda engineer Luciano Zen did extensive experiments, which included incorporating both single and double overhead-cams, along with various drive systems.

When the production model arrived, the valves were operated by double overhead-cams driven by a single chain between the second and third cylinders. The machine was known as the 3C (3 Cylinder). Other features included three Dell 'Orto carburettors, chain primary drive, a five-speed gearbox, Bosch electronic ignition and a top speed of 220kph (137mph). Unfortunately, the design still needed another year of

Laverda began its motorcycle operations in 1949 after Francesco Laverda built a prototype 75cc ohv single in his spare time. It proved so good customers wanted replicas.

Above: One of Laverda's best-loved models, the 500 Montjuic. This 1982 machine is a mark II with frame-mounted fairing and revised styling.

Right: First appearing at the Milan show at the end of 1981, the new 1000 RGS featured a 120-degree crankshaft instead of the more familiar180-degree type.

development, which it didn't get. Customers therefore suffered a spate of mechanical and electrical problems.

Most of these glitches had disappeared by 1975, by which time there were twin Brembo disc brakes up front instead of Laverda's massive drum. The 3C became the 3CL, and then one of Laverda's greatest models, the Jota (a name coined by British importer Roger Slater).

The late 1970s and early 1980s were to be Laverda's glory years, with motorcycles such as the Jota, Montjuic, RGS and V6. During this period the company also achieved considerable success in both endurance and sports-bike races with its three-cylinder

The 650 Sport of 1994 had a 668cc air-cooled parallel twin engine based on the earlier Alpino unit, but with updates and electronic fuel injection.

LE GRIMPEUR
France (Paris) c1900–32: This firm made large-capacity machines, V-twins with engines from Aubier-Dunne, Chaise, JAP, MAG and Stainless. Some smaller machines were also made until they were bought out by Dresch.

LEIFA
Germany 1924–25: Improbably, a former shipyard built these 148cc side-valve lightweights.

LELIOR
France 1922–24: This firm made a 174cc flat-twin and a two-stroke single resembling the Evans.

LEM
Italy 1974: These were mopeds and mini-bikes for young riders.

LENOBLE
Belgium 1954: This firm built the fully enclosed Kontiki scooter.

LEONARD
England (London) 1903–06: Fafnir, Minerva and MMC engines powered these typical pioneers.

LEONARDO FRERA
Italy (Tradate) 1930–34: These were typical JAP-engined machines of 173 to 348cc in Italo-English style.

LEONE
Italy (Turin) 1948–mid-1950s: This firm produced initially a 50cc two-stroke, later a 75cc lightweight.

LEOPARD
Germany (Magdeburg-Neustadt) 1921–26: This is variously reported as a one-model company making a 300cc two-stroke, or as offering a choice of 250 and 350cc, initially two-stroke, later four-stroke.

LEPROTTO
Italy (Turin) 1951–54: These were singles of 125, 160 and 200cc, two-stroke and four-stroke.

LETHBRIDGE
England 1922–23: These were Villiers-powered assembled two-strokes of 247 and 269cc.

LETO
Germany 1926–28: Rinne two-strokes of 173 and 198cc powered these Lehmann-designed machines with their pressed-steel frames.

LE VACK
England 1923: Bert Le Vack, the racer, built these JAP-powered overhead-valve 350cc singles.

intended as Italy's answer to the recent Honda NS400. It had reed-valve induction, Gilnisil plated-aluminium cylinders, liquid-cooling, six speeds and an alloy beam frame, with a claimed 201kph (125mph).

For the next eight years, Laverda met one financial crisis after another, until 1993 when local business tycoon Francesco Tognon took over and relaunched the name. The new Laverdas of 1994 – production versions of the 650 Sport – used an engine based on the earlier Alpino/Montjuic, modified and enlarged to 668cc. In 1997 the new liquid-cooled 750S appeared. In standard trim, this

748cc (83x69mm) four-valves-per-cylinder double overhead-cam twin developed 80bhp. Later in 1997, a more highly tuned Formula version arrived.

Tognon left in 1998, just after work began on a brand-new liquid-cooled three-cylinder engine as a return to the superbike league. Sadly, Laverda lacked the finances to develop this project, and were taken over in 2000 by Aprilia.

The final version of Laverda's 750SF was the Series 3 of 1976. This sported five-spoke alloy wheels and triple Brembo disc brakes.

models. Laverda also built a series of two-stroke models, including the Chott, an expensive (and another one-off) road machine fitted with an engine of Laverda's own design. Another project was the 125 and 250cc Husqvarna-powered enduro and motocross bikes. Finally, there were 125 and 175cc roadsters using German Zundapp air-, and later water-cooled, engines. Only the Zundapp-powered machines proved to be a commercial success.

Laverda's Ghost Strike, in 668cc engine size, was introduced at the end of 1996. The Strike used the sports alloy beam frame and was fitted with a small fairing.

In the mid-1980s, Laverda built the 350 three-cylinder two-stroke Lesmo. With an engine unit, the sole prototype made its only public appearance at the 1985 Milan Show. Featuring an engine layout pioneered by the DKW 350 GP racers of the mid-1950s, it was

LAVERDA 750 SFC

1971

The first Laverda 750 twin debuted at the Milan Show of 1967. By 1969 the Breganze-based company had decided to re-enter the racing arena to publicise the new model (as it had previously done with its range of small-capacity overhead-valve singles), and by 1970 it had won not only the Oss 24 Hours but also, perhaps more importantly, the prestigious 500km (311-mile) race for production machines at Monza.

The SFC (the C stood for Competizione) was launched in 1971 as an endurance racing version of Laverda's SF series. It was destined to win its first-ever event, the gruelling Barcelona 24 Horas (Hours), around the twists and turns of Montjuic Park. Although derived from the touring SF, the 744cc (80x74mm) SFC had a number of important differences. Its engine was more highly tuned and had a larger oil pump and bigger bearings. Although the frame employed the same basic geometry as the touring SF, with a spine of four 40ml tubes from which the engine was slung, visually it was quite distinct from the SF. Its chassis

incorporated a revised racing-style half-fairing, seat unit and rear-set controls. The exhaust was a two-into-one affair with virtually an

open race pipe exiting on the near side of the machine.

In 1974 a second-generation SFC made its debut. It was

The final 750 SFC was the 1975–76 18000 series with Bosch electronic ignition, a two-into-one exhaust and triple disc brakes.

instantly noticeable because of its triple hydraulically operated Brembo disc brakes (the original model sported Laverda's own massive drum brakes front and rear), stronger fork tubes, magnesium rear-wheel hub and revised styling. Initially, discs and wire wheels were used, but soon came the definitive combination of discs and cast wheels. The last major modification to the SFC was the introduction of electronic ignition. Total production was 549, and the model's final year was 1976.

Engine: 744cc dohc parallel-twin, 80x74mm, air-cooled
Power: 70bhp at 7500rpm
Gearbox: 5-speed foot change
Final drive: chain
Weight: 205kg (452lb)
Top speed: 212kph (132mph)

LAVERDA JOTA   1976

The word Jota inspired either admiration or fear from motorcycle enthusiasts during much of the late 1970s and early 1980s – depending upon whether you either owned or lusted after this ultra-rapid Laverda triple, or owned a rival marque's model. For quite simply, in its day the Laverda Jota was the fastest series-production model on the planet. The name was not a factory designation, but was coined by the (then) British Laverda importer Roger Slater, who borrowed it from a rather athletic and energetic Spanish dance! The 3C (E) had been the performance version of Laverda's standard 3C, and the Jota was a development of the former.

The first official Jota arrived at Slater's headquarters in Bromyard, in rural Herefordshire, in January 1976. This was a factory-built production bike, intended at first only for UK consumption. Compared with the 3C (E), the Jota had triple discs, alloy wheels, a different seat and tail unit, and needle-roller swinging-arm bearings.

In August 1976 *Motor Cycle* published a road test in which the Jota test bike had achieved a fastest one-way speed of 225.37kph (140.04mph), with a mean two-way figure of 221.8kph (137.8mph), making it the fastest bike ever tested by that magazine. This instantly transformed the Jota into an icon, and made it the envy of almost every other rider.

At the time, demand always seemed to exceed the strictly limited supplies. Therefore it was

The Jota was the first production bike to be clocked at 225kph (140mph). It became a legend, thanks to its high performance on both road and track.

not until 1979 that any major changes were made; unfortunately, not all of these were for the better, the result being a catalogue of engine problems. By 1980 those glitches had largely been solved, and later that year Laverda introduced a hydraulic clutch, which was a vast improvement over the old manually operated type. Previously the clutch action had been alarmingly heavy, but in truth the Jota had never been the most suitable machine for town use. Its natural habitat was the open road or the race circuit.

The 1982 model year saw the appearance of the Jota 120, using the 120-degree crankshaft from the RGS model. This provided a smoother, less harsh power delivery. However, with the motorcycle sales depression of the early 1980s, the 120 model never sold in the numbers of the original, and production of the Jota ended in 1982.

Engine: 981cc, triple dohc, 75x74mm, air-cooled
Power: 79bhp at 8000rpm
Gearbox: 5-speed foot change
Final drive: chain
Weight: 233kg (514lb)
Top speed: 225kph (140mph)

LAVERDA V6   1978

The Laverda V6 was one of the most ambitious motorcycle designs of all time. Unfortunately, it was also a very costly one which ultimately placed the company under a financial burden it could not withstand. Although it appeared only as an endurance racing prototype, the intention behind the V6 was to provide Laverda with a new range of modular models.

The project began in the summer of 1976 and, as Piero Laverda himself was later to say, 'envisaged a range of V-twins, V-fours and V-sixes covering a displacement spectrum of 350 to 1200cc'. He added that the plan was to create a series of models based around the same set of basic components, and all featuring four-valve heads, liquid-cooling and shaft final drive.

The V6 (with the other associated engines in the modular series) was placed under the joint design team of former Maserati engineer Ing Giulio Alfieri and Laverda's design boss Luciano Zen. Officially, Alfieri was employed by Laverda as a consultant, but in practice he and Zen worked as a team. The 90-degree V6 was an ideal basis for a modular series of engines because the twin and the four could also share the same 90 degrees, thus reducing the cost of tooling.

The first and only complete type to appear was the V6 endurance racer of 1978, with 995.89cc (65x50mm) and almost 139bhp. Its race debut came in that year's Bol d'Or race in France at the Paul Ricard circuit, where it was timed at an amazing 283kph (176mph) along the Mistral straight, 32kph (20mph) faster than any other bike

Laverda's amazing V6 produced 139bhp at 10,000rpm and could hit 283kph (176mph). But high development costs jeopardised the whole future of the company.

in the event. However, after eight hours the universal drive shaft failed, forcing its retirement.

Despite this speed, its weight and handling problems were to signal the model's death knell. In technical terms, the V6 proved that Laverda could build the ultimate motorcycle of its era; even so, this exercise placed the company's entire future in jeopardy.

Engine: 995.89cc dohc 4v V6, 65x50mm, water-cooled
Power: 139bhp at 10,000rpm
Gearbox: 5-speed foot change
Final drive: shaft
Weight: 216kg (476lb)
Top speed: 283kph (176mph)

LECH

ALTHOUGH THE LECH WAS only in production for less than three years, it is significant as the first Polish-built motorcycle. It was the brainchild of Waclaw Sawicki, a Polish industrialist, and Wladyslaw Zalewski, an engineer who had returned to Poland after emigrating to the United States. The motorcycle was first shown at Poznan.

The Lech 5hp V-twin – the engine was built entirely in-house – had a swept volume of around 500cc and was of up-to-the-minute design, with light-alloy pistons,

detachable cylinder heads, and positive lubrication, although the bottom end was built up and ran in roller bearings in more traditional style. Some parts were imported, such as bearings, carburettors and the Bosch electrical system, but most of the bike was purely Polish.

The cycle parts were somewhat less progressive than the engine, with an old-fashioned flat tank and no brakes on the front wheel, although there were two independent braking systems on the rear wheel, an internal

expanding drum brake and a band brake. Perhaps if, instead of visiting the United States, Zalewski had been to Britain (where brakes had been developed further) things might have been different. However, in 1930, the machine was re-designed with a front (drum) brake and a saddle tank.

A three-speed hand change was par for the period, as was an unsprung rear end, and a reported top speed of 120kph (75kph), only a little over 70kph (45mph), argues that the machine was

designed more to survive appalling roads than for 'scratching'. Apparently, there were racing versions, and there may also have been a single at one point.

It is not clear what finally ended the production of the Lech. The Depression was obviously a factor, but in predominantly agricultural Poland, such an innovation as the first home-grown machine might have been expected to survive. As it was, only a handful of machines were made – a few dozen, at most – before production came to an end.

LECTRA

FOR AROUND $4000 in 1998 – it later went up to $4500 – plus shipping, Californians (and others) were offered the battery-powered Lectra from Electric Motorbike (EMB Incorporated). The small-wheel chain drive machine was necessarily heavy at 104kg (340lb), because of the 104 Ah (lead-free) batteries that were required to propel it. This in turn required quite substantial brakes for such a slow vehicle, a dual-calliper 190mm (seven-and-a-half ins) floating disc fitted at the front, and a 100mm (4ins) drum at the back.

The 24volt 'variable reluctance' motor, of extremely advanced design, was rated at 3hp continuous, 8hp peak for acceleration. In September 1999, at the Woodburn Electric Drag Races, the Lectra actually set a

The Lectra was bulky and heavy – 104kg (340lb) – because of the sheer volume of batteries it carried, and even those typically gave a usable range of only 40km (25 miles).

couple of (highly specialised) world records for the standing 200m (one eighth of a mile): around 15 seconds, and a terminal speed of just over 64kph (40mph).

Top speed was around 80kph (50mph), but exploring such regions for long would be likely to effect a significant reduction in the the claimed range of 64km (40 miles), despite the regenerative braking, which fed power back into the battery when rolling downhill or slowing down.

In fact, most users seem to have reckoned that a distance of 40km

(25 miles), or sometimes even less, between charges was a figure likely to be much nearer the mark.

The battery life of this model was claimed at 14,500km (9000 miles), and charging time from a standard US supply was given as four-and-a-quarter hours. Intriguingly, the charging circuit was multi-voltage and multi-frequency: 90–260v, 47–63Hz. The label 'zero emissions' is a bit of a misnomer – after all, the electricity to power the Lectra has to come from somewhere: indeed it normally comes from burning fossil fuels at power stations, with the often less welcome alternative of nuclear power.

The certificate supplied to owners claims that this is the world's first electric motorcycle; this, however, is incorrect. Ome (1920), Bullo (1924–26), Socovel (1938) and Solo (circa 1950s) all made electric bikes. Nevertheless, this machine is a bold attempt to produce a modern one, incorporating interesting and innovative ideas, to take

motorcycle development away from the oil-leaking combustion engine and onto a different plane.

The VR 24 'Blue' is an odd mixture of sporting looks and pedestrian electric performance.

LEVIS

ENGLAND 1911–40

THIS FIRM HAD THEIR works in Stechford, Birmingham, which was run by the Butterfield brothers. Early in 1911, Howard Newey, designer of the Levis, was seen riding a small two-stroke model that was well able to carry a passenger, despite not having pedals. The machine was soon on the market, sold first as the Baby, but then as the Popular which became abbreviated to Levis Pop. It was indeed popular, especially for new riders, for it was such a simple machine; just a 211cc two-stroke engine with magneto ignition and direct belt drive. Inside the engine went a one-piece crankshaft but lubrication was by drip-feed from a separate oil tank which avoided the problems,

Above: The Levis Pop of 1924, a simple model that differed from most small two-strokes. It was easy to learn to ride and was capable of giving its owners years of reliable service.

Right: A Levis 247cc two-stroke engine of 1928. This motor powered much of Levis' range, and had three speeds, chain drive and mechanical lubrication.

current in those days of mixing petrol with oil. There was a ladies' model with open frame and a heavier, 269cc version with Druid forks.

The larger model grew to 293cc for 1914, then a two-speed version of this appeared and 1915 saw a 349cc model as well. However, it was the Pop that remained popular and was the only model for 1919 and 1920. Then came a 247cc TT model in 1921; the firm had taken the first three places in the 1920 Junior 250cc TT, were second in 1921, and won again in 1922, also winning the French and Belgian.

The simple Pop ran on to 1924 but other, more complex versions

were added: they had a gearbox and needed an alternative engine stretched to 247cc to keep the performance. Through this they lost the basic simplicity of the original.

By 1926 the 247cc was the only capacity, listed in two forms, increased to three and joined by a 346cc overhead-valve four-stroke

for 1927. This was joined by a 247cc six-port two-stroke in 1929, while in the new decade they moved to four-stroke power.

The 247cc two-stroke did continue through the years, joined by a four-stroke range of 247, 346 and 498cc models, most with overhead-valve, plus one of 591cc from 1937. A 346cc side-valve

model appeared in 1939 but earlier, back in 1934, there was a 247cc overhead-camshaft model. The camshaft was chain driven from a half-time pinion, but the model kept the total-loss lubrication system which the firm used for its four-strokes, claiming that the supply of fresh, clean oil was beneficial and reduced wear.

During the decade they were in production, the models followed the general trends of the time, and the machines were always well made, even though they were not manufactured in particularly large numbers.

Those who knew them were sorry to see production come to an end in 1940.

LIBERATOR

FRANCE C.1900–LATE 1920S

FRANCE LED THE WAY in private transport from the beginning, thanks to liberal laws that encouraged its development, and it was much the same in Germany and Belgium. Therefore it was in those countries that the embryonic industry began its early production of parts and machines. They were soon supplying other countries while their technical lead continued.

It was also in France that the Werner brothers established the form of the motorcycle with the engine set vertically in the frame, ahead of the pedalling gear. Liberator were just one of the many who followed in their footsteps, starting with the same primitive layout of bicycle frame and forks, engines from firms such as Antoine or Sarolea of Belgium, belt drive and cycle brakes.

They also produced tricycles, which were popular, with the engine driving the rear axle, but the uneven balance and three wheel tracks soon saw them fall from favour. The motorcycle, later attached to a sidecar after some early efforts with tricars and quads, proved to be the best answer, and developed from then on. Single and V-twin engines provided the power, gearboxes and

all-chain drive came in time, frames were designed to deal with the loads on them and girder forks were the most usual form of front suspension.

By the 1920s the format was well established but then commercial matters began to govern the fate of many firms, including Liberator, who in the era of the Great Depression, had to close down.

LILAC

JAPAN 1949–67

THE LILAC RANGE OF MOTORCY-CLES was built by the Marusho company, owned by Marashi Ito. At first single-cylinder models were offered on the market using a 148cc overhead-valve engine with two-speed gearbox and a pressed-steel chassis. Later, updated versions appeared with a more modern specification. This included tubular steel frames and Earles-type front forks. Some even featured a form of automatic transmission with a torque converter.

In 1953 a 90cc overhead-valve model with shaft final drive,

nicknamed the Baby, was an instant sales success. This led to a whole series of motorcycles with shaft final drive, a feature which would later become a Lilac trademark. The first of these horizontally opposed twins was fitted with a 339cc pushrod engine. It made its debut in the public eye in 1954.

Right: The Lilac range of motorcycles was built by the Marusho company, owned by Marashi Ito. A 1960 MF39 300cc V-twin is shown.

In time for the 1959 model year, a 247cc V-twin arrived. It had a style similar to the later Moto Guzzi V7/V75 of the late 1960s and early 1970s, and featured a very neat duplex cradle frame, telescopic front forks and swinging-arm rear suspension. Later, a larger 188cc was introduced. This larger model was

The MF39 featured a narrow angle ohv V-twin engine with front mounted alternator and shaft final drive. Suspension was by telescopic forks and swinging arm.

sold as part of Lilac's range as the MF-39 Type 300.

In 1964 a new 493cc horizontally opposed twin (again with shaft final drive) was offered, known as the R92 (intended to emulate BMW!). This model was exported to the USA and sold as the Marusho Magnum. It did Lilac no favours as it suffered from poor reliability, which of course resulted in a backlash from dissatisfied customers. Lilac never fully recovered and in 1967, Marusho closed down, taking Lilac with it.

LINTO

THE FIRST LINTO RACER – an elision of the designer Lino Tonti's name – was a double overhead-cam 75cc lightweight in the early 1950s. The later, more successful and considerably more dramatic 500cc Linto racer was the result of a collaboration between designer Tonti, racing rider and constructor Umberto Premoli and racing rider Alcide Biotti.

It was a curious machine, built up of two Aermacchi Ala d'Oro 250cc singles (72x61mm, 248cc) on a common crankcase, creating a 496cc twin. Unexpectedly, the engine was not in V formation, but was instead a (very wide) parallel twin, with the cylinders perhaps 10 degrees above the horizontal. Equally curious was the employment of a pushrod engine at a time when one might have expected overhead-cams.

It was not lacking in power; the Ala d'Oro delivered 32bhp at 10,000rpm. Tonti achieved the rare trick of nearly doubling the power by doubling up the engine, with 61bhp at 9800rpm. The bottom end was built in unit with a six-

Taking two 32bhp engines and coupling them to produce 64bhp is more difficult than it might seem – but Lino Tonti managed it.

speed gearbox. Suspension was conventional, telescopic at the front, swinging-arm at the rear. It had a distinctly vintage look with an enormously long tank that stopped above the front of the rear wheel, just short of a very tight 'bum-stop' seat.

For the 1969 season, Tonti managed to find another 3hp – the full 64bhp; two Ala d'Oros – and shaved the weight still further, from 142kg (312lb) to 134kg (295lb) by switching to a thin fibre glass tank. Alberto Pagani was second in the East German GP in that year, beaten only by the great Giacomo Agostini on an unbeatable MV Agusta. The Linto did not make much of a mark thereafter.

LLOYD

THE LLOYD MOTOR ENGINEERING CO. of Monument Road, Birmingham, began building machines in 1903 under the owner's name. He was W.J. Lloyd, a component maker, involved with Quadrant at one time, and his first machines were built up using stock parts from his own stores.

Stevens engines were used at first and the machines were typical of the time with two-and-a-half and three-and-a-half horsepower engines in loop frames with braced forks and direct belt drive. By 1908 they were being sold as the LMC and the three-and-a-half horsepower single was joined by a two-and-a-quarter horsepower vertical twin devoid of cooling fins. The cylinders were separate to allow air to flow between them. The firm claimed there were no problems with overheating, but it was not seen again. A larger single was added for 1912 which gained a two-speed gear for 1914, a V-twin model was produced in 1915 and other transmission options,

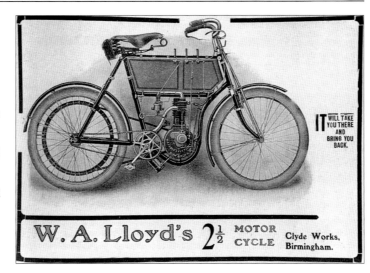

W. A. Lloyd's 2½ MOTOR CYCLE Clyde Works, Birmingham.

including a countershaft gearbox, were made for 1916.

Lloyd returned in 1919 with a 597cc single and a 842cc V-twin, both with a three-speed gearbox. There was only the twin for 1920, also available in overseas form with a larger tank and different suspension. In 1921 a 960cc V-twin

A 1905 advertisement for the 2.5hp Lloyd powered by its simple engine with automatic inlet, side exhaust, direct belt drive and braced forks.

joined the smaller one and these two ran on for one more year with all-chain drive, the belt being an option for the 842cc alone.

LUBE

ONE OF THE ORIGINAL Spanish motorcycle producers, the Bilbao-based Lube company was for many years closely connected with NSU of Germany. Luis Bojarano, the head of Lube, built NSU-powered models using both two- and four-stroke engines with frames of his own design, ranging from 49 to 247cc. Only after NSU had given up motorcycle production did the Spanish company begin building its own power units, all of which were to be two-strokes.

The well-known two-stroke engineer, Hermann Meier, had a spell at the Bilbao factory during 1962 and 1963, before joining Royal Enfield, where he was responsible for developing the GP5 racer. Meier's first efforts for Lube was a newly developed 124cc (56x54mm) engine with piston-port induction and full unit construction which, with a compression ratio of 10:1 from its German Mahle piston, produced 18bhp. The machine made its debut at the 1962 Spanish Grand

Prix, but proved no match for the latest factory bikes from Japan and Italy. In 1963 a new engine was built. This featured a disc valve driven by the crankshaft, three transfer ports and liquid-cooling. A front-facing exhaust was used so that the water inlets were positioned either side of it, and the exit was from the rear of the

cylinder head, which also featured liquid-cooling.

After Meier left Lube, a 246cc two-stroke racing twin was constructed. This was air-cooled with large areas of finning on both the cylinders and heads, a dry clutch, steeply angled carburettors and five speeds. It made several appearances in 1965, including the

Lube was one of the pioneers of the Spanish motorcycle industry. This 124cc B25 single-cylinder, twin port, two-stroke dates from 1950.

Spanish GP. It is worth recording that Ossa's star rider, Santiago Herrero, began his racing career on Lube machines.

LUTECE

BASED IN COLOMBES, Seine, this firm was one of the many that appeared after World War I but which failed to survive the financial ups and downs of the turbulent 1920s.

Lutece is remembered principally for its line of heavy-duty machines which came from a

country that ultimately went to lightweights. They are also remembered for their use of a large vertical-twin engine at a time when two cylinders invariably meant a V-twin. There were a few exceptions, but the v layout fitted so neatly into the same frame as a single that it had become the

accepted format and had better balance than a single or a 360-degree vertical twin.

The firm chose to enter the top end of the market with a luxurious model powered by a 1-litre (one fifth UK gallon) vertical-twin engine set along the frame. This enabled it to drive straight back to

the clutch and gearbox from which a shaft ran back to take the power to the rear wheel. This substantial assembly was housed in a robust duplex frame that had both front and rear suspension.

Something of an American line was given to the styling, while the sheer size was on a par with many machines coming from the USA at that time. It made a fine sidecar model but the price was against it; it was never a great commercial success, and demand gradually fell away.

Lutece produced machines until 1926. Their last model before they closed down was said to be a velomoteur which was fitted with a 100cc two-stroke engine and belt drive.

The luxurious Lutece had an in-line, vertical-twin, one-litre engine, as well as shaft drive, a duplex frame and both front and rear suspension. It was an enterprising, but ultimately expensive, machine.

MAFFEIS

ITALY 1903–35

BERNARDO AND CARLO MAFFEIS of Milan were pioneers of the Italian industry and were involved with the Belgian Sarolea firm before they built their own machines. As Carlo used a Sarolea in early Italian competitions, it was no surprise that they chose this make of engine for their first machine as it was the one they knew best, even if the rest of the machine was typically primitive.

Carlo continued to be the sporting brother in the years prior to World War I, and his competition machines followed the pattern of the period with single-cylinder and V-twin engines of their own design taking the place of the Sarolea. These engines went into a simple, rigid frame with braced forks, a cylindrical fuel tank and direct belt drive, which sufficed for the dusty road and track conditions of the times.

The road models were better equipped for general use with sprung forks and, by the start of the 1920s, the main product was a model featuring a 339cc V-twin engine with magneto ignition, a three-speed gearbox and chain final drive. This was soon dropped and during the 1920s, the firm turned to fitting British Blackburne engines of 250, 350 and 500cc with side- or overhead-valves in their machines.

Around 1931, the Maffeis began to be built and sold by Cesare Galimberti to an uprated specification, using both Blackburne and JAP engines, a combination that continued right up to 1935, when production ceased.

Above: Carlo Maffeis seated on one of the machines to carry the family name during 1912. It raced in competition events and record breaking attempts.

Below: The Maffeis was very basic with braced forks, no mudguards and direct belt drive, seen here in the typical dusty race conditions of the era.

MAGNAT-DEBON

FRANCE 1902–58

FOUNDED AT GRENOBLE in 1893 by Joseph Magnat and Louis Debon to produce bicycles, this firm became De Dion agents and used that engine for a motorcycle built in 1902. Three years later, it adopted a layout with the engine inclined parallel to the frame

A close-up of the 500cc ohv engine of a 1955 Magnat-Debon machine with its light-alloy cylinder head. The company also used engines from Moser and Moto-Rêve.

downtube; it had side valves, gear-driven magneto located behind the cylinder and direct belt drive tensioned by a jockey pulley under the lower run. The engine went into a diamond frame, and front suspension was by leading-link forks. It also built a 2hp model with an automatic inlet valve that grew in time to 2.75hp with side-valves and, in some cases, the company used engines from Moser or Moto-Rêve, as well as its own motors.

In 1912, the firm used the same layout for a 400cc engine with vertical overhead-valves opened by rockers mounted to lay across the head and moved by exposed pushrods that ran up the right side of the engine. By 1914, the range had been joined by an overhead-valve, V-twin model with the magneto at the front; all the models still retained the belt drive. The 400cc grew into a 500cc and the singles ran in competitions with some success. Magnat-Debon had some modern ideas during this period and experimented with a form of telescopic front fork and, with the rear brake working on the belt rim in the usual manner, with a cycle-type working on the deep sides of the wheel rim, acting much as a disc brake.

After World War I, the firm introduced new singles with side- and overhead-valves plus some two-strokes but, like many others, it fell on hard times and in 1923 was taken over by Terrot. From then on, the two makes began to take on the form of the Terrot, a tendency that increased over the years although, at first, Magnat-Debon used Blackburne engines while Terrot fitted JAP.

The machines followed the trends of the industry between the wars with singles in capacities from 175 to 500cc, dry-sump lubrication, with the oil tank mounted on the saddle tube, separate gearbox, four speeds, foot

The 1955 model with its unit-construction engine, pivoted-fork rear suspension and full-width front brake.

change but with rocking pedal, chain drive, rigid frames and girder forks. There were competition versions, and the fashions of saddle tanks and twin-port engines were applied with French flair.

Following World War II, the Magnat-Debon models increasingly came to resemble the Terrot, with the range extending from mopeds to a 500cc overhead-valve, single built-in unit with four-speed gearbox. In time came the modern suspension systems.

There was also a scooter but this was simply a badged Terrot with its two-stroke engines of 98cc and two speeds, or 125cc with three speeds.

By 1958, the Magnat-Debon was gone.

MAGNI

BORN IN 1920 near Arcore, the home town of the famous Gilera marque, Arturo Magni worked for Gilera before leaving with Ing. Pieto Remor in early 1950 to join MV Agusta, where he was to remain for the next quarter of a century. He served as mechanic, engineer and finally team manager until MV quit racing at the end of 1976. He then founded the Magni marque in 1977.

At first this was very much a component supplier – for MV owners – supplying wheels, chain-drive conversion kits, tuning parts and frames.

A Magni MB2. Powered by a BMW R100RS flat-twin engine with shaft final drive, the bike made its debut at the Cologne Show in September 1982.

From the early 1980s, Magni began to branch out into other marques, notably Honda, BMW and Moto Guzzi. The first such machine was the Honda-based MHI which used not only the Japanese CB900 four-cylinder engine, but also Honda forks, swinging-arm, shock absorbers, brakes and exhaust system. These were built exclusively for export, and in 1981 Magni produced a total of 150 MHIs and the later MH2s.

Next came the MB2, powered by a BMW R100 RS flat-twin engine, which made its debut at the Cologne Show in September 1982.

The success of the Magni BMW led to the introduction three years later of the Moto Guzzi-engined Magni, the Le Mans. First displayed at the Milan Show in November 1985, the Magni machine used the power unit from the Le Mans IV. This could be ordered with the standard Moto Guzzi 1000 (948.8cc) V-twin engine, or exclusively from Magni

In late 1985, Magni introduced the first Guzzi-powered model. This Magni Sfida model dates from 1990 and features classic, rather than modern, styling.

as an 1100 (1116.87cc).

The UK price in mid-1986 was £5750 for the 1000 and an additional £300 for the 1100. This was expensive, but you did get the chance to own one of the world's most exclusive and exciting motorcycles, built by someone who had managed to pack into his life motorcycle experiences that most enthusiasts could only dream about.

Since the mid-1980s, Moto Guzzi has remained the preferred engine of choice for Magnis projects.

MAICO

GERMANY 1935–87

A factory 173cc ISDT Maico in 1953, with chief designer Ulrich Pohl on the right and rider Karl Westphal on the left. Both won gold medals that year.

FOUNDED BY TWO BROTHERS as Maisch & Co, and later contracted to Maico, this firm built two-strokes for road, off-road and track with considerable success, although their beginnings held little promise of what was to come. Maico began in 1935, using a 118cc Ilo engine installed in a simple lightweight; this was quickly joined by a larger 143cc model and, in 1939, a form of moped using a 49cc Sachs engine.

As with all German motorcycle firms, Maico was rationalised in 1938 and so spent the war years producing aircraft parts. After the war, it was able to set up again and in 1948 built its first model with a Maico engine, a simple 123cc two-stroke with twin-exhaust systems and three-speed gearbox in unit, telescopic forks and plunger rear suspension.

The 125cc was soon followed by a 150cc, but real innovation came in 1950 with the launch of the Mobil at the Reulingen Show.

MAFA
Germany (Marienberg) 1923–27: This German firm was a bicycle factory that diversified into motorcycles with 120 to 250cc two-strokes bought in from DKW and 350 and 500cc four-stroke engines bought in from Kuhne.

MAFALDA
Italy 1923–28: This company manufactured sports machines powered by in-house two-stroke engines, and possibly four-strokes, of 125 and 175cc.

MAGATY
France 1931–37: This auxiliary cycle motor was a 200cc two-stroke.

MAGDA
France 1933–36: This firm produced lightweights with 100 and 125cc Train and Stainless two-stroke power units.

MAGNAT-MOSER
France (Grenoble) 1906–14: Moser engines (up to 750cc) were fitted in frames from this branch of Magnat-Debon.

MAGNEET
The Netherlands 1955 to early 1970s: These mopeds were fitted with 50cc Sachs motors.

MAGNET
Germany (Berlin) 1903–24: This firm produced unusual-looking machines with low frames and smaller-than-usual wheels. Their machines were powered by Adler, Minerva and Fafnir motors as well as Magnet's own V-twins. The company never really recovered from the economic hardships produced by World War I.

MAGNI
Italy 1928–30: Luigi Magni built a 500cc vertical single and a 350cc overhead-cam parallel twin with the cylinders pointing forwards.

The Maico Taifun, first seen in late 1953 in 348 and 400cc capacities. The two-stroke twin engine was in unit with the gearbox under the extensive enclosure.

hydraulic damping went at the front. The 35.5cm (14ins) disc wheels had their own mudguards beneath the all-enveloping body. A spare wheel was carried on the drum-shaped tail.

The Mobil was more than a scooter as it combined weather protection with good handling and came fully equipped with screen, luggage-locker, storage space, turn signals, gear indicator and, in time, a radio. At first it only had the 148cc engine and three speeds to pull it along, but for 1954 there was a choice of 174 or 197cc engines, both with four speeds. The 174cc engine soon found its way into the motorcycle and it was this model that was modified to run in the ISDT as part of the German Trophy team. It was a member of the team that won the trophy in later years.

Late in 1953, Maico sprang their next surprise in the shape of the Taifun, or Typhoon. This had a 348 or optional 400cc twin-cylinder, two-stroke engine built-in unit with a four-speed gearbox that it drove by helical gears and fed by twin carburettors. Suspension was by leading-link front and pivoted-fork rear. A light-alloy chaincase enclosed the duplex final-drive chain. Full-width hubs housed the drum brakes while the pillion footrests

Left: A late 1970s motocross Maico, available with 247 or 438cc engine, five speeds and period suspension. It was also listed in enduro form with headlights.

This had the style and enclosure of a scooter but underneath went a tubular steel frame with the engine and gearbox unit supported in a sub-frame that pivoted at a point under the crankcase and ran back to carry the rear wheel. Two exposed springs and a hydraulic damper mounted in monoshock manner controlled this rear suspension, while telescopics with

Below left: An MD250 modified to run in the 1974 Formula 3 Isle of Man TT, where its disc-valve performance and six speeds proved an asset.

Below: Maico listed this RS125 road racing single in the early 1970s. It proved competitive using a disc-valve, air-cooled engine and six-speed gearbox.

were recessed into the engine unit castings to hinge out at a touch. What really set the machine off was the degree to which the working parts were enclosed, maintaining the clean line of a motorcycle.

For 1955, the Mobil was replaced by the Maicoletta, which was in effect a re-style that retained much of the original machine and was fitted with the 174 or 247cc engine; this pair was later joined by a 277cc unit. The model continued at the top end of the scooter market, offering more performance and luxury, plus better handling. The 247cc engine was a de-tuned version of the

By the mid-1980s, the Maico enduro model had a well-advanced suspension system and 247 or 488cc engine. It was still based on the motocross model.

motocross unit Maico had run in 1954 and was also used for the touring Blizzard motorcycle that joined the 174cc models. During this period Maico had a brief fling with cars by taking over the Champion line, but this was not a success.

Back on two wheels the firm entered the moped market with the Wiesel, which had a single tube as the main frame, two speeds and both front and rear suspension.

This supplemented the range, but by the late 1950s the firm was in financial trouble, mainly offset by increased sales of off-road models that were generated by their ISDT performances.

In 1961 their fortunes improved when it won a contract to supply the West German services with large numbers of the 250cc. Against this, motorcycle sales dropped and, while the scooter kept going for some years, it was time to introduce a new generation of motorcycles. The main ones were a 125cc with disc-valve induction built-in unit with a five-speed gearbox and a similar 50cc motorcycle, while the ISDT replica and motocross models were joined by an enduro range. It was the 125cc that took Maico Germany into road racing, at first with a modified machine that progressed to six speeds and later to water-cooling and a Grand Prix win in 1972. In 1971, the road line added an air-cooled 250cc with disc-valve and six speeds; it was fast and handled well.

Another military contract for the 250cc came in 1975 but the firm gradually went downhill. Road models came to an end in 1983, leaving only the off-road line; this was still produced after the firm was sold in 1987 to a new company, who kept the name.

MAINO
Italy (Alessandria) 1902–10 and 1945–50s: Initially, Giovanni Maino used Souverain two-and-a-quarter horsepower engines, then engines of his own manufacture. After a 35-year gap, he re-entered the market with lightweights which were powered by Mosquito, Sachs and NSU engines, from capacities of 38 to 150cc.

MAJESTIC
Belgium 1928–31: JAP 350 and 500cc engines powered these English-style machines.

MAJESTIC
France (Chutenay) 1929–33: Original pressed-steel frames from this company housed JAP and Chaise singles, JAP twins up to 1000 and the 500cc Chaise four-cylinder.

MAJESTIC
England (Birmingham) 1931–35: These were basically pre-Matchless AJS machines which were assembled at the OK Supreme factory from parts left over after the Matchless take-over.

MAJOR
Italy (Turin) 1947–48: Salvatore Majorca used a 350cc engine of his own design to power this shaft-drive, fully enclosed machine.

MAMMUT
Germany (Nurnberg, later Bielefeld) 1923–32 then 1952–60: Originally, this company manufactured lightweights with 200, 250 and 300cc two-stroke engines. Then, at the new Bielefeld works, they produced mopeds of 49cc and lightweights and scooters of 125 to 198cc fitted with Fichtel & Sachs and Ilo motors.

MAMOF
Germany 1922–24: As well as 150cc Grade and DKW two-strokes, Mamof lightweights were also powered by its own 155cc side-valves.

MAICO MD250   1974

The MD250 was a development from earlier road models and a 125cc, road-racing single cylinder that appeared in 1968. This followed the form of the time with an air-cooled, disc-valve engine which had the carburettor mounted on a crankcase side door and an expansion exhaust system. It was a built-in unit with a six-speed gearbox and went into a tubular frame. The result was sold to private owners who had some successes.

This work paid off on the motocross range and led to the MD250 in 1971 with a short-stroke, disc-valve, air-cooled engine built-in unit with the six-speed gearbox. This went into a conventional tubular frame with

A Maico brochure for the MD250 in its full road form, the radial finning for the cylinder head and barrel typical of the company's design.

telescopics and pivoted-fork rear suspension, wire wheels and drum brakes. It made for a smart road machine that was revised for 1974 with sunburst fins for the head in a style running down onto the barrel sides. The single cylinder

exhausted into twin silencers, while the cycle side gained Italian forks and brakes plus turn signals.

The resulting machine was fast, handled exceptionally well and had good brakes so it could cover ground at speed. Its comfortable

riding position made this light work for the rider. It was especially at home with high-speed corners.

In this form, the Maico MD250 continued to be produced up until 1978.

Engine: 245cc rotary 2s vertical single, 76x54mm, air-cooled
Power: 27bhp at 7800rpm
Gearbox: unit 6-speed foot change
Final drive: chain
Weight: 127kg (280lb)
Top speed: 155kph (95mph)

MALAGUTI

ITALY 1930–

THIS SAN LAZZARO DI SAVERNA (Bologna) concern was set up in 1930 by Antonio Malaguti to manufacture pedal cycles and accessories.

Then came World War II, with Italy entering the conflict on the side of Germany in June 1940. Italy's industrial north suffered badly as the Allies pressed the Axis forces back during 1944 and 1945, even though the Italians had surrendered in September 1943.

When peace returned once more, Italy was in a sorry state. But for Malaguti, this meant the

Malaguti has always concentrated its efforts on lightweight motorcycles, scooters, mopeds and pedal cycles. This is an NF50 four-speed moped dating from 1977.

immediate postwar years were spent trying to satisfy a demand for its cycles, which were by now often fitted with the famous Garelli Mosquito auxiliary engine. This was followed in the mid-1950s by the German 48cc Sachs engine, which saw several years of service. Then came Italian powerplants such as the Franco

Morini unit. During the 1960s a number of lightweight motorcycles – with engines up to 125cc – and mopeds were built.

In the 1970s, the decision was taken to concentrate 100 per cent on the 50cc market. The company decided to actively seek export customers at the same time. This meant that Malaguti machines were seen in some numbers in countries such as France and Great Britain. For example, in Britain the Calvacone enduro-styled ultra-lightweight was sold during the latter half of the decade.

One of the Malguti concern's best known models was the Cavalcone, in this case used on a 125cc motocross bike during the mid-1970s.

By the mid-1980s, there were 150 workers at the firm producing 25,000 machines annually. The 1990s saw these figures more than double and, at the same time, the first scooters being sold. This trend continues today, and Malaguti is now a major player in the current European scooter boom.

MALANCA

ITALY 1956–86

FORMED IN 1956 by Mario Malanca in Pontecchio Marconi, Bologna, the Malanca marque is best known for its long-running line of parallel twin-cylinder two-strokes for both road and racing use. The racer's hour of glory came between 1973 and 1976 when Otello Buscherini gained several victories and leaderboard placings in the 125cc World Championship series.

Buscherini's mount used a 123.5cc liquid-cooled, disc-valve, twin- cylinder 43.8x41mm engine,

producing 36bhp at 14,000rpm. It was one of the few machines to match the class-leading Yamaha and Morbidelli machines. Tragically, Buscherini was to lose his life in an accident during the 1976 Italian Grand Prix, riding his own Yamaha 250cc; Malanca's challenge effectively died with him.

During the late 1970s and early 1980s, their road-going 124.9cc, 43x 43mm, piston-ported twins were well known for their high performance, particularly in liquid-

The Malanca 125cc Mark trail bike of the mid-1980s was unusual by having a liquid-cooled, twin-cylinder engine. Top speed was 120kph (75mph).

cooled form. The 'ob one 125' was *il primo della classe* (first in its class) with 25bhp and 151kph (94mph).

But this success was unfortunately not to continue. The mid-1980s saw the emergence of a new generation of 125cc machines boasting ultra-high performance from Aprilia, Cagiva and Gilera. Virtually overnight the twin-cylinder Malanca was out-classed; with it went its sales advantage.

In 1985, in an attempt to promote itself and gain customers, the company sponsored the up-and-coming Marco Lucchi on a special 250cc, twin-cylinder racer, and saw a performance that put it up with the best. But this publicity was not enough to stop financial disaster; the factory closed in 1986.

The fastest series production Malanca street bike was the 150kph (93mph) 'ob one Racing' of 1985. It was soon outclassed by bikes from Aprilia and Cagiva.

MAMMUT

GERMANY 1925–33

THIS FIRM WAS NOT to be confused with the postwar company of the same name that existed in Germany between 1953 and 1956, nor was it to be confused with the machine built by Friedl Münch from 1966 on and sold as the Mammoth in some markets. In this case, Mammut was a company that existed between the wars and it had originally been established in order to manufacture machine tools.

Mammut came into motorcycles during the 1920s with a model that followed the general format of models of the time. It was powered by a 198cc Baumi two-stroke engine that drove a separate gearbox and thence the rear wheel by chains. These items went into a basic tubular frame with girder forks, wire wheels and minimal brakes.

The company soon added models with other engines to their

Above: An early Mammut, fitted with a 346cc side-valve JAP engine, separate gearbox and all-chain drive in a rigid frame with Druid forks.

Below: By 1931, the 198cc JAP engine had its magneto at the rear. Mammut installed it in this model in a pressed-steel frame with forks also made from pressed steel.

range, and these included 197 and 246cc two-stroke units of their own manufacture.

There were also four-strokes from JAP and Blackburne of Britain and MAG in Switzerland in capacities ranging from 200 to 500cc. Later came Villiers engines and all kept to the established format up until 1929.

From 1929 onwards, the firm used pressed-steel frames for their machines. These were made under licence from the British Coventry Eagle firm. Coventry Eagle had adopted the pressed-steel frame form of construction for the previous year. These frames were able to accept a range of lightweight engines and due to their versatility, this practice continued to 1933 when production ceased, possibly due to a refusal to allow the British link to continue.

MANDILLE ET ROUX
see **MR** (France).

MANET
Czechoslovakia (Povazska Bystricka) 1948–67: Initially, this company produced a lightweight with a 90cc split single engine which had been designed by Vincenz Sklenar. Later, they manufactured two-stroke scooters of 125cc.

MANON
France (Courbevoir) 1903–06: This firm produced the usual pioneer stuff: strengthened bicycle frames, and a one-and-a-quarter horsepower engine.

MANTOVANI
Italy (Milan) 1902–10: This firm produced lightweight machines with engines of its own make from one-and-a-half horsepower to 4hp, some water-cooled.

MANUFRANCE
France 1951–55: This company manufactured lightweights of 125 and 175cc and two-stroke 125cc scooters.

MANURHIN
France 1955–62: This company took over (and improved) the DKW Hobby scooter, fitting a 75cc two-stroke.

MARATHON
USA 1910: This was a two-stroke with shaft drive; however, sources differ on whether it was a single or a twin.

MARC
France (Vincennes) 1926–51: This French firm produced English-looking machines of 250 to 500cc with Staub-JAP, JAP and LMP engines.

MARCK
Belgium 1904–08: In-house 500cc inlet-over-exhaust singles powered these pioneers.

MARS

PRIOR TO WORLD WAR I, Swiss Zedel and German Fafnir engines were used in the Nurnburg factory of the Mars concern. Then, in 1920, the chief engineer, Franzen-berg, designed one of the company's best-known models, *Der Weisse Mars* (The White Mars), with a box square section frame constructed from welded and riveted, pressed-sheet steel. Its engine – made exclusively for Mars by Maybach, famous as both aircraft and car engine builders – was a 956cc side-valve flat twin, with the cylinders pointing fore and aft. Initially, this motorcycle sold well, but Mars ran into financial difficulties in 1924 at the time of hyperinflation in Germany and production stopped until 1926. Then, Karl and Johann Muller, two leading engineers at the Mars factory, re-opened it with new financial backing. Unable to use the Mars title for a long time, the machines were marketed under the MA brand name. In the late 1920s and throughout the 1930s a variety of imported engines were used, including Sturmey-Archer, JAP, Villers, plus Germany Sachs.

Postwar production, now under the original Mars name, resumed in 1950 when Rudi Albert, normally chief designer with Allright and Phanomen, joined Mars. His first effort, launched in 1950, was the S50, a neat, 98cc Sachs-powered ultra-lightweight.

But Albert's most notable Mars creation was the Stella, with exceptionally low lines for a full-size motorcycle. It debuted in 1951, using 40cm (16ins) wheels and either 150 or 174cc Sachs engines.

The final model – the 175 DS – lasted until 1957, by which time Mars was struggling. Mars closed in June 1958, its model range being absorbed by Gritsner-Kayser.

Designed by Rudi Albert in 1950, the Mars S50 was a neat ultra-lightweight powered by a 98cc Sachs two-stroke engine, with full-size motorcycle-like appearance.

MARTIN

HARRY MARTIN WAS a well-known competitor at Brooklands and was in the TT from the outset in 1907 up to 1921. Late in 1910 he went into business from his works at

Croydon, Surrey, with two machines, a 4hp tourer and a two-and-three-quarters horsepower racer. Both had JAP engines, the tourer's standard, the racer's with a shortened stroke and overhead inlet valve. Similar in form, both had direct belt drive, a rigid frame and sprung forks, but the racer pulled a higher gear and was shorter and lighter than the tourer.

For 1912, a larger racer was added in two forms: one a single, the other a short-stroke V-twin, again with the overhead inlet valve. Six models were listed for 1913. All kept the belt final drive but transmission was to order, so any contemporary unit could be specified. Only one V-twin was

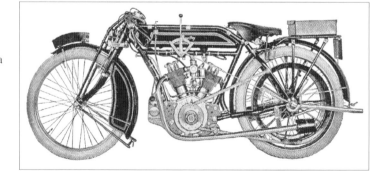

listed for 1914 but the lightweights remained available into 1915 as the only models.

In July 1920, it was announced that production was about to recommence, at the works of A.G.

A Martin Tourist Trophy model. The machine was available either with 770 or 996cc JAP V-twin engine and belt drive and was one of a range that also included a number of singles.

Millier in Willesden, on a range powered by MAG engines. Entries were made in the 1921 TT races and, for that year, included models with 293cc side-valve single engines and 498cc V-twin JAP engines fitted with Claudel Hobson carburettors – an unusual choice – driving Albion and Burman gearboxes respectively. Production then dwindled and the marque disappeared once more.

MARTINSYDE

ENGLAND 1919–23

MARTIN & HANDASYDE was an aircraft firm that turned to motorcycle production after World War I in order to utilise their facilities. They aimed for the quality sidecar market and chose to make their own V-twin engine rather than buy one from an outside source as other firms did. To this end they bought a design from Howard Newman, whose name appeared on the machines at first, and this was a 677cc V-twin with the less usual exhaust-over-inlet-valve layout. The engine drove a three-speed gearbox built under licence from AJS, with all-chain drive and typical cycle parts including girder forks.

A 498cc exhaust-over-inlet single was added for 1920 but production was much reduced for the next year as trade fell off, despite the addition of a sports version of the single. In 1922 a 738cc V-twin appeared and was listed as the Quick Six while the next year brought a 347cc single with the cylinder set vertical and the machine available in Sports and Touring form. All models continued with magneto ignition, three speeds, chain drive and girder forks.

Martinsyde had a fine, quiet running engine, a good gearbox but average cycle parts and their limited production ended in 1923 when the business failed. They had discovered that the quality market is not the easiest to satisfy. The BAT firm bought the remaining stock and rights to produce so continued to assemble machines up to 1925 and sold these under the Bat-Martinsyde name.

Above: E.H. Gifford on a 678cc Martinsyde at Brooklands in 1922. The marque was successful, taking the team award in the only 500-mile race run for motorcycles.

Below: A 1921 Martinsyde with a 677cc V-twin engine that used the unusual exhaust-over-inlet-valve layout, and drove a three-speed gearbox.

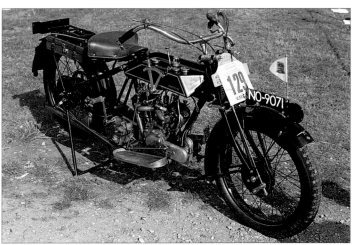

MAS

ITALY 1920–56

FOUNDED BY ING. ALBERI SEILIG, the Milanese company Mas (Motoscafo Anti Sommergibile) not only built roadsters, but also military machines. The company even went in for winning Gold medals in the ISDT, riding its range of 123cc overhead-valve models.

A huge number of different models were offered during the 1930s, ranging from a 248cc side-valve to a large, 568cc side-valve single, usually featuring inclined cylinders. Seilig departed in 1938 to form the Altea factory, an enterprise that only lasted until 1941.

Meanwhile, Mas supplied a number of 498cc overhead-valve singles to the Italian Army. After World War II, the first new model to be produced was the 122cc overhead-valve Stella Alpine, with 'suction air-cooling' as *Motor Cycle* magazine described it in its 1946 Milan Show report. It was a

MARIANI
Italy 1930–34: This machine was a 500cc side-valve of unique design, in two-valve and three-valve versions, and for petrol or diesel (or possibly naptha). The role of the third valve has been explained in several conflicting ways.

MARIANI
Italy 1924–28: This was a two-stroke lightweight: however, sources differ on whether it was 125 or 175cc.

MARLOE
England (Birmingham) 1920–22: This firm was a small assembler of 350cc Precision- and Blackburne-engined machines, and 500s with Blackburne engines.

MARLOW
England (Warwick) 1920–22: These machines were mostly Villiers 269cc powered, but 350 and 500cc JAP engines were available to order.

MARMAN
USA 1940s: This was an American belt-drive, two-stroke flat-twin moped of 110cc.

MARMONNIER
France (Lyon) 1947–51: These two-stroke lightweights were fitted with 125 and 175cc Aubier-Dunne engines.

MARS
England 1905–08: These machines were essentially Fafnir and Minerva engines in strengthened bicycle frames.

MARS
England (Coventry) 1923–26: These well-made and assembled machines were fitted with a saddle tank as early as 1923. Engines came from Villiers, JAP, Barr & Stroud and Bradshaw, and maybe others, and were mostly 250 and 350cc.

truly innovative idea: the cylinder was cast in the form of two concentric cylinders; inside this, the inner cylinder was joined to the outer one by a number of vertical fins in a single-casting operation.

This inspired idea was the work of its designer Guidetti, and it was intended to provide efficient cooling at low speeds. This would work in much the same way as a stationary engine is kept cool; in other words, the engine itself had to provide its own cooling. Nevertheless, even though this system may have been ingeniously designed, the Stella Alpine failed to make its mark in great numbers and was not a commercial success.

Next came a prototype 492cc parallel twin with single overhead-camshaft, but this never made it to production. There were also overhead-valve and overhead-cam, single-cylinder 175s which were produced during the early 1950s, but these failed to sell in any great number. This once-great marque was forced into selling 125cc two-strokes and a 49cc scooter with bought-in German Sachs engines.

The factory was finally forced to close in 1956.

This Mas model dates from the late 1920s and is typical of the marque during the period. The company also built motorcycles for the Italian Army.

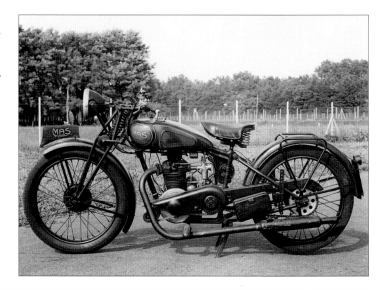

MASERATI ITALY 1953–61

After World War II came a move to Modena, more GP cars and a new venture: motorcycles. This began in 1953 with a 123cc (52x58mm) two-stroke and a 158cc (60x56mm) overhead-valve, the latter with pushrods enclosed in an integral tunnel. In 1954, these models were joined by a brace of larger-displacement, overhead-valve singles – a 175 and a 200cc – closely related to the 158cc.

At the Milan Show in late 1955, Maserati staged a surprise by offering what it claimed was the world's first production motorcycle with a disc front brake. This was fitted to a new 246cc overhead-valve, 70x64mm single. Other features included double-helical primary drive gears and twin-plug ignition. Later still came a 50cc racer.

After 1961, Maserati made only expensive supercars.

OF THE SIX MASERATI BROTHERS, sons of a railway engineer from Voghera near Milan, five became engineers: Alfieri, Bindo, Carlo, Ernesto and Ettore. Carlo, the eldest, raced motorcycles and won several events in 1899 and 1900 on a Carcano machine, which he designed, built and rode himself for the Marquis Cancano de Anzano del Parco. He also raced cars and worked as an engineer for Fiat, Bianchi and Junior. He died in 1911.

Alfieri worked as a test driver for Isotta-Fraschini and raced for the marque. Bindo also worked for Isotta and, from 1910 to 1913,

Alfieri and Ettore spent time in Isotta's Argentine factory. Having returned to Italy, Alfieri, with Bindo and Ettore, set up Officine Alfieri Maserati SpA in Bologna in 1914.

World War I saw Maserati making spark plugs and overhauling aero engines. In 1919, the youngest brother Ernesto joined the firm. From then to the late 1940s, Maserati concentrated on racing cars, but from 1938 onwards operations were based in Bologna, having been taken over by the Modenese industrialist Adolfo Orsi, who retained the surviving Maserati brothers on 10-year contracts.

Above: The car builder Maserati also built bikes between 1953 and 1961. This 1935 model created history by being the first bike with a disc brake.

Right: As well as its four-strokes, Maserati also created a number of two-strokes, including this 1956 49cc Competizione racing model.

MAUSER

GERMANY 1924–27

IN THE AFTERMATH of World War I, demand for arms at Mauserwerke in Oberndorf am Neckar was not great, so the company diversified, briefly, into vehicle production. Proceedings began with the improbable-looking Einspurauto, or single-track car, described by one German authority as '*ein karossiertes Motorrad*' (a 'motorcycle with bodywork') – and rather a lot of bodywork at that, mounted on a chassis comprising two pressed-steel channels. The picture tells the whole story, right down to the outrigger wheels. Some sources describe these as retractable, but it seems unlikely that one could successfully lower and raise the wheels in addition to performing all the other everyday tasks required to pilot the machine.

In reality, such a machine was much safer than it looked and, once under way, it worked fine. The real problem was convincing anyone this was so, especially as the big, oddly shaped handlebar cannot have inspired much confidence. The other problem was that this was very much a vehicle for the open road, and not particularly manoeuvreable at low speeds. Consequently, it tended to lurch to one side when coming to a stop, which could be awkward on a crowded city street shared with horses pulling delivery vans.

It had a 510cc side-valve single engine mounted horizontally in front of the rear wheel, with both primary and final drive by chain. Because it delivered only 10bhp at 3400rpm, requiring this modest

output to propel a vehicle weighing an impressive 290kg (638lb), performance was poor, but then the outrigger wheels would have made rapid cornering extremely interesting.

Even so, when Mauser decided to discontinue production after less than three years, Gustav Winkler, also of Oberndorf am Neckar,

The 'single-track car' (Einspurauto) has always attracted interest, but few have succeeded in building a good one. Mauser tried, but failed.

continued production until 1932. In the late 1920s, the French Monotrace (one-track) was a Mauser built under licence.

MCEVOY

ENGLAND 1926–29

IN A SENSE, THE PEDIGREE of this Derby-based company is more interesting than the majority of its products. That said, the most magnificent McEvoys, with the rip-roaring, 1000cc eight-valve Anzani V-twins, were very powerful, very fast motorcycles even by modern standards: even

The ohc McEvoy 500cc in-line four was built just before the company went bankrupt in 1929. It offered excellent performance but tended to overheat.

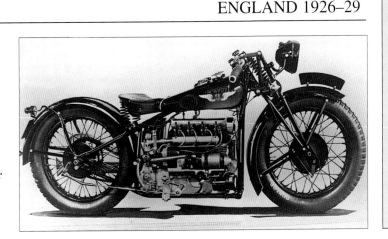

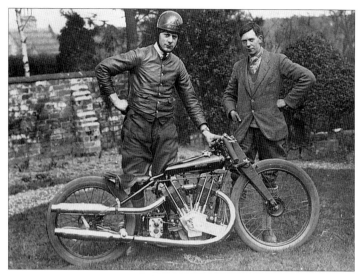

overhead-cam single and (still more intriguingly) an air-cooled, overhead-cam straight four of only 500cc. Production machines, however, ranged down from the supercharged and eight-valve big twins, through normally aspirated four-valve big twins, to side-valve singles of 498, 348 and 248cc from Blackburne and JAP, and even a 172cc two-stroke with Villiers engine. All were of a sporting mien, and were built with the benefit of racing experience, but there was a limit to how much performance could be extracted from some of these engines.

The lesser V-twins still delivered about 45bhp, which is about the same as a Vincent Rapide, and which, in the very light, slim motorcycles of the day, could give a much more sparkling performance than could normally be expected from a 45bhp motorcycle today, although the brakes would be fairly frightening by modern standards.

McEvoy machines were in many ways comparable to the Brough Superior's standard of finish but McEvoy himself was even more interested performance.

without supercharging, they could deliver in excess of 60bhp. Michael McEvoy, earlier employed by Rolls-Royce, was an expert on superchargers, and put his knowledge to good use. After he closed the motorcycle operation, he represented Zoller in England.

The undertaking was financed by Cecil Allerhead Birkin, brother of the famous Bentley racing driver, 'Tim' Birkin. The head engineer, George Patchett, came to McEvoy from Brough Superior. All three – McEvoy, Birkin and Patchett – were enthusiastic competitors in their own right: George Patchett rode a

Racing McEvoys, like this 1926 machine, followed the vintage tradition of putting a very large, powerful engine into a small frame.

supercharged 996cc McEvoy-JAP in the 1926–27 season, and in 1927 Birkin died in an accident while practising for the TT. His death led, ultimately, to the factory's demise, for he was the money man.

Even so, before the factory closed down, McEvoy built prototypes of what would have been true McEvoy engines, including a 346cc three-valve,

MEGOLA

AROUND 2000 OF THESE wildly improbable machines were made by the Megola Motoren Aktiengesellschaft of Munich, founded in 1921. The firm took its name from the first two letters of the surnames of the founding partners: Teilhaber Meixer, Fritz Cockerell, who spelled his name Gockerell for this application, and a Herr Landgraf. Before the latter joined, Meixer and Cockerell had previously founded Mego in 1920.

The five-cylinder radial had a bore and stroke of 52x60mm, for a total swept volume of 637cc. Initial power output was around 6–8bhp, though up to 14bhp was coaxed out of it later, at up to

The Megola's engine layout is very clear from this picture, as is the front stand – the only way to keep the engine running when the machine was at a standstill.

4800rpm. This was reduced by fixed-ratio planetary gearing, with no clutch or other gearbox, to a maximum of 800rpm at the front wheel: 'gear' ratios could be altered by changing the size of the front wheel. Starting was 'push and go', although it was apparently also feasible to put the machine on the front wheel stand, kick it over, using the spokes of the front wheel, and then ride off rather smartly after easing the motorcycle off its stand.

To ease maintenance – decarbonisation was often needed after as little as 2000–3000km (1000–2000 miles) – the cylinders could be removed with the spokes of the front wheel in place. Convenience was further continued by the use of butt-ended Dunlop-type inner tubes; the inner tube could be replaced without having to remove the wheel. An auxiliary petrol tank beside the front fork supplied fuel to the carburettor, which was opposite the magneto: it was filled by means of a pump from a larger,

more conventionally placed petrol tank.

The front fork was leaf sprung, and some models also had half-elliptic rear springs. The actual frame was welded and riveted pressed-steel, with bucket seats on tourers and saddles on sports models, which had rather more swooping lines.

'Sport' versions of the Megola can be distinguished at a glance by their conventional saddles, as compared with the miniature car seat on the other models.

Strange as it may seem, Megola enjoyed considerable sporting success with the works team of Baunhofer, Stelzer and Tommasi.

MEGURO

JAPAN 1937–64

THE MEGURO COMPANY began trading in 1924, its purpose being to manufacture components for automobile and motorcycle industries.

Meguro joined the ranks of the world's motorcycle producers during 1937 when it began building the 498cc overhead-valve, Z-97 single-cylinder model. This was very much a British-type design, with long-stroke bore and stroke dimensions.

Together with Rikuo, Asahi and Cabton, Meguro built motorcycles for the Japanese armed forces during World War II.

After the end of the conflict, Meguro continued its policy of building British-like machines, using either overhead-valve single or overhead-valve parallel-twin engines ranging from 248 to 651cc, the latter an obvious copy of the BSA A10 design.

Meguro also had close links with the giant Kawasaki Heavy Industries, which at that time was not building complete motorcycles

Based on the BSA A10 Golden Flash, Meguro built this 650cc Senior during the late 1950s. The firm later merged with Kawasaki.

but was instead supplying engine assemblies to other companies, including Meguro.

In late 1960, Meguro became officially affiliated to Kawasaki Aircraft. This bond was strengthened in 1961 when there was a further move to merge Meguro and Kawasaki into one

corporate industry with its financial headquarters in Tokyo. In mid-1961, Kawasaki Auto Sales was created, and then in 1962 Meguro motorcycles were pushed on to both the domestic and export market, whilst Kawasaki's first indigenous model, the 124cc B8, a single-cylinder, two-stroke, went

on sale. This leaned heavily on Meguro for much of its design.

The Meguro name lasted until 1964, at which time Kawasaki was becoming established in its own right as a bike builder. Even so, Kawasaki's first attempt to enter the big league came with the W1, a 624cc (74x72.66mm) development of the inherited Meguro, which itself was a close copy of the British BSA pre-unit A10 series. Kawasaki was still offering developments of this model for sale as late as the early 1970s.

MERAY

HUNGARY 1921–44

AT ONE TIME MERAY was the leading Hungarian make but after World War II the motorcycle industry in Hungary was nationalised and a number of firms created as a state-owned industry which replaced Meray and some others. They were based in Budapest and produced a good solid line of models which ranged in size from 175 right up to 1000cc.

In general, Meray bought their engines from other specialist firms, and also no doubt the gearboxes, along with other parts such as dynamos, lights and other electric items. They also bought in hubs and chains and thus, they were assemblers to a great extent rather than manufacturers, although they would have manufactured some items themselves.

Villiers, Blackburne and JAP motors came from Britain along with Puch from Austria and Moto-Rêve from Switzerland, or that firm's British factory. The Villiers were two-stroke units with flywheel magnetos but the others had side- or overhead-valves, both with magneto ignition. The cycle side was conventional with chain drive to a separate gearbox and chain final drive. Frames were mostly tubular in the diamond form, but sometimes cradle. All had girder forks, wire wheels and drum brakes by the end of the decade.

During the mid-1930s Meray produced their own single-cylinder four-stroke engines in 346 and 496cc capacities. These were similar to those they were already using, and took them on to the end of the decade and during World War II to 1944.

MERKEL

USA 1902–15

The Merkel, such as this V-twin version, was always an advanced and well-made machine. From around 1909, it became known as the Flying Merkel.

THE FIRST MERKEL was based on a standard bicycle with the frame braced above the bottom bracket by an added tube. The small F-head engine was mounted above this tube, and inclined to lie along the downtube to which it was clipped, with belt drive over a jockey pulley to the rear wheel. Its exhaust connected to the downtube with an outlet at the top of the seat tube via small holes, a method also used by other firms, with some variations.

The Merkel was built in Milwaukee, Wisconsin, and by 1903 had a loop frame with the engine inclined at first as before. Four years later, it was vertical, although this was done earlier for the racing model, which also had

the engine set well forward. Rear suspension appeared in 1906; this was the pivoted-fork type with the springs within the upper tubes in monoshock style. However, the front fork stayed rigid.

In 1908, the firm was taken over by the Light Manufacturing & Foundry Company, which moved Merkel production to its plant in Pottstown, Pennsylvania. Most of the 1909 line was based on the belt-driven Merkel, with some machines badged as Merkel-Light. The one Light model to remain continued with its Thor-type engine, which was made by Aurora under licence from Indian, but still had an automatic inlet valve. This type of arrangement – whereby different makes used the same engines made by other firms under licence – was common in the USA before World War I and did give rise to some confusion, as some makes were identical in all but the badge on the tank.

It was during 1909 that the Flying Merkel name came into use in company advertising and the restructured company diverted considerable resources into racing for publicity. This enabled it to hire skilled riders and, before long, it was competing with the dominant Indian machines on the board tracks, even setting records.

MM
ITALY 1924–57

THE BOLOGNA BASED MM marque, the initials standing for the co-founders Mario Mazzetti and Alfonso Morini, began trading in 1924 with the launch of a neat little 125cc two-stroke racing model.

This two-speed unit-construction device was raced by Morini, who was not only one of the company's owners, but also its first official works rider. Racing success was not immediate, but in September 1927, the 125 MM caused a sensation when it won its class at the Italian GP held at the Monza circuit.

After 1930, the 125cc category was less important following a change to the Italian Highway Code, and MM switched its attention from two-strokes to four-strokes. It was not long before the first of these new models, a 175cc overhead-valve, became popular and was followed by a sports version which had chain-driven overhead-cam.

A 1926 MM Corsa (Racer) 123cc (52x58mm) two-stroke single with horizontal cylinder, magneto ignition and side-mounted carburettor.

An MM (Mazzetti Morini) 125cc two-stroke racer of the type used by Alfonso Morini to win the Italian GP in 1927. Note the riding position for the straights.

During the early 1930s MM, along with virtually every other company in the industrial world, had to cope with the Great Depression. Even so it still managed to produce new road and racing models with chain-driven overhead-cam engines, ranging from 174 to 344cc. The chain drive remained a feature of many MM designs right up to the 1950s.

In December 1936, MM factory rider Luigi Bonazzi broke a number of world records on the Florence-Pisa autostrada with the 344cc model. Whilst in circuit racing, Bonazzi, together with Dorini Serafina and others, enjoyed considerable success.

In 1937, Alfonso Morini quit MM to set up his own business (Moto Morini).

During World War II, MM suffered enormously at the hands of Allied bombing and, by 1945, little remained of the original works. Somehow Mazzetti managed to restart production against tremendous odds.

The first new bikes arrived in 1947, and were in the 350 and 500cc classes, being simply updated pre-war designs. By 1950, the 350cc had telescopic forks and plunger rear suspension. Sadly, however, MM could never recapture its pre-war glory and it finally closed in 1957.

MOLARONI
ITALY 1921–27

THIS WAS ANOTHER Italian firm founded by brothers after World War I, but it was not one destined to survive the decade. Molaroni was based in Pesaro, and its first models had two-stroke engines, one a 300cc single mounted vertically and the other a 600cc flat twin set along the frame. The twin was based on the same bore and stroke as the single, so it was effectively a double using a common crankcase. Both engines had magneto ignition using a Bosch instrument and a semi-automatic lubrication system. Otherwise, the machines were typical of the times, with a rigid frame, sprung forks and all-chain drive.

In time, the 300cc single was revised and improved, and was soon to be joined by a 345cc model, which was essentially the 300cc, bored out but retaining the existing stroke. In order to extend the range a little, the two-strokes were, in due course, joined by four-strokes using Blackburne engines imported from Britain.

Of these, the 350cc unit was the main choice but others, with side- or overhead-valves, were also used. The design of all the models,

featuring a separate gearbox, all-chain drive, girder forks and drum brakes in wire wheels, was one commonly seen in this era.

Electric lighting arrived only gradually; many machines were sold without lights, which came as extra and were usually powered by

acetylene, not battery. This was hardly a range to make much of a mark, so it was no surprise when it came off the market.

MONARK

THE FIRM THAT INTRODUCED the Monark name made its first motorcycle in 1913, and between 1920 and 1925 built lightweight machines under the Esse banner. In 1927, the Monark name was adopted and a range of bikes was introduced using Blackburne 250 and 600cc side-valve and overhead-valve singles. By the mid-1930s, Monark had turned its attention to the moped market, turning out motorised bicycles powered by 98cc Ilo two-stroke engines. During World War II, the company supplied the (neutral) Swedish military with motorcycles fitted with 500cc Albin overhead-valve, four-stroke engines. Based on a design by Husqvarna, they were assembled by Monark. After the war production reverted to Ilo-powered 50 and 250cc machines. Monark soon became the country's biggest producer. The 1959 World Motocross Championship was won by a Monark scramble bike with a 500cc Albin engine, the only Monark four-stroke machine after 1945. The same Albin engine and Monark frame provided the inspiration for the short-lived Lito motocross bikes of the early 1960s. In 1960, Monark took over the old Nymans Verkstäder firm, responsible for assembling the Royal Enfield Bullet in Sweden as an NV. Monark also gained control of the Crescent and Apollo firms in the

This 125cc single-cylinder racer of 1973 was typical of Monark's production philosophy, being lightweight with a small engine.

Above: Among the Monark factory racing bikes in the early 1970s was this 500cc three-cylinder prototype, in action in 1973.

NV takeover, restructuring them as Monark Crescent Bolagen or MCB. Monark's production bikes of the 1960s and 1970s were two-stroke lightweights, with Sachs and Morini engines from 50 to 175cc. As well as off-road models, the company came out with its own works road-racing machines in the early 1970s, but poor sales brought about its demise in 1975.

MONDIAL

THE MONDIAL STORY began back in 1929 when four brothers (Carlo, Ettore, Giuseppe and Luigi) founded the FB (Fratelli Bosselli – Brothers Bosselli) dealership in Milan, initially to sell GD two-strokes and, later, CM four-strokes. One of the Bosselli brothers, Giuseppe, gained fame by riding a CM to win a gold medal in the

1935 ISDT. By 1936, FB had acquired an industrial workshop in Bologna and began to manufacture three-wheel delivery trucks, including a model powered by a 600cc long-stroke engine.

When war came to Italy in June 1940, FB was allowed to continue production of the trucks, but this was ended forcibly in 1944 when

the retreating German forces razed the site before fleeing the area in the face of the Allied advance. Even so, one of the brothers, Giuseppe, who had won the ISDT Gold, realised that there would be a need for basic transport in a shattered, postwar Italy. Having recently inherited his father's title of Count, he set up new

production facilities in Milan, capital of the commercial and industrial north.

Like his fellow nobleman, Count Agusta, Giuseppe Bosselli appreciated the wide publicity to be gained from going racing. Consequently, the first model of the new marque, FB Mondial, was to be produced as a double

overhead-cam, single-cylinder racing machine.

Designed by Ing. Alfonso Drusiani, this machine was to gain Mondial worldwide acclaim, winning the first three 125cc world road-racing championship titles to be staged (1949, 1950 and 1951). It not only set a new trend, but also became a legend in the process.

A single-overhead-cam version was built in small numbers for sale to private customers, but it had neither the speed nor the power of the works machines.

The success in racing also helped the development of the series production roadster models. At the 1951 Milan Show, a new 200cc overhead-valve motorcycle took pride of place on Mondial's stand. This became a vital part of the company's history, as it formed the basis for a whole series of pushrod-engined models that were to follow.

At the same exhibition came an updated version of Mondial's first street bike, a 125cc overhead-valve model based on the racer and 125 and 160cc utility two-strokes.

The 1952 Milan Show saw not only a new version of the 200 motorcycle, but Mondial's first scooter. This used an adaptation of

A high compression 125 Sport of 1951. Developed from the standard Roadster model, it was faster, but still featured pushrod operated valves, instead of the racer sohc.

the recently released 160cc two-stroke, four-speed, unit-construction engine. On the scooter version of this engine, the symmetrical, pear-shape crankcase covers that enclosed the primary transmission, generator and starter motor for the electric start (not employed in the motorcycle versions) extended to the rear and formed the swinging-arm pivot fork. Therefore, the engine, transmission and rear wheel comprised a sub-assembly pivoting under the control of the two rear shock absorbers. A duplex frame was made up of tubes welded at the joints, and steel pressings were employed for the weather shield, floor and partial rear enclosure. But even though it was technically advanced, the Mondial scooter was to suffer the same fate as Ducati's Cruiser,

FB Mondial's first street bike – a 125cc ohv single-cylinder model – made its debut in 1949. It featured blade-type forks and plunger rear suspension.

which was introduced at the same time: both were too heavy and expensive to appeal to the general public.

In the mid-1950s, Mondial had considerable success in the long-distance road events of the day, such as the Milano-Taranto and Giro d'Italia. In the latter event, Remo Venturi won the race outright in 1954 on a 175 overhead-cam Sport.

Ing. Drusiani built several new racing models around the same time, including a technically advanced 149cc (53x56mm) double overhead-cam twin, but this was to prove uncompetitive

By 1953, Mondial customers could buy this very neat 175cc ohc single, which featured telescopic front forks and swinging arm rear suspension.

chromed fittings and bright colours, was clearly aimed at the teenage market.

From 1960 onwards, Count Bosselli gradually retired to his seaside retreat, leaving the business in the hands of his nephew – and it was he, in fact, who was to preside over the gradual decline of the once-great company during the 1960s and 1970s.

Highlights of this period came with a renewed racing effort in the shape of RS125 and 250cc two-strokes designed and ridden by Francesco Villa between 1963 and 1965; and the use of German Sachs engines for the final production models from the mid-1970s, including the excellent seven-speed V778 enduro. But these final years had been difficult and Mondial shut its doors for the final time on 31 December 1979.

However, with the help of the Villa brothers the marque returned in late 1987. Its range included off-road vehicles, a super-sports 125 and a Grand Prix 125 racer but the venture failed in 1989.

due to its weight. Instead, it was down to a pair of new singles to bring back the glory days.

1957 was perhaps Mondial's greatest ever year. With a seven-speed 125 (still a single) and a brand new 249.1cc (75x56.4mm) double-overhead-cam single – with a choice of five, six or seven gears – and 220kph (137mph) maximum speed, Mondial won

A 1956 Sport Lusso model. This was both cheaper to build and buy than the four-stroke FB Mondial roadsters, while still offering many of their virtues.

both world titles. In the smaller class Tarquinio Provini was triumphant, while Englishman Cecil Sandford took the 250cc crown.

But after all the glory, Mondial, together with Gilera and Moto Guzzi, announced its retirement from Grand Prix racing towards the end of 1957. This withdrawal came because of failing motorcycle sales throughout Italy and abroad, as the small car began to replace the motorcycle as the favoured form of family transport.

Unlike many, Mondial survived the initial downturn in sales and

went on to build a whole series of either overhead-valve or two-stroke models up to 250cc. There was even a 75cc scooter named Lady which, with its many

Right: The famous FB (Fratelli Bosselli) Mondial logo. The firm had the honour of winning the first three 125cc World Championships (1949, 1950 and 1951).

Below: Cecil Sandford's championship-winning 249.1cc dohc single FB Mondial GP racer. Riders had a choice of five, six or seven gears.

MONDIAL 125 GRAND PRIX   1949

FB Mondial had the honour of winning the first ever 125cc road racing world championship title in 1949; in fact, the marque retained the title in 1950 and was to do the same again in 1951.

The motorcycle which achieved these feats was, for its day, a revolutionary design. It had been created by Alfonso Drusiani, who was the brother of Oreste Drusiani, chief designer and co-founder of the CM company.

When it made its debut in 1948, its double overhead-camshafts were almost unheard of in such a small-capacity engine. Nevertheless, in a field previously dominated by the two-stroke, the double-overhead-cam Mondial simply blitzed the opposition, which even included the famed likes of MV Agusta and Moto Morini.

The drive to the camshafts was by vertical shaft and bevel gears on the offside of the cylinder, while the 80-degree inclined valves employed exposed hairpin springs. Both cylinder and head were in aluminium, with an authentic liner and steel valve seats. Primary drive to the four-

The FB Mondial dohc 125 GP single used by Carlo Ubbiali to win the world championship title in 1951. It produced 16bhp at 12,000rpm.

speed, close-ratio gearbox was by straight-cut gears in unit with the engine. Running on a 9.7:1 compression ratio – the maximum possible with the 80-octane fuel available in those days – the 123.5cc (53x56mm) engine gave almost 11bhp at 8600rpm. At that time, the most its two-stroke opposition was able to put out was no more than 10bhp.

Factory boss Count Giuseppe Bosselli and its creator Drusiani saw the new machine roar to triumph when it made its debut at the 1948 Italian GP, ridden by former Italian 500cc champion Francesco Lama.

A month later, and still unstreamlined, the same bike was used by 'The Flying Monk' Gino Cavanna to break the world speed records for the 125cc flying and standing-start kilometre and mile distances, with a fastest run of 130kph (80.8mph) over the flying kilometre.

With the power upped to 13bhp at 9500rpm, and a top speed of 145kph (90mph), the Mondial cruised to victory in every race it contested in 1949, including the 125cc world title with Alberto Pagani at the controls.

Meanwhile Cavanna, now with streamlining, hoisted his flying kilometre record to over 161kph (100mph).

By 1951, the jewel-like double overhead-cam, single-cylinder engine was putting out a heady 16bhp at 12,000rpm for its final championship year. And although it was outpaced from then onwards by MV and NSU, the little Mondial has the distinction of being not only a triple 125cc world champion, but also the distinction of being the first ever machine to hold the coveted crown.

Engine: 123.5cc double overhead cam, 2v single, 53x56mm, air-cooled
Power: 13bhp at 9500rpm
Gearbox: 4-speed foot change
Final drive: chain
Weight: 98kg (216lb)
Top speed: 163kph (102mph)

MELDI
Italy 1927–37: These machines were racers which were powered by JAP and Rudge Python engines of capacities of 250, 350 and 500cc.

MEMINI
Italy 1946–47: In-house, 175cc two-strokes sustained this Italian undertaking, which was also known by the name Memini Electra.

MENON
Italy (Veneto) 1930–32: This bicycle factory was founded in 1875 but did not make motorcycles until much later. JAP singles powered its 175 and 200cc machines.

MENOS
Germany (Berlin) 1922–23: This was a fully enclosed machine powered by a 618cc water-cooled flat twin. It was very similar to the Aristos (see above).

MERCER
England 1961: A.C. Mercer built a two-stroke, six-cylinder radial that appears to have found no commercial takers.

MERCIER
France 1950–62: This company made lightweight and mini-scooters which were fitted with Ydral and Villiers engines of 100 to 175cc, as well as manufacturing Lavalette-powered mopeds.

MERCO
Germany (Berlin) 1922–24: This company (full name Mercur-Motoren-GmbH) made 150 and 200cc two-strokes with in-house engines.

MERCURY
England (Dudley) 1956–58: This firm produced mopeds and scooters which were fitted with Villiers engines of 50 to 100cc. Model names were eclectic and included Dolphin, Whippet, Hermes and Pippin.

MONDIAL CONSTELLATION 200

1953

The first Mondial with a 200 engine made its debut in late 1951. Unlike the same company's Grand Prix racers, it had pushrods rather than double overhead-cams.

A year later at the 1952 Milan Show, came a new 198cc (62x66mm) single, still with overhead-valve. Very much a tourer, the unit-construction engine produced 12bhp at 6000rpm.

An unusual feature of the design was the forward-operating kick-starter on the offside of the engine which, together with the traditional

Italian heel-and-toe gear lever of the period, gave that side of the engine a rather cluttered appearance. In contrast, the nearside of the power unit, with its round cover (hiding a large, outside-crankcase flywheel) was almost spartan.

The frame was a neat double-cradle affair with swinging-arm rear suspension and, at the front, oil-damped telescopic forks.

Named the Constellation, the Mondial used wet-sump lubrication, battery/coil ignition, a

dual seat and fully enclosed suspension. The engine was of all-alloy construction, and the mudguarding comprehensive. The handlebar bend was most definitely for comfort rather than for wind cheating but with the maximum speed limited to around 105kph (65mph), performance was not a priority consideration. Instead, the purpose of the Constellation was to provide its owner with a stylish commuter mount, with the benefit of a frugal thirst.

In contrast to many famous racing names – Ducati, MV Agusta, Gilera and Moto Guzzi – Mondial's production figures were always low; but there is no doubting the excellent quality of its build compared to many rivals.

Engine: 198cc ohv, 3v single, 62x66mm (2.4x2.6ins), air-cooled
Power: 12bhp at 6000rpm
Gearbox: 4-speed foot change
Final drive: chain
Weight: 112kg (146lb)
Top speed: 104kph (65mph)

MONET-GOYON

FRANCE 1917–59

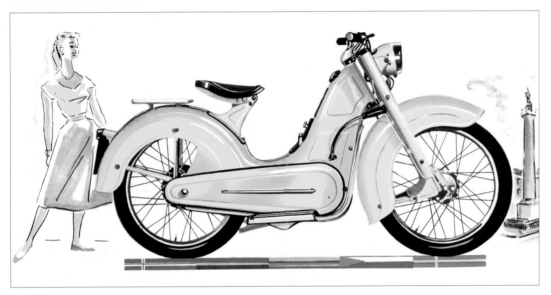

Monet-Goyon produced this Starlett scooter from 1953, using a Villiers 99cc engine with two speeds, under the extensive modern-looking enclosure.

THIS WAS AN INTERESTING firm that used Villiers and MAG engines for many years although it began with the Wall Auto Wheel, an attachment complete with engine that could be fitted to the side of the rear wheel of a standard bicycle. After World War I, the company produced a tricycle that employed a similar concept, with the four-stroke engine mounted in-board of the right rear disc wheel, while the left rear wheel was connected to the pedalling gear.

Built for war invalids, the tricycle had a wicker basket-seat, a bicycle front end and, later, a 147cc Villiers two-stroke engine.

Villiers two-stroke engines were commonly used by Monet-Goyon for their machines but some models were fitted with side-valve MAG units.

The same engine was also used for a scooter-type machine and a lightweight with direct belt drive and rocking front fork, which was soon joined by others with 172, 247 and 343cc Villiers engines with flywheel-magneto ignition and two or three speeds. In time, they all had chain drive and girder forks. The scooter was known as the Vélauto, and a Super version used the 269cc Villiers engine.

From 1926, Monet-Goyon added four-strokes with MAG engines of 346 and 496cc, with either overhead-valves or inlet overhead only and side exhaust. In the early 1930s, it built its own 350cc side-valve engine, one that continued in use for over two decades. There were also overhead-cam single engines, but these were Kœhler-Escoffier units, a firm taken over by Monet-Goyon in 1929. This engine was inclined forward with the camshaft driven by shaft and bevels on the right, while the magneto, which went behind the cylinder, was chain driven from the left end of the crankshaft. These engines were used only by the works.

The range for the 1930s continued to run from 147cc two-strokes to 500cc four-strokes, the latter with side- or overhead-valves. Two-, three- or four-speed gearboxes were employed and the models had girder forks and saddle tanks. For 1932, a velomoteur was added with a 100cc two-stroke engine mounted low down in an open frame with girder forks, and this was soon joined by a range of 100cc motorcycles based on the same power unit.

After World War II, the firm continued to use Villiers engines for its lightweight range, having built them under licence from the mid-1930s, and continued with the 350cc four-stroke in side-valve and overhead-valve forms.

In the 1950s, the Starlette scooter was added, featuring full enclosure and a 99cc Villiers engine, while 1956 saw the arrival of the Pullman 125. This had a 122cc Villiers engine, a three-speed gearbox which hung from a spine frame with telescopic front forks and monoshock rear suspension. The mechanics were well enclosed with panels on each side that just left the crankcase and part of the rear wheel open, while the front of the engine had a grill around it. The result was very stylish.

However, even this impressive machine failed to see Monet-Goyon through to the next decade, the 1960s.

MONTESA

SPAIN 1945–

ONE OF THE BEST-KNOWN producers of trials bikes internationally, Montesa was founded in Barcelona in 1945 by Francisco Bulto and Pedro Permanyer. Surprisingly, perhaps, only one notable Spanish marque was in production prior to Montesa, and that was Sanglas, which had been building heavy police bikes from 1942, and which was taken over by Yamaha in 1981.

Montesa's first offering was a 98cc two-stroke, which was followed in 1946 by a 125cc machine, both machines being used in trials competitions from the outset. Perhaps because so much of its landscape is ideally suited to bikes, Spain has spawned more specialist trials manufacturers than any other country, with Ossa, Bultaco, Merlin, Gas Gas, Mecatecno and Mototrans all contributing to a thriving market.

Francisco Bulto went his own way in 1958 to set up Bultaco (his son Ignazio was co-founder of Merlin in 1982), but Montesa carried on making off-road

From the outset, the company's production was intended primarily for trials use, though it also made machines for the road racing market.

machines powered by its own 123cc two-stroke engines.

In 1962, the company released the 175cc Impala, which proved to be one of the most successful and long-lived machines to emerge from Spain. So much so, in fact, that it spawned a racing version and a 250cc-engined model. At the same time, Montesa was building road-going two-strokes from 49 to 349cc.

In 1968, Montesa emulated Bultaco's Sherpa by coming out with the 250cc Cota trials machine which, together with its rival, dominated the market niche.

In 1973, the six-speed Cota 172 was launched; this was effectively a large-bore version of the Cota 123 and, although it was a competent off-road bike, the power delivery from its single-cylinder 158cc engine turned out not to be suitable for serious trials competition.

By the late 1970s, the market had crumbled, and the reintroduction of the Impala in 1981 coincided with the take-over of the company by Honda. Although this take-over ensured the company's survival, albeit as a Honda assembly plant for small-capacity bikes, the Montesa range itself was limited to just one trials machine, the Cota. This was a formidable-looking bike, and was very much state of the art for its time.

The mainstay of Montesa's road-going production during the 1960s and 1970s was the 175cc two-stroke Impala, one of Spain's most enduring motorcycles.

MONTESA COTA

Very much a trials competition bike, with no pretensions to road-going, the 1990s Montesa Cota was based on a Verlicchi twin-beam chassis made up of welded aluminium forgings and extrusions. Front forks were upside down tele-scopics, and the rear suspension was by single damper and rising-rate linkage. Disc brakes were fitted front and rear. The frame, ending in an extended rear mudguard, was topped by a fuel tank and a seat of the lowest possible profile. Beneath the mudguard was the silencer for the water-cooled 258cc single-cylinder

engine. This unit construction motor was allied to a six-speed transmission. Its all-up weight of 83kg (183lb) reflected its agility.

Engine: 258cc single-cylinder water-cooled
Gearbox: 6-speed, foot change
Final drive: chain
Weight: 83kg (183lb)
Top speed: 145kph (90mph)

A masterpiece of minimalist engineering, the Cota 304 exemplified the trials bike of the late 1980s, being compact, robust and relatively lightweight.

MONTGOMERY

MONTGOMERY WAS AN early maker of side-cars from 1904, and while it concentrated on these, it added motorcycles to offer complete outfits for some years. They were built initially in Bury St. Edmund's, Suffolk, and the 1905 model had a 5hp V-twin engine and a wicker-work side-car body. The side-car could be detached in two minutes, it was claimed, while the connections to the machine were flexible on some models to allow them to bank for corners. In one advertisement, Montgomery showed a machine with a side-car fitted on each side of the motorcycle, supposedly one for the wife, and the other for the two children.

For some years, Montgomery continued to list machines to suit its core business of side-cars. By 1911 it had moved to Coventry and machines were bought in or built up using bought-in parts in the firm's frame.

In 1913, the firm introduced a motorcycle fitted with a Coventry Victor 689cc flat-twin engine and intended for side-car use. Its unusual transmission was by direct belt to a three-speed rear hub, but taken from a large pulley mounted on the camshaft. For the other machines, the frame had duplex members around the engine and

The Montgomery Greyhound was fitted with a 677cc ohv JAP engine. Initially, it was only built for 1931, but returned to the company's range for 1933 and 1934.

Montgomery adopted the fashion of the time for inclined engines. This 1929 model was fitted with a 346cc ohv JAP engine and three-speed gearbox.

was fitted with Biflex forks. For 1915, the engine became 708cc but the other features remained.

After the war, the firm built a range of models, from a 147cc two-stroke to a 996cc V-twin in various forms, some aimed at the side-car market and most with three speeds and chain drive. It also built a proprietary front fork with leaf springing for its own big twins and sold it to others such as Brough-Superior and Coventry-Eagle. After modest entries in the TT, bought-in overhead-valve engines were used from such firms as JAP or Anzani.

Late in 1925, the works went up in flames, disrupting production for some time. The firm produced the same lines into the 1930s with Villiers or JAP engines. The range size varied; many models had canine names (Greyhound, Terrier, Retriever, Bulldog). The four-strokes ran from 247 to 994cc with side- or overhead-valve, and the machines progressed through saddle tanks and foot change in line with the rest of the industry. The two-strokes, from 98cc to 247cc, were simpler and fulfilled a need, but World War II brought production of the 1940 range to an end. It was never to restart.

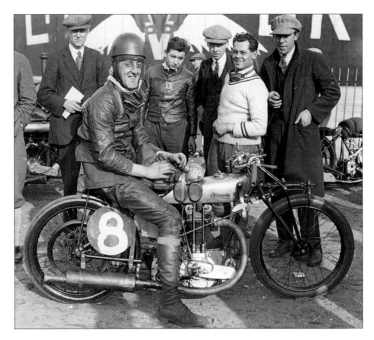

A 490cc JAP-engined Montgomery after winning a one-lap sprint race in 1924. It completed the course at an impressive average speed of 125.5kph (78.4mph).

MORBIDELLI

ITALY 1968–

BORN IN 1938, Giancarlo Morbidelli grew up with a great passion for motorcycles, racing in particular. His teenage years were spent in the 1950s, the golden years of the Italian motorcycle industry and its racing teams.

During the 1960s, the young Morbidelli built up a thriving woodworking machinery factory in his home town of Pesaro on the Adriatic coast, a short distance from the Benelli works.

A combination of enthusiasm, finance and the desire to gain publicity for his business saw Giancarlo Morbidelli join the ranks of racing entrants in 1968 when he entered a modified Benelli 60 and a Motobi that Luciano Mele used to win the Italian Junior title.

From this relatively small beginning rose a team that went on to win a total of six world championships during the 1970s.

The first all-Morbidelli machine came into being when, in late 1968, he decided to build a brand-new 50cc racer with the help of Franco Ringhini, who had recently left the Guazzoni factory. Raced in 1969, the machine featured a single-cylinder 49.8cc

(40x39.8mm) two-stroke engine with disc-valve induction and liquid-cooling. The following year, again with Ringhini, a 125cc-class machine was built (121cc, 44.4x39.8mm). Once again there was the same formula of disc-valve induction and liquid-cooling. Both machines also featured six speeds.

Most of the next few months were spent with development and race testing. Then, in 1972, Gilberto Parlotti shook the racing world by not only finishing in each of the first four rounds of the world championship series, but in the process also scoring two victories, namely a second and a third.

The next round was in the Isle of Man, which at that time still counted towards the Championship. Leading the race in extremely wet conditions, the 34-year-old motorcycle dealer from Trieste lost control of his Morbidelli and was killed instantly.

The accident was to have profound consequences within the Morbidelli team and for racing as a whole. Parlotti had been secretly testing a new four-cylinder 350cc model, which was then scrapped; only much later did another Morbidelli four-cylinder make an appearance. Parlotti's death led to the demise of the Isle of Man as a world-championship venue.

Gilberto Parlotti won the first four rounds of the 1972 125cc World Championship on his Morbidelli twin, before being fatally injured in the Isle of Man TT.

It was not until 1974 that Morbidelli finally recovered from Parlotti's death and, with a new engineer, Jorg Moller, and a new rider, Paolo Pileri, the team finished runners-up in the 125cc title race. Moller's new twin, still with disc-valves, put out 42bhp at 14,200rpm.

This was to be the beginning of a period of huge success, at first by Pileri winning the 1975 championship title. This brought demands from private owners for replicas, so a new factory was built by entering into a joint agreement with Benelli Armi (the gun-manufacturing company owned by the Benelli family). These machines were sold as Morbidelli-Benelli Armi (MBA). The customer racer was virtually a replica of the works bikes, but the engines were not quite so highly tuned (giving around 5bhp less).

It was team-mate Pier-Paolo Bianchi's turn to be champion in 1976 and, by 1977, more than half the grid of any 125 GP was Morbidelli (or MBA) mounted. By the end of the year Bianchi was the title-holder once more. Moreover, Morbidelli also took the 250cc title, thanks to the consistent riding of Mario Lega. The latter machine had first appeared midway through 1976 when,

ridden by Pileri, it had finished runner-up to Walter Villa's Harley-Davidson. The 249.7cc (56x50.7mm) twin followed the familiar Morbidelli lines with liquid-cooling, disc-valves and six speeds.

Although Eugenio Lazzarini became the new 125cc world champion in 1978 (now entered as an MBA), the team's fortunes had begun to wane, with new 350 and 500cc four-cylinder models never being able to match the performances of their smaller brothers. The 125 MBA production racer continued in production until the late 1980s when the FIM brought out a singles-only formula for the class.

Later, in 1994, Morbidelli introduced a new de luxe touring motorcycle with an 850cc V8 engine and shaft final drive. But a massive price tag and a boring styling job by Pininfarina, which ensured that customer demand was almost zero, conspired to wreck its chances in the showroom. Even a re-design by Bimota could do nothing to help.

In 1994, Morbidelli introduced a deluxe touring 850cc V8, with styling by Pininfarina. This is the revised version restyled by Bimota; both were to prove unsuccessful.

MOTOBÉCANE (MOTOCONFORT) FRANCE 1922–84

THIS WAS THE LARGEST French manufacturer for many years and is remembered for its line of reliable, sensible machines and the long-running Mobylette moped, which were sometimes sold as Motoconfort and listed under that name. Founded by Abel Bardin and Charles Benoît, the company's first prototype was built in 1922 and went into production two years later. Right from the start, Motobécane showed that high-volume production of a simple machine was the way to stay in business and turn a decent profit.

That first model had a 175cc two-stroke engine with a chain-driven magneto for the ignition, a forward-facing carburettor fitted to a manifold that curved round to

One of the fine singles range produced by Motobécane during the 1930s, the 500cc ohv model with unit construction, launched in 1934.

the right side of the barrel, sparking plug in the rear of the cylinder head and a decompressor in the front. It drove the rear wheel by belt and went into a simple loop frame that was available in two forms to suit 'ladies' as well as 'gentlemen', and had a rocking front fork. The company had sold 150,000 of them by 1929. Things changed little until 1928 when the range was extended to include more – and better – versions plus larger models. Also, four-stroke machines with 348 and 495cc Blackburne side- and overhead-valve engines were added.

For 1930, a much more complex model appeared with a 500cc, in-line, four-cylinder, side-valve engine built in unit with the gearbox. It had shaft drive, went into a substantial frame and was much revised for 1931 with a 750cc, overhead-camshaft, four-cylinder engine when it was listed as a Motoconfort. Production of the four-stroke was very limited and confirmed that small, cheap and plentiful was definitely the better business option. Throughout the 1930s, the firm built a fine range of singles that, from 1931, included a velomoteur, while its technical advances included four-valve heads and unit construction. After World War II, the range picked up again with four-strokes with telescopic forks and plunger rear suspension.

The important postwar model was the Mobylette moped of 1949 with its simple 50cc two-stroke engine with belt and chain drive. The first model had the most basic specification but other versions followed, with features such as automatic clutch, automatic variable gear ratio, telescopic front forks, plunger rear suspension, pivoted-fork rear suspension and better brakes being introduced in various combinations. Even so, the basic 50cc always held its place on the list for the market's lower end.

Above: An LT3 from the 1970s, with a 125cc twin-cylinder, two-stroke engine, five speeds, spine frame, full suspension and, later, a disc front brake.

Below: The Mobylette moped, first seen in 1949, ran for many years in a variety of basic forms. It was also built under licence outside France.

Other models came and went, while the moped just ran on. Among the other models were a vertical twin, a scooter from 1951 and, later, a 350cc two-stroke triple.

A 125cc twin developed in the 1970s eventually led to the company going racing in 1980 to take second place in the world championship. Regrettably, the recession in sales spelt an end to this run of good fortune, and not even the sales of the Mobylette could turn things around. In 1984, Motobécane sold out to Yamaha, which continued to build machines in the factory.

MEZO
Austria 1923–26: Medinger was a leading racer who (like so many other racers of that period) cashed in on his name by offering assembled machines with Villiers and JAP engines. However, production of these assembled machines was hampered by the injuries Medinger sustained in the 1924 Austrian TT.

MF
Germany (Nurnberg) 1922–25: This company, the Fahrzeugfabrik Max Fischer, offered machines powered by the 500cc BMW flat twin engine or Blackburne singles of 350 and 500cc.

MFB
Germany (Hamburg, later Munich) 1923–24: Wooden frames characterised these machines which were powered by Nabob 198cc and JAP 293cc engines. After the original firm collapsed, Hoco – based in Munich – took over production.

MFB
Italy (Bologna) 1957–64: These were mopeds and lightweights; the latter was fitted with 75 and 125cc two-stroke singles and a 175cc overhead-valve single.

MFZ
Germany (Berlin-Kopenick) 1921–28: These were excellent but unexciting machines which were fitted with in-house engines of up to 350cc. The 175 and 250cc singles from this company may have been the first German overhead-valve engines of those capacities.

MGC
France 1927–29: Ets. Marcel Guignet et Cie. used light-alloy extensively in its frames and cycle parts, and powered their machines with Chaise and JAP engines of 250, 350, 500 and 600cc.

MOTOBI   ITALY 1950–76

AT THE END OF 1949, one of the Benelli brothers, Giuseppe, left the company to form his own marque. Trading under the name Moto B Pesaro (soon shortened to Motobi), the fledgling concern debuted at the Milan Spring Fair, in April 1950.

The first model was a roadster powered by a horizontal 98cc single-cylinder, two-stroke engine, somewhat reminiscent of the German Imme design. Sales success ensured that it led to a whole series of similar models, with larger engines, with the first twin-cylinder in 1952. Known as the Spring Lasting, it was originally a 200cc unit, but was soon joined by a full-size 250cc. Both twins benefited from excellent performance, thanks to the use of rotary-valve induction, Motobi being a pioneer of the system, at least in Italy.

In June 1955, the 250cc twin, ridden by Silvano Rinandi, won its class in the Milano-Taranto race.

Then a change was made by switching to four-strokes, with a pair of 123 and 172cc singles, still with horizontal layout. Named the Catria, the larger model soon proved successful in both the showroom and on the race circuit.

In 1957, Giuseppe Benelli died. Control of the company passed to his sons, Luigi and Marco. Although the sons made peace with the rest of the family (see the Benelli entry), the two companies

A racing version of the Motobi 172cc ohv horizontal single. These machines won no less than 10 Italian Junior Championships between 1959 and 1972.

effectively joined together in 1963, Motobi kept its engineering independence for several years.

From 1959, when one of the 172cc singles won the Italian Junior Championship title, Motobi machines largely dominated the class, winning another nine championships up to their final success in 1972. Also, by boring out the cylinder to 67mm, a 203cc version was created.

The Swiss engineer, Werner Maltry, also built a number of home-brewed Motobi-based racing specials during the 1960s, including a 490cc 74x57mm, six-speed twin with which he won the national hill-climb championships.

MOTO GUZZI

ITALY 1921–

MOTO GUZZIS TEND TO be regarded by their owners in the same way that fond but intelligent parents regard wayward but loveable children: they put up with their faults, because these are far outweighed by their charms – but they recognise that the faults exist.

Of course, things have changed. No longer are nine out of 10 of the colours in the wiring-loom yellow. The panels on the faired models generally marry up pretty well, instead of being a rattling good fit. And you can no longer change the colour of the motorcycle by parking it in bright sunlight for a few days. But none of these faults has been entirely unknown on Moto Guzzis, and because they are built with passion, rather than as household appliances, they have a dimension of character that is ever rarer in the modern world. As Moto Guzzi themselves put it: 'You can measure performances,

but you have to experience sensations.'

As with many of the more traditional manufacturers, a number of models have been based on relatively few engine designs. In fact, the greatest road-going Guzzis of all have been variations on just two themes: the horizontal single and the transverse V-twin. Many people, in fact, are unaware of the company's

The flat single in military guise – this is a 1937 500cc model – was not one of the marque's greater successes from an aesthetic point of view.

Even when (relatively) cluttered, as with this 1929 racer, classic Moto Guzzi's always exhibited very clean lines. The 'flat single' was the purists' favourite.

other offerings, except in the racing field, where the famous 120 degree V-twin of 1933 and the V8 of 1955 are probably as well known as the much more successful, and far longer lived, double-knocker Norton singles.

The firm was founded by two relatively young men, Carlo Guzzi and Giorgio Parodi. Guzzi was 31 when the GP (Guzzi & Parodi) prototype was built in 1920,

The post-war two-stroke single (this machine dates from 1949) offered basic transport rather than sporting prowess but still looked good by the standards of the day.

though the name had changed to Moto Guzzi before production began in 1921. Giorgio Parodi was concerned lest the name be taken as his initials, and of course there was always the confusion of Grand Prix. A third young man, Giovanni Ravelli, had been one of the three friends who planned the new motorcycle company in the closing days of World War I, but he died in a flying accident just after the war ended; all three had met in the then new Italian Air Force. The Moto Guzzi motif of an open-winged eagle is in memory of Giovanni Ravelli.

The Normale was the first example of the first design that will forever be associated with Moto Guzzi: a 500cc over-square single, at 88x82mm for an actual 498cc, with the cylinder parallel with the ground. This 'flat single' would, with variations, be a Moto Guzzi trademark production until 1976, and the Falcone would be its apotheosis.

The other classic Moto Guzzi design is the transverse, 90-degree V-twin. This was originally designed to power a wildly improbable military vehicle, a cross between a modern three-wheeled ATV and a World War II Kettenrad. With its steering wheel, tricycle layout, and vestigial tracks on the rear wheels, it is easier to illustrate than to describe, and was nicknamed 'mulo meccanico' or

One of the greatest riders of all time (Stanley Woods) on one of the greatest bikes (the Moto Guzzi V8) at one of the greatest tracks (Monza, Italy) in 1956.

'mechanical mule'. Unlike the mule – a sterile cross between a donkey and a horse – this mechanical beast of 1960 to 1963 begat a motorcycle, the V7 of 1967, and generations of models thereafter, ranging from 350 to 1100cc.

Apart from these two designs, there have been a number of

smaller singles. The pre-war P175 of 1932 was the first road-going overhead-valve engine (the bigger singles were inlet-over-exhaust), but such had been the progress of motorcycle design that it delivered only one horsepower less than the original Normale; seven instead of eight. The PE250 (1934-39), at nine brake horsepower, was actually more powerful than the original 500cc. These were 'flat' singles, in the style of the original, and would evolve into the Egretta, Ardetta and Airone.

The other classic small single, after World War II, was the Lodola, initially (1956–58) a 175cc overhead-cam but later, (1959–66) a 235cc pushrod engine. This was the last design by

Even when their machines were more conventionally styled, like this 350, Guzzi's have almost always exhibited considerable style and flair.

Since 1967, the transverse V-twin has been a Moto Guzzi hallmark. This is a 750cc S3 from 1975. The big front discs meant that it stopped as well as it went.

(Cockerel) and the 'bargain basement' Stornello. The Galetto first appeared as a 150cc show model at Geneva in 1950 and entered production later in the same year as a 160cc 62x53mm. It grew to 175cc via a 3mm increase in bore in 1952, and again increased in capacity in 1954 via a 5mm increase in stroke.

In 1961, it was substantially re-designed and given electric starting, finally going out of production after a 15-year life span in 1965. Like the Velocette LE, which in some ways it resembled, it was an idea that failed to catch on at the time, but enjoys a cult following today. The relatively big wheels gave a far safer ride than a scooter, while the curiously mounted spare has a charm all of its own. The Stornello was introduced as a 125, but later grew to 160cc before disappearing in 1975; it was never an exciting bike, but to its credit, it did offer the Guzzi magic at a very modest price.

There was, however, a completely different strand of Moto Guzzi development after the war. In a country desperate for mechanical transport of any kind, the firm first concentrated on the tiny 64cc Guzzino, which was

Left: Styling can be a very personal matter; some people find that Moto-Guzzi's semi-scooters have the beauty that comes from form following function.

Carlo Guzzi himself, but the cylinder was inclined at 45 degrees, not 'flat', so some Guzzi purists look down their noses at it.

Actually, there were two other idiosyncratic Moto Guzzi singles deserving of classic status, the improbable-looking Galetto

Below left: The 992cc Centauro of the late 1990s was perhaps too heavily styled for the taste of the purist, but it sold well enough to the motorcycle-as-toy market.

Below: This 1996 Daytona 1000RS was a much more purposeful machine than the Centauro, though even it was a fashion victim: look at the exhausts.

later supplemented and then replaced by the Zigolo, initially 98, later 110cc. The Guzzino was not the smallest Moto Guzzi ever – it was a dubious honour shared by the 49cc Dingo lightweights and Trotter mopeds.

It is perhaps best to gloss over the badge-engineered Benellis that briefly masqueraded as Moto Guzzis after the De Tomaso take-over in 1970, although they were interesting bikes in their own right. The 125cc single may have been unremarkable, but the four-strokes – first 350, then 250cc – were fascinating.

In any case, the De Tomaso years failed to turn the company around completely, and in 1993 the management was taken over by Finprogetti, which improved matters. Then, on 14 April 2000, 79 years after the company was founded (15 March 1921), it was sold to Aprilia.

To sum up, Moto Guzzi seems, like a number of other manufacturers, to have been forced to abjure major technical

innovations such as new engines and water-cooling, in order to continue making what everyone knows it makes. Just as Harley-Davidson makes in-line V-twins and BMW makes flat twins, Moto-Guzzi makes transverse V-twins.

The extent to which these basically very old engines have been developed is remarkable, especially in the case of BMW,

Manufacturers seem endlessly willing to increase the capacity of elderly engines. This 1999 V11 Sport is around 50 percent bigger than its 1967 ancestor.

which in effect redesigned the engine completely. Nevertheless, it seems that, in many ways, we have reached 'the end of history' in this respect.

MOTO GUZZI NORMALE   1921

Although the original prototype had had a chain-driven overhead-cam and four valves, the production bike was a two-valve inlet-over-exhaust. This was before saddle tanks had become popular, so the machine looks rather old-fashioned today. It wasn't red – that would come later – but it did have the big external 'bacon slicer' flywheel that is one of the most memorable features of the classic big singles. Watching these rotate, while listening to the 'chuff-chuff-chuff' of the engine, is a hypnotic experience.

A couple of months after the company was founded, it started racing. Within half a year, at the Targa Florio, the new marque had gained the first of the 3329 victories that it would clock up before quitting racing in 1957, a case of starting as you mean to go on.

The first of them all: this 1921 Normale, with its ioe engine, dates from the very first year of production of the Moto Guzzi marque. The machine produced 8hp and could reach 80kph (50mph).

Engine: 498cc ioe single, 88x82mm, air-cooled
Power: 8bhp at 3000rpm
Gearbox: 3-speed hand change
Final drive: chain
Weight: 130kg (286lb)
Top speed: 80kph (50mph)

MOTO GUZZI GTW   1935

The Normale model gave way to the Sport 14, then the Sport 15, still inlet-over-exhaust but with over 13bhp. This was thanks to better breathing, a higher compression ratio (although it was still only 4.5:1) and, above all, more

revs: maximum power was developed at 3800rpm instead of 3000rpm.

Moto Guzzi was also very progressive in adopting rear suspension which made its debut with this model – first appearing

in 1928, with friction dampers – and foot change for the gears, with a rocking, heel-and-toe movement.

The GTW appeared in 1935, the year that a spring-frame machine first won the TT, and a model which would combine all the other

---

advances that Moto Guzzi had made with overhead-valves, for a power output that may look modest today but which was by no means bad for the time.

It was certainly sufficient to propel this light, slender machine at what, a few years before, had been racing speeds.

The other models in the same series were listed as the GTV, GTC and GTCL, these being further developed into the legendary Condor (1938), Dondolino and Gambalunga models. The Dondolino – never mind the prowess of the racing Gambalunga – was good for well over 160kph (100mph), although 170kph (106mph) is a figure commonly quoted.

Engine: 498cc ioe single, 88x82mm, air-cooled
Power: 22bhp at 4500rpm
Gearbox: 4-speed foot change
Final drive: chain
Weight: 180kg (396lb)
Top speed: 130kph (80mph)

MOTO GUZZI GUZZINI   1946

A two-stroke of any size, let alone one of 65cc (nominal) capacity, might seem somewhat infra dignitate for Moto Guzzi, but in the aftermath of World War II, there was an explosion in demand for motorised transport, and a dearth of money to pay for it. Numerous manufacturers made low-cost lightweights in an attempt to meet the demand, but few offerings were as well thought out, or as well designed, as the Guzzini.

A light-alloy head and barrel (with cast-iron liner) kept weight down, while keeping heat dissipation up. The wheels were relatively huge at 66cm (26ins), being bicycle-sized rather than motorcycle-sized. Over 200,000 were sold, and it was even possible to buy a 'big bore', four-stroke conversion kit from an after-market supplier, complete with a diminutive oil pump to replace the 20:1 petroil lubrication of the two-stroke.

The availability of this kit must have prompted the 1956 73cc, two-and-two-thirds horsepower 45x46mm version of the Cardellino, which had replaced the Guzzino in 1954: it had a strengthened frame and 59cm (20ins) wheels. Another increase in capacity, to 83cc, was made to the Cardellino in 1962, three years before production ceased.

The Guzzino/Cardolino had in any case been substantially supplanted by the 98cc 50sq.mm (0.8 sq.in) Zigolo, which first appeared in 1953. It was still a rotary-valve two-stroke but completely re-designed, in a pressed-steel frame. With 4bhp, the published top speed was 75kph (47mph). The Sport model of 1954 was good for 90kph (56mph).

The Series II Zigolo (1958) was particularly interesting for its chromed, light-alloy bores; at the same time, the petroil ratio was dropped to 50:1. A year later, for the 1960 model year, the swept volume was increased to 110cc via 2mm increases in both bore and stroke. The Zigolo survived in this form until 1966.

Engine: 64cc rotary-valve, two-stroke single, air-cooled
Power: 2bhp at 5000rpm
Gearbox: 3-speed hand change
Final drive: chain
Weight: 45kg (99lb)
Top speed: 50kph (30mph)

MOTO GUZZI FALCONE   1950

The Falcone was proof that yesterday's racer is today's road bike. At its introduction it was, to a large extent, a GTW engine in an improved, lower frame. The tank was a useful 17.5 litres (3.9 UK gallons/4.4 US gallons), and the narrow, almost flat bars were as far from the cow-horns and tillers of contemporary American heavy-weights as could be imagined.

Unexpectedly, the first variation on the Falcone was not a 'go-faster' model but a 'go-slower' model with smaller valves and carburettor, a lowered compression ratio and a lowered final drive. This reduced maximum power to just under 19bhp at 5300rpm and maximum speed to 120kph

The flat-single layout of the Falcone engine. The Falcone name survived for more than a quarter of a century and was one of Guzzi's most popular models.

(75mph), not that you would know how fast you were going, because standard fittings did not include a speedometer. This 1954 replacement for the Astore was christened the Falcone Turismo, the older Falcone having been renamed the Falcone Sport.

Astonishingly, these two distinctly vintage machines then remained substantially unchanged for almost a decade, right down to the separate magneto and dynamo and inverted brake and clutch levers. Although the Falcone Turismo was 're-launched' in 1963, it had still changed very little and was finally discontinued in 1967.

The problem was, no one except Moto Guzzi wanted to see it go, and it was more or less forced to bring it back by popular demand. As BMW was later to discover when it attempted to replace the boxer with the Brick, motorcyclists hate change, and not just the amateurs: police and the armed forces also like to stick with what they know. As a result, a substantially revised Nuovo Falcone appeared, slowly, painfully and not actually for sale to the public until 1971.

This was a very different machine, with a wet sump, a steel liner to the light-alloy barrel, fully enclosed valve gear, enclosed flywheel, much bigger and better, finned brakes (twin leading-shoe at the front), 12volt electrics – even with an electric start option – and a new frame. Power was claimed (optimistically) as 30bhp at 5000rpm and, as the Nuovo was some 15kg (33lb) heavier than its predecessor, it was hard put to get much beyond 130kph (80mph).

The net result was a machine that fell between two stools. It was functionally close enough to what the uniformed services required, but it had lost much of the vintage magic of the older machine, especially the 'bacon slicer', and the exhaust was frankly ugly. The 1974 Falcone Sahara was a bit more romantic – it was very much a civilianised version of the austere military version – but it was not even officially imported into Britain, one of the most obvious markets. The Falcone line finally ceased, for what looked like all time, in 1976.

Engine: 498cc ioe single, 88x82mm, air-cooled
Power: 23bhp at 5500rpm
Gearbox: 4-speed foot change
Final drive: chain
Weight: 180kg (396lb)
Top speed: 137kph (85mph)

MOTO GUZZI LODOLA 175

1956

The Lodola was the last of Carlo Guzzi's own designs, and occupies a slightly strange place in the Moto Guzzi pantheon. Everyone who has ever owned one is full of praises for its sweet handling and lightness (if not so enthusiastic about the electrics or the finish), but 9bhp was not particularly impressive for a 175cc overhead-cam of this vintage. This may be why, in 1959, the capacity was upped to 235cc and the expensive-to-build, chain-driven overhead-cam was replaced with more pedestrian, pushrod valve gear. Power went up to 11bhp (at 6000rpm), an increase of well over 20 per cent, which more than compensated for an increase in weight of just over 6kg (13lb).

It may also be significant that, in 1957, the year after the Lodola came out, Moto Guzzi gave up racing after more than 25 years of success. The Lodola was definitely a tourer, not a sports machine.

Engine: 175cc ohc single, 62x57.8mm, air-cooled
Power: 9bhp at 6000rpm
Gearbox: 4-speed foot change
Final drive: chain
Weight: 109kg (240lb)
Top speed: 115kph (70mph)

This is the original 175cc ohc version of the Lodola, not the later model with the technically less interesting, but significantly more practical, 235cc push-rod engine.

MOTO GUZZI V7

1967

The name derived from 'V' for the layout, and '7' for capacity (near enough) in decilitres. From its inception, the idea seems to have been to use the engine from the 'mechanical mule' in a replacement for the police and military Falcones. Its use was also considered in a 'baby' Fiat, although this came to nothing. The first prototype in a motorcycle frame appeared at the Milan Show in 1965, but a financial crisis meant that the new machine was not introduced until 1967, the year

Times change... Today, with near-limitless power available 'off the shelf', and more speed limits, fewer riders crouch down to extract the best from their bikes.

that the SEIMM was to take over the firm.

Extreme ease of access and maintenance seems to have been the aim, even where (by civilian standards) the solutions were extravagant: plated cylinder bores cannot be re-bored, but they wear very slowly, and in the relatively rare cases of damage, they can be replaced quickly and easily.

Moto Guzzi also borrowed a fair amount from BMW: the V7 is, after all, a BMW with the cylinders bent upwards at 45

degrees each. The alternators on many Guzzi V-twins and BMWs are actually interchangeable, and the car-type clutch and shaft drive are similar in concept and execution.

The low-stressed engine, with its easy power delivery, was exactly what police and military customers wanted. It soon found widespread civilian approval too, although, of course, they soon wanted more power.

Customers soon got exactly what they wanted. The V7 Special

of 1969 was given a bigger bore of 83mm to allow 758cc and it was also generally 'tweaked' to give a claimed 45bhp at 6000rpm.

Then in 1971 came the V7 Sport, with a slightly smaller bore (82.5mm) to bring it inside the 750cc racing limits, a hotter cam and 30mm Dell'Ortos for 52bhp at 6300rpm. Alongside this model was the long-stroke 78x83mm 850GT, a true 844cc with 51bhp at 6000rpm.

The first 1000cc version was the V1000 Convert, with the long-throw

crankshaft and an 88mm bore, this time with steel liners. The unique feature of the 'Old Grey Goose' was its two-speed automatic transmission, which won few friends – but those who liked it, loved it.

Engine: 704cc ohv transverse V-twin, 80x70mm, air-cooled
Power: 40bhp at 5800rpm
Gearbox: 4-speed foot change
Final drive: shaft
Weight: 234kg (515lb)
Top speed: 170kph (105mph) approx.

MOTO GUZZI V50   1977

While some transverse V-twins got bigger, others got smaller, and 1977 saw the launch of the V50 and its little brother, the 346cc, 66x50.6mm V35. The 350cc class had lost the appeal it had once enjoyed, but the 500cc offered the same (nominal) bhp as a Vincent

Rapide, even though this was from half the capacity.

At first sight, off the showroom floor, the V50 was near perfection; and indeed, it handled and went very well, apart from an intractable flat spot. Unfortunately, it also demonstrated just about all

The 'baby' twins of 350 and (as here) 500cc were popular police machines. If they had been made as well as they were designed, they would have approached perfection.

the classic Moto Guzzi faults mentioned. The paint faded where it didn't jump off; the electrics were a nightmare; it rusted; and various oil seals failed to live up to their name. Made properly, it could have been one of the greatest bikes of all time but, unfortunately for Moto Guzzi, it wasn't.

The V50II of 1979, built at the former Lambretta factory, was no better, and, by the time the (much better) V50III appeared in 1980, the damage had already been done. Increasing the capacity to 643cc (80x64mm) with the 1981 V65 failed to excite very many customers, and when the company

tried stretching the capacity yet again to 743cc via an increased stroke (74mm), the general reaction this time was one of indifference.

The variants on the small twin that did make a difference, however, were the V35TT and the V65TT: 'TT' for Tutte Terrano (all-terrain), not Tourist Trophy. These appeared in 1984, sharing the basic components of the III series, at least those with most of the bugs removed.

The 750NTX was the V75 derivative of the same series (80x74mm) but the Quota was based on the bigger engines.

Engine: 490cc ohv transverse V-twin, 74x57mm, air-cooled
Power: 45bhp at 7500rpm
Gearbox: 5-speed foot change
Final drive: shaft
Weight: 168kg (370lb)
Top speed: 170kph (105mph)

MOTO GUZZI 850 LE MANS III   1981

The Le Mans was the logical development of the V7 Sport and its successors, the 750S (1974) and S3 (1975). It first appeared in 1976 with a claimed 71bhp at 7300rpm as Moto Guzzi's answer to the BMW R90S; in its later incarnation, of course, it went head-to-head with the R100RS.

The engine was considerably reworked so that, despite a lower compression ratio, it delivered more power at a lower engine speed, while also managing to meet emissions requirements that the earlier machines couldn't.

The Le Mans 1000 followed in late 1984 with a 949cc, 88x72mm motor with big valves, big carburettors and a higher

compression ratio, for a claimed 86bhp at the crankshaft and a claimed 225kph (140mph) top speed.

This model was the last of the 1970s superbikes when it ceased production in the early 1990s.

The Le Mans was Moto Guzzi's answer to the BMW R90S and remained in production in various guises for more than a decade.

Engine: 844cc ohv transverse V-twin, 83x78mm, air-cooled
Power: 76bhp at 6200rpm
Gearbox: 5-speed foot change
Final drive: shaft
Weight: 206kg (453lb)
Top speed: 210kph (130mph)

MOTO GUZZI CALIFORNIA JACKAL

2000

To jump from the Le Mans III to the California Special may smack of bathos, and indeed, one there are plenty of other choices from the 2000 line-up. Moto-Guzzi argues that the Centauro is the true descendant of the V7, the nearest it makes to a 'universal' motorcycle. Yet there are many other, more-or-less one-dimensional machines, such as the huge Quota 1100 ES off-road bikes, the full-dress California Special and the V11 Sport 'Cafe Racer', all of which are fitted with a 1064cc, 92x80mm derivative of the long-serving transverse twin.

The Jackal is, however, an excellent illustration of the Moto Guzzi as toy. It is essentially a stripped-down California, or 'bobbed' (in the jargon of some decades ago), with bars that are slightly smaller than a full dresser but still too high and wide for serious fast riding. It may be

possible to touch the claimed 200kph (124mph) top speed, but cruising for any length of time at even 100mph (160mph) would be hard on the neck and arms, let alone the rump, thanks to the somewhat minimal saddle.

The company's promotional material describes the Jackal as being 'targeted at the more fashion conscious younger market'. This means that it is, in short, a machine to be seen on, or to ride for short distances when you want to play at being a 'tough-guy biker', rather than a machine for either serious touring or serious fast riding.

This is not Moto Guzzi's fault; it merely illustrates the state of the motorcycle business at the beginning of the twenty-first century.

Fortunately, there are also machines available on the market for those who want to ride far or

The best that can be said of the California Jackal is that it suited its styling – being neither a serious touring machine nor a sports bike.

fast (or both). The Daytona RS, with a 'mere' 102bhp (claimed) at 8400rpm from a 992cc eight-valve, 90x78mm motor, may not be any competition for the latest Japanese race replicas, but both it and the 1100 Sport Corsa (90bhp), with the same claimed top speed of around 230kph (145mph), can offer a ride fast enough for almost anyone – at least on the public highway.

Engine: 1064cc ohv transverse V-twin, 92x80mm, air-cooled
Power: 74bhp at 6400rpm
Gearbox: 5-speed foot change
Final drive: shaft
Weight: 264kg (581lb)
Top speed: 200kph (124mph)

MOTO MORINI

ITALY 1937–

A NATIVE OF THE university town of Bologna, Alfonso Morini was born in 1892. Looking at his life history, he could well be described as a self-made man.

His first manufacturing came in partnership with Mario Mazzetti with MM (Morini Mazzetti) in 1924, but he left in 1937 to start a new business under his own name.

Moto Morini's first product was not a motorcycle but a three-wheel truck. With the outbreak of war, production was switched to military equipment, including

Launched in 1946, Morini's first post-war motorcycle was a 123cc, (53x58mm) piston-port, two-stroke. This version, with telescopic forks, dates from the early 1950s.

aircraft components, which were mostly made from cast aluminium. The factory, situated in Bologna, was at the very heart of one of the world's principal centres for non-ferrous foundry work and was subject to a series of bombing raids. Late in 1943, the Morini plant was partly destroyed by aerial bombardment, for although Italy had surrendered, Bologna was still a part of the country controlled by the Germans.

In 1945, with the conflict over, Alfonso Morini could at last organise the job of rebuilding his badly damaged factory. This was a task he did well, as the company was one of the first Italian marques to resume production. Launched in 1946, the first postwar machine was clearly influenced by the pre-war German DKW RT125 two-stroke design. Like the German machine, the new Morini had piston-port induction and a unit-construction engine with three speeds. The specification was completed with girder front forks, plunger rear

suspension and 48cm (19ins) wheels.

A racing version was also constructed, both for works entry into the Grand Prix scene, and for sale to private customers. Late in 1948, work began on the design of a 246cc Jawa-like, single- cylinder roadster model with twin exhaust ports. Introduced in 1949, this was intended strictly as a touring bike, although the engine unit was subsequently used to power a series of commercial three-wheel vehicles.

It was also in 1949 that the first 125cc road-racing world championship series was run. Although rivals FB Mondial won all three rounds and took the title, Morini was its most serious challenger. Mondial had used a double overhead-cam four-stroke, so Morini, seeing the wisdom of this, followed suit and also built a four-stroke, although this was with single overhead-cam.

The new Morini racer made its debut in 1950, winning the 125cc

An early example of the 250 Gran Premio GP racer. Like all versions, it used a dohc engine. It was one of the greatest ever racing motorcycles.

Between 1947 and 1949, Moto Morini offered this 125cc over-the-counter customer racer. Like its roadster brother it was inspired by the German DKW RT125 design.

Italian Senior championship, but it simply wasn't fast enough in the GPs.

For 1951, the 123.1cc (52x58mm) chain-driven single overhead-cam engine was updated, with the power output rising from 12 to 14bhp.

By 1952, the engine had been converted to double overhead-cam, and the power increased to 16bhp. Morini was rewarded when Emilio Mendogni won the factory's first-ever Grand Prix at Monza. He also won the final GP of the season in Spain. Despite improved machinery from MV Agusta and the arrival of NSU, Morini made little impact, even though Mendogni had won the Italian championships.

On the production front, Morini had been very active, developing an all-new 175cc model with an overhead-valve, unit-construction engine. This took its first public

bow at the Milan Show towards the end of 1952 and, by the end of 1953, a similar model of 160cc had also arrived on the scene.

In 1954, an enlarged version of the 125 racer was produced for Mendogni to win the 175cc class of the Italian Senior Championship. The factory achieved considerable commercial success by then taking the decision to produce a new range of 175cc overhead-valve roadsters.

This new 175 was launched onto the market in 1955. In fact, there was a trio of models: the Briscola (Trumps), Tressette (Three Sevens) and Settebello (Seven of Diamonds), which were all popular card games in Italy.

Of the trio, the Settebello was the performance model and proved very popular for clubman's type racing and fast road work.

From the Settebello came an even higher performance model,

The stylish Tresette sprint of 1958. This 172cc ohv model sported twin Silentium silencers, clip-ons and alloy wheel rims, amongst its impressive specification.

ML
Argentina 1970s: This machine
was initially produced as a 100cc
two-stroke; then it became a 125cc;
then a 175cc, and finally it used a
Jawa motor.

MM
USA 1905-c1914: The American
Motor Company began producing
machines fitted with Thomas
singles, before moving on to
singles and V-twins from a number
of other manufacturers.

M&M
England 1914: The ubiquitous
Villiers 269cc two-stroke powered
these assembled machines.

MMM
Germany 1925–27: This German
company produced two-stroke
singles of 148cc.

MMV-Z
Soviet Union (Minsk)
1951–unknown: This Soviet
company were responsible for the
manufacture of basic machines,
initially the M1A and later in 1975,
the surprisingly powerful Minsk
with a capacity of 125cc, and
which produced 12bhp at 6000rpm.
The company also made this model
in versions which were suitable for
off-road sports riding.

MOAG
Germany (Berlin) 1924: This was a
remarkably advanced machine
compared to others being
manufactured at that time. It had an
Electron frame, overhead-valve
engine, five-speed gearbox, all-
chain drive and a choice of air- or
water-cooling.

MOBILE
England 1913: A.V. Roe of aviation
fame (AVRO) manufactured this
scooter which was fitted with a
350cc Villiers motor.

the Rebello (Rebel). Rebel by
name, rebel by nature; whereas the
Settebello and its brothers,
however successful, were still
humble pushrod designs, the
Rebello had technical features
quite different from a
conventional, production-based
motorcycle. At the time of its
introduction, in spring 1955, it was
one of the most up-to-date designs
anywhere in the world.

With a bore and stroke of
60x61mm, the Rebello had a
chain-driven single overhead-cam
and five-speed gearbox.

Mid-1957 saw the public debut
of an even more powerful single
which, although based around the
Rebello, was meant for Grand Prix
duty rather than production-type
events. The Gran Premio had first
been tested in 1956, having a
displacement of 246.7cc
(69x66mm) and put out 25bhp
(against the 175's 22bhp). When
the new machine debuted at
Monza in September 1957 power
was 29bhp at 10,000rpm from the
double overhead-cam engine.

**In 1985, Moto Morini introduced
the 501 Camel. This featured a
507cc engine, square-tube frame,
nikasil-coated cylinders and
monoshock rear suspension.**

From that time until the end of
the 1960s, the Gran Premio was to
enjoy a long run of successes, both
in the World and Italian
Championship series, with several
riders, Tarquinio Provini, Giacomo
Agostini and Angelo Bergamonti
among them.

On the standard production
front, the Milan Samples Fair in
spring 1959 saw the introduction
of the Corsaro (Pirate). Derived
from the 98cc Sbarazzino (Free-
and-Easy), which had been
successful over the previous three

**The 1981 five-speed Moto Morini
478.6cc (69x64mm) V-twin. It was
not much faster than the 3½ three-
fifty, but had more mid-range
torque.**

years, the Corsaro had a 123cc
(56x50mm) overhead-valve engine
and was capable of 101kph
(63mph). The Corsaro was to
remain in production until the
1970s and was also built in 150
and 160cc engine sizes.

Founder Alfonso Morini died in
1969; thereafter, the factory was

The 1988 350 Dart was a clever mix of bike cultures, combining a Cagiva 125 Freccia chassis with a Morini 350 engine. It was also the first Morini built under Cagiva.

interchangeable, this helping to maintain lower costs.

A turbo production of the 500 V-twin appeared at the Milan Show in November 1981, but was never put into production.

During the early 1980s, the Camel (500cc) and Kanguro (350cc) trial bikes sold well. The 500 roadster was produced in both five- and six-speed versions, while various custom versions all made use of the V-twin powerplant. So too did the first model to benefit from the Cagiva take-over of 1987, the Dart, which was produced in both 350 and 400cc guises.

Unfortunately, Cagiva chose not to develop Moto Morini as it did follow Bologna rivals Ducati, gravely allowing the name to die. However, now that Cagiva had sold Ducati, it seemed possible that the famous old marque might be re-launched, just as the Castiglioni brothers had so successfully done with MV Agusta.

run by his daughter Gabriella until it was taken over by the Cagiva Group in the late 1980s.

The early 1970s saw the Bologna factory particularly successful in the ISDT, with several gold-medal winners. Morini had always had a tradition of producing high-quality motorcycles, but none of its designs quite matched the famous V-twin series that began with the 3½ in the early 1970s. Designed jointly by Dianna Marchesini and

Franco Lambertini Jnr, production commenced in early 1973, and with it a new era in the marque's history was born.

The basis of the 72-degree V-twin was its Heron combustion chambers and belt-driven camshaft. This V-twin, and the

The Moto Morini custom bike, the 501 Excalibur, appeared in 1986. This featured a 507cc engine, chopped styling, king and queen seat and 'Comstar' type wheels.

machine that followed, carried Morini's fortunes over the next quarter of a century.

From the 3½ (a sports tourer) came the higher-performance Sport model, with disc front brake and cast-alloy wheels on later models of both the 3½ and Sport.

Then came the 500 and 250 V-twins, and 125 and 250cc singles. All were to make clever use of a modular design, which meant that certain parts were

A Settebello Formula 3 racer. This is the type used by Giacomo Agostini during the early part of his career, with a tuned engine, Oldani brakes and Ceriani forks.

MOTO MORINI SETTEBELLO   1955

The first overhead-valve Morini made its public debut at the Milan Show in November 1952. This sported a unit-construction engine,

four-speed, fast-change gearbox, telescopic front forks and swinging-arm, twin-shock rear suspension.

A revised design, in three variants, was introduced for the 1955 model year, the Briscola (Trumps), Tressette (Three

Sevens) and Settebello (Seven of Diamonds).

The Settebello won the most public acclaim. As it was the

sports model, road testers raved about it, while enthusiasts dreamed of owning it. The Settebello was an excellent fast road tool or clubman's racing mount.

In standard trim, it came complete with clip-on handlebars, a tuned engine (featuring a high-compression piston and special camshaft), a large Dell 'Orto carburettor, conical brake hubs cast in aluminium, alloy wheel rims, a bulbous 18-litre (4 UK gallon) fuel tank, sprint saddle and lightweight, pressed-steel mudguards.

The cylinder barrel of the 172.4cc (60x61mm) engine was of cast iron, with an aluminium cylinder head, whilst the crankcase formed a stressed member for the frame. The engine casing was left in a matt finish to promote cooling. In standard form, the Settebello could achieve 145kph (90mph) – an excellent performance for its time – and consequently it was very competitive in sports machine races, notably in Italy and France.

A 1955 Settebello. In standard form, this 172.4cc ohv unit construction single could achieve 145kph (90mph), an outstanding performance for its time.

Many novice racers used the overhead-valve Morini single to begin their racing careers, even the great Giacomo Agostini, who was world champion 15 times.

Besides its speed, the Settebello also possessed superb road-holding and handling characteristics, so it was at its best on a light, bumpy circuit where its lightness and handling gave it a distinct advantage over more powerful machinery, even well into the 1960s.

Engine: 172.4cc ohv 2v single, 60x61mm, air-cooled
Power: 17bhp at 8000rpm
Gearbox: 4-speed foot change
Final drive: chain
Weight: 129kg (285lb)
Top speed: 145kph (90mph)

MOTO MORINI 250 GRAN PREMIO   1963

Tarquinio Provini's love pursuit of the 1963 250cc World Championship title on his Moto Morini double overhead-cam single, riding against the might of the entire Honda team, led by Jim Redman, still remains even today as one of the true David-and-Goliath struggles in the history of motorcycle racing.

A 1963 250 Gran Premio of the type ridden by Tarquinio Provini to within two points of winning the 250cc world title that year – a fantastic achievement.

Provini had joined Morini, from MV, for the 1960 season. Over the next three years, the combination of his masterful riding talent and the patient development of the 246.6cc (69x66mm) twin-cam (gear driven), six-speed Morini single had welded into a dynamic partnership.

In 1962, the Provini/Morini combination won the Italian Senior Championship and enjoyed several notable successes on foreign soil – so much so, in fact, that Alfonso Morini gave the go-ahead for a bid on the 250cc world title in 1963.

But even Alfonso Morini could not have imagined in his wildest dreams just how close his finish would be in the 10-round championship.

After a full season of racing, Tarquinio Provini finished runner-up to 250cc world champion Jim Redman, and his mighty four-cylinder Honda, thanks to a certain amount of bad luck (cancellation of the French GP, mechanical trouble in Holland and his inability to obtain a visa for East Germany), and the decision to give the Isle of Man TT a miss. Moreover, he lost the title by a mere two points! The vital difference on the champion's side was the fact that Redman competed in the TT (which he won) and also in the East German Grand Prix.

However, Provini and Morini had the enormous satisfaction of soundly beating Redman at Monza, over the tortuous Spanish GP circuit at Montjuic Park,

Barcelona; on the ultra-fast Hockenheim track in West Germany; and over the rough Buenos Aires Autodrome in Argentina. Thus they proved the great adaptability of the design. In addition, Provini took the Italian Championship once again.

Provini then quit to join Benelli for 1964, and was replaced by the youngster, Giacomo Agostini. 'Ago' then beat Provini for that year's Italian title, before he too left for MV Agusta.

The final development of the double overhead-cam single, which Angelo Bergamonti rode to yet another Italian title in 1967, was getting it to put out yet more power. Also, the bore and stroke had been changed from the original late 1950s 69x66mm to

72x61mm, giving a displacement of 248.36cc (during Provini's time).

In addition, three- and four-valve heads had been tested, as had Desmodromic valve operation. However, the simpler and conventional two-valve system had been the one to notch up the race results.

The Gran Premio twin-cam single was finally retired at the end of 1967.

Engine: 248.36cc (early engine 246.6cc) dohc 2v single 72x61mm, air-cooled
Power: 36bhp at 10,500rpm
Gearbox: 6-speed foot change
Final drive: chain
Weight: 113kg (249lb)
Top speed: 225kph (140mph)

MOTO MORINI 3¹/₂

1973

Going on sale early in 1973 (after being shown in prototype form at the Milan Show in late 1971), the 3¹/₂ V-twin was one of the classic motorcycle designs of the 1970s.

The combined work of Dianni Marchesini and Franco Lambertini Junior, the 72-degree 344cc (68x57mm) V-twin stood apart from its rivals by the use of Heron combustion cylinder heads.

Heron heads had been used in the Repco Brabham racing car that had won the 1966 F1 world championship and also by the likes of Jaguar and Ford for their production models, but their use in the 3¹/₂ was a first for the motorcycle industry.

Essentially, the Heron principle uses cylinder heads with a flat face and parallel, not inclined, valves, and the combustion recess is formed in the piston crown.

Several other innovations were also used in the 3¹/₂'s engine. These included the toothed belt to the camshaft, a forged, one-piece crankshaft, transistorised ignition and the generally high level of the aluminium castings. Compared to the Ducati's 90-degrees, Morini's 72 degrees meant an engine length that did not over-extend the wheelbase. It was angled so that the camshaft could be located high in the crankcase in the crutch of the vee. Even so, it was necessary to space the cylinders apart at the base to allow room for the camshaft. This method of offset is known as desaxe, and in the 3¹/₂ the effect was to give a positive

Going on sale in 1973, the 3¹/₂ was the joint design of Dianni Marchesini and Franco Lambertini Jnr. The 72-degree V-twin engine had a displacement of 344cc.

bias on one cylinder and a negative bias on the other.

The unit-construction engine, with its helical primary-drive gears, dry multiplate clutch and six-speed gearbox was housed in a

particularly neat, duplex steel-tube frame. At first there were wire wheels and drum brakes for both the standard 3¹/₂ and the 3¹/₂ Sport but, by the mid-1970s, a Grimeca disc front brake and cast-alloy wheels from the same source were specified.

Both larger- and smaller-capacity versions (250 and 500cc) of the Morini V-twin were built, plus 125 and 250cc singles. All showed not only the Heron heads,

but also many other components, giving owners the advantages of a modular design, for example, availability of spares and easier maintenance.

Engine: 344cc ohv 3v, V-twin, 68x57mm, air-cooled
Power: 36bhp at 8000rpm
Gearbox: 6-speed foot change
Final drive: chain
Weight: 154kg (340lb)
Top speed: 161kph (100mph)

MOTO MORINI 500 SEI V   1982

At the 1975 Milan Show, Morini displayed two new designs: a 250 single and a 500 V-twin, both directly derived from the 3¹/₂ V-twin. The latter was described by *Motor Cycle* magazine as 'one of the prettiest bikes at Milan'.

The 500's specification included a displacement of 478.6cc, bore and stroke of 69x64mm, a compression ratio of 11.2:1 and a power output of 46bhp at 7500rpm. The gearbox was a five-speeder and other details included: cast-alloy wheels, triple disc brakes and an ultra-lightweight, 15kg (33lb) dry sump. The new single was half the capacity of the 500 at 239cc, and a maximum speed of 129kph (80mph).

As the 1980s dawned, Morini introduced yet more versions of its modular theme, including a 239cc V-twin and a 123cc single.

In 1981, most of the V-twins (except the standard 3¹/₂) were finished in a striking red paint job, black engine casings and exhausts, plus gold cast-alloy wheels. In 1982 came the Sei V, a six-speed version of the 500, in both Sport and Touring guises.

The six-speed engine in the 500 had first been used in a factory-entered machine during the 1980 ISDT, which was then put into

The Sei V, a six-speed version of the 500cc V-twin, arrived in 1982. The six-speed engine had first been used on Morini's ISDT bike in 1980.

production as the Camel (called the Sahara in the UK), an enduro-style trail bike, with leading axle, long-travel front forks and twin-shock rear suspension.

By 1985, the '500' (in trail guise only) had an improved cylinder-head layout. The valves were larger and were set further apart, the carburettor size had increased and the cylinders were bored out by a further 2mm to give 507cc.

In standard form it was good for 171kph (107mph), which for a dirt bike was excellent performance. It also sported monoshock rear suspension, which had been fitted on the 350 Kanguro dirt bike. However, despite this, the roadster 500 was only ever manufactured in twin-shock form.

The 507cc-engined bike was marketed as the 501. Production of the definitive roadster 500, the Sei V, ceased in the mid-1980s. From then on, only custom and dirt-bike versions were offered.

Engine: 478.6cc ohv 2v V-twin, 69x64mm, air-cooled
Power: 46bhp at 7500rpm
Gearbox: 6-speed foot change
Final drive: chain
Weight: 140kg (380lb)
Top speed: 177kph (110mph)

MOTOM   ITALY 1947–66

DURING THE POSTWAR BOOM years of the Italian motorcycle industry, the Milanese Motom concern was at the very forefront in supplying cheap-to-buy, cheap-to-run, small-capacity lightweights.

Having neither a famous name, nor publicity from fielding a squadron of four-cylinder racers, Motom did at least have an ultra-modern engineering plant that could be credited with producing high-quality products.

Motom's facilities – the latest machine tools, modern buildings, and even its own fully covered test track – were an ideal to which the rest of the Italian industry could only aspire.

Peter Inchley flat on the tank of his 50cc ohv single-cylinder machine at an endurance race at Snetterton, England, in 1961. He set a new lap record of 90kph (56.26mph).

Its first model, like so many models being produced at the time, was a 49cc overhead-valve, 40x39.8mm auxiliary engine.

By mid-1948, Motom was building complete machines, with the same engine. Next came the 163cc Delfino (Dolphin). Half

In 1952, a tuned version of the 49cc machine, ridden by Dalmasso averaged 75kph (46.5mph) over a standing kilometer to break the world record for the class.

Furthermore, the 50cc category of the Giro d'Italia (3057km/1900 miles in six days on normal roads) was won by Motom rider Givanetti, averaging almost 64kph (40mph).

But Motom's finest sporting achievement came in April 1958 at Monza when it succeeded in breaking several speed and endurance records. Most amazing of all, however, was the average fuel consumption figure of 232km (144 miles) per gallon (4.5 UK litres/3.8 US litres).

Before that, a new 98cc model had arrived in spring 1955. This featured an engine with overhead-cam and horizontal cylinder, which was acclaimed by *Motor Cycling* magazine as 'Italy's most advanced lightweight'.

And this model was to prove a success, too, helping Motom into fifth spot behind Vespa, Lambretta, Guzzi and Garelli in the 1956 Italian sales chart.

However, by the end of the decade, as in other European countries, sales of two-wheelers decreased in the face of competition from the small car.

Motom attempted to respond to this downturn in sales by seeking exports for the first time in their history as a company. But even though the early 1960s saw several new models, including one powered by a German Zundapp engine, Motom closed its doors in 1966.

A standard 50cc ohv Motom single-cylinder machine, with telescopic front forks and plunger rear suspension, c.1960.

scooter, half motorcycle, with overhead valve and fan-cooling, it made its debut at the 1950 Milan Show.

MOTO-RÊVE

SWITZERLAND 1904–25

THIS FIRM PRODUCED motorcycles and supplied engines to others, at first singles, quickly followed by V-twins, its core business. All had automatic inlet valves and direct belt drive in the style of the period. In 1910, the company added a 297cc vertical twin by mounting two singles in-line along the machine with a magneto in front and a clutch, bevel gears and a chain to drive the rear wheel, which incorporated a two-speed planetary gear. Both the magneto and carburettor were Moto-Rêve products.

The rest of the 1910 range comprised V-twins of 275, 297 and 334cc plus a 240cc single, all with two speeds and belt drive. The twins continued to have the engine mounted above the bottom bracket, but this proved not to be a disadvantage. The firm entered the 1911 TT races as the M.R., and altered the twin engine for the Junior to mechanical inlet valves by adding suitable cams and rockers. The Senior had an overhead-valve twin engine, which ran well enough, but belt troubles left it in 25th place. Both entries went out on the first lap.

This effort bore fruit in the 1912 range, which featured new models

By 1913, this Moto-Rêve had girder forks with side springs and other improvements to both the single-cylinder engine and its transmission.

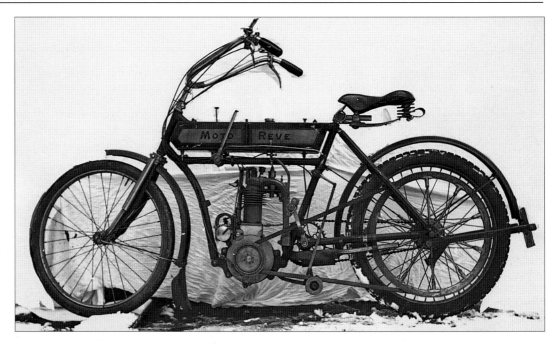

Above: An early Moto-Rêve single from the early 20th century with automatic inlet valve, front magneto, belt drive and simple leading-link front forks.

powered by 340 and 499cc overhead-valve, V-twin or 300cc single engines. These models saw the firm through to World War I, but before then Moto-Rêve got involved with a branch factory in England that manufactured the Alp motorcycle. After the war, Moto-Rêve continued to do business up to 1925.

MOTOSACOCHE
SWITZERLAND 1899–1956

FOUNDED BY BROTHERS Armand and Henri Dufaux, this was the best known and most successful of Switzerland's motorcycle firms that also supplied engines to many others under their MAG label. In their early years they also used the HADC name, an abbreviation of their company name, and introduced Motosacoche during the Edwardian period for what was essentially a clip-on unit for a bicycle.

The name meant 'motor-in-a-saddle-bag' and the 211cc engine had an automatic inlet valve and battery ignition replaced by a magneto in 1907, this skew gear driven from the circumference of one of the flywheels. The whole unit fitted easily into a bicycle diamond frame with belt drive over a jockey pulley that also acted as a crude clutch. Enclosure panels were available to conceal the power unit and they quickly offered a complete machine with sprung forks.

The clip-on was soon joined by a motorcycle with a 423cc V-twin engine and by 1909 a smaller,

Motosacoche soon added more conventional models to their range, such as this V-twin, with its separate gearbox, all-chain drive and girder forks.

297cc V-twin Motosacoche engine with side-valves was in use for a Royal Enfield model. This association led to the London manager for the Dufaux brothers, Osborne de Lissa, being involved with the British firm as well.

For 1911 the clip-on engine was enlarged to 241cc with mechanical valves and a much simpler magneto drive. That year saw the start of Motosacoche Acacias Geneva, or MAG, as a firm that supplied engines to other motorcycle manufacturers. Their range extended from 350 to 500cc

Well known for supplying their MAG engines to many other firms, Motosacoche became famous for its 211cc auxiliary engine for bicycles.

for the singles and to 1000cc for the V-twins, and they were used by many marques and in most major European countries.

In 1912 the singles had the option of a special exhaust valve patented by de Lissa. This moved the valve spring to above the valve head so there was no tensile load on the stem. To achieve this, the

valve head was extended up as a cylinder right through the cylinder head with a second valve seat at the top of a larger diameter than the main one. The spring sat in the cylinder with a screw adjuster above it to set its compression. The two valve seats were ground in so that both sealed as one, and this ingenious design became standard for 1913, but only for the one year.

That interlude aside, the firm continued with its clip-on unit and the MAG engines with side-valves, overhead inlets and side exhaust or overhead for both. Their own range of motorcycles reflected this and allowed them to build machines to suit the market along the trends of the times. They used the Enfield two-speed gear for some years but moved on to a separate gearbox after World War I but continued with dummy belt-rim brakes to the mid-1920s.

By the start of the 1930s their machines had drum brakes, saddle tanks and all the other fixtures and fittings of that period. Between the wars they built a handful of overhead-camshaft racing engines for very selected customers who had some successes, but in the main they kept to producing their range up to 1939.

Postwar, they showed a radical machine with a 200cc side-valve engine, belt drive, variable gear and many novel features, but little more was heard of this.

For 1953 they introduced a machine with a 250cc overhead-camshaft vertical twin engine built in unit with a four-speed gearbox. It had modern lines and performed well. Two years later, this model was joined by a motocross version. However, that was their final effort and they were soon gone after half a century of building both engines and machines.

A massive 1932 Motosacoche with an 846cc side-valve, V-twin engine, four-speed Hurth gearbox and US-style leading-link front forks.

MOTOTRANS

A 1979 Spanish-made Mototrans 350 Forza. It was powered by an ohc bevel Ducati single-cylinder engine, with electric start, disc front brake and 12 volt electrics.

By the mid-1960s, Mototrans was beginning to build its own designs. Two of these were racers, the '285' single, which was shared by Bruno Spaggiari and Giuseppe Mandolini when they won the 1964 Barcelona 24 hours endurance race at record speed, and the MT250 248cc 44.5x40mm four-cylinder, the latter designed by the former Benelli engineer, Renato Armaroli.

Then, in the early 1970s, Mototrans built a five-speed version of the Italian 125/160cc overhead-cam Ducatis and a version of the 250cc bevel single with new bore and stroke dimensions of 69x66mm, the 24 Horas (24 Hours). There was also a series of two-strokes, including the Mini, Pronto and Senda.

A fresh variation on the familiar bevel, overhead-cam single theme arrived in 1976 with the new 300cc Electronica. This was followed by the 250cc Strada, 350cc Forza (touring) and Vento (sport). Some of these Spanish Ducatis had features never used on the Italian models, such as cast-alloy wheels, electric start and 12-volt electrics.

MOTOTRANS BEGAN DURING the late 1950s building Italian Ducatis under licence. This was due to strict import restrictions imposed by the Franco regime, which protected Spanish jobs by banning imports of certain foreign goods, notably motorcycles. Ducati and other marques, such as Moto Guzzi and MV Agusta, were made locally.

Barcelona, home to so many of Spain's motorcycle manufacturers, was chosen as the location and, as Ducati had enjoyed a number of victories on the city's famous Montjuic Park circuit, Mototrans quickly established itself as a major force in Spanish motorcycling, a position it maintained for 25 years.

The first production models were built in 1957 and were, at first, straightforward copies of existing Italian versions, the initial batch being 175cc Sport overhead-cam singles.

In 1978, Mototrans unveiled its first completely home-grown production model, the MTV 406.61cc Yak 410. This owed nothing to Bologna; if anything, it looked more Japanese than European, with styling akin to Suzuki's SP 370, which had only recently been released.

Towards the end of 1981, Mototrans hit the financial rocks and, despite a resumption of production in 1982, died in 1983.

By 1980, the Mototrans factory had produced this sports 350 Vento model, with front and rear disc brakes, cast alloy wheels and modern styling.

MUNCH

GERMANY 1966–1980s

Above: For an engine that was never intended to be put on display, the NSU four-cylinder unit turned out to be remarkably good looking.

Below: The more you look at the 1972 TSS 1200 the more unlikely it becomes. Note particularly the huge front brake and the rear wheel.

FRIEDEL MUNCH MADE a surprisingly successful, limited-production motorcycle by putting a succession of ever larger, ever more powerful, air-cooled, in-line, four-cylinder NSU car engines transversely into a motorcycle frame.

Munch's background was with Horex, and much of his original 'Mammut' machines were made of Horex components, although later they acquired Marzocchi forks and Brembo brakes. The chain-drive machine was strikingly ugly because, of course, the NSU engine was never intended for public display in the open air. That said, it did have a great deal of power and torque; remember, in the early 1960s, the term 'superbike' did not exist and 750cc twins were among the fastest things available. The only bigger engines in normal production motorcycles were the crude, tractor-like Harley-Davidson V-twins, with their 'knife and fork' bottom ends.

Exactly when Munch built the first machine is unclear but, by about 1966, the machines were available off the shelf, initially with the 996cc engine, and later with the 1177cc version, which delivered 88bhp in carburettor form. Later still came the 100bhp model with fuel injection. The machines, assembled to order, had a 1278cc, fuel-injected engine with 104bhp at 7500rpm. Again, the precise date of the last machine is unclear, but it was probably built in the early 1980s.

Long before that, of course, it was possible to buy much lighter,

more lissome machines, which are fitted with purpose-built motorcycle engines promising the kind of power hitherto only associated with racers. These delivered the same sort of acceleration and a higher top speed.

The Munch-4 (as it was known by this time) weighed close to 270kg (600lb) and had the aerodynamics of a cathedral. There was a prototype 700cc, two-stroke triple in 1973, but it never entered production.

Today, the Munch-4 and the Mammut are sought after as powerful, well-made, distinctive, cult bikes, which you can still – just about – ride.

MV AGUSTA

THE AGUSTA NAME HAS long been associated with the aviation industry and is today not only Italy's premier helicopter manufacturer, but also one of the most important in the world. Add MV (Meccanica Verghera) to the Agusta name, however, and you have a motorcycling legend, because to many biking enthusiasts it is the Ferrari of two wheels.

MV, founded by Count Dominceo Agusta, built its first motorcycle, a small 98cc two-stroke in 1945, with the first of the glamorous four-cylinder models, a racer, appearing mid-way through 1950. This was the work of Piero Remor who had joined from Gilera the previous winter, with race mechanic Arturo Magini.

Bore and stroke dimensions of the 1950 MV four were square at 54x54mm, giving a displacement of 494.4cc. Running on a compression ratio of 9.5:1, the double overhead-cam four breathed through a pair of 28mm Dell'Orto carburettors (one pair of cylinders sharing a single instrument). Weighing in at 118kg (260lb), the four-speed machine produced 50bhp at 9000rpm, giving a top speed of almost 206kph (129mph), making it faster than either the twin cylinder AJS Porcupine or the single cylinder double-overhead-cam Norton.

MV Agusta's first motorcycle was this 98cc single-cylinder two-stroke with piston-port induction. It made its debut in 1945.

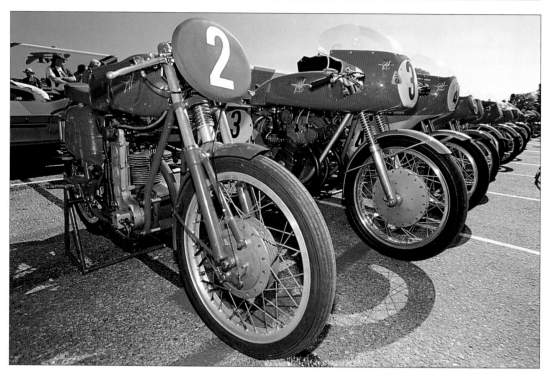

At the time many questioned how much Remor had transferred from his Gilera work into the new MV. Indeed, the MV was so similar that in today's litigious society, Gilera would have sought some form of legal redress. Remor was clearly aware that an exact copy would not be acceptable, so he introduced some features to set it apart. Most notably these included shaft- instead of chain-final drive, and torsion-bar suspension, both fore and aft. Another difference was that gear

A line-up of classic MV racers. From the left: a 1953 dohc single, a 1958 four, a 1960 four.

levers were provided for both sides of the engine. This bizarre arrangement, probably never used before or since, required the rider to use his heels, pushing downwards on the nearside for upward changes, and down on the offside to change down. In all it was an unnecessary and over-complicated system. In hindsight, it seemed merely to provide

ammunition for those who claimed it was a smoke-screen to hide an almost exact reproduction of the Gilera engine.

Other early MV racing designs were all 125cc-class machines, at first two-stroke, then four-strokes. The latter built in double overhead-cam (factory entry) and

A 1951 MV Agusta 125cc TEL Sport model, with two-stroke, four-speed engine, fly wheel magneto ignition, telescopic forks and swinging arm rear suspension.

Above: The 150RS (Rapido Sport) was built between 1959 and 1965 and used an ohv unit construction engine and twin silencers.

single overhead-cam (for paying customers). In fact, it was one of the 123.5cc (53x56mm) double overhead-cam racers that brought the MV works its first world title when the Englishman Cecil Sandford took the 125cc championship in 1952.

As with the smaller capacity racers, MV's first production motorcycles were predominantly two-strokes, the first being a single-cylinder 98cc model, which although designed during the war, did not debut until 1945. The Vespa name had to be dropped following action by Piaggio who had already registered the name for its range of scooters.

By the end of the 1940s, the '98' had become a '125', with both road and racing versions. In addition, MV had begun production of a whole family of scooters with both two- and four-stroke engines.

At the end of 1952, MV Agusta displayed a new production roadster with a 172.3cc (59.5x62mm) single overhead-cam four-stroke engine. This was to be built in a number of versions, including the CSS Supersport, but more commonly known as the Disco Volante (flying saucer) and

Squale (shark), the latter a racing-only model.

Another important design making its production debut for the 1953 model year was the Pullman. First seen in public at the Brussels Show in January 1953, it was a distinctive machine powered by the long-serving 123.5cc piston-port two-stroke engine. It combined, successfully, the best features of both motorcycles and scooters, and went on to sell in considerable numbers.

In 1954 MV offered their first overhead-valve model. This first series was a 123.6cc (54x54mm) single. It began a trend which was to see the following models gradually added: in 1956, 246.6cc (62x66mm); in 1958, 83.2cc

The 600 Quatro was the first of MV's production four-cylinder models. But between 1965 and 1972, only 135 examples were built.

(46.5x49mm); in 1958, 172.3cc (59.5x62mm); in 1959, 150.1cc (59.5x54mm); in 1959, 301cc (74x70mm); in 1962 231.7cc (69x62mm); in 1964, twin 166.3cc (46.5x49mm); in 1966, twin 147cc (53x56mm) and, finally, another twin 348.9cc (63x56mm) in 1970.

Towards the end of the 1950s, with the advent of the small and affordable car such as the Fiat 500, motorcycle production in Italy plummeted. But because of its successful return to aviation (via a licence agreement with Bell Helicopters), MV was in a much

MOTA-WIESEL
Germany 1948–52: This was a small-wheel step-through which was fitted with a 75 or 100cc engine.

MOTEURCYCLE
France 1921–24: The 206cc two-stroke engine which gave power to this machine was mounted behind the saddle, and it drove the rear wheel by friction.

MOTOBIC
Spain 1949–65: After kicking off with an 80cc lightweight, this company's product range in 1957 included 50cc mopeds, and lightweights of 60, 75, 82 and 100cc. By the early 1960s the staples of their range were a 75cc lightweight and a scooter, which came with a choice of 75 and 95cc engines.

MOTOBIMM
Italy 1969–71: These were Minarelli-powered 49cc off-road sports machines.

MOTO BIROS
Italy (Cesena) 1970s: Giancarlo Biondi and Vincenzo Rossi elided their surnames to christen these 50cc reed-valve mopeds and off-road sports machines.

MOTOBLOC
France (Vichy) 1948 to late 1960s: This company is probably best known for the 65cc SE-engined, two-stroke Sulky scooter. However, it was also responsible for the production of mopeds as well as lightweights with Aubier-Dunne and Villiers two-strokes of 125 to 200cc and AMC 125 and 250cc overhead-valve four-strokes.

MOTO-B.M.
Italy (Rastignoro Pianoro) 1952–c. 1960: This company began production of motorcycles in 1952 with Ilo-engined 125 and 160cc two-strokes; a year later, they added 75 and 100cc four-stroke lightweights with NSU engines; then produced 125 and 250cc four-strokes; and finally Minarelli-engined mopeds.

Above: The last of MV's 350 Sport ohv parallel twins was the square-case Ipotesi, which entered production in 1975.

Below: A Magni-MV 850 from the late 1970s with curved megaphone silencers, chain driven conversion and works-type dolphin fairing.

Spring 1972 heralded another variant of the four-cylinder MV750 street bike, in the shape of the very rare GT.

MV Agusta's successes on the race circuit have been unmatched, winning a record number of world championships in all the solo classes except 50/80cc. The list of those who raced the red 'fire engines' included many stars of the sport such as Les Graham, Ray Amm, Dickie Dale, Bill Lomas, John Surtees, John Hartle, Gary Hocking, Mike Hailwood, Giacomo Agostini and Phil Read, to name but a few.

MV's racing record reads: 75 world championships (riders and manufacturers), 270 Grand Prix victories and no fewer than 3027 international race wins.

The first of the four-cylinder street bikes, the R19 of 1950, remained a show prototype only. Later in 1965 Count Agusta at last authorised production of an MV four. Unfortunately, it was to be the extremely ugly 591.8cc (58x56mm) 600 touring model of which, over seven years, only a mere 135 examples were actually sold. The 750S, which was first displayed at the 1969 Milan Show, was an improvement. This was followed by the 750 GT, 750 SS, 750 (789cc) America and the 837cc Monza.

Before production ceased in 1978, MV machines had been exported to no less than 53 countries, including the US, the

UK, Argentina, Australia, France, Germany and Spain. It also had the King of Jordan as a customer.

Although MV built a number of interesting prototypes, its main production was centred around its pushrod single and twin-cylinder models. This may seem in stark contrast to its glamorous multi-cylinder racers (the roadster fours were never sold in large numbers). However, it should be remembered that for much of the original MV company's life, motorcycles were just a form of transport; the word 'superbike' had yet to be invented.

Instead, MV stuck to a tried and tested formula for its basic production roadsters. Pushrods ruled. These had largely gained five-speeds by the early 1970s and then, in the mid-1970s, a change was made from round to square outer engine covers and cylinder finning.

The end of motorcycle production was no doubt hastened by the death in February 1971 of the company's driving force, Count Agusta. Following this, the Italian Government moved in and forced the Agusta group to concentrate its efforts on the aviation sector.

Subsequently, in the 1980s, the Castiglioni brothers purchased the MV name and, with the help of the brilliant designer Massimo Tamburini, have gone on to create a modern masterpiece, the exciting Ferrari-inspired F4, which was launched to much public acclaim in 1998.

stronger position than most of its rivals who relied on motorcycle, scooter and moped sales.

MV also built a moped (between 1955 and 1959) and even a new scooter, called the Chicco (Grain). Sold between 1960 and 1964, the Chicco was powered by a newly designed 155.6cc (57x61mm) single cylinder two-stroke, with horizontal cylinder.

However, from the early 1950s until the end of the 1970s MV was best known outside Italy for its racing exploits, with an array of machinery ranging from 125cc singles through to a prototype 500cc six-cylinder model, and also including various twins, triples and fours. Yet it was to be the four-cylinder models, on both road and track, that were to capture the hearts and minds of countless motorcycle enthusiasts around the world.

MV AGUSTA 500 FOUR
1956

The first 500 four-cylinder MV racer appeared in 1950, but it was in 1956 that the design really took off, assisted by a combination of technical improvements and the signing of Englishman John Surtees. As proficient in the workshop as he was on the track, his arrival marked a turning point in MV's history.

Although 1955 had not proved very successful in terms of results in the 500cc class, MV engineers had made considerable technical progress. Streamlining (dustbin type) took a fair portion of development, while the frame was re-designed to provide a lower centre of gravity. The Earles front fork was abandoned in favour of a new MV-built telescopic assembly. Various rear shock absorbers were tried (MV and British Girling types); the double-sided front brake was equipped with massive air-scoops, while the fuel tank was also reshaped to provide a longer, lower style.

Four carburettors had first been tried in 1951 (previously only two instruments were used); then, for 1952, the engine was much revised from the previous type, including a change from shaft- to chain-final drive. The double-side gear change had already been axed in favour of a conventional lever on the offside. By 1955, with attention to detail, the power had been increased to 65bhp at 11,000rpm. For 1956 this was increased to 67bhp at the same engine revolutions.

MV Agusta first won the 500cc World Championship with their four-cylinder model in 1956. The four bowed out in 1965 after winning another eight titles.

The six-round 500cc World Championship series got underway with a victory for Surtees and MV. However, this win was not on his new 1956 bike but on a 1955 model. In the final practice session, Surtees had collided with a cow on the mountain road section of the 59-kilometre (37-mile) circuit. He was lucky to escape serious injury; the bike was too badly damaged to be repaired in time for the race. Surtees went on to win the next two rounds (in Holland and Belgium) before he crashed his smaller 350 MV Four and broke his arm. But with three different winners in the last three

rounds, he had done enough to give MV its first 500cc world crown.

Surtees also won the 500cc title in 1958, 1959 and 1960, before Gary Hocking in 1961. Mike Hailwood took over to win four times in a row from 1962 to 1965.

The Four was retired in favour of the new three-cylinder model, with which Giacomo Agustini continued MV's winning streak, taking the 1966 championship, the start of many for the new triple. Nevertheless, it was the 500 Four that was largely responsible for putting MV on the racing map.

Engine: 497.5cc dohc 2v straight four, 53x56.4mm
Power: 67bhp at 11,000rpm
Gearbox: 5-speed foot change
Final drive: chain
Weight: 118kg (260lb)
Top speed: 233kph (145mph)

MV AGUSTA 350 THREE
1965

The three-cylinder 350 MV Grand Prix machine made its public debut in 1965. First proposed during the late 1950s, the triple came to be built as a response to Honda's entry into the 350cc Grand Prix in 1962 with the 285cc Four and soon afterwards by a full-size machine.

Once the Hondas arrived, the old four-cylinder 350, itself based on the 500cc model, was quickly withdrawn. This then left rider Mike Hailwood with only the larger machine and he won the

The new 343.9cc dohc four-valves-per-cylinder three-cylinder made its debut in the hands of Giacomo Agostini (seen here) in 1965.

Blue Ribbon Senior class for four years until quitting MV to join Honda in 1965.

In that final year an entirely new combination arrived on the Grand Prix circuit: Giacomo Agostini and the three-cylinder MV Agusta. Having always dreamed of an Italian rider on an Italian bike in the larger (350 and 500cc) racing classes, this was what MV owner Count Domenico Agusta wanted.

Agostini ('Ago') had made his name with the tiny Moto Morini factory, winning the 250cc Senior Italian Championship title in 1964. Having beaten no less a rider/bike combination than Tarquinio Provini and the four-cylinder

Benelli, he was immediately signed up by the Count.

The new MV was a 343.9cc (48x46mm) across-the-frame triple with its cylinders included forwards some 10-degrees from the vertical. Other items of the machine's impressive technical specification included a seven-speed transmission, 46cm (18ins) wire wheels with Borrani alloy rims, a 16-litre (3.5 UK gallon) fuel tank, and a quad-cam 240mm (nine-and-a-half inches) drum front brake of immense power. With over 62bhp at 13,500rpm, the new MV triple could at last challenge the Japanese dominance of the class. With a maximum

speed of 241kph (150mph), it was not only as rapid as its larger four-cylinder 500cc brother, but because of its lighter weight and superior power-to-weight ratio, it was a superior racing machine.

Agusta's new paring of Agostini and the triple made a truly sensational Grand Prix debut. The race report headline in *Motor Cycling* magazine, on 1 May 1965, said it all: 'Agostini shatters Redman'. The story went on to recount: 'Undefeated throughout last season's 350cc classic races, Honda team leader Jim Redman met his match in Giacomo Agostini and the new three-cylinder MV'. The pace was so

hot that Redman crashed, while Ago's team-mate Mike Hailwood, on one of the old four-cylinder machines, was the only rider to escape being lapped in the 96-mile race.

Agostini went on to win a record 15 world titles, the majority of them riding 350, and later 500cc, versions of the MVs glorious Three.

Engine: 343.9cc dohc 4v triple, 48x46mm, air-cooled
Power: 62.5bhp at 13,500rpm
Gearbox: 7-speed foot change
Final drive: chain
Weight: 116kg (256lb)
Top speed: 240kph (149mph)

MV AGUSTA 350 SPORT   1970

The 350 twin cylinder series was launched at the Milan Show in November 1969. It was developed from the earlier 250, which had entered production in 1967. The MV engineering team created the larger engine by increasing the cylinder bore from 53 to 63mm, leaving the stroke at 56mm. This gave a displacement of 348.9cc.

Various versions of the 350 B series were marketed, the most popular being the 'S' (Sport). Early models featured battery/coil ignition, but a restyled Sport with electronic ignition was first shown to the public in 1972. This model was known as the Sport Elettronica.

There was also the GT (coil ignition) and GTE (Gran Turismo Elettronica with electronic ignition); the Scrambler with twin hi-level exhausts on the offside; and a GTE police version, with pannier bags, crash bars, windscreen, siren and direction indicator.

The 350cc twin-cylinder series was launched in 1969. Various versions of the round-case 350B were marketed, the most popular being the S (sport) seen here.

The later electronic ignition version of the Sport was available (as were some of the fours) with a fairing which closely resembled the type used by the factory's three- and four-cylinder racing models of the same period.

Although the 350 was based on the 250, the styling was much more modern and sporting, even on the touring version (except the initial batch of GT models which closely followed the 250, with its square-cut mudguards). As for the engine, this was of a very clean appearance, almost looking like a two-stroke instead of an overhead-valve unit. The cylinder head and barrel were in aluminium, and there were twin Dell 'Orto carburettors. In traditional MV fashion, lubrication was taken care of by a gear-type pump and was of the wet-sump variety.

The five-speed gearbox and wet multi-plate clutch were in unit

with the engine, while the foot-operated gear change was on the offside. All models were fitted with full-width drum brakes, front and rear.

The round-case B series 350 range was replaced in 1975 by the new Ipotesi. This still employed pushrod-operated valves, but had squared-off outer casings and finning for the cylinders and heads. The 350 S version had a very modern styling job with cast-alloy wheels and triple disc brakes. There was also a GT variant that had twin discs at the front and a drum at the rear, with wire wheels. Production ceased in 1978.

Engine: 348.9cc ohv 2v parallel twin, 63x56mm, air-cooled
Power: 28 bhp at 8400rpm
Gearbox: 5-speed foot change
Final drive: chain
Weight: 149kg (329lb)
Top speed: 155kph (97mph)

MV AGUSTA 750S   1971

Although the 750 S was first displayed on the company's stand at the Milan Show in November 1969, it did not go on sale until 1971. It was well worth the long wait because, unlike its older brother, the 600, the 'S' displayed all the style, glamour and beauty that was expected of a four-cylinder MV Agusta.

At last MV had got it right, almost two decades after the first road-going prototype-only R19 of 1950. Compared to the poor-selling 600, itself launched in the mid-1960s, the 750 S was a

stunning creation which was sleek and colourful, with its distinctive red, white and blue paint job.

As was to be expected on a four-cylinder MV, the real point of interest was the power unit, but this was now complemented by real street credibility: a bankable café-racer style, with clip-ons, rear sets, bum-stop racing saddle

Making its debut at the 1969 Milan show, the 750S entered production in 1971. This 1973 example has the optional factory fairing fitted.

(finished in red), a jelly-mould tank, a four-pipe chrome-plated exhaust with matching megaphones, and massive Grimeca-made drum brakes, with a 220mm (9in) four leading-shoe device at the front. All this was set off by an abundance of highly polished chrome and stainless steel. The castings of the 743cc (65x56mm) double overhead-cam four-cylinder engine were in a traditional MV matt 'sand cast' finish. Besides the 'S', small numbers of the touring GT and super-sporting SS versions were also built.

To this day, no one knows what caused Count Agusta to make such a U-turn. Was it lack of sales of the 600, the desire for a machine that would justify the badge, or simply common sense? The truth behind the Type 214 (the 750 S official code) will never be known, since the Count died in 1971 of a heart attack.

The most likely reason was the launch of Honda's trend-setting CB750 four at the Tokyo Show in October 1968. In 1965 MV had the distinction of being the first factory to present a modern across-the-frame, four-cylinder

motorcycle, the 600, but Honda had launched a bike that mattered commercially. Sales of the CB750 exceeded a staggering 61,000 during its first three years in the US alone, while total production of all four-cylinder MVs during the 1960s and 1970s is unlikely to have reached the 2000 figure.

Engine: 742.9cc dohc 2v four, 65x56mm, air-cooled
Power: 65bhp at 8500rpm
Gearbox: 5-speed foot change
Final drive: shaft
Weight: 230kg (505lb)
Top speed: 201kph (125mph)

MV AGUSTA 125 SPORT   1975

Following the introduction of the new 350 Sport (known as the Ipotesi) with its square-cut lines, triple disc brakes and cast-alloy wheels, MV's management also put into production a very similar and equally modernised 125 Sport overhead-valve single.

Except for its square casings and finning for the top end, the engine was very much as before, with the same 53x56mm bore-and-stroke dimensions which the Verghera-based company had used even in its earliest 125 two-stroke, and then continued over the years in its various series of pushrod-engined machines.

However, the rest of the machine was entirely new. The frame, for example, which had straight top rails, was of a full duplex cradle type, rather than the open 'banana' sub-frame affair used earlier.

On the 125, wire wheels were fitted in preference to the cast-alloy ones found on the new 350 S, and the rear brake was a drum, with a single 230mm (9ins) disc up front.

With its silver frame, red bodywork and black exhaust, the 125 Sport looked as if it was capable of a high performance but owners were to be disappointed.

Introduced in 1975, the restyled 125 Sport was the last of MV's long-running 123.5cc ohv unit singles. A disc brake and double cradle frame marked it out.

The performance was no better than that of the earlier pushrod 125 MV roadsters and it had a maximum speed of 115kph (72mph).

Like the 350 S Ipotesi, the 1975 125 Sport was also available at extra cost with a fairing based on the company's three- and four-cylinder racing models of the era, complete with matching red and silver paint work.

The 123.5cc engine ran a compression ratio of 9.8:1, a square-slide Dell 'Orto VHB 22mm carburettor, five-speed gearbox (in unit with the engine), a wet multi-plate clutch, geared primary drive, wet-sump lubrication and a Dansi electronic flywheel magneto ignition system.

Other details of the little MV included: a 19-litre (4 UK gallon) fuel tank, a length-adjustable saddle, two-piston Scarab brake caliper and a cast-iron 230mm (9ins) disc and a 136mm (five-and-a-quarter ins) diameter drum rear brake.

The wheel rims were Borrani alloys, with 2.75 section, 46cm (18ins) tyres in both the front and rear.

Engine: 123.5cc 2v single, 53x56mm, air-cooled
Power: 12bhp at 8500rpm
Gearbox: 5-speed foot change
Final drive: chain
Weight: l03kg (227lb)
Top speed: 115kph (71.5mph)

MV Agusta F4 1998

Hailed by many as the ultimate Superbike, the MV Agusta F4 could easily have been a Cagiva, a Ducati, or even a Ferrari. The fact that it was an MV represents a fitting tribute to one of the strangest true-life biking projects.

The whole F4 saga began as the result of conversations between two men – Claudio Castiglioni, the Cagiva boss and his chief designer Massimo Tamburini – with help from Piero Ferrari, son of Enzo Ferrari, and Ferrari's owners, Fiat.

First rumours concerning a brand new Cagiva-masterminded Superbike began to surface at the beginning of the 1990s. Then at the launch of the new Ferrari 465 GT car, a photograph of the new engine was shown by mistake. Claudio Castiglioni was forced to confirm that the engine was being developed in conjunction with Ferrari, and that both Castiglioni and Pieri Ferrari had actually tested the prototype machine.

Cagiva's financial hiccup of the mid-1990s slowed development at the company's secret hilltop research centre in San Marino, but in spring 1998, the first examples of this long-awaited machine arrived. For a start, it was badged

Hailed by many as the ultimate superbike, MV Agusta's F4 entered production in 1998. It was styled by Massimo Tamburini, the man responsible for Ducati's 916.

as an MV Agusta (Cagiva having purchased the brand name in the 1980s). Having sold Ducati to the American TPG finance house, it could not have used the Ducati name, even if it had wanted to.

As for the motorcycle, not only did its style place the F4 ahead of every other series production sports bike in the world, but it also had many innovative technical features.

The four-valves-per-cylinder 749.8cc (73.8x43.8mm) double-overhead-cam, across-the-frame, liquid-cooled, four-cylinder engine had the advantage of the very latest Weber-Marelli electronic fuel injection and ignition systems, a removable (cassette-type) six-speed gearbox and a radical radial valve cylinder head.

The F4's frame is made up of a 'mixed' steel and aluminium structure, while the single-sided swinging-arm is cast in aluminium and the frame's steering head angle is multi-adjustable. Front suspension is a specially built inverted Showa fork assembly. The Ohlins hydraulic steering damper mounted across the frame and an exhaust that exits under the seat are Tamburini trademarks.

Massimo Tamburini's team came up with a particularly innovative front light. The twin-stacked polyellipsoidals give the F4 an unmistakable appearance, while also allowing for a very narrow fairing for maximum aerodynamics.

Throughout, the detailing on the F4 is superb. Coupled with the flamboyant style and performance – just over 272kph (170mph) – this makes it a 'must own' for the serious sports rider.

Engine: 749.4cc dohc 4v straight four, 73.8x43.8mm, liquid-cooled
Power: 126bhp at 12,200rpm
Gearbox: 6-speed foot change
Final drive: chain
Weight: 180kg (397lb)
Top speed: 272kph (170mph)

MZ/MuZ GERMANY 1953–

MZ AND ITS MODERN successor MuZ can both trace their origins back to the years immediately following World War I, with the birth of the DKW marque in 1919. Over 25 years, DKW became one of the greatest motorcycle companies the world has ever seen.

Like other German marques, DKW suffered during World War II. When peace came in May 1945, this brought more problems. MZs Zschopau works were severely damaged by Allied bombing, and the company was left in the Soviet sector when Germany was partitioned. By order of the Soviet Military Administration, the factory was completely dismantled between 1945 and 1946. After production at Wilischthal, preparations for the re-introduction of motorcycle manufacture at Zschopau were made in 1949.

However, before this could take place, the Communist regime gained powers to nationalise large enterprises, including DKW, and on 1 July 1948 ownership of the Zschopau plant passed to the newly formed Industrieverwaltung Fahrzenbau (IFA). After

A 1957 MZ BK350 two-stroke flat-twin. Launched in 1952 under the IFA brand name, the machine had a top speed of 117kph (73mph).

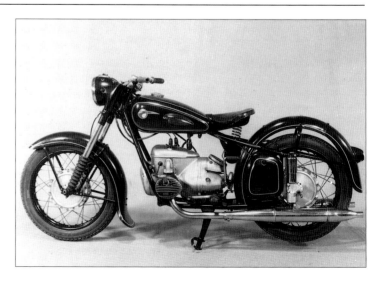

MZ dominated events such as the ISDT for much of the 1960s. The 1964 squad is seen here, on its specially-prepared ES/G two-stroke singles.

overcoming endless problems, production resumed in May 1950 under the IFA brand name. Its first model was a revised DKW RT125.

Launched in 1952, the first 'new' design was the BK350. Still a two-stroke, this looked similar to a BMW of the era with its horizontally opposed cylinders, telescopic forks, plunger rear suspension, shaft final drive and sideways-operating kick-starter. The 349cc piston port engine produced 17bhp, with a top speed of 117kph (73mph). Its seven-year production ran until 1959.

By this date, IFA was marketing the machines as MZ, or to give the full title, Motorraderwerke Zschopau. The name MZ had first been used in 1953 when engineer Walter Kaaden founded the MZ Sport department to develop competition motorcycles for both road racing and endurance trials. Although these early dirt bikes were at first little more than carefully prepared stock roadsters with knobbly tyres, the road racers were specialist designs with disc-valve induction and class-leading power output figures.

By 1955, the 125cc racing MZ single-cylinder disc-valve two-

stroke was producing 15bhp and could achieve 152kph (95mph).

The following year, a youngster named Ernst Degner joined the MZ team. Not only was he to emerge as the Eastern sector's top rider over the next decade, but at the end of 1961, he defected while racing in Sweden and went to work and ride for the Japanese giant, Suzuki.

By the 1960 model year, the MZ range of series production models comprised the 125/3, ES 175 and 250, ES 250 with sidecar, and ES 175G/250G, the latter two being complete customer versions of the factory's own International Six Day Trial bikes.

As for the 125/3, this was an updated RT125, now with six-and-a-half brake horsepower at 5200rpm, while the gearbox had an extra ratio, making four in all. Whereas the balance of the range came with

A typical MZ TS two-stroke commuter bike from the late 1970s and early 1980s. These were available in 125, 150 or 250cc engine sizes.

modern swinging-arm rear suspension and Earles-type front forks, the 125/3 retained telescopic front forks and plunger rear suspension, but the final drive chain was now fully enclosed (like the rest of the range) with rubber gaiters, a feature which would continue to distinguish MZ motorcycles for 30 years.

After Ernst Degner's defection, Alan Shepherd, Mike Hailwood and, later, Derek Woodman all rode MZs in Grand Prix. Various local riders such as Horst Fugner, Walter Musiol and the Hungarian Lazio Szabo were also under contract. MZ's star rider of the late

MOTOPIANA
Italy (Florence) 1923–31: Working backwards, this company produced an in-house 250cc overhead-valve; a side-valve version of the same motor (1927); as well as assembling machines with Villiers and JAP engines, the former 150 to 250cc, the latter, 250 to 500cc.

MOTORFLY
France (Voisin) 1920: This was an auxiliary, two-stroke cycle motor, 157cc, weighing 317kg (697lb), which had friction drive to the rear wheel.

MOTORMEYER
The Netherlands 1949–51: Two-stroke split-singles with 350cc capacity powered these machines from the Netherlands.

MOTOSOLO
Belgium 1920s: These machines were middleweights with chain-cum-belt drive.

MOTOTECNICA DELL'ITALIA CENTRALE
Italy (Florence) 1953–86: These Italian machines were initially 125cc lightweights, and later of 80cc capacity, and the company also produced mopeds. Most of these machines were pretty utilitarian, save for the occasional off-road sport model.

MOTO-V
Italy (Turin) 1927: From this Italian company, a pressed-steel frame was offered which housed a 325cc motor. The 'V' stands for Vandone, which was the constructor.

1960s was Heinz Rossner, who was backed up on occasions by the Englishman Peter Williams and the Italian Silvio Grassetti.

On the dirt, MZ excelled in events such as the International Six Day Trial, which they dominated for much of the 1960s on specially prepared versions of its ES models. Designated 'G', meaning Gelandermotor (off-road machine), these were campaigned in 175, 250 and 300cc engine sizes with great success. In the 1970s,

The limited production, high performance 1995 MuZ Skorpian could reach 200kph (125mph), using a five-valve Yamaha engine, in a British-designed chassis.

the Czech Jawas (see above) dominated the ISDT in much the same way as MZ had done in the previous decade. However, in the 1980s the East German marque staged something of a comeback with new machinery. Now known as the ISDE (International Six Day Enduro), the event had changed and favoured motocross-type machines. MZ responded to this by introducing bikes with air- and water-cooled engines, steeply angled twin rear shocks, leading axle font forks, plastic bodywork (including the fuel tank) and extremely high ground clearance. Later, a brand new 500cc with liquid-cooling, monoshock rear suspension, square section

Reformed as MuZ in 1992, this 1993 Rotax-powered four-stroke Silver Star Classic was one of the first models built under the new management.

swinging-arm, disc front brake and even upside-down (inverted) front forks came onto the scene.

Unlike their trials brothers during the 1960s, MZ's production roadsters had Earles-type front forks, which gave the machines a heavyweight look and provided great comfort, offset against which were staid, touring-bias locks.

To counteract this, in 1969 MZ introduced the new ETS 250 Trophy Sport. Indeed, it was with one of these models that the

company celebrated building its millionth bike in 1970. Although still using the same 247cc single cylinder piston-port engine, it was some 4kg (9lb) lighter and had a much more sporty appearance, at least by MZ's previous standards. The ETS was replaced in the early 1970s by the five-speed TS250, which was to run for over a decade until replaced by a new ETZ model in 1983.

The ETZ can be seen as the definitive cheap-to-buy MZ roadster, and although offering only an extra 2bhp (21 instead of 19bhp) over the TS250, it did have several worthwhile improvements, most notably in the braking department, thanks to a 280mm (11in) Brembo front disc brake. A 301 (actually 291cc) version was also offered. In July 1983, MZ built its two millionth machine, an ETZ 250. Besides these, there were TS and ETZ models with 125 and 150cc engine sizes.

A race kit for the MZ 250 was offered, originally for German MZ-Cup events. This kit comprised a new cylinder, head, exhaust, piston and gearbox components. MZ claimed 44bhp and it transformed the humble commuter bike into a machine that could provide cheap race-track thrills. MZ racing also became popular in other European countries during the 1980s and 1990s, including the UK.

After the fall of the Berlin Wall and the subsequent take-over of state-owned industries by a trust,

The prototype-only Kobra of 1994 used a Yamaha TDM 850 parallel-twin engine. It offered exciting performance and a racer-style image.

known as Deutsche Trehand, in September 1990, MZ rapidly went into decline. Sales plummeted to such a point that by the end of 1991 MZ were bankrupt.

When a brand-new company Motorrad und Zweirddwerk (MuZ) was formed on 1 July 1992, the number of employees had fallen from 3000 to a mere 80. The old factory at Zschopau had been abandoned in favour of a much

smaller, newly built plant at Hohndorf, 9.5 km (6 miles) away.

Their original plan called for the complete axing of the old two-stroke range. However, in 1990 a licence had been granted to build the ETZ series in Turkey. In addition a new 125, the Saxon Star, was to be built in Germany. MuZ concentrated on a new series of models with four-stroke engines from Rotax and then Yamaha.

In August 1996 came the news that MuZ was bankrupt. The Malaysian Hong Leong company bought the firm, announcing that it would inject eight million pounds into developing new models, while the existing five-valve Yamaha single cylinder-power Skorpian would be improved.

By 2000, MuZ's range included state-of-the-art on-off road bikes which compared with the best.

MZ 125/250 GP RACERS

1950s–1960s

The MZ racing story began back in 1951 when a private German tuner, Daniel Zimmermann, modified his home-made IFA-built, DKW RT125-based machine by means of a crude crankshaft-driven rotary disc valve. Zimmermann also changed the engine's bore and stroke from 52x58mm to the now widely used square 54x54mm dimensions. Although Zimmermann came up with the basic formula, the gifted engineer Walter Kaaden refined it into a world-beating design.

In 1953 Kaaden set up the MZ Sport department for both road racing and off-road competition, and by the late 1950s had steadily developed the idea to such a point that the 125 was producing 20bhp (160bhp/litre), while a new 250 twin cylinder model was good for 36bhp.

For 1959, MZ signed its first foreign rider, the diminutive Swiss star Luigi Taveri. Over the next 15 years, a steady flow of non-Germans rode Kaaden's bikes including Gary Hocking, Alan Shepherd, Mike Hailwood, Derek Woodman and Silvio Grassetti. This year also saw a technical breakthrough when Kaaden adopted a third transfer port (bridged like companions to prevent the single Dykes piston ring fouling the cylinder). This, together with more tuning and an increase in reliability, meant almost 2bhp extra on the 125 single. By 1960, the 123.6cc (54x54mm), six-speed engine was

In 1961, the disc-valve MZ single-cylinder GP racer produced 25bhp at 10,800rpm. This was the first time that the magic 200bhp/litre mark had been passed.

producing 23bhp at 10,700rpm, while its maximum speed had risen to 180kph (115mph). The following year, the power was up 25bhp (the magic 200bhp/litre broken for the first time) and a speed of 193kph (120mph).

Then in 1961 came controversy when MZ's top rider, Ernst Degner, quit after the Swedish Grand Prix. This enabled Honda's Tom Phillis to scoop the world title, with victory in the final round in Argentina. Many believe that Degner took MZ's secrets to his new employers, Suzuki. Certainly, the Japanese company went on to win the newly created

50cc title in 1962 with Degner aboard.

As for Kaaden and his team, this was a hammer blow from which they never fully recovered. Even though from 1962, water-cooled versions of both the 125 single and 250 twin made their debuts, after 1961 MZ's best finishes in the championships were third in the 125cc for Derek Woodman in 1965, and thirds for both Alan Shepherd in 1964 and Heinz Rossner in 1968 in the 250cc category.

Engine: 123.6cc disc valve 2s single, 54x54mm, air-cooled
Power: 25bhp at 10,800rpm
Gearbox: 6-speed foot change
Final drive: chain
Weight: 75kg (165lb)
Top speed: 193kph (120mph)

MZ WANKEL

1960s

During the early 1960s, MZ's engineering team devised a project which, although never making it to production, is still of significant historical and technical interest. This was the Wankel-engined

series of prototypes, which culminated in the liquid-cooled KKM 175W (1963) and air-cooled KKM 175L (1965). Both machines were the work of chief development engineer Herbert Friedrich,

and closely followed the engineering concept created at NSU in West Germany by Felix Wankel, the father of the rotary piston engine.

MZ's first Wankel prototype featured shaft drive and water-cooling. The engine remained oil-cooled, while the cycle parts were based around the production ES 250 of the same era. In 1965, a more advanced air-cooled version appeared from the East German factory, but this too was destined never to go into production.

The MZ design incorporated rotating pistons lying crossways to the direction of the travel, cleverly integrated into a conventional-looking engine casing and housing four foot-operated gear ratios. Its silencer was a peculiar shape due to the unorthodox positioning of the outlet at the top of the engine. The KKM 175L produced 24bhp at 5750rpm and could achieve a very respectable 129kph (80mph).

Although the 1965 MZ Wankel was claimed to have been a technical success, the factory

'shelved the concept, concentrating on its conventional two-stroke engines. The main reason was cost: MZ would have needed to

invest in a complete re-design of the production lines, in more machinery and to obtain a licence from NSU to begin production.

During the early 1960s, MZ were a decade in front of their rivals in building a Wankel-engined street bike. But they never put their 174cc model into production.

When we consider that the first production Wankel motorcycles did not appear for another decade (Hercules W2000 and Suzuki RE5) and that both were financially embarrassing for their respective companies, perhaps it was just as well MZ didn't go for the honour of this particular world's first.

Engine: 174cc, rotary single, air-cooled
Power: 24bhp at 5750rpm
Gearbox: 4-speed foot change
Final drive: chain
Weight: n/a
Top speed: 130kph (81mph)

MuZ Skorpian

1993

The first truly new MuZ was the Skorpian, powered by a water-cooled 660cc five-valve single overhead-cam Yamaha engine. It was created by a design team from the UK, Richard Seymour and Dick Powell. This London-based studio came up with several versions of the basic Skorpian theme and also of the prototype-only Yamaha TDM 850 twin-engined Kobra supersports roadster.

The mainstream model was the Skorpian Sport, with a half fairing, which left both the engine and frame in full view. Three colours were initially on offer: yellow, black and green. Putting out 48bhp, and also built in a restricted 34bhp version for novice riders, the Skorpian Sport's specification included a Delta box tubular steel frame, 41mm (one-and-a-half inch) telescopic front forks, 43cm (17ins) cast-alloy wheels, disc brakes front and rear, an electric starter, five-speed gearbox, monoshock rear suspension and a 12volt electrical system.

Soon there were other versions, such as the naked Skorpian Tour, an off-road bike and the 'hot' fully faired Skorpian Replica.

Besides having more power, the Replica boasted inverted Dutch-made White Power front forks with no less than 20 possible adjustments for compression damping and eight for rebound. The monoshock rear suspension was again of White Power origin. Other top brand-name components

The first truly new MuZ was the Skorpian, powered by a water-cooled 660cc five-valve Yamaha single-cylinder engine. It produced 48bhp at 6500rpm.

included: Brembo brakes, with four-piston Goldline callipers and twin (instead of single on the other models) 180mm (7ins) semi-floating discs at the front and a dual piston caliper and single 240mm (nine-and-a-half inches) disc at the rear. Compared with the

Sport, the Replica also had wider tyres – 120/60 front and 160/60 rear – whereas the Sport had 110/70 and 150/60 respectively.

The factory claimed the Replica could do 200kph (125mph), or 208kph (130mph) with the optional tuning kit. Its dry weight was 165kg (363lb), some 5kg (11lb) lighter than the Sport. This was surprising considering that it had a full fairing, rather than the nose-cone type which featured on the Sport.

A number of Skorpian racing models, which were used by both works-supported and private riders, have achieved considerable success throughout Europe in the popular Supermono racing class.

Engine: 660cc ohc 5v single, 100x84mm, water-cooled
Power: 48bhp at 6500rpm
Gearbox: 5-speed foot change
Final drive: chain
Weight: 170kg (375lb)
Top speed: 174kph (109mph)

The 500cc vertical single is forever associated with Norton, whether from 1927 (right), 1938 (below right) or in trials guise in 1950 (bottom).

Brooklands and elsewhere. The Model 18 overhead-valve version of the 16H engine was developed for the 1923 season (late 1922), and world records kept on falling to Norton. Yet perhaps the greatest success was an outright win at the Senior in 1924, a year before Pa's death from cancer. In 1926, the firm was financially reconstructed yet again.

The CS1 overhead-cam model appeared in 1927 as a racer, and in 1928 as a super-sports machine, still with the 79x100mm bore and stroke, for 490cc. This, in fact, (in single overhead-cam and double overhead-cam form) was pretty much what sustained Norton through the 1930s, the years of the 'Inter'. The 1940s saw both the Big Four and the 16H in military guise – still with open-valve gear – but the apotheosis of the Norton single came in 1950 with the immortal 498cc Manx Norton. This machine should have been outclassed by the twins, fours and even V-8s that were matched against it, but it went on to win races well into the 1960s.

From 1949, it had an internal rival in the form of the (equally immortal) Dominator twin. The 500cc 'Dommie' had 29bhp and an indifferent, and heavy, frame when it was introduced but when, in 1952, it was put into the Featherbed frame to create the

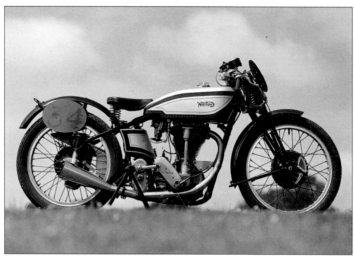

Above: It is hard to decide which decade saw the greatest Nortons of all, but many would say the 1930s: this 500cc 'cammy' Norton dates from 1938.

Dommie 88, the handling made up for the modest power output. Even so, plenty of people put the more powerful Triumph engines into the same frames to create Tritons. And at around the same time, Norton became a part of AMC, yet another indication of less than robust financial health.

AMC was by no means bad news, however, and perhaps the greatest Dommie was the 1962 650SS, with a bigger engine and 49bhp, a wonderful combination of power, 'flickability' and (reasonable) smoothness. The 750cc Atlas of 1964 was a further development of this design – Norton finally stopped making singles in that year – and the Commando (1968) was essentially an Atlas engine in an improved frame with 'Isolastic' engine

For many years, big, heavy 500cc four-stroke singles were eclipsed by buzzy two-strokes for trials and scrambles; but there is a charm to machines like this 1950 500T.

Above: A beautiful 1966 650SS. Unfortunately, the period marked a severe downturn in Norton's fortunes, from which it never recovered.

Right: The 1500cc V8 'Nemesis' was one of the greatest might-have-beens in an industry which is unfortunately well known for its might-have-beens.

Below: Although Nortons are forever associated with 500cc singles, the parallel twins were also formidable machines, from the early 1950s to the last manifestations of the Commando (pictured).

Above: The Rotary, seen here in 1990 racing guise, did well – including winning the 1992 Senior Isle of Man TT – but not well enough to ensure the continued survival of the marque.

mounting to isolate the rider from the vibration. Isolastics needed maintenance, but if in good order, they worked very well indeed.

There were lesser models: 250cc Jubilees (1958), various 350cc machines, trials versions and so on, but the only one most people remember is the ES2 pushrod version of the 500cc single, which ceased production in 1974. What they also remember is that when AMC fell apart in 1966, Dennis Poore bought out the remains to form Norton Villiers Triumph (NVT). He continued to make Commandos for a few years, including the 850 – which was altogether too big for an engine originally designed as a 500, with the result that vibration was on a Harley-Davidson scale – and the downright disastrous Combat version of the engine, which was also grievously overstressed.

When this generation went into liquidation in 1978, it was a rotary engine that kept the name alive for another 15 years or so. First, there was the Interpol 2 police bike (much admired by those who rode it), followed by civilian versions such as the Classic and Commander, and finally came the F1 race replica. The trouble was that they were not made in sufficient numbers or priced high enough to make a profit. And thus, after almost 100 years, the Norton name fizzled out.

NORTON
1902

Although the original Norton Energette had a two-speed gearbox, it had no clutch; such progressive features as gearboxes were not widely fitted to Nortons in the early years. The first Norton machine was made in 1902, which demolishes their claim to be one of the earliest makers. Norton was founded in 1898, but Marston's (who made Sunbeams) had been founded in the eighteenth century.

Engine: 169cc aise single, air-cooled
Power: n/a
Gearbox: 2-speed hand change
Final drive: belt
Weight: n/a
Top speed: 32kph (20mph)

NORTON INTERNATIONAL
1936

The Inter traced its ancestry to the 1927 CS1, but was substantially re-designed in 1929 when Walter Moore defected to NSU: the 29bhp 'Carrol' engine was good for around 160kph (100mph) in that year. The valve gear was enclosed for 1930, and the dry-sump, overhead-cam ('cammy') Norton – which was to dominate racing for decades to come – was born.

The International name – almost invariably abbreviated to Inter – referred to two models: the Model 30 500cc and the Model 40 350cc

The 'Inter' evolved steadily, and because it was a popular club racer, it was often updated. This is a 1952 example.

Engine: 490cc sohc 79x100mm, single, air-cooled
Power: 40bhp at 6000rpm
Gearbox: 4-speed foot change
Final drive: chain
Weight: n/a
Top speed: 175 kph (110mph)

(actually 348cc, 71x88mm), introduced in September 1931 for the 1932 season.

The machine evolved steadily throughout the 1930s, with race-proven technology being adopted as soon as it was appropriate for the road bikes. For example, in 1936 the plunger rear end was tried out on the works racers for the first time, and was then fitted as standard on Inters after 1938.

NORTON 16H
1942

The name 16H (Model 16, Home) first appeared in 1921 for the 1922 model year, and was chosen to distinguish it from the 17C for Model 17, Colonial, although the engine was a World War I design. It was so primitive that, until 1922, owners had to file the valve stems in order to set the valve clearance.

The 16H acquired a saddle tank (in place of the old flat one) in 1929; in 1932, the exhaust swapped sides; in 1935, it acquired a four-speed box; and in 1938 the 'Cow's Udder' exhaust was fitted, an item widely regarded as the most spectacularly ugly silencer ever fitted to any motorcycle.

Engine: 490cc sv single, 79x100mm, air-cooled
Power: 12.5bhp
Gearbox: 4-speed foot change
Final drive: chain
Weight: 177kg (390lb)
Top speed: 110 kph (70mph)

The 16H (meaning Model 16, Home) was a very long-lived, primitive design which appeared in 1921 and served throughout World War II before finally disappearing in 1954.

The wartime version still had exposed valve gear (it would be covered up after the war, although the machine would disappear until 1954) and even though it was extremely primitive – or, perhaps, precisely because it was extremely primitive – it had a reputation for being 'squaddie proof'. When you consider how many of these machines were re-sprayed in civilian colours after the war, it is amusing to see people carefully restoring the services versions. Over 100,000 of these solid machines were sold to the forces.

NORTON MANX
1950

Arguably the greatest Norton of all time, the Manx Norton derived its engineering from the International. This is a 1957 348cc example.

The reason for all the variables in the specification is twofold. First, with engines at the limits of the power available at a given time, exact power outputs vary. Second, Manxes were often tuned to give even more power, and stripped and drilled for 'added lightness'. What is more, they were made for a very long time. John Tickle bought the rights in 1969 and built a few; Unit Equipe then bought the rights from John Tickle, and Molnar Manx bought the rights from him in 1994. Although the company mainly sold engines, it also built complete Manxes in frames of its own manufacture.

The result was that, over a period of more than 50 years, these legendary motorcycles delighted riders and spectators alike, first in state-of-the-art racing – the last 'mainstream' win was probably the Yugoslav Grand Prix of 1969 – and then in classic racing. A late, well-fettled Manx was good for over 217kph (135mph) flat out.

The engine was essentially a 'double knocker' development of the Inter, with the short stroke adopted in 1938, but what really made the machine was the 'featherbed' frame, designed by the McCandless brothers. Upon its introduction, this machine became the benchmark against which others were compared. Norton won both the Junior and Senior TTs in 1953, coming in first, second and third in both events, due to the frame; brilliant riding and a good deal of design input on the engine from Leo Kuzmicki, also helped. A sweeper at the Norton factory, he was a former fighter-pilot and lecturer in internal combustion engines at Warsaw University.

Engine: 498cc ohc single, 82x94.3mm, air-cooled
Power: 45–50bhp at 6500–7000rpm
Gearbox: 4-speed foot change
Final drive: chain
Weight: n/a
Top speed: 200kph (125mph) plus

NORTON DOMINATOR
1949

The Dommie first appeared with the rather heavy and crude rear-suspension frame derived from the pre-war models; another pre-war feature was the abysmally inadequate brakes. The power output was not very impressive because the engine was designed to run on 'pool' petrol, and the compression ratio was just 6.75:1. The very mild valve-timing, however, leads one to suspect that Norton was holding plenty in reserve.

On the other hand, there is a great deal to be said for smoothness, and this first, soft Dommie was the smoothest of them all. A cruising speed of

The Dommie started out fairly 'soft' and dull: it was the 1952 Featherbed-framed Dommie 88 that really made the machine's name.

104–113kph (65–70mph) was available on almost any road, with the 145kph (90mph) top speed requiring a bit of concentration.

Engine: 497cc ohv parallel twin 66x72.6mm, air-cooled
Power: 29bhp at 6000rpm
Gearbox: 4-speed foot change
Final drive: chain
Weight: 186kg (410lb)
Top speed: 145kph (90mph)

NORTON COMMANDO   1968

The Dommie engine had gone from 500 to 600cc (the 99) to 750cc (the Atlas), and in the process it had inevitably acquired a tendency to vibrate more and more.

The solution was Isolastic mounting. The engine, gearbox and swinging-arm were assembled as a unit, along with the exhausts and rear wheel, then assembled into a new, single, top tube frame using Isolastic rubber mounts to insulate the frame (and the rider) from the vibration concomitant with an oversized parallel twin.

The result was a machine of stunning good looks, remarkable acceleration and top speed, and superb handling, if the Isolastic mounts were in good order. It soon replaced the Atlas, and variants quickly followed: the Commando S (1969) for the American market (oversize bars, undersize tank and high-level exhausts) and the Roadster (1970), an S with conventional exhausts. The original was the Fastback.

Racing variants with 68bhp appeared in 1970. In 1971 came the hideous Hi-Rider with ape-hanger bars and the Fastback LR

This Commando is a 750S from 1969: the American market was deemed by Norton to want the high handlebars and fashionable high-level pipes.

with a 25litre (5.5 UK gallon), long-range tank, probably the most desirable of all Commandos. The 1971 Combat engine with 65bhp was a less desirable innovation; pushed hard, it usually broke. The 1973 829cc 850 was an overbored, 77x89mm 750 delivering 60bhp

Engine: 745cc ohv parallel win 73x89mm, air-cooled
Power: 49bhp
Gearbox: 4-speed foot change
Final drive: chain
Weight: n/a
Top speed: 185kph (115mph)

with a reduced compression ratio. Although the new Interstate with this engine was road-tested at 194kph (121mph), vibration was a recurring problem. After 1974, all Commandos used the 850 motor.

NORTON COMMANDER ROTARY   1988

The history of the last Norton – one of the most famous – is unexpected. Research was initiated by BSA in 1969 and passed to NVT in 1973 when they bought BSA. By 1983, it had been developed into a workable, air-cooled police bike, the Interpol II, almost by accident. It then passed on again to a new company under Phillipe Le Roux in 1987, in whose care it was converted to liquid-cooling for the Commander in the spring of 1988. Further development led to a racing version giving over 145bhp at 10,000rpm (and 304kph/189mph). It finally died, only a short time after Norton's last victory at the Senior in 1992.

And that is how Nortons should be remembered: champions at the first ever Isle of Man TT in 1907, and winners in the Senior in 1924, 1926, 1927, 1931, 1932, 1933, 1934, 1936, 1937, 1938, 1947, 1948, 1949, 1950, 1951, 1952, 1953, 1954, 1961, and 1992, the last with their last ever racer. That

The Rotary Classic actually looks like a motorcycle – difficult for a rotary – but still too radical for a very conservative market.

is, not counting the Juniors, the sidecars, the GPs and the Formula 750s, on the Island alone. Overall, not too bad a record!

Engine: 588cc Wankel twin-rotor, liquid-cooled
Power: 85bhp at 9000rpm
Gearbox: 5-speed foot change
Final drive: chain
Weight: n/a
Top speed: 200kph (125mph) est.

NSU

NSU (NECKARSULM STICK-MACHEN UNION) ranks alongside BMW and DKW as Germany's most famous motorcycle marque. During the first half of the twentieth century NSU often led the world with its design, innovation and production methods, to say nothing of its sporting successes, before and after World War II.

The NSU story began in 1873 when a couple of engineers, Heinrich Stroll and Christian Schmitt, set up a business manufacturing and repairing knitting machines. At first based at Riedlingen, the fledgling concern soon moved to the town of Neckarsulm.

When Christian Schmitt died at the age of 39, his brother-in-law Gottlob Banzhaf took charge, and it was he who launched NSU into the motorcycle world.

By 1900, experiments had produced a working prototype and production began the following year. Although sturdy, the machine was crude in the extreme, with its Swiss-made ZL (Zedal) clip-on engine mounted at an incline in the centre of the frame. Engine power was transmitted via a direct drive belt, and a conventional bicycle pedal crank and chain allowed the machine to be pedalled if the engine was not working. But soon NSU switched to engines of its own design, such

as a range of V-twins with engine sizes from 496 to 996cc, which were mounted in tubular frames.

Almost instantly, the company recognised the importance of motorcycle sport as a proving ground for its technology. As early as 1905, NSU produced a purpose-built racer powered by a 402cc engine. In the same year, the marque opened a sales office in England (London). Sales exceeded even the most optimistic forecasts, with British riders purchasing almost a quarter of Germany's total motorcycle exports in 1906.

Martin Geiger, NSU's British manager, rode one of his products to fifth place in the very first Isle of Man TT races in 1907. The following year, NSU rider Liese achieved a two-way speed of 109kph (68mph), which was claimed as a world record, even though no official records were kept at the time. In 1909, Lingenfielders clocked 124kph (78mph) just outside Los Angeles to claim another record, which propelled NSU into the lucrative US market. Record-breaking was to be an important part of the NSU

The first NSU motorcycles arrived in 1901, powered by Swiss-made ZL (Zedal) engines. But soon, NSU switched to engines of its own, like this 1906 single.

story for the 50 years, culminating with Wilhelm Herz's 336kph (210mph) at Bonneville Salt Flats, Utah in August 1956, riding a supercharged double-overhead-cam NSU twin.

With the outbreak of World War I in 1914, the export market collapsed. NSU put its production into munitions. After the war, the company rapidly returned to motorcycles and by 1922 production was at full capacity and over 3000 were on the payroll.

The Neckarsulm works pioneered 'production line' techniques for the German industry, but in 1929 the famous British designer, Walter Moore, left the Norton company and joined NSU. This move aroused bitter controversy, with Moore's designs for NSU often being referred to as 'Norton Spares Used'. However, the Englishman was to stay with the German company for a decade until the outbreak of World War II in 1939. Not all Moore's NSU designs were

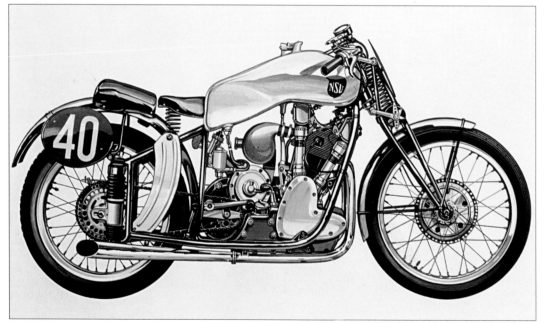

In 1938, NSU introduced this advanced supercharged 348cc dohc parallel twin Grand Prix racer; post-war, in 500cc guise, it was used for record-breaking.

four-strokes, since one of his most successful was the 98cc (49x52mm) two-stroke Quickly (see below). Between 1936 and

In August 1956, Wilhelm Herz set a new absolute world speed record of 337.02kph (210.64mph) with this streamlined 500cc NSU twin.

1953, a total of 235,411 examples were manufactured.

The peak of interwar output at NSU came in 1938 with a record number of motorcycles being produced – 62,619 – not to be bettered until 1950.

During World War II NSU built thousands of motorcycles and

A pair of single-cylinder Sportmax racing machine of the type used by HP (Happy) Muller to win the 1955 250cc World Championship.

pedal cycles for the German armed forces, as well as aircraft components, but its strangest wartime effort was the Kettenrad

NIBBIO
Italy (Milan) 1949–53: These Italian scooters were produced initially with 98 and 125cc two-stroke motors. However, the 98cc-engined model was quickly dropped.

NICHOLAS
England 1911–15: This English firm was an obscure assembler of one-and-a-half horsepower machines.

NICKSON
England (Preston) 1920–24: As well as 350 and 500cc engines from Bradshaw (overhead-valve) and Blackburne (side-valve), this English company also fitted Villiers two-strokes with capacities of up to 269cc.

NIESNER
Austria 1905–11: Fafnir and Minerva singles and V-twins powered these pioneers from Austria.

NINON
France 1931–35: This was a firm of assemblers which were responsible for fitting JAP overhead-valve singles.

NIS
Germany 1925–26: One of countless short-lived mid-1920s German assemblers, this firm was distinguished chiefly by using JAP 300cc side-valve engines, as well as 269cc two-strokes.

NISSAN
Japan 1951–56: Better known for producing cars, Nissan also made some scooters with a capacity of 60cc.

NKF
see **NFK**

NLG
England 1905–12: North London Garage believed in manufacturing powerful V-twins. Although they made 500cc singles and 750cc V-twins for road use, they also used a 2913cc JAP engine in a 1907 (or possibly 1909) racer, while a 944cc Peugeot powered another racer.

leadership NSU grew rapidly. One of his first creations was a 98cc (50x50mm) overhead-valve engined lightweight motorcycle. Named the Fox 4, this was the forerunner of a whole range of new designs which arrived over the next decade. Using a pressed-steel frame with front forks of a leading-link type patented by Roder, the Fox 4 soon became a top seller. It entered production in 1949 and soon a racing version, the Sportfox, appeared.

Also at the end of 1949 NSU concluded a licence agreement with the Italian Innocenti concern to produce the best-selling Lambretta scooter. Between 1950 and 1956, 117,000 NSU Lambrettas were produced, before NSU built their own scooter called the Prima.

Other newcomers to arrive during the early 1950s included the Fox 2, powered by a 123cc (52x58mm) two-stroke engine; the Lux, a 98cc (62x66mm) two-stroke; and most notably, the 247cc (69x66mm) Max. The overhead-cam engine of the Max was all-new and featured a type of valve gear unique in the motorcycle world. Called the Ultramax system, it was patented by its designer Albert Roder, who received a royalty for each one sold.

The early 1950s also saw NSU make a successful return to both racing and record-breaking with riders such as Wilhelm Hetz, Werner Haas and HP (Happy) Muller.

But NSU's most successful production model was without doubt the Quickly moped, which in all its variants sold an amazing 1.1 million in just over a decade. Designed by Roder, the Quickly entered the market when sales were still on an upward curve. Indeed, the Quickly deserves the title 'Father of the modern moped', even though when it appeared the term 'moped' had not been invented and it was still referred to as an autocycle.

An important part of NSU's business during the early 1950s was building Lambretta scooters under licence. From 1956, NSU marketed it own scooter, the Prima.

(chaintrack motorcycle). This was a small, tracked personnel carrier which had the steering and front wheel of a motorcycle ahead of a body which carried tracks on both sides. Power came from a four-cylinder, water-cooled Opel car engine of 1478cc (80x74mm).

With a huge choice of gear ratios (six forward and two reverse), the Kettenrad was suitable for both on and off-road use. Since it was one of the very few 'go-anywhere' vehicles in postwar Germany, the Kettenrad remained in production until 1948.

Unlike many German factories, NSU re-started production almost as soon as the war was over, and by 1948 its recovery was further accelerated by the works acting as a repair centre for the US Army.

Albert Roder was appointed chief designer in 1947. Under his

Drive better -

Drive Prima

Machines with a World-Famous Name -

Prima V · Prima III + III K   Prima D

NSU

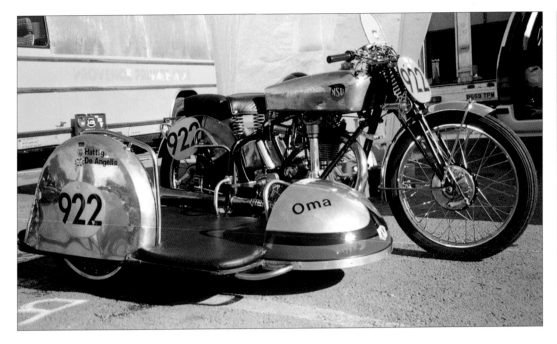

One of the most technically interesting developments of the 1950s was the Wankel engine. NSU was at the forefront of this new technology, and, in fact, other companies such as Mazda, Suzuki, Norton and Hercules had to pay licence fees to use it.

Contact with Felix Wankel first came in 1951 for NSU when its chief experimental engineer, Dr Froede, who had begun research into his own rotary valve project, needed information on sealing technology. As Wankel had been engaged in this area during the war, specifically on rotary disc

valves for Germany navy torpedo engines, it proved useful for both parties to share information.

The result was an agreement in which Wankel, Froede and NSU all became partners, and research continued in great secret throughout the rest of the 1950s. After an official announcement of the existence of the Wankel engine in 1961, the concept was to dictate much of the company's time and energy throughout the 1960s and also, ultimately, bring about its destruction.

It is apparent that NSU's management, pre-occupied with its

Englishman Walter Moore joined NSU in 1929. Throughout the 1930s, the German company built a series of ohc singles like this 1934 494cc sidecar racer.

range of rear-engined Prinz cars and the marketing of licences for the Wankel engine, allowed its motorcycle development to stagnate. Production of two-wheelers ceased in 1963.

However, it was to be the award-winning RO80 car, introduced in 1967, that was, ironically, to prove the Neckarsulm company's final, and fatal, move.

The RO80 combined a silky smooth 115bhp Wankel twin-rotor power unit with an ultra-modern styling job, which would not have looked out of place 20 years later. Unfortunately for the RO80, and most of all for NSU, the car was hampered by serious problems such as heavy fuel consumption and rapid wear of the rotor tips.

By 1969, the severe costs of warranty claims from dissatisfied customers left NSU in deep financial trouble. On 10 March of that year, the once-great marque ceased to exist as an independent body. Swallowed up by the vast Volkswagen organisation, this meant in effect that there would be no more NSU cars or motorcycles.

NSU (Neckarsulm Strickmachen Union) built a vast range of high quality motorcycles between 1901 and 1963. Today, it is part of the Volkswagen empire.

NMC
Japan early 1950s–early 1960s: These were conventional Japanese lightweights of 125 and 175cc capacity.

NOBLE
England (London) 1901–06: An early convert to the New Werner engine position (in the pedal bracket), Noble used their own engines as well as some from De Dion-Bouton, Minerva, MMC, and Coronet, from two-and-three-quarters to four-and-a-half horsepower.

NORBRECK
England (Wellingborough) 1921–24: The standard engines fitted into their machines by this company were 269cc Villiers or Arden two-strokes; 350 and 500cc Blackburnes were added as an option. The pressed-steel forks were unusual features for that period.

NORDSTERN
Germany 1922–24: This company was yet another short-lived German producer of small two-strokes which were built with in-house engines.

NORICUM
Austro-Hungary (Czech Republic) 1903–06: These were re-badged Cless and Plessing machines (see above) which were for sale in Czechoslovak territory.

NORLOW
England 1919: This English machine was a true standing-room-only scooter, with the engine over the front wheel.

NOUGIER
France 1947–c.1960: This company were responsible for producing fast, advanced designs, initially 250cc and then 350cc double-overhead-cam singles, followed by pushrod engines, twins, and even an air-cooled four. The 1957 175cc racing single could almost reach 160kph (100mph): top speed was given as 155kph (96mph).

NSU MAX/SPORTMAX

1952

The Max series of NSU singles were one of the German marques most fondly remembered set of models, incorporating the Max, Supermax, Special Max and the specialised Sportmax racer. The first model in the series, the Max, debuted in September 1952. Like the others it used a highly unorthodox 247cc (69x66mm) single overhead-cam engine.

In the pressed-steel frame and leading-link front fork design,

there was plenty of evidence of its debt to the existing Fox and Lux models, but the overhead-cam engine was an all-new unit by Albert Roder. This featured a type of valve gear unique amongst motorcycle power units. Named the Ultramax system, it drove the overhead-valve gear by long connecting rods in a tunnel cast integrally on the nearside of the cylinder. At their ends, these rods carried an eye encircling

The Max family of NSU singles comprised the Max, Supermax (a 1955 example is pictured), Special Max and the specialised Sportmax racing model.

counterbalanced eccentric discs connected to the half-time pinion and the overhead-camshaft. As the engine revolved, so the eccentrics imparted a reciprocating motion which was transferred to the valve gear. Hairpin valve springs were used and the entire mechanism was enclosed.

Only 62 of the new Max models were produced in 1952, but production hit its stride in 1953 when NSU built around 24,000.

For 1955 the Max was updated and received full-width aluminium brake hubs and a larger fuel tank; at the same time it was re-named Special Max. The same year, the company put into limited production a racing version, the Sportmax, and Hermann Peter Muller scooped the 250cc World Championship title on a semi-works version. In subsequent years many famous names campaigned

the Sportmax, including John Surtees and Mike Hailwood, to name but two. The Sportmax produced 28bhp at 9000rpm and could achieve 200kph (125mph).

In 1956 the definitive version of the Max family was announced. The Supermax differed in both engine tune and chassis details from the earlier roadsters. The biggest change was the adoption of twin shock, swinging-arm rear suspension, of the type pioneered on the off-road Gelandemax model from 1953.The engine's power output compared to the Max and Special Max, and was increased to 19bhp at 6500rpm. NSU claimed top speed to be 127kph (79mph).

When the last Supermax rolled off the production line in 1963, almost 100,000 of the Max family had been built over 11 years.

Engine: 247cc ohc 2v single, 69x66mm, air-cooled
Power: 18bhp at 6750rpm
Gearbox: 4-speed foot change
Final drive: chain
Weight: 155kg (342lb)
Top speed: 133kph (83mph)

NSU QUICKLY

1953

Designed by Albert Roder, the Quickly was in many respects the world's first real moped. It was an elegant, spindly affair with 66cm (26ins) wheels carrying narrow 5cm (2ins) tyres, a pressed-steel spine frame, pedalling gear and leading-link front suspension.

The first model, the Quickly N, arrived in 1953. When production ceased in 1962, almost 540,000 'Ns' had been sold. If this figure is added to the Quickly variants, an amazing total of over 1,111,000 is revealed, making this the world's first million-plus machine.

This 49cc (40x39mm) piston-port two-stroke single was very much the moped, until the arrival of the Honda Cub. Its success lay in combination of style, quality and price, a formula that in its day could not be matched by any other manufacturer in the world.

The weight was 37kg (80lb) and it carried 2.8 litres (0.6 UK gallons) of fuel. The engine's 1.4bhp was developed at 5200rpm and the two-speed gearbox was twistgrip operated. There were efficient drum brakes, and the

machine came complete with lights, luggage rack and stand.

In the UK, a highly publicised 1408-km (880-mile) run from Lands End to John O'Groats was made in 1955. Rider Tim Wood completed the epic journey in 37 hours 51 minutes at an average speed of 37.26kph (23.29mph). Total fuel consumption was 28.35litres (6.22 UK gallons).

Quickly variants were the S, L, TT, TTK and the Quickly-Cavallino, a lightweight motorcycle with tubular steel backbone frame, telescopic forks and twin-shock rear suspension.

Engine: 49cc 2s single, 40x39mm, air-cooled
Power: 1.4bhp at 5200rpm
Gearbox: 2-speed, twistgrip controlled
Final drive: chain
Weight: 36kg (80lb)
Top speed: 51kph (32mph)

Over 1.1 million Quickly mopeds were built between 1953 and 1962. All used a 49cc single-cylinder two-stroke engine and were noted for their durability.

NSU RENNMAX
1952

The Rennmax 250 double overhead-cam parallel twin was, in many ways, until the advent of the four cylinder Honda, the most charismatic machine of its class. It was also a beautifully engineered machine that was developed over a three-year period and appeared in a number of guises. Unlike the Roder-designed 125 Rennfox single, the R22 Rennmax was the work of Dr Walter Froede, and contrary to popular belief, was an entirely new design which didn't rely on previous NSU technology.

The first series appeared in spring 1952 and shared the square 56x56mm dimensions of both the Rennfox single and R54 500 four cylinder models, these two being the work of Albert Roder. With a displacement of 247.34cc, the power output was 25bhp at 9000rpm, improving to 29bhp at 9800rpm by season's end.

Of full unit-construction layout with a pressed-up crankshaft, early failure of the light alloy big-end cages at high revs was soon overcome, using a higher specification aluminium and by anodising the friction surfaces. Both the head and cylinder barrels were also of aluminium, and the twin camshafts were driven on the

offside of the engine by separate 'Y' shafts in the same manner as the supercharged 350/500 parallel twins. A feature of this early Rennmax was the use of torsion-bar valve springs, but these were soon dropped in favour of the hairpin type. A full duplex, twin down-bulge, steel tubular frame was specified, together with swinging-arm rear suspension and telescopic front forks.

For 1953, a brand new spine chassis of pressed steel, in which the engine was left without any support except at the rear, was used. This, together with leading-link front forks, a wrap-around aluminium tank and miniature fairing, were instant visual differences. With further engine tuning, in which the power was now up to 32bhp at 10,000rpm, the Rennmax was a potential championship winner. And so it proved, with Werner Haas riding it to become the first German to win a world title. He became a double (125 and 250) champion that year.

NSU chose to update the Rennmax again for 1954 making it 4kg (8.5lb) lighter than the 1953 bike, which weighed in at 117kg (258lb). The most noticeable difference to the engine was the

The 1953 version of NSU's Rennmax 250cc dohc GP racing twin employed a pressed steel frame, leading-link forks and a mass of aluminium bodywork.

camshaft drive which was transferred to the nearside and now operated by a single shaft acting on the axis of the inlet cam; spur gears transmitted the drive to the exhaust side.

The new engine was shorter and lighter than its predecessor, but had dimensions of 55.9x50.8mm, and an extra gear ratio was added, making six in all. Power was now up to 36bhp at 11,200rpm, giving a top speed of 216kph (135mph).

Werner Haas won two of his three world championship titles in 1953 and 1954 riding the Rennmax 250. In 1954, he won the first five rounds of the seven-round championship in succession, but retired from racing at the end of the year.

Engine: 249.3cc dohc 2v parallel twin, 55.9x50.8mm, air-cooled
Power: 36bhp at 11,200rpm
Gearbox: 6-speed foot change
Final drive: Chain
Weight: 117kg (258lb)
Top speed: 217kph (135mph)

NORVED
Germany 1924–25: This was an assembler that used Kuhne 350 and 500cc engines or (to special order) Blackburne motors.

NOVA
Hungary 1925–28: This firm of Hungarian assemblers produced sporting 250 to 500cc machines from – mostly – British parts, using Blackburne and JAP engines.

NOVICUM
Austro-Hungary/Czech Republic (Prague-Smichov) 1904–08: This Czech pioneer used the customary engines of that period, including those from Fafnir and Minerva.

NOVY
Belgium (Courtrai/Kourtrijk) early 1930s–early 1960s: These were well-thought-out assembled machines, mostly with Ilo 125 to 250cc two-stroke engines.

NSH
Germany (Hersfeld) 1923–28: A. Nodling u. Sohne of Hersfeld (hence NSH) began producing a 185cc overhead-valve single machine with an engine from Paque of Augsburg, rising to 198cc in 1924. When Paque ceased production, NSH switched to JAP (350 and 500cc), Blackburne (250 to 500cc), and Villiers (125 to 350cc) engines, the latter capacity both as a single and, in the final year of production, as a parallel twin.

NUX
Germany 1924–25: Given the date and the place, one might guess (accurately) that this firm made small, simple two-strokes. The engine was 170cc, and built in house.

NV
Sweden (Uppsala) 1926–60: Nymanbolagen AB started with an excellent 246cc single but then switched to 98cc mopeds in about 1932. After World War II, they resumed production with machines of 50 to 250cc, with a variety of two-stroke engines, eventually standardising on DKW and Sachs. They also manufactured a 38cc moped.

NYMAN
Sweden 1955: This appears to be NV (see above) under a different name.

NUT

BASED AT SOUTH BENWELL, Newcastle-upon-Tyne, this make took its name from the initials of its home town. It was backed by the Angus Sanderson firm, and its manager, Hugh Mason, promoted the name in competition with his friend Robert Ellis, who finished sixth in the 1912 Junior TT using a 344cc Moto-Rêve V-twin engine.

The company's 1913 range only used JAP engines, with a three-and-a-half horsepower single plus two-and-three-quarters and three-and-a-quarter horsepower V-twins; it was the smaller 345cc twin that both men used in the Junior TT that year. Mason had a serious accident in practice but still won, with Ellis coming eighth. Sensibly, NUT concentrated on V-twins for its production machines and built up a range extending from two-and-three-quarters to 8hp by 1916.

After the war, the company moved to Derwenthaugh, Swalwell, near Newcastle, and continued with V-twins using its own engines and three-speed

Only one NUT was listed for 1923 but in many different guises. All were fitted with a 700cc side-valve, V-twin engine.

By 1913, the year the company won the Isle of Man Junior TT, the NUT range only used JAP engines. This was one of the twins on offer for 1914.

Sturmey-Archer gearboxes. However, after losing financial backing for a period, the firm traded as Hugh Mason & Co. Ltd before a further upheaval finally steadied them as the NUT Engine & Cycle Company by 1923.

Production was affected by all this and the range shrank to one side-valve V-twin of 700cc, which was available in several specifications to meet most requirements, including colonial. The London dealer Maudes Motor Mart, was sole concessionaire by 1924, and for a time promoted them heavily. The marque's familiar cylindrically shaped fuel tank in nut-brown finish was replaced with a plated flat tank for 1927, and for 1928, in line with the trade, with a saddle tank.

A 172cc Villiers two-stroke model was added for 1928 only, as was a sports 747cc side-valve twin with specially tuned engine. In 1929 came further singles and a V-twin that were intended to be the

basis of the range for the next decade. They comprised 346cc singles with side and overhead valves, 496 and 692cc overhead-valve V-twins plus a 746cc side-valve V-twin. All the engines, specially prepared for NUT, came from JAP and went into conventional chassis with Burman gearboxes and Brampton forks. All fully equipped to a high standard.

The company then had one of its occasional moves, so no models were listed for 1930, although the

range was available later that year and went on to serve NUT well for the next two years. In 1933, the two 346cc models were replaced with an overhead-valve of 245cc, which was joined by two V-twins with overhead-camshaft engines of 496 and 692cc. It is unlikely that any of these was ever produced, for they were even more expensive to build than the existing line, and that was by no means cheap. Production was by then minimal, and came to a halt that year.

OEC

ENGLAND 1901–54

BASED IN PORTSMOUTH, England, the Osborne Engineering Company was a motorcycle firm that began with imported Minerva engines. For years, its range was unremarkable, but in 1920, John Osborne took over from his more conservative father, Frederick, and the firm's reputation grew. In 1921, OEC began making Blackburne motorcycles and engines, under the name OEC-Blackburne. The smallest model was a 147cc Villiers, whilst the largest, up to 998cc, used large, V-twin JAP engines.

OEC was best-known for its 'duplex' steering system of 1927, designed by Fred Wood. This curious mechanism was one of the factors that caused the company to

A 1938 OEC Commander. The unusual 'Duplex' steering system is clearly visible, and offered unprecedented levels of stability at speed.

Left: A detail from the 1938 500cc Commander. The 500cc ohv Clubman engine was actually made by Matchless.

be dubbed the 'Odd Engineering Co'. Other OEC oddities included a 998cc sidecar outfit, the 'Taxi', with a steering wheel. The duplex system was heavy, but stiffer than girder forks, giving unparalleled stability at speed and some of the advantages of more complex hub-centre designs.

Not surprisingly, such chassis were popular for speed record machines. Joe Wright used one to record 221kph (137mph) on his supercharged JAP record-breaker at Arpajon, France in 1930. Four years earlier, Claude Temple had taken his OEC-Temple to a world record of 195kph (121.3mph) at the same venue.

For the road, the 1930s brought single-cylinder machines from 248 to 498cc and twins up to 998cc,

Above: A 996cc JAP-engined, V-twin OEC, stripped down for competition use. OEC twins held several world speed records.

including the highly unorthodox Altanta-Duo. The duplex steering system was typified in machines such as the 129kph (80mph) Matchless-powered 500 Commander, although girder-forked versions were also built. By 1938 Commanders also featured plunger-type rear suspension with adjustable damping and around 50mm (2ins) of wheel travel.

OEC's fortunes faded after World War II. Star billing in 1952 went to the ST2 tourer, powered by a humble 197cc Villiers two-stroke. There was also an off-road competition version, the ST3, with an ingenious chain-tensioning system, but little else by way of OEC innovation. The death knell was sounded in 1954 by the Apollo, a Ducati V4.

OCM
Italy early 1960s: Franco-Morini engines powered these mopeds and light delivery vehicles.

OD
Germany (Dresden, later Sulzbach-Rosenberg) 1927–35: OD began with MAG-engined machines up to 1000cc (JAP for the racers), adding 200 and 250cc two-strokes with Bark motors; then (after 1935) Ilo three-wheeled delivery vehicles.

OGAR
Czech Republic (Prague) 1934–50: Frantisek Bartuska designed the very sporty 250cc two-stroke that made this firm's name. When Ogar was absorbed into Jawa, they made a 350cc two-stroke twin.

OLMO
Italy 1951–61: These were mopeds and ultra-lightweights with 38cc Mosquito and 49cc engines.

OLYMPIA
France 1949–54: These were primitive mopeds with friction drive from a front-wheel motor.

OLYMPIQUE
France (Courbevoie) 1922–58: These unmemorable but longlived two- and four-stroke machines were of 100 to 350cc before 1939, and postwar from 100 to 250cc, with various bought-in engines.

OMEA
Italy (Milan) 1950–53: The monoshock rear end was an interesting feature of this 125cc two-stroke lightweight.

OMEGA
England (Coventry) 1919–27: As well as their own two-stroke engines of 170 and 350cc, these machines used a variety of other engines: initially Villiers 269cc and Blackburne 500cc, then later Barr & Stroud, Bradshaw and JAP.

OMEGA
Japan 1960s: This firm built off-road sport bikes of 90, 125 and 151cc, and street parallel twins of up to 500cc.

OMNIA
Germany (Bad Godesberg) 1931–33: The Imperia works built these low-cost two-strokes with 100 and 150cc Villiers engines, and a 200cc Bark.

OMNIA
Italy 1949–53: This firm produced rebadged MT 250cc overhead-cam parallel twins. It is also reported as being named OMT.

OK (OK-SUPREME)

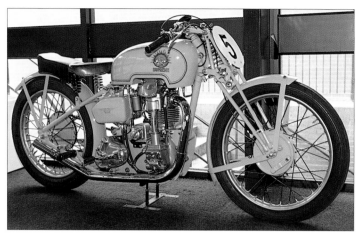

This gorgeous 'cammy' OK-Supreme racer dates from 1934. Like the Lighthouse roadster, the camshaft was bevel driven.

proprietary overhead-valve JAP engine mated to a special cylinder head but, in 1930, OK's masterpiece appeared.

The TT30 Lighthouse was a bevel-drive overhead-cam of 249cc designed by George Jones

and Ray Mason and built for OK in Gloucester. However, it was tricky and expensive to produce, and the company later reverted to a simpler overhead-cam design known as the Silver Cloud, as well as cheaper JAP-engined 'Dauntless' models of 250 to 350cc. Shortly before the outbreak of World War II, a utilitarian 250 side-valve, the 10bhp SV/39, also appeared, but it was effectively OK-Supreme's final model.

FOUNDED AS BICYCLE-makers Humphreys and Dawes in 1882, the company was called OK when it began making motorcycles in 1899. Initially, these were de Dion- and Minerva-engined models with Precision and later Green engines. A racing fanatic, Ernie Humphreys first took his OK-Precision to the TT in 1912, earning third place in the Lightweight event. In 1913 a 346cc liquid-cooled Green engine arrived, and one of the company's very few twins, powered by a fore-and aft ABC boxer engine. After World War I, OK's own two-strokes arrived, as well as Blackburne-engined models of 247 and 347cc and, later, oil-cooled Bradshaw and JAP engines.

OK's first great racing success came in 1922 when an 18-year-old

prodigy named Wal Handley set the fastest Lightweight Isle of Man TT lap on a 250 OK-Blackburne at 82kph (51mph). In this year, he won the Ulster GP, and in 1923 set the fastest Lightweight TT lap at 87kph (54mph) before crashing.

In 1927, Humphreys bought out partner Charles Dawes (whose bicycle company went from strength to strength), adding 'Supreme' to the company name. Within a year Frank Longman had validated this boastful claim by winning the Lightweight TT race. The TT-winning machine used a

The great Walter Rusk on board a factory 250cc ohc OK-Supreme at the 1938 TT. By this time, overseas machines were dominating this class.

OLLEARO

FOUNDED BY NEFTALI OLLEARO and based in Turin, this firm may have begun their manufacturing life with a simple, small two-stroke model, but this was soon replaced by a less conventional range. What set the machines apart was the use of overhead-valve, single-cylinder engines that had the gearbox built in unit with them and shaft drive to the rear wheel. Engine sizes ran from 175 to 500cc, the smallest also being listed by the company as a two-stroke.

The remainder of the machine followed the practice of the time with a rigid frame and sprung forks. The fixtures and fittings changed as the years passed by, with larger drum brakes for both

wire wheels, a saddle tank when that style arrived, electric lighting and a sturdier frame. By 1932, the smallest engine benefited from the provision of four speeds in the

The basic model from the early-1930s Ollearo range, with its 175cc two-stroke engine and conventional construction; others had shaft drive and unit construction.

gearbox, and, by 1934, both the 350 and 500cc models had followed suit. That year also saw a three-wheeled car from the firm that had the driver virtually sitting on a motorcycle within the car. It was very roomy, a feature apparently designed to accommodate the ample proportions of Italian country priests!

The existing line adopted telescopic forks in the late 1930s and, after World War II, it continued with some small improvements. It was joined by a 45cc two-stroke bicycle attachment engine, a common answer to the postwar transport needs for a few years.

OLYMPIC

ENGLAND 1903–05 AND 1919–23

PRODUCED BY F.H. PARKYN, a bicycle-maker in Wolverhampton, this was a conventional primitive that was seen at the National Cycle & Motor Show held at the Crystal Palace late in 1903. His machine was powered by a two-and-three-quarters horsepower MMC engine with automatic inlet valve and coil ignition that sat vertically in a loop frame with braced forks, cycle brakes and belt drive. Production of these machines was very limited, and ceased around 1905.

The name returned in 1919 on a quality lightweight, at which time the firm was still based in Wolverhampton, although now in Granville Street. The model was powered by a 269cc Verus engine with splash lubrication and magneto ignition set vertically in a frame that drove a two-speed gearbox by chain with belt final drive. This model continued for the next year with a change to the 261cc Orbit engine.

For 1921, the Orbit was replaced by the 269cc Villiers two-stroke, and with it came the first postwar use of four-strokes with Blackburne engines of 269 and 348cc, although the transmissions and cycle parts remained common. This range ran on for the next year but, for 1923, Olympic used the Villiers two-stroke and 292cc JAP four-stroke with a choice of transmissions, but still with belt

An Olympic two-stroke model from the early 1920s with a 269cc Verus engine, two-speed gearbox and chain-cum-belt transmission. Simple and short-lived.

final drive. The frequent change of engine supplier suggests that finances were cut to the bone and thus with this in mind, it was no surprise that production ceased that year.

OPEL

GERMANY 1901–07 AND 1921–30

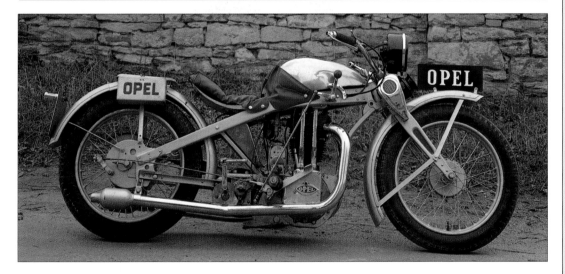

OPEL ORIGINALLY MANUFACTURED bicycles and sewing machines, adding cars in 1898. Motorcycles came in 1901 to offer a line of conventional singles until 1907. After World War I, Opel returned to motorcycles with a 138cc side-valve engine sold as a bicycle attachment that mounted to the left of the rear wheel. The company still produced bicycles, so it began to offer a complete machine with the attachment engine fitted to a

heavy-duty frame with leading-link forks. The frame had a top tube that stepped down aft of the petrol tank to run back under the saddle. The tank was cylindrical with a conical nose and chamfered tail.

Later came light motorcycles with a 148cc engine and two-speed gearbox and, in 1926, a 499cc side-valve single. In 1928 an overhead-valve version was added; both went into Motoclub models, their frames built up from

An Opel Motoclub model from 1929 with pressed-steel frame, rocking front forks and a 500cc ohv engine installed under the curious line of both tank and seat.

steel pressings in a form designed by Ernst Neumann-Neander. They were made in the Diamant factory, like the EO with a similar frame in light-alloy. The Opel retained the Neander rocking forks, separate gearbox and drum brakes.

ONAWAY
England 1904–08: This unusual-looking machine had a basketwork bucket seat and a low frame, and was powered by a 5hp Kelecom V-twin or Berkley parallel-twin.

ONOTO
France 1934–38: These were unexciting two-strokes of 100 to 175cc with Aubier Dunne engines.

OPRA
Italy (Rome) 1927–29: The Officine di Precisione Romani Automobilistiche built what may have been the world's first transverse air-cooled four, just 490cc, delivering 32bhp at 6000rpm; a water-cooled version had just 30bhp. It was subsequently developed into the Rondine 4 and the Gilera 4.

OR
Italy (Milan) 1928–31: The Officine Riunite di Costruzioni Meccaniche began with an auxiliary cycle motor and moved on to a 175cc lightweight.

ORAM
Italy 1949: The Officine Ricostruzione Automobili e Motocicli built a 125cc lightweight.

ORBIT
England (Wolverhampton) 1913–24: Before 1914, this firm built a 350cc side-valve; after the war, they built a 261cc two-stroke. Also, they fitted on request other manufacturers' motors, as long as they began with a B: Barr & Stroud, Blackburne and Bradshaw.

OREOL
France (Puteaux) 1903–14: This firm made mainly V-twins, with Moto-Reve, Zedel and other engines. The 333cc single-cylinder record-breaker ridden by Cissac seems to have been their own.

ORIENT
USA 1900–06: The Waltham Manufacturing Co. built these very early machines with Aster engines behind the steering head and a petrol tank over the rear mudguard. They may have stayed in production as late as 1910.

ORIGAN
France 1929–mid-1950s: This firm produced two-strokes of 100 and 175cc – bought in mostly from Aubier-Dunne – and an AMC four-stroke.

OSSA

SPAIN 1949–85

INDUSTRIALIST MANUEL GIRO owned a large and profitable company manufacturing film projectors and other cinema equipment, and since he also had a passion for motorcycles, he was able to realise his dream of founding his own marque.

In pre-war days, Giro was an enthusiastic rider, at first on the street, later on the race circuit. But the outbreak of the Spanish Civil War in 1936 brought an end to all peacetime activities, including motorcycle sport.

The Civil War ended in 1939 and because Spain was unable to purchase any form of transport from abroad during World War II, Giro, together with other like-minded Spaniards, began to look into producing motorcycles themselves. Giro drew up the design of a 125cc two-stroke; although it never passed the prototype stage, he was always to claim that he gave the engine to the fledgling Montesa concern, who subsequently used it as a base for its first production model.

Noting Montesa's success, Giro then set about the design and construction of another machine. This was, perhaps not surprisingly, a 123.6cc (54x54mm) single cylinder two-stroke but, unlike the Montesa machines of the period, it featured a central exhaust port. Producing 5bhp at 4500rpm, the little Ossa, equipped with a three-speed gearbox, could achieve 75kph (47mph).

From this original model came a series of machines that were used for commuting and, in specially

Designed by Eduardo Giro, the 1965 Ossa 175 Sport was capable of 145kph (90mph). These bikes scored a shock one-two in the Barcelona 24 Hours that year.

prepared versions, contested the rigours of the International Six Day Trial during the 1950s.

An improved 125 appeared in 1954, followed in 1958 by an enlarged version with a 149cc (58x56.4mm) engine. In the same year came a 175cc four-stroke roadster of Italian influence. But it was back to two-strokes in 1959, when a more sporty variant of the tried-and-tested 125 made its debut.

The early 1960s was a bad time for the Spanish motorcycle industry and, in common with other builders, Ossa found their sales severely curtailed. It was then that Eduardo Giro joined his father's firm. His engineering skills had first been demonstrated when, aged 15, he designed and built a model aircraft engine. This tiny unit would spin to over 18,000rpm and it laid the foundations for Eduardo's first commercial design – the 158.5cc (58x60mm) single cylinder two-stroke of 1962 – that was to form the backbone of Ossa production for many years to come.

From this came the 175cc (60.9x60mm) in 1965, the 230cc (70x60mm) in 1966 and then, joining two singles together, the 488.5cc (72x60mm) Yankee twin in 1972. Finally, there was the 244.3cc (72x60mm) single of 1975.

Most of these engines were not only used for the series production machines, but also for competition purposes, in road racing, motocross and trials.

The first use of the new Eduardo Giro-designed engine for racing came with the introduction of the 175 Sport in 1965. In standard road-going form, it was capable of a genuine 145kph (90mph), producing 19bhp at 7200rpm. Two of the new bikes scored a shock first and second in their class of the Barcelona 24-Hour race that year.

Spurred on by this success and realising that it was giving away some 75cc, Ossa's next move was to increase the capacity to 230cc. Overall victory of the Barcelona 24-Hours came in 1967, with a 230 Sport ridden by Carlos Giro and Luis Yglesis. Their race record distance of 662 laps was to stand for several years.

Ossa had also begun to develop a full Grand Prix machine and this,

ridden by Santiago Herrero, has its own profile.

By this time Ossa, like Bultaco and Montesa, had begun to take an interest in dirt-bike sport, spurred on by a drastic drop in domestic street-bike sales, which was brought on by a flood of Fiat-licensed designs produced by Spain's state car manufacturer, Seat.

At that time, the 250cc motocross class had been given world-championship status and there was considerable sales potential, particularly in the US, for trail and enduro bikes. Additionally, Bultaco and Montesa were already building trials bikes and exporting them to many countries, including Great Britain.

Mick Andrews became Ossa's first international star-quality trials

Ossa built this 250cc motocross machine as part of its continued interest in dirt-bike sport. This particular model was made in 1978.

ORION

Czech Republic (Slany) 1902–33: In the pioneering years, this company built singles and V-twins. After 1918, it built a 350cc two-stroke single and a 596cc split-single; after 1927, it made 500cc side-valve and overhead-valve machines, as well as a 600cc side-valve machine. All engines were designed and built in house.

ORIX

Italy (Alessandria) 1949–54: This firm produced scooters of 125 and 175cc, and a 175cc lightweight, all with Ilo two-stroke engines.

ORMONDE

England 1900–06: Kelecom and Antoine engines powered these pioneers, some of which featured partial enclosure.

ORUK

Germany 1922–24: The direct shaft drive from the 189cc side-valve single, mounted beside the rear wheel, explains the name: Ohne Riemen Und Kette (without belt and chain).

OSA-LIBERTY

France (Argenteuil) 1926–32: As well as in-house two strokes of 175 and 250cc, this firm also used JAP 350 and 500cc engines built under licence by Staub in France.

OSCAR

Italy (S. Andrea di Sesto) 1965–82: This firm produced mopeds and ultra-lightweight motorcycles.

OSMOND

England (Birmingham) 1911–24: Before World War I, this firm made 500cc Precision-engined singles and postwar, two-stroke lightweights with proprietary engines, variously reported as 102/108 and 200cc, plus a 239cc two-stroke of their own design.

OVERSEAS

England (Birmingham) 1909–15: Designed (as the name suggests) for use in the then British Empire and colonies, these solid, substantial machines had an in-house 842cc V-twin engine.

rider, and by the early 1970s, with Andrews at his peak, the combination won both the British and European Trials Championship titles. Replicas of these machines sold in their hundreds. Andrews was also seen to ride in some enduro and motocross events for the company at that time.

Ossa's famous MAR (Mick Andrews Replica) was announced for the 1972 model year and soon some 300 a month were leaving the Barcelona factory's production lines. However, in 1973, Andrews switched to Yamaha, being employed there in a development role and, obviously, using his Ossa experiences to the benefit of his new employer.

The mid- to late 1970s were not good years for Ossa, even though in 1975 a prototype 310cc (65x77mm) trials model had made its debut. This model was soon going into production for the following season.

In March 1978, Ossa was rescued from financial trouble by the Spanish Government, but from then on until its final demise in the mid-1980s, money problems were often to limit developments. But although Mick Andrews came back to rejoin the company, he could not rekindle past glories.

The last real batch of trials bikes was built by Ossa in 1983, motocross production having already been halted several years before.

This 1976 Ossa 350 Trials used a five-speed piston port single-cylinder two-stroke engine, which had a displacement of 310cc (65x77mm).

On the roadster front, a new breed of Ossa, the Urbe – a modern-day Ariel Leader – was put into production. But even this could not stop the downwards spiral for the marque.

The end of the old family-owned Ossa came in 1984, and it was relaunched as Ossamoto, a workers' co-operative. This too, like the British Triumph firm, did not succeed and was wound up towards the end of 1985. The marque with a clover leaf as its emblem was no more.

OSSA 250 GP   1969

The 250 GP's first ever race came at the 1967 Spanish Grand Prix when Carlos Giri came home sixth. But the machine's creator, Eduardo Giro wasn't happy, and for 1968 secured the services of the Spanish 250cc champion Santiago Herrero. That year was used mainly for

development purposes and for Herrero to learn the foreign circuits.

The heart of any motorcycle is its engine and Eduardo Giro moved from Ossa's traditional piston-port induction, opting instead for the greater performance

benefits of disc-valve. The air-cooled 249cc (70x65mm) featured a seven-fin barrel and head with such large fins that the top end looked more like a 500 than a 250. Its carburettor was a massive 42mm Amal, fitted to the offside crankcase. Even though, by 1969, the engine generated 42bhp at 11,000rpm, a major advantage was that useful power was available from as low as 6500rpm, making the machine's six-speed gearbox quite sufficient.

The first round was at the Jarama circuit in Madrid where Herrero raced home ahead of the field and looked certain to repeat the performance at the West German Grand Prix at Hockenheim a week later, until ignition problems sidelined him. The next time his engine failed was more than two months later, in Brno, Czechoslovakia. In the races between, the Ossa star had scored two more wins (France and Belgium), a second (East Germany) and two thirds (Isle of Man and Holland). In fact, at Spa Francorchamps in Belgium, Herrero's winning average was 188.74kph (117.96mph), faster than the runner-up in the 500cc

In 1969, Ossa rider Santiago Herrero finished a superb third in the 250cc road racing world title race, riding this disc-valve, air-cooled single.

race! His chances of being world champion ended in the Grand Prix crash he suffered in Ulster in August 1969.

For the 1970 season the power output had been pushed up to 45bhp. This figure was achieved when the engine was still in its air-cooled form, although experiments had been made with water-cooling.

As the Spanish challenger came to the grid for the 1970 Isle of Man TT, many eyes were on the sleek monocoque-framed Ossa single and its hard-riding pilot, Herrero. But tragedy struck on the final lap, when Herrero lost control and was later to die from his injuries. After his death, the firm Ossa quit Grand Prix racing,

as a mark of respect for their former rider.

Even so, the performances of the previous year had proved Ossa's 250 GP as one of the very few bikes capable of winning on such a small budget.

Engine: 249cc rotary valve 2s 70x65mm, air-cooled
Power: 42bhp at 11,000rpm
Gearbox: 6-speed foot change
Final drive: chain
Weight: 99kg (219lb)
Top speed: 229kph (142mph)

OSSA MICK ANDREWS REPLICA 1971

During the early 1970s, the 250cc Mick Andrews Replica (MAR) was the finest One-Day Trials bike in the world.

It was in 1970 that Andrews and the Spanish marque really set the trials world alight with the first of his trio of Scottish Six-Day victories. However, when Ossa should have been benefiting from the sales of the first MAR, the Barcelona factory was flooded, putting production back by a year and causing a major cash flow problem, the first of many financial difficulties.

The Mick Andrews Replica was announced in Spain by Manuel Giro in October 1971. The 24cc (60x72mm) engine produced 17bhp at 6500rpm. The ignition was by Motoplat, while the gearbox was a five-speeder, primary drive being by duplex chain. Its success meant that a Mark 2 did not arrive until 1975, with minimal changes. A Mark 3 arrived in 1976, showing that the Ossa was becoming outdated.

Engine: 244cc 2s single 60x72mm, air-cooled
Power: 17bhp at 6500rpm
Gearbox: 5-speed foot change
Final drive: chain
Weight: 95.5kg (215lb) (with lighting equipment)
Top speed: 105kph (65mph)

The Mick Andrews Replica – or MAR for short – was, at its peak, the finest trials bike in the world.

Ossa's first trials machines arrived in 1967, but it was the British rider Mick Andrews who really put Ossa on the map in the 'feet-up' trials game as the first-ever two-stroke pairing to score a hat trick in the famous Scottish Six Day Trial. He also gave this small-time manufacturer the British and European Trial Championship titles, together with many other international awards.

P&M (PANTHER)

ENGLAND 1904–68

THE FAMOUS YORKSHIRE firm, founded by Joah Carver Phelon and Richard Moore and based in Cleckheaton, was originally known

P&M machines, like this 500cc model of 1916, served Britain well during the Great War, the fully-enclosed transmission a real asset.

as P&M, its name having been derived from the initials of the partners' surnames. They came together late in 1903 to develop further the P&R that Phelon had originated with Harry Rayner in 1901, retaining its main distinguishing feature: the frame downtube was replaced by an

Lined up for the 1913 ACU Six Days trials were W.J.M. Sproulle, P. Shaw and W.C. Drake on their P&M machines. All won medals.

inclined engine. Transmission was by a simple, two-speed gear, using twin primary chains of different ratios selected by clutches, and the

The 249cc Red Panther was cheap, tough and served its owners well from 1933 to World War II, and then after it. The machine was scorned, but it was good.

Only the 555cc model was listed for 1923, but the next year brought P&M's first overhead-valve engine of 499cc. It was designed by Granville Bradshaw of ABC fame and drove a four-speed gearbox, which later became optional; the dummy rims were replaced with drum brakes. With changes to the lubrication system came the forward extension to the crankcase for the oil, another feature that was to survive to the end. The older model was dropped after 1925, leaving three versions of the overhead-valve machine for 1926.

Late in 1926 the firm stole the show at Olympia with its 242cc transverse V-twin Panthette. This was another Bradshaw design with unit construction of the engine, gearbox and final drive bevels, all housed in a horizontally split casting; the overhead-valves had leaf springs. The forks were Brampton and the engine unit was hung from a frame with forged-steel backbone. Unfortunately, it was too advanced and too expensive for most tastes, and so failed to sell in any numbers.

A speedway model was listed for 1928 along with a 247cc Villiers two-stroke in Panthette cycle parts which sold well. The same year saw the first appearance of the 594cc single, which was to enjoy a long life. The two-stroke line was extended for 1929 with 147 and 196cc models, and the big singles – listed as Redwing models – became available with a tuned engine.

In 1931, the 600s received twin headlights and, more importantly, 1932 saw the introduction of a 249cc model. The engine had the inclined cylinder and oil tank in the crankcase but it went into a conventional frame with downtube. A 348cc version was added for 1933, but the really significant commercial news was an agreement with London dealer Pride & Clarke. P&C took large numbers of the 250, which had been given a red-panelled tank and mudguards in 1939, and sold it at a cut-down price as the Red Panther. Although it was to be the object of some scorn, it proved an excellent basic machine for local work and was to win the

assembly was mounted in the bottom bracket with chain final drive.

P&M's first motorcycles were typical of the era as regards the cycle parts but were distinguished by the inclined engine and two-speed gear. The company soon made a name for itself and, from 1907, with the exception of a lightweight listed for three years

from 1910, this single model was to be the mainstay of the firm into the 1920s.

During World War I, P&M vehicles were used for despatch riding, and immediately after the war only one model was listed. In 1922, a new design of 555cc was added, although this retained the inclined engine and had four speeds, which was made possible

Bigger capacity machines were always part of the Panther range. This 645cc model with its inclined engine joined the existing 594cc version in 1959.

by combining the existing two speeds with a two-speed layshaft. In sports model form, it introduced the Panther, the name that the firm was later to adopt.

prestigious Maudes Trophy in 1934.

The same year brought a 348cc Red Panther plus Stroud trials models in both capacities. These models – along with a 498cc version of the Red Panther type introduced in 1938 plus the big singles – successfully took the firm right up to the outbreak of war in 1939. Developments included a spring frame using leaf springs, vertical engines, and a tandem-twin, in-line overhead-valve engine with coupled crankshafts, but none of these went into production as the firm turned its attention to war contracts.

After the war, P&M picked up with just three singles, very much a return to its pre-war situation. Dowty Oleomatic telescopic forks appeared in 1947 and, in 1949, the two smaller models adopted vertical cylinders and were joined by a trials version, in both capacities, bearing the Stroud name. By 1954, conventional telescopics and rear suspension had been introduced, by which time the Stroud models had gone. In 1956, the singles were joined by lightweights with 197cc Villiers engines, promptly followed by versions with the 246cc single and

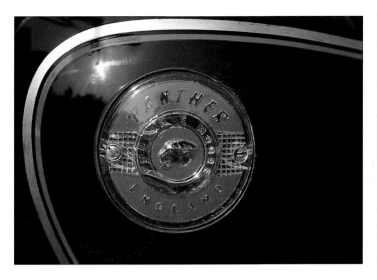

249cc twin units. In 1959, the 324cc twin was added but much more important was the appearance of a 645cc version of the big single.

The firm added the Princess scooter late in 1959. It was powered by a Villiers 174cc engine and shared body panels with Dayton and Sun. This line took P&M into the new decade but, thanks to the advent of the Mini, the market was contracting, especially for sidecars, the firm's prime market. Panther had to call in the Official Receiver late in

The Panther plastic badge was first seen in the 1950s. It continued until the company went bankrupt in 1968 on the big single and smaller two-stroke twins.

1962 and the range was soon thinned down. From 1965 onwards, P&M listed only one twin and the big single, the numbers produced slowly trickling to a complete standstill in 1968. However, from first to last, the firm never stopped using the engine as part of the frame – for at least one model.

PANTHER MODEL 100 {1954}

The one feature that P&M retained throughout its long history was the use of the engine in place of the frame downtube for at least one model. Back in 1924, the company adopted an overhead-valve for its 499cc engine, a design feature still evident in its last machine in 1968. Along the way, the engine size rose to 594cc for the Model 100 and then to 645cc for the 120.

This engine was the heart of all the company's machines; it was

tough, sturdy, reliable, long lasting and well able to pull from low down, so it was ideal for sidecar work. Aside from doing duty as part of the frame, other engine features included the semi-dry lubrication system with the oil

The 594cc Model 100 Panther was first listed for 1932, although its origins stretched back further. It gained rear suspension in 1954 and was built until 1963.

carried in a forward extension of the crankcase, and a reduced compression cam to ease starting when that long-swinging kick was all important.

The rest of the machine followed the trends of the years: at first it was a rigid frame with girder forks; later a twin-port head and two exhaust systems were standard. The girders were replaced with telescopics in 1947. These had Dowty Oleomatic legs with wheel lugs that could be reversed to give sidecar fork trail. Pivoted-fork rear suspension came in 1954, but the rigid version ran on to 1957. In 1959, when the Mini was overtaking the sidecar market, the Model 120 arrived.

Engine: 594cc ohv inclined single, 87x100mm, air-cooled
Power: 23bhp at 5000rpm
Gearbox: 4-speed foot change
Final drive: chain
Weight: 185kg (406lb)
Top speed: 120kph (70mph) with sidecar

PANNONIA

PANNONIA MACHINES WERE manufactured – together with Danuvia, Tunde and Panni – at the state-owned Csepel factory in Budapest. Production began in 1951 when the first single-cylinder, two-stroke, Jawa-like motorcycles were constructed.

As with other East European factories of the same era, Pannonia sold its products under different brand names. For example, in the USA, they were marketed under the White label.

A 250cc Hungarian Pannonia from the mid-1960s. This single-cylinder two-stroke was marketed in the American market under the White label.

During the early 1960s, the marque not only designed a neat 250 (246cc) twin (again a two-stroke), but also built a number of off-road competition bikes. With the latter, the factory posted more than one Hungarian national motocross title.

Both the single- and twin-cylinder models were sold, by White, in the USA but a major problem was that potential customers were unfamiliar with the product. At least companies such as Jawa and CZ had the advantage of international sporting success but the Hungarian make couldn't tap into this lucrative market. Ultimately, US agents spent more money on their advertising campaign than they made in profit from sales. It was a

A Pannonia 246.8cc twin dating from 1963. These machines were built at the state-owned Csepel factory in Budapest and sold well in Communist countries.

similar story in other Western markets but in the Eastern bloc countries, Pannonia scored considerable successes, at least up to the beginning of the 1970s. But from then on sales dwindled and, as was also the case at Csepel, production ceased in 1975.

PANZER MOTORCYCLES

THE CONNOTATIONS OF 'Panzer' are alarming, but the reality is rather different. The name Panzer in fact refers to the 'Neo-Pan' engine, a revised, updated and more reliable version of the original Harley-Davidson V-twin 'Panhead' engine, and it is therefore not intended to have any

military connotations with reference to the German tank.

Avowedly retro, Panzer has a slightly shaky grasp on history.

The bars of the Digger ST, and the rake of the forks, argue that 'show' was more important than 'go' – though 'go' wasn't too bad.

While conflating the 1950s and early 1960s in its advertising material, it concentrates, almost exclusively, on 1950s icons such as James Dean in *Rebel Without a Cause*, Marlon Brando in *The Wild Bunch* [sic] and Marilyn Monroe.

As usual, the publicity material is longer on lifestyle than on

technical specifications. However, the Panzer appears to be a fairly standard heavyweight; better made than many and sacrificing little in

***Easy Rider* has a lot to answer for... This is Panzer's 'Billy Bike', a mass of partially-related 'styling cues'.**

the way of modern reliability and handling (at least by American big-twin standards) in its determination to re-create the past.

When looking at this machine, reviewers uniformly agreed that throttle response, acceleration and braking were at least the equal of

2000 model year Harley-Davidsons, which means they must have been pretty good by the standards of big V-twins, at least.

PARILLA   ITALY 1946–67

GIOVANNI PARRILLA (note the spelling, one 'r' of which was dropped in the interests of easier pronunciation when used in the marque name), was born in Southern Italy in 1912, after the Parrilla family had emigrated from Barcelona, Spain. When he was three years old, the family moved to Mantova in the North before eventually moving to Milan where Giovanni spent his teenage years.

Parrilla's first business enterprise was a small workshop on the edge of the city, repairing diesel injection pumps and acting as a distributor for Bosch spark plugs. His move into the ranks of a motorcycle manufacturer began shortly after the war when, in 1946, Giovanni Parrilla set out to design and build his own racing machine. When this subsequently made its debut at Lecco, with Nino Grieco aboard on 1 October 1946, it was the first truly all-new Italian racing design of the postwar era.

In many ways, the new bike displayed Giovanni Parrilla's enthusiasm for British motorcycles (the camshaft Norton, in

particular) which, at that time, led the world.

The new bike – with the brand name Parilla – was designed by Giuseppe Salmaggi, who had been responsible for the original Gilera Saturno in 1939.

Thus Salmaggi's instructions were to build a bike which was to mirror many of the Norton's features. The result was not just a track bike, but a supersports roadster, both with a 246.3cc (66x72mm) single overhead-camshaft engine, with camshaft drive by shaft and bevels.

After a thorough test programme, production of the Corsa (Racer) – together with its road-going brother – began in 1947, after they were displayed at the Milan Show and aroused considerable interest.

The Corsa featured massive 260mm (10.25ins) drum brakes, front and rear. These were soon nicknamed *padellone* (large frying pan). With a power output of 18bhp, maximum speed was 148kph (92mph). Later a twin camshaft racing model, the

Making its debut at the Milan Show in late 1952, Parilla's first hi-cam single, the 175 Fox, went on sale in early 1953 and sold in many thousands over the next decade.

Bialbero, was built in both 250 and 350cc engine sizes.

By 1950 the Italian motorcycle industry was booming but even better was to come, with registrations in 1951 of motorcycles, three-wheelers, scooters and cycle-motors amounting to a total of 1,112,500; more than 400,000 up on the previous year.

Buoyed up by this success, the Parilla brand brought out a bevy of new models. First, for the 1950 model year came 98 and 124cc single cylinder two-strokes, then in January 1952 came a prestigious 348cc (62x58mm) overhead-valve twin. At the end of 1952, Parilla debuted the first of its trademark hi-cam models, in which the valves were operated via short splayed pushrods in the nearside of the cylinder. With a capacity of 174cc, this first model, known as

the Fox, was only the first of a family of such models over the next 15 years.

The hi-cam formula was also seen by Giovanni Parrilla as the way forward for his racing efforts. Known in Italy as *camme rialzata* (lifted camshaft), the first prototype hi-cam racer made its debut at the Italian Grand Prix at Monza in September 1952. In this engine (designed by Salmaggi and his assistant Alfredo Bianchi), the cam drive tower was on the opposite side to all the subsequent racing and production roadsters, employing the hi-cam principle. This first prototype did not go any further as it was replaced by a new 125cc double overhead-camshaft single Grand Prix bike the

following year. On this latter bike the camshaft drive was relocated (as on the production Fox) to the nearside of the engine and employed a triangular chain drive to the twin camshafts. This project was also soon axed. It was then left to a combination of the elderly Bialbero and tuned versions of the production hi-cam roadsters to fly Parilla's tarmac racing efforts.

Off-road, Parilla also put considerable effort into long-distance trials events, such as the International Six Day Trial, with success coming later in the decade.

Besides its famous hi-cam range of roadsters and, of course, the 350 overhead-valve parallel twin, other notable Parilla production models included: the 49cc

The famous hi-cam Parilla single. It employed valves operated through short splayed pushrods on the nearside of the unit construction engine.

(38x44mm) Parillino moped, the Levriere (Greyhound), a 153cc (60x54mm) two-stroke scooter, and the unorthodox Slughi (Desert Greyhound).

The Slughi was the work of Piero Bossaglia, since both Salmaggi and Bianchi had left. Bossaglia's original project had called for a choice of two- and four-stroke engines. However, when the design finally reached production at the end of the 1950s, only a four-stroke was made available, at first a 98cc overhead-

valve. A few months later, this was joined by a 114cc two-stroke. Whereas the Slughi and its naked brother, the Olimpia, had a horizontal cylinder, the new 125 Street Scrambler and 125 Sport had a new overhead-valve motor with a vertical cylinder.

By the end of the 1950s, Parilla was exporting their motorcycles all over the world, even as far as Japan. The marque also even published its own magazine, *il Levriere* (The Greyhound), the first edition of which appeared in July 1959.

When the Milan Show took place later that year, a notable guest on the Parilla stand was Ernest Wise of the newly appointed American Parilla importer's Cosmopolitan Motors.

As the 1960s began, it was revealed that Parilla's chief designer Bossaglia was working on an all-new 125cc disc-valve racing model. Although it was subsequently built, development extended for several years, resulting in it becoming outdated before it was race ready. It was this lethargic approach – in direct contrast from the previous decade – that was to prove Parilla's downfall. Some of this can be traced from the founder's decision to sell out to an investment company. Parilla did quite well in American racing for a while, but even the much-loved hi-cam unit-construction single couldn't keep the company afloat, even though by the mid-1960s it was being produced as a full 250 – 247cc (68x68mm).

Parilla finally stopped building motorcycles in 1967, although the name continued through the sale of the successful Parilla Kart engines.

PARILLA BIALBERO

1948

In 1947 work began on the Parilla Bialbero (double-cam) racer. The work of Giuseppe Salmaggi, this was developed from the earlier single overhead-camshaft racing and super-sport models. When this debuted in 1948, it reached a shade over 160kph (100mph), power output being 21bhp at 8500rpm.

Like the single camshaft versions, the newcomer sported a vertical drive shaft and bevel gears. There was also a series of gears operating the inlet and exhaust camshafts by means of

pinions. Each cam was carried by a roller race at the drive end, and a ball race at the other. The camshafts activated the valves through flat-top tappets; valve springs were of the hairpin variety and left exposed. The separate double overhead-camshaft drive box sat atop the cylinder head in much the same way as the double-camshaft Manx Norton. Both the cylinder head and barrel were cast in aluminium, the latter being sleeved with a re-borable cast-iron liner. The 7.8:1 compression three-

ring forged Borgo piston was provided with a massive dome, while the steel connecting rod was double-webbed at top and bottom for additional strength, with a caged roller bearing big-end.

To prune down weight, Salmaggi provided the Bialbero with as many engine castings in electron alloy as possible, including the crankcase assembly. This meant that its dry weight was a manageable 115kg (250lb).

One notable feature of the Bialbero was its flexibility which,

for a racing unit, was truly outstanding. The power came in at an engine speed as low as 3500rpm.

In 1950 the 250 was joined by a 349cc version. Its debut came in March that year, at Marseilles, France, in the capable hands of Nello Pagani.

One of the new 350s, together with a smaller Bialbero, was sent to Germany to be ridden (very successfully) by Hermann Gablenz and Roland Schell at circuits all over Europe for the next couple of years.

A 246.3cc dohc Parilla 'Bialbero' (double cam) single-cylinder racer from 1949. It was developed from the earlier sohc model.

Other successes gained by the twin camshaft Parillas included Piero Cavacciuti's 250cc class victory in the 1950 Milano-Taranto, as well as some good placings in the Grand Prix by long-serving factory rider Nino Grieco.

The Bialbero did much to promote the Parilla marque, both in Italy and abroad.

Engine: 246.3cc dohc single, 66x72mm, air-cooled
Power: 21bhp at 8500rpm
Gearbox: 4-speed foot change
Final drive: chain
Weight: 115kg (250lb)
Top speed: 162kph (102mph)

PARILLA 175 SPORT 1956

A family of models was developed from the Fox, the first of Parilla's hi-cam singles of 1952. But the most successful was certainly the 175 Sport which continued for a decade after its introduction in 1956.

Like the other hi-cam singles, the 175 Sport was unorthodox in that it employed valves operated through short splayed pushrods on the nearside of the engine. These ultra-short inclined pushrods were driven from a single chain-driven camshaft, mounted at the top of the timing case, and this was kept in adjustment by a Weller-type tensioner.

The valve angle was 90 degrees, while the pressed-up crankshaft featured a caged roller big-end and phosphor-bronze small-end; tappet adjustment was by a simple screw

and locknut method, and the valve springs were of the coil variety.

The gear-change and kick-start levers were both situated on the offside of the bike and there was a four-speed gearbox and helical-cut primary drive gears.

The even more sporting Gran Sport and later the MSDS Formula 3 machines gained considerable success in Italian racing events. For example, in 1957 Parilla won the 175cc class of the famous Giro d'Italia, when factory-supported rider Giuseppe Rottigni, riding a Gran Sport, averaged 97.25kph (60.78 mph) for the entire nine-

The 1957 Parilla MSDS 175 single. This machine was a specially race-tuned version of the Sport, and was capable of a genuine 160kph (100mph).

stage, 2043km (1277 mile) event. Out of the original 240 starters, only 100 finished this gruelling road marathon.

In the Gran Sport/MSDS state of tune the hi-cam Parilla could achieve 160kph (100 mph), putting it on a par with other Formula 3 models from Ducati, Moto Morini and Motobi.

In the 1960s, the 175 engine was enlarged first to 199cc (64x62mm) and finally to 247cc (68x68mm). In the latter, it was to achieve considerable success in the US.

Not only did a 250 Parilla, ridden by Ron Grant, finish runner-up in the 1964 US Grand Prix, but Norris Rancourt chalked up a string of victories from 1962 until 1965. By this time the Yamaha twin cylinder TDI outpaced even the fastest four-stroke singles. Rancourt's machine was not a factory entry, but a privately-tuned bike owned by enthusiast Orrin Hall.

Besides the larger engined versions, the 175 continued to be available and was still on sale in Europe when the factory shut its doors in 1967.

Engine: 174cc ohv 2v single, 59.8x62mm, air-cooled
Power: 14bhp at 7800rpm
Gearbox: 4-speed foot change
Final drive: chain
Weight: 129kg (284lb)
Top speed: 125kph (78mph)

PEM
USA 1910–15: Unusually, this American company built only singles, with an in-house 4hp overhead-valve engine.

PENNINGTON
England 1897: E.J. Pennington was an American engineer–cum-confidence trickster who sold a worthless design to a consortium of gullible and greedy Britons for a reported £100,000 (half a million dollars).

PENTA
Czech Republic 1992–94: This machine was a water-cooled 125cc designed for off-road competitions.

PER
Germany (Stockheim) 1924–26: Kurt Passow developed the Per from the Pawa, above. The pressed-steel frame incorporated a good deal of enclosure; the twin seats were big 'tractor-pan' types; and the 308cc two-stroke was enlarged after its introduction to 342cc. The engine was supposed to be multi-fuel but did not run very well on any of them.

PERIPOLI
Italy 1957–: Mopeds with Demm motors were supplemented in 1962 with the Giulietta 100cc lightweight, although most later machines (including the subsequent Giulietta scooter) reverted to 50cc.

PERKS & BIRCH
England 1899–1901: Also known simply as Perks, this pioneering firm used a 222cc single to propel both two- and three-wheelers.

PERMO
Germany 1952–54: This firm manufactured mopeds which were propelled by 32cc Victoria engines.

PERNOD
France 1899–1905: This French pioneer fitted their own 1hp engine behind the rear wheel.

PERNOD
France c.1980: This pastis-maker sponsored a 250cc racer.

PERSCH
Austria (Graz) 1922–25: These auxiliary cycle motors of 110cc also came with matched Krammer frames.

PARILLA SLUGHI/OLIMPIA

1959

First shown in prototype form at the Milan Show towards the end of 1957, the Slughi (Desert Greyhound) was designed by Piero Bossaglia.

Built in both four- and two-stroke guise, and also sold in a revised form as the Olimpia, the basis of the design was a fabricated pressed-steel backbone extending to form the base for the seat and rear mudguard. The horizontal engine was suspended from the backbone and detachable panels covering the sides of the power unit (left naked on the Olimpia), and continued rearwards beyond the hub. Movement of the tubular rear fork was controlled by a rubber block concealed inside the frame backbone.

In concept and appearance, the Slughi bore a striking resemblance to the Aermacchi Chimera – which had been the star of the 1956 Milan Show – even to the extent of having a horizontal, unit-construction, four-speed, overhead-valve engine!

The 1959 Parilla Olimpia used a 97.7cc air-cooled ohv engine with a horizontal single cylinder. A 114cc two-stroke version was also offered.

Additionally, the Chimera had been designed by the well-known former Parilla engineer, Alfredo Bianchi.

But whereas the Chimera was to suffer from poor sales, the much smaller and cheaper Parilla design sold well to a commuting customer base. Additionally, the major disadvantage of the Chimera – its lack of decent weather protection – was looked after on the Slughi by the availability of elegant and efficient legshields and a large windshield, all of which could be fitted quickly.

The first Slughi models went on sale for the 1959 model year and featured a 97.7cc (52x46mm) pushrod engine. The same pushrod engine was also used on the Olimpia.

Later Slughi/Olimpia models came with a choice of either a 125 (actually 114cc) two-stroke, or the original '98' overhead-valve four-stroke engines. At least twice the number of the smaller engined models sold compared to the larger two-stroke version.

The engine layout of both was particularly neat, with the two basic motors sharing many components, including gearbox, clutch and electrical items. This

obviously kept down production costs. The four-stroke engine's consumption was amazingly frugal. It was able to achieve over 2.3 litres/100km (125mpg).

Engine: 97.7cc ohv horizontal single, 52x46mm, air-cooled
Power: 6.5rpm at 7200rpm
Gearbox: 4-speed foot change
Final drive: chain
Weight: 78kg (172lb)
Top speed: 85kph (53mph)

PARILLA WILDCAT SCRAMBLER

1963

In its day, Parilla's 247cc Wildcat Scrambler was the most powerful machine in its class. Unfortunately, its excess weight blunted performance.

The Wildcat Scrambler was built by Parilla expressly for their American importer, Ernest Wise of Cosmopolitan Motors, and used the 247cc (68x68mm) version of

the long-running and highly successful hi-cam engine.

The Wildcat Scrambler was the name given by Cosmopolitan to the machine, first shown in

prototype form, at the Milan Samples Fair in the spring of 1961. It was intended as a serious competition bike, not the more normal Stateside 'Street

Scrambler' and as such, came with an open megaphone exhaust, no lighting equipment, abbreviated mudguarding, long travel, Marzocchi-made motocross front forks, a comprehensive air filtration system, massive rear wheel sprocket, tachometer and knobbly Pirelli 'Motocross' tyres. The engine was specially tuned and brake-tested and put out well over 30bhp.

These power characteristics were more suited to road racing than dirt track, however, and although it was just about passable on a dry, fast course, it most definitely did not go well on muddy conditions where low-down engine torque was needed. In a straight line the Parilla Wildcat was probably the fastest motocrosser of its day – certainly in the 250cc class – but as a serious dirt machine, it left much to be desired. This was also because of its weight: it was considerably heavier than the two-stroke opposition from the likes of Greeves and Cotton.

The frame was considerably changed from the standard roadster model, with much additional bracing required for its

new task; this didn't help its weight either. What the Parilla Wildcat is remembered for is its superb noise, a deep, mellow bark which, compared to the usual tinny two-stroke clatter, was simply marvellous.

Engine: 247cc ohv 2v single, 68x68mm, air-cooled
Power: 31bhp at 8500rpm
Gearbox: 4-speed foot change
Final drive: chain
Weight: 125kg (276lb)
Top speed: 121kph (75mph)

PATON   ITALY 1958–

In 1967, Angelo Bergamont, riding one of the dohc Paton twins, defeated world champion Giacomo Agostini to win the 500cc Italian Senior Championship.

The Paton name was derived from the first three, and second and third, letters of their surnames, although the pair went their separate ways: Tonti to Bianchi, whilst Pattoni stayed and built a whole series of racing motorcycles over the next four decades.

One of Pattoni's first customers was Stan Hailwood, whose son Mike was just taking his first steps on the path to a whole string of championships and worldwide acclaim. Hailwood Junior brought his Paton home seventh in the 1958 125cc TT. Next came the first twin-cylinder model, the first to be solely Pattoni's own work. Its best result was a third place in

THE ORIGINS OF THE Paton name date back to 1957, when FB Mondial, together with the companies Guzzi and Gilera, quit the Grand Prix racing scene. This move obviously left a number of very talented engineers out of work.

Giuseppe Pattoni, as chief mechanic for the FB Mondial squad, was one such person. Together with another Mondial employee, the designer Lino Tonti, Pattoni created a 124cc double overhead-cam racer for sale to top-line privateers for the 1958 season.

A 492cc, cross-port, liquid-cooled, two-stroke, four-cylinder Paton Grand Prix racer on display at the 1991 Milan Show. It produced 125bhp at 10,000rpm.

the 1964 250cc TT, ridden by Alberto Pagani. With backing from a Liverpool-based Scot, Bill Hannah, the model was further developed, first into a 350 and, finally, a 500.

The later 500s produced 65bhp in two-valve form, with the final version sporting four valves per cylinder for the double overhead-cam engine, putting out 70bhp.

In 1967, Paton rider Angelo Bergamonti beat world champion Giacomo Agostini, winning the 500cc Italian Senior Championship.

The twin soldiered on into the 1970s, but in 1976 Patoni designed a 492cc (45x50mm) cross-port, liquid-cooled, two-stroke, four-cylinder model. In 1984, a new twin-crankshaft, close-coupled four, consisting of two 250cc twins mounted one above the other, with the cylinders spaced at 115 degrees, caused considerable interest.

For some 20 years, Peppino Pattoni, as he was to become known around the GP paddocks, carried on with the help of Gianemillo Marchesani. However, after the Marchesani died in a car crash in the early 1980s, his place was taken by Pattoni's son, Roberto.

PEERLESS

ENGLAND 1902–08

THIS SHORT-LIVED MARQUE was a Bradbury under another name but was still made at the same factory in Oldham, Lancashire. Like the Bradbury, it was built to a Birch design with the crankcase cast around the lower end of the downtube and the bottom bracket. A door on the left side enabled the crankshaft to be installed with the one-piece head and cylinder fixed vertically to the casting.

The engine capacity was 377cc with the bore slightly larger than the stroke. A Longuemare carburettor supplied the mixture, and a Bassée-Michel coil, with the spark lever mounted on the frame top tube, fired it. Rated at two-and-a-half horsepower, the engine ran at 1500rpm and drove the rear wheel by V-belt with a ratio of 4.5:1. Pedals were fitted for starting and to help on hills.

The design meant that the engine was permanently installed in the frame, which was of the diamond type and held rigid by the crankcase. Braced forks went at the front, along with primitive cycle-rim brakes, the rear brake being a coaster type. Narrow mudguards, handlebars and a saddle completed this very basic, early pioneering machine, which continued to have 'Bradbury' and

'Oldham' cast into the side of the crankcase.

Nevertheless, the Peerless performed well for its size and era – in fact, better than many other machines – so Bradbury kept the marque going for some years. Just as it is in motorcycle production today, this was a common practice, intended to garner more sales by offering apparently rival makes.

PEUGEOT

FRANCE 1899–

PERHAPS BETTER KNOWN as the mass-producer of cars, Peugeot made bicycles from 1885 and powered bicycles in 1899. The brothers Peugeot started making their own engine with an atmospheric inlet valve in 1903, and in 1906 graduated to a range of V-twins of 345, 726 and 994cc, also selling them to other manufacturers.

Car production began in 1907 and by 1913, Peugeot's advanced 500cc parallel-twin race bikes had appeared, sporting overhead-camshafts and four valves per cylinder. A refined V-twin and a lightweight two-stroke were introduced after World War I, and in the mid-1920s Peugeot built unit-construction 350cc side-valve single-cylinder machines, followed by 125 and 500cc singles. Although the two-stroke remained on the list, the 500cc racing twin was dropped in 1927. The unit-construction cast-iron side-valve four-strokes were designed as utilitarian machines, but nevertheless, were well made and inexpensive – perfect for the market in which they were being sold.

After World War II, production did not resume until 1949. Output consisted of a line of mopeds, the S55 scooter (with a cargo deck over the front wheel), a 125cc single and 350cc twin, all using two-stroke power. Peugeot's motorcycle range was a casualty of the two-wheel recession and production came to a halt in 1959. Mopeds were a different matter, however, and these remained profitable. By 1980, Peugeot had begun to make motorcycles again with an 80cc device, working with Gilera to design and build a 125cc

The 1997 Zenith Sport scooter was one of Peugeot's offerings in the rapidly-expanding scooter market. The company was a brand leader in this field.

machine. These projects achieved little success, and a Honda-engined scooter proved more attractive.

Peugeot's products were among the brand leaders in the scooter-orientated urban two-wheeler market of the late 1990s and early 2000s. There was the compact Elyseo 100 and 125P model, a no-frills commuter with a relatively tall 830mm (32ins) seat height and a full convenience package, as well as the entry-level Vivacity and the highly popular Speedflight.

Peugeot's two-wheeled motorcycle range came to an end in 1959. Its mopeds, such as this 50cc 103S from 1978, were a different matter, remaining profitable.

PIAGGIO

ITALY 1946–

THE COMPANY THAT MAKES Vespa scooters goes back a very long way. Founded in 1884 in Genoa by the 20-year-old Rinaldo Piaggio as a general engineering business, the company prospered in the fields of shipping, railways and, from 1915, aviation. During the 1930s it built bombers and seaplanes for the Italian airforce as well as founding the country's first commercial airline. Rinaldo Piaggio was rewarded with membership of the Italian Senate, and his sons Armando and Enrico managed the company after his death in 1938. However, like so many other

Above: Named after the Italian for 'wasp', the first Vespa came out in 1946. A single seat model, the headlight was housed on the shapely front mudguard.

Left: By the 1960s, the scooter was the favoured transport of the young and trendy, the Vespa being more stylish than its Lambretta cousin. This is a 125 TS single-cylinder two-stroke machine.

factories, Piaggio's Pontedera plant was destroyed in 1945 by a combination of German sabotage and Allied bombing.

Postwar restructuring took the company in a radical new direction, providing two-wheeled transport for the people, and Enrico Piaggio entrusted the project to aeronautical engineer Corradino d'Ascanio. The prototype was up and running before the end of 1945, and was revolutionary in design. Unlike a conventional motorcycle, it had no frame, and consisted instead of a spot-welded steel chassis with mechanicals enclosed by rotund bodywork and the rider protected by legshields. The 98cc two-stroke single-cylinder engine drove the rear wheel through an enclosed gear drive, and the gearchange was by the left-hand handlebar twistgrip. Suspension was by

PHANTOM
Germany 1921–28: For their first five years, this firm used their own 150, 200 and 250cc side-valve single engines, then later added JAP side-valve engines of 175 to 500cc capacity.

PHASAR
England 1980s: A derivative of the futuristic Quasar, the Phasar enjoyed about as much success as its forebear.

PHILLIPS
England 1954–64: This subsidiary of Raleigh built mopeds.

PHOENIX
England 1900–08: As well as using Minerva engines of 211 and 345cc, this undertaking founded by J.V. Hooydonk, a well-known racer of the time, may also have built in-house motors.

PHOENIX
England 1955–64: These were scooters with a surprising range of Villiers engines from 150 to 323cc.

PHONIX
Germany (Neuheim an der Ruhr) 1933–39: see **RMW**: the machines were identical.

PIANA
Italy 1923–31: Gualterio Piana began with Villiers two-strokes of 147cc, then later added bigger Villiers engines and JAP four-strokes of 250 to 500cc. After 1928, an in-house overhead-valve 250 was also used.

PIATTI
Belgium 1955–58: The Piatti scooter was built in England to the design of the Italian Vincenzo Piatti, for sale in Belgium. The engine was a 125cc two-stroke single.

PIAZZA
Italy 1924–34: Antonio Piazza began with two- and four-stroke auxiliary bicycle motors, initially 125cc, later 175cc. They moved on, in about 1927, to 175cc lightweights, at first overhead-valve, later with an optional single-valve layout. A 500cc overhead-valve JAP engine may also have been available.

The Liberty 125 was Piaggio's offering in the burgeoning scooter market of 1997. The spindly wheels gave it the appearance of something closer to a moped.

single-sided swinging-arm at the rear and stub-axle at the front, and this enabled the wheels to be changed easily when required.

The name was taken from the Italian for wasp, and the Vespa was in production by April 1946. Some 2484 units were sold that year, and more than 10,000 in 1947. The millionth Vespa rolled off the line in 1956, with more than 15 million by 2000, making Piaggio the third largest manufacturer of motorised two-wheelers in the world. Its scooters were produced under licence in Germany from 1950 and by Bristol-based Douglas in the UK and by ACMA in France. Evolutions and increments to engine capacity were quick to follow. A 125cc four-speed version came out in 1948, with ungainly three-wheeler commercial derivatives also available. The G-model appeared in 1953 featuring a neat cable-controlled gear linkage that replaced the original rod-operated shift. Another

Right: The NRG Extreme OT fitted the prevailing style of the scooter market, with beak-like handlebar fairing and almond-shaped headlights.

capacity bike brought in the 150cc GS150 in 1955, which came with slightly larger 25cm (10ins) wheels, a four-speed gearbox and handlebar layout that incorporated the speedometer in the centre. Evolutions of the GS150 were especially popular with scooter-obsessed British Mods of the early 1960s, and although frequently festooned with chrome-plated racks, bars and baubles, the shape and proportions of the basic GS150 model endure as the classic Vespa.

In 1962 the range encompassed the 125, 150 Sportique and GS160, followed in 1964 by the 90 Standard and in 1965 by the SS180 with a rectangular headlight. The 90 was available in Super Sport trim with spare wheel and tool box occupying the step-through platform. Around this time Piaggio introduced its Automatic Fuelmix system, which governed the blending of oil and fuel according to throttle position. In 1969, Piaggio absorbed the Gilera motorcycle marque, which was unexpectedly later closed down in 1993.

For 1972, the range-topping Vespa model was the 12bhp 200 Rally Electronic with the 50cc three-speed VSA as the entry-level machine. The Vespa range received a comprehensive facelift in 1978, demonstrated by the PX 125 and 200, although the traditional Vespa 'bubbles' were still present, albeit in flattened and squared-off format. These scooters evolved into the PK Series in 1983, and were joined by the PK80 that had an electric starter, and the T5, which came out in 1986. In 1991, Piaggio began to release its new range of plastic-bodied scooters. First of these was the Sfera which won the Compasso d'Oro design award. A 125 version of the Sfera was fitted with Piaggio's first four-stroke engine. The 50cc Zip and Free models followed, with the more aggressive Typhoon launched in 1993. The Zip was available with 50cc two-stroke or electric power, while the 125cc Skipper of 1995 was the first fully automatic scooter in that capacity bracket. Bigger still was the Hexagon,

Wearing more bodywork than a Harley, the Piaggio X9 500 was a big machine by scooter standards, and required a full licence to ride.

which afforded comfort and carrying capacity with 125 and 180cc two-stroke options, or a Honda 250cc four-stroke powerplant. Recognising its lengthy heritage, Piaggio addressed the retro market with its ET2 in 1996. This machine re-captured something of its 1960s

ancestors, despite having just 50cc, but it was equipped with fuel injection for cleaner running. It was later available with a four-stroke engine. By 2000, Piaggio's range topper was the X9 250, the big single-cylinder scooter clearly requiring a full licence to ride, and providing exemplary comfort and

ergonomics. It had no visible locks or catches, and access to its cubby holes was achieved simply by pushing the key into the ignition, revealing levers within the inner fairing flap for opening the two-helmet storage beneath the seat and to open the fuel filler cap – very sophisticated.

VESPA GS150 — 1955

The machine that typified the marque was one of the earliest to come out, just 10 years after the company designed its first scooter. Piaggio introduced its Vespa GS150 in 1955, and it evolved by updates to the electrical system and auxiliary components through five phases up to the VS5 of 1962, when it was superseded by the GS160. The first GS150 had faired-in handlebars, but the brake and clutch cables were still exposed, as they had been on earlier Vespas with exposed bars.

Like all Vespas, the GS150 styling incorporated legshields, a front mudguard that turned with the wheel, and bubbles or blisters either side of the central section. The 150cc single-cylinder two-stroke motor was housed in the right-hand bubble, while the left-hand one was for storage and battery housing. Scooters were always perceived as the transport of the young and trendy, and the GS150 achieved cult status among early 1960s British Mods, as shown in the film *Quadrophenia*.

The Vespa's bubbles were frequently chromium-plated and the bikes adorned with similarly festive paraphernalia, then driven in slow-moving convoys, along with similarly bedecked Lambretta siblings, to British coastal resorts on holiday weekends.

Engine: 150cc single-cylinder two-stroke
Power: 8bhp
Gearbox: 4-speed
Final drive: shaft drive
Weight: n/a
Top Speed: 104kph (65mph)

PIAGGIO TYPHOON — 1995

The late twentieth century saw frustrated car drivers converting to two-wheeled transport. One of the front runners in the urban jungle

The 1997 Piaggio Typhoon had optional extras including top-box, screen, side-stand and headlight protector.

was Piaggio's Typhoon 125. Launched in 1995, this scooter was coveted by the style-conscious, and grid-locked motorists. Powered to a top 100kph (60mph) by an air-cooled two-stroke 123.5cc single-cylinder motor, it offered progressive brakes, excellent handling on 25cm (10in) wheels

and automatic transmission. A full-face helmet could be stored under the seat.

Engine: 123.5cc single-cylinder two-stroke
Power: 11.9bhp
Final drive: shaft drive
Weight: 96kg (210lb)
Top Speed: 100kph (62mph)

PIERTON
France 1922–25: This was an assembler offering a wide variety of engines from 100 to 500cc from Aubier Dunne, Blackburne, JAP, Train and Villiers. It was also called Pietron.

PILOT
England 1903–15: This firm began with JAP and Precision engines of 200 to 600cc, later offering their own 318cc two-stroke.

PIOLA
Italy 1919–21: This was a rare 620cc single-valve flat twin.

PIRATE
USA (Milwaukee) 1911–15: These rather old-fashioned machines had pedals, although the engines themselves – inlet -over-exhaust singles and V-twins of 3–8hp – were modern enough.

PIROTTA
Italy (Milan) 1949–55: This firm built mopeds of 40 to 75cc, then in 1954, a 160cc lightweight capable (in late Sport guise) of over 115kph (70mph) claimed.

PITTY
East Germany 1955–late 1960s: MZ two-strokes of 147cc powered these scooters.

PMC
England (Birmingham) 1908–15: The Premier Motorcycle Company of Birmingham (as distinct from the one in Coventry) seems to have used exclusively JAP engines, up to 1000cc.

POINARD
France 1951–56: Two-strokes from Aubier Dunne and Ydral, and four-strokes from AMC, powered these scooters and lightweights of up to 250cc.

POINTER
Japan 1946–62: Once a significant player, this now-forgotten company specialised in two-strokes up to 250cc.

POLENGHI
Italy 1950–55: This shortlived Italian firm were responsible for the production of mopeds.

PIAGGIO HEXAGON

1999

Only those with long memories will recall that Triumph made the 249cc Tigress TW2 overhead-valve twin and BSA the identical Sunbeam in 1959, but the modern super-scooter was born when Yamaha came out with its 250cc Majesty in 1997. Following the Japanese examples, Piaggio installed Honda's 250cc four-stroke single in its Hexagon in 1999 and joined the big-bore scooter manufacturers. Small wheels and wide expanses of bodywork coupled with a relatively hefty 140kg (300lb) were not ideal on a wind-blown motorway, but creature comforts such as mobile phone socket and rain protector for the seat were novel touches. Storage

In 1999, Piaggio followed the Japanese example and fitted Honda's 250cc four-stroke single-cylinder engine in the Hexagon GT to make a modern super-scooter.

was minimal, with just a rear boot and space behind the fairing, but none under the seat. A better machine was the Hexagon's smaller 125cc sibling, which could equal the 250's 100kph (62mph) top speed, but lacked the larger machine's novelties.

Engine: 250cc single-cylinder four-stroke
Power: 18bhp
Final drive: shaft drive
Weight: 140kg (300lb)
Top speed: 100kph (62mph)

PIERCE

USA 1909–13

THIS NAME APPEARED on the first four-cylinder motorcycles to be built in the USA, which were manufactured by the well-established car firm of Pierce Arrow located in Buffalo, New York. The motorcycles were also known as Pierce-Arrow, thanks to the form of their tank transfer, and singles were made as well as fours.

The machines were aimed at the top end of the market and, at times, it was made clear that the company had no intention of competing on price with other marques. The machines were quite distinctive, thanks mainly to the fact that their frames, as the main section, comprised three 89mm (3.5ins) diameter tubes that also acted as the petrol and oil tanks, a design that was used by both types.

Both the Pierce four and this single had extra-large frame tubes that doubled as petrol and oil tanks. The single used belt drive, the four, shaft drive.

The four was based on the Belgian FN design but its 42.5cid engine was of the T-head type with the inlet valves on the left and exhausts on the right, each with its own gear-driven camshaft. The engine followed car practice with the crankcase split horizontally to carry the three-bearing crankshaft and the cylinder complete with head bolted down to it. The head had a line of valve caps on each side; those over the inlet valves carried the sparking plugs, while the exhaust ones were blank. In the centre went another line of

caps, with those at the end designed to support the HT leads. Both the magneto and the distributor were driven from the timing gears and went at the front, and the single carburettor was located behind the block on a pipe that ran down to the tubular inlet manifold, which ran along the left side of the engine. The four exhaust pipes connected to a low-level silencer on the right.

The engine was installed along the frame and hung between the lower ends of the massive down- and seat-tubes, with a direct drive to a shaft running back to a bevel box in the rear wheel hub. Thus, there was no clutch or gearbox, and in order to start the machine it had to be placed on its rear stand and push-started; alternatively, the pedalling gear could be used. Front suspension was by leading-link forks, and the brake went in the rear wheel hub because front brakes were not then, nor for many years afterwards,

used by American riders due to the poor dirt roads outside most towns.

For 1910, the four was fitted with a multiplate clutch and two-speed gearbox, and was joined by the single. This had a side-valve engine and direct belt drive but retained the special frame, leading-link forks and pedalling gear. Apart from some minor adjustments, both models remained the same from that time onwards, the four offering smooth, vibration-free running up to 96kph (60mph), but unfortunately at a price far above the norm. They were popular with those who could afford them but that was a small market.

As sales failed to recoup the company's investment and production costs, 1913 was to be their last year.

The engine of the Pierce single was a simple side-valve with the magneto at the front. This 1911 model had bicycle-style pedals for starting the machine.

POPE

USA 1911–18

THIS NAME FIRST APPEARED in 1911 on machines built in Westfield, Massachusetts, and belonged to a firm that was part of the well-established Pope car company. Previously, the motorcycle side of the firm operated as the American Cycle Manufacturing Company and, as such, it had sold identical models under that name and also under the names Cleveland, Columbia, Crescent, Imperial, Monarch, Rambler and Tribune, all bicycle lines. Two other independent companies also used the US name.

Selling under various marque names was a good way of doing business. In any given town, each cycle agent might have his own showroom, which meant more outlets. Agents' customers were good prospects for motorcycle sales because they were already used to the idea of two wheels and therefore welcomed the notion of the same, without the hard work of pedalling. The dealers also had knowledge of the cycle side, so they could easily cope with motorcycles, even if the engines and transmissions were new to them.

From its beginning in 1912 the Pope V-twin engine had overhead valves (then rare for a major make) rear magneto and plunger rear suspension.

The Pope line began with a simple F-head single with belt drive, which was joined by a 61cid V-twin in 1912. If the single was basic and typical of the times, the twin was quite the reverse as it had an overhead-valve engine and plunger rear suspension, both unusual features for the time. Overhead-valves were generally only used for the inlet valve with overhead-valve mainly seen on competition engines or obscure makes. Rear suspension was also rare at that time; some form of pivoted fork was more common.

The Pope twin followed conventional lines in general, with

The start of the two-wheeled Pope line in 1911 was this F-head single with its forward magneto, belt drive and trailing-link front forks.

the engine installed in a tubular frame with trailing-link front forks controlled by a leaf spring fixed under the lower crown and connected to the wheel-spindle mountings by a stay running down each side of the wheel. It had a single speed, chain final drive and pedalling gear, with its brake working on the rear wheel as was usual in the USA at that time. For the rear suspension, each end of the wheel spindle was clamped to plunger rods that extended through the U-shaped frame end members. A tension spring was secured above each member and the plunger ran through to the spring top, where it was attached, so that upward wheel movement extended the springs as the rods slid through the frame ends. The method in later types differed, using coil springs in compression for both directions.

For 1914, the twin was available with a two-speed transmission option and, two years later, a three-speed gearbox was available while the single speed remained available to those who preferred it. The Pope continued in this form up to 1918.

POSDAM
Italy (Turin) 1926–29: The Possi brothers teamed up with Da Milano – hence the name – to build first a 150cc belt-drive machine, then a 125cc, followed by a 175cc with chain drive. They were as much motorised bicycles as lightweights.

POTTHOFF
Germany 1924–26: Unusually for the time and place, this firm used overhead-valve 185cc Norman engines instead of two-strokes.

POUNCY
England 1930–38: Villiers two-stroke singles of up to 350cc powered these assembled (but charmingly named) machines.

POUSTKA
Czech Republic 1924–34: A Czech equivalent of the Pouncy, with the same 150, 250 and 350cc Villiers motors.

POWELL
England 1921–26: After a 550cc Blackburne-engined single, Powell moved on to 170 and 250cc two-strokes and (in 1924) a fully-enclosed 200cc motorcycle.

POWELL
USA late 1940s: This firm produced both a scooter and a miniaturised motorcycle, the latter powered by a 400cc single-cylinder engine, which says something about 'American' and 'miniature'.

POWER WHEEL
England 1951: No less a firm than Tube Investments built this Cyril Pullin-designed 40cc two-stroke auxiliary cycle motor which delivered 0.7bhp at 3600rpm.

POW WOW
USA c.1945: This was an auxiliary cycle motor, similar in concept to the Powerbike, with its own small driving wheel.

PRAGA
Czech Republic 1929–35: When the well-known Praga car works merged with Breitfeild Danek in 1929, they also took on a 500cc overhead-cam single, sold initially as BD and later as Praga. In 350cc form, with the same 90mm stroke but a reduced bore, it powered a shaft-drive version with a pressed-steel frame after 1932.

PRINETTI & STUCCHI

ONE OF THE LEADING Italian firms at the turn of the twentieth century was Prinetti & Stucchi, whose beginnings were in bicycles. The company moved into powered transport in 1898 with a tricycle which had been fitted with a De Dion engine, in the manner of the day, behind the rear axle.

One apprentice who was involved with this work was Ettore

Bugatti. At that time, he was only 17, but he was destined to be famous all over the world for his incredible cars. Bugatti took the tricycle and added a second engine to double the power, entering the machine in a number of local races with considerable success.

Prinetti & Stucchi also built quads, essentially the tricycle with a new front fork carrying the two

wheels with a forecar mounted between them. Bugatti used one of these as the basis of his first car, fitting no less than four De Dion engines, two ahead of, and two behind, the rear axle.

The firm moved on to motorcycles and they followed the lines of most others of that time, with a single cylinder, belt drive and braced or sprung forks. In

1902, the name changed to Stucchi and, in time, all aspects of the machines were evolved to include gearbox, chain drive, sturdier cycle parts and better brakes.

After World War I the company added V-twins of various sizes, but sales were slow and a change to mid-range singles did little more than keep the firm going to the middle of the 1920s.

PUCH

THE PUCH MARQUE has a truly complex history and although Johann Puch built his first motorcycle in 1903, the background to the story is somewhat reminiscent of the Swedish Husqvarna company. Husqvarna started out with armament production, and while today its motorcycles are manufactured in Italy by Cagiva, Puch is owned by another Italian company, Piaggio.

Puch amalgamated with Austro-Daimler in 1928 and Steyr in 1934. Austro-Daimler and Steyr were in trouble and needed the prosperous Puch AG to survive. All three had the same majority shareholder, a Viennese trust bank.

The armaments connection came via Steyr, the oldest of the three organisations, which was founded in 1864 by Josef Werndl and located in the town of Steyr. As the firm was already managing another arms plant, it was no surprise that the new enterprise should be in the same field. Soon the Steyr-based outfit became the largest armaments manufacturer in Europe. By 1890, it had more than 9000 employees turning out 540,000 rifles every year. The company added bicycles in 1894, and these were soon to become a major part of the firm's output.

The outbreak of World War I caused rapid expansion, but after

The Puch S4 of the mid-1930s used a 250cc two-stroke engine and was one of the Austrian company's most successful models of the inter-war years.

the conflict had finally finished, Austria was on the wrong side, with much of its former territory gone and armaments manufacture banned.

As a result, Steyr instigated bicycle and car manufacture but was greatly affected by the Great Depression, which ultimately prompted the 1934 amalgamation.

Austro-Daimler, the second company in the group, was originally set up in 1899 to build

cars from components made at the German Daimler plant. This soon led the founder, Josef Eduard Bierenz, to construct complete cars under licence.

In 1906, Bierenz was joined by the legendary designer Ferdinand Porsche. Before long, they added buses, trucks and military vehicles, moving back exclusively to cars after World War I. In 1928, it linked up with Puch.

Puch was founded by Johann Puch at Graz in 1891 to manufacture pedal cycles. It was sold in 1897 to a German group and, in 1899, Puch opened an entirely new plant. In 1903, Puch produced his first motorcycle, followed in 1910 by the first Puch automobile.

In the very early road races (up to 1905) Puch machines were fairly active, but the most successful of its racing bikes was without doubt the Gordon Bennett of 1906. This was a four-stroke V-twin of 904.7cc (80x90mm) with belt final drive and three-and-a-half horsepower. These machines, ridden by Nikoden and Obruba, took first and second places in the 1906 European International Cup race. The marque also appeared in the Isle of Man TT, but all Puch entries in the 1913 and 1914 Senior races retired.

By the time war broke out in 1914, Puch had established itself as one of the leading motorcycle manufacturers in Europe but in the same year, Johann Puch suffered a sudden death.

The first of the marque's famous line of split-single two-strokes, the LM (Light Motorcycle), designed by Giovanni Marcelino, made its debut in 1923. This design was to form the basis for Puch motorcycles over the next half century. The first model was 122cc but the displacement soon grew, up to 250cc. Puch also had considerable success in racing events throughout Europe during the late 1920s and throughout the 1930s.

In 1931, a 500 was produced by doubling up the 250cc model to create a four-piston split-twin. Puch also built an 800cc side-valve horizontally opposed four-cylinder, which made its debut in 1936. Then came the Anschluss of 1938 and the outbreak of World War II a few months later.

After the war, Puch continued with its split-single family for both competition and street models. Exports went all over Europe and North America. In the USA, they were sold under the Allstate and Sear brand names.

A new, fan-cooled 49cc engine with sloping cylinder and pressed-steel frame arrived in the 1950s. This was subsequently built in large numbers by Puch and also, under licence, by the Yugosalvian firm, Tomos, for many years.

At the 1966 Cologne Show, Puch finally got around to replacing its ageing split-singles. Designated the M125, the first model was a 123.5cc (54x54mm) single-cylinder roadster, which featured five speeds and a striking cylinder head design. In this design, the fins arranged in a so-called 'sunburst' pattern to promote cooling and eliminate distortion.

A Puch SG split single two-stroke of 1962. The Graz firm developed this engine type over almost half a century.

From this first machine came a whole series of other models, principally intended for road racing and dirt-bike use.

The Puch engine was particularly successful as a trials unit (with the likes of Greeves and Dalesman), whilst a factory motocross bike ridden by Harry Everts won the 250cc world title in 1975. There were also the Italian Friggerio-Puch enduro bikes, which were offered for sale during the late 1970s and early 1980s.

Puch's most famous and profitable line, however, was the Maxi series of mopeds, which

were the top sellers throughout the world during the 1970s.

But then came the 1980s, and this decade was to see the beginning of a major recession that hit the two-wheel industry very badly. Although Puch didn't go under, it was badly damaged. This resulted in a merger with the Italian giants Piaggio, owners of the Vespa and Gilera brands, in 1987. Not long after this, Puch production in Austria came to an end. Piaggio also granted a licence to a Czech producer to build the venerable Maxi.

During the late 1970s and early 1980s, the Italian Friggerio company developed a range of excellent Rotax-engined Puch enduro bikes in 500 and 600cc capacities.

PRECISION
England 1912–19: Before World War I, F.E. Baker's Precision machines were for export only; postwar, his new 350cc two-stroke for the home market was produced for a short while under the Precision name before Beardmore took over and it became Beardmore-Precision.

PREMIER
England (Coventry) 1908–15: In the early years of the twentieth century, Premier claimed to be the biggest bicycle factory in the world. They made motorcycles from 1908 to 1915, and three-wheeled light delivery vehicles until the early 1920s, although after 1914 they were known as Coventry-Premier. After beginning with White & Poppe engines, they developed their own 548cc 90-degree V-twin, in 1910 a 499cc single, in 1912 a revised 548cc engine, and in 1914 a 998cc V-twin based on a doubled-up single, Vincent-fashion. Premier lightweights were used by the Allies in World War I.

PREMIER
Austro-Hungary/Czech Republic (Eger) 1913–33: The German Premier factory was moved in 1913. After the 350cc single, 1923 saw a 269cc two-stroke along with 350 and 500cc JAP-engined machines. After 1927, Premier's own 350 and 500cc singles and an in-house 740cc V-twin were used.

PREMO
England (Birmingham) 1908–15: Premier/PMC used this trademark for some of their machines, initially with Minerva engines, later with JAP singles and twins.

PRESTER (JONGHI)
France 1926–late 1950s: Prester began with Aubier-Dunne two-strokes up to 250cc, and Chaise shaft-drive four-strokes up to 500cc. They merged with Jonghi in 1939, and built a bread-and-butter 350cc four-stroke along with double overhead-cam racers up to 350cc. After World War II they made lightweights up to 250cc, and a 125cc scooter.

PUCH SGS 175/250

Built in 175 and 250cc engine sizes (one of the larger models is pictured here), the Puch SGS range of split singles spanned the 1950s and 1960s.

The Puch SGS 175 and 250 models were the final developments of the longest running split-single in motorcycle history. Puch's break from the then conventional crossflow system of scavenge came with the Harlette split-single in 1923. This was not the first to be used on a motorcycle, but it was certainly one of the most successful, staying in production for 50 years.

The Puch layout differed from the earlier Garelli and the later German Triumph (TWN) split-singles in that its pistons did not rise and fall side by side in unison. The essence of split-single scavenge is two cylinders sharing a cylinder head, and both pistons take part in both induction and power strokes. The exhaust port is in one cylinder, the transfer port in the other.

The Puch employed a 'Y'-shaped connecting rod shared by both the pistons so that as the rod began its stroke, the angle meant that one of the pistons – except at top and bottom centres – was 'ahead' of the other. This piston was used to

control the exhaust port. Thus the exhaust port could open and close early, which gave plenty of time for the exhaust gases to escape before the transfer port was opened.

The split-single had other advantages: there was no need for a deflector on the piston crown because the shared cylinder wall acted as a deflector. This meant that the pistons were lighter and free from distortion as a result of uneven heating. Also, the point where the split-single scored most was that it allowed the engine to run smoothly at all times and with superior fuel consumption, like with that of a good four-stroke.

The 248cc unit construction of the type used in SGS debuted in 1948. The design was updated in 1953; it had telescopic forks, swinging-arm rear suspension and a pressed-steel chassis. With 16.5bhp, the Puch split-single line was sold in the US as the Allstate from 1954, through the Sears Chain Store Company.

Engine: 248cc 2s split-single, 78x45x2, air-cooled
Power: 16.5bhp at 5500rpm
Gearbox: 4-speed foot change
Final drive: chain
Weight: 163kg (360lb)
Top speed: 115kph (72mph)

PUCH MAXI

Engine: 48.8cc 2s single, 38x43mm, air-cooled
Power: 2.2bhp at 4500rpm
Gearbox: single-speed automatic
Final drive: chain
Weight: 44kg (97lb)
Top speed: 48kph (30mph)

If the German NSU Quickly was the top-selling European-built moped of the 1950s, the honour for this title in the 1970s went to the Austrian Puch Maxi.

The world-famous Maxi was put

in production at Puch's Graz factory at the end of 1968. The original model had a power output of 1.8bhp at 4500rpm and the transmission was single-speed automatic. Throughout Europe the reaction to the newcomer was favourable and buyers were only too ready to pay the asking price. The Maxi went on to become Europe's best-selling powered two-wheeler for several years and so became a milestone in Puch's history. It was built in a vast

number of versions and continued in production for almost 20 years in Austria, before Puch was taken over by Piaggio in the late 1980s. Even then it continued to be built under licence in Czechoslovakia.

A secret of the Maxi's success, as with the NSU Quickly, was the quality of workmanship, which ensured years of reliable service. The machine was so well made that the finish of the castings, welding, paint work and chrome plate were a match for anything

else on the market. For city use it was first class: it was light, speedy and handled well. It was also exceedingly economical, offering over 2.2litres/100km (130mpg), which can only be described as truly cheap transport.

All Maxis shared the same basic 48.8cc (38x43mm) two-stroke engine with piston-port induction and horizontal cylinder. Weighing 44kg (97lb), the Puch moped featured an automatic gearbox and centrifugal clutch. Originally built with a rigid frame, many later models featured swinging-arm and twin rear shock absorbers. Most versions had a single seat, but on some bikes a dual seat was specified as standard equipment. Finally, as on other mopeds of the era, starting was by pedals, giving the rider a fore-and-aft foot position.

The Maxi was never glamorous but it was always extremely usable and normally the epitome of reliability.

A 49cc Puch Maxi Sport LS two-stroke moped, c.1978. Specification included a horizontal cylinder and twin shock rear suspension.

PULLIN-GROOM

ENGLAND 1920–25

AFTER HE HAD WON THE 1914 Senior TT, Cyril Pullin was to become involved with unusual designs for the next 40 years, the first of which was the Pullin-Groom produced with S.L. Groom. What set this machine apart was its frame, which concealed the engine and was built up from two steel pressings welded together with access panels for servicing, and

Rear suspension and a rocking front fork were further features of the 1920 Pullin-Groom, along with a two-speed epicyclic gearbox and all-chain drive.

which contained the petrol and oil tanks within its structure.

The machine had a rocking fork built up from pressings at the front and pivoted-fork rear suspension. Both wire wheels were quickly detachable and interchangeable, but only the rear had a drum brake, which could be operated by either hand or foot. Substantially valanced mudguards shielded both wheels. The company built its own 200cc two-stroke engine with a horizontal cylinder, flywheel magneto ignition and the mixture fed via a combined mixing valve controlling fuel and lubrication. It

drove a two-speed epicyclic gearbox with all-chain drive.

It was an ingenious design that was much praised, but was too advanced for many riders of the time. It disappeared until 1923 but was then revived by The Pullin Motor Cycle Company. The engine capacity rose to 310cc and the transmission was by a . conventional two-speed gearbox with all-chain drive. Deliveries began early in 1924 and the marque was listed in 1925 with engine capacities of 348 and 368cc, before this imaginative machine finally disappeared.

QUADRANT

QUADRANT, RUN BY W.J. Lloyd and based in Sheepcote Street, Birmingham, took the common route to the motorcycle by fitting a Minerva engine to the downtube of a heavy-duty bicycle. A forecar was soon added, and by 1903 the company had mounted an engine of its own design in a loop frame. A single lever controlled the throttle, ignition switch, spark advance and valve-lifter; this feature was intended to make the machine easier to ride, and did help to increase sales. The bike's prospects were further improved when Tom Silver set a new Land's End to John O'Groats record in June 1903 riding a 3hp model. For 1904 Quadrant added a forecar that had twin two-and-a-half horsepower engines, mounted side by side with a clutch between them so one or both could be used. Also introduced in 1904 was a short leading-link front fork for the solo models; this feature was retained for a while.

The firm moved to Earlsdon, Coventry, in 1908, when it introduced a new 550cc engine. This unit had valves at the front and rear of the cylinder in T-head style, and thus with a camshaft for each valve; the gear drive to these extended back to the magneto. The crankcase was cast as one major part, with a door on the right that

Tom Silver on his Quadrant at the end of the Glasgow to London trial held in May 1903. Except for an overnight rest, this was a non-stop run of 643km (402 miles).

served also as the inner timing case. This machine kept belt-drive with the option of a Roc two-speed gear and leading-link forks. By 1910 the exhaust valve was moved to a more standard position alongside the cylinder, but the inlet would remain at the rear for some years.

A 2hp lightweight was added for 1911, and a 4hp model for sidecar work during the year. In 1913 a more suitable V-twin appeared; its 7hp engine featured overhead inlet valves, a two-speed gear, all-chain drive and a new, centre-spring fork. There was a four-and-a-half horsepower belt-drive single for 1914, and late that year came a two-and-a-half horsepower two-stroke model with two speeds. These two, plus the V-twin, were listed for 1915, but only the big single remained for 1916.

After the war, Quadrant kept to singles, introducing a 565cc model with a three-speed Sturmey-Archer gearbox and the choice of chain-cum-belt or all-chain drive. This was joined by a 654cc version in late 1920, followed a year later by a 490cc model with a new side-by-

side-valve engine design and all-chain drive. In the spring of 1923 a similar 624cc version was added; by now the company had abandoned its idea of placing the inlet valve around the back of the cylinder. A 490cc overhead-valve model, based on the side-valve engine but with vertically positioned valves, joined the range in late 1924.

This sports type failed to last more than a year, but Quadrant made another attempt at the concept in 1926 with a re-designed overhead-valve 499cc engine. The model had twin exhaust ports, 178mm (7ins) coupled drum brakes and a three-speed Burman gearbox, by then common to all Quadrants. This machine, with the 490 and 624cc side-valve dual-purpose models, went on to 1927, the last full season for the company calling itself the maker of 'Britain's Oldest Motor Cycle'.

One of the Quadrant singles from the 1920s when the company offered a range of machines from 490 to 624cc, mostly with side valves.

QUASAR

ENGLAND 1976–83

QUAGLIOTTI
Italy 1902–07: The founder of this short-lived firm which was base d in Italy, was a man named Carlo Quagliotti. His firm was responsible for the manufacture of machines which were fitted with Peugeot engines as their powerplants. Various sources note that Quagliotti used two types of engine. What is clear is that he certainly used singles, and it is possible that he also used V-twins. The feature which they all had in common was their all-chain layshaft drive.

OBJECTIVELY, THE QUASAR had everything. It was fast, reliable and economical, and probably the safest two-wheeler ever built. Ken Leaman and the late Malcolm Newell designed the machine in the early 1970s, probably with some input from Royce Creasey: in those days, Bristol was the world centre for feet-forward motorcycles. The 850cc water-cooled engine was from the most pedestrian source imaginable, the Reliant three-wheeler. It had a mere 41bhp at 5500rpm, but thanks to the design of the machine and its excellent aerodynamics, even this was good for 176kph (110mph), with a cruising speed that was very little slower. The four-speed gearbox drove the rear wheel through a twin universal joint Kardan shaft and a spiral bevel. Braking was by triple 241mm (9.5ins) discs, two at the front and one at the back, each with Lockheed twin-piston callipers.

With its space frame of Reynolds 531 tubing, specially designed to offer maximum protection in the event of a crash, and a water-cooled automobile engine that owed its ancestry to the Austin Seven, the Quasar was necessarily heavy at 318kg (700lb), but it was also ridiculously economical at 3.75 litres/100km (75mpg UK gallons). The model performed roughly the same as a Royal Enfield Bullet with two-thirds of the top speed, half the weight, and little more

than a third of the power. It may have been the best long-distance tourer ever built, with excellent weather protection and it was very relaxing to ride at high speed.

Yet only 20 Quasars were ever built. Seven were sold between 1976 and 1980, when Romarsh Special Products in nearby Calne took over production: they built another 10 before going into receivership in 1982. Three more were built by John Malfoy, Quasar's project manager, from spares purchased from the receiver, and that was it.

There are two, or three, reasons why it failed. Firstly, motorcyclists are deeply conservative, and the Quasar was like a two-wheeled car, not a motorcycle, down to the glass windscreen with windscreen wiper as required by English law.

The Quasar looked interesting enough when it was standing still, but absolutely fascinating when in motion – though the tyres look very skinny to the modern eye.

The second problem was that the Quasar was expensive. People who buy motorcycles as toys are generally more interested in image than performance and innovation and people who buy motorcycles as transport can seldom afford expensive machines.

Thirdly, the Quasar was simply too practical. In particular, the engine was unglamorous, and although perfect for cruising, it did not offer the starship acceleration that people were beginning to expect. Paradoxically, the model might almost have done better with a low-powered engine and automatic transmission, taking it even further from its motorcycle roots, although a more powerful engine and a five-speed or even six-speed gearbox, and a reduction in weight — purely in the interests of marketing — would probably have been even more successful.

The Quasar is yet another of the countless might-have-beens that litter the history of motorcycling. However, it arguably had more potential than any of them, and was thus a greater loss.

The Quasar deserved more success than it enjoyed. Arguably, the company paid too much attention to engineering, and not enough to marketing.

RABENEICK

GERMANY 1933–63

IN THE EARLY 1930S, as Germany, like the rest of the western world, was recovering from the worst recession in history, August Rabeneick was putting the finishing touches to a new motorcycle brand. Named after its founder, the firm began trading in Bielefeld during the summer of 1933. In the inter-war years, it concentrated on building exclusively lightweights, powered usually with bought-in Sachs two-stroke engines.

After the war, Rabeneick made larger-displacement machines, including a four-stroke horizontally opposed twin in 1951. The company also built and sold a wide range of two-strokes with either Ilo or Sachs units ranging from 98 to 247cc, including an interesting 244cc Ilo-powered parallel-twin, the F250/2, between 1951 and 1957.

But perhaps the most intriguing Rabeneick was the Swiss Universal-engined 250 four-stroke overhead-valve single with shaft final drive. This debuted at the 1953 Frankfurt Show, and sold in limited numbers because it was

Above: The 50cc Binetta Super 4 lightweight motorcycle of 1960 employed a Sachs two-stroke engine and Earles-type forks.

Below: One of the company's final designs was the Sachs-powered economy commuter moped from the early 1960s.

very expensive. The Rabeneick Universal's 247cc (70x64mm) engine had a 9:1 compression ratio and produced a very respectable 15bhp. It had oil-damped telescopic forks, swinging-arm rear suspension and a Denfeld-made dual seat. Due to its sky-high asking price, the model sold badly.

Then, in 1956 and 1957, the German market suffered a great recession in two-wheel sales. Rabeneick struggled but survived.

After 1958 the Bielefeld company concentrated on smaller machinery, and by 1962 its largest model was the LM 100/4 lightweight motorcycle, with a 98cc Sachs engine. The balance of the range were all 50s: the Saxonette moped, the Binetta Super 4 (four-speed) and Super 5 (five-speed), and the R50 scooter.

In 1963 Rabeneick was swallowed up by Hercules, itself part of the Zweirand-Union group from 1960. The Rabeneick plant in the 1970s was used by Fichtel & Sachs.

RAJDOOT

INDIA 1962–

INDIA HAS A CONSIDERABLE motorcycle industry to supply its vast population and in most cases, companies in that country were

established to produce models under licence from European and Japanese firms. Although many of these models were primarily small-

capacity two-strokes, the first to be manufactured was the 1955 Royal Enfield Bullet which, to this day, remains in production and is now

exported by the company to Britain.

Rajdoot started by building copies of the Polish 175cc WFM

single-cylinder two-stroke, which was itself derived from the 1935 DKW RT125, as were several other well-known models from England, Japan, Russia and the USA. It was powered by a simple three-port engine built in unit with a foot-change gearbox. This went into a tubular frame with telescopic front and pivoted rear forks, and rode on wire wheels with drum brakes.

The model was simple, rugged and reliable, and therefore ideal for its home market, where a screwdriver and an adjustable spanner comprised a good toolkit. The same engine unit was also used for a scooter, and this level of technology proved adequate for some two decades.

By the 1980s Rajdoot moved on to manufacture the Yamaha RD350 air-cooled twin two-stroke. This

was done under licence, and it soon introduced the company to pump lubrication, reed inlet valves, disc brakes, six speeds and, in due course, electronic ignition. Later came other Yamaha models with small single-cylinder engines, all ideally designed to keep pace with an ever-increasing demand in India for small-capacity, reliable, easily serviced, private transport.

RALEIGH

ENGLAND 1901–06, 1920–33 AND 1958–71

THIS NOTTINGHAM FIRM was famous for its bicycles long before building a motorcycle; it later took over the Sturmey-Archer firm to produce engines and gearboxes of that name. Raleigh's first motorcycle was built in 1901, with an imported Schwann engine over the belt-driven front wheel.

This model was soon replaced by one in which the 3hp engine was set vertically ahead of the pedals; the new bike also incorporated a frame stronger than most available then. Although the forks were rigid, there were three transmission options: belt drive, a two-speed gear, or chain drive in two stages with a clutch. Also offered was a forecar with a three-and-a-half horsepower water-cooled engine. The motorcycle's reputation was enhanced when G.P. Mills set a new time of under 51 hours for the Land's End to

John O'Groats ride, despite many stops. The engine gave no trouble at all and the ride was a remarkable feat on the roads of the time. However, the downturn in trade led to Raleigh abandoning motorcycles for a few years after 1906 to concentrate on bicycles.

The company returned in 1920 with an interesting and totally new model that had a 698cc flat-twin, side-valve engine fitted in line with the frame. This drove a three-speed Sturmey-Archer gearbox with all-chain drive and leaf-spring rear suspension. In 1922 the flat-twin was joined by conventional singles of 348 and 399cc with two or three speeds and belt final drive. These were continued with all-chain options for the singles until 1924, when the flat-twin was replaced by 798cc V-twin models. In that year Raleigh demonstrated their

reliability with Hugh Gibson driving a combination round the British coast and Marjorie Cottle riding a solo in the reverse direction, while 1925 brought a 348cc overhead-valve model.

In 1926 Marjorie Cottle undertook another long-distance ride, this time using a new lightweight with a 174cc engine built in unit with a two-speed gearbox. The same year also introduced a 249cc single, while all models now had chain drive. A 495cc side-valve model was added for 1927, after which the 174cc single and the V-twin were dropped. This left three sizes of single, the two larger ones also in overhead-valve form, for the rest

A 1929, 348cc ohv, twin-port Raleigh. The machine was also listed with a 496cc engine; both models had a three-speed gearbox.

of the decade. By 1929 the firm was selling Sturmey-Archer engines to several other makers, and this practice continued up to 1933.

The 1930 range had side-valve models of 225, 248, 297 and 495cc plus the 348 and 495cc overhead-valve machines. The two smallest were then dropped and the others were given new, inclined engines for 1931, while 1932 brought a 598cc side-valve. At the end of 1933 Raleigh stopped motorcycle production, but continued with bicycles and a three-wheeled car and van they had introduced in 1930. These were dropped in 1935, restricting the company to bicycles for many years after that.

The name returned late in 1958 for a 49cc moped using a Sturmey-Archer two-stroke engine with V-belt drive to a countershaft. The engine was made by BSA and a version with a clutch was added for the next year.

At the end of 1960 Raleigh changed course and replaced its

From 1924 to 1927 Raleigh included a 798cc V-twin in their range. A side-valve type, it drove a three-speed gearbox and had the magneto at the front.

own moped by one built under licence from Motobécane, along with a copy of the French Mobylette. These models came in a variety of forms; during the next decade nearly a dozen types would come and go, using the same basic engine and transmission (with the exception of the Wisp). By the end of the 1960s most had gone, although one model, the Runabout, did trickle on to 1971.

In addition to the mopeds, Raleigh listed the Roma scooter from 1961. However, this was actually the 78cc Orsetto, built by Bianchi in Italy with a change of badges. Typical of the type, it had arrived on a declining market so was dropped after 1964 to leave the mopeds to carry the name into the 1970s. After that, it was back to bicycles.

RATIER FRANCE 1955–62

ESTABLISHED IN 1945 as CMR, this firm was renamed Cemec in 1948, and became Ratier in 1955. The company's machines were always based on the BMW flat-twin but gradually became more French in character, taking on a new image with the name Ratier. While for 1955 BMW changed to leading-link front and pivoted rear forks, Ratier chose the more

modern concept of telescopics and pivoted fork with a line that BMW would not use until 1969.

In other respects the two had much in common, although the Ratier was a French design. Two models were listed, with engines of 494 and 594cc capacity, overhead-valves, coil ignition and twin carburettors. The four-speed gearbox was in unit with the

engine and the shaft drive to the rear wheel ran in-board of the right fork leg. The frame featured the modern suspension system, while large drum brakes were fitted into full-width hubs front and rear. A separate headlamp appeared at the top of the forks or was blended into them.

Ratier's main customer was the French police, so most machines

were fitted with a single seat and wireless equipment. Some old Cemec bikes were badged as Ratier, and eventually only the 600 was built. This was promoted in the USA as the official motorcycle escort of President Charles de Gaulle, and for that market, as well as the domestic one, a dual seat was fitted. However, by 1962 production had ceased.

READING-STANDARD USA 1903–24

BASED IN READING, Pennsylvania, this firm entered the market with a clone of the Indian machine, with its engine laid back to act as part of the seat tube and the camel-backed tank (carrying both petrol and oil) fitted on the rear mudguard. As with several other models, the engine was an F-head Thor from Aurora and sat above the bottom bracket, which carried the pedalling gear on the right-hand side. On the left was an intermediate dual sprocket that was chain driven from the engine, with a further chain from a smaller sprocket to the rear wheel. Thus, the machine had all-chain drive in two stages.

In 1905 the tanks became separate items, with the oil carried behind the saddle and the fuel stored above the top tube. Front suspension was also added, the forks pivoting around the lower crown, against rubber. July 1906 saw a trio of Reading-Standard machines ridden to the top of the famous Pike's Peak, a feat not duplicated by any other manufacturer for some years.

For 1907 the engine was changed to the side-valve type, a first in the USA, but it still remained as part of the seat tube. The next year brought an F-head, V-twin engine that was unusual in

having cams on both sides, the left serving the front cylinder and the right the rear. There was also a forecar that could have a seat or parcel box set between the front wheels. As standard, it comprised the stock motorcycle with the front forks replaced by an assembly with the twin wheels, and was listed for several years.

A loop frame and leading-link front forks came in 1909 with the single engine set vertically, while side-valves appeared on the twins. A two-speed rear hub was offered for 1911, but this feature was never a real solution to the problem of providing gears for the

motorcycle, despite its success on the bicycle. As the power to be transmitted rose, so did the size and weight of the hub, which was then less than ideally placed. For 1912 there was reduction gearing and a clutch built into the engine; the next year brought a drum brake. A lower frame was introduced in 1914, but it was 1916 before a three-speed gearbox was used. Both frame and forks were strengthened for 1917, when electric lighting became an option, to take the firm into three good sales years.

In 1920 the twin engine was revised and Reading-Standard

tried competing with other than stock machines, but their overhead-valve singles had no success. The company also ran an overhead-cam racer that was essentially a Cyclone and fared no better. The road models were little changed after 1920, but limited production led to a take-over in 1923 by Cleveland, which sold the stocks off cheaply during the next year.

By the time this 1912 model was built, Reading-Standard had moved on from the Indian clone they had first built. The engine was now upright and suspension was by leading links.

REGAL
ENGLAND 1912–15

A Regal fitted with a Precision V-twin engine. However, the firm more commonly fitted singles from Precision or Green as well as a two-stroke from Peco.

ERNEST SMITH & WOODHOUSE of Birmingham used the Regal name for its machines, often combined with that of the engine. The 1912 range comprised two-and-a-half and three-and-a-half horsepower tourers and a four-and-a-half horsepower single with variable gear for sidecar use; all were listed as Regal-Precision (using the name of the engine make), and were typical machines, in terms of their construction and performance, of their time.

The firm entered the 1912 Senior TT with two different motorcycles, one with an air-cooled overhead-valve Precision engine with belt drive to a three-speed Sturmey-Archer hub gear and braced forks. The second had a water-cooled engine with a one-piece top half, vertical overhead-

RANZANI
Italy (Milan) 1923–31: After starting with 175cc side-valve Heros engines (German) and 170cc overhead-valve Norman engines (British), Ranzani moved on to an in-house overhead-valve 175. Both two-speed and three-speed options were offered.

RAP
Netherlands 1955–70s: This company produced mopeds, with engines from Rex, and later Puch.

RASSER
France 1922–23: This was a 100cc two-stroke in an unusual pressed-steel frame.

RATINGIA
Germany 1923–25: These machines were the usual 170 and 195cc lightweights, but were side-valve instead of two-stroke.

RAVAT
France (Saint Etienne) 1898–1950s: This firm built four-strokes of up to 500cc, and small two-strokes.

RAY
England (Nottingham, later Leicester) 1922–25: This firm initially manufactured an in-house side-valve 193cc, and later (from 1924) also a 172cc Villiers-Jardine.

RAYNAL
England 1914–53: Initially, this firm produced machines with Precision and Villiers two-strokes and in the 1920s, the ubiquitous Villiers 269cc. From the late 1930s, they made a machine with a Villiers 98cc.

READY
Belgium 1924–39: Belgian Readies offered a wide range of engines up to 500cc, variously reported as JAP, Blackburne, MAG and Rudge Python as well as a Villiers two-stroke.

REBRO
England 1922–28: This was a basic 150cc Villiers-powered two-stroke lightweight.

RED STAR
Belgium (Antwerp) 1902: This machine was a Minerva-powered 211cc pioneer.

valves and its two radiators fitted on each side of the copper cylinder jacket. In 1912 the make set records at Brooklands.

The company continued to buy-in engines from other manufacturers, and in 1913 there were two Regal-Green models, with a three-and-a-half horsepower overhead-valve engine and a choice of transmission. The Regal-Precision machines of two-and- three-quarters, three-and-a-half and four-and-a-quarter horsepower followed this pattern but for the smaller pair there were three speeds and there was chain final drive for the largest. In 1914 the Regal-Green was joined by the 349cc two-stroke Regal-Peco. A 225cc two-stroke Peco model and a four-and-a-quarter horsepower V-twin were added for 1915 before production ceased.

RENÉ-GILLET

FRANCE 1898–1957

THE FIRST MACHINES TO be made by René-Gillet were basically bicycles that had motors attached to the front forks. The company's reputation was founded on its 500cc V-twin-powered motorcycles, which were introduced in 1903, and whose engine capacity was increased by degrees to 750 and then 996cc. Frequently fitted with sidecars, these big models were favoured by the French military, where their prodigious hauling power was put to advantage. As well as the V-twins, René-Gillet also made 346cc side-valve single-cylinder bikes. After World War II, production was rationalised to small 98 and 250cc two-stroke motorcycles, and finally drew to a close in 1957.

René-Gillet motorcycles had the reputation for being sturdy workhorses, favoured by the French military and for pulling sidecars. This is a 1936 model.

REX (REX-ACME)

ENGLAND 1900–33

BEGINNING AS CAR MANUFAC-TURERS in Birmingham, England, in 1899, the Rex company moved to Coventry at the turn of the century. There the Williamson brothers, Billy and Harold, produced their first motorcycles using their own single- and twin-cylinder power units, notably a 456cc side-valve and a 726cc inlet-over-exhaust V-twin. Energetic and innovative, they produced the first telescopic forks in 1906 (helping Billy Heaton to third place in the very first Isle of Man TT one year later) and a 470cc two-stroke racing twin. Despite this, the Williamsons were ousted in 1911, although the irrepressible Billy went on to found the Williamson marque, renowned for its 1000cc liquid-cooled flat-twin.

Under new owner George Hemingway, Rex continued to make its own engines, also producing a separate range of Rex-

JAP machines for nearby Premier motorcycles. The manufacture of a sophisticated all-chain drive 952cc twin was thwarted by the outbreak of war. In 1919 the firm took over neighbours Coventry-Acme, adopting the name Rex-Acme two years later. By 1926 its range included at least 15 models, varying in capacity from a 172cc Villiers to a 746cc JAP V-twin.

The company's reputation largely derived from the exploits of Wal Handley, a precocious young racer who had first come to notice riding for OK at the 1922 and 1923 Isle of Man TT races. Less than a month after recording fastest lap at the 1923 TT, Handley was a Rex-Acme rider, winning

The legendary Wal Handley being congratulated after finished second in the 1926 Isle of Man Senior TT on the Blackburne-engined 498cc V-twin Rex-Acme.

both the Belgian and Ulster Grand Prix. He posted the first-ever TT double in 1925, winning the Lightweight (250cc) and Junior (350cc) events, and triumphed in the Lightweight race again in

1927. Although Rex-Acme campaigned a 498cc overhead-valve V-twin in 1926, it was rarely a force in the larger classes.

Rex-Acme was unable to turn track success into profit, and the

Depression of the 1930s hit the firm hard. In 1932 the bankrupt company was taken over by a sidecar manufacturer, Mills-Fulford, which stopped motorcycle production the following year.

RICKMAN   ENGLAND 1959–75

In 1970, the Rickman Interceptor was a highly desirable superbike. Power came from the 736cc Royal Enfield Constellation engine.

FOUNDED BY BROTHERS Derek and Don Rickman, Rickman was chiefly renowned for its off-road machines, but later earned a solid reputation for high-quality roadster and racing frames. The company's philosophy – based on the belief that there were 'plenty of good engines and good frames about in the '60s, but it wasn't often that you got the two together' – was to combine high strength with light weight. The result was the 'Metisse' chassis, to fit a variety of propri-etary engines.

Initially these were sold purely as chassis 'kits', but from 1970 to 1974 the firm produced some

12,000 complete off-road machines powered by Bultaco and Zundapp 125 and 250cc two-stroke engines, making Rickman briefly Britain's largest motorcycle manufacturer.

Initially, the company showed little interest in road-going machines. However, when Royal Enfield went out of business in 1969, 200 Series II 736cc Constellation engines were left over. Rickman acquired these and produced a complete motorcycle, known as the Interceptor. Its chassis was superbly executed in bronze-welded Reynolds 531 steel tubing. The finished bike cost £550 and weighed just 160kg (353lb), 43kg (95lb) less than the weight of a standard Constellation.

The quality of the Interceptor's components – including Rickman's own forks and some of the first modern disc brakes – encouraged a French magazine to call the machine 'the Rolls-Royce of motorcycles'.

In total some 205 Interceptors were built, but the story did not end there. During the early 1970s, Japanese four-cylinder machines such as the Honda CB750 had an abundance of power but handled poorly. In 1974, beginning with the CB750, Rickman adapted the Interceptor chassis to give such engines the handling they deserved.

From 1975 the company increasingly concerned itself with the production of accessories rather than chassis parts.

This 1980 Rickman CRE Endurance had a fully enclosed engine and twin front disc brakes – another high-quality machine.

REFORM
Austria (Vienna) 1903–05: Thein & Goldberger (see below) are variously reported to have used Monarch engines (from Birmingham) and Fafnir for their Reform machines. Both primary (layshaft) and secondary drive were by chain.

REGINA
England (Ilford) 1903–15: Initially (until 1907) this firm produced the usual pioneer engines: Minerva, MMC, Fafnir, from one-and-three-quarters to two-and-three-quarters horsepower. Then, after a gap, they made an in-house 292cc two-stroke.

REGINA
France 1905–15: Buchet, Peugeot, Zurcher and possibly other proprietary engines were fitted by this pioneer.

REIMA
Switzerland late 1960s: This racing 500cc pushrod twin delivered 50bhp at 9500rpm, and was made in small quantities by Werner Maltry.

RENNER-ORIGINAL
Germany 1924–32: JAP side-valve 350cc singles and 678cc V-twins were the mainstay of this company, although other engines could be fitted to special order.

RENNSTEIG
Germany (Suhl) 1925–30: These machines had Krieger-Gnading-style frames with Blackburne and Sturmey Archer engines of 250 to 600cc (one source has 200 to 500cc).

REPUBLIC
Austro-Hungary/Czech Republic 1899–1908: Laurin & Klement used this name for machines exported to Europe and the Americas.

REVERE
England 1915–22: The ubiquitous Villiers 269cc engine was fitted into Sparkbrook frames by Whitehouse & Co.

REX
Germany (Munich) 1948–64: This firm made auxiliary bicycle motors, and complete mopeds, initially 31cc, then 34cc, and finally 49cc.

RIDLEY

USA 1997–

THE CONCEPT BEHIND the Ridley is wonderful: a scaled-down big twin. The manufacturers quote it as being three-quarters the size and one-third the weight of 'the big boys' – Harley-Davidson and the like, though they are not mentioned by name – yet one might reasonably expect a bike of such dimensions to weigh just over half as much as its larger counter-parts.

At only 25bhp from a 570cc (72x70mm) 90-degree V-twin, the Ridley's standard motor is hardly over-stressed, and the constantly variable, all-belt (or belt primary, chain secondary) automatic transmission makes it smooth and easy to ride. The 305mm (12ins) wheels are perhaps a little too small from a visual point of view, but they are big enough for a real motorcycle ride. The machine weighs a mere 116kg (255lb), despite having electric start, hydraulic disc brakes front and rear, and being fitted with all modern conveniences. In fact, this diminutive 'fun bike' offers the same sort of power as would come

from a 1920s racer or a fast 1950s 500cc single.

The company's first motorcycle seems to have been the 1997–98 Cruise-Aire, which was followed by the 1999 Big Boar and Speedsters.

For the 2001 model year, the Signature Series One was made available with a 'souped up' 33hp motor, allowing well over 130kph (80mph); the standard model is good for about 120kph (75mph). The engine is coyly described as 'not Ridley's own design, but built up by Ridley'.

Based in Oklahoma City, Oklahoma, the Ridley is a very welcome twist on the Harley-clone technology, but it is impossible for a European not to wonder what the company could do if it put the 33hp motor in a 'real' motorcycle with decent-sized wheels.

It is hard to look at a Ridley without a smile and a flash of acquisitiveness: it is a superb fun bike, with surprisingly respectable performance.

RIKUO

JAPAN 1935–45 AND 1953–62

DURING THE 1920S, with its exports booming, Harley-Davidson established the Harley-Davidson Sales Company of Japan, with a comprehensive network of dealers, agencies and spares distributors. The firm from Milwaukee, Wisconsin, quickly gained such a good reputation in Japan that Harley became the country's official police motorcycle. At around the same time a quite different company, the Murata Iron Works, began building copies of the 1922 Harley-Davidson Model J, but quality was poor. Murata would later build the Meguro, a distant precursor of modern Kawasakis.

However, in the wake of the Wall Street crash of 1929, as the yen was crippled by the global slump, Harley exports dried up almost completely. It was precisely at this point that Alfred Childs, head of Harley's Japanese operation, asked the obvious question: 'Why not build Harleys here?'

The parent company was initially sceptical, but such was Childs's persistence that Harley's first overseas factory soon began production at Shinagawa, near Tokyo. Built with tooling, plans, blueprints and expertise borrowed from Milwaukee, the factory was at the time considered the most modern in the world. Initially many parts were imported, but by 1935 Shinagawa was making complete motorcycles, mainly Model VL three-speed 1216cc (74cid) side-valve V-twins.

By 1930 this model had become the official motorcycle of the Japanese Imperial Army. Later, when the army became the effective civil power, it declined the chance to convert production to the new overhead-valve Knucklehead, preferring the proven durability of the side-valve twin. It was at this point that the Sankyo corporation took over control of the factory, and began selling Japanese 'Harleys' under the Rikuo name. The 1216cc twin

was later to become the Rikuo Model 97.

Then, as Japan readied for war, Harley cut its losses and sold out. As military demand increased (especially after the invasion of China in 1937), Rikuo sub-licensed the product to Nihon Jidosha (Japan Combustion Equipment Co.). Their machines were 1311cc (80cid) versions of the Rikuo Model 97, and were called Kuro Hagane (Black Iron). That particular enterprise ended as

the war drew to a close: the Niho Jidosha factory was in Hiroshima.

Motorcycles were also produced under the Rikuo name from around 1953 to 1962. The models manufactured were singles of 250 and 350cc, as well as V-twins of 996 and 1200cc.

As well as 'Japanese Harley' V-twins of the pre-war years, a range of BMW-inspired 248 and 348cc singles was produced under the Rikuo name in the 1950s.

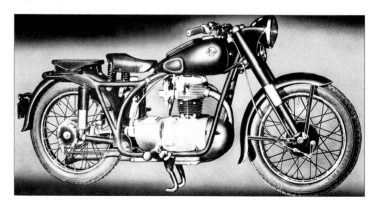

RIXE

GERMANY 1934–85

ORIGINALLY A BICYCLE manufacturer, Rixe built its first powered two-wheeler just as the Nazis were coming to power in the early 1930s. From then until the outbreak of war in 1939, a range of motorised cycles was marketed with a choice of either 73 or 98cc Sachs engines.

After the war, Rixe offered a wide variety of motorcycles, from the 98cc austerity model K98, first made in 1949, through to the final closure of the factory in 1985 with a range of lightweights headed by a sophisticated liquid-cooled 79cc sportster. In between came an array of other models.

The 1950s witnessed the KT125 (1950–52), K98 (available until 1959), KT150 (1953–55), R175 (1953–56), R200 (1953–54), R250/2 (1953–54), RS250/2 (1954–58) and finally the RS175 (1955–59).

The 1960s saw a change to smaller-capacity machines, including various Sachs-engined mopeds; one was specially adapted for tradesmen, with large front and rear carriers. There were also two

The company's last effort, the 1982 RS80W, was powered by a Sachs 79cc engine. Capable of 80kph (50mph), it was excellent, but couldn't stave off closure in 1985.

100-class motorcycles, again with Sachs power. The RS100 Tourer featured Earles forks, a low-level exhaust system, comprehensive mud-guarding, 406mm (16ins) wheels, full chain enclosure, high handlebars and a rear carrier. The sporting version was the RS100 Sport; this came not only with a tuned engine, but also a larger 13.5 litre (nearly three UK gallons) tank, a high-level exhaust, flat bars and sprint-type mudguards.

Into the 1970s, production concentrated exclusively on mopeds and mokicks (50cc motorcycles), all with Sachs engines.

Then, in 1982, Rixe introduced a new motorcycle range, headed by the RS80W. This was powered by the new Sachs water-cooled

The Rixe RS100 of 1962 sported a tuned engine, a larger 13.5 litre (three gallon) tank, hi-level exhaust, flat bars and sprint-type steel mudguards.

80SW motor, a 79cc (46x48mm) unit that provided eight-and-a-half brake horsepower at 6000rpm, giving a maximum speed of 80kph (50 mph). The model also boasted five gears, a neat duplex frame, cast-alloy wheels, a Bikini, rear carrier, twin-disc front brake, matching instrumentation and a distinctive silver finish.

However, during the motorcycle slump of the 1980s, together with such well known names as Kreidler and Zundapp, the Bielefeld factory found the going too tough to survive.

REX
Sweden 1908–57: After enjoying some success with Motosacoche engines, Rex went on to their own V-twin but soon dropped that in favour of Villiers and JAP engines from 150 to 750cc: all this was before World War I. Later they moved on to 100cc lightweights, and after World War II, a range of machines with Ilo, Husqvarna and Sachs two-strokes from 125 to 250cc.

REX-JAP
England (Birmingham) 1908–15: Predictably, this firm produced JAP engines of 300 to 1000cc in frames made – possibly – by Rex.

REYNOLDS-RUNABOUT
England 1919–22: This rather elegant scooter had mid-size wheels – about 33cm (13ins) – and a bucket seat atop a fully enclosed engine. It was propelled by a choice of Liberty 269cc or (later) JAP 350cc engines.

RHONSON
France 1952–58: These mopeds and lightweights went up to 123cc.

RHONY-X
France (Lyon) 1924–32: Wonder how many of their catalogued machines they sold: there were two-strokes of 100, 185, 250 and 350cc, and four-strokes of 250, 350 and 500cc, with engines from LMP, Stainless, Chaise and JAP.

RIBI
Germany (Berlin) 1923–25: These were relatively advanced overhead-valve singles of 200 and 250cc.

RIEJU
Spain 1952–: This firm began with a lightweight powered by a 175cc AMC four-stroke before moving on to a 125cc step-through and then mopeds and sub-100cc machines.

RILEY
England 1901–08: Riley's three-wheelers and motorcycles began in 1901 with a one-and-a-quarter horsepower model and grew to machines of up to three-and-a-half horsepower: the 9hp engine was reserved for a three-wheeler. Most engines were their own, although some were De Dion-Bouton, Minerva and MMC.

ROKON

USA 1959–

BASED IN KEENE, New Hampshire, this firm produced a truly bizarre motorcycle in its Trailbreaker, which combined a drive to both enormous wheels. Early models had a 131cc (8cid) Chrysler marine two-stroke engine with pull-cord start, driving a three-speed gearbox with an automatic clutch. From the gearbox a chain took the power up to the rear end of the frame top tube, where a cross-shaft split the drive between a chain to the rear-wheel sprocket and a shaft that ran

This strange machine was a two-wheel drive Rokon. It had drum-like hubs and massive tractor tyres, which enabled it to go almost anywhere.

up the top tube. At the steering head a universal joint took care of the steering movement of the fork and connected to a second cross-shaft that carried the chain to the front-wheel sprocket. Both cross-shaft assemblies had gear pairs within them to turn the drive.

The frame was tubular with the engine installed horizontally and the gearbox behind it, to give exceptional ground clearance. The only suspension was that provided by the large-diameter, low-pressure balloon tyres. These had tractor treads and were fitted to light-alloy wheels formed as drums so that they could carry petrol or water; when empty, they acted as buoyancy chambers. Braking was achieved by a single mechanical disc on the front cross-

A more conventional-looking Rokon from the 1970s. This trail machine featured a hi-level exhaust, for extensive off-road use.

shaft which effectively retarded both wheels. This strange machine could climb extremely steep slopes and was built in various plants, with occasional breaks in production. Later came a version with a 340cc Sachs two-stroke engine and automatic transmission.

ROTAX

AUSTRIA 1937–

ROTAX BEGAN LIFE as a small family engineering concern in the early twentieth century in the German town Dresden, manufacturing rear-wheel assemblies for pedal cycles. A century later, Rotax is based in Gunskirchen, Austria, and is one of the world's leading motorcycle engine specialists.

In 1920 it was re-formed as a public company, but engine production began in the 1930s, when the concern was acquired by Fichtel & Sachs. Still located in Germany, but now at Schweinfurt, Rotax became involved in the manufacture of torpedo components for the armed forces, leading up to World War II.

During the conflict Rotax relocated to Austria due to heavy bombing, and then moved to Gunskirchen in 1947. At first under government control and later sold to a Vienna-based

private company, Rotax was purchased by the Canadian-based Bombardier Group. This merger created Bombardier-Rotax, with the Austrian plant building a truly

This 496.7cc Rotax twin made its race debut at the Austrian GP in May 1973. The engine was based on the Canadian Bombardier snowmobile unit.

vast range of engines for not only motorcycles but also snowmobiles and agricultural equipment. Production at the Rotax factory in 1970 was 267,300 engines, with the firm employing just over 1000 workers.

Rotax began an interest in racing in the late 1960s, when a 125cc was built and raced by Heinz Krinwanek, who finished fifth in the 1969 world championships. However, it was a liquid-cooled 500cc twin, used in both solos and sidecars, that really started the ball rolling during the early 1970s. This engine was developed from the Bombardier snowmobile engine.

During the early 1980s, Rotax seemed to offer a real chance of breaking the Japanese monopoly in the 250cc racing class with the Model 256 247cc (54x54mm) disc-valve in-line twin engine, designed by Hans Holzleitner. This was supplied to a wide range of customers, including Armstrong, Aprilia and Kobas. The late 1980s saw the introduction of the air-cooled four-valve single in 500, 600 and eventually 650cc versions. A variant of this engine was also used in many street bikes, by makers such as MZ and Jawa.

In recent years, Rotax have played a major part in the rise of the Italian Aprilia concern, supplying them with both two- and four-stroke engines.

A 649cc (100x81mm) air-cooled four-valve Rotax Supermono racer at Oulton Park, England, in 1999. Maximum power was 68bhp, top speed 217kph (135mph).

ROVER

ENGLAND 1902–25

THE ROVER NAME conjures up images of the archetypal British car driven by one's favourite uncle. But in the same way as contemporaries like Humber, Rover's founder John Kemp Starley began building bicycles in 1877 at West Orchard, Coventry; the name Rover was coined in 1884. In 1888 Starley built a prototype electric tricycle, and the Rover Cycle Company was established in 1896.

The following year, motorised Peugeot cycles were imported as a feasibility study, and the first two-

This 3.5hp 1911 Rover was built after car production began. Power could be either JAP V-twin or Rover side-valve single.

and-three-quarters horsepower Rover motorcycle came out in 1902. It was powered by a 300cc side-valve engine, but was a short-lived project, as production halted in 1905 with just 1250 machines completed.

The Rover name is more associated with car production, but back in 1915, the company logo graced a 3.5hp motorcycle.

Production of Rover motorcycles resumed in 1910; they fitted some 676cc JAP V-twins, but the basis of the Rover line was a 499cc side-valve engine unit designed by the talented John Greenwood. From 1915 an Ariel three-speed transmission was used, and after 1918 a number of JAP-powered V-twins was produced.

In 1923 Rover began making unit-construction 250 and 350cc overhead-valve single-cylinder bikes, but the firm produced only cars after 1925.

RINNE
Germany 1924–32: This was a more than usually successful make, powered by in-house two-stroke motors of 125, 175 and 250cc.

RIP
England 1905–08: The main distinguishing features of this company – presumably 'Rip' rather than 'R.I.P.' – was their sprung frames. Engines came from Peugeot, Stevens and White & Poppe.

RIVARA
Italy (Colorno) 1975–: This firm produce mopeds, including the collapsible Beach.

RIZZATO
Italy (Padua) 1972–: These mopeds and lightweights go up to 125cc.

RMW
Germany (Neuheim an der Ruhr) 1925–55: Their smaller engines were in-house two strokes (132, 148 and 198cc) while the bigger engines (up to 500cc) were bought-in four-strokes from Bark, Blackburne, JAP, Kuchen, MAG, Moser and Sturmey-Archer.

ROA
Spain (Madrid) 1952–early 1960s: Industrias Motorizadas Onieva used Hispano-Villiers engines in mopeds, in motorcycles of 200 and 325cc, and in three-wheeled delivery vehicles.

ROC
England (Guildford, then Birmingham) 1904–15: A.W. Wall designed these machines with an unusually long wheelbase. Most had Precision V-twins up to three-and-a-half horsepower, although there were also in-house Roc engines. Wall was an unusually early devotee of the free engine, and also made one of the first four-speed gearboxes for a motorcycle.

ROYAL ENFIELD

ENGLAND 1901–70

THE ENFIELD CYCLE COMPANY was based at Redditch near Birmingham, and produced its first powered machines in 1899. They were actually tricycles and quadricycles, powered by De Dion, Minerva or MMC engines, and were followed two years later by motorised bicycles. The company tried out a layout in which the engine was mounted in front of the steering head.

In 1910, after a break of five years from motorcycle production, Enfield brought out a two-and-a-quarter horsepower MAG-powered V-twin, which prefaced the Model 180. This went into production in 1912 and was sold as a motorbike-and-sidecar outfit powered by a 770cc JAP side-valve V-twin engine using chain-drive and two-speed transmission. The 180 was also notable for the introduction of the rubber cushion hub, which consisted of a rubber shock absorber that was integral with the rear hub and reduced chain snatch, making for smoother getaways and gear changes.

In 1913 the company came out with another innovative bike. This time it was a 4hp 425cc inlet-over-exhaust V-twin. Not only was this a Royal Enfield-built engine, it was also endowed with an

From 1924, Royal Enfield's own 350cc side-valve engines and ohv units, like this Sports model from 1927, replaced the ubiquitous JAP engine.

automatic oil pump, contrasting with the regular manual pump that required priming by hand. To broaden the appeal of this model, the range was quickly expanded to include a 350cc machine and a 225cc two-stroke version.

Royal Enfield was still very much a bicycle manufacturer, and during World War I, it mainly supplied bicycles to the Allied forces, delivering a smaller volume of JAP-engined sidecar outfits that saw action as machine-gun carriers and field ambulances. Postwar production centred on the 976cc Royal Enfield-engined V-twin as well as the 225cc two-stroke.

In 1924, the 350cc JAP unit was supplanted by Royal Enfield's own 350cc side- and overhead-valve engines. Three years on, capacity had increased to 488cc, linked with a four-speed gearbox, and sharing many of the engine's components with the firm's V-twin. A decade on, the V-twin's capacity had gone up to 1140cc. Meanwhile, in 1928 a new 225cc

side-valve machine came out, along with a 146cc two-stroke called the Cycar.

Royal Enfield's marketing slogan was 'Made Like a Gun', because in the same way as BSA, the company's reputation came

from manufacturing military ordnance. While many competitors went to the wall during the Depression of the early 1930s, Royal Enfield survived, due to the stability of its administration and ownership.

From its early days, the firm was managed by Robert Smith, whose son Major Frank Smith was in charge right up to the 1960s. The three Smith brothers excelled in trials events, and this was reflected in Royal Enfield's later production models and off-roading successes. Behind the scenes in the late 1920s, the firm had a pair of talented designers at work: these were Ted Pardoe who designed the Bullet range, and development director Tony Wilson-Jones, who was also a trials rider.

One of Royal Enfield's best-known model ranges was the Bullet, launched in 1930, as 350 and 500cc single-cylinder machines with the cylinder barrel inclined forward. Three years later, the range expanded to include the 250cc bike, and in 1934 the 500cc

One of the company's best known models was the fine Bullet, featuring sophisticated suspension front and rear. Pictured is a 350cc model from 1955.

engine was fitted with a four-valve head. It was designated the Model JF in 1936, with the single cylinder now vertical. As well as a three-valve head, they also experimented with a twin-port head around this time.

Output during World War II was mostly in support of the Allied cause, with some 55,000 motorcycles supplied to the war office. This compares with Triumph, who made 49,700 bikes during the war, despite the destruction of its factory in the Blitz, and BSA, which managed 130,000 units. The majority of Royal Enfields were 350cc side-valve WD/C or overhead-valve WD/CO, while the Royal Navy received the 570cc side-valve model. As well as the side-valve Enfield 250cc trainer, the company also produced the Flying Flea, which was a 125cc two-stroke machine that could be collapsed and folded into a canister and dropped by parachute to provide instant mobility for its paratrooper rider. Incidentally, the machine's design was copied from a DKW, brought to Royal Enfield in 1939 by a Dutch importer of the German machines, who had been

This 250 Conti GT typified the direction Royal Enfield was taking after being taken over by the Smith Group; a large investment was made in the 250cc GPS racers.

refused delivery of the product unless it sacked its Jewish employees.

While Triumph operated from the 'Tin Tabernacle' after its Coventry factory was destroyed, Royal Enfield used an underground factory known as 'The Cave', which was situated at Bradford-on-Avon in England, for war work.

When peacetime returned, production continued in the underground factory. In addition, Royal Enfield bought back considerable quantities of its wartime production from the war office and refurbished them for sale on the insatiable postwar market.

Like other major manufacturers' offerings, big Royal Enfields were available with this bulky Airflow fairing with matching mudguards. This is a 1958 Crusader 250.

Royal Enfield's first new model was a Ted Pardoe-designed 500cc parallel twin, aimed to compete with Triumph's Speed Twin. Thanks to a design and parts commonality throughout its model ranges, the 25hp Royal Enfield 500 incorporated the sturdy and sophisticated rear suspension and swinging-arm design of the 346cc Trials Bullet. The 500 also featured two-way damped telescopic front forks. The 500 remained in production until 1958,

ROCKET
Japan 1952–late 1960s: The range from this company began with a 150cc side-valve and expanded to embrace two-strokes of smaller capacity and four-strokes of greater capacity.

ROCKET
Italy 1953–58: An attractive, intriguing, but unfortunately overly expensive machine with a 200cc transverse flat twin and shaft drive.

ROCKET
USA 1960: One of the rash of automatic (and rather crude) scooters of the time, from the Columbus Cycle Company.

ROGER BARBIER
Switzerland 1920s: Their overhead-valve 250cc machine was capable of almost 110kph (70mph) but it was overshadowed by an oil-cooled four-valve overhead-cam 500.

ROHR
Germany (Landshut) 1952–58: This firm made an Ilo-powered 200cc two-stroke scooter with a prepossessing appearance.

ROMEO
Italy 1969–75: These were Minarelli-engined 48cc tiddlers.

ROMP
England 1913–14: A Precision 500cc single powered these rare machines.

RONDINE
Italy 1923–28: These were Train-engined 100cc two-stroke lightweights.

RONDINE
Italy (Rome) 1934–35: The most famous Rondine was the supercharged, liquid-cooled 500cc straight four from Compagnia Nazionale Aeronautica. Gilera bought the design in 1936.

RONDINE
Italy (San Martino) 1952–57: These Sachs-engined lightweights were of 125 and 150cc capacities.

RONDINE
Italy 1968–early 1970s: These were off-road two-stroke competition machines of 48cc.

took advantage of the 250cc learner limit to ride it with L-plates. It provided a platform for the Meteor Minor 500cc twin that was available with a wind-tunnel developed factory-fitted Sportsflow fairing, which was a smaller version of the optional fibreglass Airflow fitted on the bigger machines.

By the early 1960s, the British motorcycle industry was in decline, and the Bullet line was dropped in 1962 when Royal Enfield was taken over by the Smith Group. They invested heavily in the 250cc GPS racing machine and the 250cc Villiers-powered Turbo. But in 1967 the factory shut down and the tooling to produce the 350 and 500cc Bullet was sold to Madras, India, where production continues apace.

From 1968, the company endured as Enfield Precision under Norton Villiers' control, operating out of Bradford-on-Avon, England.

The Meteor evolved into the 736cc Interceptor twin, which gained a good reputation but was the firm's only product. However, from 1970 Enfield Precision concentrated on fulfilling military contracts and its final batch of twin-cylinder engines went into Rickman frames.

Madras-built Royal Enfields are available new in the UK, and although quality may not be quite what it was, volumes are far higher than in the UK firm's heyday. The Bullet has proved sufficiently rugged for road conditions in India, and the modern specification includes diesel conversions, indicators and 12-volt electrics.

superseded by a 750cc version that endured into the early 1970s. The 500 was exported to the US in large volumes, where it was also marketed with the Indian badge.

To a great extent, Royal Enfield's swinging-arm rear suspension played a significant part in the company's trials successes in the 1951 and 1953 International Six Day Trial. The 350 Bullet was ridden with huge success by trials star Johnny Britain, and was top trials machine into the early 1960s. The Bullet range was Royal Enfield's best-selling line, but a measure of the

firms output can be gauged by the fact that just 9000 units were built in 13 years.

At the same time, by 1952, Royal Enfield's output was diverse, including a 125cc two-stroke and 692cc Meteor twin. With the demise of Vincent, the Meteor was the biggest bike produced in the UK, and it gained popularity as the motive power for sidecar combinations. It also had a tendency to leak oil and vibrate at speed. The Meteor was nevertheless successful in production endurance racing, especially in the hands of Syd

The company introduced this 736cc Interceptor prototype in 1964. A derivative of the Meteor, the Interceptor twin was made until 1970.

Lawton. New 250cc overhead-valve singles made their debut a couple of years later, and these were superseded by the unit-construction engine and four-speed gearbox Crusader models in 1957.

By 1964, top-of-the-range models were the 129kph (80mph) Crusader Sports and five-speed Continental GT. This caf-racer was popular with younger riders who

ROYAL ENFIELD JF

1936

It's a common misconception that the multi-valve cylinder head is a modern phenomenon, but the Royal Enfield JF had four valves in its 499cc single-cylinder head back in 1936, as did other motor-cycles.

The JF was popular with riders because of its smooth power delivery and economical use of fuel. However, the multi-valve head was more expensive to produce than a regular two-valve version, and consequently it was axed in a bout of cost-cutting. Predictably, the two-valve model lacked the urge and refinement of

The JF model from 1936 was a 500cc single-cylinder machine fitted with a four-valve head, which made for a smooth power delivery and economical running.

its predecessor. The rigid-framed JF also featured fully-enclosed pushrods and a chromed fish-tail exhaust.

Engine: 499cc air-cooled single-cylinder
Power: 19bhp
Gearbox: 3-speed
Final drive: chain
Weight: 165kg (364lb)
Top Speed: 128kph (80mph)

ROYAL ENFIELD TRIALS BULLET   1950s

The company began making its new Bullet models in 1949, and the line lasted until 1963, although the standard 346cc model continues to be built in Madras in 2000. The all-alloy overhead-valve single-cylinder motor, which was equipped with an integral oil reservoir in the same way as pre-war machines, was now relocated to the rear of the engine. The Bullet range was based on a new frame with swinging-arm rear suspension, which proved especially successful when applied to the off-road trials and scrambles machines. The Trials Bullet was equipped with different suspension and telescopic forks, small-diameter drum brakes, high-rise exhaust, special mudguards, wheels and tyres and a different state of engine tune. It was one of the 1950s' most successful trials machines.

This 350cc Trials Bullet of 1959 features the two-way damped telescopic forks and swinging-arm rear suspension that made it such an excellent machine.

Engine: 346cc air-cooled single-cylinder
Power: 17bhp
Gearbox: 4-speed
Final drive: chain
Weight: 141kg (310lb)
Top speed: 105kph (65mph)

ROYAL ENFIELD CONTINENTAL   1964

The short-lived Continental GT appeared in 1964, having evolved from the Crusader 250 of 1956 and Crusader Sports Continental. Deliberately aimed at the coffee-bar culture of the period, the Continental GT was a biker's delight. Its attractions were both practical and cosmetic, featuring competition-oriented clip-on handlebars, a racing-style fuel tank, a straight-through exhaust and fly-screen. With a top speed of 138kph (86mph), the Continental GT could easily outrun any contemporary scooters, and yet it was still learner-legal.

The Continental's five-speed gearbox was replaced with a six-speed edition in 1966, but the model was dropped altogether when the company was taken over the following year by Norton Villiers.

The Continental GT of 1964 was the culmination of a range of over-square 250cc unit-construction five-speed singles that began with the Crusader Sports in 1956.

Engine: 248cc air-cooled single-cylinder,
Power: 26bhp
Gearbox: 5- and 6-speed, foot change
Final drive: chain
Weight: 136kg (300lb)
Top Speed: 138kph (86mph)

ROSSELLI
Italy 1899–1910: The original Lilliput had a 1hp engine in front of the pedal bracket. Later machines went up to two-and-three-quarters horsepower

ROSSLER & JAUERNIGG
Austro-Hungary (Aussig) 1902–07: These machines were powered by in-house singles and V-twins of 2–4hp and had sprung frames.

ROTARY
Japan early 1950s–1961: These were two-strokes of 125cc.

ROUSSEY
France 1948–56: Initially, this firm produced an auxiliary cycle motor, and later, lightweights up to 175cc and a water-cooled scooter.

ROVETTA
Italy (Brescia) 1900–06: Giovanni Rovetta devised several machines, including water-cooled engines and an auxiliary cycle motor.

ROVIN
France 1920–34: Roaul de Rovin began with two-strokes of 100, 125 and 175cc, and in 1924 designed a unique pumping-action three-piston two-stroke for racing. In 1929 he took over San-Sou-Pap and added four-strokes to his line-up, with JAP and MAG engines of 500cc. He also built record-breakers and light cars, and raced his machines personally.

ROVLANTE
France 1929–35: These were lightweight two-strokes of 100 and 125cc.

ROWILL
France (Rouen) 1950s: These mopeds were fitted with Vap and Scoutex motors.

ROYAL
Italy (Milan) 1923–28: JAP and Blackburne 350 and 500cc four-strokes added glamour to the basic 132cc in-house two-strokes from this firm.

ROYAL
Switzerland (Basle) 1900–08: Helvetia made limited numbers of one-and-a-quarter to 2hp machines, with Zedel engines.

ROYAL-AJAX
England (London) 1901–08: The British Cycle Manufacturing Co built two-and-a-half horsepower machines.

ROYAL ENFIELD

INDIA 1955–

THE BULLET – it needs no further description to aficionados – is one of the greatest, yet most under-rated, motorcycles in the world. Almost indestructible, sweet-handling on the worst roads, extremely handsome, infinitely reparable, with a claimed 3.8 litres/100km (over 70mpg; UK gallons), it is a living fossil, a reminder of why, at one time, British motorcycles ruled the world, and also of why they lost ground to the Japanese.

In 1955 the Madras Motor Company started to import complete, knocked-down Royal Enfield Bullet motorcycles. As time went by, more and more of the parts were manufactured in India, until the bike eventually became wholly Indian-made. When Royal Enfield itself stopped making motorcycles in Britain in 1971, the Bullet remained in production in India. The company has even made the slightly exaggerated claim that 'today it is the only British bike still being manufactured anywhere in the world'.

By the start of the new millennium, there had been some innovations such as 12volt electrics, but the Bullet was still

basically the same 1955 model that had first been exported to India more than 40 years earlier.

It retained all the virtues, and all the vices, of a classic British single of the 1950s. First among the machine's drawbacks was that it was mind-bogglingly slow compared with bikes produced a couple of decades later. The 346cc – the only version in production until the 1980s – was (and is) a long-stroke (70x90mm) two-valve single with a compression ratio of only 7.25:1, giving 18bhp at 5625rpm for a weight of 163kg (359lb); these are not the attributes of a road-burner. The second clue to the model's age was its horribly frequent maintenance schedule: it was necessary, for example, to set the tappets and clean the contact-breaker assembly every 800km (500 miles); and a general lubrication was required every month or 2000km (1200 miles), whichever came first.

The Bullet was also idiosyncratic. Although the gear change was on the right-hand side, the important American market had standardised on the left. It operated up-for-down: one up, three down; again, most people expected one down, three (or four)

up. In case there weren't enough neutrals, there was also a heel-operated neutral selector.

The company did update the model, slowly. Along with the introduction of 12volt electrics, the brakes were improved, eventually using a twin leading-shoe. In 1984, principally in response to requests from overseas dealers, a 500cc version was put into production, with an 84mm bore (still under-square, though). The increase in power from the bigger engine was less than might have been expected – a mere 22 per cent to 22bhp – albeit at a mere

This 1986 Bullet still looks uncommonly like its forebear made in England a third of a century before and was still wonderfully forgiving to ride.

5400 rpm and with a compression ratio of only 5.5:1. Torque was increased by over 27 per cent, however, which made for a wonderfully smooth power delivery, and top speed rose to over 125kph (almost 80mph) from a previous 120kph (75mph). As early as 1990 there was also an overhead-cam prototype, although this was sleeved down to 250cc.

Prior to the 1990s none of this mattered very much, since the firm had never had to chase sales. Then, with the liberalisation of the Indian market, customers were no longer willing to wait – for months, or even more than a year – for a Bullet when they could simply purchase something else, often from a Japanese maker. In order to increase its competitiveness, the company gradually built up a network of contacts, including the legendary Fritz Egli in Switzerland, who agreed to make 'go-faster' versions of the engine, with swept volumes of 535 and 624cc. The gearbox was also converted to the left and made to go 'backwards' (up-for-up: one down and three up). Other strategies included investigating a five-speed transmission from Criterion

A 1995 350 Bullet, with trials-style mudguards, knobbly tyres and single seat. It is not impossible that this motorcycle will reach its centenary, in 2055.

Engineers in the UK, and, heretically, even consulting stylists.

The current challenge lies in maintaining the classic appeal of the Bullet, while incorporating necessary advances: in particular,

reducing the machine's rather demanding maintenance requirements.

At the moment, the prospects look good for a celebration of the model's centenary. If in the distant year 2055 there are any

motorcycles still being built anywhere in the world which use internal-combustion engines running on old-fashioned petrol, it seems a very likely bet that the much-loved Bullet will be among them.

RUDGE

ENGLAND 1911–39

THE RUDGE BICYCLE FACTORY had already been in business for well over four decades when it built its first prototype motorcycle in 1910. The company had been founded at Wolverhampton in 1868, but (as its badge proudly proclaimed) the motorcycles were made in Coventry. Actually, a few were made in Hayes at the very end of the company's involvement with motorcycles, but that is a minor footnote.

For such a legendary company, it made surprisingly few models, and even those that made its name tended to have just one or two innovations in an otherwise conservative – even old-fashioned – machine. The first Rudges, designed by John Pugh, were well made and fast, but not particularly original. The 500cc singles had inlet-over-exhaust valvegear, which was bang up to date for the time, but not exactly new: bore and stroke were slightly under-square at 85x88mm, giving an actual swept volume of 499cc. Likewise, spring forks were modern, but not unheard of. The starting arrangements were, however, novel: pedals, connected to the engine by a chain, were used to start the engine, after which they could be folded down and used as footrests.

Rudges came dramatically to public notice when, on 25 May 25 1911, Victor Surridge lapped Brooklands at around 107kph (66.47mph) and

covered 97.5km (60.45 miles) in one hour, the first 500cc motorcycle ever to do so. In the same year, several machines were entered for the Isle of Man Senior TT, and although only two finished (and 21st and 22nd at that), the race entries were the beginning of the first legendary Rudge motorcycle, the Multi, with its infinitely variable gears (thanks to a variable-diameter engine and rear-wheel pulleys). Actually, even this was not entirely new: Zenith's famous 'coffee-grinder' Gradua had featured something similar since 1908.

After the introduction of the Multi, there were surprisingly few

This 1937 Rudge 'Rapid' dates from the days of the decline and fall of the once-great company, but it was still a good-looking and reasonably quick machine.

changes for well over a decade. This was partly due to World War I, but in addition (as with so many great motorcycle companies) finances were shaky and there was insufficient money for innovation. A second place at the Senior TT in 1913 helped, but even Cyril Pullin's win at the 1914 Senior did little to boost sales, given the state of the motorcycle business for the next five years or so. A V-twin emerged on the eve of the war, but it came to nothing, and after peace was declared, the inlet-over-exhaust Multi single continued to be sold, with 499 and 750cc displacements.

By definition, the Multi depended on belt drive, and by the early 1920s this was beginning to look distinctly old hat, so Rudge made another great leap forward, with the Four of 1924. This referred to both the four-valve head and to the four-speed gearbox, both of which gave the model a significant advantage over the two-valve, three-speed competition. In fact, the four-speed gearbox had appeared a year earlier, on a 998cc V-twin, but Rudge was always best known for singles, and 85x88mm singles at that.

The cylinder head layout of this 1930s 'Special' is clear enough in this close-up shot: good cooling and good breathing added up to good performance.

The first Fours had parallel valves, but by 1927 the racing machines already featured radially disposed exhaust valves, for better gas flow and a bigger valve area. They had also acquired saddle tanks, making them look much more modern. It was the 1928 version of this model that won the 1928 Ulster Grand Prix by some 183m (200yds) at a record speed of 128.87kph (80.078mph) – the first-ever win of an international road race at more than 128.75kph (80mph) – and thereby gave rise to the most famous name of all among Rudges, the Ulster.

This engine design was further developed, in capacities from 250 to 500cc, and it was without question the high point of the company's career. In 250cc form, with all-radial valves in a hemispherical head, Rudges took first and second place in the Isle of Man Lightweight TT in 1931, and would have taken third place as well, had not the race leader (Ernie Nott) had a tappet lock-nut come loose on the last lap, when he was four minutes ahead of his team-mate Graham Walker. Lacking tools to tighten it, he held it in place with his finger for the remainder of the lap – and still finished fourth!

The true full-radial layout (with a forest of rocker arms) was used only in the 250 and 350cc machines, with the 500cc remaining a hybrid with parallel inlet valves and splayed exhaust valves. There was also a two-valve 250cc side-valve, advertised in 1929 with the claim: 'will attain 50mph [80kph] and will maintain 40mph [64kph] indefinitely' – which is some way from the Ulster legend. Rudge sold not only its own excellent motorcycles but also four-valve engines under the Python name to other manufacturers, in Britain and abroad.

Unfortunately, racing was simply too expensive, and even

while Rudge was at its peak the firm went into receivership, to be bought (improbably enough) by His Master's Voice, the gramophone and radio company. To its eternal credit, HMV continued to make fine motorcycles, which by now had such refinements as pressure lubrication, positive-stop foot change and enclosed valvegear, but after the 1932 season there was no more official racing. The Graham Walker Syndicate – Graham Walker, Ernie Nott and Tyrell Smith – raced Rudges as a private team in 1933 and 1934,

and Tyrell Smith continued to race (with success) in 1935, but the end of Rudge's glory days was sealed in 1936 by the death of John Pugh, who had been the driving force behind the company since it first started to build motorcycles.

Even so, there were new machines under development: an overhead-cam 350cc, and an overhead-valve 250cc (albeit only with two valves) as a possible Army 'Don R' bike. There was also a 98cc autocycle, with a two-stroke Villiers motor, but that eventually appeared as a Norman, not a Rudge.

The very purposeful looks of this 1930 TT model are brought into perspective by the size of the brakes, which are terrifyingly inadequate to a modern rider.

Despite the military potential of the 250cc bike, World War II brought Rudge's motorcycle production to a close. The company built wireless sets during the war, and never went back to motorcycles afterwards. Nevertheless, for the 28 years they were in production, Rudges were among the stars of the motorcycling firmament.

RUDGE MULTI

1911

The Multi's gearing worked in a simple but ingenious way. The engine and rear-wheel pulleys were each made of two flanges, intersecting as a V-form that drove the belt. If the two flanges were moved closer together, the effective diameter of the pulley increased; if they were moved

further apart, the effective diameter decreased. By a clever system of linkages, the effective diameter of the two pulleys could be varied in a way that kept the belt tension constant as one expanded and the other contracted, which was, of course, what provided the different gear ratios.

Gear changing was effected by a hand lever with a very long throw. Although in theory the gear ratios were infinitely variable between the limits set by the maximum and minimum diameters of the two pulleys, a set of notches in the gear-lever 'gate' meant that certain ratios could be

set and held without the rider keeping his hand on the lever.

Some historians have excited themselves unnecessarily about the precise number of notches, but the simple truth is that 'gates' are known with anything from 19 to 23 notches, and that no one now alive seems to know whether this

was to suit personal preferences, or for different engines, or simply pure chance. The last seems the most likely, as the practical differences between 19 steps and 23 steps would seem to be fairly trivial.

The Multi first appeared in 1911 but was still in production in 1922. The total range of (continuously variable) gears, selected by a lever on the side of the tank, was actually not all that many.

Engine: 499cc ioe single, 85x88mm, air cooled
Power: n/a
Gearbox: infinitely variable
Final drive: belt
Weight: n/a
Top speed: n/a

RUDGE FOUR

1924

The impact of the all-chain Four, after so long with the Multi (from 1911 to 1923), must have been considerable. The early machines were still flat-tank, which makes them look old-fashioned, and there were plenty of other vintage features, too: non-unit gearboxes, a dummy-rim brake on the back wheel, a rigid rear end (which survived to the end of Rudge's motorcycle production), total-loss lubrication and exposed valvegear (these would be remedied in 1930). But the two big-bore exhaust pipes sweeping back from the upright cylinder were eye-catching, as was the cast-aluminium silencer bearing the legend 'RUDGE-FOUR'.

The 'Four' referred, of course, to the number of gears – quite unusual at the time, when three-speeds were the norm even for sporting bikes.

The Four was introduced as a 350 and a 500cc, and it was on a 350cc that Col and Mrs Stewart covered 2093.98km (1301.14 miles) in 24 hours at an average of 87.24kph (54.21mph), breaking a string of records. However, the 350cc was dropped the following year leaving only the 500cc.

Engine: 499cc ohv single, 85x88mm, air-cooled
Power: 25bhp approx
Gearbox: 4-speed hand change
Final drive: chain
Weight: n/a
Top speed: 150kph (90mph) approx

RUPP
Germany 1928–32: This firm produced as a staple product an in-house 200cc side-valve, and for glory, a 500cc overhead-valve three-valve Kuchen.

RUPPE
Germany (Berlin) 1925–28: This was an auxiliary cycle motor of 98cc.

RUSH
Belgium 1922–34 or 1921–34: Mijnheer Van Geert won the Monza 250cc with one of his own (Blackburne-engined) overhead-valve 250cc machines in 1924; a Blackburne 350cc was also available. He later made his own side-valve and overhead-valve engines, at least 350 and 500cc, and possibly 600cc as well.

RUSPA
Italy (Turin) 1926–29: The Ruspa brothers, Luigi and Franco, brought out their first 125 early in 1926, and the pushrod 175 later in the same year. Their overhead-cam 350cc was built in very limited numbers.

RUSSELL
England 1913: This was an obscure manufacturer of 175 and 500cc machines – altogether an unlikely combination of sizes.

RUT
Germany 1923–24: This firm made the usual basic two-strokes, but unusually with an outside flywheel.

RUTER
Spain 1957–60: Hispano-Villiers two-strokes of 100 and 125cc powered these lightweights.

RUWISCH
Germany 1948–49: Victoria 38cc auxiliary-cycle motors were adapted for these mini-scooters.

RWC
Austria 1949–60: A Rotax-Sachs 100cc motor was used by this bicycle manufacturer to build a lightweight.

R.W. SCOUT
England (London) 1920–21: As well as building Blackburne-powered Weatheralls, R. Weatherall used two-strokes – 318cc Dalm and possibly 269cc Villiers – in the R.W. Scout.

RUDGE ULSTER

Since 1927 the Four had featured a saddle tank and (for its time) quite large brakes: a 203mm (8ins) drum at the front. The Ulster name came with the 1928 win at the Ulster Grand Prix, but the greatest year for the Ulster (and for Rudge in general) was 1930, when it won the Ulster TT (Graham Walker), the Dutch TT (Ernie Nott), the German Grand Prix (Tyrell Smith), the Czechoslovak Grand Prix (Tyrell Smith again) and the Brooklands 200-mile solo (Ernie Nott). The last victory was the only time that the Brooklands 200-mile solo race was won at over 160kph (100mph), albeit just marginally over, averaging around 161.05kph (100.07mph).

These wins were quite apart from all the second and third places that Rudge picked up all

The greatest Rudge of them all, although devotees of the Multi might disagree: the immortal single-cylinder Ulster, here seen in 1936 guise.

over Europe, and while one should not disparage for a moment the skill of the three riders, the fact that the wins were so evenly shared among them suggests that the machines they rode were far from secondary to their victories.

Although Rudge had a sound policy of selling ready-to-race Ulster replicas, the company still maintained a non-racing model, the 500 Special, which was effectively a somewhat downrated version of the Ulster, but still a very fast machine by the standards of the day. Production of the Ulster ended in 1933.

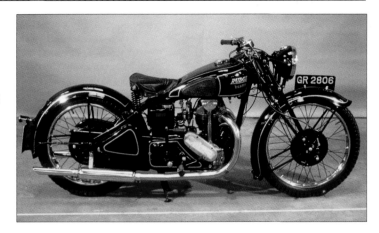

Engine: ohv single, 85x88mm, air-cooled
Power: 33bhp approx
Gearbox: 4-speed hand change
Final drive: chain
Weight: n/a
Top speed: 170kph (105mph) approx

RUMI

The Rumi twin-cylinder 125 Junior Gentleman was a fast road or racing motorcycle. With race kit fitted, it could excess 160kph (100mph).

The sportster was only the beginning. Soon a whole string of new bikes arrived, thanks to their much travelled designer, Giuseppe Salmaggi.

One such machine was an experimental 247.36cc (54x54mm) double overhead-cam racing twin with shaft final drive. Another was Rumi's first scooter, the Scoiattolo

(Squirrel). These were soon followed by a new 125 over-the-counter racer, 175 and 200cc variants of the horizontal 125 roadster twin. In 1954, the definitive Rumi, the Formichino (Little Ant) scooter, appeared. This machine went on to become a best-seller and also won the French Bol d'Or endurance race on more than one occasion. The engine was used to power the Junior Gentleman sports/racing motorcycle which, when it was race kitted, could top 160kph (100mph).

OFFICINE FONDERI RUMI was founded by Donnino Rumi in Bergamo, just before World War I. During the inter-war years, the company built textile machinery, then during World War II, specialised in the design and construction of midget two-man submarines and torpedoes, which explains the anchor as part of the marque's logo.

After the conflict, as other firms such as Agusta and Macchi who had built military equipment were to do, Rumi diversified into motorcycles. The first model was a 180-degree crankshaft, twin cylinder two-stroke with vertical cylinders. Displacing 124.68cc (42x45mm), this engine was to become a Rumi trademark

throughout its life as a motorcycle and scooter constructor.

By 1950 the company was exhibiting its products outside Italy in both Geneva and Paris Shows and in the following year Rumi made its sporting debut in the 1951 International Six Day Trial.

In January 1952 the Bergamo marque launched a sports version, featuring twin Dell'Ortos, a tuned engine and patented bottom-link front forks. With 8bhp at 7000rpm, Rumi claimed 116kph (72mph).

Rumi made its mark with its Formichino (little ant) scooter. Like the motorcycles, these used a horizontal, twin-cylinder, two-stroke engine.

SANGLAS

FRANCE 1900–03

FROM THE COMPANY'S foundation in Barcelona in 1951 to its take-over (and extinction) by Yamaha in 1981, the mainstay of Sanglas was a 500cc single of uncompromisingly upright appearance, which sold mainly to the Spanish police.

Sanglas's earliest motorcycles included 248, 347 and 423cc overhead-valve singles, all with conventional unit-construction four-speed gearboxes and chain primary and final drive. The line-up saw little change until 1962, when the firm added (under the Rovena name, not Sanglas) a range of two-strokes with proprietary Zundapp and Hispano-Villiers two-stroke engines from 49 to 325cc; these were made until 1975. From 1978 to 1981 Sanglas also made a 392cc twin with a Yamaha engine; it was presumably this alliance that killed the planned four-valve double overhead-cam single, with belt-driven cams and an impressive 747cc swept volume, that had been intended for introduction in 1978.

The definitive Sanglas must be the late 496cc single 500S

Right: The 500-S boasted proudly on its side panel that stopping was taken care of by a disc brake, 'freno de disco'.

Above and below: A late but 'real' and handsome Sanglas (above) – the 500cc 500-S single from 1978. This was the year of Sanglas's alliance with Yamaha which produced the relatively short-lived and extremely ordinary-looking Yamaha-engined Sanglas 400 twin (below).

(89.5x79mm) delivering 32bhp at 6700rpm, enough to propel the slim, neat bike to 160kph (100mph) despite the added weight of an electric starter. Police bikes, as is often the case, were rather 'softer', with 27bhp at 6000rpm and a top speed of around 144kph (90mph). The square-finned vertical cylinder is very distinctive, though the machine looks a great deal better with traditional wire-spoked wheels than it did with the cast-alloy wheels that were fitted to the last S2 models: the 180mm (7ins) drum brakes were also much more attractive than the discs of the S2.

Although they were good, workmanlike machines of modern

The 1980 S2 might have sold better with retro, rather than modern, styling. Its design was a vain attempt to attract the youth market.

design when they were introduced, by the time of their demise, these big singles were looking distinctly long in the tooth, and had more to offer to the nostalgia market than to either the young, speed-obsessed rider or to the fleet buyer. Unfortunately, they were not marketed with much acumen, perhaps because they had enjoyed a protected domestic market for so long. They deserve to be better known, since the choice of 160kph (100mph) classic singles is limited.

SANYANG

TAIWAN 1962–

THIS IS ANOTHER FIRM that began by assembling chassis parts for Honda; Taiwan was popular in this role with Japanese companies. At first work was restricted to the simpler tasks using parts made in Japan, but in time this extended to more complex units (although, for many years, excluding engines). Sanyang then started to manufacture some basic detail parts, and acquired the knowledge needed for both production and assembly.

The machines carried their own badges but in most other respects

Above: Based closely on the Honda scooterette, the Sanyang 80KC8E had the usual 72cc ohc single engine built in unit with its three-speed gearbox.

were small models from the existing or older Honda range. The scooterette was the most popular, although other models using the same engine units were also available. Small two-strokes eventually appeared, but the reliable scooterette, with its overhead-camshaft engine and

three speeds, remained the favourite on local roads.

Later years brought more sophistication and a larger range. However, the company's offerings always centred on the small capacities, from 50 to 125cc,

Below: Sanyang offered the 125CB1 as their small capacity motorcycle. It was essentially the Honda CB125 with a 122cc ohc engine and five speeds.

which were very well suited to the South-east Asian market. Scooters were produced in the same sizes as the motorcycles, and once in production, would run for years with little alteration. Even so, technical advances such as electronic ignition, electric start, disc brakes and pump lubrication for the two-strokes, arrived. Styling changes, were minimal, restricted to paintwork, but with the basic parts unaltered.

SAROLEA

BELGIUM 1896–1963

LIKE RIVALS FN, Sarolea began as a weapons manufacture. The factory produced precision armaments, and subsequently

switched to bicycles, then motorcycles. Originally founded by Mainson Sarolen in Liège during 1850, the company became a

pioneer of the once-large Belgian motorcycle industry.

Like FN (and Minerva), Sarolea was heavily publicised abroad.

Early models were powered by a mixture of single and V-twin engines up to 750cc, all of which were bought in. After the end of

World War I, the firm launched a major sales offensive, and to promote this entered the racing scene. Its first major competition success came in 1923, when Sarolea won not only the prestigious Liège–Nice–Liège endurance event but also the Belgian Grand Prix. This triumph was garnered by an overhead-valve single with a vertical cylinder. In the following year a production version, the 23M, scored a highly acclaimed victory in the Tour of Italy, an extremely demanding race contested by the majority of Continental European manufacturers. The Italian rider Guido Premoli rode the 23M to a hugely popular victory, with Luigi Arcangeli third, Erminio Visioli seventh, Dall 'Oglio 13th and Gambarini 18th. Sarolea also won the manufacturers' team prize.

During 1925 Sarolea totally dominated the domestic scene in Belgium, winning the national championship title, and also won no fewer than 23 major races in Italy. Again, the basis of this success was the tried and trusted 493.6cc (80.5x97mm) long-stroke pushrod single, with its vertical-cylinder layout and separate three-speed foot-change gearbox, the latter a rarity in those distant days. Other features of the 23M racer included a single-cradle steel

The first Sarolea racer to hit the headlines was 23M 500 single from the mid-1920s. The 350cc racing single shown here is of 1936 vintage.

tubular frame, rigid rear and sprung front suspension, and expanding drum brakes front and rear.

The marque's final major racing exploits came in 1926, when it sent an official works team to contest the Tour of Italy. After dominating the first four stages, the Sarolea entries were sidelined by locals throwing nails on the road. Even so, the Belgians went on to win the Italian Gentleman's Championship (for production-derived models) that year. Sarolea then announced its retirement.

All this racing glory made the Sarolea name widely known, at least in Continental Europe, and nearly 20,000 machines were built each year during the late 1920s. Then, in October 1929, came the Depression, triggered by the Wall Street crash in New York. Sarolea, like other European companies,

For many years, Sarolea was a major marque in European motorcycling, both on road and track. The 493.6cc ohv single dates from 1933.

was badly affected. However, through good business sense it survived and in 1932 introduced a new cheap-to-build, cheap-to-buy utilitarian two-stroke model. Sarolea hadn't forgotten their sporting past, and continued to build motorcycles like the Monotube, a high-performance 500-class single with an overhead-valve engine and a top speed of over 128kph (80mph).

With war clouds looming, Sarolea's engineers then began producing military motorcycles for the Belgian Army, including a 980cc side-valve horizontally opposed twin for both solo and sidecar use. After 1945 Sarolea continued to build its traditional overhead-valve singles, up to 600cc, while in 1950 a new series of models was introduced, headed by a brand-new 498cc parallel twin four-stroke. At the other end of the scale came a 125cc two-stroke commuter bike.

By the mid-1950s Sarolea was beginning to struggle, leading to an agreement in 1955 with fellow Belgian producers FN and Gillet-Herstal. 1956 saw a moped, with a 49cc German Ilo two-stroke engine, added to the range. In 1960, following more financial problems, Sarolea merged with Gillet-Herstal; production of Sarolea machines ended in 1963.

SCOTT

SCOTT MOTORCYCLE PRODUCTION began in 1908, initially at the Bradford premises of the Jowett brothers, later famous for their cars. The first Scotts used a patented frame, which was to survive substantially unchanged until 1930, and a new 333cc engine. This was of the same liquid-cooled, two-stroke, parallel-twin-cylinder design with which the Scott name will forever be associated (although some very early examples were air-cooled).

Alfred Angas Scott was an energetic genius and one of the great innovators of motorcycling's infant years. As early as 1897 he had patented a form of calliper brake, a fully triangulated frame, rotary induction valves (the equivalent of modern two-stroke power valves), unit engine construction, the first motorcycle kick-start and much, much more. Patents for his first engine date from 1904. This two-stroke twin was installed on his Premier bicycle, and occasionally powered a small boat, the Petrel.

Scott's original 330cc engine shortly grew to 450cc, with later versions displacing 498 or 596cc. All were of the 'classic' Scott design, with overhung two-bearing crankshafts with the drive taken from a central flywheel. Coolant was circulated through the large honeycomb radiator (another Scott patent) by natural thermosiphon effect, rather than pumped.

By the time the company moved into new premises at Shipley in 1912, the 'yowling two-strokes' had a string of competition successes behind them. Scott's twins had proved, over half a century before the Japanese demonstrated it again, that the lightness and simplicity of the two-stroke twin were potent features. As well as innumerable wins in trials and hill climbs, Scott machines won the Isle of Man Senior TT in 1912 and again in 1913, ridden by Frank Applebee and Tim Wood respectively.

Early Scotts used a simple but effective two-speed transmission. The first three-speeder appeared on TT machines in 1926 and later on roadsters of both 498 and 596cc form. However, four years earlier Alfred Scott himself had died at the age of just 48, from pneumonia contracted after a caving trip. Although Scott's

Alfred Scott's genius is still with us in many things modern motorcyclists take for granted, such as this, the first kick-start, dating from 1910.

attention had increasingly focused on non-motorcycle projects, with his departure much of the initiative went out of the company, which was having difficulty competing with the ever-more powerful four-strokes. In 1931 the official receiver was called in.

Albert Reynolds, an industrialist from Liverpool, stepped in to save Scott, but the undercapitalised company never fully recovered from its financial problems and the loss of its guiding light. Plans for a 650cc twin never reached fruition. An even more exciting prospect, a 986cc three-cylinder two-stroke, did reach production but only a handful were made. A 596cc Clubman's Special appeared in 1938; although its top speed of over 144kph (90mph) aroused considerable interest, the outbreak of war prevented it reaching the street.

A Scott from the 1930s. The period was a difficult one for the company, starting with the appointment of an official receiver in 1931. The marque never really recovered.

Production of the 596cc rigid-framed Flying Squirrel continued after the war. Unfortunately, at that time four-stroke parallel-twins were ruling the roost, so sales were poor and production ceased less than 12 months later. However, the story does not end there. As the famous Shipley works closed down, the Scott rights were secured by Matt Holder's Aerco Jigs and Tools company of St Mary's Row, Birmingham.

One of Holder's problems was his passion for accumulating the remnants of other marques. As well as Scott, at one time or another he owned tooling for Royal Enfield, Velocette and Vincent, which tended to distract his attention.

Somehow, Aerco continued to build Squirrels in very small numbers – practically to bespoke specification – including a revised Flying Squirrel with a swing-arm frame.

Although the bikes retained Scott's name into the 1970s, his sparkling influence ended even before his death in 1922, and the range became moribund by the 1930s.

A new 500cc model, the Swift, was announced by the company in 1958, but just six prototypes of this machine were ever built. A further 344cc prototype appeared in 1963, followed by an experimental racer in 1965, and yet another

roadster, of 498cc, in 1969. The last Aerco Scott was built in 1972. From 1972 to 1979 around 140 Silk (q.v.) roadster specials were built near Derby, using an extensively modified Scott engine in a Spondon frame.

SCOTT FLYING SQUIRREL   1929

Scott had dabbled with three-speed transmission as early as 1923, but this was perfected only for the factory TT machines of 1926, and was applied to roadsters one year later. Of all Scott twins, the three-speeds of the late 1920s have the reputation of being the finest, and of these the 'TT Replica' models are the most prized, with the 1929 Flying Squirrel perhaps greatest of

them all. For 1929 the model employed a long-stroke engine, as used to finish in third place by Tommy Hatch at the previous year's Isle of Man TT races.

The three-speed Flying Squirrel of the late 1920s was considered by many to be the finest of all Scott roadsters. This 596cc example dates from 1928.

These machines were made in 498cc (RZ) and 596cc (RY) capacities. In unsilenced racing trim, even the smaller engine developed a giddy 24bhp. The frame was fully triangulated, while the solidly mounted engine further enhanced stiffness. The rear end was rigid, but at the front a pair of forks looked very much like girders but were in reality more like slim telescopic forks braced fore and aft.

By 1930 the Flying Squirrel's porting and crankshaft design had been revised; the engine became the 'Powerplus' PZ (500cc) and PY (600cc). TT Replica versions left the range in 1934, but much the same engine continued into the 1970s, albeit with the introduction of detachable cylinder heads (DPZ and DPY motors) in the mid-1930s.

Engine: 498/596cc two-stroke parallel-twin, 66.6/73x71.4mm, liquid-cooled
Power: up to 24bhp at 5000rpm (498cc)
Gearbox: 3-speed hand change
Final drive: chain
Weight: 165kg (364lb)
Top speed: 137kph (85mph)

SAUND
India 1962–88: DKW-inspired machines werer based ever more loosely on the 100cc original.

SCARAB
Italy 1967–85: These were off-road competition machines from Ancilotti, with engines of 50, 125 and 250cc from Sachs, Hiro and Franco-Morini.

SCARABEO
Italy (Noale) 1968–: These typical Italian off-road competition machines came from Aprilia, with engines of 50 and 125cc.

SCHEIBERT
Austria (Vienna) 1911–13: The engine of this machine was built into the steering head, after the fashion of the Original Werner.

SCHICKEL
USA (Stanford, Connecticut) 1912–15: The cast light-alloy frame of this machine housed a big two-stroke single.

SCHLIHA
Germany (Berlin) 1924–33: Predictably, this was a 175cc two-stroke at first. Later models offered 200, 300, 350 and even 500cc.

SCHMIDT
Germany 1921–24: Their own in-house side-valve motors powered this 200cc lightweight; there was also an auxiliary cycle motor.

SCHNELL-HOREX
Germany 1952–54: 'Schnell' refers both to the speed and to Roland Schnell, the racing rider/designer. Based on Horex parts, these 250, 350 and 500cc singles had gear-driven overhead-cams and were sold to privateers.

SCHURHOFF
Germany 1949–53: These mopeds had 50cc Sachs and Ilo engines, and lightweights up to 175cc, with Ilo engines.

SCHUTT
Germany 1933–34: Paul Schutt's 200cc two-strokes were set in a Duralumin frame.

SCHUTTOFF
Germany 1924–33: This firm produced 250, then 350 and 500cc in-house engines, both side-valve and overhead-valve. They were taken over by DKW in 1933.

SCOTT 3S

1936

Bill Cull's three-cylinder two-stroke design had the potential to be one of the superbikes of its era. Originally produced as a 747cc prototype, by the time three such machines were unveiled to an enthralled public at the 1934 Olympia Show, the model had grown to a mammoth 986cc.

The liquid-cooled engine which had been fitted into this machine featured a 120-degree crankshaft house in magnesium alloy cases, mated to a car-type clutch and four-speed transmission. This would have made it ideal for shaft final drive, but instead bevel gears drove a conventional sprocket and chain to the rear wheel.

The running gear comprised Webb girder front forks and a DMW swinging-arm rear end. Fuel was carried in pannier-style tanks above the rear wheel, unlike the show bikes, which carried theirs below the main frame rail.

The first production example left the factory in 1936, listed at the high price of £115. Only eight machines were ever manufactured in total.

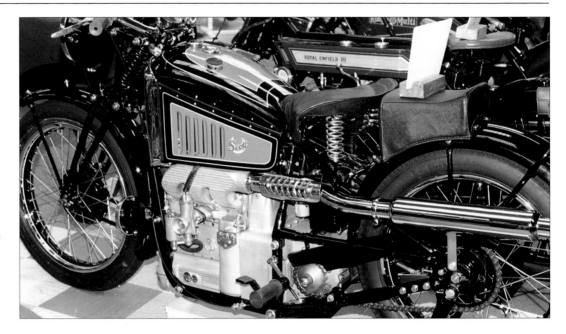

Although 23 years later, in 1959, a further batch of 3S triples which had been adapted for marine use was shown at the UK Boat Show, these too failed to make the further step into actual volume production.

In 1938, the astonishing 986cc three-cylinder 3S was one of many failed attempts to launch a new range of Scott machines. A marinised version of the engine surfaced briefly in 1959.

Engine: 986 two-stroke triple, 75x68.25mm, liquid-cooled
Power: 40bhp approx
Gearbox: 4-speed foot change
Final drive: chain
Weight: 222kg (490lb)
Top speed: 153kph (95mph) approx

SCOTT SQUIRREL

1950

The 1950 Squirrel was one of the last machines to be built at Scott's Shipley works. Later versions, like this 1957 model, were built in Birmingham until 1972.

problems that by the time motorcycle production ceased at Shipley, Scott had been dead for 27 years.

The last of the Squirrel models still continued to rely on the familiar 596cc two-stroke twin, and it also still used deflector pistons.

Work beginning at East Germany's MZ (formerly DKW who, ironically, had once borrowed from Scott's designs) was about to revolutionise two-stroke technology. But neither Scott, nor its successors, would share in the spoils.

Engine: 596cc two-stroke parallel-twin, 73x71.4mm, liquid-cooled
Power: 30bhp at 5000rpm
Gearbox: 3-speed foot change
Final drive: chain
Weight: 170kg (375lb)
Top speed: 137kph (85mph)

If the postwar Squirrel looked little different from a Flying Squirrel of the mid-1930s, this was scarcely surprising, since it was at heart the same machine. The first examples

to be made after World War II continued to employ girder forks, although these were later replaced by Dowty telescopics, while coil ignition ousted the old magdyno.

In other respects, there was little about the machine that would not have been instantly recognised by Alfred Scott himself, and it was an indication of the company's

SEARS

USA 1912–16

THE FAMOUS SEARS ROEBUCK firm was briefly involved with motorcycles prior to World War I and made a return in the 1950s, when it sold Austrian Puch machines in the USA under the trademark Allstate. Sears was no more involved in manufacturing these then it had been in 1912: at that time, its engines had come from Spacke of Indianapolis, Indiana, and the rest, including the assembly, was done by the Excelsior Cycle Company of Chicago, Illinois. This was not the widely known company of that name, also based in Chicago, but an obscure outfit that built the De Luxe machines and De Luxe clones, which were sold as Crawford, Dayton and Eagle as well as Sears. This type of multiple manufacture and marketing, with just a change of tank transfer, was quite common in the USA in the years prior to the outbreak of World War I.

Both singles and 1147cc (70cid) V-twins were produced, and the Spacke F-head engines had some unusual features in their valve operation. The camshaft was positioned to run along the side of the engine and was driven from the crankshaft by skew gears; a second set of these was at the front

end to drive the magneto, which sat across the front of the crankcase. For the singles, a pair of conventional cams moved the valves, but in the V-twin, face-cams were used. These moved small rocker-followers, which then transmitted their motion on to the valves (via tappets for the exhausts, and tappets plus long pushrods and rockers for the inlets). The twin crankshaft was also unusual in that it had a master connecting-rod for the rear cylinder, the front rod being a slave attached to the master.

The Sears V-twin had a 1147cc capacity and unusual valve gear. The machine was built by an obscure Excelsior firm and also sold under four other names.

Either engine went into a loop frame, with girder front forks for the singles and a trailing-link with leaf spring for the twins. This spring was fixed to the underside of the bottom fork crown to extend forwards, with a stay running from its front end down to the wheel spindle link on each side of the wheel. Direct chain final drive was

This Sears single-cylinder engine shows the shaft drive to the magneto of the Spacke engine. It also carried the cams for the valves – an unusual feature.

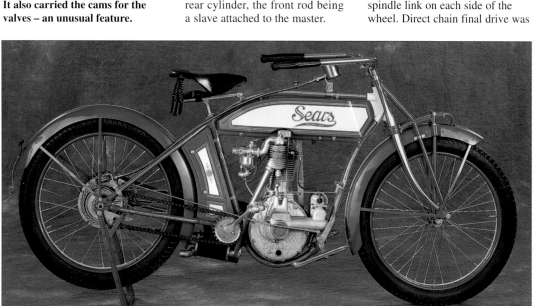

SCHWALBE
Germany (Aalen) 1922–24: The Spiegler brothers made a 125 or 150cc flat-twin, as a complete lightweight and as an auxiliary cycle motor, then added a 200cc lightweight.

SCHWALBE
Switzerland 1901–05: These machines featured Zedel two-and-three-quarters horsepower engines in strengthened bicycle frames.

SCHWEPPE
Germany 1949–50: This Ilo–powered scooter, with 143 to 184cc engines, was the precursor of the Pirol.

SCOOTAVIA
France 1951–56: These were AMC-powered overhead-valve 175cc scooters.

SCORPION
England 1951–56: Villiers 200 and 250cc motors in pressed-steel frames ensured that these had less sting than their name implied.

SCOTO
France 1949–early 1950s: Mosquito 38cc engines powered these mini-scooters.

SCOTT-CYC-AUTO
England 1934–50: This long-lived moped had an in-house 98cc motor.

SCYLLA
France 1931–37: These were two-stroke lightweights with 100 and 125cc Aubier-Dunne motors.

SEAL
England 1912–23: It is disputable whether this was a motorcycle or a three-wheeled car. The driver and passenger sat in the enormous, permanently attached sidecar, and steering was by wheel. Power came from a 6hp 1000cc JAP V-twin.

SEILIG
Italy 1938–39: These were rather handsome machines, with the single 250 or 350cc side-valve cylinder set well back in the frame.

SEMIOR
Spain 1952: This was quite an advanced 175cc two-stroke lightweight, with good suspension.

SENIOR
Italy 1913–14: Moser singles (300 and 330cc) and V-twins (500cc) powered these sporting machines.

fitted so both models had a single-speed transmission with pedalling gear for starting and light-pedal assistance where needed on hills.

The fuel tank sat between the two frame top tubes and the oil tank tucked in behind the seat tube, just ahead of the rear mudguard. The

brake was fitted to the rear wheel, as was American practice at that time. Other fixtures and fittings were of the period. For 1914 the

single adopted a trailing-link front fork, and the two models went on until 1916. After this, they were dropped from the Sears catalogue.

SEELEY

ENGLAND 1966–81

COLIN SEELEY WAS, and still is, a man of many talents: a motorcycle dealer at the age of 18, British sidecar racing champion (twice), a championship-winning team manager, and a constructor of both racing and street bikes (and even Brabham racing cars). After a successful sidecar racing career with Matchless- and BMW-powered outfits, Seeley took over the rights to manufacture AMC's (Associated Motor Cycles) AJS 7R and Matchless G50 racers in 1966. From the first Seeley-Matchless with its Mark 1 frame, the Seeley empire – at its peak employing a total of just 67 workers – built a

The 1978 Seeley-Honda superbike used an overbored four-cylinder engine displacing 1000cc. Specification included triple disc brakes and cast alloy wheels.

truly vast array of machines, culminating in the Seeley-Honda TL200 trials bike of 1980.

In between these years, there was a Seeley-framed URS four-cylinder racing solo (there were also URS sidecars) in 1967, followed by the 1968 Mark 2 Seeley-frame model (again housing either 7R or G50 single-cylinder engines) and the 1969 Kuhn-Seeley with a Norton twin-cylinder engine in a Mark 3 chassis. Then in 1970 came the QUB (Queens University Belfast) 500cc two-stroke single, the engine of which was designed by Dr Gordon Blair. However, the most successful Seeley machine of the era was the Yamsel (Yamaha two-stroke twin engine/Seeley frame).

In 1971 the firm Ducati asked Colin Seeley to build a chassis for

its new 500cc V-twin GP engine. Ducati also chose to fit and equip its standard production bikes with a method of chain adjustment which had been developed by Seeley. Also in 1971, a Seeley

A 1970 Seeley G50. This 496cc sohc single-cylinder racer used a development of the 1950s Matchless engine in Seeley cycle parts. It was the last of the big British singles.

frame transformed the previously poor-handling TR500 Suzuki, while in the same year the Seeley Condor roadster, using a G50 single-cylinder engine, made its debut. More commissions came in 1972, with Seeley frames being used for both the 750cc Westlake parallel-twin and Kawasaki 750cc three-cylinder two-stroke power units.

The 1973 Seeley Monoque, with a Suzuki twin-cylinder engine, also sported Seeley-made wheels, discs and front-fork assemblies. The same period also saw the 750cc three-cylinder Suzuki engine built to complement the earlier TR500-engined machine.

The mid- to late 1970s were spent in co-operation with Honda, and these years of partnership yielded the 1975 big-bore (820cc) Dixon-Seeley single overhead-cam Honda four roadster and the 1978 Seeley-Honda Superbike.

Success with these machines led to an ill-starred plan to build 1000 Seeley-Honda TL200 four-stroke trials singles. Only 300 were subsequently built and the whole exercise proved to be a financial disaster; ultimately, it brought Seeley's 15-year reign as a motorcycle builder to a close.

SERTUM

THIS FAMOUS MILAN factory originally manufactured precision instruments, but in 1922 its owner, Fausto Alberti, decided to enter the motorcycling world. The company's first design was a 174cc side-valve model, which was soon followed by a cheaper 119cc two-stroke. Thereafter, throughout the mid- to late 1930s, Sertum manufactured a wide range of strong, dependable single and twins with not only a side-valve, but also an overhead-cam engine. The Milanese concern was involved in motorcycle sport, too, most notably the International Six Days' Trial (ISDT) and long-distance road races such as the Milano–Taranto event.

After the war, Sertum was one of the first Italian manufacturers to resume production, and at the 1947 Milan Show it could boast of being the only Italian company to support that year's ISDT. At the exhibition, Sertum showed two basic models: a girder-fork rear-sprung 250cc overhead-valve single and a similar 500. There was also a 500cc vertical twin, but the firm was undecided about production. The most striking bike on Sertum's display stand was a new sports 250 with a pressed-steel frame.

A 1950 Sertum 250cc side-valve single. The famous old Milanese works became the first major post-war casualty of the Italian motorcycle recession, in 1951.

One of the factory-entered Sertum side-valve vertical twins used in the 1939 ISDT held around Salzburg, Austria, on the eve of World War II.

The following year, together with Gilera, Bianchi, Parilla and Moto Guzzi, Sertum was responsible for 97.74 per cent of all Italian motorcycle registrations, with the remaining 33 manufacturers having to divide a measly 2.26 per cent between them!

Sadly, from this high point, sales declined rapidly, until eventually Sertum was forced to close its doors. The company was to be the first major postwar casualty of the Italian motorcycle industry.

SILK

DERBY-BASED GEORGE SILK had long been a Scott enthusiast, but in 1971 he took this a stage further by entering a Scott-engined special in the 1971 Manx Grand Prix. The frame of this original motorcycle was a sturdy duplex affair built by the local firm Spondon Engineering, headed by former racer Bob Stevenson.

A number of Scott-engined bikes was produced before Silk turned to building his own power unit. Laid out on similar lines to the Scott, this was a water-cooled 653cc two-stroke twin, with deflector pistons and primary drive taken from the centre of the crankshaft. A machine was displayed at the London Racing and Sporting Show in January 1972, but production did not start

until 1975. Marketed as the 700S, a total of 138 were sold between 1975 and 1980.

The crankshaft of the 700S was supported by a combination of two

Based in Derby, England, the Silk was a limited production liquid-cooled twin-cylinder two-stroke modelled around the earlier Scott theme, but brought up to date.

SERVICE
England 1900–12: Connaught, and Wartnaby & Draper, actually built these machines, sold as Service.

SESSA
Italy (Milan) 1951–53: These were two models of Ilo-powered 150cc lightweight.

SETTER
Spain 1954–56: These ultra-lightweights had an in-house 60cc motor.

SFM
see **JUNAK**

S-FORTIS
Czech Republic 1929–31: These English-looking 600cc pushrod singles had Sarolea engines.

SFW
Germany 1924–26: As well as a 200cc two-stroke of their own manufacture, this company also offered a 500cc with the BMW proprietary flat twin.

SGS
England (Macclesfield) 1926–33: Gleave Engineering built Sid Gleave Special racers and sporting roadsters with JAP 250 and 500cc four-strokes, and 175 and 250cc Villiers two-strokes.

SHANGHAI
China 1964–unknown: This firm began with two machines copied from others' designs. One was a 750cc BMW-like sidecar hauler, the Donghai 750 A, and the other was a CZ-based 250cc two-stroke single.

SHARRATT
England 1920–30: These machines were fitted with JAP engines of 300 to 1000cc, and some Villiers and MAG engines.

SHAW
England 1898–1909: Sidney Shaw built his first 250cc chain-drive Gazelle motorcycle in 1898 but he seems not to have kept ahead of the times; production ended in 1909.

SHAW
USA 1909–23: These were simple, direct-drive machines with single-cylinder in-house engines, giving two-and-a-half and three-and-a-half horsepower.

ball and four roller bearings. On the offside of the crank was sited the throttle-operated oil pump, as well as the infrared triggers of the Lumenition electronic ignition system. The 100th example of the 700S came off the factory floor in November 1978. Silk production continued until February 1980, during which some 140 engine/gearbox units were made, together with 138 chassis. The first 30 were Mark 1s, featuring a polished engine, and the remainder Mark 2s, with engines that were partly black.

Another development was a 325cc trials engine. This unit was virtually a 700S, but was air-cooled, with a four-speed gearbox that included a shaft to produce two-speed final drive, giving four low ratios for trials work, and four for road use.

One of the 700S models built by the George Silk-owned marque, the engine was a 653cc two-stroke twin, with deflector pistons.

SIMONINI

ITALY 1973–83

MARANELLO, NEAR MODENA, is well known as the home of car giants Ferrari, but for several years during the 1970s and 1980s it was also the site of the Simonini factory. Founded in 1973 by Enzo Simonini, the company was little more than a workshop, hand-building very small numbers of competition bikes, almost exclusively for motocross. Demand increased, and in 1974 the firm moved to Torre Maina, just outside Maranello.

Above: A Simonini 50cc SF Enduro of the late 1970s. The company was based near car giants Ferrari and specialised in high quality dirt bikes.

In addition to the construction of special motocross and a small number of enduro bikes – each machine being made to suit the individual requirements of its rider – the marque also offered tuning kits for most Italian dirt-bike engines. At this stage Simonini

relied exclusively upon German Sachs engines, which, with the help of Simonini tuning components, proved both fast and reliable.

Success led to an influx of orders, but there were not enough funds to pay for expansion. This led, in spring 1975, to a commercial marriage between Simonini and another local company, Fornetti Impianti SpA, based nearby in Maranello. The result was a brand-new factory (with the Torre Maina facilities retained for research and

development purposes) and a brand-new range of motorcycles. Engines from Kreidler and Minerelli supplemented the Sachs motors, while a pure Simonini 125cc motocross unit, called the Mustang, was also designed and built. Another new model was the 250 Shadow motocrosser, powered by a seven-speed Sachs engine. A

Small numbers of the high performance 125SS single-cylinder sports roadster with a tuned 123cc two-stroke engine were built in the late 1970s.

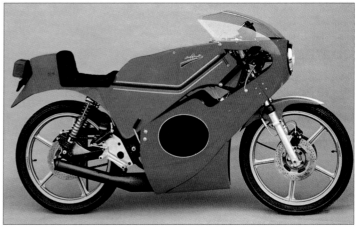

feature of this machine was its cast-alloy wheels and disc brakes, both front and rear.

During 1975, Giuseppe Fazioli won the 125cc Junior Italian motocross title on a Simonini.

The following year, Sergio Franco contested some of the 125cc World Motocross championship rounds for the marque, while in 1977 the British rider Andy Ainsworth was signed up. A team of Swedish riders rode Simonini machines in the 1977 International Six Days' Trial (ISDT).

The company expanded further in 1977, introducing new Sachs water-cooled engines for the 50 and 80cc models. However, as the 1980s dawned, Simonini's sales fell. The marque never fully recovered, and was forced to close down finally in 1983.

SIMSON

GERMANY 1938–

The origins of the Simson marque can be traced back to 1856, when its predecessor, the Ernst Thalmann Hunting Weapon Works, began manufacturing armaments in the East German town of Suhl, in the Thuringian Forest. In 1896 production of pedal cycles began; these were innovative for their day, being fitted with pneumatic tyres, when much of Europe was still having its bones shaken.

While many bicycle manufacturers made the transition into motorcycle production, the East German firm moved into cars. It was in this new field that the name Simson-Supra first appeared, under which various forms of touring and sporting vehicles were offered in the mid-1930s.

In 1938 Simson made its first powered two-wheeler, a 98cc

Above: Large numbers of the S50B Simson ultra-lightweight motorcycle were built during the 1970s and exported all over the world.

Below: A Simson for the modern era. The 50cc Sperber model made its debut in 1997 and had many advanced features in its comprehensive specification.

SHAW
England 1918–22: This auxiliary 115cc cycle-motor was actually made in Galesburg, Kansas.

SHIN MEIWA
Japan 1955–mid-1960s: The 250cc Pointer Ace was soon followed by the Pointer of the same capacity, then the 123cc Senior, 60cc Junior, 175cc Pointer Comet and Pointer 90. In 1960 they restructured their line-up. The last new model, the Pointer Sports KS1 of 1963, was good for 130kph (80mph) from its 16bhp (at 8500rpm) 125cc motor.

SHL
Poland (Kielec) 1935–: Before 1939, Villiers 125cc two-strokes powered these machines; postwar, they had 125, 150 and 175cc two-strokes.

SHOWA
Japan mid-1950s–early 1960s: In the 1950s, this firm produced mopeds of 50cc, 125cc lightweights, and a 250cc scooter, then in 1961, a 125cc scooter, all two-strokes.

SIAMT
Italy 1907–14: Luigi Semeria was 26 when the first machine to bear his name appeared, a 260cc single. Later came 350cc singles and 500, 688 and 731cc V-twins.

SIAT
Italy (Senegallia) 1924–26: The Societa Italiana di Applicazioni Techniche built a 75cc auxiliary cycle motor, followed by lightweights of 100 to 200cc, both two- and four–stroke.

SIATA
Italy 1954: Once known as an automobile pioneer, Siata made the 160cc two-stroke Dinghi lightweight and was also known for the Cucciolo moped.

SIC
France (Paris) 1921–25: Initially Aubier-Dunne, Train, Zurcher and possibly other motors powered these machines, in capacities from 100 to 350cc; they switched to a DKW 160cc two-stroke just before the end.

SICRAF
France 1947–53: These assembled machines of 50 to 250cc had Ydral and AMC (France) motors.

SIDEMOTOR
France 1925: This was an integral combination of sidecar and motorcycle, with the engine alongside the frame and driving between the two rear wheels (one motorcycle, one sidecar).

Sachs-engined ultra-lightweight. With the intervention of World War II, and the subsequent partitioning of Germany, it was late 1952 before Simson resumed motorcycle production.

First of the new models was the SR-1, a very basic commuter moped with a 49cc engine. It was sold under the AWO brand name, as were all Simsons until the late 1960s. The next model was the SR-2, which became the biggest-selling East Germany two-wheeler in the 1950s and early 1960s.

Building on these successes, the first real motorcycle was the AWO 325, powered by a 247cc overhead-valve single-cylinder engine. Very similar to a BMW R26, it not only spawned a series of roadsters, but was also used by the company for racing.

Launched in 1958, the double overhead-cam Simson RS 250 was an amazing product, featuring every modern feature, including a six-speed gearbox. Hans Weinert won the national title riding just such a bike in 1958 and 1959.

Simson subsequently abandoned four-strokes and ever since has concentrated its efforts on the smaller classes (not exceeding 100cc), in moped, motorcycle and scooter form.

SOKOL

POLAND 1934–39

THE POLISH SOKOL COMPANY produced at least four models: a 200cc single (the 200 M411), a 1000cc V-twin (the 1000 M111) and a couple of long-stroke single 'thumpers' (the 500RS M311 and 600RT M211). The smallest was 199.2cc (62x66mm) and delivered 7hp at 4000rpm. It weighed 100kg (220lb), and was good for about 85kph (53mph). The 1000cc V-twin was also known as a CWS, but no further information is available.

The 'thumpers' had tall, inclined cylinders. The 500RS was 502cc (78x105mm) and (depending on the type) delivered 18hp at 4500rpm or 22bhp at 5000rpm; it weighed 160kg (353lb) and was good for 125kph (78mph). It seems to have been a later sporting development of the 600RT, which was 575cc (83x106mm), weighed 146kg (322lb) and had only 15hp for a top speed of 110kph (68mph). With a claimed oil consumption of 100ml per 100km (281 miles per pint), it appears also to have had total-loss lubrication, although it may simply have been a prodigious oil-burner.

Reputedly, Sokol's motorcycles were intended primarily for military use. However, the company seems to have had a genuine programme of development that, had Poland not been invaded, might have resulted in an interesting line of machinery.

SOS

ENGLAND 1927–39

Always giving that little bit extra than the usual run of British two-stroke models, the SOS (a 1934 249cc water-cooled model is shown) was built in relatively small numbers between 1927 and 1939.

IN 1999, AT THE AGE of 100, SOS's remarkable founder Leonard Vale-Onslow was still riding motorcycles. His company's name at first stood for 'Super Onslow Special' and later 'So Obviously Superior', and its bikes were considered to be more exclusive and higher in quality than the standard Villiers-powered machines so common in the 1930s.

Ironically, SOS originally used a variety of JAP four-stroke and Villiers two-stroke power units, but from the 1931 season only the latter were fitted, ranging from 172 to 346cc. In addition, Vale-Onslow made its own 148cc (53x 67mm) and 172cc (57.15x67mm) engines with water-cooled cylinder and head. SOS's machines were initially manufactured at Hallow, near Worcester, but by late 1931 production had been transferred to Birmingham. The company's most sporting model was the 172cc (57.15x 67mm) AA, later known as the Brooklands. This was available in track, road racing or trials specification to special order.

In October 1933 control of SOS passed to Tommy Meeten, a Villiers specialist from Redhill, Surrey; production, however, remained in Birmingham. During 1936 Meeten opened a dealership in London, named Meetens Motor Mecca, which became the centre for Villiers parts in southern England for the next 50 years. When World War II broke out in 1939, Meeten offered his services to the government, but was turned away. He closed the Birmingham factory, which was destined never to re-open. As for the original owner, Vale-Onslow, he continued as a motorcycle dealer in Birmingham.

SPRING

BELGIUM 1910–24

LA SA DES ATELIERS SYSTÈME SPRING, of Streupas-Angleur et Tilff-Liège, produced unusual machines in small numbers with multi-cylinder engines. The first, in 1910, had two or four cylinders set across the frame in 'V' format, with the drive set back and turned to run to the rear wheel. The motorcycles were intended for sidecar work rather than solo use, and further differed from the usual specification of the day in having both front and rear suspension.

After World War I, at the 1920 Brussels Show, the firm revealed a new suspension system for its models, using a duplex cradle frame. Into this went V-twin engines of 498, 749 or 998cc installed across the frame, with side-valves at the front and the magneto on top of the crankcase at the rear. The engine was set well forward and built in unit with the transmission, final drive being by chain. Legshields running down into footboards were a feature.

The marque established a reputation for its type of layout and construction, and undertook some tests and trials for promotion purposes. However, after some years, production was abandoned as the whole of the motorcycle market moved away from large and unusual sidecar-dedicated machines to a more traditional design for both sidecar and solo use. Nevertheless, the company remained in existence up to 1939, but only undertook general mechanical work.

SUN

ENGLAND 1911–61

SUN WAS ORIGINALLY a maker of bicycles in Birmingham, and took up the manufacture of motorcycles in 1911. Its output consisted of 270 and 590cc Precision-engined machines, with the adoption of a 346cc inlet-over-exhaust Villiers unit in 1913. This unusual powerplant was superseded by the Villiers 250cc two-stroke. After World War I, Sun entered the Isle of Man TT with models powered by the 269cc Vitesse VTS (Valveless Two-Stroke, or rotary disc-valve), while its road-going bikes were equipped with a

selection of Villiers, Blackburne, JAP and Vitesse engines, ranging in size from capacities of 98 to 650cc.

Sun stopped making motorcycles in 1932, but bicycle production continued. It came back again with powered two-wheelers in 1948, introducing the 98cc Villiers-engined Autocycle and Sunwasp scooter.

During the following decade, the 1950s, a number of motorcycles, scooters and off-roaders were manufactured. As with many small British firms, all

The Sun marque began and ended with utility two-strokes, fitted with a variety of engines from manufacturers such as JAP, Villiers, Vitesse and Blackburne.

models were Villiers-powered and no more than 250cc in size. Among these was the 250cc Overlander twin of 1957, which was noted for its ample weather protection.

The Sun company was acquired by Raleigh in 1961, and only bicycles were made from then onwards.

SIEG
Germany 1922–30: Success was not prolonged for Jungst's ambitious machine that could be had with a wild variety of engines from 110 to 600cc, from many different manufacturers.

SIGNORELLI
Italy 1928–30: These lightweights had in-house 175cc two-strokes.

SIL
India 1978–: These were Lambrettas for which Sil bought the tooling when Lambretta ceased production.

SILVER PIDGEON
[sic] Japan early 1950s–1965: This improbably-named scooter, with its choice of 87cc two-stroke or 192cc side-valve engines, was a separate marque within the Mitsubishi group.

SILVER PRINCE
England 1919–24: This assembler had a 350cc Blackburne for a flagship and Villiers two-strokes from 150 to 269cc for the lesser models.

SILVER STAR
Japan 1953–58: In-house 125 and 150cc overhead-valve engines powered these lightweights.

SIM
Italy (Milan) 1955–60s: The Societa Italiana Motori began with a 48cc four-stroke moped, and the Pegaso with a pressed-steel frame.

SIMCA
France 1935–39: From a choice of 250, 330 and 350cc prototypes, the French War Department ordered 40,000 350cc two-stroke, shaft-drive twins. Only about 250 were built before Hitler interfered with the delivery schedule.

SIMONCELLI
Italy 1927–35: These 175cc lightweights were initially powered by Train strokes, then by JAP four-strokes.

SIMPLEX
Italy (Turin) 1921–50: Luigi Pellini (of Pellini & Ferrari) began with a 124cc auxiliary cycle motor and in 1927 moved on to 150 and 175cc overhead-valve lightweights. Enclosed valve gear followed in 1930, along with bigger engines.

SUNBEAM

ENGLAND 1912–57

ALTHOUGH SUNBEAM MOTORCY-
CLES sprang from the company's
Sunbeamland Cycles business,
founded in 1887, the firm could
trace its roots back to 1790 as
Marston Ltd. Its owner John
Marston decided to take Sunbeam
into motorcycle manufacture in
1912, by which time many of its
rivals were established producers.
Another member of the family,
Charles Marston, started Villiers
Engineering in 1898 to build
bicycle components. Villiers
engines would play a crucial part
in motorcycle motivation for more
than 50 years. Yet another facet of
the family business was Marston
Radiators, which still existed as
Marston-Excelsior in the late
1900s. Sunbeam built a prototype
car in 1899 and launched the
Sunbeam-Mabley car in 1901.
Production of two- and four-wheel
vehicles was separated in 1905.
The company's car-making days
began in 1909 when Louis
Coatalen joined the firm.

The Sunbeam motorcycles
introduced in 1912 were finished
in black livery similar to the

bicycles, with a nine-layer
weatherproof coating developed
from Marston's japanning (metal-
lacquering) treatment for kitchen
utensils. Designed by John
Greenwood, the Sunbeam was
powered by the company's own
347cc side-valve single-cylinder
engine, in which the crankshaft
was balanced by eccentric internal
flywheels. It had a two-speed
gearbox and multi-plate clutch,
with chain final drive
incorporating the Sunbeam oil-
bath chaincase – originally a
bicycle feature and also taken up
in early Sunbeam cars – rather
than belt drive. A V-twin was
introduced, using 770cc JAP,
MAG and AKD engines, mated to
a Sunbeam three-speed gearbox,
and a 499cc version of the single-
cylinder model followed late in
1913. This machine was ridden to
joint second place in the 1914 Isle
of Man TT, marking the
company's first competition

**The Model 9 ohv single from 1939
was part of Sunbeam's new line of
bikes, produced in London. The
company was now part of
Associated Motor Cycles.**

**The 1916 Sunbeam pictured here
in black with gold coachlines
didn't look so different from the
Model 5 a decade later. The oil
bath chain case is prominent.**

success. The model was supplied
to the Allied forces during World
War I and run by the French Army
in belt-drive format.

John Marston died in 1918, and
his family sold the motorcycle
business to Imperial Chemical
Industries (ICI) in 1922. The car
company became part of the
French Sunbeam Talbot Darracq
alliance, maintaining an illustrious
racing history. However,
competition successes on two
wheels included two Senior TT
race wins in 1920 and 1922.
Following the introduction of new
350 and 500cc overhead-valve
singles in 1923, Graham Walker
became Sunbeam's competitions
manager in 1924; the marque
became active in European races.
The most consistent performer was
the overhead-valve 493cc Model
90; winning the 1928 and 1929
Senior TTs, it was the last two-
valve overhead-valve engine
to do so.

Meanwhile, Sunbeam's overhead-cam engine proved a disappointment, and the company was slow to react to trends with its road bikes such as the fitting of saddle tanks and girder forks, retaining flat fuel tanks and Druid front forks instead. This restraint may have contributed to Sunbeam's survival of the Depression, eased further by the rationalisation of its product range. Eventually the saddle tanks and a positive-stop foot shift were adopted, while the oil-bath chaincase was dispensed with.

ICI sold off Sunbeam in 1937 to Matchless and, together with AJS, it became part of Associated Motor Cycles. Sunbeam bicycles were sold to BSA the following year. Production of motorcycles was relocated from Wolverhampton to London, and by 1938 the old Sunbeam range began to be phased out, to be replaced by a new line, which included 250, 350 and 500cc overhead-valve, high-camshaft singles. Further advancement was stymied by the outbreak of war, however. Then, in 1943, Sunbeam was acquired by BSA, and postwar production took off in 1946 with the extraordinary-looking Erling

The company logo was always 'The Sunbeam', and its history encompassed both motorcycle and car manufacture, although the two aspects were divorced in 1922.

Poppe-designed S7, which was powered by a 487cc in-line twin with shaft drive. This innovative machine was revised for 1949 and relaunched as the S8 model with much BSA componentry. Production lasted until 1957, but the Sunbeam identity was then applied to BSA's largely abortive venture into the scooter market. The 175 and 250cc BSA Sunbeams were identical to products from their Triumph

The Model S7 from 1946 and S8 of 1949 were designed by Erling Poppe. In terms of style and powertrain the model differed from traditional British bikes.

stablemates, but although they were on a par with the Italian market leaders, the British models failed to catch the wave of popularity.

By 1964, the Sunbeam motorcycle marque was defunct.

SUNBEAM MODEL 90

1924

The first Sunbeams to be powered by the firm's own overhead-valve engines were the racing machines of 1923, run alongside the stock side-valve 499cc Model 5s. The competition machines were based on the cycle parts of their road-going siblings, and extra power was gained by tuning the engines and by weight-saving measures, which included dispensing with the 'little oil-bath' chaincase and standard equipment such as lights and a stand.

The John Greenwood-designed 347cc Model 80 and 493cc Model 90 introduced in 1924 were offered as racing bikes, and as such bore few concessions to creature comforts. Even the kick-starter was absent, although four years on, the inventory had graduated to full road-going specification.

Twin-port cylinder heads were optional equipment on the Model 90 in 1926, and standard in 1927. The 80mmx98mm dimensions

Introduced in 1923, the 493cc Model 90 was offered at first as a competition bike. Charlie Dodson won the 1928 and 1929 Senior Isle of Man TTs on this machine.

typified British single-cylinder engines of the period, and the internals included a pair of cams with hollow pushrods that were exposed, with hairpin valve springs. Valves were angled at 90 degrees in the finned cast-iron cylinder head, while race bikes came with steering dampers, and the exhaust pipes were splayed out to either side of the bike for improved cooling and gas flow. Druid-pattern girder forks and a three-speed crossover hand-shift gear change were common to road and racing machines.

Riders to excel on Sunbeams were George Dance, who was a sprint and hill climb specialist, and Charlie Dodson, who won the 1928 and 1929 Senior TTs on a Model 90. For 1929, this model

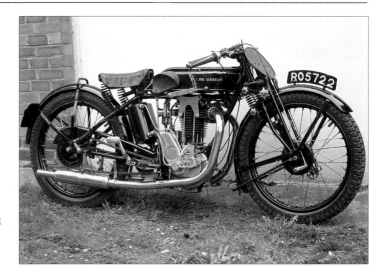

featured a saddle tank, which was a stylistic advance on its predecessors, which used flat-side tanks.

Without exception, all vintage Sunbeams were finished in elegant black enamel featuring gold coachlines.

Engine: 493cc single-cylinder, air-cooled
Power: 5hp
Gearbox: 3-speed hand change
Final drive: chain
Weight: 136kg (300lb)
Top speed: 121kph (75mph)

SUNBEAM MODEL S7

1946

The Model S7 had a 487cc ohc, in-line, all aluminium, twin-cylinder engine, four-speeds and shaft drive mounted in a duplex cradle frame. This is a 1948 bike.

modest 25bhp, however, and the S7's top speed was just 116kph (72mph).

The S7 came with telescopic front forks, tyre-enveloping mudguards and bulbous 127mm (5ins) section tyres, plus big drum brakes. It was slimmed down in 1949 and redesignated the Model S8 with BSA suspension, wheels and other cycle parts.

The Model S7 De Luxe version that appeared in 1950 was an S8 with S7 running gear and front forks and rear plunger units which had been introduced from the BSA A7.

Production continued until 1957 and, although scooters followed, this was the last Sunbeam motorcycle.

Engine: 487cc twin-cylinder, air-cooled
Power: 25bhp
Gearbox: 4-speed foot change
Final drive: shaft
Weight: 197kg (435lb)
Top speed: 116kph (72mph)

The Sunbeam name was bought from Associated Motor Cycles by BSA in 1943 and applied to the S7, which came out in 1946. Designed by Erling Poppe, the upmarket S7

was quite a radical departure from accepted practice in the British motorcycle industry. From its duplex cradle frame hung a massive 487cc twin-cylinder all-alloy

engine, mounted longitudinally with shaft drive from its four-speed gearbox. The overhead-camshaft was chain-driven from the rear of the cylinder block. Output was a

SUZUKI

JAPAN 1952–

SILKY-SMOOTH FOUR-CYLINDER engines are the norm from Japanese producers, and in fact Suzuki's origins lay in the silk industry. Founder Michio Suzuki was born in 1887 in Hamamatsu, and Suzuki is still located there.

The silk industry was widespread in Japan, and in 1909 Michio set up in business building silk-weaving looms. It wasn't until 1937 that Suzuki created a prototype engine and entered an agreement to manufacture Austin 7 cars under licence. However, the country was on a war footing and Suzuki was obliged to commit to ordnance production instead. When the war was over, Suzuki

Launched in 1963, the 250cc T10 had a pressed steel frame and ran with a two-cylinder two-stroke engine and four-speed gearbox. It was mild mannered.

began making looms again, but a shortage of silk led to the company's manufacture of farm machinery and heaters.

Now in his 60s, Michio Suzuki was well aware of the advantages of powered transport, and elected to produce a motorised bicycle. Construction of the prototype was underway in November 1951. It was powered by a 36cc two-stroke engine, which could be clipped on to the frame of any bicycle,

nestling above the bottom bracket in the base of the frame diamond. In June 1952, the first Suzuki was sold, known as the 'Power Free'. In March 1953 the Power Free Suzuki was followed by the 60cc Diamond Free, and this model won its class in the 1953 Mount Fuji hill climb. The company's first recognisable road bike was the Colleda, unveiled in May 1954. This 90cc four-stroke single-cylinder machine promptly won the Mount Fuji hill climb against 85 rivals. In 1955 the 125cc two-stroke Colleda ST showed the direction that Suzuki's production would take. A new plant was opened in 1957, providing the capacity to bring Suzuki closer to Honda in production volumes. Meanwhile, Shunzo Suzuki, son of the founder, toured the USA and returned convinced of the North American market potential.

In 1959 the company built a special 125cc Colleda RB race bike, with a four-speed gearbox, telescopic forks and swinging-arm. It came fifth in the Asama races behind the Hondas, but after prompting by Soichiro Honda,

In the early 1960s, Suzuki made its mark in the West through its racing machines. This is the 125cc RS67 racing machine from 1967.

The Suzuki T305 of 1968 and T316 were uprated versions of the long-running 250 twin range, and remained in production until 1973.

early 1960s included the Twinace and the 246cc T10, an evolution of the twin-cylinder Colleda TT from 1956, with a pressed-steel frame and relatively bland styling. The 1963 T10 was equipped with an electric starter and flashing indicators, reinforcing the Japanese commitment to user-friendly machines.

On the racing front, Suzuki's forays into the 1960 and 1961 Isle of Man TTs reaped only a 15th place. Top Suzuki rider was Mitsuo Itoh, who would become racing manager. However, the defection of East German rider Ernst Degner from MZ in 1961 provided Suzuki with intimate details of MZ's rotary-valve two-stroke technology. From that point there was no stopping Suzuki, and Degner won the 50cc championship in 1962, while New Zealander Hugh Anderson took the 125cc title in 1963 and 1965. Up to the end of the decade, the 50cc series belonged to Suzuki, whose riders Anderson and Hans-Georg Anscheidt added four more titles.

Suzuki's road bike range had been essentially unsporting until 1966, when it released its first true sports machine, the T20 Super Six, known as the X6 in the USA. It was powered by an all-new 247cc

Right: Suzuki's two-stroke GT750J and GT750B triples inherited much of the company's racing heritage and created a big impact on the sports bike market.

Suzuki entered the Isle of Man TT races in 1960.

Racing didn't bring in money, however, so along with other Japanese makes, Suzuki built small commuter bikes. Typical were the K- and M-series two-stroke singles of the early 1960s, which were made in huge numbers. The K10 and K11 accounted for more than 500,000 units. One of the attractions of these machines was their oil-injection system, which negated the need for the rider to mix the fuel and oil himself, as was the case with other two-strokes such as Vespa and Lambretta. Suzukis had separate oil tanks that supplied lubricant via the CCI (Controlled Crankshaft Injection) system according to engine revs and throttle opening.

In 1964 the K- and M-series were replaced by the B100P, or 'Bloop', sufficiently popular to remain in production until the mid-1970s, when it was known as the B120 Student. The smaller A100 of 1967 endured into the 1980s. Other models from the

Powered by a 497cc Wankel rotary engine, the high-spec RE5 was introduced in 1974, but being different as well as thirsty, it was largely ignored by riders.

two-stroke twin fitted in a tubular steel frame, with alloy barrels and 24mm carburettors, and driving through a six-speed gearbox. The electric starter was omitted in order to save weight. The Super Six developed 29bhp and was capable of 145kph (90mph), setting new standards for the 250cc category. It did wonders for Suzuki's image on the export markets, and the company capitalised on its success by bringing out the T200 and 177kph (110mph) T500 Cobra – or Titan in the States – a year later. The

The DR350 of 1991 was Suzuki's mid-range dirt bike, and was a good compromise between on- and off-roader. It combined speed with lightness and agility.

T500 remained in production as the GT500 until 1977, by which time it came with a front disc brake and electronic ignition.

In 1972 the popular 500 twin was joined by a couple of two-stroke triples, the six-speed GT380 and GT550, together with the GT125 and GT185 twins, featuring 'Ram Air' cylinder cowling. The GT550 lasted until 1977 and the GT380 just two years more.

Suzuki's first real trail bike was the TS125 of 1971, a dual-purpose machine for on- and off-road use, which sired a family of TS trail bikes, including the TS50 and TS100 with rotary-valve induction, as well as the TS250, TS185 and TS400. The latter went out of production, but the smaller-capacity

The water-cooled disc-valve RG500 was first raced in 1974 by Barry Sheene, whose 1976 and 1977 championship-winning bike was run by the Texaco Heron team.

bikes were gradually upgraded during the 1980s and 1990s.

One of the range's key machines was the two-stroke GP100/125, which replaced the old B120 in 1978. Suzuki specialised in two-stroke engines, and these powered its 50 and 70cc step-through mopeds. At the other end of the scale, Suzuki sought a more fuel-efficient power unit than the air-cooled two-stroke for its bigger machines, such as the GT750 triple of 1971, known as the 'Kettle' in the UK and the 'Water Buffalo' in the USA, on account of its innovative water-jacket cooling system. In 1974 the firm tried a rotary engine in the flawed RE5, which proved to be heavier than the GT750 because of its water-cooling, and more thirsty yet less powerful. Four-stroke engines were the only other alternative, and during the second half of the decade, Suzuki replaced all its mid-range two-strokes with four-strokes. In 1976 it came out with the 68bhp GS750, which was a big air-cooled four-cylinder twin-cam machine, in a similar mould to products from Honda and Kawasaki, but somewhat quicker. It had a stiffer frame than the Honda and handled better. In 1977 Suzuki capitalised on the success

SPARTA
Netherlands 1931–: Sparta moved from bicycles into lightweights, initially (and to this day) with auxiliary cycle motors and later 49cc mopeds, but also until about 1960 Sachs, Villiers, Ilo and Victoria engines, from 100 to 250cc.

SPARTON
Wales (Caernarfon) 1976–unknown: These were limited production racers, four-cylinder four-strokes of 500 and 750cc, and two-strokes of 500 and 525cc, all water-cooled.

SPHINX
France 1933–39: This assembler used Stainless and other engines.

SPIEGLER
Germany (Aalen) 1923–32: The successor to Schwalbe, this firm made a pressed-steel box section, incorporating the tank, stretched from the steering head to the rear wheel: the rest of the frame was tubular. As well as their own engines, JAP and MAG were also used. All were singles; capacities varied from 200 to 600cc.

SPRITE
England 1965–unknown: These off-road two-stroke competition machines came in kit form, up to 400cc.

STADION
Czech Republic 1958–66: These mopeds were fitted with Jawa engines.

STANDARD
Germany and Switzerland 1925–52: Wilhelm Gutbrod founded Standard in Germany in 1925, but also bought Zehnder in Switzerland in 1929. After starting with JAP 250 and 350cc overhead-valve motors, Standard switched to MAG 350 to 1000cc engines of varying types. In 1930, Standard introduced their own 200 and 250cc engines.

STAR
England 1898–1914: Star were early motorcycle producers, first using De Dion-Bouton engines, and then JAP 625cc singles and 770cc V-twins.

STAR
Germany 1920–22: In-house 400cc flat twins powered these precursors of the D-Rad.

The RF series was available in 600 and 900cc format, and represented Suzuki's effort in the sports-tourer market. With 125bhp, it was very fast and good value, too.

were fitted with the new four-valve TSCC (Twin Swirl Combustion Chamber) cylinder head, which had a square-profile combustion chamber, configured to maximise swirl and improve combustion. The bikes came with telescopic forks and adjustable air damping, and a massive rectangular headlamp. The following year Suzuki introduced the Katana, fitted with low bars and small cockpit fairings, and available with a number of different four-cylinder 16-valve engines ranging from 250 to 1100cc.

The four-cylinder 550 engine was also given four valves per cylinder in 1983, increasing power to 65bhp, fitted in a new square-section alloy frame, with a half-fairing, monoshock rear suspension and anti-dive front forks. Four-valve heads were also fitted to twin-cylinder units. Reflecting other motor manufacturers, Suzuki came out with the XN85 Turbo, with a turbocharger fitted to the air-cooled four. The resulting 85bhp did not justify the additional complication.

Race replicas are nothing new, with Grand Prix copies going back to the earliest days of motorcycling. In the mid-1980s, however, Suzuki unveiled its road-going GSX-R series, which was very close to the works endurance racers of the early 1980s. Suzuki had already established a commendable racing record with the square-four RG500 in Grand Prix racing in the late 1970s and early 1980s with Barry Sheene, Keith Heuwen, Graeme Crosby

of the GS750 with the 997cc GS1000, the company's biggest bike so far. Developing 87bhp, it could hit 217kph (135mph), with adjustable suspension and handling to match. The GS sportsters were dropped in 1981 in favour of the four-valve GSX series, while the shaft-drive GS850 tourer was replaced by the GS1000G in 1980, and that by the 1100G in 1983.

Another of Suzuki's staples was a GS400 air-cooled two-valve twin with a gear-driven balancer-shaft, which spawned the GS425 in 1979, the GS450 in 1980 and the GS500 in 1989. They represented basic motorcycling, but were cheap and reliable with average performance. Suzuki's four-stroke trail bikes were led in 1984 by the DR600, running a twin-plug four-valve head, and producing 44bhp. By 1987 the DR750 was available, and this evolved into the 780cc DR800, which had the distinction of being the biggest single on the market. Bigger isn't always better off-road, and the DR350 released in 1991 was a handier size for mud-plugging, also being lighter and easier to recover if dropped in the dirt. The DR125 was even better in this respect. For basic road-going machines, Suzuki also offered the custom GN250/400 and GS125 commuter, as single-overhead-cam four-stroke singles.

Above: The Bandit 600 came out in 1995 and was an accessible all-rounder, powered by a de-tuned 80bhp GSXR600 oil-cooled four.

Right: The VS800 Intruder and VZ800 Marauder V-twins were Suzuki's rendition of the classic Harley and Indian look.

The GSX range that epitomised Suzuki's sports bikes was launched in 1980 with the 100bhp GSX1100 and 750 models. They

Launched in 1999, the SV650S V-twin was meant to replace the traditional-looking Bandit as Suzuki's new all-rounder. It was sold both half-faired and naked.

and Franco Uncini, and, later, Kevin Schwantz with the V4 RGV500. Suzuki's victory in the 1983 World Endurance Championship prefaced the launch of the GSX-R in September 1984. Now built around an aluminium beam frame, the GSX-R's lightweight four-cylinder engine was part air-cooled, part oil-cooled, the latter by means of an oil cooler and two oil pumps that doubled the flow rate, coating the underside of each piston crown with an oil jet. The disadvantage was a peaky power delivery that came in at 7000rpm, with peak torque at 10,000rpm. Revisions made it more rider-friendly, and by 1998 the 135bhp 750 was fuel-injected with water-cooling.

On its introduction, the GSX-R750 set new standards and established the race replica as a popular genre. It was a successful clubman's racer and, by fitting factory racing parts, it was competitive in Superbike and Superstock racing. It was followed by 250, 400 and 600cc versions, and although the smaller machines were retained by the restricted

Japanese market, the 600cc performed well in the European Supersports 600 category. At a more down-to-earth level were the GSX600F and 750 sports tourers, introduced in 1989 as competition for the Honda CBR600, and heavily revised in 1998.

The GSX-R1100 of 1987 was less highly strung than its 750 sibling, with a broader power

New for 1997 was the TL1000S, a 996cc 256kph (160mph) V-twin that developed a reputation for tank-slappers, which made it cheap on the secondhand market.

band, making it easier to cope with in everyday riding. It could also top 249kph (155mph). Image counts for a great deal in the marketplace; as the GSX-R's appeal was based on the endurance race bikes, so the RG250 imitated the V-twin two-stroke Grand Prix machines campaigned by the factory in 250 and 500 GP racing. In 1990 Suzuki introduced the 60bhp V-twin RGV250, which could do 217kph (135mph), and was about as close as you could get to a Grand Prix race bike.

In 1995 Suzuki introduced another machine that became a

The race-replica GSX-R1000 hyper-sports machine first appeared in 1986. With an alloy beam frame, the liquid-cooled four evolved from 1052cc to 1127cc.

bench-mark bike. This was the Bandit 600, an all-rounder running a detuned 80bhp version of the GSX-R600's oil-cooled engine, mounted in a tubular steel frame. It was neither retro nor cruiser, street-fighter or race replica, and had an upright riding position, with a half-faired option available. It therefore attracted customers from all areas, and was an instant best seller. The Bandit 1200 was also available in unfaired and half-faired formats. Late in 1999 Suzuki came up with its own lighter and more glamorous option to the Bandit 600: the SV650 V-twin, available either half-faired or unfaired.

All the Japanese manufacturers were in a position to challenge the smaller-volume European and US makers, and Suzuki issued the V-twin TL1000 in 1997 as a direct threat to Ducati. Powered by a 125bhp fuel-injected eight-valve twin-cam V-twin, the TL1000 was not only cheaper but also more user-friendly than a Ducati, yet more stimulating than Honda's VTR1000 Firestorm. Suzuki followed up with the more powerful TL1000R in 1998, as a basis for the company's V-twin Superbike.

By the late 1990s, the scooter market was burgeoning and along came a plethora of new models from a host of producers. Of

course, at this important point, Suzuki was right up there with the best of them.

In 1998 it announced the 250cc Burgman superscooter. Not content with such a relatively powerful commuter, the company

came out with the 400cc edition in 1999, which at the start of the new millennium was the largest scooter available, offering commuters 161kph (100mph) performance. Capable of going almost twice as fast was the 173bhp GSX1300R

Hayabusa – a supersports machine named after a Japanese falcon, launched the same year – it could clear 0–97kph (0–60mph) in 2.75 seconds, steaming on to reach a high 225kph (140mph) in 10 seconds.

SUZUKI T20 SUPER SIX
1966

The T20 Super Six was launched in 1966 and placed Suzuki well and truly on the map as an international player.

Known as the X6 in the USA, the Super Six was powered by a 250cc air-cooled two-stroke parallel-twin, allied to a six-speed gearbox, from whence came its name. The engine incorporated a sophisticated Posi-Force lubrication system, and developed 29bhp at 7500rpm, making it good for 153kph (95mph).

The slant-forward power unit was mounted in Suzuki's first dual cradle frame, with coil-over telescopic dampers and big drum brakes, endowing the model with good handling and light weight.

Cosmetically, it was just right, with chromed tank sides and silencers and two-tone mudguards, although the headlight design was somewhat quirky. Curiously, Suzuki supplied a bike pump to inflate the tyres.

Engine: two-stroke parallel-twin, air-cooled
Power: 29bhp at 7500rpm
Gearbox: 6-speed foot change
Final drive: chain
Weight: 138kg (304lb)
Top speed: 153kph (95mph)

The 144kph (90mph) T20 Super Six, or X6 as it was known in the US, was Suzuki's first true sports bike. It featured a tubular steel frame and a new 247cc engine.

SUZUKI GS1000   1978

Introduced in 1978, the GS1000 was capable of outperforming even Kawasaki's already legendary Z1. It thus set new standards for sports bikes of the period, owing to its exceptional handling and powerful 997cc four-cylinder engine, whose specification included twin overhead-cams and four valves per cylinder. It was based on a sturdy tubular-steel cradle frame, with adjustable suspension and twin front disc brakes, running on alloy wheels with ample-sized tyres. The GS1000 proved comfortable and reliable, stable at high speed in a straight line and relatively agile in corners. The straightish handlebars required more of an arms-forward posture than other machines, and styling was unremarkable, despite the chromed megaphone exhausts. Only marginally slower was the model's 750cc sibling, the GS750

Below: The GS1000 was powered by a 997cc air-cooled, eight-valve, twin-cam four, mounted transversely in the tubular frame – already proven by Kawasaki.

Above: Released in 1978, the GS1000 was Suzuki's biggest ever offering, and proved that big-engined Japanese bikes could handle well.

Four, introduced a year earlier and capable of 201kph (125mph), with a realistic 145kph (90mph) cruising speed, if given a moth screen to improve aerodynamics. In race trim, with cockpit fairing, a Suzuki GS1000 with Yoshimura tuning took Wes Cooley to the 1980 US Superbike title.

Engine: 997cc 8-valve dohc transverse-mounted four-cylinder, 70x64.8mm, air-cooled
Power: 87bhp at 8000rpm
Gearbox: 5-speed
Final drive: chain
Weight: 241kg (531lb)
Top speed: 217kph (135mph)

SUZUKI GSX-R750   1985

The GSX-R750 – with the emphasis on the R for 'Race' – was unleashed in 1985, and promptly fostered a generation of race-replica bikes. Many riders wish to emulate their racing heroes to a certain extent, and the GSX-R750 was a close approximation of the works endurance bikes from the early 1980s; these had been highly

successful under team leader Hervé Moineau.
Devastatingly fast, with handling to match, the GSX-R750 outperformed all other mass-produced machines, thanks to a specification orientated for high-speed riding.
The powerplant was the 16-valve oil-cooled twin-cam four,

which had a magnesium cam-cover and developed 100bhp at 10,500rpm. It delivered most of its power above 7000rpm, giving a theoretical top speed of 233kph (145mph). The motor was housed in a new aluminium perimeter frame that weighed half that of the old GSX750, and the front end consisted of a pair of stout 41mm

STUCCHI
Italy 1901–27: See **PRINETTI & STUCCHI**.

STURM
Germany 1923–25: More of a light shower than a full-blown storm, these were Alba-powered 150cc two-strokes.

STYLSON
France 1919–39: This idiosyncratic assembler used JAP (and Staub-built JAP-licensed) engines up to 1000cc. Some were shaft drive; some had transverse-mounted V-twin engines.

STYRIA
Austria 1905–08: Fafnir singles and V-twins powered these pioneers.

SUBLIME
France 1954: This was a 350cc pushrod twin with four-speed box and telescopic forks that was reasonably up-to-the-minute.

SUDBRACK
Germany 1949–51: Ilo engines were used by this bicycle factory to make 98 and 123cc lightweights.

SUECIA
Sweden 1928–40: JAP engines of 250, 350 and 500cc powered these assembled machines. Two-strokes built by Sparta were also sold as Sucias.

SULKY
France 1954–57: These were mini-scooters with AMC (France) engines of 100 to 125cc.

SUMITA
Japan 1951–55: In the usual Japanese style, these machines had in-house 125 and 150cc overhead-valve engines.

SUPERBA
Italy 1928–35: JAP and Piazza engines, both 175cc, powered these sporting lightweights.

SUPERB-FOUR
England 1920–21: This was a longitudinally mounted overhead-cam straight four of 1000cc made, sadly, in very small numbers.

SUPERIA
Germany 1925–28: These sporting machines were mostly overhead-cam Kuchen-powered with 350 and 500cc engines, plus a few 500cc ECE side-valve machines.

(1.6ins) diameter forks, containing a pair of drilled disc brakes. Much of the bike was concealed by a race-derived fairing, fronted by a pair of headlights and emblazoned with the Suzuki nomenclature.

The road-going machine was equipped with a comfortable pillion saddle, and the four-into-one perforated silencer was set lower than the racer's.

Over the succeeding years, the chassis was refined to give the GSX-R750 even better handling, and in 1992 it was fitted with a water-cooled 116bhp engine in a stiffer frame with upside-down forks and sleeker fairings.

The first true Japanese race-replica, the GSX-R750, was launched in 1985. It developed cult status.

Although there were few components in common with the original model, the GSX-R750 remained essentially the same in spirit.

Engine: 749cc 16-valve dohc transverse four, 70x48.7mm, oil-cooled (later water)
Power: 100bhp at 10,500rpm
Gearbox: 5-speed foot change
Final drive: chain
Weight: 176kg (388lb)
Top speed: 233kph (145mph)

SUZUKI GSX1300R HAYABUSA
1999

The distinctive but bulky looks of the Suzuki GSX1300R Hayabusa belied its potential as the fastest road-going bike on its debut in 1999. Sensationally, it was suggested that the magic 'double ton', 322kph (200mph), would be possible to achieve on this machine. Under the right circumstances, road-testers showed that it was.

The Hayabusa was powered by a 1299cc transverse four-cylinder motor with 16 valves, developing 173bhp. Engine timing was by eight 'trigger poles' at the end of the crank, doubling the number found on the 750. The water-

cooled engine was based on Suzuki's latest 750 range rather than the outdated 1100. Fuel injection was controlled by maps individual to each cylinder, improving the balance between each cylinder and making cold starts and high temperatures less power-sapping. A computer-activated flapper valve in the air box monitored the air flow through the rev-range, shutting at under 4000rpm and reducing air intake; above 4000rpm it was wide open, giving maximum air flow.

Like the GSX-R750, the Hayabusa made use of SRAD

(Suzuki Ram Air Direct) to boost top-end power. The narrow, stacked headlight allowed the top fairing air intakes to be placed as close to the centre line of the bike as possible, in order to pass the greatest volume of air through. At the other end of the combustion cycle, to cope with emission laws, the model carried twin catalysts in the main pipework just ahead of

In 1999, the fastest bike on the road was the GSX 1300R Hayabusa, named after a falcon that could reach 320kph (200mph) in a dive. The bike could do it on the level.

the cams, and PAIR (Pulsed-secondary AIR), which introduced air downstream of the exhaust valves, diluting the unburned hydrocarbons and carbon monoxide.

The Hayabusa was based on a twin-spar aluminium frame, with fully adjustable inverted 43mm (1.7ins) front suspension and progressive monoshock at the rear. Suzuki claimed 15 per cent higher rigidity in both frame and swing-arm for the Hayabusa over the GSX-R750. Bridgestone extended its BT56 range to suit the Hayabusa, having submitted 15 different combinations of tyre, based on the 190 rear. Suzuki engineers favoured the BT56 type J, which became the only recommended tyre for this bike. Its actual width is 198mm (7.8ins) with a more shallow crown radius, and in 1999 it had the distinction of being the flattest, fattest rear tyre yet seen.

To achieve the goal of a potential 322kph (200mph) top speed, aerodynamics were a principal consideration. The machine had to be able to slice cleanly through the air, hence the sculptured bodywork. Suzuki engineers used their wind tunnel to define the most 'slippery' shape, and the front mudguard was critical for initial penetration. With its deep sides, the mudguard channelled the passing air onto the fairing sides, which stretched as far forward as possible to keep air moving to the back of the bike. The belly-pan extended up to the rear wheel to clear the air flow under the bike, while the top fairing benefited from the shaped

headlight, and even the mirror backs were contoured for maximum slice. The Hayabusa's fairings culminated in a TL1000R-style hump at the rear, although it failed to offer similar storage potential as the twin. Suzuki didn't classify the GSX1300R Hayabusa as a true 'R' model, which was why the 'R' was placed only at the end of the bike's designation. It was also the reason why the traditional GSX-R blue-and-white paintwork was absent.

Engine: 1299cc 16-valve transverse four, 81x63mm, liquid-cooled
Power: 173bhp at 9800rpm
Gearbox: 6-speed
Final drive: chain
Weight: 215kg (474lb)
Top speed: 322kph (200mph) est.

SWM

ITALY 1971–85

SWM (SPEEDY WORKING MOTORS) was one of the real commercial and sales success stories of the Italian motorcycle industry during the 1970s, but its life at the top was relatively short. Founded by Pietro Sironi, SWM built a series of extremely competitive off-road machines for both motocross racing and enduro use. Many of the latter were also bought by style-conscious (and affluent!) Italian teenagers during the mid- to late 1970s, when the enduro bike was viewed as an icon of its era. Together with the Austrian KTM, SWM was one of the few motorcycles to win gold medals in the ISDT (International Six Days' Trial) and also to be seen on the street.

Using either German Sachs or Austrian Rotax power units (when the vast majority of other Italian

SWM (meaning Speedy Working Motors) was founded in 1971 by Pietro Sironi. A 125TC trials model dating from 1978 is shown here.

marques bought their engines from domestic suppliers such as Minerelli, Franco Morini or Hiro), SWM grew rapidly. In fact, this growth was to be the very reason for the company's problems in later years.

In 1980 SWM's purchase of the rival Gori concern led to an overcapacity in the dirt-bike market. When a major sales recession occurred in 1981 and 1982, the firm was left dangerously exposed.

Left with mounting debts, SWM president Pietro Sironi was forced to close the business in 1985. He re-formed the company under the SVM title that same year, but it had foundered by 1987.

Besides enduro and trials models, SWM also built motocross racers, such as this 1977 RS250MC, powered by a 247cc single-cylinder Rotax two-stroke engine.

TAURUS

ITALY 1933–66

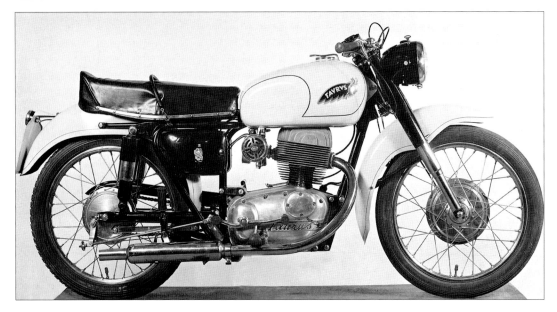

Aermacchi, Ducati and MV Agusta).

The firm realised that it needed more modern designs, and the mid-1950s saw a brand-new overhead-valve 250cc single. This featured full unit construction of the engine and transmission and also telescopic front forks and swinging-arm rear suspension with twin shock absorbers.

Nevertheless, compared with its rivals, the new Taurus seemed solid and staid rather than swift and stunning. Clearly, it was a machine for the commuter rather than the sports enthusiast. This lack of sporting pretence affected sales; although the company clung on until 1966, it didn't make the sales breakthrough it needed to survive in the longer term.

DURING ITS 33-YEAR existence, Taurus built a number of different models powered by two-stroke and four-stroke engines. In 1938 it also constructed a superbly engineered 499.34cc (85x88mm) double overhead-camshaft single. Solely for racing use, this machine could with more development have posed a real threat to the larger manufacturers such as Bianchi, Gilera and Moto Guzzi. But lack of funds and the outbreak of World War II conspired to seal its fate.

Taurus struggled to get back on its feet when the conflict was over; by the late 1940s full production had been resumed. In fact, in those

Above: The mid-1950s saw a new Taurus ohv 250cc single. This not only featured a unit construction engine, but telescopic forks.

Right: Taurus began making motorcycles in 1933. Its logo was often written in the Roman style as 'Tavrvs'.

immediate postwar years it was very much a seller's market. However, there were still problems, including a shortage of components needed to meet production demands, and the sheer number of new companies entering the market (among them

TERROT

FRANCE 1902–61

CHARLES TERROT BUILT TRICYCLES and quads powered by De Dion engines before building his first motorcycle in 1902, using a Swiss Zedel engine with the cylinder inclined forward but its fins parallel to the ground, a style he was to use for some years. A side-valve V-twin followed, in which the rear cylinder was vertical and the front inclined forward with the same arrangement of fins as for the single. Both models featured belt drive and a rocking front fork, while later machines had a three-speed rear hub gear.

After World War I, Terrot's company produced a two-stroke range using its own inclined

engine with a large external flywheel, and four-strokes with side- and overhead-valve JAP and Blackburne engines. All models eventually had three speeds, and by the late 1920s sported saddle tanks and girder forks. They had more of a British character during that period, albeit enhanced by French chic and flair, which was reflected in design details such as the silencer, headlamp shell, mudguard line and (sometimes)

Terrot ran in the Isle of Man TT during the late 1930s using their ohv singles. Manuel Simo from Spain is seen here about to start the 1936 Lightweight race.

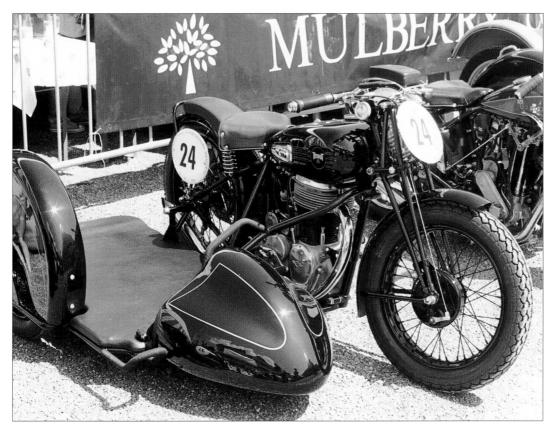

enclosure of the gearbox area from the engine back to the rear mudguard.

In the 1930s Terrot added its own unit-construction engines, with the gearbox in a cylindrical shell within a rear extension of the crankcase, this being rotated for chain adjustment. For the new line, the valvegear was fully enclosed (the overhead-valve engines having a hemispherical combustion chamber), and the generator was chain-driven from the left-hand end of the crankshaft and located behind the cylinder, while the ignition points were in the timing chest. A 100cc velomoteur appeared in 1932, the same year as a 680cc side-valve V-twin, and this stretched to 750cc in 1934. By the end of the 1930s, the range included small two-strokes,

side-valve or overhead-valve models from 175 to 500cc, plus the 750cc V-twin.

There was also a line of racing models with overhead-valve engines of 175, 250, 350 and 500cc. All were rather similar and each were fitted with Amal carburettor and magneto ignition. These motorcycles had a four-speed gearbox and used a rigid frame with side-spring girder forks.

After World War II, Terrot continued with the 100cc two-stroke and a neat 125cc overhead-valve model with a unit-construction four-speed gearbox. A scooter was added in 1951; this had a 98cc engine and a bulbous body that called to mind an American car design. It was usually finished in two-tone

A 1939 French Terrot with a racing sidecar attached. The machine was powered by a single-cylinder ohv engine.

colours and had both front and rear suspension forks enclosed. The original engine drove a two-speed gearbox, but later examples were 125cc and three-speed; these machines led to the Scooterrot, which had a pre-selector gearbox.

The larger singles continued with telescopic forks and plunger rear suspension, later replaced by a pivoted-fork system. Talbot's line included the unit 500 overhead-valve, which ran on to the late 1950s, while the 125 was joined by an appealing 175. In 1954 the firm joined Peugeot, and Terrot production ceased in 1961.

TESTI

ITALY 1951–83

UNTIL IT WAS STRUCK DOWN by the motorcycle sales recession of the early 1980s, Testi had enjoyed considerable success for over 30 years in the fiercely competitive ultra-lightweight motorcycle and moped market. The Bologna-based company used a variety of bought-in engines from Sachs, Franco

Morini and Minerelli. Testi's best-known models included the Trail King, the 125cc Minerelli-engined Corsa 2000 and the ultimate sports moped, the Champion Special P6.

But the most interesting Testi was certainly the eight-speed Militar. A full-blown military motorcycle with a fan-cooled

49.6cc (38.8x42mm) Minerelli engine, its accessory list included a ski attachment, gun-holder (in civilian use a fishing-rod attachment) foglamp, and even a bottle for fast inflation and repair of damaged tyres! The Militar was used by both the Italian and Finnish armies.

The 1980 model line was Testi's most comprehensive ever, with 10 machines, all using 50cc-class powerplants. In addition to the Militar and Champion Special, there were the Monocross P6 (trial bike), Monocross Corsa CR (motocross), Monocross Regolarita (enduro), Amico (scooter), Pull (small-wheeled moped), Cricket (de luxe moped), Mini Cricket (moped), Comfort (three-speed moped) and OKS V1 (commuter moped). The most powerful was the 15bhp Monocross Corsa CR, which needed a road-racer riding style to keep within the power band. Testis were sold under the Horex name in West Germany by the Roth organisation, and in the UK by the Mick Walker Group.

Testi's Executive Cross enduro from 1974 was equipped with a bought-in 125cc Minerelli single-cylinder two-stroke engine.

THOR

USA 1903–15

THE THOR WAS PRODUCED by the Aurora Automatic Machinery Company of Aurora, Illinois, whose motorcycle involvement began in 1902 when it started supplying Indian with engines. This contract allowed the firm to supply other companies with the same engine, which led to a number of Indian clones appearing, all using the Aurora engine and including a Thor in 1903. Among the others were Manson, Moto-Racycle, Rambler, Reading-Standard and Warwick. The deal with Indian lasted to 1907, and Aurora continued supplying engines to others for another year or two.

The first Thor was simply an Indian clone with the F-head engine, with an automatic inlet valve, inclined back to act as part of the seat tube but located above the bottom bracket that housed the pedalling gear, with its chain on the right. An intermediate dual sprocket went on the left; this was chain-driven from the engine with another chain from a small sprocket to the rear wheel, which gave the machine all-chain drive in two stages. As usual, the camel-backed tank carrying both petrol and oil was fitted on the rear mudguard and the diamond frame had rigid forks.

For 1909 Thor set the unaltered engine upright and installed it in a loop frame with sprung forks, and changed to direct chain drive to the rear wheel. That year also saw the introduction of a Thor V-twin that had one vertical cylinder and the second inclined forward by 45 degrees. The twin magneto sat at the same angle on the rear of the crankcase, while the carburettor went behind the rear cylinder. From there, a long inlet pipe ran to a manifold located between the cylinders to serve them both. This model also had the same loop frame and sprung forks.

Mechanical overhead inlet valves went into the V-twin in 1911, lifted by pushrods curved to clear the cylinder fins, and the carburettor was moved to a much better position between the cylinders. The twin was further revised for 1912, when the engine was tilted back so that the cylinders inclined fore and aft in

The V-twin Thor from 1913, by which time it was well-established and no longer had the vertical rear cylinder. A fine make but only built until 1915.

the usual (and much more pleasing) manner, while the pushrods became straight.

At the same time, the magneto was moved to the front of the crankcase and the entire timing side was cleaned up and better styled. In 1914 the twin's capacity was increased from 1000cc (61cid) to 1245cc (76cid). However, motorcycle production ceased in 1915 as the firm decided to concentrated from that year on other products.

Aurora engines bore many names cast into the crankcase, including their own or the name Thor, and sometimes (but not always) that of the user marque, with numerous variations appearing over the years.

TOHATSU

JAPAN 1949–64

THIS COMPANY CAN TRACE its history back to 1922, when the Takata Motor Institute began carrying out research into various forms of internal-combustion engines. Throughout the inter-war years the business continued to expand, and in May 1939 it was renamed Tokyo Hatsudoki – or Tohatsu for short. During the war years, the company was a major supplier of generator sets to the Japanese armed forces, and it survived the conflict with both its Tokyo and Osaka works intact.

Production after the war was to centre around fire pumps and motorcycles, the latter marketed under the Tohatsu brand name. By 1957 there was a four-model line-up of street bikes with engine sizes of 86, 123 and 199cc, all piston-port two-stroke singles.

Sales grew, until in 1961 Tohatsu claimed some three per cent of the vast Japanese domestic market. But the company realised that to make further progress, it would have to follow Honda and build competition bikes.

That year's Tokyo Show saw the first of Tohatsu's efforts: a couple of motocrossers (125 and 250cc) and an entirely new 50cc road racer. The latter machine, the Runpet CR50, was a single-cylinder two-stroke producing almost 7bhp at 12,000rpm. Other details included a close-ratio four-speed gearbox, a beam-type frame and telescopic front forks. Tohatsu engineers had also been busy developing a 124cc (43x43mm) twin-cylinder model with five speeds. Its maximum speed was around 145kph (90mph).

This work led to the definitive racing Tohatsu models: a 49.8cc (31x33mm) twin and a completely revamped 125. The latter machine was

The definitive racing Tohatsu was this 49.8cc (31x33mm) twin – the only twin-cylinder machine of its size ever offered for general sale.

Tohatsu (Tokyo Hatsudoki) built a series of high performance road and racing bikes. The 1962 50cc Runpet Sport produced 6.8bhp at 10,800rpm.

notable because of its unusual three-piece, vertically split crankcases, which allowed owners to strip and rebuild the engine with a bare minimum of tools.

The engine's unique construction was matched by the innovative chassis. While other Japanese manufacturers, such as Suzuki and Yamaha, produced simple top-tube frames, Tohatsu created a neatly crafted twin-duplex affair which provided superb roadholding. In fact, for many years after the original engine was no longer competitive, Tohatsu cycle parts were used to house other powerplants, a trend that continued well into the 1970s. Resembling its larger brother, the Tohatsu 50 was the only twin-cylinder machine of its displacement ever to be offered to private buyers.

Future world champion (in 1969, riding a Kawasaki 125cc) Dave Simmonds was probably the most famous Tohatsu rider, scoring many victories on both the 50 and 125cc twins.

At the 1963 Japanese Grand Prix, Tohatsu announced that it

TECO
Germany (Stettin) 1920–26: Based in the 'Polish Corridor' this Polish manufacturer of Alba-powered 200cc lightweights also offered a Kuhne-powered 350cc single.

TEDDY
France 1922–24: A 203cc side-valve engine, apparently of their own manufacture, powered these lightweight machines.

TEE-BEE
England 1908–11: This company apparently used their own engines as well as 300cc JAPs.

TEHUELCHE
Argentina (Santa Fe) 1958–62: These small machines – initially 75cc, later 100cc – had overhead-cam engines.

TEMPLE
England 1924–28: Claude Temple, record-breaker, racer and tuner, lent his name to these machines from the OEC stable, mostly 350 and 500cc singles, but also 1000cc Anzani V-twins.

TEMPO
Norway 1949–: There mopeds of 49cc and lightweights of 123cc had a range of bought-in two-stroke motors.

TERRA
Germany 1922–24: Simple three-port two-strokes, Terra's in-house engines were 125, 150 and 175cc.

TERROT
Czechoslovakia 1933–35: This short-lived subsidiary of the French company built 350cc singles.

TETGE
Germany 1923–26: These firm made MAG 600cc V-twins at the top of the line, and 150 and 175cc singles for everyday fare.

was considering backing a factory team (which was headed by Simmonds) in the 1964 European Grand season. Unfortunately, this idea would remain only a dream, as in subsequent months, Tohatsu was to find itself struggling from yet one financial crisis to another.

Finally, in February 1964, the company (or at least its motorcycle division) went into liquidation. All the remaining racers – including spares, jigs and tools – were purchased by John Honda (no relation to the other Mr Honda), who then set up Japan

Racing Motor Cycles. The manufacture of the Tohatsu standard production roadsters was never resumed, although rumour had it that the rights to produce the 1964 model line were to be sold to the nationalist Chinese Government in Formosa (now Taiwan).

Meanwhile, after the factory had finally closed, almost all Tohatsu's engineering staff moved to the rival company Bridgestone, whose subsequent models benefitted from technology that had been developed in the Tohatsu factory.

TOMOS

YUGOSLAVIA 1954–95

BASED IN THE SMALL fishing town of Koper (now in Slovenia) south of Trieste on the Adriatic coast, the state-owned Tomos concern built its business on the manufacture, under licence agreements, of Puch machines from Austria and automobiles from Citroen of France.

Tomos first sprang to the notice of foreigners when, in 1961, the FIM staged the Coupe d'Europe (European Cup) championship series for 50cc racing motorcycles. This was to serve as a forerunner

The Tomos 90 Electronic of the late 1970s used a Puch-derivative, single-cylinder, two-stroke engine, Italian Grimeca brakes and full cradle frame.

to full world championship status for the class, achieved the following year. A total of eight race organisers ran rounds for the Coupe d'Europe during 1961: three in Belgium, two in Germany and one each in the Netherlands, Spain and Yugoslavia. Kreidler

and Tomos were favourites for the title. Kreidler and its star rider Hans-Georg Anscheidt emerged as champions, but the Yugoslav team put up a tremendous performance, including winning on the Germans' home ground at the ultra-fast Hockenheim circuit.

For 1962, and a full tilt at world championship honours, Tomos engineers created something quite different. Coded D7-62 (for seven-speed, 1962), the machine had an

One of the 50cc Tomos racing motorcycles with which the Yugoslav factory contested the 1966 Coupe D'Europe championship.

entirely new engine with a vertical cylinder and the unusual feature of a piston with no rings. Although this particular design proved a flop, Tomos developed its earlier work and competed successfully in the 50cc racing class until the category's demise in the early 1980s. The last European champion, Zdravko Matulja, rode a Tomos to victory in 1982.

For many years, Tomos had a division in the Netherlands (its best export market), from whence it distributed its production mopeds in Europe, including the UK, but the struggle for independence in the former Yugoslavia sealed Tomos's fate in the mid-1990s.

TORNAX

GERMANY 1922–55 AND 1982–84

TORNAX BUILT UP AN ENVIABLE reputation in the years preceding the outbreak of World War II as makers of quality motorcycles, using JAP and Columbus (Horex) engines. The Wuppertal-Langerfeld concern also designed and built a small sports car that was sold from 1934 to 1936, with a three-cylinder DKW two-stroke engine.

Following the war, production did not resume until 1948, when the company was reorganised by its new owner, Ernst Wewer. In

that year, the first of an entirely new breed of Tornax models made their debut, powered by 125 and 175cc Ilo single-cylinder two-stroke engines.

Unlike any of their contemporaries, these bikes had an air of glamour rather than of

Reformed after World War II by Ernst Wewer, the famous Tornax marque offered a range of models, including this 1954 175cc, twin-port, two-stroke single.

During the 1980s, the revived Tornax marque built a range of small two-strokes, such as this RX80 trail bike, powered by a 79.81cc six-speed engine.

austerity. Both models sold well, not just in the home market, but also in Belgium and the Netherlands. But by 1952 the management had become aware that the prevailing seller's market was almost over, and that the firm was under increasing threat.

An intensive and expensive development programme produced new 200 and 250cc Ilo-engined machines (the larger model being a parallel-twin). However, the star model – and the one that had swallowed up most of the investment – was a 250cc four-stroke twin, with pushrod-operated valves.

Unfortunately, although this latter bike sold reasonably well,

Tornax was still unable to recoup the high development costs. This led to a cash-flow crisis and, together with the Hoffman marque, Tornax became an early casualty of the recession that was to decimate the German motorcycle industry. The company

shut down in 1955. Almost three decades later, the name was briefly revived on a range of 50 and 80cc machines using Italian components, including Minerelli engines. This line was launched in 1982, but two years later it, too, was a memory.

TRITON ENGLAND 1952–

TRITON WASN'T A MAKE. Or rather, it was, but made by hundreds, maybe even thousands of different manufacturers, usually young men working in garden sheds or spare rooms. The premise was simple. Norton's Featherbed frame, designed by the McCandless brothers, was not only the most comfortable frame on the market, but also had the sweetest handling,

and it was used for the vast majority of Nortons, including some that were fairly sluggish.

Triumph's frame wasn't a patch on the Featherbed, but its 500cc parallel-twin was affordable and an exceedingly fine motor in its own right – better than most of the Norton line-up, with the exception, of course, of the Manx. For that matter, even the Manx sometimes

Alloy tank, bum-stop seat, no surplus weight: the Triton, with its Featherbed frame and Triumph engine, was very much a motorcycle for the purist.

provided 'donor' frames, because Norton would not sell Manx engines to just anyone who wanted to build, for example, a single-seat four-wheeled racer. Customers had

TGR
Italy (Bologna) 1980s: This electric moped with 60 Amp-hour batteries had a top speed of 30kph (20mph).

THIEM
USA (St Paul, Minnesota) 1903–14: These typical US singles (550cc inlet-over-exhaust) and V-twins (900 and 1000cc) came from that brief era when US motorcycle design led the world.

THEIN & GOLDBERGER
Austria 1903–05: These were typical pioneers with Fafnir and Minerva engines of two-and-a-quarter to 3hp.

THOMANN
France 1912–39: This was part of the Alcyon group, which built two-stroke machines of 100 to 250cc.

THOMAS
England 1904: The usual pioneering bought-in engines – Minerva, Sarolea, maybe others – powered these rare machines.

THOMAS
USA 1907–08: The Thomas automobile works built 3hp singles with their own in-house engines.

THOROUGH
England 1903: MMC and Coronet engines powered these assembled pioneers.

THREE-SPIRES
England (Coventry) 1931–32: The three spires is a common Coventry logo: these lightweights had a 147cc two-stroke engine, priced at the time at eighteen guineas (£18 and 18 shillings).

THUMANN
Germany (Hanover) 1925–26: In-house 250 and 350cc side-valves powered the products of this small factory.

THUNDER
Italy 1952–54: Offering more of a loud buzz than rolling thunder, nevertheless this was a well-made, fast, and overly expensive 125cc overhead-valve parallel twin.

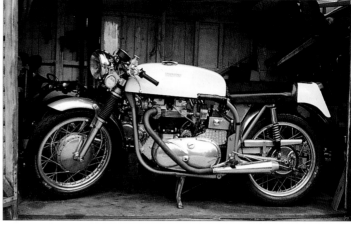

to buy whole bikes, and then dispose of the frames.

Add to this the almost inevitable combinations of blown-up engines and bent frames – a spare engine from a bent frame, a spare frame from a blown-up engine – and there was the possibility of building a fast, smooth and fine-handling motorcycle. The Triton was born: TRIumph, norTON.

There were very nearly as many Triton specifications as there were Tritons. As well as being a blend of Triumph and Norton components, the machines incorporated all sorts of other parts – depending on what came with the donors, what the builder had lying around (or could scrounge from his friends), or what he could afford in the way of after-market parts, such as light-alloy mudguards, clip-on handlebars, rear sets and seats (although many Tritons had home-made seats tolerable only by fit young men who cared more about speed than anything else).

Silencers were as close to straight-through as the local police

The Isle of Man, and a lap or two of the famous circuit on a Triton during the free-for-all 'Mad Sunday': motorcycling heaven.

would allow (assuming they could catch the Triton rider, of course). Engines were normally 'breathed on' to a greater or lesser extent, and 'added lightness' was the order of the day, with extraneous items omitted. Everything possible was drilled, often overzealously – more than one kick-start broke from being too enthusiastically lightened – though the true aficionado might well eschew the kick-starter altogether.

Numerous freelance interpretations of a Triton logo existed but the ultimate Tritons had no logos, just bare, light-alloy racing tanks.

preferring a racing push-start. Brakes ranged from the terrifyingly inadequate to full-house twin-leading-shoe racing kit.

The natural habitat of the Triton was London's North Circular road, and (above all) the Ace Café, the premier hang-out for what came to be known as 'café racers' in the days when riders genuinely did race one another from café to café. Tritons did not, by modern standards, have a very high top speed, and besides, in those pre-motorway days, there were relatively few public roads on

If you cross a Triumph and a Norton you get a Triton; but mercifully, a Thunderbird engine in a Featherbed frame, as here, is not a Thunderbed.

which there was room to achieve the magic 'ton' – 161kph (100mph) – even at five o'clock on a summer's morning when there was no other traffic about. Nevertheless, the bikes were superb 'scratchers', and probably the best-handling home-made machine ever built in such a piecemeal fashion.

Other motorcycles were constructed from a similarly odd medley of parts, but only the Triton really warrants the dignity of being described as a marque in its own right, on the grounds of quality and quantity. Magnificent a Norvin may have been, with its (slightly hacked about) Vincent motor in a Norton frame, but there were not many of them. Tritons were another matter; and even today, there are still young men who come across an old Triumph engine and an old Norton frame, and build a brand-new Triton.

TRIUMPH

ENGLAND 1885–

TRIUMPH'S EXTENSIVE HISTORY divides neatly into four main periods. The first was under the company's founder Siegfried Bettmann, and lasted from 1885 to 1936. This was followed by Edward Turner's reign (1936–73). Then came the brief NVT Norton-Villiers-Triumph phase, leading to the formation of the Meriden Workers' Co-operative, which endured between 1973 and 1984. The renaissance of the modern company under John Bloor's ownership began in 1990, with

state-of-the-art machines rolling off the Hinckley production line.

Back in 1883, Siegfried Bettmann arrived in Coventry from Nuremberg, Germany, and together with partner Mauritz Schulte was soon making Triumph bicycles at his Much Park Street factory. Triumph produced its first motorcycle in 1902, a strengthened cycle frame powered by a Belgian 239cc Minerva engine. Power output was two-and-a-quarter brake horsepower at 1500rpm, and its top speed was 40kph (25mph).

Triumph also used British-made JAP and Fafnir engines.

By 1906 Triumph had relocated to its new Priory Street premises. The machines they produced were still based on an uprated bicycle frame with direct belt drive from a 3hp single-cylinder side-valve 363cc unit. In 1907 Jack Marshall took second place on his three-and-a-half horsepower Triumph behind Charlie Collier's Matchless in the single-cylinder class of the very first Isle of Man TT. Marshall won the class in 1908, setting

fastest lap at 68.36kph (42.48mph). Other Triumph riders came in third, fourth, fifth, seventh and 10th, prompting the company to offer a TT Racer in its 1911 catalogue. That year saw the introduction of the 499cc Hub Clutch model; bump-starts were no longer necessary. The front forks incorporated Triumph's unique rocking-spring system, hinged at the base of the headset and controlled by a horizontal spring fitted on the handlebar stem.

In 1914, when World War I broke out, the War Office commissioned Triumph to supply 100 motorcycles for army use, and around 30,000 Triumph motorcycles went into service during the war. These were mostly 4hp belt-drive Type H models, known as 'Trusty Triumphs', powered by the standard 550cc side-valve engine with a three-speed Sturmey-Archer gearbox and chain primary drive.

Triumph's post-war five-and-a-half horsepower Type SD model was not that different from the 550cc Model H, although belt drive was replaced by an all-chain system, supplemented by spring drive or 'SD', a transmission shock absorber incorporated in the clutch to provide a smoother drive. Pedals were by now banished, and a kick-starter was fitted.

In 1922 Triumph released the 499cc Type IR Fast Roadster or 'Riccy', designed by engine specialists Ricardo & Co; its advanced specification featured a four-valve head and an aluminium piston. Power output was 20bhp, making a top speed of 121kph (75mph) possible. In 1923 the cycle-producing side of the firm was sold to Coventry Cycles, and Triumph went into car production

The Tiger 100, launched in 1939, used the Speed Twin frame fitted with a tuned parallel-twin engine to give smooth acceleration and good performance.

Like every other pioneering manufacturer, Triumph's early products – like this 1903 Minerva-powered machine – relied on strengthened cycle frames.

with the 10/20hp Super Seven light car, a direct rival to the Austin 7. Production rose to around 1000 motorcycles a week, and the all-new 500cc Type TT topped the range in 1927, its engine designed by Brooklands racer and Triumph dealer Victor Horsman. By now, the motorcycle was starting to look more like the modern machine rather than a motorised bicycle.

As the worldwide Depression in the 1930s put sales in decline, Triumph recruited noted engine designer Valentine 'Val' Page from

Ariel to design a completely new range, including 250, 350 and 500cc overhead-valve singles, 350 and 550cc side-valve singles, a 650cc overhead-valve vertical twin, and a 147cc overhead-valve lightweight. These were fitted with four-speed gearboxes. The 500cc model came in three different guises, designated the 5/2, 5/5 and 5/10 racing bike. The 6/1 pushrod 650cc vertical twin was a sturdy bike, with a heavy-duty duplex cradle-frame chassis, girder front forks and a substantial pair of mudguards. In 1933 it won the prestigious Maude's Trophy for completing the ISDT (International Six Days' Trial) – with sidecar attached.

Col Claude Holbrook took over from Siegfried Bettmann as

TICKLE
England 1967–73: John Tickle bought the right to make Manx Nortons after they were discontinued by Norton.

TIGER
1903–14: These were uncannily reminiscent of Allright and Vindec machines of the same period.

TIGER
USA (Chicago, Illinois) 1915–16: Unusually for the US, this was a 241cc two-stroke lightweight.

TIGLI
Italy 1950: Twenty-three years after his last 125cc Italian championship win, racer Amedeo Tigli (in partnership with Franco Morini) offered a 75cc two-stroke.

TIKA
Germany 1921–24: This assembler of lightweight four-strokes used Herko 150 and 200cc side-valve engines.

TILBROOK
Australia 1950–53: Villiers two-strokes of 125 and 200cc powered Rex Tilbrook's advanced but short-lived machines.

TILSTON
England 1919: This assembler used 225cc Precision two-stroke engines.

TINKLER
England 1920s: The improbably named Almond Tinkler, a maker of timepieces, built his first 'bitsa' in 1914 and announced the Tinkler Special in 1927. His machines – including a three-cylinder radial – do not appear to have entered series production.

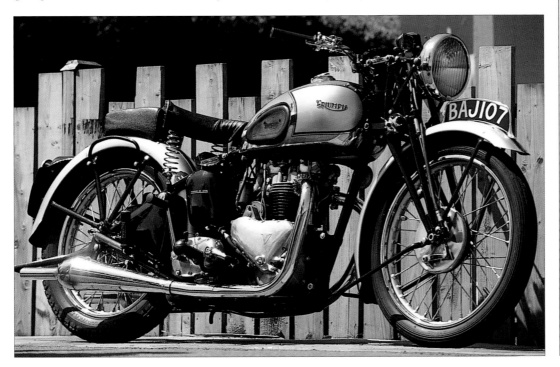

Triumph's wartime production majored on the 350cc sidevalve 3TW, ridden by dispatch riders like these WRNS. Initial output was 300 units a week.

managing director and entered into a joint venture with Alfa Romeo to build the Triumph Gloria Dolomite, a Coventry-built version of Alfa Romeo's 8C 2300 Monza sports car. In return, Alfa Romeo had the rights to produce Triumph's 6/1 vertical twin, but only three Gloria Dolomites were made. Triumph had produced 17,000 Super Seven cars in seven years, but now the car-manufacturing side of the business divorced itself from the motorbikes; the latter concern was sold on 22 January 1936 to John Young (Jack) Sangster of Ariel Motorcycles, for just over £41,000. Then aged 70, Bettmann had retired, but Sangster reinstated him as chairman of the new Triumph Engineering company, ensuring continued goodwill from component suppliers. Bettmann died, aged 88, in 1951.

Edward Turner had succeeded Val Page as chief designer at Ariel in 1932, and in 1936 Turner was brought in by Sangster as general manager. Born in London in 1901, he had set up as a Velocette dealer

after World War I. Jack Sangster signed Turner up as a draughtsman at Ariel, and he popularised Val Page's Red Hunter range by using bright colours for the tanks and adding chrome plating to the exhaust pipes. It was clear to Turner that the cosmetics that had worked for the Red Hunters would do the same for the Triumph singles – the 2/1, 3/2 and 5/5 – and they were re-designated the 250cc Tiger 70, 350cc 80 and 500cc 90. A sales operation was established in the USA around Bill Johnson's Pasadena-based Johnson Motors Inc dealership.

Edward Turner's masterpiece was the Speed Twin model, launched in July 1937. It developed 27bhp at 6300rpm, could do 150kph (93mph), and cost £75. Its standard finish was a rich shade of maroon known as amaranth, with chromed tank, exhaust pipe, headlight and wheel rims, plus gold coachlines and amaranth-coloured panels on the tank sides. The wheel-rim centres – 483mm (19ins) front, 508mm (20ins) rear – were similarly decorated, and the overall effect was little short of sensational. Competition success was also just around the corner: in 1938 the Speed Twin captured the Maude's Trophy, a timed run between Land's End and John o'Groats, covering the entire length of the British mainland, from south-west to north-east.

The sporting version of the Speed Twin, the silver-liveried Tiger 100, was announced in 1939. Its acceleration and quiet running, together with its reliability, made it a highly desirable machine. It was selected for the London Metropolitan Police's motorcycle fleet, and set the scene for British parallel-twin production during the postwar period. More than that, it served as the basis for the Triumph range for more than 40 years. The Speed Twin format was used with 250, 350 (3T), 500 (5T), 650 (6T) and 750cc engines; rivals took years to match these machines.

By 1939 the Speed Twin's girder forks had been replaced by telescopic forks. The Tiger 100 sports derivative also featured polished ports, forged slipper

The 149cc Terrier of 1952 embodied the latest styling cues of its bigger brethren but with such a small engine, it provided much greater fuel economy.

The first model to benefit from the fresh post-war styling and nacelle headlamp and clocks was the T6 Thunderbird, introduced in 1950. This is a 1956 bike.

pistons and a higher (8:1) compression ratio. It replaced the Tiger 90 in the Triumph range, and was just as attractive as the Speed Twin, featuring a pair of megaphone silencers. In 1939 Triumph's engine development manager Freddie Clarke equalled the 750cc-class record at Brooklands on a Tiger 100; his time of 189.93kph (118.02mph) remained a track best, since the circuit was later abandoned.

Triumph's wartime production gradually transferred to military equipment, including a winch for target-towing aircraft, which was powered by the 500cc Speed Twin motor. By May 1940 Triumph was producing 3TW bikes for military dispatch riders at the rate of 300 a

Left: In production from 1954 to 1974, the T20S Tiger Cub was Triumph's entry-level model, also available as the T20C/S trialler.

Below: One of Triumph's most famously successful bikes was the 750cc Trident triple known as Slippery Sam, a production racer that covered everyone in oil at the 1970 Bol D'Or.

TITAN
Austria (Puntigam, near Graz) 1927–33: After the two-stroke 144cc twin Austro-Motorette, Titan introduced a reed-valve 350cc of their own design as well as offering 350 and 500cc JAP and Blackburne four-strokes.

TITAN
San Marino 1975–: These mopeds in various guises came from Curio Rinaldi and Gianfranco Mularoni.

TIZ-AM
Russia (Kharkov) 1931–40: As well as a solid 600cc side-valve single in a sprung frame, Tiz-Am sold a 2hp lightweight after 1936.

TM
Italy (Pesara) 1968–92: These were typical – but unusually successful – Italian lightweight machines for off-road competition use, with 48cc (Franco-Morini, Zundapp) to 125cc (Yamaha) engines.

TOMASELLI
Italy 1931–39: These JAP engines of 167 to 500cc were fitted into sporting assembled machines.

TOMMASI
Italy 1926–27: One Della Ferrera 123cc motor powered the smaller machine: two, coupled together, powered the 246cc machine.

TOREADOR
England (Preston) 1924–26: Although JAP and Blackburne singles, and even a 500cc MAG V-twin, were also used in these machines, most Toreadors were powered by Bradshaw oil boilers, including the rare double overhead-cam 350cc.

TORPADO
Italy (Padua) 1950–70: This firm produced 50cc mopeds with a Minarelli engine.

The 1994 Tiger rekindled an old name in the guise of a big traillie, powered by the Hinckley 900cc triple. Tall and heavy, it could be a handful off-road.

twins were mostly Bonnevilles produced between 1976 and 1988, and they were followed by the modern era of Hinckley triples and fours from 1991 to the present day.

The first bike to receive the unit-construction engine was the 3TA, a 350cc twin, also known as the Twenty-One. The engine was finished to look like an alloy unit in order to match the gearbox section, and was the first production Triumph with extensive body panelling. The area below the twin saddle and the rear wheel was shrouded in a curved fairing, and the generous front mudguard echoed the 'bathtub' bodywork. The first unit-construction Tiger was the T100A of 1961, which shared the now-familiar enclosed look, although by 1964 the 3TA's metal cloak had been cut back to more of a skirt, and these claddings had completely disappeared by 1966.

While the bikes sported bathtub fairings, Triumph entered the scooter market in 1959 with the single- and two-cylinder Tigress models. The Tigress TS1 was powered by an air-cooled two-stroke 172cc BSA Bantam-derived

week. However, on the night of 14 November 1940, the centre of Coventry was blitzed in a German air raid. Triumph's Priory Street factory did not escape. Any serviceable plant equipment was relocated temporarily in a foundry in Warwick, and the firm was making motorcycles again by June 1941. A new factory was built in 1941–42 on the outskirts of Coventry at Meriden, and by 1944 output had reached 11,000 bikes.

The pre-war 3T, 5T Speed Twin and Tiger 100 carried Triumph into the postwar period, with most of their componentry in common. The first all-new postwar model was the 500cc Trophy, followed by the 6T Thunderbird, announced in 1950; this was the first bike to benefit from the modern styling, incorporating a headlamp nacelle. In 1951 Jack Sangster sold Triumph to BSA for nearly £2.5m. Turner, who held a 10 per cent stake in Triumph, remained in charge, and the two firms remained competitors.

Postwar Triumphs are categorised as pre-unit-construction twins, running from 1946 to 1962, including the T100

Tiger and early Thunderbird models. After the all-in-one unit-construction engine and gearbox assembly was adopted in 1957, production consisted of small unit-construction twins until 1974; machines like the T100A Tiger and Daytona are examples. The large unit-construction twins, such

as the Thunderbird and Bonneville, were built from 1963 to 1975. The T160 Trident and short-lived Hurricane three-cylinder triples ran between 1968 and 1976. There were also smaller single-cylinder Terriers and Tiger Cubs, made from 1953 to 1974. The Meriden Co-operative and Devon-built big

Privateer Taylormade Racing's 1995 production racer was based on the 900 Daytona. The factory also ran its own Speed Triple Challenge series.

engine, while the TW2 and TW2S used 249cc overhead-valve twins. These were identical to the contemporary Sunbeams made by BSA. However, Triumph's scooters never matched the popularity of their Italian counterparts. Production of the TW2 continued until 1964 and the TS1 finished a year later. In 1962 Triumph launched the 100cc Tina. This machine was smaller than the Tigress, and had automatic transmission.

In 1955 a specially built 650cc Triumph engine powered Texan Johnny Allen's 4.27m (14ft) long 'Cigar' to 311kph (193mph) on the Bonneville salt flats in Utah. An NSU raised the record to 340kph (211mph) the following year, and Allen returned months later to retake the honours with an amazing 344kph (214mph). Another Triumph-powered streamliner returned to Bonneville in 1962, and Bill Johnson – not the Pasadena distributor – set the record at 361.41kph (224.57mph). The location of these successes held considerable significance, so when a name was sought for the powerful new twin-carburettor 650 machine, 'Bonneville' was the obvious choice.

The T120 Bonneville was launched at the 1959 Earls Court

Show in London, and was an overnight sensation. Customers were quick to take advantage of its performance potential, and although it was equally at home as a two-up tourer, the T120 was the dominant force in production racing for many years. Malcolm Uphill won the 1959 Isle of Man Production TT at 160.92kph (99.99mph), achieving the first-ever 161kph (100mph+) lap on the Manx course in the process, and Uphill and Percy Tait shared a Bonnie to take the honours in the Thruxton 500-mile race in 1965. This success spawned a special factory-tuned limited edition, known as the Thruxton Bonneville, which was a regular winner. It developed 54bhp at 6500rpm, and was capable of 225kph (140mph).

In the early 1960s there were three machines in the Triumph range to suit sports and touring riders, and drivelines for the 6T Thunderbird, TR6 Trophy and T120 Bonneville went over to unit construction in 1963. Three years on, 12volt electrics came in, followed in 1968 by twin leading-shoe front brakes for the Bonneville, which got a front disc brake in 1973.

In the late 1960s off-road versions of the Trophy and

The original T150 Trident was announced in 1968, powered by a 58bhp three-cylinder triple, with distinctive fuel tank and exhausts.

Bonneville were made for the US market, featuring high-level exhaust pipes and chunky tyres. The US-spec Bonnie – the T120TT – was a scramble bike with no concessions whatsoever to road use. Similarly, the North American version of the Trophy, the TR6C, was built as an off-roader, and there were even different specifications for eastern and western states.

Following Jack Sangster's retirement as BSA chairman in 1961, Bert Hopwood returned to Meriden as general manager after 14 years at Norton. Meanwhile, Triumph was well aware of the threat posed by the emergent Japanese makers with their high standards of build quality, advanced specifications, large production volumes and, crucially, low showroom prices. Edward Turner travelled to Japan in 1960 to visit Honda, Yamaha and Suzuki, and was impressed by the levels of mechanisation, machine tooling and use of rolling roads for testing. Triumph had never made 1000 units of any particular model

TORPEDO
Austro-Hungary/Czech Republic (Kolin) 1903–12: This unusually self-sufficient company even made its own carburettors. Engines were singles of three-and-a-half and 4hp, and V-twins of 6hp and 8hp.

TORPEDO
England (Barton on Humber) 1910–20: F. Hooper used Precision singles and twins of 300, 350 and 500cc.

TORPEDO
Germany (Geestemunde) 1901–07: Ernst Weichelt bought in the usual proprietary motors, including Fafnir, Minerva and Zedel.

TORPEDO
Germany (Rodelheim bei Frankfurt) 1928–56: Before World War II, these were fitted with Blackburne 200cc side-valves, and after it, Sachs and Ilo 125, 150 and 175cc.

TORROT
Spain 1960–85: This firm produced mopeds. The name is a Spanish readjustment of Terrot, of which the company started as a subsidiary.

TOWNEND
England 1901–04: These were pioneer singles.

TOYOMOTOR
Japan 1957–early 1960s: Adler apparently provided the inspiration for these 250cc two-stroke twins.

TRAFALGAR
England 1902–05: This firm was a pioneer in sidecar manufacture, originally to accompany their own machines with MMC and Minerva engines.

TRAFFORD
England 1919–22: The famous 269cc Villiers two-stroke was found in this company's only model.

Launched to rave reviews in 1999, the TT600 swept Triumph to the top of the ultra-competitive 600cc sports niche, vying with the benchmark Honda CBR600.

stopped making its own bikes and, instead of its Rocket 3, was producing T150V and, later, T160V Triumph Tridents. With their disc rear brake, left-hand gearshift and electric start, these bikes were popular with police forces, and the T160V lingered on until 1977, when NVT crashed.

Faced with sackings and the unceremonious hand-over of its product line to a rival firm, the Triumph workforce was understandably furious and took matters into its own hands. Instead of the intended shutdown, the gates of Meriden were locked from the inside in September 1973, and the workers began an implacable 18-month sit-in. During this time, only a trickle of machines left the factory, mostly T120V Bonnevilles. The Labour government, however, was receptive to the concept of a workers' co-operative, and Meriden Motorcycles became a reality in March 1975 when the government granted a £4.2m loan and the factory gates opened once more.

Both Meriden's new 1976 models, the TR7V Tiger and T140V Bonneville, had to satisfy

from one week to the next, yet the Japanese were producing small-capacity machines in these volumes in a single day.

In response to Honda's CB 750, Bert Hopwood and Doug Hele designed a three-cylinder unit for the new Triumph model for 1965, which had its tank and livery styled by the British design house Ogle. The shape of its fuel tank was likened to a loaf of bread and, for obvious reasons, the flared silencer and triple tailpipes were known as 'Ray Guns'. The oil cooler was mounted at the top front of the frame, and although the triple weighed 18kg (40lb) more than a 650 twin, the new engine fitted neatly in the regular frame. The brakes were similar to the Bonneville's, and were less than adequate for the heavier machine, but the engine was a success, delivering reliable 193kph (120mph) performance. Triumph beat Honda to the punch, as the Trident Triple was launched in September 1968, just a month ahead of the Honda CB 750. A Trident could outperform the big new Japanese machines, thanks to better handling, and was just as quick in a straight line. Tridents twice won the Isle of Man 750 Formula event, and the victorious Trident at the 1970 Bol d'Or race at Circuit Paul Ricard was

The Hinckley plant's early Trophies were sporting, but by the mid-1990s the model was a supreme touring machine, available as a 900cc triple or a 1200 four.

awarded the nickname 'Slippery Sam' after covering everyone in oil. Slippery Sam went on to win the 1971 and 1972 Production TT as well. The Trident evolved alongside its twin-cylinder siblings; revisions included a brand-new frame in 1971, in which the enlarged top and seat tubes acted as the oil tank, a five-speed gearbox, and a front disc brake in 1973.

In July 1973 Triumph was conscripted into the BSA merger with Norton-Villiers to form NVT.

(Norton-Villiers had its origins in the former Associated Motor Cycles corporation, which collapsed in 1966, taking with it a number of famous marques, including AJS, Francis Barnett, James, Matchless and Norton.) It was NVT's intention that Triumph's Meriden plant would shut down and that production of the remaining Triumph models – the T100R, TR5T, T120V and T140V – would be carried out at BSA's Small Heath factory in Birmingham. By now, BSA had

stringent US Environmental Protection Agency legislation. Both bikes used the familiar 744cc engine (with two carburettors for the Bonneville and just one for the Tiger), while the gearshift was swapped over to the left, and a rear disc brake fitted. In 1977 Triumph received £1m from GEC, and Meriden was given a clean slate towards the end of 1981 when the Labour government wiped out the co-op's debt. This enabled Triumph to become a limited company, with the workforce its shareholders.

A new model, the TR7T Tiger Trail, was launched at the 1981 Paris Show; this still had the old frame and 744cc engine, but with a high-rise exhaust system and knobbly tyres. The base-model Thunderbird was reintroduced, powered by the single-carburettor short-stroke 649cc motor and fitted with a drum brake at the rear. However, by mid-1983 Meriden's money had run out, and the liquidators auctioned off the plant and machine tools. The factory was eventually bulldozed to make way for a housing estate, and the Triumph name was bought by an astute entrepreneur named John Bloor. A brand-new Triumph plant was built on a 4-hectare (10-acre) site at Hinckley, between Coventry and Leicester, and a new modular range of bikes was designed.

In September 1990 the new Triumphs were launched at the Cologne Show, headed by the

The cruiser look of the early 1970s was typified by the 1973 X75 Hurricane, featuring megaphone pipes, wide bars and BSA Rocket engine.

In 1996, Triumph unveiled its extruded aluminium beam chassis, replacing the steel spine frame, for the T595 Daytona and T509 Speed Triple, shown here.

range-topping Trophy 1200. Three pairs of models were listed – the Trophy, Daytona and Trident – and by September 1991 the whole introductory range was in place. The six models in the line-up were the unfaired Trident in 750 triple and 900 triple form, the fully faired sports Daytona in 750 triple and 1000 four-cylinder format, and

the fully faired touring-biased Trophy as a 900 triple and 1200 four-cylinder machine. Production was slow at first, at just eight bikes a week on average, compared with a new machine rolling off the line every six minutes in 1996, when production totalled 15,000 bikes. All six models in the range shared many common features, including chassis frames, fuel tanks, engine components and running gear.

Another name from the past was revived in 1993 with the launch of the Tiger 900. It was styled as an enduro machine, and had avant-garde graphics on its plastic tank and fairing. This was followed by the Trident Sprint, which was no more than a Trident 900 embellished with elegant swooping side and rear panels and a cockpit fairing that featured Daytona-style twin round headlights. Along with the Trident, the Sprint was later equipped with an aluminium rear suspension unit, adjustable for preload and rebound damping should the bike become heavily laden. The Trophy got a major facelift in 1995 and was fitted with a set of rotund body panels and twin headlights. The John Mockett-designed fairings were derived from wind-tunnel

477

experiments and gave the Trophy a unique identity in the big touring category.

Triumph unveiled its retro Thunderbird in 1994. It proved sufficiently popular for Triumph to launch the similar Adventurer, which had a virtually identical frame but was made as a cruiser-style single-seater, with an upswept duck-tail rear mudguard, even higher bars, megaphone exhausts and lots of chrome.

From 1996 the range included a faster, lighter, limited-edition version of the Daytona 900, known as the Super III. It had a hand-finished Cosworth-cast cylinder head with gas-flowed ports and high-lift cams, matched by six-piston calliper aluminium front brakes acting on fully floating twin discs. Only 805 units

were made, and the additional cost over a standard Daytona was a cool £5500. The Speed Triple café racer appeared in 1995, based on the Daytona frame with a minimal tail fairing, and powered by the 900 triple engine. It was the subject of a highly successful race series in the UK, known as the Speed Triple Challenge, with rounds held at the major circuits, frequently in support of large meetings such as the British Grand Prix.

In October 1996 Triumph unveiled a pair of innovative new models in Cologne. One was the new T595 Daytona, a super sports machine with a new 955cc triple engine based around a stunning, curvaceous oval alloy-tubing perimeter frame. The other was the T509 Speed Triple, which had the

same frame but embraced the street-fighter look with an absence of frontal fairings. The new fuel-injected 955cc triple produced 128bhp at 10,200rpm, with a massive 72.3ft/lb of torque, and the Daytona was now a match for state-of-the-art icons like Honda's 900 FireBlade and the Ducati 916. At 915cc, the T509's triple had a 3mm shorter bore than the Daytona, but both models had six-speed gearboxes and a sophisticated fuel-injection system that was superior to that of any other production bike.

The range was continuously updated, with wholesale revisions to certain models like the Tiger enduro, which was entirely reworked for 1999.

Brand-new bikes included the Sprint ST – good enough to take

on the Honda VFR750 for the bench-mark sports-tourer accolade – and the four-cylinder T600, which was announced in November 1999 and was pitched directly at the Honda CBR600, doyen of the popular 600cc sports class.

By 2000 Triumph had produced over 90,000 motorcycles, and output at the factory had reached around 100 units a day, which was the maximum capacity at the first Hinckley plant.

Construction of a new factory – which is scheduled for opening in the middle of 2002 – began in May 1999 on a nearby industrial site. Set to occupy over 46,452sq.m (500,000sq.ft), the factory's intended production capacity is around 50,000 motorcycles per year.

TRIUMPH FAST ROADSTER   1922

Triumph introduced the 499cc Type IR 'Fast Roadster' in 1922. Designed by piston and combustion chamber specialists Ricardo & Co, its cylinder head configuration consisted of four pushrod-actuated overhead-valves with centrally positioned spark plugs and both sets of valves arranged at 90 degrees to one another. The piston was

aluminium, running in a bore machined from steel billet, and there was a single inlet manifold from the carburettor, while exhaust emissions passed away down two

Triumph's Type IR 'Fast Roadster' was based on regular cycle parts like that of the SD shown here, with a 499cc engine designed by tuning specialists Ricardo.

separate pipes. The IR's frame and cycle components were directly descended from the Model H, although the druid-pattern girder forks were a slight improvement.

The 'Riccy' engine contained four pushrod-actuated valves, a central spark plug, an aluminium piston, a single inlet manifold and two exhaust outlets.

Power output was 20bhp, giving a top speed of 121kph (75mph). The Type IR was affectionately known as the 'Riccy' (after Harry – later Sir Harry – Ricardo, the well-known engineering guru) and it took the all-new 500cc.

In 1927 the Type TT displaced the Type IR in the Triumph range. The engine of the two-valve TT was designed by the Brooklands racer Victor Horsman, and featured a twin-port overhead-valve head, enclosed lubricated valvegear and roller-bearing rockers, driving through a three-speed gearbox with traditional crossover drive. The hub brakes were the expanding internal type front and rear, while new front forks incorporated large fabric-friction discs and a steering damper.

Engine: (Type R) 499cc single-cylinder 4-ohv four-stroke, air-cooled
Power: 20bhp
Gearbox: 3-speed
Final drive: chain
Weight: 109kg (240lb)
Top speed: 121kph (75mph)

TRIUMPH SPEED TWIN   1937

Edward Turner's masterpiece was the Speed Twin, unveiled in July 1937. Its strong point was its lightness, weighing in at 171kg (378lb), which was 2.3kg (5lb) less than the Tiger 90 single, whose frame it used. Yet, at £75, it cost

just £5 more. And, with its twin pipes tucked neatly under the engine, it was also slightly narrower and could be leaned over further during cornering.

The block and head were cast-iron, and the single-throw crank

had a central flywheel, split-alloy connecting rods and white-metal lined big-end caps. Twin camshafts were located ahead of and behind the block, while the valvegear was mounted in separate alloy casings bolted to the head,

and operated by pushrods housed in chrome tubes running between the cylinders. The pistons went up and down together, an arrangement which Turner believed provided better torque and more efficient carburation than

a twin with a two-throw crank, and better balance than a single-cylinder unit of similar capacity. The inlet camshaft pinion also drove the Lucas Magdyno lighting and double-plunger oil pump. An instrument panel was set in Bakelite plastic and mounted on the tank top. It included a three-position light switch, ammeter and oil-pressure gauge.

In standard finish, the Speed Twin was spectacularly attractive – chromed tank, exhaust pipe, headlight and wheel rims, amaranth paintwork and gold coachlines. The bike also won the 1938 Maude's Trophy, a timed run spanning the British mainland. Such was the model's success that it dominated Triumph's line-up for over 40 years, being produced in

250, 350 (3T), 500 (5T), 650 (6T) and 750cc forms.

Early Speed Twins were known as six-stud models, a reference to the bolts securing the cylinder block to the crankcase. When at maximum speed, these were prone to coming undone, but by 1939 the problem was cured. At the same time, telescopic forks replaced girder forks. In 1939, the sporting version, the Tiger 100, was announced. It had a higher (8:1) compression ratio than the Speed Twin and matched the 750cc-class record at Brooklands with a time of 189.93kph (118.02mph).

Engine: 498cc parallel-twin, 63x80mm, air cooled
Power: 27bhp at 6300rpm
Gearbox: 4-speed Triumph, foot change
Final drive: chain
Weight: 171kg (378lb)
Top speed: 150kph (93mph)

TRIUMPH BONNEVILLE 1959

Launched at the 1959 Earls Court Show, the powerful T120 Bonneville featured a twin-carburettor 650cc two-cylinder engine, and became the dominant force in production racing for many years. When it came out, the 'Bonnie' was fitted with the familiar headlamp nacelle, but Triumph quickly reverted to the traditional unfaired headlight arrangement so that it could be detached when the bike was ridden in competition.

Manufacture of engines and gearboxes went over to unit construction in 1963. Most engine internals remained as before, the significant difference being the rearward extension of the crankcase to incorporate the gearbox, like the smaller-capacity machines. The T120 was given 12volt electrics and a revised tank badge in 1966; two years later, it was equipped with twin leading-shoe front brakes for better stopping power, with a front disc fitted by 1973.

The US-spec Bonnie – the T120TT – was a no-nonsense scramble bike completely untailored for road use. A small batch of T120RT production racers was constructed to contest the US-

based AMA series in 1970 using bored-out 744cc engines. Gene Romero rode one to victory in 1970, and came second on another in 1971. In a major relaunch in 1971, the Bonneville TR120R unit twin was built up on a brand-new frame. The enlarged top and seat tubes of the new frame acted as the oil tank, which paradoxically had the undesirable effect of raising the height of the seat and thus the centre of gravity. There were new slender forks and

conical hubs, as well as flashing indicators. Cosmetic changes included new side panels and megaphone-style silencers.

The Bonneville was dubbed the T140 in 1973, when it was fitted with a new engine, initially of 725cc and later rising to 744cc,

The T120 Bonneville was crucial to Triumph's sales, particularly in America. Specification was gradually upgraded, with a new frame in 1971 and engine in 1973.

like the American T120RT racer. There were also major revisions to the cylinder head. All Triumph models now had the option of a five-speed gearbox – indicated by a Roman 'V' for '5' in the designation, as in T140V – while the existing cycle parts and running gear of the old T120 were retained. At this time, the Bonneville was struggling to keep pace with the new wave of big four-cylinder Japanese machines, such as the Honda CB750 and Suzuki GT750, which were stealing the limelight with affordable, reliable performance.

The Bonneville was the mainstay of Triumph's sports production from 1960 to 1983, and the torch was rekindled by the launch of a retro version for 2000.

During the Triumph workers' 18-month sit-in, beginning in September 1973, only a small number of machines left the factory. These were mostly T140Vs, and most Bonnevilles produced during the protest were delivered only in its final months, between March and May 1975.

The new 1976 T140V Bonneville used the familiar 744cc engine in twin-carburettor format, but the gearshift was swapped over to the left-hand side and a rear disc brake fitted. The following year, Triumph launched a special edition of the Bonneville to mark the Queen's Silver Jubilee. Appropriately liveried in red, white and blue, just 2400 units were built. An upgraded model, the T140E, was introduced for the USA in 1978, fitted with a new cylinder head and carburation that was better suited to American emissions requirements. This bike replaced the T140V on the UK market in 1979, when it went over to electronic ignition. The T140ES was equipped with an electric starter from 1981, and an Executive model appeared in 1980, complete with a Sabre faring, Sigma panniers and a top-box. Triumph launched another limited-edition special to celebrate Prince Charles' marriage to Lady Diana Spencer; called the T140 Royal, it had alloy wheels and Bing carburettors. The rubberised anti-vibration engine mountings tried on police-use Bonnevilles were productionised in 1982, in conjunction with an all-alloy eight-valve engine fed by twin Amals, fitted in the T140 TSS Bonneville. A custom version called the T140 TSX was also

available, sporting brighter colours, a two-level seat and high-rise bars.

Another all-new water-cooled eight-valve twin with chain-driven overhead-cams was announced in early 1983. This machine was known as the Phoenix 900. The engine was code-named 'Diana' and acted as a stressed member of the frame, which had monoshock rear suspension, alloy wheels, disc brakes and telescopic front forks.

In its final incarnation, the Bonneville was produced by the Newton Abbot-based Racing Spares concern of Les Harris, who was granted a five-year licence to make Bonnevilles. Although the frame and cycle parts were much as before, the engine components were made on new CNC lathes for greater accuracy. Kick-starters and Amal carburettors were used once more, while newly sourced parts included Paioli forks, Veglia instruments and Brembo brakes from Italy. The last of the Devon Bonnevilles came out in 1988.

Engine: (T120) 650cc parallel-twin, 71x82mm, air-cooled
Power: 46bhp
Gearbox: 4-speed foot change
Final drive: chain
Weight: 183kg (404lb)
Top speed: 177kph (110mph)

TRIUMPH TRIDENT

1990

Engine: (T375) 750cc 12-valve ohv triple, water-cooled
Power: 90bhp
Gearbox: 5-speed foot change
Final drive: chain
Weight: 209kg (461lb)
Top speed: 201kph (125mph)

The renaissance of Triumph began in September 1990, when the new range was launched at the Cologne Show. The entry-level model was the unfaired Trident, which was available with two variations of the three-cylinder triple engine – 750 and 900cc – designated the T375 and T309. All six bikes in the modular range shared many common features, including chassis frames, fuel tanks, engine components and running gear. The three-cylinder triple was a water-cooled twin-cam, with a horizontal joint in the crankcase, and the top section of the casting combined with the wet-liner block. There were four valves per cylinder in the one-piece cylinder head, and

these were chain-driven from the right-hand end of the crank via a tunnel in the casting. The electronic ignition was triggered from the same end of the crank, while the oil filter cartridge was underneath the crankcase. The one-piece crank was allied to a vibration-damping balancer shaft ahead of the crankshaft. Compression ratios were 11:1 for the short-stroke engines and 10.6:1 for the long-stroke, while the 36mm (1.4ins) Mikuni carburettors used unleaded fuel. Nissin disc brakes were fitted, with twin 296mm (11.7ins) discs and two-piston callipers at the front, and a single 255mm (10ins) disc at the rear. At the front were Kayaba 43mm (1.7ins) telescopic forks, and at the rising-rate rear was a single Kayaba damper.

By October 1994 the Trident was Triumph's second-best seller after the Trophy. The Trident Sprint, released that year, was essentially a Trident 900 with

elegant swooping side and rear panels and a cockpit fairing featuring the contemporary Daytona-style twin round headlights. Both the Sprint and the

The unfaired Trident was one of the first Hinckley-built Triumphs, with steel spine frame and 750 and 900cc triple engines. It was the basis of the firm's modular range.

Trident were later equipped with an aluminium rear-suspension unit that was adjustable for pre-load and rebound damping, making the bikes capable of carrying heavy loads.

The Sprint was also available in Executive and Sports formats.

Both of these were available with appropriate accessories, such as imitation carbon exhausts and low bars.

TRIUMPH T595 DAYTONA   1997

The ground-breaking T595 Daytona, introduced in 1997, placed Triumph right back at the top of the world's motorcycle manufacturing tree. It differed from its modular predecessors, the T309 and T400 Daytonas, in having as its basis the curvaceous oval-tube aluminium frame designed by Chris Hennegan. Almost as radically, the T595 was powered by a new variant of the Hinckley triple, a 955cc three-cylinder unit that produced 128bhp at 10,200rpm, with a massive 72.3ft/lb of torque. The T595's engine casings were cast in magnesium for lightness, and the crank, gearbox and clutch were also lightened. The gearbox sprocket cover was plastic, while bores were lined to reduce drag on the aluminium pistons. The Daytona was equipped with a sophisticated fuel-injection system that was superior to that of any other production bike, and it also had a six-speed gearbox. The single-sided swing-arm on the left

of the bike allowed the three-into-one exhaust system to be tucked in tightly on the right-hand side, thus showing off the three-spoke Brembo wheel, which was shod with sticky Bridgestone BT56 tyres. Suspension front and rear was by Showa of Japan, with fully adjustable 45mm (1.8ins) front forks and a rear shock absorber. Brakes were Nissin four-piston calliper at the front and two-piston at the rear.

The T595 was quickly compared with state-of-the-art icons such as Honda's 900 FireBlade and Ducati's 916, and, priced at £9800, it was only £500 more expensive than the FireBlade, and a significant £3000 cheaper than the Ducati. In 1999 it was superseded by a new model, the 955i. This was a supersports bike powered by the liquid-cooled, double overhead-cam, in-line 955cc three-cylinder unit. Bore and stroke was 79mmx65mm, and the compression ratio 11.2:1. The fuel system was multipoint

In 1996, Triumph raised its game with the aluminium-framed T595 Daytona, which proved a match for the front-running Honda FireBlade and Ducati 916.

sequential electronic fuel injection, while the throttle bodies were 41mm (1.6ins) in diameter. Transmission was via a six-speed gearbox with a wet multi-plate clutch.

The list of improvements included a modified exhaust camshaft, revised throttle bodies, a new air bypass system, revised engine management tuning, new exhaust header pipes, a rear suspension unit, an air-box, revised wiring and hoses, and new paintwork.

Engine: 955cc fuel-injected ohv triple, 79x65mm, water-cooled
Power: 128bhp
Gearbox: 6-speed foot change
Final drive: chain
Weight: 198kg (436lb)
Top speed: 257kph (160mph)

TRUMP

ENGLAND 1907–23

FRANK A. MCNAB, the force behind the Trump firm, was successful at Brooklands from 1909, setting a new one-hour record of over 77km (48 miles) in May that year. First based in Liphook, Trump moved to Birmingham in 1912, but retained the Foxdale Works at Byfleet, Surrey, convenient for the track.

Since the company used JAP engines, its machines were sometimes listed as Trump-JAPs. By 1910 its three-and-a-half horsepower model was offered with a 6hp V-twin, both with Druid forks and belt drive, joined in 1913 by three-and-a-quarter and

An early Trump prepared for competition work. Such machines had many successes at Brooklands.

8hp V-twins, and in 1914 by a Trump-Peco with a 349cc two-stroke engine with two speeds and belt drive. A 208cc version was added to the 1915 list.

Trump returned in mid-1921 as Trump Motors Ltd, with a 976cc JAP V-twin sports model, soon joined by a 548cc JAP side-valve single with a Sturmey-Archer gearbox and close ratios as an option. By 1922 the range comprised 292, 346 and 490cc side-valve singles, plus 747 and

976cc side-valve V-twins, all JAP. For the next year there were the 346cc side-valve single in standard or sports trim, and the two sizes of

V-twin, plus another with a 994cc overhead-valve Anzani engine. This was to be Trump's swan song; McNab retired early in 1923.

TWN (TRIUMPH)

GERMANY 1903–57

ALTHOUGH THIS COMPANY WAS known as TWN (Triumph Werke Nurnberg) in Germany's export markets, to avoid confusion with the British Triumph marque, in many ways the German Triumph arm had as much claim to the name as its English counterpart. It was two Germans, Siegfried Bettmann and Maurice Schulte, who founded the British company in Coventry during 1897. For the first few years, its output concentrated on bicycles, but in 1902 the first motorcycle appeared. The following year, in 1903, when Triumph officially entered the motorcycle business, it also opened a German factory in Nurnberg.

In the early days, most of the German-built Triumphs had engines and other components supplied from Coventry. This arrangement continued until 1929, when the two firms went their separate ways. Following the break, the Nurnberg factory built its own 198 and 294cc two-stroke engines, together with a range of Swiss MAG engines ranging from 347 to 742cc. Very soon TWN secured a licence from MAG to build these engines in Germany.

In 1931 the Nurnberg concern employed Otto Reitz as chief designer. He created most of the numerous two-strokes that TWN built over the next quarter of a century. One of his most

interesting designs was a 198cc with shaft drive, a unit-construction engine and a pressed-steel frame. These features on such a small machine were most unusual for the period. TWN also participated in racing, with 348 and 493cc overhead-cam singles being ridden by the likes of Fleischmann and Ley.

By the late 1930s almost all of the company's production was under the direction of military authorities. Among the models manufactured was TWN's first split-single two-stroke, the BD250, featuring two pistons carried on a single, forked connecting rod, and having a displacement of 248cc (2x45x78mm). Over 12,000 of these were purchased by the Wehrmacht alone, and in army service the machine was known as the BD250 W. During wartime, Triumph also developed prototypes of a scooter, powered by a 125 engine, that could be dropped by parachute, and a TWN-engined NSU tracked personnel carrier, but neither went into production before the war ended.

TWN was among the first motorcycle manufacturers to resume production after World War II. The bulk of its output in

Sold in export markets as TWN, the German Triumph firm introduced the 350 Boss in March 1953. It employed a 344cc split-single two-stroke engine.

the late 1940s was centred upon two models: the BDG 125 and BDG 250. Both were directly descended from the larger machine powered by the same 248cc split-single engine, with dual exhausts and a fully enclosed final drive chain. Except for the substitution of telescopic front forks for girders in 1949, the bikes were to their pre-war specifications.

The BDG 125H 123cc (2x35x62mm) split-single was launched in 1950, and was the first of the Nurnberg factory's products to employ plunger rear suspension. A 250 version followed a year later. Many of the following months were spent in the development and testing of a new, larger-capacity machine. Designated the 350 Boss, this made its world debut at the Geneva Show in March 1953.

The engine of the Boss was new, but still of the split-single variety. Its capacity was 344cc (2x53x78mm) and it employed hard-chrome cylinder bores. Two carburettors were used to ensure (or so TWN claimed) that both pistons were properly cooled by fresh incoming gases. Twin exhaust pipes were fitted, although the exhaust outlet ran from the left-hand bore only. Part of the exhaust gas travelled through the exhaust pipe on the left, while the remainder passed through an internal passage across the front of the cylinder barrel and then into the exhaust port on the right. The

exhausts were specially manufactured for TWN by Eberspacher and were designed to both improve performance and reduce noise. This innovation led to TWN being known as the 'Producers of the Whispering Motorcycle'.

July 1953 marked the company's Golden Jubilee, and to commemorate 50 years of motorcycle production it introduced the 197cc (2x45x62mm) Cornet. The model's most notable feature was its full swinging-arm rear suspension, which was a first on a TWN design. Oil-damped telescopic forks and a sturdy frame made it a supremely comfortable bike.

In 1956 the Cornet was updated with 12-volt electrics and press-button starting. However, the following year TWN (along with Adler) was taken over by Grundig, and from then on made only office equipment.

July 1953 marked TWN's Golden Jubilee, and to commemorate this event it launched the 197cc Cornet. This was the first TWN to feature swinging arm rear suspension.

UNIVERSAL

SWITZERLAND 1928–64

THE FIRST MOTORCYCLES from Universal were built using the Helvetia name and a 190cc two-stroke engine from PA. Soon the company turned to its own name, and began combining a variety of two- and four-stroke engines from Anzani, Ilo and JAP (and the Python from Rudge) with cycle parts that were conventional for the day. Universal also built racing machines, powered by 248cc

Near the end of the company's life in the mid-1960s, the Swiss Universal firm produced a 250cc single that retained the shaft drive and other features of their twin-cylinder machines.

Python and 996cc V-twin JAP units. By the mid-1930s, Universal was making its own 680 and 990cc side-valve V-twin engines for the Swiss Army.

After the war, the company introduced a new design with an overhead-valve flat-twin engine built in unit with the gearbox. It was extremely neat, with the single carburettor, electrical equipment and air cleaner all enclosed, and featured shaft final drive, a duplex frame, telescopic front forks and plunger rear suspension. First seen early in

A typical Universal flat-twin, a 580cc model with shaft drive, duplex frame, plunger rear suspension and pan saddle.

1946, the 500cc model was also offered in side-valve form.

Later, the twin grew to 580cc and was joined by a 250cc single with similar features. In the early 1950s a 250cc two-stroke twin model had an Ilo engine, while a similar single used a 147cc Sachs. In time, Universal concentrated on the flat-twins, building them primarily for army and police use.

UT

GERMANY 1922–59

A UT Sachs-powered moped from the early 1950s. Compared with many rivals it had the advantage of both front and rear suspension.

singles of 123 and 174cc. Sold under the model designation KTN, these machines debuted in 1951.

With sales roaring ahead, a major push for increased production was made in 1953, accompanied by the arrival of the newly released KTV 175, featuring both front and rear suspension. The success of this venture led to the introduction of a larger-engined version, the KTV 200. Three new models also emerged with swinging-arm rear suspension, in contrast to the KTVs' plunger frames. These were the TS 200, TS 250 and TS 252 (the latter having twin cylinders).

The TS 175F and TS 175J arrived in 1955, while 1956 brought the VS 100; this, like the TS 175J and VS 252 twin, used a Sachs engine. However, from 1957, sales nose-dived and Universal spent the next two years selling off remaining stocks.

ONE OF THE MORE IMPORTANT of the lesser-known German marques, UT at first built its own 246cc two-stroke engine featuring a horizontal cylinder. Then, to save development costs and to speed model introduction, it began buying power units from Bekamo, Blackburne and JAP, the two latter companies supplying large-capacity overhead-valve singles. At the same time, during the late 1920s, the UT works gained a considerable amount of publicity by taking part in road-racing events throughout Germany.

Notable riders included Blind, Frenzen and Kohfink.

Then came the Depression, but somehow UT weathered the storm, making a switch to Bark and Kuchen engines for the company's series production bikes. During the subsequent war, UT was inactive in making motorcycles. When manufacture resumed afterwards, the first models used Ilo two-stroke

A top-of-the-range UT, the 1955 VS252. Its kilometre-eating urge came from its Ilo-made twin-cylinder, two-stroke engine.

VAN VEEN

NETHERLANDS/GERMANY 1975–82

DUTCHMAN HENK VAN VEEN began his motorcycle activities as the Kreidler importer for his home country. This soon proved so successful that he took over the running of the Kreidler works racing team at the end of the 1960s.

During most of the 1970s, the Van Veen Kreidlers were some of the fastest 50cc racing machines around, with riders Alt Toersen, Jan De Vries, Angel Nieto and Rudolf Kunz not only collecting several world titles, but also breaking a number of speed

The Van Veen OCR 1000 super-bike of the late 1970s was a joint Dutch–German venture and was powered by a Wankel engine.

records at Elvington, Yorkshire. Then, in the late 1970s and early 1980s, Van Veen set up a new factory in Germany to produce his own Superbike. Named the OCR 1000, it used a liquid-cooled 996cc twin-rotor Wankel engine developed in conjunction with Audi and NSU (it was NSU that owned the patents, and Audi's involvement came because its parent company VW Group had taken over NSU in 1969). With its four-speed gearbox developed by Porsche, the suspension specially created by Koni, and braking equipment which came from the Brembo company of Italy, the OCR 1000 was a true Eurobike, as it featured input from several nations.

Hand-built exclusively to order, the Van Veen sold only in small numbers, and the last was delivered in early 1982. Yet as far as its technical merits, it was one of the best Wankel-engined vehicles ever, proving (unlike many) durable in service. This 100bhp machine had staggering acceleration and is today highly prized. Examples that appear for sale fetch a high premium, in part because of their rarity value.

Van Veen also built, in Germany, limited runs of Grand Prix Replica 50cc racing machines, and from 1978 the Gelandesport (Off-road Sport), a 12bhp 49cc enduro bike. By 1979 this had been renamed the GS50; production ceased in 1981.

VELOCETTE

ENGLAND 1904–71

THIS FAMILY-RUN COMPANY was founded by Johannes Gutgemann, who settled in Birmingham, England, in 1884 to avoid national service in his native Germany. Gutgemann initially assumed the name John Taylor, and under the title of Isaac Taylor & Co, set up a

pill-making business. He then, somewhat improbably, began making bicycles in the early 1890s at premises in Great Hampton Street. After joining forces with William Gue, bicycles were built under the Hampton name from 1896. By 1900 Taylor Gue Ltd was

also making rickshaws and forecars, its first powered vehicles.

In 1904 the company took over London-based Kelecom Motors, which had been making Ormonde motorcycles using its own 3hp engine in a frame built by Taylor Gue. Within a year, the trade name

---

Veloce was adopted but, despite a new 2hp motor, Taylor Gue went bankrupt in October 1905.

Undaunted, Gutgemann resumed bicycle-making under the Veloce name at Spring Hill, Birmingham. In 1910, in concert with sons Percy and Eugene, he resumed motorcycle manufacture, using Percy's design for a clever two-speed unit-construction 276cc engine. These powerplants were built at Spring Hill, while the chassis were crafted at nearby Fleet Street. (In 1908 Percy had founded New Veloce to manufacture cars, but the enterprise failed to prosper.) In the event, the four-stroke 276cc machine proved too novel for public taste and a more conventional 500cc model was soon added, marketed as a VMC (Veloce Motor Company).

Although chiefly associated with 350cc racers, this ohc 500cc Velocette carried the great Stanley Woods to second place in the 1937 and 1938 Isle of Man Senior TT.

The first model to carry the Velocette name was a 206cc two-stroke in 1913. Gutgemann/Taylor was also dabbling again with personal names. Having taken British citizenship in 1911, he and his family changed their name to Goodman by deed poll in 1917.

A plan for a V-twin engine was thwarted by World War I, leaving the company with a range comprising small-capacity two-strokes until the mid-1920s. First were the 220cc D1 and DL1 (the L denoted a ladies' model, with a cut-down, skirt-friendly frame). In 1919 a works derivative took a gold medal in the ACU Six Days' Trial.

However, despite occasional adventures in later years with twins, scooters and odd two-strokes, Velocette will always be associated with classic four-stroke singles. The first of these arrived in 1925. Again designed by Percy Goodman, it was an overhead-cam 348cc single, and was to become the blueprint for the company's most prized machines. Perversely, the first examples were badged Veloce, although this was quickly changed to the more recognisable Velocette. Three such bikes were entered in the 1925 Junior (350cc) TT race, but all retired. One year later Alec Bennett made ample amends by taking a 'Velo' to victory by an astonishing margin of 10 minutes at an average speed of 107.34kph (66.70mph). In the same year, having previously moved to Aston, Birmingham, the company relocated to the former premises of OK Supreme at Hall Green, which was to remain its home until the end.

Roadster versions of the overhead-cam machine were sold from 1925 under the model designation K. Later that year a sports version appeared, capable of 129kph (80mph). This was the immortal KSS, which endured in modified form for another 23 years. From 1928 this bike (along with its sister models, the KS, KE and KES) was provided with the first positive-stop foot gear change, designed by development engineer Harold Willis.

In 1929 a production racing version of the KSS was offered for public sale. The KTT, as it was called, swept the first eight places at the following year's 'amateur TT', the Manx Grand Prix. Not surprisingly, these were to become the ultimate clubman's race tools

From the 1920s to the 1950s, the ohc KTT was a potent 'over-the-counter' racer. This is one of the last of the line, a Mk8 KTT, dating from 1948.

for a generation, rivalled only by Norton's International and Manx. Yet even at the highest level, Velocette's track record was

Black with gold pin-striping was as much a part of Velo lore as their ohc and ohv singles, as with this detail of the 350 MAC.

remarkable for a relatively small company, totalling eight Junior TT wins between 1926 and 1949. Although Velocette was always associated with the 350cc class, a rare prototype 495cc model was ridden by the great Stanley Woods to second place in the 1937 and 1938 500cc Senior TTs. Woods

The 350 MAC was introduced in 1954, a year before this example was built. Note the trademark 'fishtail' silencer.

also took fastest lap on a 348cc in the 1936 Senior TT.

For good measure, Velocette claimed the first 350cc world

machines arriving from Italy, yet Velocette was still wedded to sporting singles, invariably in classic black with gold pin-striping. Throughout the 1960s it made what became the epitome of British road-going singles, the 350cc Viper and 500cc Venom. Derived from the MAC and MSS respectively, these machines were to evolve into ever more potent models, named the Clubmans and Thruxton Velos. Along with BSA's Gold Star, they were to become the ultimate expression of the sporting British single.

However, by the late 1960s the market was demanding more from motorcycle manufacturers. Yet what finally brought Velocette down in February 1971 were the development costs of, of all things, the Viceroy scooter. Like much that the company produced, this two-stroke twin with reed valve induction was way ahead of its time, but sadly it was to prove the last roll of the Hall Green dice.

championship in 1949 and retained the crown in 1950, with riders Freddie Frith and Bob Foster respectively. As early as 1921, Velocette's modified roadsters were habitual record-breakers. Precisely 40 years later, the marque claimed a further hatful of honours, including, at Montlhèry, France, becoming the first 350cc machine to average 100mph (161kph) over 24 hours. The Goodmans were motorcycle enthusiasts as well as manufacturers, and if the family firm had a lasting commercial handicap (the company rarely showed much profit), it was this sheer addiction to racing.

Of course, there were humbler Velocettes available. A reworking of the old two-stroke single, the model U, appeared on the market in 1928, while the next year brought a supersports variant, named the USS. This was replaced in 1930 by the enduring 249cc GTP.

In an attempt to broaden the range still further, a budget overhead-cam 350 called the KTP was introduced by the company in the same year, but it was to prove troublesome and therefore unpopular. The niche was filled far more effectively with the arrival of the overhead-valve 248cc Velocette MOV in 1933.

The MOV was followed 12 months later by the similar 349cc

The ohv Venom in tuned 'Clubmans' trim was introduced in 1958 and became the forerunner of the raucous Thruxton model. This model dates from 1961.

MAC, and then by the 495cc MSS in 1935. These 'cooking' models did much to offset the Goodmans' expensive preoccupation with racing, which culminated in the ambitious 500cc twin-cylinder 'Roarer'. This machine was yet another British racer killed off by the postwar ban on supercharging. In 1938 a prototype parallel-twin, the Model O, failed to reach production.

During the austere years immediately following World War II, the emphasis passed to machines which were simpler, yet often reflected Velocette's customary need to be different, notably with the novel (but ill-fated) LE, which was built with a steel monocoque. This led in turn to the air-cooled Valiant and scooterish Vogue, neither of which enjoyed any greater commercial success.

By the1950 overhead-cam singles were no match for the wave of multi-cylinder racing

The 250cc Viceroy was another failed attempt to cash in on the Sixties scooter boom. It was good, but expensive at £200 (US$320) and not remotely Italian enough.

VELOCETTE 250 GTP 1930

Despite an enduring preoccupation with racing, such commercial success as Velocette enjoyed was largely founded on more 'everyman' machines such as the GTP roadster, launched in 1930. Although undoubtedly far humbler than its overhead-cam stablemates, the GTP had the finish and proportions of a geniune motorcycle, and (Scott excepted) was of higher quality than most British two-stroke fare of the period.

The air-cooled engine relied on deflector pistons rather than the

Two-stroke or not, the 250 GTP was a classic. This example is from 1936, the year after four-speed hand-change transmission replaced foot-change gears.

later Schnurle loop technology, breathing through a single carburettor but twin exhaust pipes. Unusually for that time, coil ignition was preferred to magneto, and a novel oil metering arrangement linked delivery to throttle opening. Initially launched with an iron cylinder head and

barrel and a three-speed hand gear change, by 1935 it boasted an all-aluminium engine and a Harold Willis four-speed foot change. Although production effectively ceased in 1940, a few GTPs were produced for export after 1945.

Engine: 249cc two-stroke single, 63x80mm, air-cooled
Power: n/a
Gearbox: 4-speed foot change
Final drive: chain
Weight: n/a
Top speed: 97kph (60mph)

VELOCETTE 250 MOV 1933

During the 1930s Velocette's showcase models were their overhead-cam bikes, yet they were difficult and costly to produce and returned very low profit margins. Eugene Goodman's first attempt at a more affordable four-stroke was a 350cc side-valve machine that proved a disappointingly poor performer. The overhead-valve MOV, unveiled in 1933, was the logical next step. The name came from type M, Overhead-Valve.

The 250 MOV was the prototype for future 'high camshaft' models. Its rugged versatility is shown in this shot of trials ace David Jones in action.

This was a 'high camshaft' design of a broad type which would last until the company's demise. The cams were driven by gears and were mounted high in the timing chest on the right-hand side of the engine, allowing the use of short, stiff pushrods. The powerplant was housed in a chassis originally intended for the

350cc side-valve, with Webb girder forks and a rigid rear end.

The 349cc MAC (MAF when produced for the British forces) was essentially an MOV with the stroke enlarged to 96mm, while the 495cc MSS was a MAC with an 81mm bore. Although the MOV reappeared only briefly after World War II (finishing in 1948),

both the MAC and MSS continued in production, being redesigned in 1953 and 1954 respectively with swing-arm rear suspension. The Venom and Viper ranges later derived from the MSS.

Despite their lack of cachet compared with the overhead-cam models, the MOV and its larger derivatives were perhaps the most

commercially successful models in Velocette history.

Engine: 248cc ohv single, 68x68.25mm, air-cooled
Power: n/a
Gearbox: 4-speed foot change
Final drive: chain
Weight: 125kg (275lb)
Top speed: 116kph (72mph)

VELOCETTE KSS
1925

The K 'Super Sports' bike arose out of Velocette's all-conquering TT exploits. A true sister model to the KTT racers, the Mk 1 of the early 1930s offered prodigious, free-revving performance that was remarkable for its day. It was dropped for 1935, but a revised Mk 2 version appeared in 1936 (along with a 'touring' sister, the KTS, as before), with a much-improved engine less prone to leaking oil. Regrettably, the bevel-drive overhead-cam engine was prohibitively expensive to produce, and although the model reappeared after the war as the company's sole 'cammy' roadster in 1946, it was withdrawn after another two years.

From then on, only the pure racing KTT – which culminated in the Mk 8 – continued to fly the overhead-cam flag for the Velocette company.

Engine: (Mk 1) 348cc ohc single, 74x81mm, air-cooled
Power: n/a
Gearbox: 4-speed foot change
Final drive: chain
Weight: 191kg (420lb)
Top speed: 129kph (80mph)

If the KTT was one of the most desirable 350cc privateer racers, the KSS was its equivalent amongst sports roadsters. This is one of the last Mark I's, dating from 1934.

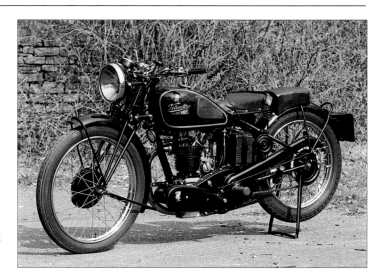

VELOCETTE LE
1949

First appearing in 1949, the curious LE was an enterprising but unsuccessful attempt at bringing a note of civility to commuter motorcycling. Although a side-valve, it was powered by a

near-silent 149cc engine (192cc from 1950) of unusually advanced specifications: liquid-cooled, horizontally opposed, with a four-bearing crankshaft, alloy heads and a pull-handle starter.

There was no conventional frame; instead, a fabricated sheet-steel monocoque formed the chassis, with integral mudguards and leg-shields. The bikes were hugely economical (2.2L/100km, or

130mpg), sedate and sensible. Yet although they enjoyed some success as police vehicles, as far as the public was concerned, Velocette could scarcely give them away.

Despite the LE's failure, Velocette plugged on with the same basic engine in a succession of different machines. The first, in 1956, was the Valiant, a far less radical derivative, with air-cooling and almost double the power. This was followed by the Vogue, which reverted to full-coverage bodywork, but now made from fibreglass. Unfortunately it sold even less well than its predecessors.

Engine: 149cc sv flat-twin, 44x49mm, liquid-cooled
Power: 6bhp at 6500rpm
Gearbox: 3-speed foot change
Final drive: chain
Weight: 120kg (265lb)
Top speed: 89kph (55mph)

Even 50 years on, it is clear that the LE 'Noddy Bike' exemplified all that was unconventional about Velocette.

VELOCETTE VENOM THRUXTON

1965

With a history so track-orientated, Velocette could never resist producing special performance machines. By 1958 even the basic Venom, launched two years earlier, was available with factory extras such as racing wheels, carburettor, ignition, exhaust, rev-counter and close-ratio gears. The 'Thrucky', as it was soon nicknamed, was effectively a factory-built model utilising the available performance parts, and was in turn derived from the slightly less potent Clubman model, which was itself a tuned Venom. The new name celebrated a similar machine's 1964 victory in the prestigious 800km (500 mile) race at Hampshire's Thruxton circuit. From mid-1965 around 1000 'replica' Thruxtons were built.

The 500cc Thruxton Venom was descended from endurance racers and was effectively a race bike on the road. It was many sports riders' idea of the ultimate ohv Velocette.

Powering the Thruxton was a highly tuned version of the standard 499cc Venom overhead-valve engine. Modifications on the machine included an Amal racing carburettor, high-compression pistons, special cylinder heads with larger inlet valves, improved gas flow and more radical valve timing. The bike was also equipped with close-ratio gears, uprated forks, clip-on handlebars, rear-set footrests, a humped seat and a long-distance fuel tank.

Although many Thruxtons were raced, others were used on the road, where they were exciting but were wildly impractical, as they demanded time-consuming care from their owners.

The high point of the model's track career arrived when it won the first 500cc Production TT in 1967. At this event, it was travelling at an average speed of 144.66kph (89.89mph). In full race tune, a good Thruxton was capable of 193kph (120mph), which was well up with even the fastest twins.

Engine: 499cc ohv single, 86x86mm, air-cooled
Power: up to 41bhp at 6500rpm
Gearbox: 4-speed foot change
Final drive: chain
Weight: 177kg (390lb)
Top speed: 171kph (106mph)

VELOSOLEX

FRANCE/HUNGARY 1946–

WHEN THE FOUNDER of Velosolex died, his sons sold the company to Yamaha, which closed it down shortly afterwards. Fortunately, a Hungarian concern bought all the tools and resumed manufacture of the Velosolex, one of the most successful powered two-wheelers of all time. Over eight million were made and sold in the first 54 years of production, with

The earliest 45cc Velosolexes – this is a 1948 model – made few concessions to elegance, but offered 30kph (17mph) from 0.5bhp at 2000 rpm.

remarkably little change, and there is little sign of any future plans for alteration, even down to the 483mm (19ins) wheels.

The biggest fundamental differences between a 2000 model and a 1946 model, apart from regional variations for specific markets, were that a square-section frame (instead of round-section) had been adopted in the 1960s, and that the incredibly low-powered motor could run on a leaner petrol-oil mix than when it was first introduced: 1+30 to 1+50.

With a fuel tank of only 1.4 litres (about two-and-a-half pints imperial; 3 pints US), the Velosolex still has a range of around 100km (over 60 miles) between fill-ups, thanks to a fuel consumption surpassing 1.4L/100km (200mpg). It has a miniature 6volt electrical system, with a glow-worm-power 15W headlight bulb and a 4W tail light.

Memorably described as looking 'like a very heavy bicycle with a large dead snail on the front mudguard', the Velosolex does not have a clutch in the conventional

sense: more a 'free engine' in the vintage style. To start, the machine is pedalled, and once it is under way, the friction drive to the engine is engaged by pulling a lever; the engine should then catch. Thereafter, the whole assemblage buzzes merrily along, even on quite steep hills, though the dreaded 'light pedal assistance' may be required with heavier riders or steeper hills. A centrifugal automatic clutch takes care of stops and starts along the way; to stop the engine, there is a decompressor.

In most of Europe, the Velosolex is not subject to the normal taxes or restrictions that affect motorcycles – such as road fund or insurance – since it is regarded (not unreasonably) as more akin to a bicycle. After two generations of popularity despite a rather unfashionable image, it was relaunched in the late 1990s as a trendy, convenient, environmentally friendly and cheap mode of urban transport. Certainly, a solo machine with such fuel economy compares

Later (and indeed current) Velosolexes may be slightly more stylish than the original, but they are still wonderfully utilitarian.

favourably with a small bus having fewer than six to 10 passengers, or with a full-sized double-decker bus carrying under 20. The seemingly endless life of a light bike like the Velosolex means that the energy expended in its manufacture and the cost of its materials are rapidly amortised; it is perhaps more environmentally friendly than an electric moped.

VICTORIA

GERMANY 1899–1966

FOUNDED IN NURNBERG by Max Frankenburger and Max Offenstein, the Victoria bicycle factory began trading in 1886. After 13 successful years, the company switched to motorcycles. Victoria's first machines to use the internal-combustion engine

featured either Fafnir or Zedel single-cylinder units. These were sold until 1918 with only minimal change, but after the war, production concentrated on a series of motorcycles powered by a 493cc horizontally opposed twin-cylinder engine. As the engine

layout might suggest, Victoria used proprietary power units built by BMW. These were the early M2B15 assemblies with fore-and-aft cylinder, not the more familiar transverse flat-twin configuration.

In 1923, when Munich-based BMW decided to build complete

motorcycles, Victoria quickly engaged BMW's former designer, Martin Stolle. He developed a family of new overhead-valve engines with a very similar layout; these were built for Victoria at the Sedlbauer factory in Munich. In the late 1920s Victoria bought the factory and continued producing 498cc flat-twins. A 598cc version was added later.

Stolle remained with the company for only two years and was succeeded by Gustav Steinlen. In 1925 Steinlen designed the first supercharged German racing machine, using a 498cc flat-twin engine. Once again, the cylinders were in line with the motorcycle, and in 1926 one of these models set a new German speed record of 167kph (almost 104mph).

New single-cylinder models were introduced in 1928, using Sturmey-Archer engines of 198 to 498cc, with upright cylinders, and Victoria also fitted a 348cc

Victoria was one of the pioneers of the German motorcycle industry. This 1901 model feaured an upright cylinder, single speed and belt final drive.

overhead-valve version of the Sturmey-Archer unit built by Horex (Columbus) under licence.

Besides Stolle's efforts, Victoria also used designs by Albert Roder and Richard Kuchen. Among the series-production models built during the interwar years were several two-strokes, ranging from 98 to 198cc, a 497cc inlet-over-exhaust single and some overhead-valve twins designed by Stolle. These featured triangular pressed-steel frames and completely enclosed unit-construction engines.

During World War II Victoria concentrated mainly on its four-stroke single, the KR35WH, which was produced virtually throughout the war and was widely used by the Wehrmacht. After 1945, production initially focused on small-capacity two-strokes, ranging from a 38cc engine (for attachment to conventional pedal cycles) to a 247cc motorcycle, the KR25 Aero. Like other manufacturers of the period, Victoria soon discovered that demand outstripped supply, and by the end of the 1940s the company was firmly re-established and in full production.

In 1951 an improved 250 appeared, but the biggest news was a completely new smaller machine, the KR125 Bi-fix. Its 123cc (51x60mm) single-cylinder engine produced four-and-a-half

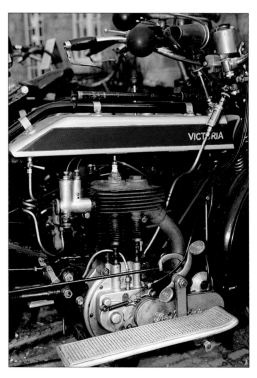

Above: Victoria's first internal combustion engined machines used either Fafnir of Zedel single-cylinder units. These were sold until 1918.

Below: Several Victoria models, including the 1937 KR9, featured triangular pressed-steel frames and completely enclosed unit construction engines.

brake horsepower at 3000 rpm, and could achieve 80kph (50mph). Next was Victoria's first postwar four-stroke, the V35 Bergmeister (Mountain Master). First displayed in 1951, this was an unusual narrow-angle V-twin.

The Bergmeister didn't go on sale until 1953, when the KR26 Aero also became available. With a twin-port single-cylinder two-stroke engine, this model was sold in both touring and sport versions. That same year, at the Frankfurt International Show, Victoria introduced a scooter called the Peggy. This was not only luxurious but also practical, with excellent weather protection and a lusty 198cc horizontal engine (again, two-stroke). Other features of the design included 406mm (16ins) wheels, leading-link front forks and swinging-arm rear suspension.

A new lightweight, the Vicky III, debuted in 1954. Although

An Aero 250cc built in 1938. Post-war, Victoria's production initially centred around small capacity machines. At that time, the Aero was the largest bike it made.

unstable because of higher living standards combined with the availability of small cars. In an attempt to counter this slide, Victoria entered into a sales agreement with the Parilla concern. Bikes made using the Italian maker's engines were known as Victoria-Parillas. After a period of indecision, Victoria also decided to relaunch the Peggy

scooter, but with the same power unit as the new Swing motorcycle. The revised Peggy had a 'live' rear axle and push-button gear change. Other newcomers in 1956 included the Avanti and Tonyl mopeds and the Spatz micro-car.

Unfortunately, all these new offerings were not enough to keep the Victoria ship afloat. In 1958, the company amalgamated with DKW and Express to form the Zweirad Union. From then until 1966, models such as the Avanti, Peggy and Vicky continued to be available for both domestic and export consumption.

classified as a moped, the design was much more like a scooter, and indeed a Vicky finished first in a scooter rally at Merano, Italy, that year. The course, laid out in the Tyrolean Alps, attracted entries from all over Europe. The victor, Wilhelm Steiner, won the event by covering 605km (376 miles) on only 8.6 litres (1.9 gallons) of fuel! The Vicky had a 48cc (38x42mm) two-stroke single-cylinder engine, with a hand-starter and a two-speed gearbox.

At the Brussels Show in January 1955 there was an interesting

exhibit from Sparta, then the Netherlands' largest motorcycle manufacturer, featuring a new 250cc model with a Victoria KR26 Aero engine in place of the previous Ilo unit. The same month brought news of an exciting new Victoria 200, the KR21 Swing.

By 1956 the German motorcycle industry was becoming financially

By the end of the 1950s, Victoria was reduced to manufacturing lightweight motorcycles and mopeds. Typical of the breed was the 1959 Avanti 50cc model.

VICTORIA V35 BERGMEISTER
1951

The Bergmeister (Mountain Master) was a fine motorcycle, let down by an overlong development process, high price and small engine size (350cc).

filter. Hidden under another cowling was the Noris dynamo, the battery and the components of the coil ignition system. There were several interesting features, including a gear-driven camshaft located between the 'V' of the cylinders, and pushrod tunnels cast into the cylinder barrels and heads.

The frame was extremely modern, with telescopic forks and swinging-arm rear suspension. The 483mm (19ins) wheels were laced to 180mm (just over 7ins) full-width driven brakes, and offered excellent stopping power. There was just one snag: for two years after its public debut, customers were not able to buy it.

Ultimately, however, it was the Bergmeister that nearly bankrupted the company, since it took four years of development before serious engine vibration problems could be fully rectified.

The V35 Bergmeister (Mountain Master) had an unusual narrow-angle (28-degree) V-twin engine, a chain-operated four-speed gearbox and shaft final drive. Victoria claimed that it could reach 130kph

(81mph), but it was the wide spread of power from the 347cc engine that really impressed. On paper, 21bhp at 6300rpm might not seem much, but the Victoria V-twin could often be seen hauling a

single sports sidecar. The closeness of the cylinder layout and the exceptionally clean lines of the castings for the massive crankcase completely concealed the 26mm (1in) Bing carburettor and its air

The first Bergmeister models went on sale in 1953 and were well received; only a slow-operating throttle spoiled the bike's otherwise impressive performance. There was no sign of the dreaded torque reaction, then a feature of almost all transverse engines. Even

with the machine at a standstill, blipping the throttle failed to produce a noticeable reaction.

The Bergmeister was a fine motorcycle but was hampered by a combination of high price, a long development period and the fact that it was only a 350.

Engine: 347cc ohv V-twin, 64x54mm, air-cooled
Power: 21 bhp at 6300rpm
Gearbox: 4-speed foot change
Final drive: shaft
Weight: 176.5kg (389lb)
Top speed: 130kph (81mph)

VICTORIA SWING   1955

The Victoria Swing was one of the most unusual German motorcycles to reach production in the postwar period. First seen at various shows around Europe in 1955, it featured a unit-construction engine of extremely advanced design, which borrowed heavily from existing scooter, rather than motorcycle, practice. This was mounted almost horizontally in a duplex cradle frame. The 197cc (65x60mm) power unit was fixed rigidly to an internally ribbed cast-iron strut that carried the rear wheel. This wheel was linked to the spindle of the four-speed gearbox by an enclosed final drive chain tensioned by an eccentric jockey sprocket. In order to provide rear suspension, the engine unit pivoted from the frame below the crankcase. The upper rear portion of the frame and the rear mudguard were integral welded-up pressings, reinforced to take the upper mountings of the twin, adjustable, rear shock absorbers. Since this system precluded the use of a conventional foot-controlled gear change,

In 1956, the Swing was truly revolutionary. This 197cc single-cylinder two-stroke had push-button gear change and a unique form of rear wheel suspension.

buttons on the left handlebar served instead.

The rear of the engine was concealed under detachable panels fitted to the frame. Front suspension was provided by leading links, connected by covered links to a bridge piece that bore on a coil spring, with a co-axial damper placed in front of the steering head. A small fairing was built into the top of the forks, and this carried the headlamp and speedometer. Both wheels had 406mm (16ins) rims and 3.25-section tyres.

Other details included a large dual seat (in two sections) and a huge, but nonetheless very effective silencer. From 1956 the specification was updated to include an electrically operated fuel gauge and brake warning lights.

However, the really innovative feature of the Swing was its new method of gear-changing. From a small panel on the left-hand handlebar, the rider changed gear at the press of a button. The system was remarkably simple, consisting solely of a powerful electromagnet which operated the gear selector pushrod. There was even an emergency circuit for use when the battery was flat.

It is a great pity that this novel machine appeared at a time when the industry was entering a period of poor sales. It could well have achieved much greater success, rather than meeting its end in 1962. The Swing could also have influenced other, later designs, a loss not just for Victoria, but for motorcycling in general.

Engine: 197cc two-stroke horizontal single, 65x60mm, air-cooled
Power: 11.3 bhp at 5300 rpm
Gearbox: 4-speed press-button change
Final drive: enclosed chain
Weight: 131kg (289lb)
Top speed: 97kph (60mph)

VILLA

FRANCESCO VILLA AND HIS younger brother Walter were both road racers of world-class standing. Francesco was also a highly gifted engineer, with a speciality for two-stroke engines. After working for FB Mondial and Montesa, his first autonomous effort was the design of a single-cylinder over-the-counter 125cc racer with square bore and stroke measurements of 54x54mm (although the prototype employed 56x50mm). Liquid-cooled with disc-valve induction, it produced 30bhp at 11,200rpm. Top speed was 190km (118mph).

The Villa brothers, Francesco and Walter, were not only successful racers, but motorcycle builders in their own right. This is a 1969 50cc racing model.

The tarmac racer was soon joined by no fewer than seven dirt-bike models. All were orthodox air-cooled singles with piston-controlled induction, and were available in trials or motocross form, ranging from 50 to 250cc. Other production Villa competition machines of the same era included a purposeful disc-valve single-cylinder racer of either 174 or

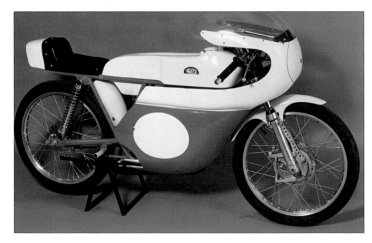

247cc, suitable for Italian Junior Formula events. There were also a 125cc narrow-angle 125 V-twin and a 250cc four! Intended for Grand Prix events, the larger model soon became a victim of new FIM restrictions and the Villas withdrew from direct involvement in GP racing.

Villa motorcycles were campaigned in the classics by not only the brothers, but also riders

A 1983 Villa 250 MC (Moto-Cross), with a 247cc liquid-cooled engine, long-travel Marzocchi forks and single-shock rear suspension.

such as Mandolini and the British star Charles Mortimer. This resulted in considerable publicity during the early 1970s. Since then, Villa has mainly concentrated its efforts on the manufacture of motocross and enduro bikes, latterly with liquid-cooling, as well as monoshock frames. Even so, the Monteveglio company has also offered some street models, notably the 125 Daytona and Italia (roadsters), the 125 Scrambler (trail) and the 350 Rommel (trail). The off-road bikes were imported into Britain during the 1970s by the Cleveland-based John Burdon Engineering concern.

VINCENT

IT IS DISPUTABLE WHETHER there is – or can be – a single 'best motorcycle in the world'. Although the Vincent had its shortcomings (and of course, having ceased production in 1955, it was slower than many, more modern, machines), there are thousands of motorcyclists – perhaps even hundreds of thousands – who, if asked to name the best motorcycle of all time, would reply, without hesitation, 'Vincent.'

Why? In brief, everything comes together with this marque. Firstly, the looks of the Vincent (at least, Series B and C examples) cannot be bettered: a purposeful combination of immaculate black gloss, silvery light-alloy, and sparkling chrome and stainless steel; a massive engine; and not an ounce of unnecessary weight. Secondly, once the engine is

started (this is not easy: the kick-start has been known to throw light riders over low walls), it emits that evocative V-twin sound. Thirdly, there is the ride ...

By modern standards, 55bhp – the output of a Series B Shadow – is modest, but this is a very light motorcycle for its power. The ride from the hinge-in-the-middle frame, with its constantly varying saddle angle, is odd at first, but soon curiously natural, more like riding a horse than a motorcycle. With around 177kph (110mph) in third gear and over 193kph (120mph) in top, if you can find a road long enough to wind it up all

This is about as far as it is possible to get from a classic Vincent motorcycle: a 48cc Firefly auxiliary cycle motor, dating from 1954.

the way, this is still a fast machine today.

What's more, the Vincent just keeps going. To cover nearly 161,000km (100,000 miles), you will need to replace the tyres and chains from time to time, and reline the brakes. You may well find that the exhausts rust through and must be replaced, and you will probably have to reline the clutch. Yet you won't wear the engine out, as long as you stick to the manufacturer's service schedule. However, you might need an engine rebuild at anything between 300,000 and 800,000km (200,000 and 500,000 miles). The design life of the frame is about 1.6 million km (a million miles).

When you do need to work on the bike, the tool kit required is ridiculously small. Philip Vincent thought of this, too: he deliberately kept the number of fastener sizes to a minimum, so that everything could be fixed with just a few tools, and everything on the engine was designed to be easy to work on.

There is more. You may not care to subject your Vincent to such stresses, but others modified theirs to break world records: at one

time, Vincents held the flying-mile records both for motorcycles and for sidecars. Fifteen years after production ceased, the supercharged Super Mouse could still pull an 8.5-second standing quarter and a terminal 273.1kph (169.7mph).

So, this was not only the fastest motorcycle of its day, and the basis of numerous record-breakers, but also the most reliable, and the easiest to repair – a very rare combination! Small wonder that people will still say today that the Vincent is the best motorcycle in the world, even if they were born long after the last example was built.

The actual history of the marque begins with the original HRD firm. In 1928 Conrad Vincent, father of Philip Vincent, put up roughly £30,000 to buy HRD and finance a new machine.

The main feature of the first Vincent-HRD was the sprung frame; the engine was a JAP 500cc single, later with Rudge Python and Sport Python alternatives. The model sold in tiny numbers: 24 in 1929, 36 in 1930, 48 in 1931 and 60 in 1932. Vincent's own 500cc single was shown in 1934, offering

The 35bhp Vincent Grey Flash machine, which was a racing derivative of the Comet single, flourished in the days of the full or 'dustbin' fairing.

approximately 130–160kph (80–100mph) in Meteor (basic), Comet and TT forms.

Famously, the genesis of the V-twin was two overlapping drawings for this engine, which was built with offset cylinders (much better for cooling than the 'knife and fork' approach). The resulting Series A Rapide appeared at London's Olympia Motor Show in 1936. This model continued to 1939, and was followed after the war by the far superior Series B, C and D machines. Other Vincent products, mostly undertaken in an attempt to keep the company solvent, included a three-wheeler car, the Picador engine for a target drone, the Firefly auxiliary cycle motor (which required altogether too much 'light pedal assistance') and an industrial two-stroke (also fitted to what would now be called a jet-ski in 1956–58). In addition, Vincent acted as a distributor for the NSU Quickly. None of these side ventures was a success.

VIPER
England 1919–22: Despite its name, the 293cc side-valve engine which was bought in from JAP meant that this assembled machine lacked bite.

VIRATELLE
France 1907–24: This individualistic French assembler used a very wide variety of bought-in engines in the production of motorcycles.

VIS
Germany 1923–25: The in-house 250cc two-stroke single from this company was more successful than its other machine, the in-house longitudinally mounted 500cc two-stroke flat twin. In the latter machine, the rear cylinder overheated.

VITTORIA
Italy 1931–80: Before the outbreak of World War II, this was an assembler which used a wide variety of engines in different capacities, from 100 to 500cc: these engines were bought in from Sachs, JAP, Kuchen and Rudge Python. Postwar the company produced for the most part small two-strokes of capacities of under 100cc.

VOLLBLUT
Germany 1925–27: These motorcycles from Germany were full-blooded machines designed for sporting use. They had been fitted with 250 and 350cc overhead-valve engines, bought in from Blackburne.

VINCENT RAPIDE   1936

The 47.5-degree angle of the original 'plumber's nightmare' was reputedly chosen to allow the new engine to be fitted into an existing

frame – and a legend was born. Certainly the Series A Rapide, produced between 1936 and 1939, has its faults. The clutch is heavy

and prone to creep, and the machine rather generously shares its oil with the rest of the world. Full torque in intermediate gears can defeat the clutch or the gearbox, or both. On the other hand, the brakes are surprisingly good – an accusation seldom levelled at Brough Superiors, the most obvious competitor – and the motorcycle's very first speed test yielded 174kph (108mph).

It is hard to remember, because so many of us have seen a Series A, that only 78 of these machines were made, of which perhaps two-thirds survive. Compared with the later Rapides it was, however, a most unrefined beast. Postwar Series B (1946–50), Series C (1948–54) and Series D (1954–55) models had a 50-degree included angle and internal (and much more leakproof) oil passages, and are much better bikes in every way.

Engine: 998cc ohv in-line V-twin, 84x90mm, air-cooled
Power: 45bhp at 5300rpm
Gearbox: 4-speed foot change
Final drive: chain
Weight: 206kg (455lb)
Top speed: 190kph (118mph) approx

Post-war Rapides – this is a 1951 Series C – were vastly superior motorcycles to the pre-war Series A, and a great deal more oil-tight.

VINCENT SERIES C BLACK SHADOW
1948

The differences between the basic Series C Rapide and a Series C Black Shadow were remarkably small. The compression ratio was raised, of course, from 6.45:1 to 7.3:1 – the standard back-yard tuner's trick.

The carburettor was bigger, but this was only by 1.5mm (one-sixteenth in) at 28.58mm (one-and-an-eighth in), with slightly different jetting. Ports were smoothed, and connecting rods polished: again, basic refinements. Today, most of this would be done as standard on any high-performance motorcycle.

The result was an extra 10bhp, an increase from the original power output of well over 20 per cent.

The distinguishing marks of the Shadow were black enamelled engine cases and the 242kph (150mph) speedometer.

Apart from that, the model's huge, beautiful engine cases were enamelled black. This was done not for any real engineering

advantage (heat loss from the bare alloy was at least as good), but simply to announce to those in the know that this was the fastest off-the-shelf road-going motorcycle in the world.

There were no speed limits in those days, on the open road. Nor, in Britain, were there any motorways: these were still a decade in the future. The last Series C Black Shadow would be produced in 1953.

Engine: 998cc ohv in-line V-twin, 84x90mm, air-cooled
Power: 55bhp at 5700rpm
Gearbox: 4-speed foot change
Final drive: chain
Weight: 208kg (458lb)
Top speed: 201kph (125mph) approx

VINCENT SERIES C COMET
1948

To quote one Vincent dealer, 'It may only be half a Vincent, but it's the best half'. The 500cc singles are inevitably overshadowed by the V-twins, but they were very

fine (and fast) machines in their own right, especially in Grey Flash form (1949–51) with 35bhp at 6200rpm and 27kg (60lb) lighter, offering 177kph (110mph) –

although the aluminium bottom ends of Flashes were suspect.
Of course, from 1948 to 1955, the 1000cc Rapide/Shadow V-twin was also available in super-tuned

form, as the Lightning. This had 70bhp at a mere 5600rpm, thanks to fiercer cams, a higher compression ratio, 32mm (one-and-a-quarter ins) carburettors –

up from 28.58mm (one-and-an-eighth ins) on the Shadow – and a lot of hand work. It also weighed 35kg (78lb) less than a Shadow, and 4.5kg (10lb) less than a standard 500cc Comet. The latter were made until 1954.

Engine: 499cc ohv single, 84x90mm, air-cooled
Power: 28bhp at 5800rpm
Gearbox: 4-speed foot change
Final drive: chain
Weight: 177kg (390lb)
Top speed: 145kph (90mph) est

The 500cc Comet, seen here in 1949 Series C guise, was not outstandingly fast by modern standards but it was a solid mile-eater.

VINCENT BLACK PRINCE   1954

The Black Prince was a fully enclosed Shadow, and really did look like some caparisoned warhorse from the Middle Ages. Astonishingly, it weighed only 6kg (13lb) more than the unfaired Series D Rapide, and only 2lb (1kg) more than the Series C Shadow; the Black Knight was a Black Prince with a Rapide engine instead of a Shadow unit.

Alas, the Series D was the last of the line, not least due to

Argentine politics. Philip Vincent's father was unable to get capital out of Argentina, and a contract with the Argentine police had been lost in 1948 (prior to this, Vincent had been selling 10 machines a week to Argentina). The company went bankrupt in 1949, and although it did recover, the sad truth was that despite high price tags on its bikes, Vincent lost money on every machine sold, and the public wanted an even faster motorcycle.

Engine: 998cc ohv in-line V-twin, 84x90mm, air-cooled
Power: 55bhp at 5700rpm
Gearbox: 4-speed foot change
Final drive: chain
Weight: 209kg (460lb)
Top speed: 185kph (115mph) approx

Even good photographs rarely do justice to any motorcycle, and you really have to see the Series D Black Prince to appreciate its sheer magnificence.

VINDEC

VINDEC WAS A MARQUE designation used by Brown Brothers of London, a supplier of parts and fittings as well as the Brown motorcycle. The Vindec name was rarely advertised or used until late in 1914, when it appeared on a 225cc two-stroke model that had a two-speed gearbox and chain-cum-belt transmission. At the same time, Brown Brothers listed a 4hp V-twin having an overhead-inlet-valve, Bosch magneto and various transmission options. The two-stroke was included in the line-up through to 1916, when the V-twin was given a 6hp JAP engine.

After the war, the company promoted a 225cc two-stroke single, and then added a 976cc side-valve JAP V-twin for 1920. These were continued until 1922; the following year, the two-stroke was replaced by a 292cc side-valve JAP model. Since Brown Brothers was a trade wholesaler, most Vindec machines were probably bought-in badged designs from established firms, and models from this era bore a strong family resemblance to those of the Rex-Acme factory.

In 1924 only a 170cc two-stroke joined the JAP single for that season, the twin returning for 1925 only, with the 292cc side-valve model (enlarged to 300cc for 1926). Another lightweight two-stroke, (147cc) was also launched for one season. The 300cc side-valve JAP that carried the Vindec name into 1929, its final year.

A fine Vindec V-twin from 1915 with three speeds, belt drive and period sidecar complete with spare wheel, typical of the marque in that period.

VULCAAN

SOMETIMES SPELT AS VULKAAN, this Dutch firm was based in Venray and had its roots in bicycle manufacture, as did many firms in that country. Then as now, cycling was a very popular form of personal transport, thanks to the flatness of the native terrain and a benevolent government attitude.

Before World War I Vulcaan decided to enter the motorcycle market with a range of models powered by single and V-twin side-valve engines. The company had a close connection with the Swiss concern of Zürcher & Lüthi, which produced the Zedel range, and naturally turned to this source for its needs. With plenty of power units to choose from, the machines were constructed with heavy-duty bicycle parts that were easy for

Vulcaan to design and make. The models were conventional, featuring a tubular frame, girder forks, wire wheels and belt drive, with some form of gear and minimal brakes.

In later years, Vulcaan built some engines itself using a combination of Zedel parts that were in stock as spares and other components manufactured in-

house. Engine construction became more difficult as the war progressed, although the company's facilities were adequate for the rest of the production process, being bicycle based. In time, supplies of the essential Zedel parts ran out and production ceased. The firm continued with bicycles and postwar imported motorcycles from Britain.

WANDERER

THIS MARQUE WAS EARLY on the scene, and its first machines were built by Winkelhofer & Jaenicke in Saxony. They were typical primitives with a single-cylinder engine mounted vertically in a loop frame with belt drive to the rear wheel. The 308cc engine had an automatic inlet valve and magneto ignition located in front of the cylinder, while the carburettor went at the rear on the end of

a long inlet pipe. The rest of the design incorporated what were essentially the forks, brakes, bars and saddle of a heavy-duty bicycle.

Wanderer's range soon expanded to include more singles as well as V-twins in several different capacities. Side-valves replaced the automatic, while the cycle parts became heavier to take the increased loads, and the models assumed a typical pre-

World War I form. During this time the company did offer rear suspension on some models, using a pivoted system controlled by coil springs.

After World War I came a 185cc overhead-valve single with a horizontal cylinder, but of more importance was a range of V-twins. All were of unit construction with either side- or overhead-valves, and some of the latter type had

eight valves. For the twins the frame had duplex members; these ran parallel to the ground along the top of the crankcase to the rear-wheel spindle, but were otherwise typical of the period. Front suspension was by leading-link forks and chain final drive.

In 1928 the range was replaced by a unit-construction single with shaft final drive. The 498cc engine had overhead-valves and the crankshaft set along the frame, and drove straight back to the three-speed hand-change gearbox, its output shaft having a contracting-band brake fitted to its front end and a coupling to the bevel box at the rear. The engine unit went into a rigid duplex pressed-steel frame fitted with tubular trailing-link front forks controlled by a single leaf spring. There were good-sized drum brakes, while the fuel tank was tucked in under the top frame member. A battery and electric

lighting, along with a horn, were provided; the speedometer was driven from the front end of the gearbox via the output shaft.

Unfortunately, this innovative model came at just the wrong time and overextended the firm, which had insufficient capital to remain afloat until sales began to match investment.

Wanderer failed and was taken over by German rival NSU, for which it produced a Sachs-engined lightweight for a time. However,

the company's shaft-drive single design, drawings and production equipment were sold to F. Janacek of Prague, who began building the Janacek-Wanderer. The name of this model was soon abbreviated to Jawa, spawning a whole new marque.

A Wanderer V-twin from 1911. By this time, the bike had leading-link front forks and changes to the transmission to improve its efficiency.

WERNER

FRANCE 1897–1908

THE WERNER BROTHERS were Frenchmen of Russian extraction who lived in Paris and worked as journalists. They became involved with powered transport in its very early days; their first attempt combined a standard bicycle with a Labitte engine mounted horizontally over the rear wheel, which it drove by chain.

This was an experiment, but in 1897 they began to sell a revised machine with the three-quarters horsepower 116cc engine mounted

A famous tile picture, one of many originally housed in Michelin House, London. This one depicts a Werner competing in the 1902 Paris-Vienna race.

LE PNEU MICHELIN BOIT L'OBSTACLE

PARIS-VIENNE 1902

BUCQUET sur WERNER

from France and Arnott from England were the riders, and Bucquet, on a three-and-a-half horsepower Werner, arrived first. His machine was stripped of all non-essentials to meet the weight restrictions; hence the mudguards were removed, although a band brake was kept for the rear wheel.

Models for 1904 were the 2hp Tourist, two-and-three-quarters horsepower Paris-Vienna and a three-and-a-quarter horsepower Paris-Madrid, all much as before in their established lines, with a vertical engine and belt drive. A leading-link front fork appeared for the 1905 range, and was based on the braced forks. To these were added the links, on pivots at the base of the fork, with the wheel held at the front end of the links and tension springs at the rear; the springs were connected to lugs on the main fork tubes, which were to stretch as the wheel rose.

above the front wheel of a standard bicycle. The engine had an automatic inlet valve, hot-tube ignition and the Werners' own system of surface carburation, and drove the front wheel by a twisted belt. This smoothed the drive in comparison with other designs, although the layout did make the machine top-heavy – and any fall usually meant a fire caused by the ignition arrangements. The power was limited, supplementing the efforts of the rider on the pedals rather than replacing them.

The machine was sold as the motocyclette, and battery and coil ignition soon replaced the hot-tube system. However, the design's inherent instability remained and became more noticeable in 1899, when a heavier 217cc engine appeared to offer more power. That year also saw the machine made under licence in Britain at works in Coventry run by Harry Lawson.

Overcoming the weight distribution problems required a radical rethink, which resulted in the brothers introducing their 'New Werner' design in 1901. This would set the basic layout for their motorcycles for decades to come. They moved the engine from above the front wheel to a position ahead of the frame bottom bracket, and used the crankcase as a stressed member to join the lower frame sections together. The Werners also added an extra frame tube above the engine to brace the

structure, thus creating the diamond frame. In a stroke, they both greatly lowered the machine's centre of gravity and moved it back to between the wheels, much improving the weight distribution on them. The layout was soon being used by others under licence, and was protected by patents. Attempts to circumvent these led to the development of a loop frame that ran under the crankcase, which no longer had to hold the frame together.

The new design featured a 225, later 262cc, engine which retained the automatic inlet valve but had hand-pump lubrication and was fed by a spray carburettor. The improved frame kept its bicycle form, and also the rigid front forks, which were braced in later years. The pedals were moved back slightly to allow more room for the crankcase, and kept their chain run to the rear wheel. Braking was minimal, using a block against the belt rim at the rear and cycle calliper brakes at the front.

Werner began to gain success in major road races in 1902, with Bucquet running in the Circuit du Nord and Paris–Vienna events. Labitte also appeared in the latter race, where both men rode 2hp machines and finished first and second among the motorcycle

A Werner advertisement from October 1903 showing the engine details, its controls, carburettor, the mounting and belt drive.

entries. In 1903 Werner had four bikes in the ill-fated Paris-to-Madrid race that was stopped at Bordeaux because of accidents. Bucquet, Maillard and Rivierre

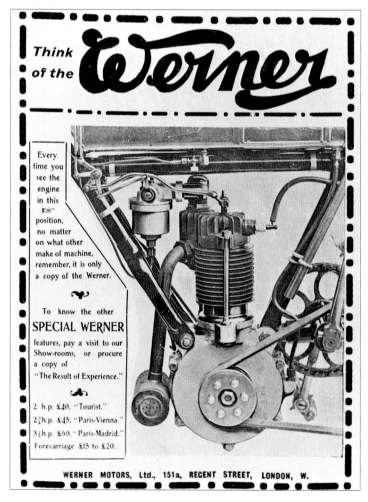

Think of the **Werner**

Every time you see the engine in this ☞ position, no matter on what other make of machine, remember, it is only a copy of the Werner.

To know the other
SPECIAL WERNER
features, pay a visit to our Show-rooms, or procure a copy of "The Result of Experience."

2 h.p. £40. "Tourist."
2¾ h.p. £45. "Paris-Vienna."
3¼ h.p. £60. "Paris-Madrid."
Forecarriage £15 to £20.

WERNER MOTORS, Ltd., 151a, REGENT STREET, LONDON, W.

The main news for the 1905 line-up was the addition of a vertical-twin engine of three-and-a-quarter or 4hp with the cylinders side by side, and the exhaust valves and camshaft at the front. Since the pistons rose and fell alternately, the engine had a 180-degree crankshaft, unlike later twins in which the pistons moved as one. The inlets continued to be automatic, but they were governed by a lever that varied their lift and at the same time introduced a piece of gauze into the inlet pipe

to prevent backfires. In other respects, the twin copied the singles, with belt drive and the option of sprung forks.

The Werner motorcycle was not to progress much further, as it would be overtaken by other, improved designs. However, in 1906 the company used the twin-cylinder engine for a tricar, which had two drive chains on different-sized sprockets to give two speeds.

Sadly, the two brothers who had contributed so much to the basic design of the motorcycle did not

This Werner was from 1902 and was typical of the early models. The deep tanks were set between the frame tubes and there was no suspension.

prosper from their work and enterprise. They invested a very considerable sum which they were expecting to receive for their interests in the firm, but this proved worthless. The Werner motorcycle business collapsed; only the car-manufacturing arm went on to 1914.

WERNER 1901

Before the new Werner design appeared, opinion was sharply divided on where to position the engine. The brothers themselves had tried it above the front wheel, as had others, with either wheel driven. There were three solutions to this problem. One strategy was to hang the engine unit from or above the frame downtube using a clip-on, with the drive to the rear wheel either direct or over one or more jockey pulleys. A second, less typical, arrangement was to hang the engine out behind the rear wheel or to tuck it in behind the seat tube, either low down towards the rear of the bottom bracket or high up under the saddle. A third, even more unusual solution was to build it into either the front or rear wheel. All these options were explored, but the original Werner layout, with minor variations, proved to be the best for most machines and it remains so today.

This 1901 Werner displays, in rudimentary form, the engine position copied by almost all motorcycle manufacturers since. This 2hp model was capable of delivering a top speed of 40kph (25mph) from its 225cc engine.

Engine: 225cc aiv vertical single, 64x70mm, air-cooled
Power: 2hp
Gearbox: direct drive
Final drive: belt
Weight: 41kg (90lb)
Top speed: 40kph (25mph)

WESLAKE

ENGLAND 1974–

THIS FIRM, BASED AT Rye in Sussex, was best known for its work on cylinder heads for major car companies. Then, in the early 1970s, Weslake took its expertise into the two-wheeled world to build a speedway engine. Success with this soon led to the unit being used for grass- and long-track events.

The Weslake engine was a 495cc overhead-valve single with four valves, constructed robustly to withstand the loads generated from the high compression ratio. It also had to cope with hard use,

races in quick succession and meetings often following hard on one another. Despite the four valves, there was only one carburettor and one exhaust pipe, the ports joining internally. The tried and tested total-loss lubrication system was retained, with an external pump bolted to the timing chest, while ignition was either electronic or via battery-powered points.

From the start, the Weslake powerplant was a success and it was soon dominant in speedway racing, followed by grass- and

Left: One aspect of Weslake work was this exotic sprint machine fitted with two 850cc engines, each with a supercharger and running on special fuel.

Above: Weslake were involved in many projects and this was a typical road racing one. The company supplied the 500cc twin-cylinder, twin-cam engine.

long-track events. Much later there were also single and twin overhead-camshaft engines, to suit riders' demands, and a 998cc overhead-cam V-twin that was used for sidecar grass-track events and had five-valve cylinder heads.

In the 1970s the company collaborated with John Caffrey to

build the Weslake Vendetta. The engine was a 492cc eight-valve vertical twin and drove a five-speed gearbox installed in a duplex frame. Later came larger versions of the same engine, but in most cases with limited chassis involvement for Weslake, which concentrated on power units.

WHITE & POPPE

ENGLAND 1902–22

COVENTRY-BASED WHITE & POPPE was more celebrated for its motorcycle engines, although the machine that endures most in people's minds was actually a Sunbeam designed by the son of one of the founders. From 1902 White & Poppe found a ready market for its engines in the emergent car and motorcycle industries, having produced its own complete bikes, including

498cc vertical twins and 347cc two-strokes.

The company's most notable scion was Erling Poppe, who began designing motorcycles in 1922. Poppe's aim was to improve the lot of the motorcyclist in areas such as silencing, comfort and cleanliness, and he went on to design cars and heavy vehicles before presenting his magnum opus, the Sunbeam S7. From 1943

the Sunbeam name belonged to the BSA group, and Erling Poppe was hired from the bus-building division of Bristol Tramways to design the new motorbike for the postwar years. The result was the S7, and in some ways its imposing bulk and manner of construction bore witness to its designer's previous theatre of work. The 487cc in-line twin-cylinder engine was bolted solidly in the frame,

and the test riders found the vibrations so severe that, although initial output was sold in this format, subsequent production was based on a vibration-free rubber-mounted engine.

Nevertheless, Poppe's Sunbeam S7 and its De Luxe and S8 derivatives which appeared from 1949 onwards were regarded as the epitome of the gentleman's motorcycle.

WHIZZER

USA 1939–62

THE WHIZZER MAKE BEGAN with a simple 138cc (8.4cid) side-valve engine designed to fit into a standard bicycle frame, with the carburettor located behind the unit and the exhaust running into a finned manifold. The engine had belt drive to a friction roller fitted

under the bottom bracket and in contact with the rear tyre, to offer cycling without too much work and at minimal cost.

After the war, a complete machine became available and had the same engine mounted low down, its crankshaft fitted with a

large flywheel on the left-hand end. Outboard of that was a starter pinion, which was rotated by a gear segment formed as part of the kick-starter. From the engine a belt ran to a jockey pulley positioned up in the corner, between the seat and top frame tubes. A further belt

ran to the rear wheel so that the jockey pulley was able to tension both belts, and a clutch was incorporated in this transmission. The frame was rigid, but the forks were sprung with a rocking action at first, changing to telescopics in later years.

A second Whizzer model, retaining more of the original design, used a Schwinn frame with a different telescopic front fork. The engine was mounted higher, and there was direct belt drive with the pedalling gear retained. The Whizzer was popular for over 10 years, until the new breed of mopeds and small motorcycles came from Europe and Japan.

The curious Whizzer, pictured in early post-war form, with a Schwinn loop frame, 138cc side-valve engine and two-stage belt drive.

WILKINSON

ENGLAND 1908–15

The air-cooled TAC of 1908 was the civilian redesign of a very long wheelbase military scouting machine that (not entirely surprisingly) was unsuccessful.

THE BEAUTIFULLY MADE Wilkinson is as eccentric a machine as one could wish for. The very first eccentricity is the manufacturer, the Wilkinson Sword company of London, a long-established firm of military cutlers, now razor blades. One could make jokes about the cutting edge of design, but swords to motorcycles is not an obvious transition.

Or perhaps it is not so odd: the original 1908 design by P.G. Tacchi was intended as a military scouting vehicle, which at least preserves the link with arms manufacture. Then again, perhaps it is all the more eccentric, since one is hard put to imagine a theatre of war in which the Wilkinson might thrive. Indeed, military orders were not

The water-cooled TMC of 1911 was the most rational of the Wilkinson designs, though in reality, it was still a very bizarre machine.

forthcoming, despite the Maxim gun, part of the specification.

The four-cylinder inlet-over-exhaust machine therefore underwent its first redesign, as the Wilkinson TAC, or Touring Auto Car. The initial version had a steering wheel instead of handlebars, which must have been interesting to use, and was

powered by a 676cc air-cooled engine. For 1911 it was re-designed again, as the TMC (Touring Motor Cycle) with 848cc and cooling switched from air to water, a much more rational choice for a straight four mounted in line with the frame. The water tank was behind the steering head, while the fuel tank was over the rear wheel. The sight-glass for the total-loss lubrication system can be seen clearly on the top tube; oil was pumped up from the tank using a foot pump. There was no front brake, but there were twin drums at the back. Suspension was featured both front and rear, with Saxon forks and quarter-elliptic rear springs.

Although the TMC was a casualty of World War I, the engine survived in the Deemster car.

WELLER
England 1902–05: In-house one-and-three-quarters and two-and-a-quarter horsepower engines drove the machines which came from this pioneer, also known for cars.

WELS
Germany 1925–26: Kuhne 350cc and JAP 500cc overhead-valve engines powered these machines with their clean, elegant lines.

WELT-RAD
Germany 1901–07: Their own singles of three-and-a-half horsepower, and V-twins of 7bhp, were used in these sturdy and (for the time) reliable machines.

WESTFALIA
Germany 1901–06: These pioneers used the customary engines: De Dion-Bouton, Fafnir and Zedel, of one-and-three-quarters and two-and-a-half horsepower.

WIGA
Germany 1928–32: These were good assembled machines with JAP and Kuchen engines, the latter three-valve.

WILHELMINA
Netherlands 1903–15: A variety of engines, most notably the two-and-a-half horsepower Precision, powered these machines from this leading Dutch importer.

WILIER
Italy 1962–c.1970: This mini-bike was powered by a 48cc motor.

WILKIN
England (Sheffield) 1919–23: An enclosed drive chain was the principal remarkable feature of these 350 and 500cc Blackburne-powered machines.

WILLIAMS
USA 1912–20: The power unit for this machine was built into the rear wheel.

WILLIAMSON
England (Coventry) 1912–20: For most of their career, Williamson used 996cc flat twins, both water- and air-cooled, specially built for them by Douglas of Bristol, but in the last year or so, they used a 770cc JAP V-twin.

WINDHOFF

THE FIRST MODELS FROM this firm had 122 and 173cc water-cooled two-stroke engines with a secondary pumping piston and a horizontal cylinder, built under licence from Bekamo. They were conventional, having a separate gearbox, all-chain drive, a rigid frame, girder forks and drum brakes. In 1927 the company introduced a sensational new design with a 746cc overhead-camshaft, in-line four-cylinder, oil-cooled engine. The engine formed the basis of the machine with the headstock bolted to its forward end and the gearbox and rear frame to the back. The three-speed, hand change gearbox had shaft drive to the rear wheel, which was supported by pairs of tubes running back from the cast-alloy,

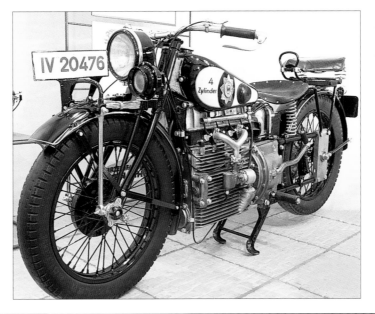

This massive shaft-drive Windhoff from 1929 had a four-cylinder, in-line engine that acted as the centre of the frame and connected headstock to rear end.

one-piece engine block. At the front went trailing-link forks controlled by a pair of leaf springs; both wire wheels had drum brakes.

The four sold badly; a 996cc version stayed at the prototype stage. In 1929 a flat-twin replaced both. It had a 996cc side-valve engine built in unit with the gearbox and shaft drive, a similar frame to the fours but with added bracing, and the same trailing-link forks. It found no buyers, and the Depression years saw Windhoff producing Villiers-powered lightweights made under licence.

WOOLER

JOHN WOOLER WAS A MAN on a mission who spent nearly half a century trying to launch a series of almost unique motorcycles. It would have been much more easy – and profitable – to conform, but Wooler wanted to do things his way, or not at all. His first bike was a two-stroke with double-ended pistons, the purpose of which was to avoid crankcase compression. Mounted horizon-tally, the engine made use of a variable-ratio belt-drive system. A form of plunger suspension was fitted both front and rear.

In 1911 John Wooler designed and built a fore-and-aft flat-twin

with a 348cc inlet-over-exhaust engine mounted in line with the frame. By 1923 this design had been updated to an overhead-valve layout. Wooler also entered machines in the Isle of Man TT, painted bright yellow, and these were soon nicknamed 'flying bananas'.

In 1926 Wooler constructed a 500cc overhead-cam engine with the camshafts on the top end of the vertical shafts. Horizontal tappets and rockers transferred the movement to the valves, while the cylinder had twin exhaust ports. That same year, he purchased the London-based P & P marque,

formed in 1920 by Erling Poppe (later to design the Sunbeam S7) and Gilmour Packman. However, the subsequent Depression decimated sales, and Wooler was forced to close down P & P in 1930.

Little more was heard of John Wooler until 1945, but he certainly had not forgotten motorcycles, and of course his latest design was nothing if not unusual. This time it was a flat four, the cylinders being stacked like a pair of bunk beds on either side of the crankcase. This

Wooler's first motorcycle was a two-stroke with double-ended pistons. Mounted horizontally, the engine had a variable-ratio belt-drive system.

John Wooler was a man who went his own way. His designs were in many ways unique. This fore-and-aft flat-twin has a 348cc engine and dates from 1920.

alone was far from conventional, but the really unique feature was the way in which the pistons were connected to the crankshaft, for this featured rods, a T-beam, a master-rod and gudgeon pins. The valves were mounted in parallel to each other. The first postwar bike had curious duplex suspension units, but by the final model in 1956 a more conventional swinging-arm and telescopic fork were fitted. John Wooler's death that year signalled the end of further development.

WSK

POLAND 1947–95

THE FIRST MODEL FROM the Polish WSK marque leaned heavily – as did so many others around the world – on the German DKW RT125. Hermann Weber's design must rank as the most copied motorcycle of all time, and one of the reasons for this is that, with Germany a defeated nation, other countries were able to claim their engineering creations as war booty.

In the case of the RT125, the spoils comprised an exceptionally fine bike.

WSK was state owned when formed in 1947. Its product range at first consisted of solely the 123cc single-cylinder DKW-derived two-stroke, but by the mid-1950s this had been joined by a similar 175cc model. These motorcycles were mainly for the

A Polish WSK 175cc single-cylinder trail bike of 1977 vintage. It featured telescopic front forks, swinging arm rear suspension and hi-level exhaust.

home market and export to other communist states, including the Soviet Union. They sold well, though not quite in the same numbers as similar 'Iron Curtain' makes such as CZ, Jawa and MZ. Yet, like these, WSK concentrated its production on cheap-to-buy, easy-to-service commuter machines. From time to time, models were exported to the West, but only in very small numbers.

In 1977 Roy Cary of Barron Eurotrade in Hornchurch, Essex, entered into an agreement with WSK for the Polish concern to supply cycle parts for a 125cc-class motorcycle to be assembled in the UK, using a five-speed piston-port Italian Minerelli two-stroke engine. This unlikely union did not prove to be a sales success and Barron soon stopped production, concentrating upon its various Italian import concessions. No new WSK models appeared after the 1970s, though the firm only stopped trading in 1995.

In the late 1970s, the British company, Barron, built a series of motorcycles using WSK cycle parts, or in some cases (as here) the WSK 175cc engine.

WIMMER
Germany 1921–39: This bicycle factory started out with an overhead-valve 175cc engine, then switched to a 200cc two-stroke, supplemented with 250, 300 and even 500cc singles. All were built in house. Bicycle production, but not motorcycle production, was resumed after World War II.

WIN
England 1908–14: Precision singles of 500 and 600cc were the choices for this assembled machine.

WITTLER
Germany 1924–53: This was yet another German two-stroke manufacturer, albeit with in-house engines of 249cc. After World War II, they produced mopeds with Zundapp or Fichtel & Sachs engines, and a 175cc Sachs-engined lightweight.

W.M.R.
Germany (Rottenburg am Neckar) 1926–32: The Wurtttemburger Motorfahrzeug Werke began with side-valve and overhead-valve Kuchen engines of 500cc, later adding 250 and 350cc Blackburnes, initially side-valve but then (for the Sport models) overhead-valve.

WOLF
England (Wolverhampton) 1901–39: From the same factory as Wearwell, this was a wide range of machines with engines from 100 to 750cc, all powered by proprietary engines. Early models had engines from Moto Reve, Blackburne, JAP, Peco, Stevens Brothers (later of AJS) and Villiers; later machines (after a break in production) mostly used 250cc Villiers two-strokes.

WOTAN
Germany (Chemnitz) 1921–22: This was a rare 600cc V-twin.

WURRING
Germany 1921–59: August Wurring (also of AWD) used a wide variety of proprietary motors of 150 to 600cc from Bark, Columbus, DKW, Ilo, Kuchen, Kuhne, Sachs and Villiers.

WURTTEMBERGIA
Germany 1925–33: Good frames characterised these solid Blackburne-powered 200 to 600cc machines which came from this agricultural machinery manufacturer.

YAMAHA

IT IS MORE THAN PROBABLE that the man whose name identifies millions of motorcycles did not actually ride one himself. Torakusu Yamaha died in 1916, and may never even have seen a motorbike. Born in Nagasaki in 1851, Yamaha was first an apprentice clockmaker, then a trainee in the manufacture of medical equipment, moving to Hamamatsu in 1883 as a self-employed engineer. An early commission to mend a school organ led to the founding of the Yamaha musical dynasty. The musical instrument business was called Nippon Gakki and was soon a huge success, using as its logo a trio of tuning forks. With Yamaha the founder long gone, and the company having survived strikes, earthquake disaster and major changes of management, its president Genichi Kawakami set about utilising a wartime plant in 1948 to make small motorcycles for the blossoming home market. Whereas other firms launching into

The shaft-drive XS1100 from 1978 was Yamaha's first big four, but it was flawed: the frame was not strong enough to cope with the 95bhp twin-cam engine.

bike production for the first time erred on the side of caution, Nippon Gakki had the benefit of a secure financial foundation and took its time building a new factory at Hamamatsu while perfecting the new bike. The fledgling motorcycle division was named Yamaha after the company's founder.

With an absence of Japanese precedents to follow, Nippon Gakki took as its inspiration the DKW RT125 which, by coincidence, had also influenced BSA when it designed the Bantam, and Harley-Davidson when designing the Hummer. The first Yamaha was the 125cc YA1, launched in 1955 and built at a rate of 200 a month. The following year, a larger 175cc version was released, and the YA series continued until the early 1970s. To create a 250cc machine, Yamaha studied the Adler MB250 twin, and came up with the pressed-steel frame YD1, whose only concessions to the Adler were its basic layout and dimensions.

The company built a racing version of the YD1 on a lightweight tubular frame fitted with a short-stroke engine, and Yamaha riders filled the first three places in the 250cc races at Asama in 1957, also coming first and second in the 125cc event. Demonstrating the old adage that racing success is good for sales, the YD1 was an instant hit with customers. Yamaha was the first Japanese manufacturer to race in the USA, entering the European Grand Prix arena in 1961 and finishing seventh in the 125 and 250cc French GPs.

By this time, Yamaha also owned the Showa company (which had no connection with the suspension components

The 250cc YDS2 of 1963 and its successors was the mainstay of Yamaha's road-going production bikes of the Sixties, evolving into the RD series in 1973.

manufacturer) and inherited its 125cc racer, from which Yamaha engineers gleaned much about disc-valves. In the same way as Suzuki adhered to the two-stroke principle, Yamaha, too, built two-stroke engines for racers and commuters alike. In 1966 it came out with the twin-cylinder YL1, which could do 113kph (70mph) in standard trim and perhaps twice that when fitted with a factory race kit. A series of 250 twins ran concurrently, beginning with the YDS1 in 1959 and evolving through the YDS2 of 1962 and YDS3 of 1964. Via the DS7, these basic road-going machines became the long-running RD series in 1973. The TD series consisted of ready-to-race machines and included the 250cc TD1 from 1962, while the 350cc FR series evolved into the liquid-cooled TZ in 1969.

Yamaha's first period of Grand Prix success came in the 1960s, in the smaller classes. In 1963 Yamaha returned to the European GP series with its 45bhp 250cc RD56, and took its first Grand Prix victory at Belgium's high-speed Spa-Francorchamps circuit. Second places followed at Assen and the Isle of Man. Yet major success was only a year away, and in 1964 and 1965 Phil Read clinched the 250cc World Championship for Yamaha on the parallel-twin RD56 – the first time it had been won by a two-stroke. The next two seasons belonged to Mike Hailwood and Honda, but Yamaha came back to take the 125 and 250cc titles in 1968.

In order to capitalise on the craze for off-road trail bikes that was sweeping the US, Yamaha announced the DT1 in 1968. Prior to the arrival of this no-nonsense scrambler, Japanese trail bikes had been merely adaptations of road bikes fitted with high-level exhausts and knobbly tyres. The DT1 (DT = Dirt Trail) was powered by a 175cc two-stroke single that could cruise on-road at 97kph (60mph) and was entirely competent off-road; with the lights removed and a factory race kit fitted, it became a serious competition option. Before long, the major players offered similar machines, and the range of all-terrain Yamahas was expanded to include the DT50 and DT400. An interim step on the ladder was the

Following on from the DT, the single-cylinder XT500 trail bike was released in 1977, opening up a new market for off-road bikes. However, it was too heavy.

DT175, in production from 1973 to 1985; this represented a sound alternative to the 250 and 400cc machines because it was more nimble off-road and more economical to run. By 1974 Yamaha was offering an out-and-out motocross bike called the YZ250.

In 1969 Yamaha introduced a four-stroke vertical-twin model, the XS1, which was the largest bike it had yet made. It encroached quite deliberately on traditionally British territory occupied by stalwarts like the T120 Bonneville. The XS1 was powered by a 653cc overhead-cam engine mated to a five-speed gearbox with an electric start, but its immediate

The FZR750 evolved from the FZ750 of 1985, the first bike to have five-valves per cylinder. The FZR1000 of 1989 featured electronically operated exhaust valves.

shortcomings were inferior roadholding and handling. A revamped model designated the XS650 handled better, and was put to use as a sports bike in the esoteric world of US sidecar motocross and flat-track racing, continuing in production until the early 1980s. Yamaha tried a 750 version equipped with two contra-rotating balancer weights in the rear of the crankcase to minimise vibration, but these had the effect of diminishing the machine's

X-ALL

England 1902–c.1906: Accounts of this English machine vary in their details: not only are there several slight variations in the dates during which the machine was manufactured, but the name of the model is also reported as being XL-All. What is clear is that it was a V-twin. It may have been the first engine to offer the option of shutting down one cylinder when the full power of the engine was not absolutely necessary. Alternatively, the second cylinder may have been a spare, to which ignition and carburation were transferred in the event of a failure of the first cylinder. Reports suggest that there may have been two models offered for sale, one of which had a power output of 2hp, and the other a power output of 4hp. However, these figures might have referred to the power output, the former on one cylinder and the latter on two.

XL

England (Worthing) 1921–23: This English motorcycle was manufactured in the early years of the 1920s in Worthing. Reports which were written about the machine ultimately conclude that it was strong and well-made, and that it was fitted with an engine with a capacity of 500cc, which was a side-valve.

X-TRA

England 1920–22: This English machine – which was manufactured during the early years of the 1920s – was accompanied by a sidecar. Unusually, this sidecar was so firmly incorporated into the machine's design that it was effectively a three-wheeled car which had handlebar steering of one wheel, and chain drive to another.

RD stood for 'Race Developed', and the RD200 that appeared in 1973 pioneered the use of reed valve induction in production bikes in place of conventional piston ports.

main advantage of a broader power band. In the case of the new RD250, it began to take off at 4000rpm instead of 6000rpm, so it was more tractable and economical. The RD range encompassed 125, 200, 250 and 350 versions, and the two larger models came with a six-speed gearbox, which was utilised by the TZ racer. The RDs got a face-lift in 1975; this included a squarer tank and seat, plus new graphics. The following year, the RD350 metamorphosed into the RD400, while electronic ignition was introduced in 1978. However, the feisty RD two-strokes met their demise in 1980, when prevailing

US emissions regulations ruled them out of contention in the environmental stakes.

Midway through the 1970s, Yamaha unveiled its four-stroke XS500 twin. The specification included twin overhead-camshafts, four valves per cylinder and a balancer-shaft to iron out vibrations. The unit developed 48bhp at 8500rpm to give a top speed of 175kph (109mph). However, the heavy XS500 was impaired by indifferent handling and poor performance, and it was shaded by its lighter siblings, the XS twins. These included the single overhead-cam, 180-degree crankshaft XS360 from 1976, and the XS250. The 360 was bored out to become the XS400, which eventually ran with a backbone frame, a twin overhead-cam cylinder head and monoshock rear suspension, and remained in production until 1983.

performance, and were quickly dropped.

At the other end of the scale, it was obvious that Yamaha would have to provide motorcycles similar to the commuter bikes made by Honda and Suzuki. Yamaha's small reed-valve, two-stroke, step-through commuter machines were exemplified by the V50 and V80, fitted with two- and three-speed automatic gearboxes with manual selection. The two-stroke oil-fuel mixture was blended automatically, and the bikes had the benefit of enclosed chain drive. They were later replaced by the four-stroke shaft-drive T50 and T80, and in 1972 Yamaha brought out the FS1 sports moped, which combined a disc-valve engine and motorcycle images to woo the teenage market. Despite being restricted to 48kph (30mph) in the UK, the model remained on sale to the end of the century as the FS1 with drum brakes and the FS1DX with disc brakes.

The RD or 'Race Developed' series replaced the long-running YDS in 1973, using Yamaha's improved version of reed-valve induction – known as 'Torque Induction' – instead of conventional piston ports, with the

The SR500 was the road-going version of the XT500 trail bike, which had the advantage of 12-volt electrics, larger valves and bigger carburettor internals.

YALE
USA 1902–15: Initially, this company – which hailed from the USA – was responsible for the manufacture of a single. In this machine, the engine was mounted over the pedals within a strengthened bicycle frame. Later, the company was responsible for the manufacture of an all chain-drive V-twin which was a two-speed with a capacity of 950cc.

YAMAGUCHI
Japan 1953–64: Always confusingly named, Yamaguchi models, which came originally from Japan, began with the Super 200 and Super 100 two-strokes. These machines had capacities of 83 and 60cc respectively. However, the 1956 Model 600 was fitted with an engine with a capacity of 147cc. The biggest engine ever produced was the 250cc four-stroke T92, which appeared shortly afterwards, while their Super 350 had an engine capacity of 125cc and the AP10 moped a capacity of 50cc. The date of the commencement of production is also reported in places as being as early as 1941, but this date is almost certainly wrong.

A new market for big trailies was opening up in the late 1970s, and the eagerly awaited XT500 arrived in 1977. It was powered by a four-stroke, single-cylinder, single overhead-cam engine displacing 499cc, with two valves, one carburettor and no electric starter. The road-going equivalent was the SR500, which used the same engine but with larger valves and carburettor internals, plus a front disc and 12volt electrics in contrast to the XT's 6volt system.

In 1977 Yamaha launched the XS750, its first successful four-stroke and an initial, tentative foray into the emergent Superbike category. The power unit was the 747cc double overhead-cam triple, allied to shaft drive, which made for an easier maintenance schedule if not such sporting pretensions. Three years later, capacity was lifted to a performance-enhancing 826cc and 79bhp at 8500rpm. The XS850 could better its 177kph (110mph) predecessor by 24kph (15mph), and fully adjustable suspension back and front ensured that it could handle well, too. The

Intended to rival British stalwarts like the Bonneville, the XS1 from 1969 was a 653cc ohc four-stroke vertical twin. After initial handling problems, it became the XS650.

four-cylinder XJ900 superseded it in 1983.

Meanwhile, Yamaha's two-stroke twin-cylinder production racers were making a name for themselves, winning the 250cc World Championship four times – in 1970, 1971, 1972 and 1973. They took the 350cc category the following three years, as well as two 125cc titles, having won the 500cc class in 1973. Kenny Roberts wore the 500cc crown for Yamaha from 1978 to 1980, too.

The YZ400 motocross bike was descended from the YZ250 of 1974, the first to feature a single long-travel rear suspension unit mounted beneath seat.

The LC, or 'Elsie', was a reincarnation of the RD, with more rounded contours than its predecessor and launched in Europe as a liquid-cooled two-stroke twin, which made for a quieter engine and a more even-running temperature than the old

RD. It still used reed-valve induction and a six-speed gearbox, with rubber engine mounts and a new monoshock rear suspension derived from the YZ motocross bike. The LC turned out to be particularly effective in production racing, winning the 250 and 500cc classes in its first TT. In 1982 its major innovation was introduced, the Yamaha Power Valve System (YPVS), consisting of a variable exhaust port, whose size and position changed automatically according to engine revs and which lifted power to 59bhp at 9000rpm. The same system was applied to the 499cc RD500LC 80bhp V4 of 1984, a 217kph (135mph) machine calculated to bask in the reflected glory of Kenny Roberts' Grand Prix success. This engine contained a pair of crankshafts and drank through four carburettors, while the four YPVS valves were mechanically linked and activated by a servomotor.

Yamaha was late to join its rivals in making a four-cylinder four-stroke, and after its unconvincing vertical twins and triples its next big four-stroke was the TR1, which came out in late 1980. Powered by a 981cc 75-degree V-twin with single overhead-cams and two valves per cylinder, the TR1 was based on a steel backbone frame and came with an enclosed chain drive, a

Built around its huge water-cooled 1200 V-four motor, the 1985 V-Max was a factory custom machine with great power, but questionable handling.

vertically split crankcase and a five-speed gearbox. It was a roadster in the traditional Western idiom, with electronic advance for the ignition timing and monoshock rear suspension the only concessions to a sophisticated specification. The TR1's stablemate was the similar 740cc Virago, which featured shaft drive with its custom styling. The Virago concept was sufficiently popular for Yamaha to offer 125, 250 and 1100 versions as well.

A motorcycle that was potentially more adventurous in its make-up was the XZ550, released in 1982 and powered by a 70-degree 552cc V-twin with liquid-cooling and double overhead-cam

For those who admired classic American style, the Drag Star 1100 delivered build quality, performance and value, but without the authentic character.

four-valve cylinder heads, each with twin exhaust ports. Surprisingly, a balancer-shaft was suspended from the cradle-frame downtubes, and the bizarre specification also featured shaft drive and trailing-axle front forks. It was not a pretty bike to look at, and performance was less than enervating. More conventional fodder available at the same time was the double overhead-cam four-cylinder XJ series, which included the XJ550, the shaft-drive

XJ650 and the XJ750. Just as Honda did with its CX, Yamaha fitted the XJ650 with a turbocharger to create the eponymous XJ650 Turbo, as a means of obtaining performance similar to that of a bigger-capacity engine. As it turned out, bigger was better, and the XJ900 from 1983 proved to be a more flexible – and more straightforward – tourer. It was powered by an 853cc double overhead-cam, air-cooled, four-cylinder engine with shaft-drive transmission. In FJ900 form, with the capacity increased to 891cc to produce 91bhp, the concept was sound enough to still be in the showrooms at the turn of the twentieth century. The FJ1100 of 1984 made more of an impact and, having been raised to FJ1200 level in 1986, it was hailed in 2000 as one of the best long-distance tourers on the second-hand market, despite having been discontinued. Power came from an air-cooled shaft-drive four, producing 125bhp and good for 238kph (148mph), with monoshock rear suspension, an alloy frame and belly pan, and cockpit fairing. From 1991 it even had an ABS option.

Yamaha entered the market with a smaller four-cylinder machine in 1991. This was the Diversion 600, an unpretentious model that used an air-cooled slant-forward 600cc block with two valves per cylinder, and was available in naked and half-faired formats. Yet if the Diversion was bland, the

V-Max was certifiable. Unveiled in 1985, this muscle-bound cult bike oozed aggression from its hunky, frame-filling liquid-cooled 1198cc V4. This car-sized motor was adapted from Yamaha's big XVZ12 tourer and fitted with bigger carburettors, valves and valve springs, plus a toughened bottom-end.

Off the beaten track, Yamaha's trail bikes now came with four-stroke single-cylinder engines; the range was exemplified by the XT550, with a four-valve twin-carburettor 558cc engine, and its junior sibling, the XT400. These gave way to the XT600 and the XT600Z Ténéré, which captured the wave of popularity enjoyed by desert rally-raids such as the Paris–Dakar event. The bike's requisite ingredients included capacious fuel tanks and tall suspension. By 2000 Yamaha had refined the concept of the dual-purpose model to the extent that the XT600E was probably the best machine available. The lighter XT350 made a better job of riding off-road, however. The road-going SRX600 used the same four-valve 608cc single as the XT, and was popular with elements of the racing fraternity.

In 1985 Yamaha attacked the sports bike market with the FZ750.

Based on Yamaha's aluminium Deltabox frame, the YZF600R Thundercat was comfortable to ride and handled well, but lost out in performance to rivals.

Yamaha model numbers are generally prefixed by DT, XJ, YZ or FZ, but occasionally single models have separate designations like this 1998 WR400F traillie.

Its liquid-cooled 749cc, four-cylinder, five-valves-per-cylinder engine was canted forward at 45 degrees for a lower centre of gravity and optimum inlet and exhaust porting. It was fed by four downdraught carburettors, and pushed out 106bhp via a flat torque curve. Two years later, the company consolidated its class superiority with the FZR1000 Genesis. This machine ushered in the alloy box-section frame, called the Deltabox, which enabled a lower seat height and promoted better handling. Engine capacity was enlarged to 1002cc to produce 135bhp and a top speed of 266kph (165mph).

The Deltabox chassis wasn't the only new concept that Yamaha came up with in the late 1980s. The exotically-named Exhaust Ultimate Power Valve or 'EXUP' concept introduced in 1989 consisted of a valve in the exhaust collector-box that controlled the gas-pressure wave, and was featured on the FZR range. This now included the 750, which came with a Deltabox chassis, and the new 90bhp 16-valve FZR600, to vie with Honda's CBR600. Slotting underneath the Japanese 400cc capacity break was the FZR400R, a neat race replica in the popular mould. In 1996 the FZR600 and 1000 models were revised and redesignated the Thundercat and Thunderace, both attractive machines which featured full fairings.

In the late 1980s Yamaha's smaller bikes, such as the TZR125,

Introduced in 1998, the bargain basement FZS600 Fazer with its four-cylinder 16-valve 94bhp twin-cam engine brought pace and handling to a wider market.

powered by a 849cc twin-cylinder engine with the Genesis five-valve layout. Its identity was a mixture of big trailie, half-faired roadster and sports bike, which Yamaha described as 'New Sport'. The TRX850 was a café racer spin-off using the same running gear.

Yamaha ended the twentieth century with a trio of milestone motorbikes: the YZF-R1 and R7, introduced in 1998; and the R6, which was launched the next year.

The 1000cc 150bhp R1 was an immediate standard-bearer in the supersports category, as it was more compact, lightweight and powerful than any of its rivals.

Like the R1 and R6, the new R7 was a no-compromise supersports motorcycle featuring extremely advanced engine and chassis

components developed using technology from Yamaha's Superbike and Grand Prix race machinery.

In the 1998 World Superbike Championship, Noriyuki Haga put in some remarkable rides on his factory YZF750SP, and the R7 offered the performance-minded supersports rider the opportunity to experience sophisticated factory-racer technology in a street-legal motorcycle. This development came at a price, however, for the YZF-R7 cost a cool £21,000 in the UK in 1999.

The hothouse that is the 600cc sports-bike playground was then rocked by the arrival of the 120bhp Yamaha YZF-R6, whose 274kph (170mph) top speed made it class leader in terms of sheer velocity. It could be cornered at up to 56 degrees from the vertical, and wound up to 15,500rpm, while its devastating mid-range power was as accessible on the track as on the road.

mostly ran with the reed-valve two-stroke single, which was fitted in the Deltabox frame and these models were available with or without fairing.

Offering trail-bike looks along with on-road performance, the

twin-cylinder two-stroke TDR250 was something of an enigma. It cashed in on the TDM850's stance, and was capable of over 161kph (100mph) on tarmac.

The TDM came out in 1990, based on a Deltabox chassis and

YAMAHA YR5 350 1970

Yamaha's successful series of 250cc YDS models from the 1960s led to the introduction of its first 350cc twin, the YR1. Then, in 1970, the neatly styled YR5 350 was unveiled, powered by an air-cooled parallel-twin that produced 36bhp, sufficient to take the light-weight screamer to 153kph (95mph). It also had the advantage of good handling and effective brakes, while reliability was excellent. The YR5 350 was competitively priced and became very popular. Its descendants included the six-speed RD350 of 1974 and the 161kph (100mph) RD400 of 1976. Evolutions were the water-cooled single-shock RD350LC from 1981 and the 1983

YPVS or Power Valve model, whose exhaust power-valve brought mid-range performance to 53bhp. The RD350LC F2 was still made in Brazil in the mid-1990s.

Engine: 347cc reed-valve two-stroke parallel-twin, 64x54mm, air-cooled
Power: 36bhp at 7000rpm
Gearbox: 5-speed, foot change
Final drive: chain
Weight: 150kg (331lb)
Top speed: 153kph (95mph)

Yamaha's YR range first appeared in 1967, ushering in a line of bigger-capacity two-strokes, the first to have horizontally split engine cases and five port cylinder barrels.

YAMAHA YZR500 1984

Engine: 498cc 80-degree reed-valve two-stroke V-four, 56x50.6mm, water-cooled
Power: 165bhp at 12,500rpm
Gearbox: 6-speed. foot change
Final drive: chain
Weight: 130kg (287lb)
Top speed: 306kph (190mph)

The YZR was the dominant 500cc Grand Prix machine during the decade spanning 1984 to 1993, winning six world championships. It also provided the basis for the

ROC and Harris-framed privateer V-fours of recent seasons. Wayne Rainey took over from Eddie Lawson to win three cups for Yamaha, while Frenchman Christian Sarron triumphed in the 250cc World Championship on Yamaha's TZ twin in 1984. Kenny Roberts captured world titles riding a Yamaha and, more recently, as a team manager.

The Japanese factory's success with 500cc V-fours took off with

Roberts' disc-valve OW61 of 1982. The YZR, with its crankcase reed-valve induction system, was introduced as the OW81 model in 1984. Its engine used twin crankshafts that were geared together, a layout that had also been adopted by Suzuki and Cagiva, which left only Honda's NSR as a true V-four. The YZR's power output rose gradually over the years to top 180bhp from the most recent 'big bang' unit.

Chassis layout remained typical of a Grand Prix 500, based on a thick twin-beam aluminium frame, with suspension provided by Ohlins, the Swedish specialist firm owned by Yamaha. The YZR may not always have been the fastest bike, but it was tractable and good all-round.

Among the great race bikes of the 1970s were the Yamaha's TZs, ranging from the TZ250 twin to the TZ750 four. After winning its first event in 700cc form in 1974, it dominated Formula 750 racing for the rest of the decade. The TZ750 won four F750 titles, including a win at Daytona in 1982. Giacomo Agostini won

Yamaha's first 500 World Championship on a four in 1975. Most successful of all was Kenny Roberts, who rode the four to three titles between 1978 and 1980.

Introduced in 1984, the YZR500 won six world championships up to 1993. Eddie Lawson (left) won three of them and is pictured with the 1986 machine.

YAMAHA FJ1200 {.clearfix}
1986

The ingredients for an ideal touring bike are: ample range, good comfort, a torquey engine, luggage capacity and weather protection. The FJ1200 possessed all of these – a huge seat, big tank, half-fairing and belly pan, and pulling ability from low and medium revs. In road tests it frequently outstripped rivals such as the Kawasaki GPZ1100, BMW K1100 and Triumph Trophy 1200. It handled better than the Kawasaki, was faster than the BMW, and was less ponderous than the Triumph. Power for the FJ1200 came from a double overhead-cam, air-cooled, in-line transverse four-cylinder engine, canted over for optimum porting and a better centre of gravity. This unit gained a reputation for being unburstable, and FJ Owners' Club members cited bikes that had clocked up 193,121km (120,000 miles) and required nothing more serious than routine servicing. Launched in 1986, the big Yamaha was quite at home carrying panniers as well as other luggage. It was no beauty, but it was exceedingly practical.

Engine: 1188cc, dohc four-cylinder, air-cooled
Power: 125bhp
Gearbox: 5-speed foot change
Final drive: chain
Weight: 238kg (525lb)
Top speed: 238kph (148mph)

A superb long-distance tourer, the FJ1200 was in production from 1986 to 1994. Extremely reliable, the specification was improved in 1988 to include 42.5cm (17in) wheels and better brakes.

YAMAHA XT600E

1985

The doyen of big single-cylinder trail bikes, Yamaha's XT600E evolved from the DT dirt-trail series of 1976, refined over 25 years into one of the best dual-purpose on/off-road machines available. Although it could reach 161kph (100mph) on tarmac, the aerodynamics and riding position mitigated against anything over 121kph (75mph), with sufficient seating comfort to undertake long journeys. The seat was lower than previous incarnations, and the air-cooled single-pot motor was slimmer than water-cooled rivals. While not as powerful as the Aprilia Pegaso or Kawasaki KLR650, the XT600E's four-valve twin-carburettor engine possessed

a smoother power delivery, with a gear-driven balancer-shaft minimising low-down transmission snatch. Aftermarket tuning acces-

The big traillie category was virtually created by the XT600E. It later proved more capable off-road than Honda's rival Dominator.

sories meant that more power could be accessed than the standard 45bhp. With suitable tyres such as Avon Gripsters fitted, the XT600E could be cornered with aplomb, on the road. Off-road, it was not as handy as the DT125R. The malleable plastic panels were resilient in spills, and from 1995 improvements were made to the colours, fuel tank and front brake.

Engine: 595cc, ohc single-cylinder, air-cooled
Power: 45bhp
Gearbox: 6-speed
Final drive: chain
Weight: 155kg (342lb)
Top speed: 161kph (100mph)

YAMAHA YZF-R1

1998

The flagship machine that took Yamaha into the twenty-first century, the R1, was powered by a four-stroke in-line four-cylinder motor with five valves per cylinder. The state-of-the-art chassis included front suspension by telescopic forks and at the back a swinging-arm and monoshock.

Up front were 298mm (11.75ins) diameter dual disc brakes. In 1998 the R1 was voted 'Machine of the Year' in many countries by journalists and readers of the specialist press, and in 1999 it was the top-selling model in the over-600cc supersports category in Europe. For 2000 the star of the YZF-R

series underwent a major redesign, incorporating over 150 components, making it the benchmark sports bike.

Engine: 998cc four-stroke in-line four-cylinder, 20 valves, 74mmx58mm, liquid-cooled
Power: 150bhp at 10,000rpm
Gearbox: 6-speed foot change
Final drive: chain
Weight: 175kg (386lb)
Top speed: 286kph (178mph)

No question, the 150bhp R1 was a milestone bike, redefining super-sports handling and performance. Its R6 and R7 siblings were equally impressive.

YAMAHA YP125 MAJESTY

1999

Yamaha's most effective offering for the burgeoning scooter craze at the turn of the millennium was the YP125 Majesty. Its sharp handling qualities made it a strong competitor against rivals from Honda and Piaggio. Top speed was 105kph (65mph), with a relatively high seat height of 774mm (30.5ins). The Majesty was styled with an appealingly aggressive attitude, with more weight forward than the Honda Pantheon, and it

The 125cc Majesty four-stroke single was a lot of body for the money, and while the 250cc version offered more open-road go, the 125 was adequate for commuting.

could be turned into corners with greater enthusiasm. Its punchy four-stroke single sounded refined at idle, but was prone to send jarring vibrations up through the bars and seat. The front brake was particularly effective and had good feel, but the back brake seemed wooden. Altogether, the Majesty was a well-made machine, despite certain vices.

Engine: 125cc ohc four-stroke single-cylinder
Power: 10bhp at 8000rpm
Gearbox: automatic
Final drive: n/a
Weight: 128kg (282lb)
Top speed: 105kph (65mph)

ZANELLA

ARGENTINA 1957–

AMONG SOUTH AMERICAN MARQUES, Zanella is the only one that is wholly owned by South Americans, with a factory to have built and raced its own machines in track events. Others have had their stockholders overseas or have made only roadsters and dirt bikes.

The Zanella brothers were of Italian origin, hailing from Belluno, just north of Venice. They left their native Italy to settle in Argentina during 1948. That year they formed Zanella, specialising in metallurgy. Then, in 1955, the brothers began to manufacture components for the fledgling native car industry.

Two years later, in 1957, the first motorcycles were built, with 80 per cent Italian content and the balance manufactured by Zanella. The following year, a licence agreement was signed with the Italian Cecceto company for Zanella to manufacture a 100cc two-stroke machine.

In 1959 construction of a new factory began; this was completed the following year. That same year saw the first Zanella motorcycle wholly manufactured in Argentina.

Exports of motorcycles (and three-wheeled trucks) began in 1961, the first customer being Paraguay, and by 1963 Zanella was shipping bikes to other South American nations, as well as to the USA. Zanella also began a racing programme with the sale of over-the-counter 'customer' machines.

The Italian Zanella brothers settled in Argentina in 1948 and began building bikes in 1957. This example is a 200 J-R model from 1986.

By the mid-1960s Zanella was building a full range of motorcycles, including the popular SS125 roadster and a larger version with a 168cc (60x59.6mm). Racing developments dominated Argentine competition for the next 20 years; water-cooling was later adopted.

Zanella came to Europe in the early 1980s with a successful 80cc Grand Prix racer, and also exhibited at the biennial Milan Show. This resulted in an agreement whereby the Zanella commuter moped was marketed in Italy by Cagiva. There were many occasions when Italian bikes were imported into South America; this was a first the other way around.

During the 1980s, Zanella started an export drive, which included racing in Europe, with a new 80cc model. It also displayed this 49cc moped at the 1987 Milan Show.

ZENITH

ENGLAND 1905–50

ZENITH BEGAN IN LONDON with one of the strangest of machines, called the Bicar, said to be 'a revolution in motorcycles'. The design was first seen early in 1905

at the Crystal Palace Show, where it was called the Tooley Bicar after its inventor, and was shown by Bitton & Harley of Great Yarmouth. By July that year, it had

been improved and was produced by the Zenith Motor Engineering Co. of London.

The Bicar had a novel frame, with its main tube running from

the rear-wheel spindle along the machine, round the front wheel and back again. Below this, on each side, ran a second tube to carry the weight of rider and engine, with this hung from joints to eliminate vibration. Hub-centre steering was used, so there were no front forks in the normal sense, the handlebars being connected to the wheel axle by stays. The engine was a 3hp Fafnir with a free-engine clutch and belt drive to the rear wheel, which had a drum brake. Zenith also offered the Tricar, with a 5hp engine and two speeds, both of which were soon options for the Bicar.

The company was run by Freddie W. Barnes, who in 1907 patented his Gradua Gear system, combining a variable engine pulley with movement of the rear wheel to maintain correct belt tension. The system used a series of rods connected to a single handle so that the gear could be altered while on the move. So useful would this prove in hill climbs that some clubs prohibited Zenith machines from their events, and the firm profited from this with its 'barred' trademark.

Before this came about, the original Bicar was revised to become the more conventional Zenette. This had the looks of the period, but retained the sprung frame concept of the Bicar. Braced front forks and the Gradua Gear were fitted. Late in 1908 the Zenette was joined by a rigid

model that had sprung forks and improved hill-climbing ability, thanks to its lower weight. At the end of the year, the company moved to Weybridge, Surrey, close to Brooklands, where Freddie Barnes set the first record for the Test Hill early in 1909. After the relocation, the firm was to become much more successful.

For 1910 the entire motorbike was tidied up and took on the typical style of the time with Druid forks. The Zenette continued to be offered for that year, but the 1911 range also included the Zenith Gradua with single or V-twin JAP engines; during that year, the 'barred' advertisement appeared to promote the ease with which the Gradua Gear disposed of hills. Although more models appeared for 1913, they were much revised by 1914, with a chain-driven countershaft, complete with clutch and kick-starter, mounted in front of the crankcase. The countershaft carried a large pulley to drive the rear wheel by a lengthy belt, while retaining the Gradua Gear and rear-wheel movement. The power units were now all JAP twins.

During 1914 the firm moved to Hampton Court, Middlesex, and after the war production resumed

An interesting Zenith fitted with a water-cooled single-cylinder engine. The radiators were fitted to each side of the cylinder.

For 1914, Zenith listed only models with V-twin JAP engines, including this 550cc example. Transmission was by the famous Gradua Gear by chain and belt, or belt alone.

with the JAP twin models, still with the countershaft and Gradua Gear. However, by November 1919 these were joined by a 346cc flat-twin with the same transmission.

In 1921 a model fitted with a 494cc oil-cooled Bradshaw flat-twin engine was introduced, and this was soon listed with the choice of the Gradua Gear or a three-speed Sturmey-Archer gearbox and all-chain drive. This was to be an option for most models in 1922. For 1923

conventional singles were added to the line-up.

Chain drive was the order of the day for 1924, the Gradua Gear having run its course, and the firm offered a range of singles and V-twins that increased annually and were typical of the decade. One model launched that year used an overhead-valve single-cylinder Bradshaw engine; by 1926 there were 348cc Blackburne units, 490cc JAP singles and 680 and 980cc V-twin JAP engines of this type. A 175cc side-valve lightweight was added for 1927 only and was replaced the next year by one using a 172cc Villiers two-stroke.

The company had not forgotten its sporting history, and in 1928 O.M. Baldwin set the motorcycle world speed record at over 200kph (124mph) riding a 996cc Zenith-JAP. Two years later Joe Wright used a Zenith and not the OEC, as had been publicised, to take the figure to over 241kph (150mph).

However, Zenith did not sell many machines in 1930, after which the firm was taken over by Writer's, a large London dealer. The new owner listed a reduced range for 1931, all with JAP engines, but soon expanded this, using Blackburne engines as well for a few years. This conventional, perhaps slightly old-fashioned, format continued through the rest of the decade, up to World War II. After the war, only one model was ever listed, and this used the 747cc side-valve JAP V-twin engine in pre-war form with Druid girder forks. In time, these were changed for Dowty Oleomatic telescopics, before production ceased altogether in 1950.

ZENITH GRADUA   1910

ZEPHYR
England 1922–23: This 131cc two-stroke, was sold in two forms: as an auxiliary cycle motor, and already installed in a lightweight.

ZETA
Italy 1947–54: This scooter, with its 33cm (13ins) wheels, was initially powered by a 48cc Cucciolo motor and possibly later by a 60cc Ducati engine.

ZETGE
Germany 1922–25: One source reports this machine as having two-stroke engines of 150 and 175cc, another reports side-valve singles of 500cc and twins of 600 and 750cc.

ZEUGNER
Germany 1903–06: This assembler used the usual range of pioneering proprietary engines: Fafnir, FN, Minerva, Peugeot and Zedel.

ZEUS
Austro-Hungary (Czech Republic) 1902–12: These machines were singles of three and three-and-a-half horsepower and V-twins of four and four-and-a-half horsepower. They were also sold as Linser, after the name of the designer, Christian Linser.

In the Edwardian era, most motorcycles had direct belt drive from the engine to the rear wheel and therefore a fixed ratio, with no means of changing this for hills.

Adjustable engine pulleys helped with this problem, but meant a stop at the foot of each hill to lower the ratio, and another at the top to raise it again. This was a major problem, so Freddie Barnes devised the Gradua Gear.

By 1910 the original design was refined so that a tank-top handle turned a vertical shaft with a bevel gear at its lower end. This meshed with one on a shaft that ran back

Zenith continued with the Gradua Gear up to 1923. This 1921 680cc V-twin also had the option of push starting and belt drive, or kick starting and chain-cum-belt drive.

in the right-hand frame tube, and that shaft was connected to a similar one on the left. These two moved the wheel back and forth, and this movement was linked to the engine pulley so that as it expanded or contracted, so the rear wheel moved to maintain belt tension.

The infinitely variable gear actually worked from 3:1 to 9:1,

which was a great advantage in competition, so much so that the marque was banned by some organisers. This was fine publicity for Zenith and soon led to its 'barred' advertisements and trademark. The remainder of the machine was conventional and much like others of the period.

Engine: 499cc sv vertical single, 85x88mm, air-cooled
Power: n/a
Gearbox: variable hand change
Final drive: belt
Weight: 82kg (180lb)
Top speed: n/a

ZUNDAPP   GERMANY 1921–84

FOUNDED IN SEPTEMBER 1917, Zunderund Apparatebau, better known as Zundapp, began as a joint venture between three established firms at the height of World War I. Based in Nurnburg and employing 1800 workers, the commercial stimulus was war production, and they manufactured fuses for artillery guns. At war's end the company struggled to find a needed product.

Zundapp was acquired by Fritz Neumeyer in 1919 and the task of discovering a new product line was solved in 1921 when it built its first motorcycle, forerunner of three million machines that would be made over the next 63 years.

The first model was the Z22, powered by a bought-in 211cc British-made Levis two-stroke. By October 1922, 1000 had been made.

Neumeyer quickly realised how important motorcycle sport was to the company's prestige. The very first Zundapp built was ridden in

Zundapp built a whole series of horizontally opposed twins for both civilian and military use. This machine dates from World War II.

During the 1930s, Richard Kuchen designed the first of Zundapp's flat-twins, with capacities of 398 and 498cc. He also created this 598cc four-cylinder model.

the North Bavarian reliability trials in September 1921 by the German champion Metsch, who later became a legend within the Zundapp organisation for his exploits on the company's product during the 1920s.

By November 1924 other models powered by Zundapp's own engine designs had been added to the range, including one which used a 249cc version of the original Levis. At the beginning of 1924 Zundapp commissioned its first modern assembly line. By the year's end more than 10,000 machines had been assembled on its conveyors.

The German public first bought motorcycles in high volume in

1924. This boom was greatly helped by a national 17-day touring race that aroused the interest of millions; in it, Zundapp scored some impressive successes.

From 1926 onwards Zundapp established branches in all major

This swinging-arm version of the KS601 was built in 1958, expressly for the American importers, the Berliner Corporation of New Jersey.

commercial centres throughout Germany beginning in Berlin, and in the process set up a nationwide dealer and service network.

By 1928, after record sales, the four separate Zundapp plants in Nurnburg were swamped, so a new plant at Nurnburg-Schweinau was constructed. When it opened the following year it was hailed as the most modern in the world. In seven short years Zundapp had risen from nothing to take its place amongst the market leaders. In April 1929 a new monthly record output of 4200 units was achieved. A couple of months later Hans-Friedrich Neumeyer joined the company, but by the end of the year sales had fallen dramatically to a mere 300 units per month.

The Great Depression had arrived. Over 5.5 million Germans were soon unemployed. Zundapp, unlike many other companies, survived and much of this was due to the management skills of the Neumeyer family.

By 1933 Zundapp was making a massive recovery. It produced the first of its four-stroke horizontally opposed twins, with capacities of 398 and 498cc and also brought out a flat four of 598cc. These models were the work of Richard Kuchen and were introduced as unconventional, but were very successful.

A new small displacement two-stroke was launched in 1934. Called the Derby, it had a 174cc unit producing five-and-a-half brake horsepower, which introduced a new three-way scavenging system. This was later incorporated into other Zundapp two-stroke models.

For a few short years sales were expanding so fast that dealers were complaining about their machine allocation; Zundapp simply couldn' build bikes quickly enough. Moreover, by the late 1930s, military requirements were starting to rule industrial life more and more in Hitler's Germany. Even so, Zundapp introduced several new models, including the KS600 flat twin with a 597cc engine. Another new model, the DS350, was the first of the marque to feature a foot pedal gear change.

From March 1940 all supplies to civilian customers were discontinued but, unlike many of its rivals, Zundapp retained a large part of its wartime production facilities for the manufacture of

motorcycles. It was thus able to celebrate its 250,000th bike, a KS750, which left the assembly line on the 13 March 1942.

The KS750 was designed expressly for military purposes. It had an integral sidecar with the wheel driven via a lockable differential. The power unit was an air-cooled flat twin and the gearbox featured two sets of four forward and reverse gears. With the similar BMW R75, the KS750 was one of the definitive German motorcycles of World War II.

By 1945, Zundapp had lost one third of its production facilities. The US Army of occupation made use of the main office block, repair shops and service premises and only 170 workers remained, compared to 4000 in 1944. Motorcycle production did not resume until the summer of 1947, when some updated pre-war models were built. The first truly new bike was the DB201, a two-stroke single.

Memories of pre-war Zundapp flat-twins were stimulated by the appearance of the KS600. With its

During the late 1970s, Zundapp built the KS125 and KS175 (the latter is shown here). These used a liquid-cooled two-stroke engine; Laverda also used this engine.

pressed-steel frame, inter-connected hand and foot change and dated looks, this model soon gave way to the much more sporting KS601 (nicknamed the 'Green Elephant') in 1951. Its 597cc (75x67.6mm) overhead valve engine produced 28bhp, giving a top speed of nearly 141kph (88mph), making it the fastest German street bike when introduced.

Besides their solo performances, these flat twins also made ideal sidecar tugs and were in great demand. A KS601 could top 120kph (75mph) and it could also achieve considerable success in

For many years, Zundapp had considerable success in the ISDT. This GS125 enduro bike with a single-cylinder two-stroke engine dates from 1972.

long-distance trials such as the International Six Day Trial.

Zundapp moved production to Munich in early 1950 and under the leadership of Dr Mann Zundapp went from strength to strength. Development concentrated on small capacity two-strokes, and the last of the KS601 twins was built in 1959. A major seller for Zundapp was the Bella scooter of which 130,680

ZEUS
Germany 1925–27: Kuchen 350 and 500cc three-valve engines powered these well-designed machines.

ZIEJANU
Germany 1924–26: This common story featured 211 and 246cc two-strokes, which were produced in house and were supplemented by bought-in 350 and 500cc four-strokes, from JAP.

ZIRO
Germany 1919–24: These two-strokes of 150 and 350cc had rotary valves in the crankcase. Albert Roder, the designer, later worked with Ermag, Zundapp and Victoria, before becoming chief designer at NSU.

ZM
Poland 1959: Zakladt Motolowa built a 49.8cc two-stroke, which was called the S38.

ZURTZ-REKORD
Germany (Darmstadt) 1922–26: This shortlived German assembler of the 1920s used a variety of engines as powerbases. They were two-stroke and four-stroke, and were bought in from firms such as DKW, Paque and Columbus, as well as from JAP. The JAP engines went up to a capacity of 500cc.

A Zundapp KS 750 from 1939 with Stoppa sidecar. The machine was powered by a flat-twin engine and was one of the definitive German motorcycles of World War II.

units were to be built. On the motorcycle side, the Elastic (so called because of its luxurious suspension system) was also a massive seller, and was built in several engine sizes.

The 200S arrived in 1955, the father of its own family of machines and ultimately a replacement for the Elastic model range. The final 250 Trophy S was made in the late 1960s.

For many years Zundapp had considerable sporting success in the International Six Day Trial, and on several occasions provided the machines which won the coveted Trophy and Vase trophies for the West German national squad. Unlike many others, Zundapp was not greatly affected by the sales depression which hit the German motorcycle industry in the late 1960s. By 1965 sales of mopeds, lightweights and scooters were at near record levels for the Munich-based marque, and as a result Zundapp made a big effort in the sporting arena. This included one-day trials and

endurance events and also led to a successful world record attempt at Monza in 1965. Zundapp, with Gustav Franke, became European Trials champions that same year.

Zundapp's first water-cooled production bike was the KS50 of 1972. The company also exhibited

the prototype-only KS350 water-cooled two-stroke twin at the Cologne Show in September 1976. This advanced and superbly styled machine never reached production, however, a KS125 with liquid-cooling did go on sale, followed later by the larger KS175. These

engines were also used by the Italian Laverda concern from 1977 until the mid-1980s.

From a high point of 115,000 machine sales in 1977, Zundapp declined in the next few years. By 1981 sales fell below 60,000 and by the 1982 Cologne Show, it was definitely struggling, having lost some 41 per cent of the previous year's figure. This was despite new models such as the KS80 and a brand new world-beating 80cc RSM racing motorcycle, a horizontal single which developed 30bhp at 14,800rpm and could reach an amazing 219kph (137mph). Zundapp even won (with Stefan Dorflinger) the 1984 80cc world title, but the company was declared bankrupt on the eve of the 1984 Cologne Show.

A buyer was found from the People's Republic of China and it resulted in the tooling, stock and designs being shipped there.

World champion Stefan Dorflinger won the 80cc title in 1984, riding this Krauser-backed Zundapp RSM, which could top 219kph (137mph).

ZUNDAPP KS601   1951

The flat-twin Zundapp, with its chain and sprocket gearbox had been around since the early 1930s and was the work of the legendary German designer Richard Kuchen.

There was even a flat four before the outbreak of World War II. During the conflict, Zundapp built the KS750 military model, which together with the BMW R75, was

one of the most well-known of Germany's wartime motorcycles.

After the war, the company built the KS600, which with its pressed-steel frame, blade girder forks and

rigid rear end was extremely old-fashioned. But Zundapp enthusiasts were able to ride proudly once more, with the introduction in 1951 of a new sports version of the flat twin theme, the KS601, soon nicknamed the Green Elephant, due to its colour scheme and the toughness.

The KS601 had a 597cc (75x67.6mm) overhead-valve engine with a separate 25mm (1in) Bing carburettor for each cylinder, cast-iron barrels and light-alloy heads. Power output was 28bhp at 4700rpm, with its electrical power coming from a 6-volt, 90W system.

The four-speed foot-operated chain and sprocket gearbox was in unit with the engine and there was

With a single seat sidecar, the 597cc KS601 Green Elephant was able to reach 120kph (75mph). In solo trim, maximum speed went up to 141kph (87.5mph).

shaft final drive, with plunger rear suspension matched to a new telescopic front fork. With a maximum speed of 145kph (90mph) in solo guise, the Green Elephant was the fastest German production bike at the time of its introduction. Even more impressive was its ability as a sidecar machine, since it was able to reach 120kph (75mph), and it won most admiration in this latter role – as well as a clutch of International Six Day Trial gold medals during the early 1950s.

The KS601 was a superb machine, in many ways superior to the BMW R51/2, but Zundapp's attempts to match BMW in showroom sales were badly affected when BMW launched the Earles-fork R50/60 series in 1955.

Manufacture of flat-twin Zundapps was halted in 1959 when the last Green Elephant left the factory's gates late that year. A total of some 5500 machines had been built. Finally, when the famous German motorcycle journalist and writer Ernst Leverkus was looking for a name for his winter rally at the Nurburging circuit, he chose to call the event the Elephant Rally; a fitting tribute to one of Germany's greatest ever motorcycles.

Engine: 597cc ohv 2v flat twin, 75x67.6mm, air-cooled
Power: 28bhp at 4700rpm
Gearbox: 4-speed foot change
Final drive: shaft
Weight: 202kg (445lb)
Top speed: 141kph (87.5mph)

ZWEIRAD-UNION
Germany 1958–74: Three motorcycle firms amalgamated in 1958; these were DKW, Express and Victoria. The Hercules company was to join later, in 1966. These four concerns were combined and went on to end up as part of Fichtel & Sachs. They were responsible for the manufacture of two-strokes – mainly of 50 and 100cc capacity – which were enclosed in their pressed-steel frames.

ZWERG
Germany 1924–25: This shortlived German firm was yet another manufacturer of that period who was responsible for the production of in-house two-stroke lightweights. The company used engines with capacities of 147 and 187cc as powerbases for their machines.

ZWI
Israel (Tel Aviv) 1952–55: This shortlived make was based in Israel during the early 1950s. It was founded by the Hungarian racer Stefan Auslaender. He used two-strokes which were bought in from JAP and Villiers to act as the powerbases for his machines. These engines were of 123cc displacement.

ZZR
Poland 1960–unknown: Exact dates of this Polish company are difficult to obtain, but what is clear from various sources is that they were reponsible for the production of mopeds.

ZUNDAPP BELLA

1953

One of Zundapp's best-selling models ever was the Bella scooter which made its debut in May 1953. Designated Bella Motor Roller (Motor Scooter), this was to prove a major success story for the company, with the basic design

continuing until 1964, by which time a total of 130,680 scooters had been built in a number of versions during its 11-year life.

The first model was the Bella 150, or R150, with a displacement of 147cc (57x58mm), seven-and-a-

third bhp, a 20mm Bing carburettor and top speed of 80kph (50mph). Its piston-port two-stroke engine featured a three-ring piston, cast-iron cylinder and alloy head.

The Bella featured geared primary drive to a four-speed

A 1954 Zundapp R200 Bella scooter. Powered by a 198cc single-cylinder two-stroke engine, it boasted several changes from the original smaller-engined version.

gearbox in unit with the engine and controlled by a foot-operated rocking pedal, while the final drive chain was fully enclosed in a case arranged to pivot with the swinging fork rear suspension assembly.

Open coil suspension springs were employed, controlled by a single hydraulic damper fitted on the nearside of the fork. The front wheel was mounted in leading axle telescopic front forks, and the relatively large diameter 30cm (12ins) alloy wheels with 150mm (6ins) drum brakes front and rear were shod with 3.50 section tyres.

The frame took an unusual form, principally consisting of a large diameter downtube and two backbone members arching over the engine and rear wheel. Over this frame was fitted pressed-steel bodywork offering a large expanse of protection both front and rear. Included in the body was a fuel

tank with a capacity of 8.5 litres (two UK gallons).

A cooling duct allowed air in at the front and directed it over the cylinder through to a vent behind the rider's seat. An optional pillion seat could be fitted. Cast aluminium grilles on each side of the rear wheel were hinged so that they would fold down to become pannier luggage supports, and a spare wheel and carrier could be bought at additional cost.

By May 1954 no fewer than 10,000 Bella scooters had been sold, but to meet a demand from customers for improved acceleration and a higher maximum speed, Zundapp introduced the R200, which was powered by a 198cc (64x62mm) engine with several changes from the original smaller-engined version.

Engine: 147cc 2s single, 57 x 58mm, air-cooled
Power: 7.3bhp at 6000rpm
Gearbox: 4-speed foot change
Final drive: chain, fully enclosed
Weight: 158kg (350lb)
Top speed: 80kph (50mph)

ZUNDAPP B250 CONCEPT

1953

At the International Frankfurt Show in 1953, Zundapp stole much of the thunder, thanks not only to its Bella scooter and 250 Elastic motorcycle, but to a brand new overhead-valve horizontally opposed 247cc (54x54mm) twin, the B250.

Although at the time, this newcomer was expected to enter production the following spring, it never happened. Instead, it was a Concept Bike, launched in a blaze of glory for publicity purposes only.

It had been influenced by the similar Hoffman 250 flat twin of 1951, and only built by Zundapp specifically to create a show sensation, since it would have been far too costly to build in production form.

The engine of the 250 Zundapp twin had an exceptionally clean design with alloy heads and barrels with reborable cast-iron liners. The bore and stroke dimensions were square and the three-ring pistons gave a 6.8:1 compression ratio. Power output with twin Bing 24mm (1in) carburettors was 18.5bhp at 7000rpm.

Perhaps the model's most notable feature (one usually found only on expensive large capacity models) was the use of shaft final drive. The engine featured needle roller big-end bearings of a similar type to the KS601 Green Elephant. To the forward end of the three-bearing crankshaft was attached the armature shaft of the Noris DC dynamo. A four-speed gearbox was flange-fitted to the rear of the crankcase, and the drive was via a large diameter, single-plate car-type clutch. The gearbox, like that of the larger flat twins, was actually of the chain and sprocket type, linked by duplex chains.

A novel approach to frame design saw the transverse flat twin engine slung below two widely spaced, large-diameter tubes which ran downward and rearward from the steering head. The tubes terminated above and slightly in front of the rear wheel spindle to form upper supports for the rear shock absorbers. As the engine mounts were close to the horizontal plane through the crankshaft axis, the arrangement was claimed largely to counteract the effects of torque reaction.

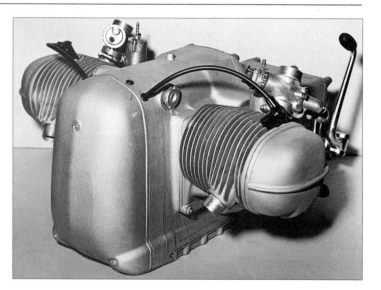

The ohv 247cc horizontally-opposed twin-cylinder engine from the 1953 B250 machine. The bike was very much a concept design, for attracting press attention only.

Both wheels had 180mm (7ins) full width aluminium brake hubs, with 40cm (16ins) rims and 3.50 section tyres. Other component parts included a 15 litre (3.3 UK gallons) fuel tank, a deeply

Engine: 247cc ohv 2v flat twin, 54x54mm, air-cooled
Power: 18.5bhp at 7000rpm
Gearbox: 4-speed foot change
Final drive: shaft
Weight: n/a
Top speed: n/a

valanced front mudguard and an almost totally enclosed rear section which was positioned aft of the engine unit.

GLOSSARY

ABS Anti-lock braking system
AC Alternating current (as produced by an alternator)
Acceleration Rate of change of speed, commonly expressed in terms of standing-start quarter mile times
Accelerator pump Carburettor feature which enriches the fuel/air mixture when the throttle is opened quickly
Air-cooling Cooling in which the passage of air over the engine takes away combustion heat
Air-box A pre-chamber of still air feeding the engine, surprisingly important for performance
Air filter A screen, usually of paper or oiled rubber foam, for keeping dust out of an engine
Aise An engine with an Auto Inlet, Side Exhaust valve
Alternator The electricity generator on most motorcycles, producing alternating current which must be rectified to DC
Ammeter Instrument which measures electrical current flow
Automatic Gear-less transmission, favoured on commuter machines, in which some sort of fluid drive or variable belts transmit power to the rear wheel
Automatic inlet valve Early type of valve in which the suction of the piston opened and closed the inlet valve
Automatic tensioner Spring-loaded self-adjusting tensioner, usually used on cam chains or belts

Beaded-edge tyres Early tyre in which a hard edge (the bead) is located into a channel on the wheel rim
Bellmouth Trumpet-shaped tube designed to improve air-flow into a carburettor
Belt drive Flexible toothed belt which takes the drive to the final wheel (e.g. modern Harleys) or drives the camshafts (Ducati), or other components such as super-chargers. Many early machines used a simple leather belt from the final drive
Bevel drive Drive in which drive is turned through 90 degrees from one shaft to another via bevel gears
bhp Brake horsepower, the horsepower developed by an engine
Bias-belted Tyre construction with two or more fabric belts at different angles, effectively a half-way house between cross-ply and radial construction
Big end The eye in the lower end of a connecting rod and its associated crankshaft journal
Bore The diameter of the cylinder in which the piston travels
Butterfly Rotating disc acting as a throttle valve in some carburettors and most fuel injection inlets

Calliper Disc brake component in which one or more pistons press friction pads against the disc rotor
Camshaft Shaft, usually with several cam lobes which control the opening of valves, either directly or via some intervening mechanism
Capacity The displacement of an engine
Carbon fibre Very strong, light composite of fine filaments of carbon, woven and bonded in a matrix such as epoxy resin
Carburettor Device, usually working on the Venturi principle, for mixing fuel and air in the correct quantities to enable combustion
Cardan shaft The final drive shaft in shaft driven motorcycles
Cable On a motorcycle, usually a Bowden cable with a stiff outer and flexible steel inner which transmits linear movement (e.g. clutch cable) or rotation (speedometer cable)
Castor See 'rake'
Cc Cubic centimetres, the units for measuring engine displacement (1 cu.in (cid) = 16.4cc)

A beautifully-made post-World War I small capacity engine. It features a two-speed gearbox, but is powered by a belt drive, typical of its time. This motor was fitted in a Calthorpe machine.

Soldiers line up on their Ariel 350cc W-NG machines. These militarised motorcycles were made by the thousand and sold successfully to the British Army during World War II.

Choke Refers both to the carburettors venturi diameter (or fuel injector trumpet bore), and to any mechanism for richening the mixture for cold starts

Clutch Device for controlling the transmission of power from engine to gearbox, usually by means of friction plates

Coil Electrical windings which turn a low-voltage current into the high voltage required by the spark plugs

Combustion chamber The space (usually in the cylinder head) above the piston at top dead centre in which combustion begins.

Compression ratio The ratio of maximum cylinder and combustion chamber volume at bdc to that at tdc

Connecting rod (Con rod) Metal rod which joins the piston to the crankshaft

Contact breaker (Points) Pairs of mechanically-controlled electrical contacts which, with high-tension coils, create the current for the spark plug

Crankcase Commonly split in two, the cases in which the crankshaft (and often the gearbox) are located

Crankshaft Shaft (one-piece or pressed up) which turns the up-and-down motion of the pistons into rotational movement.

Cross-ply Tyres having fabric layers with cords lying crosswise, as opposed to radial tyres

CV Constant Vacuum, Constant Velocity: carburettor in which the choke is controlled by depression rather than a direct mechanism such as in a conventional slide-type carburettor

Cylinder The usually cylindrical chamber in which the piston travels

Cylinder head The crown of an engine. In two-strokes it is little more than an inverted metal dish with a spark plug; in four-strokes it contains the valves, and usually the camshafts.

Damper Device for slowing the movement of components relative to each other. Usually hydraulic, but friction dampers were once common

Desmo (Desmodromic) Valve system in which a cam rather than a spring controls the closing of the valve, such as on many Ducatis

Disc brake Brake in which pads of friction material are squeezed against a spinning rotor

Disc valve Type of valve using a rotating disc with a window to permit flow, sometimes seen on two-stroke inlet ports

Dohc An engine with a Double Overhead Camshaft

Drag racing Sprint-type racing, usually over a measured quarter mile

Drum brake Brake in which shoes of friction material are moved radially against the inside of a cylinder (the drum)

Dry sump Four-stroke engine in which the lubricating oil is contained in a special tank rather than in the crankcases

Dry weight The weight of a motorcycle without fluids

Duplex Literally, double. Used of frame design and double-row chains, etc

Dynamo Simple device for converting rotation of a shaft into electricity, now almost unknown on motorcycles

Dynamometer (Dyno) Instrument for measuring engine torque (from which power can be extrapolated).

EFI Electronic fuel injection

Enduro Off-road motorcycle racing over an unseen course

Engine braking The braking effect of an engine when the throttle is closed

Eoi An engine with Exhaust Over Inlet valve, as on some Indian fours

Exhaust The pipes which conduct spent combustion gases away from an engine; the gases themselves

Expansion The characteristic of almost all materials to grow larger as they are heated.

Expansion Chamber Bulbous portion of two-stroke exhaust system, designed to maximise exhaust pressure-pulses and so improve engine efficiency

Fade Lose effectiveness, especially of overheated brakes

Feeler gauge Precision metal strip of marked gauge used to measure fine clearances

Fender American expression for mudguard

Fin/finning Cooling extensions, on cylinder, crankcase, brake drums and some electrical components

Fishtail silencer Silencer with flattened, wedge-shaped end portion

Flathead Cylinder head offering flat combustion chamber face, such as many sidevalves and 'Heron' head ohv

Flat twin Boxer engine layout with two cylinders opposed at 180 degrees, e.g. BMW, Douglas

Float Bouyant object in carburettor used to actuate a petrol cut-off valve

Flywheel Rotating mass, commonly in crankshaft assembly, used to store energy and smooth power delivery

Flywheel magneto Magneto mounted directly on the crankshaft, rather than driven remotely

Footchange Gearchange mechanism operated by the foot (early bikes were hand-change)

Footrest Fixed or hinged rest for the rider or passengers foot

Forced induction Engine using a supercharger or turbocharger

Four stroke Engine operating on the Otto cycle (named after its inventor, Dr Nicholas Otto), requiring four piston strokes for each power stroke

Fuel injection Positive metering and introduction of fuel by mechanical or electro-mechanical means, now often integrated into comprehensive engine management systems

Gaiter Flexible protective shroud, usually around a suspension unit or control linkage

Gap Space between two elements, especially contact breaker points or spark plug electrodes

Gasket Sealing between two joint faces. May be of paper, metal, composite or 'plastic'

Gas tight Seal or joint which is impervious to gas, used especially of cylinder head to barrel face

Gas welding Joining materials by heating with burning gases, usually oxygen and acetylene

Gauge Measuring device; measure of thickness

Gear tooth Projection on a gear designed to mesh with a complementary indent on another gear

Gear ratio Ratio of turning speeds of a pair of gears, or the aggregate ratios of a train of gears

Gel coat Thin, uppermost coat used in glass-fibre lamination to give a smooth finish, with or without colour

Girder fork Front suspension comprising rigid beams, movement being allowed by links at the steering head

Girdraulic Vincent's proprietory form of girder forks employing light alloy blades and hydraulic damping

Gland Joint, usually in a pipe, with either jointing material or a preformed seal

Glass fibre Fine strands of spun glass, usually pressed or woven into sheets and treated with a chemically-setting resin

GP Grand Prix; type of Amal racing carburettor

Grand Prix Blue-riband motorcycle road racing competition, began in France in 1913 but was not incorporated into a world championship until 1949

Grass track racing 'An accident looking for a place to happen' on an oval grass circuit

Grease Stabilised mixture of a metallic soap and a lubricating oil

Grinding paste Abrasive compound of carborundum powder and oil, used to bed-in valves and mating surfaces

Grommet Doughnut-shaped item, usually rubber, preventing chaffing of control and electrical cables passing through a hole

Ground clearance The distance between the lowest sprung point of a motorcycle and the ground

Ground joint Face joint made by lapping two surfaces together

Gudgeon pin (wrist pin in USA) Hard steel tube linking the piston to the small-end

Guide Component that directs, aligns or positions another, e.g. valve guide

Gusset Piece used to strengthen any open structure, such as steering head assembly

Gyroscopic precession The effect in which gyroscopic forces give a rotating wheel both a self-centering effect and the capacity for counter-steering

Hairpin spring Commonly a valve spring, hairpin-shaped but often with coils at the closed end

Half time pinion Crankshaft gear or sprocket sized to drive ignition or camshaft at half engine speed

Halogen bulb Light bulb using one of the halogen family of gases, e.g. iodine, to increase light output

Handlebars Projections from the steering column used for mounting controls and steering by the hands

Harden To toughen, usually by heat, mechanical or chemical process

Head angle Angle of the steering axis with reference to the horizontal or vertical

Head steady Tie-bar between cylinder head and frame

Heat sink Usually metallic mass used to absorb heat away from another component (e.g. brake, rectifier) until it can be shed

Helical gears Gears having spiral or part-spiral meshing faces

Helicoil Brand name for a type of threaded female insert, used in alloy to repair or strengthen a fastening

Hemi head Hemispherical head, favoured in some older engines, in which the combustion chamber is roughly half a sphere

Heron head Type of cylinder head in which combustion chamber is formed in the piston rather than the head itself, e.g. Morini

High tensile Material, commonly steel, of high 'stretch' strength

High tension 'HT', the high-voltage secondary phase in an ignition system

Hill climb Standing-start speed competition over a twisting uphill course

Honing Achieving a fine finish to precise size by abrasion, typically in cylinder bores

Horizontally opposed Engine layout with pairs of cylinders opposed at 180 degrees, e.g. BMW Boxer, Honda Gold Wing

Hose Any flexible pipe, e.g. hydraulic brake lines

Hot spot Area of a combustion chamber which gets too hot, causing pre-ignition. Often caused by incandescent carbon deposits

Hot tube ignition Primitive ignition system in which a platinum tube is heated by spirit burner

H-section Shaped like a letter 'H' in cross-section, e.g. con-rod

HT leads High tension cables, from coil to spark plug or coil to distributor to spark plug

Hub Centre part of a wheel

Hub centre steering Steering system in which the axis of wheel movement lies within the wheel hub

Hugger Lightweight, racing-style rear mudguard which moves up and down with the wheel; Harley-Davidson models with very little ground clearance

Hunting Erratic tickover, often caused by incorrect carburation

Hydraulic Mechanism using the flow or pressure of a liquid through valves and orifices, such as with motorcycle brakes and suspension dampers

The V-twin engine is synonymous with the legendary Harley-Davidson marque. This Twin Cam engine dates from 1998 and is the latest incarnation of a much-loved power unit.

Hydrometer Instrument for measuring specific gravity of a liquid, e.g. to test state of charge of a battery

Hygrometer Instrument for measuring humidity, such as to calculate jetting for racing engines

Hygroscopic Substance which attracts water, such as (most) brake fluids

Hysteresis Literally, lag. Of tyre rubber, high-hysteresis compounds (invented by Avon) have less internal bounce and more grip

Ice racing Racing on oval ice tracks with speedway-like machines fitted with metal-spiked tyres

Idiot light Slang expression for an instrument warning light

Idler gear Gear interposed between two others to avoid using overlarge working gears

Ignition advance Extent to which the ignition spark precedes TDC, necessary because combustion is not instantaneous but takes a finite time to occur

Import, grey motorcycle imported into a country which dos not officially import that model

Import, parallel motorcycle which is imported in direct competition with official imports

Index mark Vehicle identification number (VIN) of a vehicle; also reference point for adjustment, e.g. of wheel alignment or ignition timing

Induction Drawing-in of fuel-air to an engine, although correctly it is mainly pushed in by atmospheric pressure

Inertia The tendency of all things to carry on moving in the same direction once started. Everything in an engine – the pistons, even the air in the carburettor – has inertia

Injector Pressurised nozzle for squirting fuel or oil into an engine

Inlet Place of entry, as in inlet valve, inlet tract

Instant gasket Plasticised substance, sometimes hardening, for sealing joint faces

Instrument Device which measures or controls a function

Intake Inlet

Integral Belonging to a complete whole

Inter 'Between', as in inter-cooler

Internal combustion engine Any heat engine in which energy is developed in the engine cylinder and not in a separate chamber

Inverted forks Upside down forks, in which the sliders are at the top rather than the bottom.

Theoretically stiffer than conventional forks, and with less unsprung weight

Ioe Inlet Over Exhaust - engine with overhead inlet valve and side exhaust valve

ISDT Former name of the ISDE, the International Six Day Enduro (Trial), an international team off-road endurance event

Isle of Man Island in the Irish Sea which first allowed motorcycle road races in 1905 and has hosted the motorcycle TT since 1907

Isochronous Occurring at the same time, e.g. two-stroke induction and exhaust phases

Isolastic Proprietory name for the rubber-mounted engine/swinging fork system of Norton's Commando

Jampot Slang for the fat rear dampers of 1950s AJS and Matchless machines.

Jet An orifice, usually of precise size, through which fuel passes

Jet needle Tapered needle in a carburettor which rises and falls to vary fuel flow at medium throttle openings

Jig Cradle used to manufacture or check the dimensions of an assembly such as a motorcycle frame

Jointing compound Material applied to joint faces to assist sealing

Journal Accurately machined portion of a shaft on which a bearing (e.g. big end) engages

Jubilee clip Originally branded hose clips, the title is now generic

Kadency Effect, using pressure waves to enhance cylinder filling and scavenging

Keihin Japanese brand of carburettor

Kevlar A synthetic (para-Aramid) fibre with enormous tensile strength, used in exotic motorcycle components and protective clothing (including bullet-proof vests)

Triumph's X75 Hurricane had the cruiser look so typical of machines from the early 1970s. It also used a bought in engine, from BSA.

Kick back Brief but often fierce reverse rotation of an engine during starting

Kickstarter Foot-operated crank for starting an engine

Kilowatt kW, now becoming the standard ISO measure of horsepower. 1kW equals 1.3596PS or 1.341bhp

Kneeler Usually a low-profile sidecar outfit in which the rider kneels; more rarely special solos such as the 1953 Norton kneeler

Knee slider Slippery attachment to racing leathers allowing the rider to drag his inside knee on the ground in corners

Knurling Machine tool rolling process for cross-hatching components

Laminar flow The tendency of fluids near a solid surface to stick with the surface and lubricate the movement of fluids farther away. The principle relates to mixture in an inlet tract as much as to motorcycle aerodynamics

Lap Complete circuit of racetrack; bed-in by lapping with abrasive compound

Latent heat Heat needed to change a solid to liquid or liquid to gas. Methanol's high latent heat gives excellent engine cooling

Lathe Machine tool with rotating workpiece and fixed cutter

Layshaft Gearbox shaft parallel to the mainshaft, carrying the laygears

Leaded Petrol bearing tetra-ethyl lead, an anti-knock compound and neuro-toxin

Leading link Form of front suspension using a pivoted link with the wheel spindle in front of the pivot

Leading shoe In a drum brake, the brake shoe with its actuating cam at its leading edge

Leaf spring Suspension spring comprising one or more narrow strips of spring steel

Lean Ingoing fuel-air charge which has too little fuel

Lean-out Make fuel-air mixture more lean; extent to which the steering head leans away from the vertical in a sidecar outfit

Level plug Plug, usually screw-in, which marks the desired upper level of fluid in a chamber

Lever Handle for achieving a mechanical advantage, typically a brake or clutch lever

Lift Amount something is raised, e.g. a valve off its seat

Light alloy Loose expression for a multitude of aluminium alloys

Aprilia's RS250 was hailed as the best 'miniature' superbike on the market. Its braking and handling were racer like – a classic in sports bike design.

Liner Detachable insert, commonly a steel cylinder liner in an alloy barrel

Linkage Typically an articulated joint, such as in a gearchange mechanism

Lobe Raised part of a cam

Lock (Maximum) steering deflection

Lockheed Generic term for hydraulic fluid, taken from the company of the same name

Locking wire/lockwire Strong, usually stainless steel wire used for securing items against loosening

Locknut Nut tightened hard against another to prevent loosening

Lock stop Abutment to the steering gear limiting amount of steering lock

Lock washer Washer with anti-loosening feature

Lockwire pliers Special pliers with jaws capable of locking onto and twisting lockwire

Loctite Proprietory liquid used for securing threads, bearings, etc

Long reach Term for a spark plug of ³/₄in (19mm) reach

Long stroke Undersquare engine, in which the stroke exceeds the bore

Lubricant Any substance interposed between rubbing surfaces to reduce friction

Magdyno Unit combining a magneto and dynamo in a common housing

Magic box Anything electrical which you don't understand. See black box

Magnesium Metal (36 per cent lighter than aluminium) expensively used for some motorcycle castings

Magneto Ignition spark generator requiring no external electrical power source

Main bearing Any principal bearing, but usually those carrying the crankshaft

Main jet The principle fuel jet in a carburettor

Mains Crankshaft main bearings

Mainshaft Principle shaft, usually in gearbox

Manifold Branched system conducting mixture to, or exhaust from, an engine

Marque Another word for make of motorcycle

Marshal Usually unpaid safety official at race meeting

Master cylinder Reservoir and pump at the operator end of a hydraulic system

Maudes Trophy ACU trophy infrequently awarded for feats of unusual machine endurance

Megaphone Megga, outwardly tapering four-stroke exhaust chamber capable of increasing power and power spread

Metalastik Flexible bush acting as both pivot and vibration insulation

Mikuni Japanese carburettor manufacturer, began making Amals under licence

Mixture Ingoing fuel-air charge

MON Motor octane number, arrived at by a more severe test

than RON and more relevant for racing purpoes

Monobloc Amal carburettor with float bowl and mixing chamber formed in one casting; any such carburettor

Monograde oil Oil with a viscosity defined by a single SAE number

Monoshock Rear suspension system employing a single shock absorber. Although a Yamaha trade name, now commonly used

Moped Pedal-assisted motorcycle

Motocross Off-road circuit racing, formerly called scrambles

Motocross des Nations Annual international team motocross championship

Mudguard Shroud designed to prevent road dirt being flung from wheels onto machine and rider

Multigrade oil Oil with viscosity characteristics encompassing two or more SAE numbers

Multi-rate A spring which changes length unequally for different increments of load

Needle roller A bearing roller very much longer than its diameter

Negative earth Connecting the negative battery terminal to earth; the usual convention

NGK Nippon Geika Kaisha, Japanese spark plug manufacturer

Nikasil Proprietory process for applying a thin, hard coating to alloy cylinder bores

Nimonic Nickel-rich iron alloy favoured for exhaust valves

Nipple Boss with a hole in it for admitting grease

Nitriding Process for hardening steel

Nitro Nitro-methane, an oxygen-rich fuel of low calorific value

Non-unit Engine layout in which the powerplant and transmission as separate units

Normally-aspirated Engine charged by atmospheric pressure, rather than forced induction

Nyloc Nut with a nylon insert which resists loosening through vibration

Nylocable Bowden cable with 'self-lubricating' nylon inner sheath

Observed section Part of a trials course in which penalties can be incurred

Observer Official stationed at observed section to monitor competitors' performance

Octane rating Measure of the knock resistance of fuel, higher numbers being more knock resistant. Usually given as average of MON and RON

Odometer Mileage recorder, usually inset into the machine's speedometer

Ohc An engine with an Overhead Camshaft

Ohv An engine with an Overhead Valve

Oil Natural or synthetic fluid with good lubricating properties

Oil bath Protective oil reservoir into which a component dips

Oil cooling Where oil is used to collect engine heat and transport it

to cooling surfaces. Although all engines are partially oil cooled, Suzukis GSX-R series has taken this to extreme lengths

Oil cooler A radiator containing engine oil rather than water

Oil pump Mechanical device for pressurising oil in an engine

Oil seal Lipped, semi-elastic oil barrier on a shaft

Oil thrower Shaped ring or plate designed to throw oil away from a particular site

O-ring Rubber sealing ring, typically in oil feeds

O-ring chain Final drive chain using O-rings to seal in grease

Otto Cycle The four-stroke cycle

Outside flywheel Flywheel carried outside the crankcases, where it can be wider and thus more effective with less weight

Overlap Time when the inlet and exhaust valves are simultaneously open

Over-square Engine in which the bore is greater than the stroke, as in most modern engines

Pannier Component hanging down either side of a motorcycle, as in luggage bags or fuel tanks

Patent Protection granted by the state to an inventor

Pattern parts Replacement parts not authorised by the original manufacturer

Pawl Catch meshing with a ratchet wheel

Peak Highest point, as of cam lobe, power output, revs

Peak revs Maximum safe revs for a particular engine

Penetration Consistency of a grease; infiltration of a freeing agent; depth of a weld

Pent roof An efficient combustion chamber form in multi-valve heads, shaped like a pitched roof

Petrol Petrol and oil mixture used in some two-stroke engines

Petroleum jelly Waxy petroleum product used to protect battery terminals; 'Vaseline'

Phased piston Large 'super-charging' piston in machines such as DKW and early EMC racers

A 250cc overhead cam Benelli racer from the late 1930s. The machine was part of a successful racing venture that was ended by World War II.

Phillips Proprietary form of crosshead screw, often wrongly used generically

Phosphor-bronze Copper-tin alloy with excellent bearing qualities, often used for small-end bushes

Piggy-back Often used of the pressurised gas reservoir attached to a modern suspension unit

Pigtail Short length of conducting wire connected to a pickup brush

Pilgrim Simple type of double-ended pump using a single plunger to supply and scavenge

Pillion Seat behind the rider; person on it

Pilot jet Auxilliary jet in a carburettor which governs fuel flow at small throttle openings

Pilot light Small, low-wattage bulb; parking light

Pinking Metallic tinkling noise produced by pre-ignition

Piston Moving plunger in a cylinder, accepting or delivering thrust

Piston ring Springy metal hoops in groove on a piston, designed to promote gas seal or scrape oil from bore

Piston slap Audible contact of piston skirt against cylinder bore, worse in cold or worn bores

Pitch Distance between two repeating characteristics, such as rollers on a chain or teeth on a gear

Pinchbolt Bolt pinching two elements of a part together, such as on a fork yoke

Plain bearings Plain metal bearings (such as some big-ends and mains) which effectively suspend the moving components on a microscopic oil film

Plating Electrolytic deposition of a metal onto a dissimilar material for protective or cosmetic purposes

Plug cap Spark plug cover acting as protection, HT conductor and often radio suppressor

Pocketing Valves sunk into the cylinder head by repeated hammering effect, to the detriment of performance

Polarity Positive or negative, as of electrical connections

Polycarbonate Lightweight, resilient plastic used for crash helmets

Pop rivet Deformable metal pin used for joining two components

Poppet valve Reciprocating valve (as in cylinder head), essentially a disc on a stick

Popping back Spitting back through the carburettor

Porous Material allowing the passage of fluids. Often this is unwanted, as in porous castings

Parilla's famous 'hi-cam' single-cylinder engine. The prototype motor made its racing debut in 1952 and appeared in Parilla's production machines the same year. It brought the company instant recognition.

Port Any opening, now commonly applied to two-stroke's cylinder windows and their associated tracts

Positive earth Electrical system in which the battery's positive terminal is connected to earth

Pot Slang for cylinder

Power The rate of work, as measured in horsepower; more loosely, an engines peak power output

Power band The range of rpm in which an engine is making useful power

Power-slide Cornering with deliberate power-induced wheelspin, as in speedway

Power valve Two-stroke exhaust mechanism which alters the height (and thus duration) of the exhaust valve, usually known by manufacturers trade names

Pre-ignition Spontaneous combustion of the fuel-air mix before sparking

Pre-load Compression applied to a spring in installation. It has no bearing on the spring's rate

Pre-'65 Class of trials and motocross competition for machines built before 1965

Pressure gauge Instrument used for measuring air or oil pressure

Pre-unit Description of a layout with separate engine and gearbox, but of a model type which later had them in unit

Primary chain Chain transmitting drive from crankshaft to gearbox

Primary gears Gear train transmitting drive from crankshaft to gearbox

Progressive rate Spring compressing at a rate which decreases with load

Prop-stand Retractable side-stand

PS Widely-used German measure of horsepower (equivalent to French cv). 100PS equals 98.6bhp

PTFE Poly-tetra-fluoro-ethylene, a low-friction plastic often used for bushes

Pudding-basin Early, abbreviated form of crash helmet, cork-lined with leather temple protection

Pulling power slang term for an engine's ability to work under heavy load at low rpm

Push rod Metal rod used to transmit motion, such as from cam follower to rocker arm or in a clutch mechanism

Quench To Cool; used of metal treatments, and combustion chambers in which a large area of metal is in contact with combustion gases, restraining pre-ignition

Quietening ramp Gradual slope between base circle of a cam and the lobe proper

Radial tyres Radials have plies lying across each other radially (c.f. cross ply), allowing greater flexibility and grip.

Radial valves Multi valves radiating from the centre of the head rather than in parallel pairs

Radiator Device for dissipating heat through a large surface area, usually used for engine coolant

Rake Effective slope of the front forks relative to the vertical. Also known as castor. Usually, but not necessarily, the same as head angle

Ram Air The use of forward-facing air-scoops to pressurise an air box. At most speeds, the intake air's coldness is of more benefit than its supposed pressure

Ramp cam Cam fitted with quietening ramps

Reamer Fluted tool used to cut a hole to an exact final size

Rear wheel steering Steering a motorcycle by deliberately drifting the rear wheel

Rebore Machine a cylinder to accept an oversize piston

Rebound damping The damping which resists the spring's tendency to recoil after compressing

Reciprocating Moving backwards and forwards along a single path, such as a piston

Rectifier Electrical device passing current in one direction only, thus converting AC to DC

Recoil The bouncing back of a spring to its unloaded position

Reed valve A 'flapper' valve in a two-stroke's induction system, comprising flexible plates housed in a reed cage

Reflector Polished bowl of a light unit; passive safety reflector in rear light units; element in some exhaust systems designed to maximise exhaust wave harmonics

Regulator Electronic component which maintains the desired voltage; sometimes the voltage control unit

Rev counter Tachometer: Instrument for measuring the rotational speed (rpm) of an engine

Reverse cone Extension to some megaphones having a steep taper in the opposite direction to the megaphone

Riffler Small fine-toothed file, especially used in porting work

Rich (mixture) Fuel-air mixture with excess fuel

Rim Edge of a wheel carrying the tyre

Ring gear In engines with a longitudinal crankshaft, the gear engaging with the starter motor

Ring pegs Small metal keepers preventing piston rings from rotating, especially in two-strokes

Rising rate Suspension in which linkages cause the rate of movement to decrease as wheel travel increases

Rocker Pivoting arm translating rotational cam action into linear valve movement

Rockerbox Closed compartment housing the rocker gear

Rocking couple Lateral rocking motion set up in some types of multi-cylinder crankshaft

Roller bearing Bearing having cylindrical rollers rather than balls

RON Research octane number

Rotary Spinning, rather than reciprocating. Usually applied to Wankel engines

Rotary valve Rotating, rather than piston-port or poppet valve, which opens and closes gas passageways as it spins

Rpm Revs per minute, the rotational speed of a shaft or engine

Rumble Low-pitched noise emitted, especially, by worn crankshafts

The Triumph 1R Fast Roadster was introduced in 1922. Nicknamed 'Riccy', its engine was designed by tuning specialists Ricardo & Co.

Running on Phenomenon of an engine continuing to run after the ignition has been switched off, usually due to local hot spots

Run-out A shaft or wheel that is out of alignment

SAE Society of Automotive Engineers, USA; standards established by them

Sand racing Racing on beaches, often on speedway-type courses

Sand casting Metal component made by pouring molten metal into pre-formed sand mould

Scavenge Clear away, especially of exhaust gases from a combustion chamber

Schnurle Loop Two-stroke scavenging process in which transfer ports direct gases up and away from the open exhaust port, propelling exhaust gases ahead of them

Schraeder Design of tyre valve core, also used for air suspension

Scraper Tool for scraping; piston ring designed to clear oil from bores

Sealed beam Light unit with lens, filament and reflector in one piece

Security bolt Clamped rubber pad designed to prevent creep of tyres running at low pressure

Seizure Binding together of inadequately lubricated parts, especially pistons in cylinders

Selector fork Fork-shaped prong, controlled by a cam-plate or drum, able to slide gearbox pinions and thus change gear

Serrated Toothed, as in a serrated or 'Shakeproof' washer

Set screw Bolt threaded almost to its head, with no plain shank

Shim Tough metal insert of known thickness used to achieve desired clearances

Shock absorber Device for smoothing transmission impulses; also applied less correctly to suspension dampers

Shorrock Brand of rotary, vane-type supercharger

Short reach Spark plug hole of half-inch depth

Short stroke Markedly oversquare

Shot blasting Bombardment of parts to de-scale or work-harden them. Bead blasting is similar but less destructive

Shuttle valve Valve free to move to and fro, often found in telescopic forks

Siamese Two pipes joined into one, especially in exhausts

Sidevalve Engine with valvegear at the side and below the combustion chamber, rather than above

Sidewall That part of a tyre between the tread and the bead

Silencer (Muffler in USA) Portion of an exhaust system concerned with reducing its noise, now very sophisticated with modern noise limits

Silentbloc Proprietory part made from rubber block bonded to metal

Silver solder Solder with high silver content giving much stronger joint than ordinary tin solder

Simmonds nut Precursor of the nyloc nut, with fibre anti-loosening insert

Sohc Single Overhead Camshaft

Single leading shoe (SLS) Drum brake with one actuating cam, and hence one leading and one trailing shoe

Sintered Formed by heat and pressure, usually of metallic powders

Skimming Removing metal to achieve a flat or straight surface, e.g. of cylinder head face

Skirt Hanging portion, particularly of the piston below the gudgeon pin

Slave cylinder The end of a hydraulic system remote from the operator

Slick Treadless racing tyre

Slickshift 1950s Triumph gearchange mechanism which automatically disengages the clutch. Not to be confused with the modern racing mechanism which cuts the ignition momentarily between gearchanges

Slide Moving piston in a slide carburettor which both opens the venturi and governs the flow of fuel through the main jet

Slider The moving lower part of a telescopic fork leg

Slipper piston Piston with its skirt cut away to reduce weight and friction

Slipper tensioner Tensioning device employing a synthetic blade, typically on a cam drive chain

Slip ring Rotating part of a magneto on which the brushes bear

Sludge Accumulation of oil-insoluble material in an engine, sometimes centrifuged into a sludge trap

Small end Bearing on a con rod through which passes the gudgeon pin, sometimes called little end

Snail cam Chain adjustment eccentric

Socket Cylindrical spanner fitted with a positive square drive

Socket head screw Fastener with a recessed head taking hexagonal 'Allen key'

Sodium-filled valve Hollow valve containing sodium which melts at working temperature, aiding heat transfer to the cooler end of the valve

Solder Tin alloy of low melting point, typically used to join electrical components

Solenoid Electrical device using a magnetic field to move a soft iron core and thus engage a mechanism

Spark arrestor Silencer component designed to reduce fire risks from some off-road motorcycles

Spark erosion Process for discreet removal of hard components from softer ones by bombardment with high tension sparks

Spark plug Device for arcing HT current across two electrodes to initiate combustion

Spectacle head Cylinder head with iron element comprising valve seats and spark plug boss, onto which is cast a skull of light alloy

Speedometer Instrument for measuring speed

Spigot Protrusion, e.g. of cylinder liner into crankcase mouth

Spindle Fixed rod about which another part turns, e.g. wheel spindle

Spine Backbone, especially of spine-type frame

Splayed head Four stroke twin cylinder head with widely splayed inlet and/or exhaust valves

Spline Grooved shaft allowing longitudinal but not radial movement of a complementary part

Split single Two-stroke engine with two pistons sharing a common combustion chamber

Spring Anything which deforms to permit movement and recoils elastically

Spring washer Spring steel washer of interrupted circle, designed to prevent loosening

Sprung hub 50s Triumph suspension with the springing located in the rear hub

Square four Cylinder layout using two crankshafts to place four parallel cylinders at the corners of a square; Ariel Square Four

Squat Extent to which the rear suspension of most motorcycles sags under power. Anti-squats are designed-in features intended to reduce this

Squish band Area of cylinder head almost touched by the piston at TDC, promoting quenching and turbulence of combustion gases

Stainless Corrosion-resistant steel, often non-magnetic, having some 25 per cent of alloyed metals such as chromium

Stall Stop an engine by over-loading it

Stanchion Rigid structural member; in telescopic forks, the static tube clamped by the yokes

Steering damper Friction or oil-damped device for combatting tank-slappers

Steering head The section of frame into which the front forks engage

Stiction 'Static friction' — initial resistance to movement especially in suspension systems

Stinger Relatively narrow-bore pipe to the rear of two-stroke exhaust systems, important in exhaust resonance control

Stoichiometric ratio Theoretical air:fuel ratio for perfect combustion at molecular level, 15:1 by weight

Straight (oil) Mineral grade oil without additives, and thus monograde

Stroboscope an instrument using an intermittent bright light to freeze rotating markers and so determine ignition timing

Stroke Linear travel of any component, especially a piston

Stoppie Monowheeling on the front wheel under extreme braking

Stud Threaded rod

Subframe Framework secondary to the main frame, usually at the rear of a motorcycle

Sump Oil reservoir, below or integral with the crankcase, in wet sump engines

Supercharger Mechanically-driven air pump for used in forced induction engines, now rarely used

Suppressor Electrical resistance in a spark plug to suppress TV and radio interference

Sv An engine with a Side Valve

Swan neck S-shaped tube linking sidecar to motorcycle

Swarf Scrap metal from machining processes, sometimes present destructively in new engines

Swept volume The volume covered by a piston's travel, cylinder displacement

SWG Standard Wire Gauge, a measuring convention in which smaller numbers refer to thicker wire

Swinging arm Pivoting rear suspension member carrying the wheel at its free end. More accurately called a swinging fork unless single-sided

Alfred Scott, founder of Scott motorcycles, was one of the industry's great innovators during its infant years. In 1910, he invented the kick starter, years ahead of his time.

Synthetic Substance such as oil or paint based on artificial rather than organic materials. Synthetic oils can be finely tuned and offer greater performance and longevity

Tab washer Washer with one or more tabs capable of being bent to secure a nut

Tachometer Rev counter

Tank rail Frame tube on which sits the petrol tank

Tank-slapper Violent lock-to-lock wobble of a moving motorcycle

Taper A narrowing, especially of a shaft onto which another component is pressed

Taper roller Tapered roller bearing, adjustable and able to take loads radially and axially, such as at the steering head

Tappet Part interposed between cam and valve or pushrod, often with provision for valve clearance adjustment

Tappet clearance The free play allowed at a cold tappet to allow for thermal expansion

TDC Top Dead Centre, the highest position reached by the piston, opposite of BDC

Telescopic Paired tubes, one able to slide within the other, as in telescopic forks

Terminal A battery post to which connections are made

Thackaray washer Spring washer with three coils

Thermal efficiency Ratio of an engine's output to the potential energy of the fuel it consumes

Thermo-syphon Water-cooling system using convection rather than a pump

Thermostat 'Switch' responding to temperature, typically one which opens a valve in a water-cooling system

Throttle A variable restriction in, usually, a carburettor; the twistgrip

Thrust bearing Bearing whose working face takes up the thrust and any rubbing action of associated shaft

Thrust washer Washer which operates as above.

Timing The opening and closing points of valves, and of spark occurrence, expressed in degrees of crankshaft rotation or distance from TDC; adjusting the same

Timing cover Access cover to the valve timing mechanism

Timing gears Gears driving the valvegear and/or ignition

Titanium Strong, grey metal, 43 per cent lighter than steel, used in exotic motorcycle applications

Toe-in Extent to which the path of a sidecar wheel converges with that of the motorcycle

Tolerances Allowable variations in manufacturing dimensions

Tooth Meshing projection on a sprocket, gear or rack

Torque The twisting force exerted by the crankshaft. Horsepower is a measure of torque over time

Torque converter A fluid coupling using oil and rotating vanes in some automatic transmission systems

Total loss System of lubrication, usually in two-strokes, in which the oil is lost after delivery to the

working surfaces; racing ignition systems with a battery but no charging system

Tract Passageway in an engine, as in 'inlet tract'

Traction control Electronic system which reduces power to the driven wheels in the event of wheelspin. Rare on motorcycles

Trail The distance by which the steering axis, extended to the ground, lies in front of the tyre's contact patch. Its effect is to make the bike run straight when upright, but to turn the bike in the direction of lean when cranked over

Trailing link Form of front suspension using a pivoting link with the wheel spindle behind the pivot

Trailing shoe Brake shoe with a cam at its trailing edge

Transmission The general term for the drive chain from crankshaft to final drive, including clutch and gearbox

Tread Part of a tyre intended to clear water from the road

From its introduction in 1987, Honda's CBR600F quickly established itself as a great all-rounder on road and track in the super sports category.

Trial Motorcycle competition over off-road hazards in which penalty points are incurred by a rider putting his feet down, falling or failing a section

Trickle charge Slow charge given to a battery

Trigonic Triangular-section race tyres developed by Dunlop in the 1960s

Triplex chain Chain with three parallel rows of rollers

Trumpet Inlet tube (bellmouth), typically applied to fuel injection applications

Tubeless Tyre needing no inner tube

Tungsten Rare metal used as alloy with tough steels and as filament in conventional light bulb

Turbocharger A forced air pump, broadly similar to a supercharger, but driven at very high speed by exhaust gases, rather than mechanically

Turbulence Agitation in a fluid, especially of inlet charge, where it can promote combustion

Twistgrip Rotary throttle control on the right handlebar

Twin leading shoe (2LS) A brake with two actuating cams and hence two leading shoes

Under-square Engine with stroke greater than the bore

Unit construction Engine in which the powerplant and transmission are formed in one integrated unit

Universal joint (UJ) The double knuckle joint in shaft drive which allows play in the driven shaft to permit suspension movement

Unleaded Petrol devoid of tetra-ethyl-lead, deriving its anti-knock capability from other ingredients

Unsprung weight That part of the wheels, brakes and suspension which lies the road side of the springs

V-twin Twin-cylinder engine having its cylinder axes arranged in a 'V' formation, both big-ends usually sharing a common crankpin

Valve Any device for regulating flow

Valve bounce Destructive condition where a poppet valve is travelling faster than its spring can control it

Valve gear The timing gear, cam(s), pushrods, rockers, valves and associated parts in a four-stroke engine

Valve lift The distance a poppet valve is raised from its seat

Valve lifter Mechanical device, sometime automatic, for reducing compression during starting of a four stroke single

Valve seat Insert of harder material into an aluminium cylinder head on which the poppet valve sits when closed

Venturi A narrowing in a gas passage, especially in a carburettor

Venturi principle The basis on which carburettors work: gas moving through a narrowing creates a partial vacuum able to lift fluid (fuel) into the venturi

Vernier Precision measuring device comprising parallel-jawed sliding caliper

Veteran Any motorcycle made before 1915

Viney bones Rubber bands cut from old inner tubes, named after trials ace Hugh Viney

Vintage Any machine made before 1931

Viscosity Runniness, indicated by SAE number. Higher number denotes more viscous

Volumetric efficiency Ratio of the actual mass of charge drawn into an engine to that which the cylinder could hold at atmospheric pressure. Can exceed unity in racing engines

Vulcanising Hot curing of rubber

Wankel Rotary engine invented by Felix Wankel, operating on four-stroke cycle but without reciprocating parts

Washer Disc of, usually, metal, placed under a nut or bolt head to prevent scouring, loosening or to seal

Water-cooling liquid cooling; transmission of heat from an engine to atmosphere via a liquid intermediary

Watt Unit of electrical 'volume' — volts times amperes

W-clip 'W'-shaped clip securing headlamp unit to shell

Weight distribution Ratio of a vehicle's weight which bears on the front and rear wheels respectively

Weller tensioner Self-adjusting spring-loaded blade tensioner, such as used on camchains

Weld Join materials by melting

Werner Position The (now) usual site for a motorcycle engine in a frame; the name of two brothers who first put one there in 1897

Wet liner Cylinder liner which bears directly against the cooling liquid

Wet sump Engine in which the oil is carried in a well below the

The G80 Matchless single-cylinder engine. Matchless took over the AJS marque in 1931 and their engine designs then dovetailed.

crankcase, rather than in a remote tank

Wheel Any circular object rotating on an axle at its centre

Wheelbase The distance between front and rear wheel spindles

Wheelie Monowheeling on the rear wheel under excess acceleration.

White metal Applied to various alloys of a whitish colour, typically used in plain bearings

Whitworth Type of thread of coarse pitch

Winding Coil of wire around a core in a solenoid or generator

Wire-wound piston Vintage piston with split skirt wrapped in coils of steel wire, eliminating differential expansion with an iron bore

Woodruff key Half moon-shaped piece of hard steel locating a component onto a shaft

Worm gear A uni-directional gear set in which a gear-wheel meshes with a screw-type thread, such as in speedometer drives

Wrist pin (gudgeon pin in USA) Secondary big end pin found in radial and some V-twin and split single engines

Y-alloy Hiduminium, a brand of light alloy which casts well and retains strength at high temperatures

Yoke Component connecting two or more others, usually called a fork yoke

Zener diode Voltage regulator allowing excess voltage to leak to, commonly, an associated finned heat sink

Zinc Grey metal used in galvanising

Zoller A Vane-type supercharger

INDEX

PICTURE CREDITS

American Quantum Cycles: 38 (all).

Derek Avery: 82 (b), 83 (b).

Roy Bacon: 27 (both), 34 (b), 35 (m), 51 (t), 55 (b), 143, 157 (b), 158, 160 (t), 161 (b), 162 (t), 163 (b), 166 (t), 167 (t), 176 (b), 177 (t), 244 (tl), 265 (t), 285 (b), 287 (b), 288 (t), 292 (b), 293 (both), 294 (t), 295 (both), 296 (tl), 302 (tl), 314 (m), 315 (b), 319 (b), 320 (t&bl), 329 (b), 338 (bl), 365 (both), 410 (all), 426 (b), 495, 502 (b), 503 (b).

Murray Barnard: 24 (t), 50 (t), 142 (b).

Derek Beattie: 35 (b), 132 (m).

Big Dog: 72.

Roland Brown: 21 (b), 44 (b), 47 (b), 49, 54 (m&b), 59 (t), 62 (t&m), 80 (tl), 81 (both), 82 (t), 84 (b), 91 (m), 99 (b), 101 (b), 104 (t), 109 (m), 112 (t), 114 (t&b), 117 (t), 134 (m&b), 141 (t), 171 (t), 178 (t), 183 (t), 186 (bl), 189 (b), 191 (b), 200 (t), 245 (b), 246 (tl), 248 (t), 249 (t), 250 (br), 252 (both), 253 (both), 254 (b), 263 (t), 269 (t), 270, 271 (t), 291 (b), 292 (t), 309 (t), 311, 319 (t), 329 (t), 344 (t), 348 (t), 349 (t), 351 (b), 366 (b), 382 (m), 385 (t), 401 (both), 411, 412 (t), 454 (b), 456 (m), 459 (b), 461 (b), 462 (b), 469 (b), 470 (tr), 480 (both), 481, 487 (both), 490 (b), 491 (b), 508 (t), 514 (b), 515, 516 (m).

California Customs: 118 (t).

Cannondale: 120 (b), 121 (t).

CSA: 140 (both).

De Agostini: 14 (b), 16 (t) (both), 18 (t&m), 24 (b), 25 (both), 31 (t), 34 (t) (both), 45 (b), 46 (b), 54 (t), 56 (b), 58 (all), 65 (both), 74 (br), 77 (t&b), 85 (t), 95 (t), 97 (b), 104 (b), 105 (b), 110 (b), 112 (b), 119 (both), 120 (t), 124 (b), 125 (both), 126 (m&b), 128 (both), 130 (both), 131 (t), 132 (b), 135 (t&b), 136 (t), 144 (b), 145 (both), 147 (t), 148 (b), 149 (both), 150 (b) (both), 151, 152 (b) (both), 153 (both), 154 (t&m), 160 (b), 163 (t), 164 (t), 176 (t), 181 (t), 190 (all), 192 (both), 193 (m), 195 (b), 198 (m&b), 200(br), 201, 202 (t), 203 (t), 205 (both), 206 (t), 207 (b), 208 (m), 214 (b), 215 (m), 226 (m), 228 (all), 231 (t), 235 (b), 236 (b), 237 (b), 238 (b), 239 (b), 243, 245 (t), 262 (bl), 263 (b), 266 (m&b), 267 (b), 276 (tl&b), 282 (b), 285 (t), 286 (both), 287 (t), 294 (m), 298 (b), 300 (b), 304 (m), 305 (tl&m), 308 (all), 310 (m), 317 (t), 320 (m), 322 (tr&tl), 323 (m&b), 326 (b), 328 (m), 330, 331 (both), 332 (t, m, br), 334 (t), 345 (m), 346 (m&b), 357 (b), 358, 361 (both), 366 (m), 371 (b), 375 (both), 376 (tl&mr), 377, 378, 379 (b), 380 (b), 381 (t&m), 386 (both), 392 (both), 396 (b), 399 (both), 409 (t), 412 (m&b), 413 (b), 417 (b), 418 (both), 423 (t), 425 (b), 429 (m&b), 437 (t), 438 (m&b), 439 (all), 442(b), 443 (m), 445 (t), 446 (b), 448 (t), 451, 452 (t), 453 (b), 454 (t), 455 (t), 461 (t), 470 (m), 482 (b), 498 (b), 499 (both), 508 (bl), 509 (b), 510 (both), 511 (t), 519 (both), 521 (b).

M. Decet: 46 (t), 57 (b), 91 (m), 102 (bl), 103 (t), 105 (b).

Ducati: 184 (t).

Excelsior-Henderson: 194 (both).

Clive Garman: 106 (b), 138 (b).

Geeley Motorcycles: 213 (both).

Harley-Davidson: 231 (m).

Indian: 271 (b).

Italjet: 273 (both).

KTM: 302 (tl).

Lectra: 312 (b), 313 (t).

Jaques Maertens: 303.

Mac McDiarmid: 20 (t), 21 (t), 30, 40 (b), 41 (t), 43 (t), 45 (t), 48 (m&b), 56 (t), 57 (t), 60 (b), 61 (both), 64 (t), 66 (tr), 71 (b), 74 (t), 75 (both), 78 (tr), 80 (t), 87, 92 (both), 93 (both), 95 (b), 96 (b), 97 (t), 101 (t), 102 (br), 103 (b), 107 (t), 109 (both), 123 (both), 137 (b), 138 (t), 162 (m), 167 (b), 169 (b), 170 (t), 173 (b), 193 (t&b), 216 (t), 229 (t), 234 (t), 242 (ml), 247 (b), 248 (b), 249 (m), 250 (t&bl), 251 (b), 254 (m), 255 (both), 256 (t&m), 276 (tr), 278 (b), 288 (t), 291 (b), 328 (b), 342 (b), 366 (t), 372 (t&br), 376 (tr), 380 (t), 382 (tl&b), 383 (b), 393 (m), 394 (t), 400 (b), 414, 425 (m), 446 (t), 455 (b), 457 (b), 458 (t&m), 459 (t), 460 (both), 462 (t), 471 (both), 473 (t), 475, 476 (both), 477 (both), 478 (both), 479 (b), 486 (both), 488 (t), 491 (b), 493 (b), 498 (t), 506 (t), 509 (t), 511 (b), 512 (b), 513 (both), 514 (t), 520 (t).

Millers Publications: 122 (t), 150 (t), 316 (t).

Andrew Moreland: 14 (t), 15 (b), 26, 28, 33 (t), 44 (t), 48 (t), 51 (b), 52 (t&br), 79 (b), 80 (tr), 84 (t), 88 (b), 90 (m&b), 91 (b), 96 (t), 98, 99 (t), 102 (t), 106 (t), 107 (b), 108 (t), 110 (m), 113 (t), 116 (b), 124 (m), 136 (b), 137 (b), 139 (b), 141 (b), 142 (t), 169 (t), 170 (b), 172 (both), 177 (b), 178 (b), 184 (b), 185 (t), 186 (m&br), 188 (both), 191 (b), 219 (t), 222 (t), 225 (t), 229 (b), 230 (t), 231 (b), 233 (both), 234 (b), 237 (tl), 242 (tr&b), 246 (tr&b), 251 (b), 257 (t), 262 (t), 269 (b), 272 (b), 276 (m), 279 (t), 290 (t), 294 (b), 309 (m), 313 (m&b), 318 (t), 340 (b), 344 (b), 347 9T7m), 348 (m, bl, br), 350, 352 (m), 362 (t), 376 (ml), 383 (b), 384 (t), 393 (b), 400 (t), 422, 450, 452 (b), 470 (tl), 473 (b), 474 (both), 489 (t), 490 (t), 494 (t&b), 506 (b), 512 (t), 518 (t), 520 (b), 521 (t), 522 (t).

Don Morley: 31 (b), 71 (t), 76, 89 (b), 90 (t), 166 (b), 171 (b), 173 (t), 196 (t&tl), 204 (b), 232 (both), 235 (t), 236 (t), 239 (t), 259 (t), 268 (both), 277 (t), 297 (t), 298 (t), 306 (b), 317 (b), 325 (b), 337 (t), 338 (m&br), 346 (t), 351 (t), 360 (b), 364 (t), 368 (m), 369 (t), 379 (b), 381 (b), 384 (b), 385 (t), 390 ((t), 406 (b), 415 (t), 430 (both), 431 (b), 432 (both), 433 (b), 435 (b), 436 (b), 437 (b), 441 (b), 442 (t), 443 (b), 444 (b), 447 (b), 453 (b), 457 (b), 467 (b), 472 (b), 488 (b), 489 (t), 492 (b), 493 (t), 496 (b), 497, 501 (both), 516 (t&b), 523.

Motorcycle Hall of Fame: 32 (t), 445 (b), 456 (t&b), 466 (b), 473 (m), 505 (t).

Munch Technical GmbH: 363 (m).

Musée Henri Malartre: 424 (t).

National Motor Museum, Beaulieu: 34 (m), 67 (both), 129 (m), 135 (m), 144 (t), 152 (t), 160 (b), 244 (t), 281, 325 (t), 326 (t), 327 (both), 328 (t), 343 (t), 360 (m), 505 (m), 506 (m), 518 (b).

Ladislav Neubert / A. Kudlac: 78 (tl&b), 79 (t), 88 (t), 278 (t), 307 (both), 395 (b), 502 (t), 503 (t).

NSU: 387 (t).

Panzer Motorcycles: 402 (bl&br).

Piaggio: 408.

Ridley: 426 (t).

Science and Society Picture Library: 53, 55 (t).

SR Keig LTD: 464 (b).

Suzuki: 458 (b).

Matt Swindlehurst: 29 (both).

TRH Pictures: 15 (t), 52 (b), 86 (b), 89 (t), 129 (b), 202 (b), 226 (b), 230 (b), 261 (t), 300 (t), 310 (t), 377 (t), 394 (m).

Vintage Motorcycle Club: 198 (t), 203 (b), 204 (t), 206 (tl, m, b), 207 (t&m), 208 (t), 212 (b, bl, br), 282 (t), 304 (tl), 316 (b), 317 (m), 324 (bl&br), 394 (b), 395 (t).

Mick Walker: 17 (b), 18 (b), 19 (both), 20 (b), 22 (t), 23, 41 (b), 42 (both), 43 (b), 50 (b), 59 (b), 60 (t), 62 (b), 63, 64 (b), 66 (b), 68 (both), 69, 70 (both), 73 (both), 86 (t), 100, 113 (b), 114 (m), 115 (both), 116 (t), 117 (b), 124 (t), 131 (b), 133, 147 (b), 161 (b), 164 (b), 165 (both), 172, 174 (t), 179 (both), 180 (both), 181 (b), 182 (both), 183 (b), 185 (b), 187, 189 (m), 195 (t), 197, 204 (m), 209 (m), 210 (both), 212 (b), 216 (m), 217 (b), 218 (both), 219 (b), 220 (t), 221 (both), 223 (t), 225 (b), 238 (t), 240 (t), 247 (t&m), 248 (m), 257 (b), 258 (t), 259 (b), 260 (both), 261 (b), 264 (t), 265 (t), 266 (t), 272 (t&m), 274 (t&b), 275 (t), 280 (both), 283 (b), 289 (t), 296 (tr&b), 297 (b), 299 (t), 305 (tr), 306 (t), 310 (b), 312 (t), 314 (b), 315 (t), 318 (b), 320 (br), 322 (b), 324 (t), 326 (m), 332 (bl), 333 (both), 334 (b), 335 (both), 337 (b), 341 (b), 342 (t), 347 (b), 349 (b), 352 (b), 353, 354 (ml, mr, br), 356 (t&br), 357 (t), 359 (t), 360 (t), 362 (b), 363 (t), 364 (br&bl), 367 (both), 368 (b), 370 (b), 371 (t), 372 (b), 373, 374 (t), 382 (tr), 388 (both), 389 (both), 390 (t), 391 (b), 396 (t), 398 (t), 402 (tl), 403, 404, 405 (b), 406 (t), 407 (both), 415 (b), 416 (t), 428 (b), 429 (t), 431 (t), 433 (t), 438 (t), 447 (t&m), 464 (t), 468 (b), 483 (t), 485, 494 (m), 507 (t), 508 (br), 517 (b), 522 (b), 524 (both).

Wayne Woodruff: 33 (b), 77 (m), 94.

Mick Woollett: 32 (t), 40 (t), 47 (t), 118 (b), 126 (t), 134 (t), 168 (both), 222 (t), 222 (t), 226 (b), 227 (t), 237 (tr), 256 (b), 277 (b), 284 (both), 289 (b), 290 (b), 304 (b), 336 (both), 338 (t), 339 (t), 341 (b), 342 (m), 343 (b), 359 (b), 393 (t), 419 (both), 421 (b), 423 (b), 424 (b), 434 (b), 435 (t), 440 (t), 441 (t), 444 (t), 465, 472 (t), 479 (t), 500, 504 (both), 505 (b).

The World's Motorcycles News Agency (Doug Jackson): 16 (b), 17 (t), 22 (b), 35 (t), 36 (both), 39 (both), 66 (ml), 74 (mr&bl)), 83 (t), 85 (b), 108 (b), 111 (both), 121 (m&b), 122 (b) (both), 127 (both), 139 (t), 146 (both), 148 (t&m), 154 (b), 155 (both), 156 (both), 157 (t), 159 (both), 174 (b), 175 (both), 196 (b) (both), 199 (both), 200 (ml), 208 (b), 209 (t&b), 211 (all), 212 (mr), 214 (t&m), 215 (t&b), 216 (b), 217 (t), 220 (t), 223 (b), 224 (all), 227 (b), 240 (b), 241 (both), 242 (t), 244 (bl&br), 254 (t), 258 (b), 262 (br), 264 (b), 274 (tr), 275 (m), 278 (m), 279 (b), 283 (t), 301, 302 (m), 305 (b), 309 (b), 321 (both), 340 (m), 345 (t), 355 (both), 356 (bl), 370 (b), 374 (t), 387 (b), 397 (b), 398 (b), 402 (tr), 405 (t), 409 (m&b), 417 (t), 420 (both), 427 (both), 428 (tr&tl), 434 (t), 440 (m&b), 448 (m&b), 449 (both), 463 (both), 464 (m), 466 (both), 467 (t), 468 (m&t), 469 (t), 482 (b), 483 (b), 484 (all), 492 (b), 496 (t&m), 507 (b), 517 (t).

544